ANIMAL ENCOUNTERS

ANIMAL ENCOUNTERS

Human and Animal Interaction in Britain from the Norman Conquest to World War One

ARTHUR MACGREGOR

REAKTION BOOKS

For Heather
for
continuing
indulgence

Published by
REAKTION BOOKS LTD
33 Great Sutton Street
London EC1V 0DX
www.reaktionbooks.co.uk

First published 2012

This book has been published with the support of
The Paul Mellon Centre for Studies in British Art

Printed and bound in China by C&C Offset Printing Co., Ltd

British Library Cataloguing in Publication Data
MacGregor, Arthur, 1941–
Animal encounters : human and animal interaction in Britain
from the Norman conquest to World War I.
1. Human-animal relationships – Great Britain – History.
2. Animal culture – Great Britain – History.
3. Working animals – Great Britain – History.
I. Title
304.2'7'0941-dc22
ISBN 978 1 86189 849 4

Contents

Preface

I should have been wonderfully qualified by birth to compile this book. My ancestors – or such few as may be named – were Highland shepherds until my father, after war service with the Royal Horse Artillery, broke with tradition to become a cattleman. It did me no good at all: all that accumulated wisdom ought to have enriched the following pages, but it's clear that I learned next to nothing on the farm; I never put a rod in the river, never shot a grouse, stalked a deer or snared a rabbit. The following account must therefore be declared immediately to be largely a literary exercise rather than the distillation of a lifetime of carefully assembled animal lore and personal observation, although it may prove to be leavened here and there with occasional insights into the material culture of animal exploitation gained from my own career, spent largely in archaeology.

It was only with undergraduate study of the beginnings of agriculture in prehistoric Europe that the missed opportunities of childhood began to dawn on me; some later research on bone, antler and horn as raw materials for a range of artefacts required a certain amount of reading on the donor species, reinforcing my growing curiosity, which came to find expression in a number of essays touching on aspects of animal exploitation or husbandry. These disjointed experiences left me with a sense that there was a very disparate range of evidence to be gathered from different disciplines and that inevitably many practitioners in each of these areas were less familiar than they might have been with the work of their counterparts in other fields; neither was there much writing that looked across this broad subject-area in an accessible manner.

Animal Encounters has given me the opportunity to expand my own isolated areas of familiarity in an attempt to form a coherent overview of the relationship (or rather the many relationships) experienced in the British Isles between the human population and the natural world over the past millennium. This is not a work of zoology and neither is it a simple history: it might best be described as being more historiographical in nature and also as concerning itself with the materiality of these encounters. For the historian it is enough to know the quantity and the value of furs being traded, or the numbers of wildfowl being supplied to urban markets at a given time: here I have looked at the techniques of capturing the donor species, whether by traps, nets, weapons or hot pursuit, and their evolving technologies and methodologies through the ages. The names of fish appearing on menus from the early years of the Norman Conquest are well enough known: here the methods of breeding them in captivity, transporting them around the country, harvesting them and preserving them are traced to the point where the advent of the railways changed the whole basis of supply and demand. The progress of some species is pursued in individual detail: the rabbit is followed from high-status exotic, cosseted in specially constructed and jealously guarded warrens, to national pest in the century before it fell victim to myxomatosis; the long-held taste for bear- and bull-baiting is investigated, as is cockfighting – not only in terms of chronology and social context but with due consideration for what was involved in breeding, training, controlling and presenting the animals involved and the staging of these spectacles. Insights from early historical sources are combined with illustrations from manuscripts, artefactual remains, architectural surveys and late-surviving practices, in an attempt to form a rounded picture of this progress. The practicalities and dynamics of agriculture and husbandry in the pre-industrial age are examined, as are the many and crucial supporting roles played in society by the horse. The impact of the steam train and the petrol engine on our dealings with animals is addressed.

Although I have gone to considerable lengths to make the illustrations as numerous, as apposite and as telling as possible, the book itself can make no claim to be a historical survey of animal art. Effective integration of the images into the narratives presented has nevertheless been treated as a matter of basic importance: they are here accorded treatment on equal terms with the other forms of evidence presented. On the other hand, some of the drawings, paintings and engravings reproduced are of indifferent artistic merit and quite naturally have not attracted the attention of the art-historians; they none the less prove invaluable as repositories of otherwise unrecorded detail and no apology is made for including them alongside works of independent artistic value.

Many of the encounters described below were bloody and their end predictably violent. No moral standpoint is taken here – not out of lack of conviction but because it would be inappropriate and counter-productive in such an investigation.

Wherever possible, contemporary voices are left to introduce topics and to explain the mundane (or occasionally adrenalin-charged) means by which particular relationships were consummated; many were conducted in a highly formalized manner, and these conventions too are traced through the ages. There is an extensive literature from the late medieval period, on through the likes of Izaak Walton to the late nineteenth and early twentieth centuries, in which expert sportsmen purport to share their experiences and prejudices by means of reported dialogue with inexperienced beginners; although the genre has fallen from critical favour, it forms a treasure-trove of information from which I have borrowed extensively without myself having any pretension of writing a how-to-do-it manual. The observations of diarists and travellers such as William Harrison, Daniel Defoe, Celia Fiennes and Per Kalm provide valuable eye-witness accounts of practices that were never deemed worthy of more formal record.

Inevitably then, what follows is to a large extent culled from the library rather than from experience in the countryside – a poor contrast to the authorship of many of the books I have come to admire in recent years. There is, none the less, some advantage to be gained from a more detached perspective: what I have attempted to provide is a broad view of the interaction between human society and the animals with which we have shared the British Isles over the past thousand years. There are no means by which such a survey could hope to be comprehensive: I have merely tried to identify some of the more acute instances in which man (and it was usually men) has been brought into some sort of direct relationship with the animal world, to summarize the practical measures through which these encounters were resolved, and to chart the outcome in a balanced way. Exotics (in zoos, parks and menageries) have been specifically excluded, as have domestic pets; sea-fishing has similarly been deemed beyond my scope. So much of present-day society is now isolated from the rural practices recorded here by (extensively urbanized) topography as much as by history: what follows may help to re-forge some of those broken links.

A word should be said about the system of referencing adopted here. Having spent my entire writing career making use of detailed footnotes (my last book had just short of 1,300 of them), I have decided here to do away with them altogether in an attempt to make the primary text as self-sufficient and as enjoyable as possible to a wide audience. None the less, all the bibliographical sources used are listed for each chapter and indebtedness for specific information is indicated by naming particular authors in the text; inevitably, much of the more general background is repro-

duced in a variety of earlier works, which should be identifiable from the references quoted in the lists of sources. Students will doubtless find it tedious not to be provided with chapter and verse for every assertion made and I readily apologize for any inadvertent failure adequately to acknowledge other authors, but it is hoped that the general reader will be content with the level of information provided and will be glad not to directed at every other line to further sources that must be consulted in order for particular points to be validated. The primary aim here is to provide an accessible overview of aspects of the interface between the human and animal worlds – a companion for those seeking a more detailed picture of any given facet of this interplay, for whom the bibliographies may prove helpful in the early stages of their own researches.

1 Paul Sandby, *Englefield Green, near Egham*, c. 1800, bodycolour on paper. Both landscape and livestock betray the effects of human intervention, yet all retain a sense of harmony at this period.

Introduction: Human Engagement with the Animal World

Until the very threshold of our own era, which for present purposes is taken to date from the increasingly mechanized carnage of World War One, the lives of the human and animal populations in Britain as elsewhere were interlinked to an extent that today seems scarcely imaginable. Our largely urbanized society may fret about the (vanishingly small) menace from dangerous dogs or take to the streets in protest at the hunting of foxes – creatures many of us will glimpse only as late-night scavengers that vanish with the daylight; we may be well-read on the threat to the survival of the red squirrel or the perceived role of badgers in spreading bovine tuberculosis, but they are problems imbued with an inescapable sense of remoteness. Keeping up with the columns of the nature correspondent can be akin to reading the reports of theatre critics on plays we are never going to experience at first-hand: we may form a media-inspired and highly impressionistic view of the animal world, but for the majority it is a world now remote and disconnected from daily life.

It was not always so. Animals and birds undoubtedly were present in greater numbers and in wider diversity in earlier centuries, but more significant is the degree to which they inhabited on more equal terms a landscape that remained as yet thinly settled by the human population and consequently was less altered from its natural state. This is not to imply, of course, that the countryside of the last millennium was in any sense virgin territory, for the effects of pastoralism, agriculture and embryonic extractive industries had already imposed far-reaching changes over the preceding 5,000 years (illus. 1). The pace of those changes would quicken over the period under review, however, and would be bound up in an intimate way with many of the animal histories explored here; in their wake came the inexorable processes of alienation alluded to above. Before attempting to recapture on paper something of the experience that helped shape the everyday lives of our ancestors as they interacted with the animal world, a few words may be dedicated to some of the broader considerations that lie behind these encounters.

Environmental Change: Conditioning and Consequences

To some extent, the changes witnessed in the course of animal history over the past millennium have taken place independently of human involvement, with climatic fluctuations playing possibly quite a significant role in parallel with changes wrought in the course of human progress. The advent of the 'Little Ice Age' followed on some centuries of higher-than-average warmth, making its effects all the more keenly felt: a significantly cooler regime set in from the middle of the fifteenth century, with episodes of exceptional cold recorded in the mid-seventeenth, mid-eighteenth and mid-nineteenth centuries. During these extended periods, not only did the winters become markedly more severe but summer growing seasons too were shortened and rainfall increased. In the realm of agriculture, productivity was adversely affected to the point where famine took hold on more than one occasion as crops failed and animals died; the local effects of this downturn on rural populations may have been as dramatic as those wrought by the Black Death itself, for in the absence of a highly developed transport network individual communities were largely abandoned to their fate. The impact on animals is largely unrecorded, but at the least they would have come under unprecedented pressure from the ever more desperate human population and just occasionally – for instance, in anecdotal accounts of fish being frozen solid in their ponds and birds falling stone-dead from the trees as a result of intense frosts – the fate that must have been overtaken countless unregarded creatures falls under the spotlight.

To a considerably greater degree than the changes imposed by climatic factors, the face of the landscape was permanently altered by human intervention in ways that impacted profoundly on the environment occupied by the animal population. The countryside gradually became overlaid with ever more intricate patterns of ownership, a process that was already well under way by the time the intrusive Norman monarchy so comprehensively rewrote the rule-book in the second half of the eleventh century. Great swaths of forest, together with their animal inhabitants, were at successive strokes of the pen placed beyond the reach of the ordinary population from the reign of William I onwards, as the monarchy and its supporting aristocracy progressively consolidated their grip on these resources by means of

exclusive legal instruments. While the swineherd and his pigs might continue to be granted grudging (though not unprofitable) access to the important food resources of the forest, common grounds came to form almost the only resources to which the landless peasant might continue have free access with his domestic animals, though even these were under constant pressure from landlords eager to expand their portfolios of real estate and to assert their rights over game wherever it might be found. The forest – always a valuable economic resource in its own right as well as a haven for animals – found itself progressively diminished by a variety of pressures: agriculture expanded at the expense of the territory designated as forest (only parts of which were indeed tree-covered) while grazing by beasts placed a limit on the natural processes of regeneration. The trees themselves were harvested, not only for building houses and ships – the latter increasing considerably from the sixteenth century onwards – but also for fuel, both domestic and (increasingly) industrial. Game-reserves in the form of enclosed deer-parks were created within the forest at an increasing rate from the late medieval period onwards; these might potentially have offered some relief from the pressures described, but in practice their expansion was a symptom of a deer population already in crisis from over-exploitation and destined never to recover its former numbers.

Having drifted for centuries towards progressive degeneration, much of the most depleted land not under cultivation was stabilized in a state of semi-wilderness in the nineteenth century with the creation of extensive shooting estates employing professional game-keepers to breed and protect artificial populations of birds and animals (and ruthlessly to exterminate their natural enemies), in order to provide sport for the guns whose economic value came to outweigh any other form of return that could be gained from heaths and moorland.

Meanwhile the march of agriculture had by no means progressed at the expense of the forest alone. While open field systems struggled to produce crops, with their harvests constantly pegged at low levels by soil exhaustion (an inevitable result of two-course rotation), the establishment of vast monastic estates from the twelfth century onwards introduced a new element to a landscape in which sheep began to occupy a dominant position, their insatiable appetite for grass determining that open grazing would increasingly come to form one of the most characteristic features of the countryside. Following the demographic collapse wrought by the Black Death in the mid-fourteenth century, depletion of the agricultural workforce led to an even greater reliance on a sheep-based economy and to the abandonment of many established rural settlements. Further changes in topography were brought about in the later medieval period by the first wave of enclosures, prompted by the passage of an increasing proportion of land into private hands, a process that accelerated considerably when the monastic estates were seized for the Crown in the mid-sixteenth century and were redistributed in a process that saw ownership of these tracts fragmented and cascading down to growing numbers of increasingly prosperous yeoman farmers.

Enclosure had the effect of promoting efforts towards improving the quality of now well-defined properties in a way that had never been practicable in the days of open-field cultivation. 'Landscape plotted and pieced' became a cipher for the settled countryside – good news, in some ways, for the domesticates which began to benefit from closer attention from farmers anxious to maximize their returns but with mixed implications for the rest of the animal world: bustard, for example, that had continued to flourish among the open fields found the increasingly enclosed landscape inimical to

their tastes and faded from the scene; rabbits, on the other hand, which had been straying tentatively from their warrens for some centuries now took advantage of the increased cover offered by the dense networks of hedges to determinedly colonize the countryside as never before.

At a regional level, a more fundamental impact was made on the Fenland landscape and in the Somerset Levels by measures undertaken initially in the medieval period (notably by the Benedictines) but at an increased pace from the seventeenth century onwards, aimed at draining waterlogged territory and converting it to agricultural land. In economic terms the exercise must be considered one of the triumphs of the age of improvement, but the effect on existing wildlife populations was devastating. East Anglia and Lincolnshire still attract considerable numbers of migrating wildfowl on an annual basis, but they represent only a tiny fraction of those formerly overwintering on the watery medieval landscape, teeming with fish, eels and frogs and with all the insect life associated with its reed-filled character.

The sandy heath lands interspersed with the marshes similarly underwent widespread transformation as attempts were made to improve them by marling – a process not always as successful as drainage and in some cases abandoned after a few years of experiment, but not before existing ecosystems had been extensively interfered with in a manner that frequently proved irreversible.

And finally, the march of industrialization in the eighteenth and nineteenth centuries transformed tracts of rural landscape into wastelands, their woodlands swept away to power the furnaces, their meadows dumped with sterile waste, their rivers polluted and rendered lifeless. The spread of manufacturing and mineral extraction over the face of the landscape can be mapped with some accuracy in terms of its buildings, installations and associated communities, but its impact on surrounding ecosystems can be inferred to have been significantly more widespread. It is hard to conceive of any positive benefits that might have devolved to the animal world through any of these developments.

ANIMALS AS CURRENCY

A repeated theme in this book is the way in which animal populations came to be viewed as resources so integral with the territory they occupied as to feature commonly in contractual arrangements for the granting of land by a lord to his tenants or in the obligations due from tenants to lords. A striking example is formed by the initial reservation by the monarchy of hunting rights over deer irrespective of where they might be in the king's forests and the ultimate devolution of these rights to certain favoured lords in a system that might operate independently of (but in parallel with) the normal obligations between landlord and tenant. Similar arrangements were developed for other beasts of the chase and of the warren, all of them forbidden to the ordinary populace, who might none the less have to turn out periodically to assist in the more mundane duties associated with the hunt.

Rights over swans on open waters were similarly claimed by the Crown: these were devolved to a much greater extent and gave rise to an elaborate bureaucracy designed to register ownership of the entire population of swans over large areas of the country, while maintaining monarchical rights and privileges whenever the opportunity arose. Royal officials proved opportunistic whenever moments of uncertainty arose over ownership, or during the transfer of power from one landowner to another: any delay in the appointment of a new bishop, for example, seems to have provided

the monarch with the opportunity to ransack the fish-ponds of episcopal estates, either for the benefit of his table or in order to transfer the fish to royal ponds elsewhere. Regular supplies of horses featured in the obligations to be observed by many recipients of royal favour, from the constables of medieval castles to the Gentleman Pensioners who benefited so handsomely from the break-up of monastic estates under Henry VIII.

The holding of lesser offices and serjeanties from the Crown brought with it similar obligations in terms of animal revenues. These might be in the form of pest control, as in obligations to exterminate any wolves that threatened a particular district, or they could involve body-service in joining the royal boar-hunt when the monarch visited local forests for sport. They might demand the supply of hawks for the royal mews – or indeed the keeping of birds at the holder's own expense for use by the king in the event of being in need of sport and without his own establishment of falcons and falconers.

Further down the social scale similar obligations at times required tenants to provide accommodation and care for the lord's young hunting hounds before they graduated to the field, or for his fighting cocks before they had been entered to the cockpit for the first time. Early feudal obligations frequently required tenants to perform services with their oxen and horses for their lord; alternatively their wives and daughters might be required to help with milking or with sheep-washing prior to shearing.

Animals also fuelled the common round of gift-giving that both lubricated and cemented relationships between those of more equal status. Horses, falcons and hunting hounds formed acceptable presents between royal courts of the medieval period and by the sixteenth century live deer had come to be exchanged in a similar manner. Venison formed the gold-standard of the internal market, distributed by lords to their family members and to favoured members of their retinues. Fish such as pike and bream were equally acceptable as gifts in aristocratic circles; chubb occupied a curiously ambivalent position for a time, accorded a value as a prestige fish in the system of gift exchange but with eating qualities so negligible that their value on the open market remained minimal. Time and changing fashion altered the dynamics of these relationships: rabbits, counted in the early Norman period amongst the gifts fit for a king, became a staple of the urban poor by the nineteenth century as their numbers soared.

INSULARITY AND INTERPENETRATION

A conscious effort is made in the following pages to focus attention on the interaction between animal- and human-kind, specifically within the British Isles. Inevitably, Britain's status as an off-shore island at the north-western periphery of Europe dictates that much of the practice involved in encountering animals was influenced by experience on the Continental mainland – most visibly, perhaps, in the context of the fashion-conscious royal and aristocratic hunt. The indebtedness of all early hunting tracts to those produced by Continental authors shows all too clearly the derivative nature of much English writing on the subject at this time, and in any more general treatment of the subject precedence would inevitably have to be given to the influential French, German and other texts, both in terms of their authoritative content and of their frequently superior level of illustration. Here a more narrow view is deliberately adopted, in order that the distinctively insular contribution may be allowed to emerge more effectively than otherwise it would.

For every debt of this kind that is clearly manifested in the literary and historical record, there were, moreover, many more shadowy but ultimately influential ways in which the lessons offered by Continental practice were transmitted to these islands. Already in the centuries immediately preceding the period reviewed here the introduction of the horseshoe and the stirrup had transformed the effectiveness of the horse as an instrument of war, and would place it at the very centre of the feudal system that characterized the early medieval centuries; similarly, the adoption of the padded shoulder-collar in preference to earlier harnessing systems that had threatened to strangle horses used in any form of traction not only enhanced their pulling power but placed the horse in a position to alter the entire course of agriculture, notably in conjunction with the heavy wheeled plough (perhaps a Danish introduction) that appeared about the same time. In later centuries, the adoption of Dutch methods of constructing decoys to capture wildfowl further illustrates Continental-inspired technological change: evidently firmly established in eastern England well before their better documented 'polite' introduction at the hands of Charles II, decoys exemplify the manner in which technological innovation often ran ahead of the historical record, perhaps especially so in the rural context. In the same way, the extensively recorded aristocratic craze for newfangled Prussian coaches that swept London in the later sixteenth century can be seen to be have been paralleled by the independent adoption in the countryside of more mundane Dutch-style wagons with steerable fore-carriages whose arrival is nowhere formally documented, although in economic terms they represented a development of equal value to the coach since they transformed the usefulness of wagons for the farmer. A burgeoning demand from both of these communities for heavy horses to draw each of these types of vehicles is duly registered in the record of those animals as given below.

And it was not only ideas but also animals themselves that made their way on occasion from the Continent to be absorbed into the domestic fauna. Horses were amongst both the first such imports and the longest-continued, for the lengthy story of the evolution of British horses as world-class contenders is influenced at every stage by cross-breeding with imported stock, from early medieval destriers from France, through sixteenth-century coursers from Italy, the Near East and North Africa, to draught horses from Flanders and Germany. Dutch cattle emerge as having had an important but largely undocumented impact on English dairy herds well before their role came to be acknowledged in print in the seventeenth and eighteenth centuries. The pig population similarly benefited at some unrecorded stage from the introduction of a Continental strain that contributed to the emergence of the 'Old English' breed, with a character quite distinct from the native swine that preserved so many of their formerly wild characteristics (and which James I tried to perpetuate for sporting purposes with imported wild boar in the early seventeenth century). Pigs from the Far East would play a similarly influential role in the more purposeful attempts at improving the profitability of stock witnessed from the 1700s onwards. The sheep population, on the other hand, gives the appearance of remaining more substantially unadulterated at this time (although a large measure of Scandinavian blood had flowed in during the centuries immediately preceding the Norman invasion), until the Merino made its entrance by royal command in the late eighteenth century.

Less expected, perhaps, are imports of species other than those constituting the standard domestic stock. The history of the rabbit is perhaps the most spectacularly successful of these, its numbers growing from carefully husbanded handfuls of imported exotics to epidemic proportions that threatened the very viability of agriculture. One of the rabbit's greatest enemies, the fox, proves to have an even more unexpected history, being persecuted by hunters to the point where it was threatened with extinction before the same hunters took to encouraging native populations and even swelling them with foxes brought from overseas in order that their sport should not be extinguished – for all that fox-hunting was commonly presented with a positive spin in terms of vermin control carried out in the public interest. Deer prove to have a similarly ambivalent history, being shielded from the population at large so that they could be hunted by the elite, brought so low in numbers that they had to be protected in deer parks and pursued repeatedly without being killed, decanted from one end of the country to the other and being supplemented in the sixteenth and seventeenth centuries with new stock brought from as far away as Brandenburg and Denmark. From the early medieval centuries, falcons arrived as high-status gifts or as purchases from an even wider range of sources stretching from Iceland and Scandinavia to north Africa. Clearly the domestic livestock population was by no means alone in its repeated adulteration (or rather its enrichment and diversification) with foreign blood.

URBANIZATION AND INDUSTRIALIZATION

In the growth of towns we can detect both a reflection of the developing national economy and one of its principal driving forces. In 1400 there were fewer than twenty provincial centres with populations of 3,000 or more, and even London harboured at that time no more than 40,000 citizens. Then the population of England as a whole has been estimated at just over two million, a figure that would more than double by the 1650s; urban dwellers were by now much more numerous and continued to form an increasing proportion of the total as the national figure climbed from the 1740s to reach over 20 million by 1870.

In order that these expanding urban populations could be maintained, it was necessary for a parallel revolution to take place in both agricultural and livestock production and in the supply systems that enabled produce to be delivered to urban markets in a consistent and predictable manner. Horsepower provided the means by which flour, vegetables and dairy products were channelled to the growing population centres; in the matter of meat supply, while the carcasses of small mammals, birds and fish might similarly be consigned to the carrying trade, all the larger beasts capable of making their own way to the urban meat-market were expected to do so. The process was most highly developed in the case of cattle: from the seventeenth century onwards, when the general consumption of meat grew at a steady rate, a high proportion of the beasts sold at Smithfield and elsewhere might have begun their lives as far away as the Scottish highlands, the Welsh Marches or in Ireland; their progress to market involved epic journeys in herds of perhaps some hundreds along the green drove roads that formed an alternative communications network proliferating over hundreds of miles of countryside, and would generally be punctuated by several seasons in the hands of intermediate graziers who would bring them to prime condition after their long trek and would 'finish' them for the market in order to achieve the best possible price. Sheep underwent a similar process, and for centuries even geese and turkeys were driven considerable distances from their breeding grounds in East Anglia to the poultry markets of London. Only the advent of the railway system would bring an end to these enforced marches, adding undreamed-of levels of efficiency to the process of drawing in fowl, fish and flesh – by now mostly killed at source and transported in the carcass – to satisfy urban appetites.

From the early medieval period a whole raft of professional entrepreneurs emerged who took it upon themselves to source these supplies and to oversee their sale in the market place. The principal players were to be found in the formally constituted guilds: in London the forerunners of the Butchers', Poulters' and Fishmongers' Companies all occupied influential positions in the regulation of trade by the 1300s. Ancillary trades relying ultimately on the same rural resources for their raw materials included the skinners, tanners, horners and leathersellers, as well as others further down the supply chain including saddlers, harness-makers and shoemakers, all reliant on leather, fletchers whose trade depended on the supply of goose-quills, felt-makers whose industry consumed the bulk of the rabbit fur, and wax chandlers who processed beeswax into candles and tapers. Wool merchants, who must be considered amongst the earliest commodity brokers, were more likely to conduct their business at arm's length, perhaps buying unseen the fleeces from entire flocks (sometimes several years in advance) and either selling them on through the London staple or having them delivered to the Channel ports for export or to the spinners and weavers who supplied the home market and who came to build an impressive export market of their own.

Whatever their destiny, few animals entering the towns profited from the experience. Cattle and sheep met their end in the shambles and slaughterhouses whose reputation for squalor and inhumanity was legendary. The lives of urban horses were pitifully impoverished compared even with those of their overworked country cousins: so great was the toll taken by the relentless grind of city life that the average horse, having spent its early years on the farm being conditioned for its coming labours, might be lucky to survive the rigours of city life long enough to be sold back for some further years of work on the land after it had been deemed worn-out and unfit for further toil in the town. Cities consumed horses as voraciously as their citizens consumed cattle: by the nineteenth century, measures for the disposal of those that had died in harness – and there were many – had been developed to the level of an efficient and independently profitable industry.

CRUELTY, COMPASSION AND DOMESTIC PETS

One consequence of the distancing of the animal world from everyday human life has been the transfer of our responses to animals to a largely abstract plane: few of us would consciously espouse attitudes that were less than benevolent towards them, but on the other hand our values are seldom put to the test. A great deal of the frankly brutal treatment formerly meted out to animals, as documented in the following pages, would be classed today as inhuman, immoral and frequently illegal too, but it would be simplistic merely to assign those shortcomings to an age when wanton cruelty and indifference were universal.

Pets form the most common means by which many of us maintain our most direct links with the animal world, and although they fall outside the scope of the following chapters the role played by pets in establishing present-day attitudes to animals in general is of some importance. The degree to which some owners bond with their animals is notorious – anthropomorphizing them to a great extent and forming deep emotional bonds of affection. These remarkably close relationships stand at

the extreme end of a spectrum of experiences in which animals emerge initially as more distant symbiotic partners in human society, with dogs, for example, appreciated for the role they might play in hunting and herding and with cats valued for their effectiveness in controlling the rats and mice that threatened stores of grain and other foodstuffs. These were essentially arrangements of mutual convenience, however, carrying with them no perceived responsibilities for feeding or for providing more than minimal shelter: giving food to a cat would, indeed, only have compromised its keenness as a hunter, while many dogs too would have been expected to scavenge for themselves. With the emergence of the post-medieval world a degree of change can be detected, coinciding, perhaps, with the migration of an increasing proportion of the population away from direct involvement with the land and with a new period of growth in towns and cities.

Amongst the factors conditioning the responses of society as a whole was the biblical notion that humankind had dominion over the animal world – that it had been created purely for our benefit. In time, more thoughtful theologians and others came to assert that biblical authority provided no sanction for the ill-use of animals and from the sixteenth century Puritan writers in particular began to campaign against mistreatment. The more overt forms of deliberately orchestrated cruelty – bear-baiting, cockfighting, bull-baiting – formed early targets for the growing volume of protest that began to make itself heard from the 1500s onwards. From the time of the Restoration, polite society as a whole began to distance itself from the worst of these excesses, although it was a process that would take many years more to run its course – if indeed it can be said to have done so entirely by our own day.

The view that past relationships between man and animal were characterized by unmitigated and wilful mistreatment of one by the other may be, in any case, easily overstated. Indeed there are simply no records on which to build a trustworthy picture of patterns of behaviour between, say, the average farm labourer and his charges: it seems entirely possible that recognition of the benefits to be achieved by sympathetic treatment rather than by unbending harshness were never limited to, for example, the falconers whose training regime for hawks was amongst the first such relationships to be extensively documented and who recognized that their charges could never be brought to the peak of perfection without much patient and gentle handling. It may well be that what the 'progressive' authors of the sixteenth and seventeenth centuries claimed as novel developments were already far more widespread in popular culture than they cared to acknowledge: the peasant at his plough, after all, had nothing to gain from mercilessly tormenting his ox, for their destinies were quite literally yoked together and the best that life could bring them would emerge from recognition of their mutual interest.

What is perhaps most striking is that the earliest documented intimations of a benign attitude emerging in the treatment of animals precede considerably any formal recognition that children too might respond to the carrot as well as the stick, for it was only in the course of the seventeenth century that educational reformers began to advocate more gentle methods of discipline in schooling. In terms of the social norms of the day, attitudes to animals were perhaps more narrowly in line with interpersonal relationships than they might appear from our twenty-first-century perspective.

Plenitude

Also exercising an influence on the way that natural resources of all kinds were viewed was a widely held sense that the resources of the animal kingdom were virtually limitless. While a few prescient souls may have noted and regretted the loss of the crane and the bustard from the English countryside, no one claimed to see in their extinction any danger-signals for the wider natural world. British beavers faded from the scene just as access to the richer resources of northern Europe came to be organized on a wider international scale, so that their passing was scarcely noticed: by the time the last scattered communities died out, the fur trade (the only major consumers of beaver products) had long since realigned its supply networks on the countries of the Hanseatic League and on Scandinavia, and from the seventeenth century would look as far afield as Canada. The time had not yet arrived when the loss of indigenous species such as these was a matter for wider concern, least of all when alternative sources could be plundered in such a way that the market felt no impact whatever.

More prevalent was a general confidence that God would provide. Fieldfares and seabirds could be netted by the hundred with complacency and wildfowl blasted in swaths from the water by giant punt-borne scatter guns, all in the confident belief that divine providence could be relied on to replenish the stock and make good losses in time for the coming season.

Considerations of this kind impinge repeatedly if tangentially on many of the themes treated in greater detail in the following pages, but are not the primary concern here. Others have delved in greater depth into the moral and philosophical dimensions of human involvement with the animal world: from this point it will be rather the physical dimensions – the material culture – of these relationships that occupy us and which form the primary concern of this study.

2 John Fernley, *The Council of Horses*, 1840, oil on canvas. Included here to illustrate something of the range of British horses, Fernley's romantic image was inspired by a tale by John Gay in which the horses planned a revolt, in a manner later reworked by George Orwell in his *Animal Farm*.

ONE

The Ubiquitous Horse

A Horse-Driven Society

In their variety of appearance, size, shape and occupation, the horse population of the medieval and early modern periods mirrored human society: there was a horse for every occasion and for every station in life. Equine society was quite as stratified as its human counterpart, with enormous differentials in monetary value between high-bred aristocratic mounts at one end of the scale and the undersized, underfed and overworked jades that eked out a miserable existence at the other: in the late seventeenth century, for example, a packhorse might be had for under £3 while a racehorse could change hands for £3,000. From a Europe-wide perspective, British breeds early in the period were generally undistinguished in character and small in stature; after a slow start, advances were eventually made in improving their conformation, to the point where a sizeable export trade developed in horses suited to all manner of uses and British mounts came to be widely sought after by horsemen overseas.

Although present-day perceptions of the horse are of a primarily agricultural animal, there may never have been a time when more horses were employed on the land than were engaged in the myriad other activities in which they served. Large numbers were engaged in construction, for example: the logistical challenges involved in assembling masonry for major ecclesiastical buildings and for civil and military defences in an unmechanized age seem from today's perspective to be almost insurmountable, but undoubtedly were overcome simply by the application of massive man – and animal – power; similarly, the mining and quarrying industries were entirely dependent on the engagement of the horse, both in the extraction of raw materials and in their distribution, while the industrial revolution that transformed Britain's fortunes from the eighteenth century onwards would have been still-born without the presence of a correspondingly dynamic transport network.

A number of arbitrary divisions are made below in order to allow examination of different aspects of the horse, but few of these categories were in any sense mutually exclusive. Farm horses have been treated separately here (pp. 488–94), but the countryside and the towns were in reality constantly engaged in a process of exchange that might see a farmer work his younger horses for some years on the land before selling them for heavy draught work in the town; after some further years of service, the urban drayman was likely to find them no longer up to the heavy demands made on them in the town at an age when they could still give further years of service in the field, at which point they might be sold back to the farming community at advantageous rates.

Progress in systematic horse-breeding was painfully slow before the eighteenth century and while nearly all earlier efforts at improvement had been directed towards horses for warfare (and later for sport) it was only when more insightful procedures were developed for other domestic animals that lasting improvements were made also to the horse. At the same time, the prejudices that had grown up since the early days when stallions and mares were simply allowed to run free together – for example, the belief that a stallion should not be put to service until he was at least seven years old, and then only with two or three mares at a time – were swept aside in favour of what might be called an industrial-scale organization. Professional stallion owners appeared, serving farms within an accessible range of their homes or advertising their presence at particular places on fixed days, so that mares could be brought to them. The owners of the mares, on the other hand, took to arranging regional shows with prizes for the best stallions, in order to attract the attention of stallion owners – and the services of their animals – to their localities.

The inordinate demands made on perhaps the majority of horses are reflected in their all-too-short life expectancy, held at far below their maximum potential. Even the writers of manuals in the sixteenth and seventeenth centuries acknowledged that, properly looked after, a horse might be expected to survive perhaps 25 years, but the combination of poor diet, breaking at an early age and unremitting overwork thereafter meant that most had reached the end of their useful working lives at half that age. Writing of Cornish horses at the turn of the seventeenth century, Richard Carew observed that

> very few of them (through the owner's fault) retain long . . . their natural goodness, for after two years age they use them to carry sacks of sand, which boweth down and

weakeneth their backs, and the next summer they are employed in harrowing, which marreth their pace, two means that so quail also their stomachs and abate their strength as the first rider findeth them overbroken to his hands.

John Evelyn was equally aware of the way their usefulness was compromised and their lives habitually shortened by:

> The Tyranny and cruel Usage of their Masters in tiring Journeys, hard, labouring and unmerciful treatment, Heats, Colds, &c which wear out and destroy so many of these useful and generous Creatures before the time. Some as have been better us'd, and some, whom their more gentle and good-natur'd Patrons have in recompense of their long and faithful Service, dismis'd and sent to Pasture for the rest of their Lives . . . have been known to live forty, fifty, nay (says Aristotle) no fewer than sixty-five Years.

Such an optimistic estimate (which in reality could never have been reached), or indeed the prospect of spending their declining years in pasture was utterly denied to the vast majority of horses, as reiterated by John Flavell, a near contemporary of Evelyn's, in his *Husbandry Spiritualized* (1669):

> Though some men be excessively careful and tender over their beasts . . . yet others are cruel and merciless towards them, not regarding how they ride or burden them. How often have I seen them fainting under their loads? wrought off their legs, and turned out with galled backs into the fields, or high wayes to shift for a little grass? Many times

have I heard and pitied them, groaning under unreasonable burdens, and beaten on by merciless drivers, till at last by such cruel usage they have been destroyed, and then cast into a ditch for dogs meat!

Retirement was indeed a concept unfamiliar in the horse world, most working animals being driven until they dropped and buried where they died, generally after being relieved of their hide for use in covering carriages, weaving into traces or plaiting into whiplashes for chastising the next generation of drudges. The large numbers of horses living and dying within the medieval cities caused major problems of disposal: simply throwing their carcasses into the city ditch was a solution evidently resorted to so frequently that well before the end of the medieval period legislation was widely enacted to outlaw the practice. By the end of the horse-drawn era, at the turn of the twentieth century, the process had gained nothing in sentiment but had been greatly streamlined: Gordon describes seven major depots established in London by that time where carts for the recovery of horses that had failed in the streets were kept in readiness 'like fire engines' and where their cargoes would be dispatched, flayed, butchered and boiled down for cat's meat in the space of an hour or two. Horseflesh, incidentally, seems never to have been eaten in England, except under the extreme conditions imposed by famine: Edwards records that at the Parliamentary siege of Banbury (Oxfordshire), news that the defenders were considering eating their horses put the besiegers 'in great hopes of speedy obtaining the castle', so convinced were they that their adversaries must be in extremis. Neither was it considered profitable to export horsemeat to countries lacking in these finer sensibilities before the very end of the nineteenth century, when a considerable trade in worn-out horses developed with the horse butchers of the Netherlands and Belgium in particular.

By that time, the international trade in horses, which will be seen below to have had a lengthy history, had reached its peak: Gordon records that in 1890 just short of 20,000 animals were imported, including draught horses from Denmark, Holland, Belgium and France; ponies from Norway, Sweden, Russia, Poland and Finland; riding and driving horses from Hanover and Hungary; and others for unspecified tasks from the USA and Canada. At the same time, high-grade English horses were exported for breeding purposes, and for the prestige end of what had become a truly international market.

THE HORSE POPULATION

Although human intervention may already have wrought some degree of change on the character of the various breeds (or rather geographical races) of horses to be found in different parts of the British Isles at the opening of the Norman era, the animals themselves retained a large part of their respective group identities, forged by generations of perfectly natural selection in response to regional and environmental factors – marsh or mountain, windswept Atlantic coastline or sandy forest floor – and not greatly affected by human intervention. These individual characters were ascribed no intrinsic value to be preserved and nurtured by a population that saw the horse in purely functional terms, and since one type of animal was readily appreciated as being suited to one task and another to some other purpose, users tended to divide them primarily according to function: the fixed breeds familiar today would emerge only in the course of the period reviewed here.

Throughout the medieval period, by which time horses had come to occupy a central place in the functioning of society, much of the horse-breeding up and down the country remained unstructured in nature, characteristically taking place on common land: breeding mares ran semi-wild with the stallions, their progeny being rounded up once a year for apportioning amongst the respective owners. Already in the *Domesday* survey, however, some areas of East Anglia are seen to possess horses in sufficient numbers to indicate the presence of deliberately assembled breeding populations in which, one might imagine, more purposeful targeting of particular character traits might already have begun to make some impact; on the other hand, in view of the dearth of appreciation of the most basic principles of breeding for maintaining (let alone improving) the quality of stock amongst contemporary keepers of sheep and cattle (p. 426), it might be over-optimistic to ascribe too much insight to these breeders. By the following century the monasteries had also made an entry into horse-breeding: R.H.C. Davis records that Burton Abbey (Staffordshire) had a stud (*haraz*) with 70 mares and foals before 1114, with another 85 mares at Whiston in the same county shortly afterwards; Shrewsbury Abbey was given tithes of forest mares in Shropshire and both Bardney Abbey (Lincolnshire) and Byland Abbey (Yorkshire) owned pastures for mares in north Yorkshire. Giles Worsley notes that by 1269–70 Beaulieu Abbey (Hampshire) possessed nearly 300 adult horses of various kinds plus nearly 100 colts and foals, all distributed over seventeen granges. It would be entirely in keeping with everything we know of the running of monastic estates if these were to have been amongst the most progressive and orderly establishments of their day – their stock protected to some degree from the haphazard sexual encounters of the common land that resulted in the horse population at large having such an undistinguished character. Indeed, following their suppression in the sixteenth century, the Venetian ambassador would ascribe to the destruction of the model studs formerly associated with the monasteries the poor state in which he found English horses. Finding their way on to the domestic market, the progeny of these monastic studs would have helped raise the quality of the stock, while the advance of the process of enclosure meant that increasing numbers of private owners could also exercise a degree of control over access to their mares. The royal studs and those of the nobility and gentry no doubt benefited from even more strictly imposed isolation as well as from the introduction of carefully selected foreign breeding stock, but to a large extent their efforts were concentrated specifically on the production of warhorses (pp. 38–40).

By the time we learn anything of common practice, it seems that foals were normally weaned at about six months, although the royal stables favoured running them with the mare for a year; in the mid-sixteenth century Thomas Blundeville went so far as to recommend weaning at three years, but a generation later Gervase Markham asserted that one year was sufficient while their mid-seventeenth-century successor the Duke of Newcastle thought any longer was likely to adversely affect the breeding capacity of the mare. Mares were generally covered for the first time in their third year, after which owners with any sensibility thought that foaling every other year was quite enough. For the vast population of ordinary mares, however, the annual attentions of the stallion and an eleven-month gestation period combined to ensure that they spent much of their lives in foal. The spaying of mares was little practised, but colts not destined for breeding were castrated at ages ranging from nine days (as recommended by Markham) to two years (as favoured by Blundeville).

Two other initiatives were important in forwarding the methodology of horse-breeding. A belief that the seventeenth-century 'gentlemen of the turf' at Newmarket exhibited a precocious understanding of the principles involved had a wide currency and certainly an early interest was shown there in recording the lineage of successful 'gallopers' and in conspiring to bring together the most propitious combinations of features from both stallion and mare. More importantly, however, the great eighteenth-century agricultural improvers, amongst whom the name of Robert Bakewell stands supreme, finally grasped the method by which these inherited characteristics could be fixed in succeeding generations of offspring, namely by in-and-in breeding (p. 428). With the benefit of this insight, it now seems clear that the character traits inherited by the offspring of all the expensive imported bloodstock in previous centuries were doomed to be dissipated in subsequent generations, but having once established his working methods with sheep and pigs (whose life cycles were conveniently brief by comparison), Bakewell and his followers were soon applying the same procedures to horses with equal success. Chivers observes that since it was common in horse-breeding to bring together stallions and mares of widely different breed or type, in-and-in breeding was all the more important in fixing the character of succeeding generations. It may be, as he suggests, that the taint of incest that was inherent in the consummation of these relationships had been simply too repugnant to earlier and more pious generations of breeders for it to have gained much ground, and even in the enlightened eighteenth century Bakewell found it prudent not to make too much of these practices in public. Such was the success of his methods, however, that in time they came to be universally adopted.

HORSE TYPES: REGIONAL VARIANTS

As suggested above, points of difference in character were of secondary interest to a human population that saw horses essentially according to the functions they might perform – and there were many. To the average smallholder at the opening of our era, an all-round animal was required that might be yoked to the harrows one day and to the dung-cart the next, before carrying his wife and her dairy produce to market the next: he had no interest in its pedigree (which was likely to be undistinguished and miscellaneous in the extreme), would afford it the very minimum of resources to keep it functioning, and would expect to work it until it dropped.

A number of broad regional populations had already come to be recognized as having particular qualities (see illus. 2), to be sought out by those who had access to them and had the financial means at their disposal. 'The good breed of the north' comprised some of the best saddle horses available anywhere in England. The countryside of the Yorkshire dales and of Durham proved ideal territory for raising horses, both by secular and monastic breeders, while the grooms from these same areas earned themselves a country-wide reputation for the attention they lavished on their charges. Daniel Defoe comments that:

> As this part of the country is so much employed in horses, the young fellows are naturally grooms, bred up in the stable, and used to lie among the horses; so that you cannot fail of a good servant here, for looking after horses is their particular delight; and this is the reason why, whatever part of England you go to, though the farthest counties west and south, and whatever inn you come at 'tis two to one but the hostler is a Yorkshire man.

Although the situation described by Defoe is that of the turn of the eighteenth century, the long-term benefits of this sympathetic relationship between man and animal had doubtless contributed significantly to the emergence of this region as prime horse territory from the early medieval period – notably with the contribution of the abbeys of Fountains and Jervaulx.

Mention should also be made of the Cleveland bays, which emerged as the coach-horse of choice for fashionable carriage owners in the eighteenth and nineteenth centuries, displacing the bulkier black horses that had struggled with the heavy vehicles of late Tudor and Stuart date. Commonly the Clevelands appeared not in pure-bred form but crossed with three-quarter or thoroughbred horses: the larger stallions formed, in Youatt's words, 'the coach-horse most in repute, with his arched crest and high action', while from horses of lighter build came 'the four-in-hand and superior curricle horse'.

Wales was also the source of good quality riding horses of moderate size, including the so-called 'merlins' of Monmouthshire, reared in a semi-wild state and sold at three years, while the 'hobbies' of Ireland formed an early reputation for themselves both in civilian life and later as the standard light cavalry mount of the army.

The Midlands area achieved early notice for its 'black horses' from the Trent valley, Derbyshire and elsewhere, which made sturdy farm horses and cavalry mounts; later they would also serve as handsome coach-horses while intensive breeding in the eighteenth century transformed them into the ultimate heavy horse, to become known as the Shire. (The name derives originally, it is suggested, from the 30 shires and other districts in which Henry VIII sought to improve the breed by his legislative measures introduced in 1540: see p. 46.) Defoe wrote of Leicestershire, for example, that:

The horses produced here, or rather fed here, are the largest in England, being generally the great black coach horses and dray horses, of which so great a number are continually brought up to London, that one would think so little a spot as this of Leicestershire could not be able to support them.

Black horses or Shires were extensively cross-bred with other stock, ranging (rather improbably) from the pit-ponies of south Wales, to which they added strength and bulk, to the Clydesdales of south-west Scotland.

The romantic version of the Clydesdale's foundation myth ascribes its rise to a Flemish stallion imported by the 1st Duke of Hamilton in Cromwell's era, but more sober historians are unwilling to venture its origins beyond the early decades of the eighteenth century. At that time two more-firmly documented Flemish horses undoubtedly made a positive impact, one imported c. 1715–20 by John Paterson of Lochlyoch (Lanarkshire), whose stud retained an unrivalled reputation for several generations thereafter, and the other acquired some 30 years later by the 6th Duke of Hamilton, an enlightened landlord who rendered its services free to all his tenants. Individual stallions undoubtedly had it in them to bring about major improvements in the stock of a region well provided with serviceable mares and to become, in Marshall's words, 'a treasure to the whole district', but more significant, perhaps, in the longer term were the larger numbers of black horses from the English Midlands that were interbred so extensively with the Clydesdale population that at times it was difficult tell the two populations apart.

The most noteworthy products of East Anglia were the sorrel horses that began to emerge in the seventeenth century as an already coherent breed that emerged ultimately as the Suffolk Punch. As draught horses they were confined almost entirely to farm work: their stocky fore legs were perfectly proportioned to allow them to throw all their weight into traction, but (perhaps fortunately for them) they were never greatly favoured as dray horses for the town or for coach work – although Arthur Young, who thought they could 'only walk and draw, [and] could trot no better than a cow', noted disapprovingly that by his day (that is, in the 1780s) breeders had taken to selecting them for lightness and good looks, 'for using in coaches and chaises as well as carts'. Mostly, however, they travelled little beyond their native territory, where one strain was recognized on the sandy loams of Norfolk and another – perhaps the definitive type – from the Sandlings of south-east Suffolk.

The native horses of southern England as far north as the Thames were the ancestors of those now confined to the New Forest area – ponies rather than full-sized mounts – so that the development of a vigorous market in horses from other, better provided regions became a matter of necessity in order to answer the more differentiated demands of the growing population of the south-east in particular. The smaller native horses proved well suited to pack work, however, as did their south-westerly cousins on Exmoor.

Perhaps the bulk of the packhorses belonged to the type known as Galloways, named originally for the region of south-west Scotland that produced the best exemplars of the type but ultimately a name applied to much of the pony population of the northern half of England irrespective of their lineage. Defoe waxed lyrical about the qualities of these horses in their native land, where, he asserted,

> they have the best breed of small low horses in Britain, if not in Europe, which we call pads, and from whence we call all small truss-strong riding horses Galloways: these horses

are remarkable for being good pacers, strong, easy goers, hardy, gentle, well broke, and above all, they never tire, and they are very much brought up in England on that account.

HORSE FAIRS AND MARKETS

Throughout much of our period the majority of horses changed hands at regularly constituted horse fairs and markets. In country districts these were likely to be seasonal, but in London a weekly market for horses had been established at Smithfield as early as the twelfth century. William fitz Stephen's description in 1174 alludes to the full range of types regularly traded there, ranging from destriers or warhorses (*dextrarii*), through amblers or pacing horses (*gradarii*) and sumpters (*sumarii*) to modestly priced mares:

> Earls, barons and knights, who are in the town, and many citizens come out to see or to buy. It is pleasant to see the high-stepping palfreys with their gleaming coats, as they go through their paces, putting down their feet alternately on one side together. Next, one can see the horses suitable for esquires, moving faster though less smoothly, lifting and setting down, as it were, the opposite fore and hind feet: here are colts of fine breed, but not yet accustomed to the bit, stepping high with jaunty tread; there are the sumpter horses, powerful and spirited; and after them are the war-horses, costly, elegant of form, noble of stature, with ears quickly tremulous, necks raised and large haunches . . .
>
> By themselves in another part of the field stand the goods of the country folk . . . There also stand the mares fit for plough, some big with foal, and others with brisk young colts closely following them.

Doubtless the practice of horse-trading earned its status as a byword for ruthless bargaining over centuries of shady dealing. Horse-stealing was rife, and every attempt to secure a horse by lodging it with a caretaker or by locking it up with fetters was countered by schemes to circumvent these measures, just as every method of registering the identity of a horse by marking or branding or by cutting distinctive patterns in its ears produced further means to disguise these same features. (Samuel Pepys describes 'a little crop black nag' [that is, one with the points of both ears cut off] recovered after it had been stolen in 1663, 'being found with black cloth eares on and a false mayne, having none of its own'.) Buying a horse on the open market was a risky business throughout the medieval period, and in a series of attempts to control abuses the Tudor monarchs introduced measures that sought to impose tighter controls on the conduct of markets. Under the terms of the Act against the Buying of Stolen Horses (1555) all transactions were required to take place in 'market overt' and all details of the deal had to be entered in a toll-book; to counter clandestine dealings taking place in 'houses, stables, back-sides and other secret and privy places', all horses were now to be 'openly ridden, led, walked, driven or kept standing by the space of one hour together at the least, betwixt ten of the clock in the morning and the sun-setting, in the open space of the fair or market wherein horses are commonly used to be sold'. In a well-tried Tudor ruse, those who denounced the owners of illicit horses could claim half the value of the horse while the other half went to the Crown. The preamble to further measures set out in the Act to Avoid Horse Stealing (1589) acknowledges that, despite previous legislation, 'stealing is grown so common, as neither in pastures or closes, nor hardly in stables, the same [horses] are to be in safety from stealing'; now it was decreed that sellers of horses had to be known to the warden of the market, or had to have witnesses to vouch for them, and that details of the colour and 'one special mark at the least of every the same horses' had to be recorded in the toll-book. While no doubt open to abuse – Anthony Dent observes that almost every one of these provisions gave employment to a range of shady characters eager to alter brands, disguise natural markings or offer themselves as witnesses – these measures did eventually contribute towards the emergence of flourishing horse markets over the following century and more.

The Duke of Newcastle, the greatest English authority on horsemanship in the seventeenth century, singled out in his *New Method, and Extraordinary Invention, to dress Horses* (1667) a number of markets offering horses for a variety of purposes:

if you would buy for the Mannage at Fayrs, you must go to Rowel Fayr, Harborow Fayr, and Melton Fayr, to Northampton and Leicester-shire; but Northampton, they say, is the Best . . . At Molten Fayr, for the most part, they are young Stone-Horses, and some Geldings, but fitter for the Padd, and Hunting, than for the Mannage; Rippon Fayr is but the remnant of Molten Fayr, and commonly but Geldings and Naggs; those Fayrs are in York-shire; Lenton Fayr is in Nottinghamshire, and is a great Fayr of all Sorts of Horses, but especially Geldings and Naggs, Fitter for the Padd, and Galloping, than for the Mannage; you may also find some Stone-Horses there.

His list continues with approbation for Penkridge (Staffordshire), especially for colts and young horses; the many other fairs in 'the Northern Parts' he considers not worth mentioning in detail, but gives general approval to Worcestershire for strong carthorses. In Cornwall, he says, 'there is good Naggs, and in Wales excellent good Ones; but in Scotland the Gallowayes are the best Naggs of them all'. An account of Penkridge fair, recorded by Defoe at the opening of the eighteenth century, gives a vivid impression of the character of these occasions:

> We expected nothing extraordinary; but was I say surpriz'd to the see the prodigious number of horses brought thither, and those not ordinary and common draught-horses, and such kinds as we generally see at country-fairs remote from London: but here were really incredible numbers of the finest and most beautiful horses that can anywhere be seen; being brought hither from Yorkshire, the bishoprick of Durham, and all the horse-breeding countries: we were told that there were not less than an hundred jockies and horse-kopers, as they call them there, from London, to buy horses for sale. Also an incredible number of gentlemen attended with their grooms to buy gallopers, or race-horses, for their Newmarket sport. In a word, I believe I may mark it for the greatest horse-fair in the world, for horses of value, and especially those we call saddle horses, and draught horses; though here were great numbers of fine large stone horses for coaches, &c. too. But for saddle horses, for the light saddle, hunters, pads, and racers, I believe the world cannot match this fair.

In a study of the horse trade in the Midlands in the sixteenth and seventeenth centuries, Peter Edwards observes that the whole area formed a nexus for the movement of horses around much of the country, drawing in young animals from the breeding areas in the north and west in particular and redistributing them among rearers such as those in the Bedfordshire and Hertfordshire areas who trained them up for service in London. More mature horses also passed through the Midlands, with different markets serving different interests: Edwards notes that at Brewood (Staffordshire) in the late seventeenth century a significant majority of both sellers and buyers lived within ten miles of the town, while at Rothwell (Northamptonshire) at the turn of the eighteenth century one-third of the horses sold went directly to London. Just as Penkridge emerged as the principal market for saddle horses (with over half its sales being to dealers in London, especially in the Smithfield area where a market continued to be held weekly as it had been in fitz Stephen's day), Northampton came to be noted as the source of strong carriage- and coach-horses, while Market Harborough and Melton Mowbray (Leicestershire), as well as Northampton and Rothwell, dealt in more utilitarian draught horses. Many smaller markets, operating perhaps fortnightly or monthly, sprang up to satisfy local demands and to act as feeders to the major fairs.

Areas not actively involved in the commercial breeding of horses might none the less take part in rearing foals which were bought and exchanged at fairs such as these. Transactions could take place over considerable distances: Edwards records that, in the seventeenth century, horses bred on the Somerset Levels were being sold in Winchester and bought by dealers in Staffordshire and Leicestershire, at a time when the East Midlands had developed a reputation as the foremost rearing area in the country and was drawing horses too from Yorkshire, East Anglia and Worcestershire.

HORSEGEAR AND STABLES

As well as those who depended directly on riding, working, training or driving horses for their livelihood, a number of secondary crafts and trades depended on the horse population for the livelihood of their practitioners. Amongst the most ubiquitous were the farriers – known as marshals in the medieval period – continually employed in an endless round of shoeing but also expected to be knowledgeable in 'physicking' or maintaining the health of the horse in an era before the emergence of the professional veterinary surgeon.

Shoeing had been practised to some degree in the centuries immediately preceding the Norman conquest but became more widespread thereafter (illus. 3). Although shoes were essential for road work, not every farm horse would be shod and those that were would not necessarily be shod on all four feet: economics had to be balanced against the nature of the terrain on which the horse operated. A set of shoes might cost 6d. or 8d. in the mid-fourteenth century, plus a small charge for each 'remove', a service demanded by an average working horse every two months or so – not necessarily as the shoes had worn out but because they

would no longer fit the horse's continually growing hoof, which had to be pared back to form a well-fitting bed for the shoe. No impecunious peasant would embark on this routine if he could avoid it; he might even alter the shoeing pattern at different times of the year. The service to be rendered by a tenant at Minchinhampton (Gloucestershire) in the fourteenth century, included a statement that 'he keeps shod one horse fore and hind or two horses fore, throughout the year'. John Clark notes that if this were to have been a widespread custom more fore horseshoes should be found than those from the hind feet, but the difficulties of distinguishing one from the other have so far made it impossible to demonstrate that this is the case.

Sufficient horseshoes, however, have been recovered from archaeological contexts for a general typology to have been constructed, although the variety of shoes (many of them designed to remedy or compensate for various faults) contained within Blundeville's *Fower Chiefyst Offices belongyng to Horsemanshippe* (1565) (illus. 4), is wide enough to indicate that our understanding is likely to remain at a rather generalized level for some years to come. Shoes were fitted by means of nails passing through the hoof at an angle and being clenched

3 A marshal (farrier) shoeing a horse, from an English treatise (*c.* 1200–1250) on horse management.

or bent-over (sometimes forming a hook or spiral) on the outside surface; they were removed again by cutting off the clenches and withdrawing the nails. Calkins or thickened terminals of various forms are not uncommon on medieval shoes, but the practice of fullering – forming a medial groove within which the nail-holes are placed – is unknown before the nineteenth century. The nails were commonly forged with 'fiddle-key' heads and the nail-holes counter-sunk to accommodate them: the narrow shoes characteristic of the Norman period are frequently expanded by the punch in the process of counter-sinking, giving them a wavy outline. Later medieval types are wider and flatter and the nails have rectangular or 'eared' heads.

In the countryside and small towns the blacksmith undertook the duties of the farrier, but in the capital and perhaps in other cities the professions were distinct. The London Brotherhood of Farryers, which received its royal charter in 1674, expended considerable energy in defending its territory from the blacksmiths in the city. In truth, both groups shared many of their skills and much of their equipment, though the prudent farrier might invest in a travis (*travellum*), a sturdy wooden framework erected outside his premises within which a restive horse could be confined while undergoing physicking – the administration of drenches, medicines or horse-pills, generally by means of a horn funnel inserted in its mouth – or shoeing.

Saddlers and harness-makers make up the next most widespread craft. The medieval saddle was frequently worn with a breast-band and a crupper in addition to the girth, to stop it sliding forwards or backwards. Surviving early examples tend to be war-saddles made for destriers, with a high pommel and cantle to protect the rider and to hold him securely on his mount: they are built around a wooden framework that elevates the rider from the horse's back (illus. 5). In its ultimate form in the

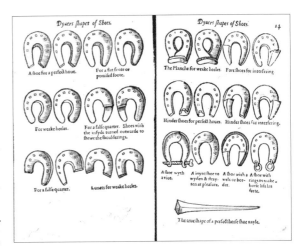

4 'Diverse shapes of Shooes', from Thomas Blundeville's *Fower Chiefyst Offices belongyng to Horsemanshippe* (1565). Starting with 'A shoe for a perfect horse', the author shows something of the variety employed by the farrier to mitigate various faults in the gait.

seventeenth century, the 'great saddle' lost something of its defensive role but continued to enclose the rider, with pads on either side of his leg to hold him in position. The modern form of riding saddle seems to have been well developed by the end of the seventeenth century.

For women the side-saddle was developed – or rather was introduced – towards the end of the fourteenth century when, according to John Stow's *Survey of London*, Anne of Bohemia (Richard II's queen) 'first brought hither the riding upon side saddles'. At first its use was confined to the court, but within a generation side-saddles had become so widespread that, for example, both the prioress and the nun illustrated in the Ellesmere manuscript edition of Chaucer's *Canterbury Tales* (executed c. 1405) are depicted riding in this way (the Wife of Bath, on the other hand, adopts the traditional mode of riding astride: see illus. 6). In the centuries that followed, the adoption of one style of riding or the other was determined according to class: Richard Carew describes the horses of Cornwall at

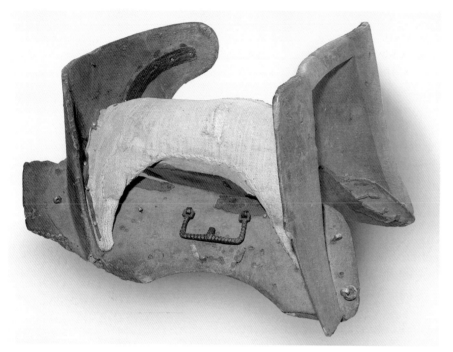

5 Henry v's funeral saddle, preserved at Westminster Abbey. The padded seat is raised clear of the rigid framework, while the high pommel and cantle provide protection for the lower abdomen in front and behind.

the turn of the seventeenth century as being 'shod only before, and for all furniture a pad and halter, on which the meaner country wenches of the western parts do yet ride astride, as all other English folk used before Richard II's wife brought in the side-saddle fashion of straw'.

For the first 200 or 300 years of their currency, side-saddles had neither a horn to support the thigh nor a stirrup on which to brace the foot, but had instead an integral shelf or ledge known as a planchette, on which the rider could rest her right foot. A long saddle-cloth, suspended from under the saddle, protected her dress from being splashed by the horse's hooves. For spouses of a less independent turn of mind, the pillion saddle (also known as a cushion or pad) was developed so that she could ride behind her husband (illus. 7). Once again, a planchette provided the only form of independent support.

Although leather formed the raw material for all good-quality harness in the medieval period, it was by no means uniform in appearance. Black and brown leather would both have been in use, but the best quality harness was more likely to be coloured – usually red – and was often further embellished with rich textile coverings and with decorative gilt-bronze bosses. Harness pendants of cast bronze are also well known, many of them enamelled and heraldic in character, expressing allegiance to one or other of the great households. Spherical bells (rumblers) were in wide circulation, not only amongst those of a gentle and romantic inclination but also on horses of the most mundane kind: carters and wagoners were notably fond of them, while they were a virtual necessity for the owner of a string of packhorses, since these were invariably led by a bell-mare whose tinkling bell unfailingly drew all the other horses in her wake without the need for them to be roped together.

As mentioned elsewhere (p. 15), the breast collar was already coming into use for draught horses by the time of the Norman conquest. In its essentials it probably differed little from the modern collar, except that the hames, the wishbone-shaped framework that takes the load, would invariably have been of wood in early collars, being replaced by metal perhaps as late as the nineteenth century. The long traces by which the leading horses of a team delivered their pulling power were perhaps normally of rope for working teams but could also be of leather. During the latter part of the sixteenth century, the explosive demand for coach-harness lifted a great deal of the harness-maker's craft out of the realm of the carthorse and into that of conspicuous display, where it would remain until the advent of the motor car.

Along with many of the other metal fittings described above, stirrups and bits were produced by a distinct body of craftsmen, the loriners. Originally subservient to the saddlers, the loriners gradually exerted their independence as a separate craft, working both in iron and in bronze. The highly polished nickel surfaces of today's fittings were unknown before the nineteenth century. Everyday riding involved the use of a snaffle-bit, whatever the variety of horse involved. Curb-bits, with trailing arms that cause a loop or port in the centre of the bit to be pressed against the roof of the horse's mouth when the reins are pulled, evolved to incorporate also a curb-chain which passed around the

6 Two female riders illustrated in the Ellesmere edition of Chaucer's *Canterbury Tales* (*c.* 1405) – an invaluable index of horse types at the turn of the 15th century. The Prioress, modest and coy, adopts the fashionable new side-saddle, while the more forthright Wife of Bath rides astride.

7 'A Citicen riding with his Wife': the fashionably dressed rider sits well forward on the withers while his wife perches on a pillion with a foot-cloth below. From the *album amicorum* of Tobias Oelhafen von Schöllenbach (1623–5).

horse's chin and was again constricted by pressure on the reins. Curbs, which could be savagely used in the wrong hands, were adopted primarily for military and ceremonial use as well as for the manège (the arms of the Loriners' Company incorporate 'three manage bits'), but evidently had some wider private use for a fourteenth-century huntsman shown in Queen Mary's Psalter makes use of a curb and it may be that in hunting in general this harsher form of control was more widely used; generally, however, a snaffle was considered adequate for this purpose. In the course of the sixteenth and seventeenth centuries, curbs were produced to increasingly elaborate and baroque designs under the influence of Federigo Grisone and other influential Continental writers; although favoured by sixteenth-century authorities like William Blundeville, they were dismissed a century later by the Duke of Newcastle as 'very Ridiculous'.

Spurs, although part of the horseman's equipment rather than the horse's, were also produced by loriners as well as by specialized spurriers: early examples are invariably prick-spurs, with a single point, while later rowel-spurs evolve into a variety of extravagant forms whose effect on the horse scarcely bears thinking about.

As for their accommodation, little detail has survived concerning the design and fitting out of early stables, although Giles Worsley, who eloquently surveyed their whole history, notes that those of the medieval period could already be as extensive as their more recent successors: Edward I, for example, is recorded as having erected stables for 200 horses at his hunting lodge at Clipstone (Nottinghamshire), while the accommodation for 50 horses at Pickering Castle (Yorkshire), used chiefly as a royal stud, was an impressive 240 feet in length. At the other end of the scale from these luxurious premises would have been structures of the most wretched character, with a continuous spectrum of intermediate types.

With the age of the Tudors and Stuarts the quality of the record improves just as stables and stable practice were being overtaken by a new and more purposeful set of values. Closer thought was given to the design of the building, while the horses began to be provided with individual stalls separated by planking partitions. Hitherto the only barrier between one stall and its neighbour had been a suspended 'bale' or pole, hanging by a rope or a chain from the roof structure or from the wall facing the horse and the heel-post delimiting its territory to the rear. These survived in military stables and in the more extensive commercial stables up to the nineteenth century, but enlightened horse-owners saw that there were advantages in allowing the horses to rest undisturbed by their neighbours; hence the partitions between the stalls were frequently made to sweep up to their maximum height at the horse's head, shielding them from one another's presence. Hay-racks and mangers also became more substantial in design, and floors in the best stables were planked; only in the seventeenth century did paved floors come to be favourably looked upon in stables. Effective drainage, with running water, kept the best establishments more wholesome from the 1600s onwards. For the ordinary working horse, however, these innovations took a long time to filter through. In a description of the typical inn or livery stable at the turn of the nineteenth century, the *Sporting Dictionary* writes:

> Here stand rows of poor patient animals, absolutely fumigated with the perspirative transpiration of their own bodies, broiling with heat, and panting with thirst, in a degree beyond the temperature of a common hothouse, in the severity of the winter season. Each horse is observed to stand upon a load of litter (clean at top, and rotten underneath) very little inferior to a common cucumber-bed in height, with all the advantages of equal warmth from the dung below!

Not every new development worked to good effect. Worsley records that a fashion emerged for constructing stalls with a steep slope to show off the horses to best advantage, a feature deprecated by more enlightened spirits: Markham thought these were 'not to be tolerated in any place but Smithfield and among horse copers', while de Grey asserted that they 'begetteth in the poor beast much paine and griefe', resulting ultimately in the horse going lame.

SADDLE HORSES

The saddle horses on which the bulk of the equestrian population travelled displayed a great deal of variation in conformation and bearing, in accordance with their origins and with the social status of their owners. Up to the period of the Civil War, coursers represented the upper end of the range for the assertive masculine rider, while both sexes opted for the palfrey as the horse of choice for comfortable and stylish travel over any distance.

Most of these everyday riding horses were characterized by one feature that distinguishes them from the vast majority of those encountered today, in that they were trained for the comfort of their passengers not to trot but to amble or pace. (If any distinction can be read into the latter terms, it may be that pacers were capable of a greater turn of speed than amblers, but they moved in an identical manner.) All such horses, whatever their breed, were marked out by their easy-going gait (remarked upon by fitz Stephen in his account of the Smithfield horse fair in the late twelfth century, quoted above), in which first the fore- and hind-leg on one side were moved forward in unison, followed by the legs on the other side similarly swinging forward together – in contrast to the horse's 'normal' gait in which diagonally opposite feet move synchronously. A capacity to amble recommended particular horses for travelling or for a long day's hunting, for both high-born and low, and for women as well as men: the minimal degree of security offered by side-saddles and pillions of the medieval period (having no stirrups) has already been commented on, so that the smoothest possible ride was much to be desired. By the same token, litters (p. 65) were assigned to ambling horses in order to ensure maximum comfort for the occupant. Most ambling horses would never break into a trot – they simply increased their speed while maintaining their much-prized smooth movement – although, as shown below, a capacity both to trot and to amble was positively encouraged by some trainers.

The ambling gait was a capacity common in some horse populations (though absent in others) and was readily passed on by a mare to its foal;

generally it was considered enough for a youngster to follow in its mother's footsteps during the early months of life for it to be permanently endowed with the same means of locomotion. The training of foals in this way was a routine that normally fell to the breeder or rearer, so that most horses were already accustomed to the gait by the time they came on the market. Nicholas Morgan's *Perfection of Horse-manship* (1609) includes the following advice on 'The manner to teach a colt to amble without handling':

> You are to begin the lesson the next day after the [colt] is foaled. Put on a halter on the mare's head: in the morning early lead her forth, let the colt follow her so gently and soft a pace as she can go, into some even, plain and hard ground, and be sure that the colt be not enforced to go faster than you lead the mare, and then observe and you shall find the colt going by her that he doth altogether go and train his legs in an amble. Thus continue leading the mare in soft and slow going about halfe an houre, and the colt himself will not go faster than his dam.

This routine was to be repeated three times a day for ten days,

> and as the colt increaseth in swiftness of pace in his amble, so increase the pace of the mare, and he will amble most swiftly and perfectly: if you begin with that maner aforesaid, and never force him to go faster, use will bring him unto all perfection.

There was a widespread assumption that an ambling mare would produce an ambling foal: the tendency might indeed be inherited, but the process of encouraging imitation as outlined above was important in maintaining it; some horses proved impossible to teach. Having been schooled in this manner, most animals probably went through life knowing no other means of locomotion, but by the sixteenth century, at least, by which time there was, perhaps, a greater degree of confidence among rearers in what they could achieve, it is clear that horses could be persuaded to adopt either form of gait at will. Such is the implication of William Browne's *Fiftie Yeares Practice* (first published in 1574), the lengthy sub-title of which declares it to be useful 'for Trotting and Ambling of all manner of Horses whatsoever, from one degree to another, till they be perfit both for the Trot and the Amble'. Browne shows how a foal that is not itself a natural ambler can be taught how to amble by means of a special harness of straps termed 'traves' or trammels, which link the legs fore and aft on either side, so that only by moving its legs in the prescribed manner could the horse make any progress. With infinite patience and a variety of combinations of trammels (illus. 8), Browne asserts that the horse can be brought to perfection in ambling as well as trotting, so that the rider may decide 'Now I will ride of an ambling horse one mile, and of a trotting horse another mile, and of a galloping horse the third mile.' It is clear that not all horses proved equally versatile, however: Edwards quotes a letter of 1664 from Francis Denzil Holles expressing a need for a new set of 'seaven stone horses' for his

coach, stipulating that all should 'trot and not amble' as one of his current team persisted in doing. Rising demand for trotting horses for harness work may have been one of the factors leading to the ultimate demise of the ambler.

A further family of easy-going horses progressed by means of racking rather than pacing, a system in which the feet were advanced one at a time in sequence around the body, again holding their rhythm while increasing their speed. Like the amblers, these mounts were particularly suited to purposes requiring a smooth gait, such as conveying produce to market in panniers or carrying a lady on a side-saddle or pillion. References to racking are encountered only infrequently in the literature, so that it would seem to have been more limited in use.

Saddle horses which trotted in the manner most prevalent today were, it seems, in a minority throughout the medieval period, but by the fifteenth century they were beginning to displace the pacing and racking types and had acquired a name of their own – hackneys – a term that evolved with their increasing popularity to take on the meaning simply of an everyday riding or road horse.

8 Stages in the instruction of a horse learning to amble, with the aid of trammels. From William Browne, *Fiftie Yeares Practice* (1624).

HORSES FOR CROWN AND COUNTRY

During the centuries following the Norman invasion, in which feudal custom stressed the importance of the mounted warrior and in which the supply of horsemen formed a primary contractual mechanism for the expression of allegiance between landholder and overlord, mounts for military use formed the supreme creatures in the hierarchy of horses. In a very real sense, horses formed the common currency on which the feudal system operated, for grants of land from the Crown commonly came not merely with generalized obligations but with specific quotas for the supply of cavalry being imposed by the monarch on his barons and by them in turn on their tenants – all in the interests of national security.

With their larger and more powerful mounts shipped over from the Continent, the Norman overlords not only sent out powerful signals of their dominance but also showed the way to future improvement by means of crossing native horses with fresh blood from the European mainland, a process that was at first confined to the production of increasingly impressive chargers but which, after several centuries, began to filter down to saddle horses in general and latterly to draught horses up and down the roads and fields of the British Isles.

From the closing decades of the thirteenth century the strategic necessity of a reliable supply of warhorses was recognized and a formalized breeding programme was implemented, based on a network of estates belonging to the royal castles that spanned the country. Among the primary duties of the constable (originally the *Comes stabuli*) of each castle was the requirement that he should keep a number of brood mares (usually numbering about two dozen) on the estate, to be served by selected royal stallions that were rotated at intervals from stud to stud. As a result of these measures, reserves of good-quality horses were built up, although they were always liable to be jeopardized by losses in military campaigns that might take years to make good.

Attempts to maximize the potential of the native stock came comparatively late in the day, however, and all early efforts to bring about improvement were conducted on the basis of cross-breeding with imported horses. While the countries immediately across the Channel provided some of the livestock through which these strategies were implemented, the history of the horse is remarkable for the extraordinary lengths to which breeders were willing to go in order to achieve their objectives. In time these efforts brought about improvements to the point where British horses would be counted amongst the more desirable in Europe.

THE DESTRIER

The true nature of the destrier or 'great horse' (a term that first appears at the end of the thirteenth century) has been much disputed: current opinion characterizes it as a more modestly proportioned animal than the veritable heavy horse of 17 or 18 hands envisaged by earlier historians: while contemporary manuscript illustrations seem to support such a heroic stature (illus. 9), other less overtly hagiographical images show horses generally standing at about shoulder height to their riders – that is to say, about 15 hands. Confirmation of these more modest estimates has been provided by Ann Hyland through measuring surviving horse armours from the Tudor period. This is not to deny that sustained efforts were made throughout the medieval period to maximize size, but it is significant that when Henry VIII sought to give them the force of law he settled for a realistic minimum of only 15 hands for stallions. The greatness of the great horse, therefore, was to be found in its

9 Sir Geoffrey Luttrell, mounted on his fully caparisoned destrier, towers over his diminutive wife. Dramatic licence has here obscured the fact that most warhorses were more modestly proportioned. From the Luttrell Psalter (*c.* 1340).

bearing, its noble breed and bloodline, rather than in outright size. Those bred in England ultimately shared most of their genes with the general type familiar across the Channel and the North Sea, though with a reputation for being deficient in the speed and stamina of the best Continental horses.

The destrier was essentially a specialized warhorse, chosen for its ability not only to convey its rider in an appropriately heroic manner but also to lend its weight to the charge and to batter, bite and kick its way into the enemy lines – hence the premium placed on its overt masculinity: every warhorse was a stallion throughout virtually the whole of the medieval period. Such an assertive creature could be a liability off the battlefield and hence it was customary for even the most highborn horseman to make use of an altogether different type of animal for his everyday conveyance, while his charger was preserved for its primary role: even on its way to the field of battle it would have been led rather than ridden, with its own armour carried by a packhorse.

Once on the battlefield the destrier carried a considerable load, not only in the form of the fully armoured knight – initially clad in a heavy mail shirt (hauberk) and great helm, and later in overall plate armour – but also its own metal armour. Davis notes a reference to 200 horses captured by Richard I from the French as early as 1198 of which 140 were already 'clad in iron'. Horse armour became increasingly heavy and more elaborate in the later medieval period, bringing about a demand for correspondingly heavier and stronger horses. A full set of armour (which no doubt comparatively few horses ever wore) would include a shaffron to protect the face, a crinet for the neck, a peytrel or bard for the forequarters and a crupper for the hindquarters – not to mention steel plates reinforcing the reins and other exposed elements of the harness.

Needless to say, early attempts at engineering improvements in the conformation of the warhorse were hampered by a lack of understanding of the first principles on which modern breeders operate. There was a general belief, for example, that only the male horse contributed any qualities to the characteristics of the offspring: the mare was merely the vehicle by which it was brought into the world. The degree to which this misconception held back progress can only be guessed at, but it may be contrasted with the attitude adopted by the Moorish owners of the Barbary horses (Barbs) after which the English lusted so passionately in the sixteenth and seventeenth centuries, for they were resolute in their unwillingness to part with mares. Virtually all the influence wrought by Barbs in England was brought to bear through the male line and the principal fruits of their blood were manifested in first-generation crosses, beyond which any benefit passed on to succeeding generations would have been highly unstable. If there were widely held beliefs about the processes involved in selecting desirable characteristics they were unscientific in the extreme: as with every aspect of life and every other animal, there was a general acknowledgement that astrology played perhaps the defining role in deciding matters of

gender and character for the foal, according to the phase of the moon during conception. These remained as widely held beliefs up to the sixteenth century and were not wholly eradicated before the Enlightenment.

IMPORTED HORSES UP TO THE TUDOR PERIOD

Recognition of the superior quality of the best animals from continental Europe and of their potential for improving English stock can be detected from the earliest phases of the medieval period. Undoubtedly the Crown played the major role, first of all taking the lead in importing animals for cross-breeding and later by setting up more formal networks in order to ensure a continuing and reliable supply of the best quality warhorses. No doubt the bulk of these were initially acquired by way of France, while the Norman conquest of Sicily, begun in 1061 and completed in 1091 (and which also brought with it territories in Puglia and Calabria), opened up an awareness of the qualities of horses from the Mediterranean and provided a channel through which Arab and North African blood would begin to flow directly to the studs of northern Europe. It is also noteworthy that for 300 years, from the mid-twelfth to the mid-fifteenth century, the English Crown held the duchy of Aquitaine, which territory lay on the threshold of Spain, providing access to another primary source of precious horseflesh.

That the lords and barons were no less eager than the Crown to improve their stock is confirmed by a reference in Giraldus Cambrensis who, in 1188, found to the south of Lake Bala (Merioneth) a number of 'most excellent studs put apart for breeding, and deriving their origin from some fine Spanish horses', imported by Robert de Belême, Earl of Shrewsbury. Undoubtedly the Earl would have had no thought of sharing this precious blood with his turbulent neighbours in the Marches, although Davis suggests that the 'Powys horse' which gained such a favourable reputation in the course of the following century may ultimately have drawn something of their breeding from these superior animals.

From the reign of King John (1199–1216) there survives a record of 100 stallions of large stature being imported from the Low Countries and in the course of the following two centuries there are repeated references to imports of prized heavy horses from northern Italy, Brabant and Germany. In terms of their bulk and strength, these approached most closely the ideal of the medieval charger and perhaps contributed most to the evolution of the 'great horse' of the battlefield. When in 1232 three 'horses from Lombardy' came on the market in London, Henry III was alert to their value and immediately took steps to recruit the mayor and aldermen in his determination to acquire them; a further record from 1359 mentions 48 horses being bought by Edward III from a named Lombard dealer. These reports should be regarded as chance survivals from more regular importations of stallions in particular, that must have gone a considerable way to maintaining the high quality of the stock in the royal stables.

Under Edward I the framework of a purposeful programme began to emerge, with 158 horses being imported through Wissant and Dover for the king and with 45 others approved for importation by the barons. Edward I invested freely in his studs until he was forced to curtail his spending, but under Edward II a new impetus was launched. Even before he acceded to the throne, Edward had acquired the Earl of Warenne's stud at Ditchling (Sussex); thereafter Davis finds him sending another Lombard merchant, William Persona, to buy stallions and mares in Lombardy, and William de Toulouse to Spain in search of 30 destriers. Further expansion took place under Edward III

with more horses brought from Spain until, with an alliance drawn up between the Castilians and the French in 1342, this source declined in favour of the Low Countries and Lombardy.

Many of these gains were in any case definitively dissipated in the course of the 30-year carnage of the Wars of the Roses, which racked the country between 1455 and 1485 and devastated the stock of horses, with the result that when Henry VII, the first monarch of the Tudor dynasty, came to power in 1485, the quality of English mounts stood once again at a low ebb.

From the time of Henry VIII (illus. 10), a somewhat altered perspective emerges. Certainly, the heavy horses of northern Europe continued to maintain their appeal, notably with two of the most sought-after heavier breeds: German horses known to the English as Almaines – 'comonly a great horse, & thoughe not finely, yeat very strongly made' according to Thomas Blundeville, '& therefore more meete for the shocke [of battle] then to passe a cariere' – and the Flanders horse, which, 'in his shape, disposition, and pace, differeth in a maner nothinge from the Almayne horse: saving that for the most parte he is of a greater stature and more puissant'. An influx in 1544 that must surely have made an impact was a consignment of 200 Flanders mares, destined, presumably, for the royal stud. At the same time, however, a more intense interest manifests itself in horses from the Mediterranean. At his marriage to Katherine of Aragon in 1509, Henry VIII had solicited his new father-in-law for a Spanish, a Neapolitan and a Sicilian horse, demonstrating an interest in testing lighter, more agile and swifter animals – coursers rather than destriers – instead of the heavy cavalry mounts that hitherto had formed the principal focus of English desires. There was nothing frivolous in this new taste, however, for they still made formidable warhorses: in his league table of horses 'mete to

10 A meeting in 1513 on the field in France between the young King Henry VIII and Emperor Maximilian I, c. 1545, oil on canvas. The warhorses are accoutred in the ultimate development of plate armour, but the solid squares of pikemen behind signal the imminent end of heavy cavalry as an unstoppable force.

serve in the fielde', for example, Blundeville places the Neapolitan stallion in the first place.

Three primary sources can be identified for this new style of mount that came to obsess the Court. As early as 1517 Sir Griffith Donne was dispatched to Turkey in search of mares for the King: Henry's long-term ambitions are made clear in his choice of mares in particular, since these would have had no other function than to breed. Although 'Turkey horses' were considered by Blundeville to be 'indifferent fayre to the eie', rather small and not very strongly made, yet he estimated them 'very light and swyfte in their running and of gret courage'. Arab horses, principally from Syria and the Levant, were equally prized for their beauty and speed, as well as their courage. Virtually every Arab horse arriving in England in the Tudor period was a stallion, since the mares were never sold. Barbary horses were perhaps the most sought-after of all, being esteemed by Blundeville as 'excellently well breathed, & thereby are bothe able to

mayntayne a very long cariere, and also to abyde anye kind of laboure & travayle'; importantly, they also made excellent cavalry horses.

The earlier contribution of Barbary blood in particular to the development of the Neapolitan courser elevated Italian horses to a position of especial admiration. As well as coming directly from Naples and Sicily, many of the most outstanding Italian horses reaching England during the reign of Henry VIII came from the Gonzaga stables at Mantua, which were similarly heavily penetrated by Turkish, Arab and especially Barbary blood. In 1514 alone the English sources mention a particularly valuable consignment of twelve Mantuan brood mares secured for Henry's stud, while records for the same year in the Mantuan archives speak of four horses, individually named and described as 'the flower of our stables', which received an ecstatic welcome from Henry at Eltham Palace. Soon he was again making importunate demands for fresh blood, as when Federico II Gonzaga was approached by Gregory Casalis on the King's behalf in search of mares and stallions with which to establish in England a breeding population of Barbary horses.

Continuing to rival the Italians in refinement and mettle were the Spanish horses known to the English as genets (or jennets) and now called Andalusians, of which race the most esteemed specimens came from the royal stud at Cordova. English hostilities with Spain in the latter part of the sixteenth century placed a limit on the numbers of these horses that might then be obtained, however, although under the Stuarts these difficulties would evaporate, leading in 1623 to a personal visit to the Spanish court by the future Charles I (then Prince of Wales), primarily with a view to winning the hand of the Infanta: although his marriage plans came to naught, the prince was consoled on his return by some 60 of the prized Spanish horses and his Master of the Horse (the Duke of Buckingham) with a further 30.

Within the narrow circle of the court, the royal stud provided a focus for the efforts at improvement by judicious breeding strategies involving horses from these varying origins. The stud system was thoroughly reformed by Henry VIII, who concentrated his resources at a few specialized centres, most notably Hampton Court (Middlesex), Eltham (Kent), Malmesbury (Wiltshire) and Tutbury (Staffordshire). It was here that these immigrant horses could make their most lasting impact on the native stock and concerted efforts were made to conserve and to perpetuate the benefits of their several bloodlines. A survey of the studs at Malmesbury and Tutbury carried out by Prospero d'Osma in 1576 reveals a high proportion of horses with Neapolitan, Spanish, Barbary and Turkish blood in their veins amongst both the mares at stud and the stallions which served them.

Not everyone was convinced of the wisdom of these strategies. Richard Holinshed in his *Chronicles* of 1586 took a dim view of 'such outlandish horsses as are dailie brought over unto us': Henry VIII's 'noble studderie' had for a time 'verie good success with them', he tells us, 'till the officers waxing wearie, procured a mixed brood of bastard races, whereby his good purpose came to little effect'. D'Osma, too, had no very high opinion of such 'bastard horses'. There is indeed noteworthy evidence, as surmised by Malacarne, that the most prized horses bred in England at this time were of pure oriental parentage rather than of mixed race.

The principal test of Henry VIII's efforts to elevate the quality of the royal horses came not on the battlefield but in 1520 at the lavish, extended tournament between the English and French courts, staged in a splendid temporary encampment in the Pas-de-Calais, which has entered the history books as the Field of Cloth of Gold (illus. 11). Here Henry and his arch-rival François I measured themselves against each other over the space of eleven days, the two kings and their courtiers striving to outdo each other in feats of arms, courtly refinement and conspicuous consumption. Horses featured largely in these manoeuvrings, matched against each other for bearing and performance, decked out in the most magnificent manner, displayed proudly at one moment and given away or exchanged the next in elaborate displays of largesse: any expression of admiration from one side tended to be met (according to Russell) with the animal in question immediately being relinquished by the other. In preparation for the event the Netherlands had again been scoured by English agents in search of outstanding mounts; Henry himself was well supplied for the occasion with Neapolitan and Mantuan horses, while François too was mounted on Mantuan stock. However magnificent the mounts brought with them by the

English on that occasion (and Edwards observes that the royal party had a staggering 3,000 or more horses in its train), they can scarcely have returned any the worse for these encounters and every effort would have been made to capitalize on the new blood in the studs at home.

Within two years these short-lived fraternal relations between England and France were a thing of the past and the ensuing hostilities greatly inflated the demand for cavalry mounts. The equine reserves of southern England were once again drained during Henry's reign and the north too was greatly impoverished, in the process nullifying much of what might have been achieved by way of improvement. In this context continental Europe came increasingly to be viewed as an inexhaustible reservoir from which replacements could be purchased to compensate for the wastage of native beasts. On one occasion in 1544 the Queen Regent of the Netherlands received a demand for 4,100 draught horses, which she was asked somewhat brusquely to deliver to Calais for shipment to England within six days. Within a month a further 7,200 draught horses were required from her by Henry, again to be delivered to Calais. In the end he received 9,600 horses from his hard-pressed ally, but only at the cost of catastrophically depleting the domestic resources of her own territory: further requests made two years later were met with the response that there were simply no more horses to be had there.

Some of these animals may never have left the garrison in France, but others were undoubtedly intended for shipment to England. Amongst the latter, some part would have been pressed into immediate service as working horses but others were certainly destined for the stud. On one occasion a consignment of 200 mares destined for England got caught up in diplomatic wrangling: such a large number was clearly extraordinary, causing the

Queen Regent to assert that their loss was likely to 'strip the country, which partly depends upon the rearing of horses and would easily be deprived of them if they could be carried away which from all time has been strictly forbidden'. The fact that the mares had already been assembled at Calais before knowledge of Henry's intentions reached her caused further irritation to the Queen Regent, as did intelligence that the ships she had sent to transport the King's army had already illicitly carried off some 700 mares, numbers of which were not yet even of serviceable age. Other records of this period contained in the *Letters and Papers of Henry VIII* show horses being sought as far away as Speyer and Kassel.

The importance to the English of these fresh resources and the low ebb to which the protracted hostilities had brought the native stock are underlined in a report sent from France to the Council, dated 1544, in which the complaint was made that the draught horses sent from England were by then 'so evil' that it took fourteen or fifteen of them to draw a single wagon. This was where the Flanders horses in particular made such an outstanding contribution. The mares, according to Blundeville, were of 'a great stature, stronge, longe, large, fayre and fruytfull, and besydes that, will endure great labour, as is wel seene, for that the Fleminges do use none other draught, but with those mares in their wagons, in whiche I have sene twoo or three Mares to go lyghtly away with suche a burthen, as is almost incredible'. Small wonder that Henry was prepared to resort to deception in order to obtain them.

For the remainder of the sixteenth century and up to the period of the Civil War, perceptions remained unchanged that for good warhorses as well as sumpters (or packhorses) high-grade European stallions were needed for crossing with English mares. The list of breeds admired by contemporaries such as Markham includes Hungarian, Italian, French,

11 Henry VIII and his entourage enter the Field of Cloth of Gold, 1520 (detail). British School, *c.* 1545, oil on canvas.

Swiss, Polish, and Flemish as well as Irish, with little confidence being placed on native stock. Not until the era of the Duke of Newcastle in the following century would equestrian opinion begin to acknowledge the qualities of the stock at hand – even if it had by now, in his words, been 'Bred out of all the Horses of all Nations'.

MEASURES TO IMPROVE NATIVE HORSES

It would be false to suggest that no account was taken under the Tudors of the equine resources of England and indeed the sheer numbers of horses required for daily life and for military adventures abroad meant that any impact made by foreign imports was likely to remain superficial or patchy at best. The generally low opinions passed on English horses at the higher end of the market also need to be balanced against the evidence that everyday working horses were sufficiently well regarded on the Continent for there to be a continuous drain on resources to satisfy a fairly buoyant export trade. When the Crown came to take steps to improve this situation it did so both by seeking to control the outflow of horses and later to improve the quality of those that remained.

First among these measures was the Acte agaynst transportinge of Horses and Mares beyounde ye Seas of 1495 which acknowledged the poor standards and high prices that had resulted from an unregulated export trade and now prohibited the export of mares under three years of age or above the value of 6s. 8d., and male horses of any value whatever. This new measure evidently was less than wholly effective, for under Henry VII's successor it had to be re-enacted in 1530–31, when it was recognized that due to the continuing and illicit conveyance of great numbers of animals out of the country 'the good brede of Horses of this Realme is greatly decayed'. A further Act of 1531–2 directed these measures more specifically against Scotland – still an independent and volatile neighbour: here the export of a 'greate multitude' of mounts was recognized not only as having brought 'strength and boldnesse to the Scottisshemen' but also as bringing about 'a greate enfebling of the Kinges said subjectes' in the defence of the realm.

Right-minded citizens were encouraged to profit from seizures made in enforcing these measures, the normal formula being that 'the moytie or one halff of the price of the said Horse Gelding or Mare shalbe to the use of the seysour and arrestour of the same . . . and the other Moitie to the Kinges Highnes'. Further re-enactments followed in 1540, in 1547 and in 1558–9, while in 1562–3 new legislation repealed provisions that had allowed the export of certain horses for private use abroad provided they were not sold, since 'many evill disposed persons of a covetous and gredy desire doo daylie transporte out of this Realme verye greate nombres of Horses and Geldinges, and doo exchange and sell the same in parties beyond the Seas for their owne pryvate Lucre and Gayne'.

Henry VIII had introduced further measures that sought both to increase the numbers and to improve the quality of serviceable horses throughout the land. His Acte concerning the Breade of Horsys of 1535–6 recalled (perhaps over-optimistically) the 'swyfte and strong Horsis whiche here to fore have benne bredde in this Realme', but acknowledged that due to the fact that 'commonly little Horses and Naggis of small stature and valeu be suffered to depasture & also to covour marys and folys of very small stature, by reason whereof the brede of good & strong Horsis of this Realme is nowe lately dymynyshid alterid & decayed & farther is lyke to decaye if spedy remedye be not the soner providid in that behalfe'. By way of response, the Act decreed that all owners of game parks 'enclosid with hedge diche walle or pale' to the extent of one mile in compass, should henceforth keep 'two Mares being not spayed apte and able to beare foles, each of them of the altitude or height of xiij handfulles at the lest'. Landowners of parks of four miles compass or above had to keep four such mares and no owner was to allow the said mares 'to be covered or lepte with any stonid [ungelded] horse under the stature of xiiij handfulles'. Owners in the northern counties of Westmorland, Cumberland, Northumberland and Durham were exempt from these measures.

Also excluded from these controls were the vast majority of horses, pastured by their owners on common ground up and down the land. A new statute 'For bryde of Horses' of 1540 brought these animals under control by recognizing 'that in forrestis chaces moores marrishes hethis Comons and Wasted groundis . . . little stoned horses and nagges of small stature and of little value' were wont to 'cover and leape mares feading there, whereof cometh in maner no profitte nor commodity'. Thereafter no stoned horse over the age of two years and under the height of 15 hands (14 hands in some counties) was allowed to be so pastured. Subjects suspecting that certain horses might fail to meet these requirements could report them to the king's officers and, if found to be justified, could seize the horses for their own purposes. The provisions were to be further enforced by annual 'drifts' of all such territories, during which any mares, fillies, foals or geldings thought 'not able or like to growe to be able to beare fooles of reasonable stature or not hable or like to grow to be hable to doo profitable labours' were to be culled. These drifts were already part of the established practice of forest regulation, during which, as recorded by Manwood, 'The Officers of the Kings Forest do use to Drive the Waste soil of the Forest in every place where there is commoning with Beasts, to the intent to avoid the surcharging of the same with many Beasts by those that have right of common therein, and also to avoid the commoning of foreigners, that have no right of common at all within the Forest'. Now the owning or putting out to pasture 'any horse gelding or mare infect with scabbe or mange' was similarly prohibited.

In the preamble to the 'Bill for great Horses' of 1541–2 the claim is made that as a consequence of the measures introduced in 1535–6 'ther is begon a good nombre of brede of horses whiche by contynuance is like in shorte tyme muche to encreace for the suer defence of this Realme'. Henceforward, to ensure the continuing generation of horses 'hable for the Warres', every archbishop and duke was required to maintain seven 'stoned trotting horses for the sadill' of at least fourteen hands; marquises, earls and bishops with bishoprics worth £1,000 a year had to maintain five such horses; bishops, viscounts and barons with estates worth 1,000 marks or more three horses and all those with estates of 500 marks or more two horses; those with estates worth £100

or more 'and every other person temporall not afore mencyoned whos Wiff . . . shall were any goun of sylke or . . . any Frenche hood or bonnet of Velvett, wt any habiliment past or egge of gold perle or Stone or any chayne of gold about ther nekks or in their partletts or in any apparell of their bodie', had to endure the further expense of keeping one such horse. The Bill concludes by stressing that 'cart horses or sumpter horses shall not be takyn reputed or recknd' for any of the horses specified in the regulations.

Perhaps as a result of the depredations made by Henry's foreign adventures (mentioned above), little progress seems to have been detectable in the decade following his death – at least if we are to believe the testament of the Venetian ambassador. The *Calendar of State Papers Venetian* records that in writing of Britain to his Senate in 1557, Giovanni Michiel reported that:

> that island produces a greater number of horses than any other region in Europe; but the horses being weak and of bad wind, fed merely on grass, being like sheep and all other cattle kept in the field or pasture at all seasons, the mildness of the climate admitting of this, they cannot stand much work and they would do much better if they were fed.

Twenty years later the Neapolitan Prospero d'Osma, brought in to survey the royal studs maintained by Elizabeth I, found that even there the brood mares were woefully malnourished. From d'Osma's survey (published *in extenso* by Prior) it is clear that there had not yet emerged in England – even within the royal stables – an appreciation that all the careful breeding in the world would fail to produce horses capable of reaching their full potential unless they received a well-balanced diet. In other ways too the English appeared backward in

Continental eyes in their lack of appreciation of the essentials of good management: in 1511, for example, Polydor Vergil had written to the Marquis of Mantua of the difficulties of finding good horses in England, due to their frequently being spoiled by being trained too early and worked too hard. It takes five years for a filly to reach maturity and six for a colt, but all too commonly their adult lives began two or three years before these ideal times.

Although much of Henry's legislation remained in place for the next century or so, not all of his measures proved universally sustainable. In 1566, for example, a new Act recognized that some of his regulations had brought 'great and manyfold Hurtes and Hinderaunces and Losses' to the inhabitants of the fens around the Isle of Ely, Cambridge and Huntingdon, 'for that the saide Mores Maryshes and Fenne Groundes, because of their rottennesse infirmness moysture and wateryshnes, were never able ne yet are to breede beare or bringe foorthe suche great breede of stoned Horses of such bignesse and heigh Stature as wthin thaforesayd Statute are expressed, wthout daunger and peryll of the mireyng drowning and perishing of the same'. Accordingly, the measures were repealed for the said counties, although stoned horses pastured on open ground there had to be at least thirteen hands in stature.

In other ways the Elizabethan administration tightened its control on the equine population by instituting six-monthly musters of horses and geldings apt for war service and by appointing a Special Commission for the Increase and Breed of Horses to oversee its implementation. Its operation depended on the appointment of a large number of sub-commissioners who, on a given day, were responsible for reviewing simultaneously all the horses in every county.

The long-term effectiveness of all of these measures is most eloquently witnessed by the rising demand for British horses from the Continent. Large numbers of them continued to be shipped from Rye, Dover and Sandwich – many of them without official sanction or record – and the government, after years of trying to suppress this irregular trade, decided instead by the mid-seventeenth century that 'if restraints were taken away and customs made easy, it would advance trade and manufacture'. Consequently, from 1 January 1657 horses could be freely exported at specified customs rates; thereafter exports flourished, with some 500 horses a year passing out through the port of Sandwich alone.

GENTLEMEN PENSIONERS AND ITALIAN RIDING MASTERS

As far-reaching as the efforts to improve the physical lot of horses in the sixteenth century may have been, the changes of attitude brought to bear in the breeding and more particularly the training of horses represent an equally significant revolution, bringing about a set of more mature and thoughtful attitudes than hitherto had been manifested in England. Once again the impetus for some of these improvements would come from the Continent, and particularly from Italy and France. Their successful reception, however, depended on the presence of a community that was both sympathetic and independently knowledgeable – a role performed in particular by a body set up by Henry VIII under the name of the Gentlemen Pensioners.

Amongst the properties that fell to the Crown at the dissolution of the monasteries from the 1530s onwards was a huge acreage of former monastic parkland and, in a carefully thought through policy, large tracts of it were redistributed amongst the Gentlemen Pensioners (who were 50 in number), with a clear mandate that the estates in question should be dedicated specifically to boosting the numbers of horses available for royal service. This body had a further role in serving as intermediaries between the king and the gentry in ensuring that the wider national policies with regard to horses, as outlined above, were duly fulfilled. The generous grants of land they received and their closeness to the court rendered them instantly influential and effective as instruments of royal policy, and it is a measure of their well-judged professionalism that this body became so closely identified with a rise not only in the numbers of horses available to the Crown but also in the introduction to England of new attitudes to all aspects of horsemanship.

The ultimate source of these innovative responses can be traced to the books on horsemanship that had begun to emerge on the Continent from the turn of the fifteenth century and which from the mid-1500s came thick and fast. The principles of horsemanship which they embodied, together with novel attitudes to rearing and training, carried messages unfamiliar to English ears concerning the achievements that could be made in training horses. (The – principally Italian – authors from whom these writers drew their inspiration were in turn indebted to classical sources stretching back to Vegetius and ultimately to Xenophon, so that the revival of interest in equestrianism may be seen essentially as an aspect of Renaissance culture.) In turn, these attitudes were promulgated in a number of books that emerged from the circle of the Gentlemen Pensioners, all of them showing an indebtedness to some degree – a debt they were eager to acknowledge – to the Italian masters who came to be recognized as the arbiters of equine fashion. The latter included several experts employed at various times in the royal stables and in the households of the English nobility, including Alexander de Bologna (a pupil of the acknowledged master Federigo Grisone),

Jacques de Granada and Matthew de Mantua, brought to England by Henry VIII; Sir Philip Sidney brought over two more to instruct his nephew (later the Earl of Pembroke); Robert Dudley, Earl of Leicester and Master of the Horse, brought Claudio Corte for a year; and Lord Walden brought one 'Hannibal of Naples', a skilled farrier. Influential as they undoubtedly were, especially in the introduction of fashionable styles of riding, by no means all of the wisdom committed to print from the mid-sixteenth century onwards was dependent on the example set by the Italians: Grisone and de Bologna in particular were singled out by the English writers for the cruel methods by which they achieved results, whereas a great deal of the English writing from this era stresses the benefits to be gained from sympathetic and sensitive treatment rather than from unbending discipline and harshness.

A prime example amongst the Gentlemen Pensioners is formed by Nicholas Arnold of Highnam (Gloucestershire), recorded as having imported horses from Flanders in 1546, having travelled to Italy in the reign of Edward VI and thereafter as having kept in his own stables a stud of Neapolitan horses for war service. Arnold is said not only to have bred the best horses in England but also to have written a tract on the manner of their breeding and care: his manuscript has not survived but, as Joan Thirsk observes, it is almost certain that some of his wisdom is incorporated in the books of the next generation of Pensioners.

The first-published of these tracts, titled *The Art of Riding*, appeared *c.* 1560 under the authorship of Thomas Blundeville, a Norfolk gentleman who had spent his youth at court. His work is part translation and part adaptation of Grisone's *Gli ordini di cavalcare* (1550), but Blundeville found Grisone 'a far better doer than a writer' and incorporated many additions of his own. His volume owed its appearance to William Cecil (later Lord Burghley), who read it in draft. Blundeville next published a larger work, *The Fower Chiefest Offices belongyng to Horsemanshippe* (1565), made 'more perfecte' by adding new sections on each of the 'offices' concerned – those of the 'Breeder, of the Ryder or Breaker, of the Keeper, and of the Ferrer'. It was less reliant on Grisone or on the 'most excellente Ryder, called Maister Claudio Corte', but gathered material from 'a great nombre of [other] Authors, whose sayinges and experiences' were combined with 'mine owne small knowledge gotten by travelling in forreine countreies' and adapted (as he emphasized) to English conditions. Above all it abhorred the use of force in training, recommending instead gentle handling and sympathetic treatment.

In 1584 John Astley, whose father had been a Gentleman Pensioner in Henry VIII's day, produced a new text with the same title – *The Art of Riding* (1584). His text was prepared in consultation with the other Pensioners, including his friend Blundeville; Astley too combined the fruits of his own long experience with a close reading of Grisone and lessons gained directly from Alexander de Bologna. His text, addressed 'To our verie loving Companions, and fellowes in Armes, her Majesties Gentlemen Pensioners: and to the gentle Reader whosoever', acknowledges that there were by his day two kinds of 'service in the warre or field on horsebacke': 'the one in troops and companies, and those be likewise of two sortes, either in the maine battell, or skirmish: the other, when men being singled out by chance or of set purpose, meete & fight hand to hand, which is most proper to this art'. The first was certainly the order of the day in the sixteenth century, with single hand-to-hand combat by now reduced to a fiction that would be played out in the formalized setting of the tournament rather than the battlefield, even if it continued to preoccupy the authors of these volumes.

Also in 1584 yet another volume with the title *The Art of Riding* appeared, compiled by Thomas Bedingfield at the instigation of Henry Mackwilliam (both Gentlemen Pensioners) and comprising a translation of Claudio Corte's *Il cavalerizzo* (1573).

Gervase Markham, one of the most prolific and popular writers of his day, was not himself a Gentleman Pensioner although one of his forebears, Henry Markham, had been so appointed under Henry VIII. In his youth Markham had served some time in the household of the Earl of Rutland, where he had gained his knowledge of horses, supplemented with a course of training at Thomas Story's riding school at Greenwich, which was staffed by several celebrated Italian riders. Markham committed his accumulated knowledge to print with his *Discourse on Horsemanshippe* (1593), which he reworked more successfully in the popular *Cavelarice, or the English Horseman* (1607).

Together, these widely circulated printed works disseminated to a national audience an appreciation of the finer points of horsemanship that increasingly would be counted amongst the unmistakable marks not only of professional cavalrymen but of gentlemen at large.

THE REFORM OF THE CAVALRY

Although they long held iconic and heroic status, heavily armoured and caparisoned to match the display of their knightly riders, it may be emphasized that 'great horses' never formed more than one component (albeit the most important) of the medieval battle-group: Dent and Goodall have calculated that for every warhorse in the front line, up to five further mounts would have been engaged in supporting it, including a second destrier held in reserve for the knight, a palfrey for him to ride whenever the army was on the march, a cob or rouncy as a mount for his squire while leading one or both of the knight's horses, and perhaps two sumpters to carry the heavy armour for man and horse whenever they were not engaged in combat. The immediate preamble to an engagement would therefore be marked by a considerable amount of frenetic re-equipping by all those concerned.

None of these mounts were interchangeable in their functions and all would in turn be dependent on further pack- and carthorses carrying stores and provisions, tents, kitchen equipment and the other paraphernalia without which any body of fighting men would quickly grind to a halt. Horses involved in military expeditions at any given moment, therefore, were liable to be of a variety of kinds.

Of course, not everyone observed the formal etiquette of the battlefield. The Scots, for example, made early use of mounted infantry in order to harass their better mounted English opponents while they were on the move and hence not fully equipped. These guerrilla tactics proved highly effective and frequently allowed the attackers to make their escape without getting involved in full-scale set-piece engagements. From the end of the thirteenth century Edward I responded by hiring a company of 260 Irish 'hobelars' – troopers mounted on hobbies – in order to counter like with like; they saw regular service for about half a century, before mounted archers came to be deployed in their stead.

From the middle of the fourteenth century the proportions of heavy cavalry in the English forces were reduced in favour of these highly effective supporting troops. Heavily armed foot-soldiers armed with pikes had also served to diminish the effectiveness of the all-powerful cavalry charge during this period and rendered the cumbrously armoured knight terribly vulnerable once he had been unhorsed (or likely as not had his horse disabled or mortally wounded under him). From the mid-1400s artillery and handguns made further inroads into the effectiveness of the massed charge, and by the end of the sixteenth century light cavalry had effectively replaced the fully armoured knight on his great horse. Although it is nowhere spelled out, it seems likely that this transition was accompanied by the universal adoption of trotting horses as cavalry mounts and the extinction for military purposes of the pacing horses on which the heavily armoured warrior had relied.

In the early 1600s Sir Edward Harwood might still draw unfavourable comparisons between the English cavalry and that of France, and although his statement that 'it is a question, whether or not, the whole Kingdome could make 2000 good Horse, that might equall 2000 French', strictly refers to horse-soldiers rather than mounts, his opinion of either was equally scathing. According to Harwood, a major factor contributing to the decline of horses and horsemanship that he perceived in contemporary England was the national obsession with hunting and racing, to the exclusion of any exercise designed to promote military prowess. He suggested that the reform of this lamentable state of affairs was 'a worke worthy of his Majesty' and claimed that the problem lay 'chiefely in want of fit horses, and fit men to be horse-men'. By way of remedy, he suggested that steps should be taken anew to promote 'a stronger breed of horses through the Kingdome', while at court the king should reform his bands of Pensioners into a troop of professional cuirassiers; the Lords and other officers and counsellors would be expected to follow his example, maintaining numbers of great horses and fighting staff. The colonel's words evidently fell on deaf ears, however, for no new legislation was forthcoming and in any case the impending Civil War rudely overtook any such long-term designs.

In the early stages of preparation for the war Harwood's bleak observations were confirmed by the noticeable want of recent experience of open warfare amongst both men and horses. Reese records that a meeting of the Council of War in 1628 resolved to put into operation

> the four advices of Mons. La Broue, how to make horses acquinted with war – vizt. that the groom dressing him should be in armour, that provender should be given him on a drum-head, that while he is eating a piece should be discharged, and that he should be ridden against a suit of armour, which he may overthrow and trample under his feet.

There was confusion too about the kind of horses required: both sides are said initially to have sought out troop horses and chargers of the heavy build that reflected traditional rather than contemporary military values, but in reality the tactics of warfare had long since changed to the point where it was cavalry mounts of lighter and more manoeuvrable build that were specifically required – the 'middling-sized horses' so favoured by the Duke of Newcastle. Arab and Barbary horses as well as those of Spain fitted these requirements perfectly, but naturally these expensive animals were appropriate only for the officers who owned them privately. The initial requirements of the two sides in terms of mounts is estimated by Edwards to have stood around 10,000 saddle horses, but quickly escalated to the point where over twice that number (including those hauling guns and supply wagons) might be fielded for a single set-piece battle. The vast majority of these would have been native-bred and as both sides attempted to forestall or to raid the markets within their respective spheres of influence the horse population was once again thinly stretched. The Parliamentarians tended to contract-out the supply of warhorses, while their seizure in 1642 of a Dutch ship carrying a consignment of 42 Flemish horses 'trayned up for warr' illustrates Royalist attempts to look abroad for mounts – at least until the eastern ports were closed to them.

Blackmore has typified the Civil War cavalryman – or at least those in the uniformly equipped Parliamentarian forces – as riding a horse of some 15 hands and carrying with him a short-barrelled flintlock (a harquebus or caliver) and a sword; additionally, he would have a pair of pistols on his saddle. What these troopers lacked in refined horseflesh compared to the royalists, they more than made up for with discipline and commitment. Companies of dragoons also took to the field, mounted on rather inferior nags that would carry them to the field of battle, where they would dismount in order to engage the enemy.

In the course of the later seventeenth and eighteenth centuries the distinction between cavalry and dragoons became blurred to the point where there was little to tell them apart, although in the later nineteenth century new companies designated mounted infantry were formed, equipped with smaller ponies of 14 hands, which would prove particularly valuable in the colonial service.

THE CARRYING TRADE AND THE POST

In a country without a developed road network, it was not only people but also goods that were constrained in their movement: industry and trade could never expand beyond the most parochial level without reliable means of distribution and indisputably the mercantile economy that delivered the prosperity on which modern society is built could itself never have taken shape without the emergence in parallel of an effective system of transportation. Without the carrier and his packhorse – or rather team of horses – the country would have been stuck in the isolation of Dark Age provincialism, but in the event they facilitated a remarkable degree of progress even before the development of long-distance carrying by means of wheeled transport on the well-made turnpike roads that underpinned the industrial expansion of the eighteenth century. At the opening of that era, Daniel Defoe could note with admiration in his *Complete English Tradesman* (1725) the enterprise already shown by northern manufacturers who, notwithstanding their comparative prosperity (they might be travelling, he estimated, with £1,000 worth of goods), journeyed 'not to London only, but to all parts of England . . . the Manchester men being, saving their wealth, a kind of Pedlars, who carry their goods themselves to the country shop-keepers everywhere, as do now the Yorkshire and Coventry manufacturers also'. To convey their wares to the annual fair at Stourbridge (Cambridgeshire) alone, Defoe was told that 'near a thousand horse-packs of such goods' came there from Lancashire and west Yorkshire; they returned home laden with hops. The packhorse is clearly one of the unsung heroes of early modern Britain.

Those engaged in carrying were perhaps too diverse to emerge as a well-defined body at an early stage. Many of the smaller operators pursued their trade on a part-time basis, combining carrying with farming or innkeeping or some other occupation. John Crofts notes that formally designated 'common carriers' existed (albeit in shadowy

fashion) from at least the fourteenth century, but there were advantages to independence that were not lightly given up in return for official recognition. He observes too that when John Taylor went round the inn-yards in 1637 collecting information for his *Carriers Cosmographie* – the first attempt at a printed guide to the regular carrying services offered from London – he found himself 'suspected for a projector, or one that had devised some tricke to bring the Carriers under some new taxation': it was feared that anyone who had his name published in this way might find himself deemed willy-nilly to be a common carrier and thereafter to be encumbered by additional duties and liabilities as such, and to a man the freebooting carriers preferred anonymity and independence.

Passenger traffic also played some part in boosting the carrier's income. Although not primarily specialized in human carriage, the carrier might occasionally undertake delivery of travellers unfamiliar with the route, sometimes providing a 'pad nag' for the traveller to ride, at other times transporting baggage while the traveller himself kept pace on foot alongside – not an option for the physically challenged. There were advantages in accompanying the carrier in this way, both from the point of view of security and simply for wayfinding in an unfamiliar landscape largely destitute of signposts and characterized by stretches of featureless heath and flood-prone marsh. Ultimately much of this traffic would be lost to the expanding coaching network, but in many a smaller community the arrival of the traveller continued to provide, in Crofts's evocative image,

the only regular means of contact with the outside world, and the recurring freshets of news that he brought stirred the sleeping pool of local opinion like the return of the tide, enabling its inhabitants to glow momentarily with a sense of the open sea.

PACKHORSE AND CARRIER

The small size of the average English pony was no bar to its employment as a packhorse: indeed the best of them were perfectly suited to the task, since excessive height would have been a disadvantage during loading and unloading, while sure-footedness and stamina were the qualities most sought-after. No doubt the respective regional horse populations produced most of the ponies involved, but those of the south-west, of the Welsh mountains and of the region of the Scottish border – Galloways in the widest sense of the term – came in for particular praise in this role.

There were no rules as to the size of a packhorse team, and indeed one of its advantages was that it could expand or contract to suit the demands of a particular consignment – whereas the carrier with a wagon would incur virtually the same expenditure whatever his load. A typical team might be composed of, say, twenty horses, but some were substantially bigger and some freelance carriers may have operated with only three or four. Estimates of the horses' carrying capacity vary, but fall within the range of 200 to 300 pounds; by comparison, a modern Shire horse might carry four times as much. A normal load for a pony carrying textiles in the eighteenth century (illus. 12) was reckoned at 240 pounds.

The trappings of the packhorse were invariably functional in the extreme and adapted according to the load they were destined to carry. At its simplest they might have no more than a 'wanty' or belly-band to which the pack was secured (illus. 13); some of these were supplied with hooks to which the load was lashed or on which baskets or 'pots' could be suspended. Panniers might be provided for a variety of loads, varying from farm produce or bread to lime, coal or iron ore. Celia Fiennes noted in 1698 that in Cumberland 'a sort of pannyers' were used,

> some close some open that they strew full of hay turff and lime and dung and every thing they would use, and the reason is plaine from the narrowness of the lanes: where is good lands they will lose as little as they can and where its hilly and stoney no other carriages can pass, so they use these horse carriages; abundance of horses I see all about Kendall streetes with their burdens.

Hey characterizes the panniers used to transport coal in Lancashire as some 30 inches deep, 20 long and 10 wide. He quotes from the diary of one John Hobson of Dodworth Green (Yorkshire), in an entry from 5 May 1732, as follows:

> Will Lindly, of this town, now basket-maker, aged near 90, says that he was bound apprentice to a bannister maker, which was a large sort of hamper, then in use, for the carrying [of] charcoal to the furnaces on horse-back, one on each side of the horse. They were made with a bottom to pull out, for the convenience of emptying. They were wide at the top and narrow in the bottom . . . this was in the year 1660.

If graced with a saddle, the packhorse merited only a rudimentary affair at best, composed of two wishbone-shaped wooden elements joined by braces, all set on a padded cushion to prevent chafing.

Fiennes's comments on the narrowness of the tracks frequented by packhorses were echoed by a number of observers, all of whom were struck with admiration for the skill of the horses and

12 Cloth-makers carrying textiles to market. Etching and aquatint with hand colouring by R. & D. Havell after George Walker (fl. 1803–15). From Walker's *Costume of Yorkshire* (1814).

with dismay at the difficulties of negotiating such a track when confronted by a team in a hurry. Charles Vancouver noted in his *General View of the Agriculture of Devon* (1808) that:

> It is truly surprising to see with what speed and security the native horses of the county will pass over . . . rough and broken places, whether burthened or otherwise . . . The rapidity with which a gang of packhorses descend the hills, when not loaded, and the utter impossibility of passing loaded ones, require that the utmost caution should be used in keeping out of the way of the one,

and exertion in keeping ahead of the other. A crossway fork in a road or gateway is eagerly looked for as a retiring spot to the traveller, until the passing squadron, or heavily loaded brigade, may have passed by.

Much of the carrier's success depended on his knowing the roads and pathways by which his team could reliably come to their destination in the shortest possible time. Open, rocky hillsides presented no problems for his sure-footed animals, but flood-prone and marshy areas where they could easily become bogged down were to be avoided at all costs. River crossings mostly took

13 A variety of loads secured to packhorses by 'wanties' or belly-bands. Detail from Michael Loggan's *Oxonia illustrata* (1675).

the form of fords until, perhaps, the seventeenth and eighteenth centuries when increasing numbers of bridges in timber and later in stone were built: Hey and Crofts both quote a petition of 1718 in connection with a ford at Alport near Youlgreave (Derbyshire), mentioning the 'great gangs of London carriers as well as drifts of malt-horses and other carriers' making use of that route despite the fact that 'carriers with loaden horses and passengers cannot pass the said ford without great danger of being cast away'; it was proposed on that occasion that a bridge should be built, though not one that could accommodate wheeled traffic. Many present-day bridges would have had their origins in this way, starting as timber and later as steep stone packhorse bridges, only later being made wide and flat enough to handle vehicles.

A cracking pace was generally set by such teams. Defoe singles out the carriers from Workington (Cumberland), who 'carry salmon (fresh as they take it) quite to London. This is perform'd with horses, which, changing often, go night and day without intermission, and, as they say, very much out-go the post; so that the fish come very sweet and good to London, where the extraordinary price they yield, being often sold at 2s. 6d. to 4s. per pound, pay well for the carriage'. Similar fish-trains are said to have operated from Newcastle in 1592 and from Rye and Lyme Regis in 1608, with such effectiveness that they brought about a great decline in the market for pond-bred fish. A reference from 1817 reproduced by Hey to a string of packhorses, 'each muzzled, to prevent their stopping to graze by the Road sides', hints at the unrelenting pace they were expected to keep up.

CARTERS AND WAGONERS

Carts undoubtedly played a part in the carrying trade from an early date, but initially there were comparatively few routes on which they could operate regularly; the speed and flexibility of the pack-train, meanwhile, rendered it by comparison highly competitive. Even the introduction of 'long wagons' in the sixteenth century failed to change matters overnight, since their size and unwieldiness meant that even fewer routes were available to them. When the Turnpike Acts (the first of which was passed in 1663) began to bring about improvements in the roads and hence in the operation of wheeled transport, the justices attempted for a time to discriminate against pack-trains by taxing them at a higher rate, but even then their faster mode of travel gave them a competitive edge over the increasingly efficient wagons. Also, each wagon had of necessity to have a driver, whereas a large team of packhorses could be managed by one or two men at the most: what they cost in extra provender for the horses was more than compensated for by savings in the wages bill. In a study of one such transport company, Russell's London Flying Waggons, Dorian Gerhold finds that it was almost a century after the introduction of the first wagon services to the West Country before the proprietors were persuaded that the economics had tipped decisively in favour of the four-wheeled wagon (though local distribution of goods to their final destination continued to be effected by packhorse up to the nineteenth century).

In the southern half of England, and especially in the east and south-east, easy terrain and a higher volume of demand resulted in the early adoption of two-wheeled carts to supplement the pack-trains and ultimately in their displacement. Elsewhere in the country carts also began to make an appearance, but here their adoption seems to have been more patchy: amongst the earliest evidence found by Langdon, for example, are references from the end of the twelfth century to the nuns of Yedingham (Yorkshire) having the right to take a horse and cart annually to a wood in Staindale in order to cut timber for their ploughbeams, and of two horses (together with two oxen) being used to cart turves or peat at Fraisthorpe in the same county. By the following century, services with horse and cart were commonly included amongst the duties to be performed by tenants (even those with quite minor smallholdings) on their respective demesnes, with horses performing some four-fifths of all demesne hauling by the late 1200s. Thereafter a comparatively rapid shift in favour of wheeled transport took place in the lowland zone, but even in the more testing terrain of the Peak District evidence is produced by Hey to show that carts displaced at least some of the packhorse carrying. Even within the area around London itself, wheeled transport was by no means universal: as late as 1607 the parish of Weybridge (Surrey) petitioned to be excused from supplying transport for the queen's progress to Oatlands since there was 'but one cart in the parish'. Nonetheless, the southern counties proved more progressive in the adoption of the cart and by the early decades of the seventeenth century larger, four-wheeled wagons had firmly established themselves in this area, drawing a further contrast with the north. Gerhold finds wagon services plying regularly between London and Dorchester (Dorset) by 1620, Sherborne (Dorset) by 1638 and Exeter (Devon) by 1642.

As on the farm, teams of three horses were commonly harnessed in tandem to a single cart. John Clark notes a reference from 1337 to a fatal accident involving such a team in Bishopsgate, London, in which the trace (middle) horse was described as being blind in both eyes – a striking reminder of the way that the maximum service was wrung out of every animal. The expanding population of London exerted an ever-growing attraction for produce and materials of all kinds from the surrounding counties (notably malt from the Home Counties and textiles from the West country), while finished goods from its manufacturing base and products such as beer filled the carts on their return journeys. To these were to be added the large numbers of carts employed in private service rather than in commerce: by 1356 the city authorities were differentiating between, on the one hand, carts and packhorses bringing goods and produce into the city for sale, which were charged a toll, and on the other hand the horses and vehicles of 'great people and other folks' laden with goods and victuals for their own use, which entered free of charge.

Around the year 1564, according to John Stow, 'began long waggons to come into use, such as now come to London from Canterbury, Norwich, Ipswich, Gloucester, &c with passengers and commodities'. Within two generations of this novel development, wagons and coaches had become so numerous that a proclamation against the use of four-wheeled wagons was issued in 1618; on that occasion, Crofts notes, carriers from Sussex, Hampshire, Wiltshire, Berkshire, Oxfordshire and Northamptonshire were amongst the objectors in a petition drawn up in protest against the restrictions. Twenty years later, in Taylor's *Carriers Cosmographie* (1637), wagons and coaches coming from Essex, Suffolk and Hertfordshire were added to these comparatively local counties, while 'The Waines and Waggons doe come every weeke from sundry places in Glocestershire'. But more striking still are the numbers of long-distance destinations now served on a regular basis from the capital:

The Carriers of Bar[n]stable in Devonshire, doe lodge at the starre in breadstreet, they come on fridaes and returne on saturdaies or mundaies . . . The Carriers of Denbigh in Wales, doe lodge at Bosomes Inne every Thursday . . . The Carriers of Preston in Lancashire doe lodge at the Bell in friday street, they are there on fridayes . . . [etc].

Doncaster, York, Halifax and Wakefield were all catered for on a weekly basis, while the carrier for Edinburgh left the King's Arms or the Cradle in Cheapside every Monday. Towns in Kent, Sussex and Surrey were served by services operating from Southwark.

Even the comparatively lightly constructed carts of the medieval and early modern periods (illus. 14) doubtless encountered difficulties from time to time (and especially during the winter months) with the condition of the roads, but the appearance of heavy wagons introduced problems of an entirely new dimension. Acts for repair of the roads, introduced in 1555 and 1563, gave responsibility for the highways to parish overseers, a system that proved sufficiently workable to survive in some country places up to the nineteenth century, but as Crofts points out, it failed to establish any uniform standards to be observed, with the result that they were patchy in the extreme. Even the line of the road was imprecisely established in many places, while in others it could move with the rotation of crops in the fields through which it passed. 'Repairing' the carriageway was at times a matter of ploughing and harrowing the surface in order to re-establish some superficial uniformity, but this proved to little purpose when it was

14 A London carrier of 1614. The bed of the cart is extended by a ladder-like framework over the horse's back, throwing the weight well forward of the more comfortable centre of gravity.

15 Eight less-than-adequate horses struggle (on a comparatively good surface) with a heavily laden broad-wheeled wagon. From William Henry Pyne, *Costume of Great Britain* (1804).

exposed again to wheeled traffic. Heavier horses in greater numbers came to be harnessed to wagons and, when these were for a time forbidden by Proclamation (in 1618), to carts, which began also to reach an impressive size. (Five horses to a cart was the maximum number allowed under this regulation, but frequent prosecutions show that twice as many were commonly being used.) The use of broader wheels was also encouraged, with a minimum width of 4 inches being prescribed in 1662; this proved short-lived on lighter vehicles, for narrow wheels were found to travel better and came to be shod with iron plates with projecting bolt heads (which proved even more destructive of the roads). Broad wheels with multiple rims also continued to proliferate on heavy wagons (illus. 15): on the largest of these, weighing in at 8 tons gross, the wheels not infrequently reached 12–14 inches in width. The Act for the Amendment and Preservation of the Publick Highways (1753) virtually made broad wheels mandatory, specifying 'fellies . . . of the breadth of gage of nine inches' while an amendment to that Act in 1755 suspended

this provision for a period of three years since it had 'not answered the good purposes intended thereby'. In theory, wheels of this design should have preserved the road surface by rolling it flat, but in practice they generally had been made with a conical rather than cylindrical form, which wreaked even greater havoc on the carriageway; the 1753 Act specified that 'the sole or bottom of all such fellies shall be flat and even from side to side, or as near as maybe'.

Beyond the privileged areas within the ambit of London and off the main roads (progressively turnpiked from 1663 onwards), the introduction of wheeled transport took a great deal longer. As late as the mid-eighteenth century there were reportedly no carts whatever in Cornwall nor indeed in Northumberland, while in 1698 Celia Fiennes noted in Cumberland that 'Here can be noe carriages but very narrow ones like little wheelbarrows that with a horse they convey their fewell and all things else'. Those she encountered around Windermere were small tumbrels of primitive construction:

the wheeles are fasten'd to the axletree and so turn altogether, they hold not above what our wheele barrows would carry at three or four tymes, which the girles and boys and women does go about with, drawn by one horse to carry any thing they want.

Even within the areas where roads had improved, seasonal weather could still play an important part in determining the form of transport used, with wagons simply being laid up for the winter: a petition of 1631 quoted by Crofts mentions that the Hertfordshire maltsters had formerly used packhorses from Michaelmas to May Day as a matter of course; in their over-eagerness to supply their markets, the maltsters had more recently abandoned that pragmatic custom with the result that all the roads were now 'daily torn up by malt carts' to such a degree that it proved impossible to maintain them. Although it was possible that transport costs could be significantly reduced by use of the wagon, Chartres has shown that it was profitable only when the roads were open both in winter and summer, and where the demand was both substantial and regular. The same author has analysed the services operating out of London and identified a substantial increase in the later seventeenth century, during which time the population of the capital almost doubled in size: agricultural and horticultural produce was drawn into the city in ever greater quantities, while luxuries of various sorts flowed out. The Home Counties benefited most significantly from this traffic, but its benefits were felt as far as the east Midlands, the south coast and westwards as far as Devon. By 1750 virtually every major trunk road out of London had been turnpiked, though wagons remained limited in their effectiveness by the numbers of horses needed to draw them and the method of their harnessing. In 1748 Per Kalm observed that

for other wagons on which all sorts of things are carried, and for carts, where they are large, the horses are harnessed or spanned in quite a peculiar manner, viz., not in pairs or abreast, as for the coaches, but all in a single row one after the other. I have once seen as many as eight such horses spanned all in a row after one another, nevertheless, it is rare to see so many. Commonly five or six horses are used for one of the large baggage wagons, so harnessed *tandem*. They are bound to and after one another with strong iron chains, one of which goes on each side of the horse, and where it comes sometimes to rub against the horse's side it is covered with leather, so that it may not gnaw the horse. The weight and thickness of these chains is such that any other than English horses would with difficulty be able to support it, for the horses which are used here in England for these wagons, are as large as the largest cavalier-horses in Sweden, fat, and of an uncommon strength.

Further from the metropolis, on the more demanding roads of the deep countryside, the road surface was for a long time deliberately left soft for the benefit of the oxen that frequently substituted for horses there in heavy haulage, but this measure resulted all too often in wagons becoming bogged down while the pack teams trotted by on the hardened pavements or causeways created in many places for them, so they still maintained their advantage. Even without such a causeway, the packhorse team was recognized as a less destructive force than the wagon, as William Marshall makes clear in the following observation:

a horse path may be poached in wet weather, yet in dry it is, in the nature of the tread of horses, trodden level again, to receive with benefit the water of heavy showers: but not one soil in a hundred is capable of affording materials sufficient to bear the wheels of laden carriages; which, in the action of wheeled carriages, tend, not to fill up and level, but to deepen the holes and gutters made by running water; and of course act in concert with it to render the road impassable.

Extra horses (or oxen) might be necessary to help on uphill stretches. Hey quotes the Revd J. C. Atkinson, who was amazed to encounter in the 1840s a team of ten horses and ten oxen on the Yorkshire moors,

drawing a huge block of fine freestone up the terribly steep 'bank' or hill-side road, which runs like a house-roof on the eastern side of Stonegate Gill. At the foot of the bank, on the limited level space available, there were standing four other waggons similarly loaded. The full complement of animals dragging each of these 'carries' was a pair of horses and a yoke of oxen; and when they reached the foot of one of these stupendous hills, the full force of animal power was attached to each of the carriages in succession, and so the ponderous loads – five tons' weight on the average – were hauled to the top; and then, when all were up, the cavalcade proceeded on its slow march again.

Inevitably, there came a point beyond which some loads proved immovable – or at least could be moved only with the greatest difficulty. Writing of the countryside around Lewes (Sussex), Defoe records that:

The timber I saw here was prodigious, as well in quantity as in bigness . . . [but] was so far off any navigation, that it was not worth cutting down and carrying away . . . I have seen one tree on a carriage, which they call here a tug, drawn by two and twenty oxen, and even then, 'tis carry'd so little a way, and then thrown down, and left for other tugs to take up and carry on, that sometimes 'tis two or three year before it gets to Chatham; for if once the rains come in, it stirs no more that year . . .

The coming of the railways by no means rendered carts and wagons redundant on the roads but it changed immeasurably the way they operated. Much of the long-distance carrying trade was indeed displaced in this way, but the numbers of horses employed by the railway companies to gather in freight to the terminuses and to distribute it at the other end of its journey greatly exceeded those rendered redundant by the steam engine. The same companies also took control of a large proportion of local trade that never went near the railway. The Great Western Railway's depot at Paddington, for example, included a stable arranged over four floors connected by ramps, housing some 500 horses; another 140 were stabled under the railway arches nearby. Gordon considered this one of the best-run establishments in London, with the immaculately kept horses separated by colours so that teams always looked at their best; each horse was branded with a number and each had its own stall. No teams worked in tandem by this time, but some worked three abreast, causing difficulties in the congested streets; the company's most powerful four-horse teams pulled wagons of up to 9 tons laden weight. The GWR horses participated in the cycle described above, being brought up on country farms, broken to light work at two years and sold to the railway company at about four; after two months of acclimatization and training they worked until the age of seven, when they would often be sold to end their days back in farm work.

The other major employers of horse labour in the capital by this time were the brewers, whose handsome Shires and Clydesdales were amongst the most impressive animals on the streets. A full load of 8 tons gross would be shifted by three such animals, harnessed 'unicorn fashion', with one walking ahead of the other pair.

HACKNEYS, STAGES AND THE POSTS

Perhaps inspired by the example of France and the Holy Roman Empire (which had a network of posts from as early as 1491), Henry VIII appointed Brian Tuke to be Master of the Posts, with authority to establish a certain number of 'standing Posts in pay'. Local authorities were now to produce 'an able bodied man well horsed', who could take up further horses when necessary, but it clearly took some time for the situation to be improved. Twenty years after his initial appointment, we find Tuke writing to Thomas Cromwell, in 1533, in revealing terms: 'Sir, ye know well that except the hakney horses bitwene Gravesende and Dovour, there is no such usual conveyance in post for men in this realme as in the accustomed places of France and other parties'.

The service referred to on the Dover road had already operated entirely under private enterprise for a century or more by this time and the Tudor postal service was launched by means of absorbing this remarkably busy route (carrying cross-Channel mail to the ports) and by providing royal patents to protect the hackneymen on what was now Crown business. As well as being equipped to carry mail, the service on the Dover route also provided means by which the traveller could reach his destination with the aid of relays of horses operating between recognized staging posts. In order to regulate this trade and to minimize the opportunities for fraud, it had been ordained by a patent granted as early as 1396 that

> there shall be taken for the hire of a hakenei from Suthwerk to Rocester 12d, from Roucester to Canterbury 12d, and from Canterbury to Dover 6d, and from town to town according to the rate of 12d and the number of the miles; that the petitioners be in nonwise compelled to let their horse for hire unless paid promptly; and that for the better security of the horses a branding-iron be kept in each of those towns by an approved person for branding, without payment, horses on hire.

As Crofts points out, the fact that Chaucer, in writing the prologue to his *Canterbury Tales* only a few years earlier, makes no mention of hackneys, suggests that they may have been a comparatively recent innovation – though evidently it was already subject to perversion. John Clark quotes the instance of one Thomas Bastard of Essex who, in 1365, had hired a horse to carry a sick woman from London to Canterbury but had got only as far as Singlewell near Gravesend when it died: not only did poor Bastard have to lay out 10s. on the hire of further horses in order to reach his destination and return to London, but there he found himself being sued for 30s. by the original horse's owner for allegedly riding it too hard and too fast. Whatever the justification on this occasion, it is certain that many such complaints would have been well founded, for the hired hackney received scant consideration from riders, whose only thought was to complete the allotted stage in the shortest possible time.

Despite these pitfalls, the service as it developed under the Tudors soon attracted the favourable attention of foreigners. Paul Hentzner took one of these hackneys in 1598, posting to London, and was quite impressed: 'It is surprising how swiftly they run', he writes; 'their bridles are very light, and their saddles little more than a span over'. The 'false gallop after some ten miles an hour' with which Fynes Moryson credits the English post horses came to be called 'a Canterbury gallop', which, Crofts tells us, has left us the term 'canter'.

The regular carriage of mail (as opposed to 'posting' services for travellers) took considerably longer to emerge. By the end of the sixteenth century it was still limited to a large extent to dispatches to and from the court and on those routes busy enough to merit standing posts the horses had a reputation for being frequently overburdened and 'evilly used'. The early decades of the 1600s brought some reforms, but most of them were mired in the increasingly chronic financial difficulties of the early Stuarts; under Cromwell an Act for Settling the Postage of England, Scotland and Ireland established in 1657 'one general Post Office' for the whole of the Commonwealth, although the 'common known' carriers of goods were exempted from the government's monopoly. In 1660 Charles II effectively refounded it with a new Act, widely regarded as the Post Office's 'charter', and with many new personnel; its effectiveness, however, remained limited by the condition of many of the roads.

By the mid-eighteenth century the situation had been transformed, with the posts commonly consigned to coaches for longer-distance deliveries and with licensed postmasters providing relays of horses both for the mail coaches and for travellers at large. In the 1780s the business of posting in the broadest sense was thrown open to contract, although the carriage of mail remained a royal monopoly. Bird identifies four principal types of mail (all of them limited to letters only): through mails or London letters, all directed to the capital; country letters, routed via London; bye-letters, taken up and set down at intermediate points along given routes; and cross post, directly linking the major provincial cities. One of the earliest of these services was that offered by John Palmer between Bristol and London, instituted in 1784. In addition to the mail, his coaches also carried a limited number of passengers – normally four, all inside – and together with the security offered by an armed guard and a padlocked strongbox they offered one of the fastest and most reliable services of its day. Two years later Palmer was appointed Surveyor and Comptroller-General of the Post Office and quickly introduced the first specially constructed mail-coaches – the 'improved wheel carriage' patented by John Besant in 1786. With this new generation of vehicles the mail coaches set the gold standard of the coaching world: their horse teams matched the smartness of the coaches in their standard of maintenance and the efficiency of their operation became a byword for effectiveness. Anthony Bird mentions that five minutes were allowed for changing the teams between stages, but such was the sense of urgency with which these proceedings were conducted that the changeover was often completed in two. At its peak around 1835, around 700 coaches were deployed in maintaining a mail service that was the envy of the world (illus. 16): Gordon recalls that one of the most popular events of the London calendar at that time was the annual procession of mail-coaches that took place on May Day between Millbank and the General Post Office, when the turnout of freshly varnished coaches, scarlet-coated coachmen and immaculately presented horses stood comparison with any military parade.

16 Royal Mail coaches thronged about the General Post Office, St Martin's-le-Grand, London. The coaches, serving destinations from Hastings to Edinburgh, are individually identified. In the foreground are also shown a clarence four-wheeled cab, an early Hansom cab, two back-door cabs and a hackney cabriolet. Print by James Pollard, 1830.

COACHES AND COACH-HORSES

Throughout the medieval centuries, wheeled transport of a sort had been available to the seriously well-to-do, though perhaps made use of only by the more delicate women of the household, small children, the elderly and the sick. Variously designated chares, chariots and whirlicotes, these vehicles were little more than four-wheeled wagons of the most primitive design, covered over with a tilt and upholstered internally as well as might be in order to absorb the spine-jarring jolts transmitted by the unsprung chassis. An example illustrated in the Luttrell Psalter accurately reflects the combination of unsophisticated construction mediated by sumptuous furnishing met with in these vehicles (illus. 17). The small numbers of

these on the road declined even further when side-saddles were popularized in England with the example set by Anne of Bohemia, under whose influence, according to John Stow's *Survey of London*, 'the riding in Whirlicotes and Chariots' was foresaken by the fashionable, 'except at coronations and such like spectacles'. On the evidence of certain inventories, however, the type survived in the provinces until the sixteenth century: the Earl of Northumberland retained in the early 1500s a 'chariot' to which were assigned seven 'Great Trotting horses', reserved by that time for transporting the Earl's 'Chappel stuff', while in the household of his neighbour the Earl of Cumberland there survived in 1572 an 'old chariett with 2 pair of wheeles bound with iron, and cheynes belonging thereto', valued at 30s. Such vehicles would by this time have been the cause of considerable mirth in fashionable circles in the metropolis.

Apart from those on the farm and in use in the carrying trade, harness horses – and certainly those of desirable quality – were therefore little known before the Tudor era. Up to the reign of Elizabeth I the more delicate members of the royal household and of the noble families were generally transported by litter, a lightly built framework with a tilt and with curtains for modesty, shouldered by a pair of docile ambling horses. Elizabeth is shown riding to her coronation in such a litter (illus. 18), and as late as the reign of Charles I provision is made in the stable inventories for litters as well as for coaches, and for designated litter-horses with appropriate harness and braces to carry the supporting poles.

A fairly precise date can be given for the introduction of the coach to the English scene. The very earliest record is of one imported during the reign of Mary Tudor, as relayed to the Venetian senate by the ambassador, Giovanni Michiel, on 13 May 1557 when he mentions

a number of things of no little value presented by me at several times, not from personal vanity but because they were all asked of me for her Majesty's need and service by the said Mistress of the Robes, besides a coach and horses and all their furniture presented in like manner from necessity owing to the wish for it of the said Mistress of the Robes, to whom the Queen subsequently gave it. I had the coach sent to me from Italy for my convenience, and used it all that summer.

John Stow was evidently unaware of this vehicle when, in his *Annales* (1615), he confidently placed its introduction a few years later, in 1564, when, he says, 'Gwylliam Boonen, a dutchman, became

the Queenes Coachmanne and was the first that brought the use of Coaches into England'. Mirroring Mary's evident indifference to the ambassador's expensive gift, Elizabeth too displayed a degree of coolness towards her new acquisition, and indeed customarily placed it at the disposal of visiting foreign envoys rather than submit her own person to its jarring progress, but Stow continues that 'within twenty years began a great trade of coach making', and fashionable society showed remarkable alacrity in seizing on the new form of conveyance. So avidly were they adopted, indeed, that within two generations Henry Peacham could characterize the streets of London as so crowded with coaches that, 'like mutton pies in a cook's oven; hardly you can thrust a pole between [them]'.

At their first introduction in the sixteenth century, coaches were invariably cumbersome and uncomfortable, necessitating large teams of horses and performing services that had as much to do with prestige and ceremony as with practicality; it would take 100 years before any form of springing was incorporated that would ease the ride and over 200 before the road system would be fully brought up to a standard that made long-distance travel both predictable and moderately comfortable. Many of the coaches to be found in Elizabethan London are said to have been of Pomeranian origin, selling in London for something over £40. Although the bodywork on a coach for this price might have been transformed into a work of art by the German manufacturers, fitting out and furnishing were more often left up to the buyer and would be carried out in London – at a cost frequently exceeding the original purchase price. A common modification amongst early imports, it seems, involved raising the roof in order to accommodate the tall hats then favoured in London. Crofts finds a reference of 1576 relating to such a coach, purchased for Sir Henry Sidney:

17 Ladies of the court riding in a whirlicote drawn by five horses in line, two of them with postilions. The primitive form of the vehicle (no springing, no turning ability) is well conveyed. From the Luttrell Psalter (*c.* 1340).

In primis for sending one man into the country of Pomerland by my said lordes appoyntment to provide a strong cowche with all maner of furniture therto belonging and covered with leather, and viij wheles for the same cowche: which cowche being made with furniture for iiij horses . . . £XLII.

Item the same cowche was att Smithfield in London uncovered and made higher, the doing thereof cost £VIII. 10s.

New forms of coach appeared as quickly as the changes in fashionable headgear: a bill of 1625 mentions two new caroches for the royal stables, one in the Spanish style and one of the German fashion 'with the roof to fall asunder at his Majesty's pleasure . . . The like of them were never made before in England.' Other technical innovations followed, especially in the manner of suspension, with springs being incorporated in the leather slings on which the body was hung. Another late refinement was the introduction of glass to the windows instead of the screens

that had been the most that could be expected on earlier models: once again, a fairly precise date can be advanced for their introduction, for John Aubrey records in his *Brief Lives* that 'The first glasse coach that came into England was the duke of Yorke's when the king was restored. In a very short time they grew common, and now [1681], at Waltham or Tottnam high crosse, is sett-up a mill for grinding of coach-glasses and looking glasses'. None the less, glass remained so expensive (and so vulnerable) that the windows were commonly removed when a coach ventured into the countryside.

An attempt was made in 1601 to introduce an Act through the House of Lords proposing that 'Noone under the degree of Knight, Privy Counsellor, Queen's Counsel etc or paying £50 to the subsidy shall ride or travel in coaches under penalty of £5 for every offence, and no person shall let a coach or coach-horses, to any but those herein authorized to use them.' It came to nothing, and attempts to ban the use of coaches on the Sabbath similarly failed in the face of burgeoning popular

demand. For all their blatant extravagance and their unquestioned role as the status symbol of the age, the coach could also be a shrewd buy: Crofts observes that it offered the possibility of considerable saving to the gentleman with a wife and a large family who formerly would have travelled everywhere on horseback with numbers of footmen and servants but who could now be transported *en masse* with no more than a coachman and a couple of grooms.

Initially much of the coach traffic was limited (by the road system as much as by ambition) to the immediate environs of the capital. Even within London, opportunities for coaching were severely limited: there was no bridge across the Thames capable of taking wheeled traffic at this time. By 1617, however, Fynes Moryson records that 'one or two daies any way from London' the roads were 'sandy and very faire, and continually kept so': coaching for pleasure expanded within this radius, while the remainder of the country remained largely inaccessible – especially to the lighter caroches or pleasure-coaches which were most fashionable. For the countryside a more robust type of vehicle was developed, with heavy wheels

reinforced with iron strakes in the manner of contemporary wagon-wheels, and slowly the country opened up: Hey finds a reference as early as 1599 to the Earl of Shrewsbury's coach completing the journey from London to Sheffield, though most noblemen at this time were content to keep their coaches for use at their London townhouses rather than their country seats. Writing over a century later, Daniel Defoe shows how the ambition to own a coach could still outrun the provision of an appropriate carriageway:

> going to church at a country village, not far from Lewis [Lewes, Sussex], I saw an ancient lady, and a lady of very good quality, I assure you, drawn to church in her coach with six oxen; nor was it done in a frolick of humour, but meer necessity, the way being so stiff and deep, that no horses could go in it.

Another telling incident, recounted by Anthony Bird, concerns the visit of the Emperor Charles VI to England in 1703, when he undertook the 55-mile journey from London to Petworth (Sussex) by coach: three days after setting out he arrived at his destination with a party of Sussex labourers in tow, retained to right the coach (which had been overturned a dozen times along the way) and to extricate it when necessary from quagmires in the road.

The earliest private coaches might carry as many as six passengers plus a further two lodged in the (open) doorways with their feet outside, protected from the weather by an enveloping leather bag known as a boot: customarily the lady's gentle-woman occupied the offside door and her maid the more hazardous nearside position. Despite the cool reception given to it by Queen Elizabeth herself, it seems that ladies took effortlessly to the coach but amongst gentlemen a more equivocal attitude prevailed long after its introduction. John Aubrey writes that 'in Sir Philip Sidney's time 'twas as much disgrace for a cavalier to be seen in London riding in a coach in the street as now 'twould be to be seen in a petticoate and Waist-cote'. This prejudice was gradually overcome in the capital but it remained ingrained in the prov-inces into the last quarter of the seventeenth cen-tury. Here we have the personal testimony of the Leeds antiquary Ralph Thorseby, who records that

following a serious illness in 1678 he had been brought by his father from Hull to York in a coach: 'it proved a mortification to us both', he writes, and his father 'was as little able to endure the ef-feminacy of that way of travelling, as I was at pres-ent to ride on horseback'; none the less, 'weak and crazy' though he was, Thorseby was persuaded by his father to ride the last leg of the journey, from York to Leeds, on horseback, rather than expose himself to further ignominy in front of the neighbours. And quite right too, some contempo-raries would have said: an anonymous tract pub-lished in 1673 with the title 'The Grand Concern of England Explained' (quoted at greater length below), fulminates against the spread of wheeled transport, asserting that it tends to 'effeminate his majesty's subjects' to the point where they are rendered incapable of serving their country on horseback, preferring to ride 'lolling' in a coach and protecting their clothes.

It was in this still-evolving context that coaches for public use gradually emerged. In Taylor's *Car-riers Cosmographie* (1637), all but one of the stage-coaches listed plied to places within 30 miles of London – the exception being Cambridge, which

18 Queen Elizabeth I in procession. 'The Quenes maiestie' is shown in her accession day parade, occupying a litter under a canopy, but in reality she preferred to ride side-saddle.

took two days. The majority of these vehicles were also six-person coaches (although some may have offered little more in the way of comfort than the contemporary stage-wagons in which passengers shared the accommodation with miscellaneous cargo or were housed in a special compartment slung precariously from standards within the body of the wagon), but in time they came more closely to resemble private coaches, except for the additional provision for baggage. At the time much of this was consigned to a fore-boot under the driver's seat and to a large basket known as the 'conveniency', slung between the back wheels; passengers paying the lowest fares might even share the latter space with the luggage and could still be required to walk up the steepest hills in order to ease the burden on the horses. No seats were provided on top before the middle years of the eighteenth century, although for a consideration the enterprising coachman might allow illicit passengers to cling on to the roof as best they could. By the late 1700s the fore-boot and the conveniency had been incorporated into the structure of the coach while both forward- and backward-looking seats for passengers had been added to the roof. Predictably, these developments risked making the coach top-heavy and prone to overturning; accidents were frequent. Legislation of 1788 limited the number of passengers on the roof to six (later reduced to five) on a coach with three or more horses, although up to twelve external passengers were at times carried on six-horse coaches. In this form the stagecoach offered the principal means of long-distance transport until the introduction of the railways, their only competition coming from the mail-coaches. The first services had been able to average some 30 miles a day; early improvements tended to be achieved by the expedient of spending more hours a day on the road, rather than by any increase in speed. An advertisement of 1658

announces coaches reaching Stamford in two days, Newark in two and a half days, and Wakefield in west Yorkshire in four days; by the turn of the eighteenth century over a hundred towns were being served and coaches were being patronized by the business community and by gentlemen.

The effect of these developments on the saddle horse population was considerable. Far from viewing the efficiencies won by travelling in this way as an unmitigated bonus, the anonymous (and it must be said somewhat perverse) author of 'The Grand Concern of England Explained' (1673) found the consequences entirely deleterious:

> There is not the fourth part of saddle horses, either bred, or kept, now in England that was before these coaches were set up . . . there is no man; unless some noble soul, that scorns and abhors being confined to so ignoble, base and sordid a way of travelling, as these coaches oblige him unto . . . that will breed and keep such horses.

Calculating that some 936 passengers were then being carried annually from London on return visits to York, Chester and Exeter in coaches requiring a total of 120 horses, he reckons that without this innovation work would have been provided for at least 500 horses. Quite apart from the loss to manufacturers of riding clothing as well as 'swords, belts, pistols, holsters, portmanteaus, hat-cases', there were 'not so many horses by ten-thousand kept now in these parts [the London region] as there were, before stage-coaches set up'.

On the other hand, with these developments there had emerged a demand for a whole new class of horses suitable for harness work: in 1590 the queen had 28 coach-horses in her stables; 59 of them are recorded in the inventories of Charles II in 1668, while William and Mary between them had 82 by the end of the seventeenth century. The demand from society at large was in proportion much greater – so much so that the suppliers of appropriate horses must have had difficulty in satisfying the public appetite. It was fortuitous that this new market developed just as the demand for the 'great horses' that had formed the bedrock of the cavalry in earlier centuries was beginning to fall off, and many of the first generations of coach-horses must have found themselves suffering a career change in order to satisfy the new market – especially those that had proved in any way unsatisfactory for the saddle. These were increasingly likely at this period to be geldings, and indeed a team of entire stallions must always have presented a challenge for even the most formidable coachman; the emergence of the coach-horse and the rise of the gelding were developments that went hand-in-hand, for a docile temperament was now at a premium. The other principal requirement of the privately owned team was that it should be as handsome and well matched – and as sumptuously turned out – as could be achieved. The horses that regularly drew the public coaches in stages over considerable distances and in all weathers were doubtless of less refined stock, but the task was a demanding one and stamina and quality remained at a premium.

While the assiduous horseman was provided at this time with a growing literature to help him master the latest riding techniques, there were no such handbooks for the coachman. Having broken one team to harness, it seems that coachmen generally trained up additional horses by the expedient of yoking them between those already accustomed to the harness team. Lightly built brakes (originally 'breaks', for breaking horses to harness) allowed the trainee coach-horse to become accustomed to its role without burdening it excessively with a load. Four horses quickly came to form the standard team for town work, although six and even eight were favoured by the more precocious. The coachman on the earliest vehicles occupied a bench slung fairly low between the standards supporting the body; from this position he could exert little control over the leading pair, so it was essential to mount one of these with a postilion (illus. 19). Later developments placed the coachman in a higher and more advantageous position, from which by the first half of the eighteenth century he could begin to control single-handedly a team of six; this process was completed, according to Bird, by the introduction of coupling reins and bearing reins in the later eighteenth century.

By this time, increasing numbers of wealthy private citizens had become coach owners. In London the expansion of the city northwards and westwards carried much of the population away from the main artery of the river that previously had provided a convenient means of communication and to cope with the explosive demand for coaches rows of mews came to be incorporated as standard features in new housing developments of the Regency and Victorian periods, interspersed within the regular terraces so that coaches and horses could be accommodated within easy reach of dwellings. Outside the capital, during the 1800s the numbers of coaches on the road increased exponentially, while Telford's and MacAdam's smooth and durable road surfaces encouraged the development of lighter, faster and more stylish machines. Stagecoaches reached speeds undreamed of a century or two earlier: by 1836 the combination of improved roads and well-planned relays of horses had reduced the journey time from London to York to a mere 20 hours, though not without an enormous investment in horsepower: Worsley notes that similarly fast times on the 158-mile journey from Shrewsbury to London were achieved with the employment of no fewer than 150 horses.

19 A coach with low-seated driver and with a postilion on the offside lead horse. A detail from Michael Loggan's *Oxonia Illustrata* (1675).

The varied nomenclature applied to private carriages from the eighteenth century onwards conjures up a picture of bewildering complexity. The principal types included the chariot – a two-seat forward-facing coach – and its long-distance version, the post chaise; the landau with two folding leather heads (or hoods), and its two-seater version, the landaulette; and the brougham, an everyday closed carriage, and its open version, the victoria. For all of these, two-horse teams were standard although they could be boosted to four on occasion; by the later 1800s a single horse had become more general for the lighter varieties. Over this same period a range of sporting carriages also appeared, designed to be driven by the owner himself. Phaetons were particularly popular, especially in an improbably tall version termed the highflyer phaeton, as favoured by the Prince Regent and his contemporaries; while two horses were generally sufficient for these, for maximum effect they would sometimes be drawn by four or even six. Dictated by fashion rather than practicality, sporting carriages changed in appearance with frequency, before falling casualty in turn to the new fad for motor cars, which quickly saw carriage-driving reduced to the competitive (and largely off-road) sport still practised today.

The internal combustion engine also brought about the end of the most democratic form of horse transport, namely the omnibus. Credit for the introduction of the bus goes to an Englishman named George Shillibeer, who first set up business in Paris and later, when two eighteen-seater vehicles ordered from him in 1819 were well received, returned to London in the hope of repeating his success. There his first two buses ran between Paddington and Bank on 4 July 1829, each drawn by a well-matched pair of horses and carrying 22 passengers inside. For a time a service drawn by three horses was experimented with, but this proved too much for the narrow streets and ultimately two-horse omnibuses became standard, initially carrying fourteen passengers but later increasing again; extra horsepower was provided for some of the steeper hills on the expanding network of routes. Within 25 years 1,000 buses were plying the streets, by now with a 'knife-board' longitudinal seat to carry additional passengers on an open upper deck, an arrangement superseded in the 1880s by more congenial 'garden seats'. By the death of Queen Victoria the London General company alone operated nearly 1,400 buses, serviced by a stable of over 10,000 horses.

The demands made on the omnibus horse were considerable, so although they were well cared for their working life on the streets was short: Gordon records that the normal sequence of events was for them to be bought at five years of age for about £35, worked for five years and resold for a mere £5. Twice as many years might have been expected from them in a less demanding role, but the constant stopping and starting with a full load approaching 3½ tons, pulled over all manner of surfaces and inclines, made heavy demands on them. Injuries were also common, rendering some unfit for further work; two out of three horses died in service, at which point they might fetch 35s. from a cat's-meat man.

The introduction of the tram, the first one of which ran in Birkenhead in 1860, provided yet further demand for horsepower. The reduced resistance offered by the tram's wheels ought to have made life easier for the horse, but inevitably the transport companies merely used the opportunity to increase the load. The fact that an extra 1s. a week was spent on their feed reveals something of the extra productivity expected of tram horses, as does their even shorter working life of four years.

At a price intermediate between that of a coach and an omnibus the traveller in town could hire a cab, the earliest of which were rather primitive, two-horse vehicles controlled from the back of the nearside horse: these four-wheeled vehicles had a reputation for being unsavoury in the extreme and were avoided by anyone who could find an alternative means. In 1823 a lighter and more satisfactory design was introduced, two-wheeled, with a leather apron and screens to protect the passengers and with the driver on a dickey-seat on the outside; these proved much more popular, although four-wheeled 'growlers' (otherwise known as clarences) continued to operate in competition with them. Even within the cities, the occupants of these cabs were placed at considerable risk from the effects of collisions and numerous designs were tested which sought to protect them by increasing the size of the wheels and suspending the bodywork as close to the ground as possible. Joseph

Aloysius Hansom was one of those who sought a solution to the problem of lowering the centre of gravity of the cab in this way; in the event his own design proved excessively cumbersome, but he had the good sense to recognize the superiority of a model developed by one of his competitors and to buy him out, so the Hansom cab that ultimately proved such a success owed its production but not its design to the entrepreneur whose name it bore. (Barker estimates that some 7,500 hackney cabs were licensed during the period immediately before the introduction of the petrol engine.)

The life of the cab horse was amongst the least enviable of all the urban livestock. Cabbies frequently hired their horses (many of them Irish in origin) from commercial stables on a daily basis, and while the driver's day might be a long one the horse could be unfortunate enough to find itself working double shifts and Sundays as well. Again the wear and tear was considerable, the horses frequently retiring 'fractionally', as Gordon puts it – ending up pulling the shabbiest of cabs or being sold on to end their days pulling a tradesman's cart.

By comparison, one might have expected the life of a carriage-horse at the turn of the twentieth century to be one almost of luxury, but here too the picture was all too often one of hard work and early exhaustion. Gordon points out that while the weight they had to pull was a light one, the pace demanded of them was frequently excessive. Of the 40,000 coach-horses he estimated to be in use in London at the close of the nineteenth century, many were not in private ownership but on hire from jobmasters, an arrangement that saw the average horse clocking up perhaps 14 miles a day at the trot. Cleveland bays remained the animal of choice, or Clydesdale / Cleveland crosses, although the less discerning end of the market was served by more miscellaneous horses, many of them imports. For their part the jobmasters took care to offer a full range of horses of all qualities to suit the needs of their clients: one of the largest, Messrs Tilling of Peckham, is said to have had a stable of some 2,500 horses of all kinds, but of uniformly good quality: each was given some months of training appropriate to its station, whether it be for funerals (invariably black horses, usually Flemish, much in demand during periods of epidemic), weddings (greys preferred), carriages of state, or fire engines.

The Horse in the Industrial Age

Throughout the period reviewed in outline above, the role of the horse as the primary means of motive power was undisputed, while it also provided the means of driving a limited number of simple machines. With the advent of developing mechanization, the horse population had the misfortune to find (for a time, at least) that a whole new range of duties had been invented for it in providing the driving force for a new range of industrial devices. Many of the machines that ultimately would be powered by steam were originally driven by treadmills – the very word has come to signify unremitting toil – and the fact that horsepower is even today the unit by which mechanical output is measured tells us all we need to know about the former universality of the pony in powering virtually every device that could not be more efficiently driven by wind or water. Cranes were amongst the most common devices incorporating treadmills (or more strictly tread-wheels – large diameter wheels incorporating an internal walkway, as opposed to the external steps on a treadmill) on which the pony, by constantly attempting to walk up the slope of the interior circumference, caused the wheel to turn and the machine to which it was

attached to function. Quarries and mines were amongst the most numerous users, but they were also found in dockyard cranes and on large-scale construction sites, as well as in manufacturing plants: Worsley notes that in Arkwright's first mill, established in Nottingham in 1768, were 1,000 spindles powered by nine horse-wheels, requiring some 36 horses to operate them.

An alternative principle involved harnessing the pony to a horizontal beam which formed a radius around which the animal, whether pony, donkey or mule, was forced to walk interminably. The practice was already thousands of years old, having been used to turn millstones and olive presses in the ancient world, and in its simplest form it survived in Britain up to the nineteenth century for crushing apples for cider-making, gorse for animal feed, ore for smelting and stone for building purposes (illus. 20). A development of this idea saw the horse harnessed to a capstan or drum, which might serve as a winding device for raising men, materials and water from the depths of coal, iron or lead mines, or it might transmit its momentum to a machine such as a pump or a pile-driver; on the farm similar devices drove threshing machines and devices that chopped straw or turnips. The power applied directly to the machine could be increased simply by hitching further animals to the device, but by the later 1700s efficiency was also being improved by the addition of gearing, at first in timber and increasingly in the course of the following decades in cast iron.

Hoists using either one of these principles were already in common use in the construction of large-scale buildings in the medieval period: examples survive at a number of cathedrals, including Canterbury and Peterborough, at Beverley Minster and Tewkesbury Abbey. In sheer numbers 'horse-gins' spread in unprecedented fashion over the industrialized parts of the country from the eighteenth

20 A one-horse mill for crushing flints. Drawing by William Henry Pyne, *c.* 1804.

century onwards. A record from the Lowther pits at Whitehaven (Cumberland) from 1793 gives a glimpse of the gin horses going 'at full trot' for an eight-hour shift, three shifts in a day.

The material output of the mines and quarries was increasingly transported on site by means of tubs running on rails and pulled by horses. Coal mines in particular sent ponies underground in large numbers, hauling the mineral from the coal-face to the base of the shaft, where others would raise it to the surface for processing. Thereafter yet more horses, initially packhorses (recorded as transporting lead from the Peak District as far as Boston (Lincolnshire), Waltham Abbey (Essex) and even to Southampton for export to France) but increasingly those pulling carts, would deliver it themselves or would transfer it to ships or barges, the latter to be hauled yet again by horses. A great deal of freight travelled by the canal system,

instituted in the 1760s: within 60 years Messrs Pickfords employed some 4,000 horses to pull their barges between Birmingham and London – a fig-ure that would increase further before the railways began to siphon off much of this trade.

Even after the national railway system took over much of the long-distance transport, there remained ample employment for horses in feeding the railway trucks with freight and in the final dis-tribution of materials of all sorts – but principally, perhaps, coal – to domestic and industrial custom-ers. The railway companies themselves employed large numbers of horses in both in collection and delivery (see pp. 61–2) and in shunting operations. In time many of the latter were replaced by light locomotives designed specifically for the purpose, but Coulls tells us that the last shunting horse retired from the railways only in 1967.

Horses for Sport and Leisure

For a society that spent so much of its time in the saddle, it was perhaps inevitable that the horse would feature heavily too in its recreational activities. Apart from hunting, which is treated separately here (pp. 101–33), the earliest activities known in any detail are those which took place on the tournament field, in which the arts of equestrian warfare were practised in an increasingly formalized setting. In the course of the sixteenth century interest (and ability) in the practice of these skills began to wane as the role of the heavily armoured knight on his great horse was progressively rendered obsolete on the battlefield, and although it would survive in ritualistic form up to the eve of the Civil War it had long since lost any claim to military significance.

Coinciding with this decline, an entirely new interest in horsemanship as an art in its own right began to emerge, observing an elaborate set of conventions designed to demonstrate grace and poise rather than martial invincibility on the part of the rider, and schooling to the ultimate levels of agility and precision on that of the horse. The manège was essentially a solo performance art, in which horse and rider were provided with an opportunity to demonstrate what might appear to be a complete harmony of interest and ability but which more accurately displayed the total dominance of one will by the other.

Competitiveness by no means died out at this time, but found a new expression in racing, at first with the owner as likely as not mounted on his own horse and only at the turn of the eighteenth century becoming a sport more likely to feature professional jockeys rather than gentlemen of all-round sporting ability. Polo, the fourth sport considered here, is a more recent introduction, arriving only in the latter half of the nineteenth century but ultimately taking firm root in Britain and being re-exported around the world.

THE TOURNEY, JOUST AND TOURNAMENT

War games provided equal measures of entertainment, training and the opportunity to attract favourable attention to the medieval warrior as they continue to do for today's soldier. In their earliest recorded form they were hazardous in the extreme – the equivalent of field exercises with live ammunition – but in time increasing formalization and control led to a greater emphasis on their entertainment value and a consequent diminution of the risks involved.

In the form in which it is first encountered, the tourney or *mêlée* did indeed resemble the kind of manoeuvres still practised by the Army, ranging as it did over a wide expanse of countryside and engaging the participants in series of strategic decisions with a view to outwitting or simply overwhelming the opposition. Generally these combats, which emerged around the turn of the twelfth century and might involve large bodies of participants – sometimes numbering in hundreds – continued until a clear winner emerged or until darkness overtook the proceedings; there was no playing dead or impounding by referees, for the principal aim was to take prisoners (both men and horses) with a view to extracting ransom. Inevitably, these were games in which participants got seriously hurt or even killed from time to time. No one bothered to comment on what happened to the horses, but casualties must certainly have been common and severe for the tactics then in favour relied on the shock and sheer weight of a massed assault to dominate the opposition, with horse and rider effectively forming a living battering ram. So great indeed were the human as well as the animal costs in these events that by the early twelfth century the Church declared tourney-ing to be morally repugnant: in 1130 the Council of Clermont prohibited all such engagements and even denied ecclesiastical burial to those who fell as a result. Nevertheless, they continued to take place for at least another century: Juliet Barker identifies the 'Dunstable tournament' of 1342 as the last occasion on which such an exercise took place in England.

Over the same period, a more formalized form of combat emerged in which all attention was focused on a single pair of knightly combatants – normally armed with a heavy lance, although in its earliest manifestations the struggle was likely to continue on foot with a variety of hand-held weapons. The joust seems to have emerged first as an event for junior participants wielding blunted lances, before being adopted as an adult exercise in which the skills of the respective participants could more easily be judged as they fought in a series of knock-out engagements. After some decades when it was viewed with suspicion by the monarchy, the sport received formal blessing from Richard I (himself an adept from years of partici-pation in France), who established under a decree of 1194 five named places where jousts could offi-cially be held under royal licence, respectively in Wiltshire, Warwickshire, Northamptonshire, Not-tinghamshire and at a site 'near Stamford' which may have been in Lincolnshire or Suffolk. Under Richard and later under Edward I and Edward II the practice firmly took root, with little opposition from the ecclesiastical authorities in England.

Over the following three centuries, these sports with the lance ('hastiludes') took on an increas-ingly recreational character as a growing social dimension was added to (and eventually largely displaced) military considerations. Some of the most elaborate meetings came to be referred to as 'Round Tables', at which the chivalric ideals of the court of King Arthur began to oust the increas-ingly obsolete tactical preoccupations of the heav-ily armoured knight on the battlefield. Elaborate codes of conduct, generally overseen by the her-alds, emerged to govern these engagements, so that by the time Henry VIII took his turn in the lists little direct military relevance remained in the exercises performed on the tiltyard: it is significant that in the great festival of peace between England and France held on the Field of Cloth of Gold jousting should have played so great a part, for by that time it had shed any significant military connotation. The primary importance accorded to horsemanship may also be detected in the way that Henry drew a steady supply of competitors from within the ranks of his Gentlemen Pensioners, helping to swell the numbers of competent cavalry-men in a field whose participants were otherwise drawn from the nobility.

During his brief reign, Edward VI never reached the age where he might personally have participated in jousting, although the practice per-sisted at court, as it continued to do under Mary Tudor. With the monarch excluded from involve-ment in the tilts, some attempts were made during Mary's reign to integrate more fully the Spanish courtiers who clustered around her consort and formed a potential source of tension with the Eng-lish nobles – a further example of the tilt acting as a mechanism for peace rather than preparation for war.

Under Elizabeth too it was necessarily the courtiers rather than the monarch who disported themselves on the tiltyard, where they competed intensively with each other to catch the eye of the Queen with their dash and elegance. It was here that Robert Dudley, later 1st Earl of Leicester, first attracted her attention in the early years of her reign, and where Dudley's stepson, Robert Dev-ereux, 2nd Earl of Essex, would do likewise. In his eagerness to gain complete domination in this field, Essex also ended up by shouldering most of the considerable financial burden imposed by the annual tournaments mounted (almost always at Whitehall) to mark the anniversary of the Queen's accession; others were arranged to mark events such as important victories (including that over the Armada), weddings, visits by foreign dignitaries and even religious festivals.

By the time the Stuart dynasty replaced the Tudors the original ideals of the tiltyard were becoming a distant memory, though they continued to be preserved in a self-consciously archaic and formalized manner. Almost every tilt recorded during the reign of James I took place on the 'King's Day', 24 March, marking the anniversary of James's accession, although the king himself displayed a marked reluctance to enter the lists on his own account. The few other occasions on record from this period (numbering no more than nine or ten) were arranged to mark royal weddings, visits by foreign princes, and other celebratory occasions. Some twelve to sixteen participants are usually listed, including the royal princes as they came of age. The practising that went on beforehand seems to emphasize the infrequency of these events and the need of the courtiers (and their mounts) for regular refreshment of their martial skills: on 10 March 1605, for example, Sir Dudley Carleton noted that 'much practising' was going on at court, but evidently to little effect for two weeks later Samuel Calvert records that 'The tilting on Sunday last . . . was not performed with the accustomed solemnity.' By now entry had (perhaps necessarily) become extended beyond the nobility and even seems to have included a number of professional horsemen. Alan Young singles out the Zinzan family for special mention: Sir Robert Zinzan, he suggests, may have been employed within the royal stables under Elizabeth and was a regular

participant for 25 years, while his sons, Henry and Sir Robert, made their first appearances during the last years of the Tudor reign and continued to participate regularly under the Stuarts, possibly having some additional role in the organization of the same tournaments. Young suggests that they may have acted as practice partners for James I's two sons, for when he reached retirement age Henry Zinzan sought a pension from Charles I on the grounds of the 'long service and extreme hurts he has received by Prince Henry and His Majesty'.

The arrangement of a particularly splendid tilt at Whitehall to mark the creation of Henry as Prince of Wales in 1610 serves to underline the resonances of ancient princely virtue which such an occasion consciously evoked, while contributing to the iconographical programme with which the Stuarts sought to consolidate perceptions of their inherited birthright to the English throne:

> Uppon Wednesday in the Afternoone, in the Tilt-yeard, there were divers Earles, Barons, and others, being in rich and glorious armoure, and having costly caparisons, wondrous curiously imbroydered with pearls, gould, and silver, the like rich habiliaments for horses were never seen before. They presented their severall ingenious devices and trophies before the King and Prince, and then ran at Tilt, where there was a world of people to behold them.

It was indeed around Henry rather than his notably uncombative father that attachment to the tradition seemed set once more to crystallize, for the tournament field provided a peculiarly appropriate forum for development of the image of the Warrior Prince on whom the kingdom's hopes came to rest. In the years following Henry's early death, Prince Charles never managed to attract the same measure of adulation, although he acquitted himself with distinction in the Accession Day tournaments of 1620 and 1621 when he drew the admiration of the Venetian ambassador: '[The prince] is practising in order to take part in a tilting match in a few days. The public and solemn combat will take place first, although many of the Lords of the Council are humbly trying to dissuade him, owing to the risks run and a reasonable regard for the preservation of his life.'

Charles's failure to capture the public imagination may be counted among the contributory factors that led to the extinction of the tournament in favour of more introverted and exclusive forms of courtly entertainment under the Stuarts. Young identifies a number of other considerations, including James I's distaste for public spectacles in general, the decline in participants sufficiently skilled in the handling of arms on horseback and their reluctance to invest in costly new caparisons, so that the spectacle took on an increasingly amateur and tawdry air. Also, he suggests, the rise of the courtly masque, with specially designed scenery and costume and with subtle employment of lighting, music and dialogue by the best talents of the day, gradually displaced the ritualistic and propagandist roles of the tournament; the consequent removal of the formerly public spectacle to an exclusive, indoor setting also contributed to the alienation of the court from the populace at large. Following the jousts arranged to celebrate Charles's marriage in 1625 to Henrietta Maria and the royal couple's ceremonial entry into the capital in the following year, no further royal tournament was ever held.

Away from the battlefield, the finer points of breeding had become a matter of greater interest when horses appeared in the tournaments and jousts which celebrated and ritualized the art of warfare: here the participants adopted ever more elaborate flourishes to their great helms and evolved extravagant heraldry to decorate their shields and armour, while their mounts, chosen for their striking appearance and caparisoned as elaborately as their riders, were elevated to similarly heroic status (illus. 21). The tiltyard provided the only opportunity off the battlefield for the chivalric knight to display the qualities of his mount, and indeed it was here that the destrier was itself raised to the status of a heraldic beast of heroic proportions and appearance. Young points out, however, that the galloping steed of legend would have been of little use to the heavily armoured knight squinting from within an all-enveloping helm, for he would have been shaken so violently by the movement as to have had difficulty in maintaining control. Instead, the destrier (or from the turn of the sixteenth century the courser) had to be a pacing horse, providing a smooth ride that allowed the rider to extend his legs almost straight in the stirrups with a firm seat that enabled the lance to be held in steady aim at the opposing knight.

The horse too would have been well armoured, its chest protected by a bard, originally of quilted cloth and/or mail or else of leather, but later of plate armour, sometimes lavishly wrought. Less decorative but probably more useful in absorbing shocks was the buffer, a crescentic pad of leather filled with straw, developed in the late fourteenth century to protect its chest. The horse's face was covered by a protective 'tester' or shaffron of either metal or *cuir bouilli*, to which the crinet protecting the neck was attached. A flowing caparison or trapper of linen, velvet or silk, often richly embroidered or painted with heraldic or other devices, covered the whole of the horse's body.

The heavy saddle (also gilded, painted, embroidered or otherwise decorated) that provided a degree of protection for the rider (p. 81) put an additional burden on the horse. In order to cope

78

21 Two knights (Richard Beauchamp, Earl of Warwick, and Sir Hugh Lawney) shatter their blunted lances in a tournament watched by the king and his courtiers (to the rear) and by a more numerous public in stands (in the foreground); a herald acts as referee in this image of *c.* 1483–7. Note the substantial barrier separating the contestants and the elaborate armour and trappings of both horsemen and mounts.

with the shock of any impact, double girths were fitted to ensure that it stayed in position, but as Barker points out, the horse's breathing was restricted in this way – just as it was required to throw everything into a desperate sprint – so that periodically the saddle would have had to be loosened or removed.

One aspect of the tournament that undoubtedly did contribute to the preparation for warfare was the accustoming of the horse to charging an unwavering line almost head-on towards what it knew would be a certain impact, accompanied by an explosion of noise and violence. As was the case for the knight himself, however, the tiltyard must have gone only part way towards replicating the chaotic conditions of the pitched battle. No one bothered to record the numbers of horses injured or accidentally killed in the lists, but

Crouch asserts that casualties were high and anec-dotal evidence supports the suggestion that these encounters carried no less danger for the horse than for its rider.

The tiltyard

In its earliest form there may have been little more to the jousting ground than a suitably open and flat area where the opponents could get a good run at each other: the combined closing speed of the two participants was likely to be in the region of 50 miles per hour. A finely judged line had to be run in order to get close enough for them to strike each other with their lances, a proximity that carried with it the additional possibility that the horses might collide, with potentially disastrous results. By the first half of the fifteenth century this eventuality had been minimized by erecting a length of canvas – a tilt – suspended over a rope running the length of the course, acting as a guide for both horses and the horsemen, who aimed their lances at each other across the top of the tilt, the lance being held under the right arm (furthest from the partition) and carried across the body and behind the horse's head towards the opponent.

Timber barriers soon replaced those of canvas on the most prestigious tiltyards. A height of 6 feet emerged as the standard and a length of about 100 yards – as at Whitehall – although some could be shorter (at the Field of Cloth of Gold it was 80 yards) or longer (as at Greenwich Palace, where it was 150 yards). It became customary too for the barriers to be provided with a short, angled sec-tion at either end designed to guide the horses to the appropriate side at their run-up to the barrier and to send them off at an angle at the other end so as to avoid collisions with the surrounding palisades – the lists – which eventually gave their name to the tournament ground they enclosed.

Weapons

While 'feats of arms' with sword, dagger, axe or mace continued to be practised up to the sixteenth century, either on horseback or on foot, or both, it was the couched lance (that is, held under the arm) that emerged as the standard weapon for the tournament. Normally the lances used in tour-naments were 'rebated' or blunted, but combats in which sharp lances were used also lingered on. Needless to say, jousts with these potentially lethal weapons, termed *à outrance*, could easily result in death or serious injury: they survived longest wherever the army found itself on the edge of po-tential combat zones – as in Calais or on the border with Scotland – where occasional fatalities during interludes in open hostilities could be tolerated without attracting too much official displeasure (although normally the object of the exercise was to gain the surrender of one's opponent rather than his death). Under the eye of the court, how-ever, they gradually dwindled: one of the latest manifestations of the old form of combat was seen at the celebrations mounted at Westminster to mark the marriage of Katherine of Aragon to Prince Arthur, when a charge of massed knights armed with sharp lances was arranged – apparently without loss of life.

In the less deadly form of combat, termed *à plaisance* or 'jousts of peace', the lance was fitted with a blunt head or 'coronel', comprising multiple short spikes spread out rather than forming a point. In time these 'weapons of courtesy' entirely dis-placed sharp lances on the jousting field, initially in an attempt to limit the damage wrought acciden-tally on the flower of the aristocracy and ultimately reflecting the recreational rather than military role which the tournament gradually adopted. Perhaps the ultimate expression of this movement was seen on the Field of Cloth of Gold, from which Henry VIII and François I intended to launch a new era of fraternal relations: the rules of engagement for this event decreed that 'In consequence of the numerous accidents to noblemen, sharp steel not to be used as in times past, but only arms for strength, agility and pastime'. Young notes that among other conspicuous expenditure for this occasion was the cost of purchasing in Flanders 2,000 blunted lance-heads appropriate for this activity.

In addition to the security afforded by the blunt lance, further attempts to limit the potential for injury resulted in the shaft of the lance being made to shatter on impact, so that if a palpable hit was made the recipient would be likely to escape injury. Before the development of this convention participants were always at danger from the impact – even if (from the early thirteenth century) they had the advantage of a metal breastplate – and even more so if, as frequently happened, they were unhorsed: the high back on the saddle should have minimized this possibility, but it by no means eliminated it. As the design of jousting armour was developed so as to give additional protection to the vulnerable left side, the use of shields in tournaments was abandoned. Up to the sixteenth century, points could be gained for striking the opponent's helm or the tip of his lance, for breaking a lance against him in a permissible place or for unhorsing him; points were deducted if the lance struck the opponent's horse or his saddle (or indeed the tilt), while striking below the waist was also penalized. The possibility of an improper strike with the sharp lance was limited by the high-fronted war saddle, in use up to the fourteenth century. Thereafter, specially made jousting saddles appeared, which might have a notably high front (and protection for the legs) or it might be of a lower design particularly associated with jousts *à outrance*, allowing the rider to be unhorsed rather than run through, as the lesser of two evils. Doubtless the horse remained no less vulnerable.

RUNNING AT THE RING AND THE QUINTAIN

In order to improve his eye and the steadiness of his grip (and to train his horse to run a true line), the knightly warrior might practise riding at the quintain, a device originally involving no more than a target of some sort fixed to a post. The sport was in fact a widespread one, played on village greens up and down the country and not linked exclusively to the noble pastime of jousting. When practising at the quintain (also known as the peacock (*pavo*) or pile), novices were encouraged to use heavier-than-usual arms in order to develop their facility on the field. Ultimately a more interactive form evolved, in which the target formed one end of a bar mounted on a counterbalanced pivot; John Stow in his *Survey of London* (1633) gives a diagramatic sketch of one of these, with the crossbar expanded at one end and counterweighted with a pendant bag:

> he that hit not the broad end of the Quinten, was of all men laughed to scorne; and he that hit it full, if he rode not the faster, had a sound blow in his necke with a bag full of sand, hanged on the other end.

An alternative sport requiring just as steady an eye was running at the ring, in which the horseman aimed his lance-point at a suspended hoop. Like the experience of the quintain, there was ample opportunity here for the novice to get it wrong, as James Cleland wrote in his *Institution of a Young Nobleman* (1607):

> to run at the ring with a comelie fashion is as honourable for a Noble man in al honourable companie as it is shame for him, to run his Lance against the post, turning his face awry, or not to be able to keep his horse within the rinck.

The king himself might safely participate in such a pastime: Edward VI was anxious to display his prowess on horseback in this way, and it provided welcome respite from an incessant programme of hunting for Christian IV of Denmark during his visit to England in 1606, when James I and Prince Henry also participated in a contest. In March 1609, 'to please the prince', James accepted a further challenge to tilt at the ring with five gentlemen on either side. Tilting and running at the ring were frequently combined in chivalric contests; in 1610 it was recorded that 'The King's Day passed over with the ordinary solemnity of running and ringing' and on the same anniversary in 1620 Prince Charles 'got all the praise' by running twelve courses at the ring. Other occasions could also be so marked, as when Charles and his new brother-in-law the Prince Palatine competed following the latter's marriage to Princess Elizabeth.

By 1628 there is evidence that more attention at court was being directed to the demands of contemporary battlefield tactics (p. 52), and before long the remnants of courtly nostalgia for the chivalric virtues of medieval England were ridden into the dust by low-born troopers of the Parliamentary cavalry, consolidated by military discipline and backed by firearms that took no account of gentle breeding.

THE MANÈGE

Displays of virtuoso horsemanship as embodied in the manège, an early and rather demanding form of dressage, formed an essential element of the new forms of equestrian culture as it developed on the Continent in the course of the sixteenth and seventeenth centuries. Castiglione's influential *Book of the Courtier*, first published in Italy in 1528, makes it clear that in courtly circles there

the tournament had already been abandoned as the favoured means of displaying equestrian prowess in favour of this new and more self-conscious form of individual exercise. Within a short space these principles were being promoted in England by Sir Thomas Elyot in *The Boke named The Governour* (1531) in which he addressed the king with his conviction that

> The most honourable exercise in mine opynion, and that becometh the estate of every noble personne, is to ryde surely and cleane on a great horse and a roughe, which . . . importeth a majesty and drede to inferious persones beholding hym above the common course of other men, daunting fierce and cruel beast.

In Italy riding academies sprang up to teach these new conventions, the most famous of them opened in Naples by Federigo Grisone in 1532, and within a few years the first graduates of these schools made their appearance on the English scene. As a result of these influences, the great horses that hitherto had been reserved for war and in practising for war, began instead to be paraded on occasions of state. Whatever their accustomed style of riding, it was essential for participants in these events to present a brave and increasingly an elegant figure, hence the popularity with which the Italian instructors in particular were met when they came to England, promoting these new values (see p. 49). Now the nobleman could aspire to attract the approbation of his monarch (and the watching crowds) by having his horse execute complex airs and graces in displays known as gambading. Henry VIII himself evidently was an adept: Young finds a reference to a tournament in 1517 at which, 'between the courses, the King and the pages, and other cavaliers, performed marvellous feats, mounted on magnificent horses, which they made jump and execute other arts of horsemanship'.

These techniques would be practised away from the public gaze, increasingly commonly in a private riding house – a new phenomenon in English architecture where horse and rider could perfect their moves under the close eye of the instructor (illus. 22). Early examples were built at St James's Palace and at Sheen Palace and were also taken up by the nobility, for example at Petworth (Sussex); perhaps the most famous of all were those built by the Duke of Newcastle at Welbeck Abbey (Nottinghamshire) and at Bolsover Castle (Derbyshire), the latter completed on the very eve of the Civil War. An elaborate vocabulary of terms and conventions governed the practice of the manège, which had no connection with battlefield manoeuvres and had no other purpose than to demonstrate the mastery of the rider over his horse.

Although the intricacies of the manège attracted their adherents in sixteenth-century England – perhaps especially during the regime as Elizabeth's Master of the Horse of Robert Dudley, Earl of Leicester, its practice seems never to have attracted quite the dedicated following it had on the Continent. Its greatest English exponent, in the person of William Cavendish, Duke of Newcastle (1592–1676), was not to emerge until well into the mature period of the art under the Stuart monarchs, but the values embraced by adherents of the manège exerted a significant influence on the choice of horses imported into England from the middle decades of the sixteenth century onwards. By the 1600s French rather than Italian masters dominated the scene, notably Antoine de Pluvinel, Salomon de la Broue and the Chevalier de Saint-Antoine, who instructed both Prince Henry and the young Charles I. The Civil War saw an end to

the popularity of the manège in England, so that Newcastle, on his return from exile in Flanders at the Restoration, found himself master of an art that effectively had been abandoned by his countrymen: his failure to engage the interest of Charles II sealed its fate in England. Although it continued to attract adherents on the Continent, the reformed *haute école* promoted most famously by François de la Gueriniere, director of the French royal manège in the second quarter of the eighteenth century, found few followers in England. Continental masters continued to make an appearance at court, however, where Henri Foubert and later Domenico Angelo instructed the Hanoverian princes, but their regimes concentrated on mastering the essentials of horsemanship rather than pursuing the complexities of the manège.

Outdated military values evidently continued to exert some attraction up to the middle of the seventeenth century: William Stokes's *Vaulting Master* (1652), for example, purports to address itself to those 'who cannot mount a Palfrey, unless you have a convenient block and stirrup too', but proceeds to describe improbably athletic exercises for springing into the saddle of a veritable destrier in full armour. Not surprisingly, there is no evidence that Stokes attracted any followers whatever.

RACING

The tradition of matching horses against one another in races doubtless goes back to remote antiquity, and no doubt the swiftness of medieval coursers – and indeed horses of much less distinguished lineage – was regularly put to the test. Early races were almost always, it seems, two-horse contests, usually with one designated the leader and the other the follower and the result determined by how successfully they could maintain or improve on their relative positions. By the

22 The Duke of Newcastle observes while his companion Captain Mazin puts his horse through a series of manoeuvres in the riding house. Illustration by Abraham van Diepenbeke from Newcastle's *La Methode et Invention Nouvelle . . . de dresser les Chevaux* (1658), published in English as *A New Method and extraordinary Invention to Dress Horses* (1667).

mid-sixteenth century, however, indications of a more purposeful approach to horse-racing emerges, with horses being sought out specifically for their speed and stamina, and within 50 years the breeding of swift-running horses was to become a major preoccupation of the English.

At this time owners still looked overseas for horses of suitable conformation, preferably those of unalloyed oriental origin. Blundeville, for example, counsels that 'if any man desyre to have swyft runners, let hym chouse a Horse of Barbary, or a Turke to be his stallion', and up to the time of the Restoration opinion remained largely unchanged.

The Duke of Newcastle was equally trenchant in his views on this matter: 'Your stallion, by any means, must be a Barb . . . for a Barb that is a Jade, will Get a better Runing-Horse, than the best Running-Horse in England.' The Duke's own stud, which he re-established at Welbeck following the Restoration (illus. 23), was composed largely of Arabians, Barbs and Turkish horses.

By the opening of the second decade of the sixteenth century, racing was already being organized at a number of centres: Chester and Durham, as well as Richmond and Beverley (both Yorkshire), had emerged as recognized meeting places.

By the mid-1500s half a dozen references to recognized courses are found by Edwards, a number that had increased to about three dozen by 1625. As early as 1585 a horse race was organized at Salisbury, attended by noblemen and gentlemen and offering prizes including a golden bell and a golden snaffle. In the early years of James I's reign further races are recorded at Croydon, Epsom and Richmond (Surrey), at Enfield (Middlesex) and at Newmarket (Suffolk). The support of the king was undoubtedly an important factor in establishing racing as a polite recreation, but it quickly took on a momentum of its own, with not only the gentry but also civic bodies taking on responsibility for its organization, as when Salisbury corporation took charge of a fund in 1619 designed 'for the encouragement of the races', a practice that would become more widespread in racing towns in the eighteenth century.

Not everyone approved of this frivolous preoccupation with speed, and the rise of horse-racing was seen by some as being positively antithetical to the more serious business of breeding and preparing horses for war. Thomas de Grey would write in 1639:

> Since the laying aside of the great Saddle and Cannon [the curb bit], and the neglect of the Horse of the Menage, since the applying of our Breed only to Racing or (as I may better say) in furnishing our Selves with Horses of speed to runne away from our Enemy, the most ancient honour of Horseman-ship peculiar to this our Kingdome, and for which all other Nations highly esteemed us, is now almost vanished and lost.

By mid-century the sport was still sufficiently closely identified with the court for it to be banned altogether for periods under Cromwell, for example

with his Proclamation prohibiting Horse-races for Six Months of 24 February 1654, at which time it was noted that 'several Horse-Races are appointed in divers parts of this Commonwealth'. Later, with the restoration of the monarchy in 1660, racing found a dedicated supporter in the person of Charles II, who not only presided over the re-establishment of Newmarket as a social and sporting centre but also on more than one occasion successfully competed there on his own account. Although succeeding monarchs were never so closely identified with the course, their enthusiasm can scarcely be questioned. Soon after his succession William III appointed William Tregonwell Frampton effectively as his racing manager, naming him Keeper of the Race Horses or Running Horses at Newmarket (a post that survived until 1782) and awarding him 'for the Maintenance of 10 Boys their lodgings, &c., and for Provisions of Hay, Oats, Bread, and all other necessaries for 10 Race Horses, £1,000 per annum'. In the succeeding decades the popularity of the sport continued to rise, until Francis Drake could write in 1736 that 'It is surprising to think to what a height this spirit of horse-racing is now arrived in this kingdom, when there is scarce a village so mean that has not a bit of plate raised once a year for this purpose'. So widespread, indeed, had racing become that there was a perceived danger of the sport suffering from over-extension, and accordingly in 1740 an Act to Restrain and Prevent the Excessive Increase in Horse-Races was passed. The legislation was couched in terms not only of economics but also of social improvement, asserting that 'the great number of horse races for small plates, prizes, or sums of money, have contributed very much to the encouragement of idleness, to the impoverishment of many of the meaner sort . . . and the breed of strong and useful horses hath been much prejudiced thereby'. By stipulating a minimum

23 A manège horse from the stable of the 1st Duke of Newcastle, pictured before the east front of Welbeck Abbey, *c.* 1630.

purse in prize money of £50, the Act quickly brought about a reduction in the number of races to some two-thirds of their former total, a situation that only rising prosperity in the later Georgian period would begin to redeem. As racing became increasingly a fashionable social device, the spa towns to which the well-heeled habitually retired for the season rose to new heights of popularity, so that centres like Newmarket came to find themselves in growing competition with towns

like Epsom and Cheltenham. Other activities were added to broaden the appeal of the occasion, with cockfighting forming a popular on-course activity (p. 250) and lavish balls providing evening entertainment that brought large numbers of women as well as men to the races. In a review of racing practice at this time, Peter Edwards notes that racecourses themselves began to take on a more permanent air, with the posts and ropes that had marked out earlier courses beginning to be replaced by more permanent markers and the formerly linear courses (sometimes stretching over several miles) being superseded by circular tracks that kept the field constantly within view of the spectators; purpose-built stands also became more numerous. The introduction of subscription races with large purses further extended the appeal.

At Newmarket the races continued to be run on a knock-out basis in a series of heats, the best horses having to perform several times in a day with little more than a brief rub-down between matches, sometimes in a specially built rubbing house (illus. 24). At some other venues this practice also continued, often in heavy going which made the routine even more punishing for the horses; elsewhere prizes for single races were by now becoming more common, shifting the emphasis away from the head-to-head competitions formerly favoured in aristocratic competitions. A range of ages and abilities among the horses was catered for, with some races restricted to mounts under a certain age (normally six) and others known as 'Galloway races' for those under 15 hands. Edwards equates changes in the weight restrictions applied to jockeys to an increasing tendency for these to be professional 'hirelings' rather than gentlemen owners: earlier races had more usually featured owner-riders and some were open only to gentlemen, but these would lapse in the course of the eighteenth century.

From the reign of Charles II until about 1750, a new wave of intensive cross-breeding involving perhaps as many as 150 Middle Eastern stallions both with English mares (many of them from Yorkshire) and with mares imported from the same sources brought about a transformation in the English racehorse and established the template within which modern thoroughbreds are classified to this day. The process was evidently well under way when, in April 1682 the Moroccan ambassador, who had brought with him to England a number of magnificent horses, visited Newmarket; while declaring himself 'extreamly satisfied with the Divertisements of that place', he evidently found that 'his little Barbs were much inferior in swiftness to our Racers', suggesting that the tide had already begun to turn. The origins of modern thoroughbred racing can be traced to this period, although races continued to be held in heats over a distance of some four miles until the later 1700s. The three great horses which stand at the head of the bloodline from which present-day thoroughbreds trace their descent all make their appearance at this time. (The pedigrees of all thoroughbreds are recorded in the *Stud Book*, published regularly for the Jockey Club from 1808 onwards.) First among these is the Byerley Turk, which was foaled *c.* 1680 and which, by the time it had reached ten years of age, was said to have seen service as 'Captain Byerley's charger in Ireland in King William's wars'. The Godolphin Arabian (which Juliet Clutton-Brock judges to have been more probably a Barb) was imported to England by a Mr Coke, who had found him in Paris drawing a cart. Coke gave him to a Mr Williams who in turn presented him to the Earl of Godolphin. Even then his exceptional qualities evidently remained unrecognized, for the Earl made use of him as a teaser, and it was only when on one occasion the stallion refused the mare (named Roxana) that the Arabian was allowed to cover her: the resulting foal stands at the head of one of the most successful dynasties in racing history. But the influence of the Byerley Turk was perhaps overshadowed by the third of this trio of great horses, the Darley Arabian, which arrived directly from Aleppo around 1704. According to the *Stud Book*, 'Darley's Arabian was brought over by a brother of Mr Darley of Yorkshire, who, being an agent in merchandise abroad, became a member of a hunting club, by which means he acquired interest to procure the horse'. Over 90 per cent of modern racehorses trace their descent from the Darley Arabian through Eclipse (foaled during an eclipse of the sun in 1764), a great-grandson of the Darley Arabian which became probably the best-known horse of all time. He was bred by the Duke of Cumberland and sold on the Duke's death to Mr Wildman, a sheep salesman, for 75 guineas; Colonel O'Kelly bought a half-share in him for 650 guineas and then the remainder for a further 1,100 guineas. Eclipse ran for only two seasons from 1769 when he was five years old: during 21 races he was never beaten. When he retired to stud he sired 334 offspring that went on to become winners and made £25,000 for his owner in service fees before dying at the age of 25.

Formalization of the conduct of horse-racing can be traced to the founding of the Jockey Club in 1750. Two years later the Club began to acquire land around Newmarket and to lay down the rules which gradually came to be accepted throughout the country; today it owns a dozen more racecourses, operates the National Stud and continues to regulate horseracing throughout Britain. With the establishment of three of the classic races – the St Leger in 1776, the Oaks in 1779 and the Derby in 1780 – the transition to the modern form of racing, as a sprint for young thoroughbred horses carrying lightweight jockeys, was essentially completed.

POLO

Although possibly the most ancient equestrian sport (apart from racing) in the Middle and Far East, polo was a late introduction to the West, a process engineered by British cavalry officers and documented with surprising precision. It was first reported to an English-speaking audience from

24 George Stubbs, *Hambletonian*, 1799–1800, oil on canvas. The scene is at Newmarket, with several rubbing-down houses visible in the background.

the court of Shah Abbas, King of Persia, at Isfahan in 1599, during an embassy by Sir Anthony Sherley, who witnessed there a six-a-side game, but thereafter polo remained no more than a literary curiosity until the second half of the nineteenth century, when the game itself was transmitted to England from the northern territories of India. In particular, the province of Manipur, a mountainous region wedged between Assam and the Burmese border, was especially influential: British-owned tea plantations were established there in the Cachar valley in 1854 and evidently the planters soon began to join in the game played so enthusiastically by the villagers. It also attracted a young subaltern in the Bengal Army, Lieutenant Joseph Sherer, who played his first game in Manipur in 1856 and who, three years later, along with Captain Robert Stewart, Superintendent of Cachar, was to establish the first European polo club there.

The game soon spread to the British military in India: Captain (later General) George Stewart of the Guides Cavalry, brother of the Superintendent of Cachar, formed a club at Barrackpore in 1862 which within a year was challenging another club founded at Calcutta. By the mid-1860s the game was firmly established in Bengal and by 1870 was played throughout the British garrisons in India. The movement of servicemen to and from India provided plenty of potential for knowledge of and enthusiasm for polo to be spread, but curiously it was first played on British soil by cavalry officers who learned of the game only through reports in the press. One of the participants in the first-ever game in England, T. A. St Quintin, recorded the event in his memoirs:

It is ancient history now that one day in 1869, when the 10th Hussars were under canvas at Aldershot for the summer drills, Chicken Hartopp, lying back in a chair after luncheon, reading *The Field*, exclaimed, 'By Jove! this must be a good game,' and read us a description of 'hockey on horseback' in India. Some five or six of us who were in the tent then and there sent for our chargers, and routed up some old heavy walking-sticks and a cricket-ball, and began to try to knock the ball about – a somewhat difficult thing to do properly, as may be imagined, on a tall horse with a short stick, as, of course, we could not reach the ball. However, it appealed much to us, and resulted in our improvising a sort of long-handled mallet and having some wooden balls turned about the size of a cricket-ball. We then deputed Billy Chaine to go over to Ireland and get us some ponies, impressing upon him that they must be very quiet and handy, and under 14 hands, and that we did not mind their being a bit slow, for nobody at that time had any idea you would be able to 'go the pace' at the game. He returned with about seventeen ponies, and we set to work to fashion out a suitable ball and sticks to play the game. That started polo.

The 10th Hussars introduced the game to a rival cavalry regiment, the 9th Lancers, and each put up a team for what was to be the first inter-regimental match played in England. The *Morning Post* reported as follows:

Nearly all fashionable London journeyed from town to Hounslow on Tuesday, to witness a new game called 'Hockey on Horseback' between officers of the 9th Lancers and the 10th Hussars . . . The game took place on Hounslow Heath; the various equipages quite surrounded the space allotted to the players.

Four upright posts, some twenty feet apart marked the goals through which the ball (a small sphere of white bone) had to be driven by the players before either side could claim any advantage. The sticks used were like those for hockey, of ash and crooked at the end, and with these the ball was often struck a considerable distance. The distance between the goals was a little under 200 yards, and the players having taken up their position in front of their respective goals, the ball was thrown into the centre by a Sergeant Major of the 10th Hussars, who then galloped off, when each side immediately galloped for the ball at the best pace of their ponies . . . The game, which has been imported from India, and which has for a long time been in vogue among the Munipoories, one of the Frontier tribes, was watched with the keenest interest by the numerous and aristocratic company present.

By the following year the Household Cavalry had raised a team to challenge the two originators. This time they met in Richmond Park, and once again 'all London came to see it'. An early encounter between the 9th Lancers and the Royal Horse Guards at Woolwich Common, was recorded by the *Illustrated London News* (illus. 25). By 1876 a formal inter-regimental championship had been established.

Perhaps no one individual was more influential in developing the game than Captain John Watson (1852–1908), an Anglo-Irishman dubbed 'the father of modern polo', who revolutionized it with his skilful playing of a standard never seen before. Watson, who had taken part in the first formal match played in Ireland, in 1872, was posted to India with the 13th Hussars. He played a leading role in transforming the pace of the game

by introducing the back-handed shot (hitherto direction was changed only by dribbling the ball around) and he was also instrumental in welding the team into a single coordinated unit rather than a collection of freelances, each eager to pursue his own game. Watson's return to civilian life in England brought these developments to the English game.

The role of the military in forwarding polo in England is indisputable, but from the 1870s its popularity spread rapidly among the civilian population, leading to the formation of numerous private clubs. The origins of the most illustrious of these, the Hurlingham Club, lay in a pigeon-shooting club which secured a lease in 1868 on the Hurlingham estate at Fulham in west London (p. 263). Polo began to be played there five years later and by the turn of the century had become the club's defining activity. So popular did the Hurlingham become in its new guise that other clubs soon sprang up to cater for the demand for polo. The Ranelagh Club opened in 1878, adjacent to Barnes and Putney commons to the west of London. It is a measure of contemporary enthusiasm for the game that on 29 May 1880 a Saturday evening match between the Ranelagh and Hurlingham clubs was illuminated by electric light, during which 'operators with concave reflectors turned the rays of the light upon the players as they galloped about the field. The effect as a spectacle was exceedingly picturesque' (illus. 26).

Another (short-lived) club flourished at Wimbledon in the 1890s, and others followed at Roehampton, Beckenham and Crystal Palace before the end of the century. The London garrisons fielded a further 500 players between them and the total numbers of ponies stabled in the Greater London area at this time has been estimated at a staggering 10,000. However, by the eve of World War Two all of them had closed for polo

25 'Officers playing polo (hockey on horseback) on Woolwich Common' – a match between the 9th Lancers and the Royal Horse Guards (Blues). *Illustrated London News* (1872).

with the exception of Roehampton, where it lasted only just into the post-war years. The game was also popular in the provinces: a its height the County Polo Association listed a further 63 clubs outside London (including one in Scotland and nineteen in Ireland), fielding between them over 750 players.

The earliest rules published in England were those of the Monmouthshire Polo Club, which appeared in April 1873. Two years later they were overtaken by the first *Hurlingham Club Rules for Polo*, which formalized many of the conventions that had come to be observed and which have remained influential (with only slight modifications) to the present day. They included, for example, stipulations on the numbers of players – not more than five players being allowed on either side – on the goals – to be 250 yards apart and 8 yards wide – and the size of the ball – 3 inches in diameter – as well as conventions for the size of the ponies (see below) and the rules of engagement between

players. Although initially intended for internal use by the club, the Hurlingham rules came to be increasingly widely followed. By the time the edition of 1905 appeared in print, they were expected to apply to all polo played in England. (Many senior members of the provincial clubs were also members of the Hurlingham, easing the wide diffusion of a uniform set of rules.)

A Polo Pony Stud Book Society was established, with the aim of encouraging breeding to an agreed type, with a thoroughbred as the foundation, mixed with Arab, Barb, Welsh and English pony strains, although a willingness to jostle was judged to be more important than fine breeding. Thoroughbreds were deemed to form the best sires, and Arabs the best mares. A valuable new outlet for undersized thoroughbreds was provided by polo, although clearly there were mixed views on the appropriateness of these smaller-sized animals: in 1905, for example, we find T. F. Dale extolling the virtues of mounts with true pony blood rather

26 'Polo match by electric light, at the Ranelagh Club'. *Illustrated London News* (1880).

than the 'thoroughbred dwarfs and misfits' that had been favoured only a few years earlier.

The mounts used at the first game on Hounslow Heath were described as 'active, wiry little ponies about 12½ hands high'. The collision between the small-sized ponies adopted from the Indian game and the often over-sized frames of early European exponents undoubtedly brought about some unfortunate juxtapositions of horse and rider. One correspondent in *The Times* in 1877 remarked:

Any one who has watched a game of polo must have remarked how severely the strength and endurance of the ponies are taxed. Limited to a certain height, they must be possessed of a fair turn of speed, and require to be wonderfully active, qualifications by no means easily combined. Strong cobby ponies are seldom fast enough; and quick, active ponies are just as seldom possessed of the requisite strength. The consequence is that heavy men – and unfortunately the size of the players is not limited in proportion to that of the ponies – are often mounted on ponies either quite unable to carry their weight in safety or bestride thick-set, clumsy animals, which blunder about unable to twist and turn quickly enough to avoid collisions. The light active animal and the clumsy one are soon fagged alike, the first by overweight, the latter by undue exertion, and in either case accidents are likely to occur.

By the time Moray Brown came to compile a list of clubs around the world in 1895 the total exceeded 200, not including regimental clubs. From its origins as an Oriental courtly and military pursuit, polo had had truly become a world sport: perhaps its apotheosis came in 1908 when it was recognized as an Olympic event (repeated in 1922 and 1936).

Mules and Donkeys

The relative lack of impact made by mules and donkeys in British agriculture is mentioned elsewhere (pp. 494–5), and, it seems, they were equal rarities on the road. In his 'Historical description of the Iland of Britaine', reproduced in Holinshed's *Chronicles* (1577), William Harrison asserts that 'Our lande doth yielde no Asses, and therefore the most parte of our caryage is made by [horses]' – a statement that perhaps too readily dismisses this form of transport while surely confirming its uncommonness. Three centuries later the situation remained largely unchanged, causing those well aware of the appreciation extended to the mule in particular in other societies, in terms of its endurance, capacity for hard work, economy and longevity, to wonder why this should be. Writing at the end of the nineteenth century, Tegetmeier and Sutherland could only conclude that it was due to

the unfounded prejudices which are based upon the most extraordinary ignorance of the merits and characters of the animal. It is difficult to conceive or overstate the want of knowledge and false ideas that prevail

regarding them, and this not only among persons who have little knowledge of the subject, but amongst those who are regarded as authorities upon equine subjects.

Since the internal combustion engine was already making an appearance on the roads at that time, their crusading zeal came too late to persuade British readers that they had deprived themselves of an asset of enormous value. Only the military seem to have been convinced, with the result that thousands of mules were sent to perform unimaginable feats of labour in the quagmires of Flanders, from which few if any of them would return.

The donkey (*Equus asinus*) is, of course, a viable species in its own right. Mules, on the other hand, are the offspring of a male donkey and a female horse, while a hinny (sometimes also termed a jennet) is the progeny of a male horse and a female donkey; both mules and hinnies are sterile, and hence incapable of producing offspring of their own. Of the two, mules are generally the stronger and hence were favoured over hinnies. Being generally docile animals, mules responded well to working in trains – especially, it seems, when led by a bell-mare – and the reputation widely given to them for ill nature reflects on the misuse they commonly suffered from their earliest years, rather than forming an inherent character trait.

The *Husbandman, Farmer, and Grasier's Compleat Instructor* (1697) writes as follows of the 'ass' – evidently meaning the donkey – which it considers as 'the hardiest of all Domestick Creatures, seeming by Nature, to be framed for Labour':

its Feed is indifferent to it; and anything that is proper to be eaten by Cattle, it will make a good Meal of . . . The Ass likewise brouses on Briar-staks, will eat Chaff pleasantly; and indeed by reason of his hardiness, and the few Diseases incident to him, requires little looking to, although his Labour is considerable; for though here, (by reason of the abundance of good Horses) riding on him is accounted scandalous, and not used but by the meaner sort; yet in other Countries, they are used by great Ladies, as Palfreys, with Imbroidered Carpets, and guilded Trapings thrown over them . . . Then, for drawing Burthens in a Cart, they are very serviceable; as also at the Plough, in light ground, or where there is no roots of Trees, stiff Clay, or large Stones . . .

The passage here referring to it as a mount for foreign ladies might suggest that the author had in mind the mule rather than the donkey, but elsewhere he continues with a separate discussion of the mule: 'The Moile or Musle, among other Domestick Cattle, I conceive necessary to treat of, as being a Beast commendable for its enduring much labour and Travel.'

Anthony Dent has drawn attention to the lengthy tradition that deemed mules to be appropriate mounts for ecclesiastical use, whether by those in holy orders or (by extension of early custom in which most lawyers in the probate and divorce courts were also churchmen) by the legal profession and especially to officers of the state, including the Lord Chancellor. The lawyers distinguished themselves from other churchmen, it seems, by riding specifically a docked mule. It may be noted that already by Bede's day bishops and other clergy had taken to riding rather than walking on urgent errands: at that time they used only mares, as a mark of humility, the mare generally not being esteemed or valued for riding – a consideration that would apply equally to the mule, whose wider use may date from the time of the Normans.

No other person of gentle birth or of high status in England would be seen on such an animal – a marked contrast, incidentally, to Continental practice where not only senior churchmen (including the pope and his cardinals, as well as bishops and abbots) regularly travelled by mule but so too did the Doge of Venice and the rulers of all the kingdoms of the Iberian peninsula. These were invariably magnificent animals in their own right (usually the products of Andalusian mares and Catalan jackasses), far superior to the stunted creatures more familiar in England, although even here some estimable animals appeared. Cardinal Wolsey, whose household included a formally designated 'mewlyter', rode an animal (illus. 27) described by his gentleman usher as 'trapped altogether in crymosyn velvet and gylt stirropes . . . and his spare mewle followynge him with lyke apparel'. Furthermore, his baggage train consisted of 'sumpter mewles which were 20 in number, with his carts and other cariages of his trayne'.

In his capacity as Lord Chancellor, Lord Burghley evidently adopted the same mode of transport: an equestrian portrait in the Bodleian Library (illus. 28) shows him mounted on what is judged to be a jennet, caparisoned with a magnificence that would have stood comparison with Wolsey's mount. Whether he rode this animal in the execution of his office, however, seems less certain: tradition has it that in his later years, to which the portrait belongs, he took his exercise in the walks at his manor at Theobalds (Essex) riding in this way on a mule presented by the French ambassador. When this animal died in 1586, it was replaced by a younger one.

Such systematic mule-breeding as took place in England – never on a large scale, it would appear, despite England's sovereignty for several centuries over Poitou, home of one of the most famous breeds of donkeys on the Continent – may have

27 Cardinal Wolsey rides out on one of his mules of state, accompanied by his entourage. From a manuscript copy of the *Life* by Wolsey's gentleman-usher, George Cavendish (1578).

been largely in the hands of the monasteries. In 1116, for example, the abbey of Burton on Trent (Staffordshire) is recorded as keeping six brood mares and three Spanish jackasses, evidently with a purposeful breeding programme in mind. All such enterprises would seem to have ceased with the Reformation, after which the few references that occur – as to an incident in 1612 when the Spanish ambassador is recorded as 'riding in his carrosse with his six mules over Holborn Bridge' – may well have involved imported animals. There were some, at least, like Richard Carew in his *Survey of Cornwall* (1602), who appreciated the contribution the mule might make: in deploring the negative effects that Henry VIII's statute of 1540 had exerted on the population of ponies there, he was caused to 'entertain a conceit that ordinary husbandmen should do well to quit breeding of horses and betake themselves to mules, for that is a beast that will fare hardly, live very long, draw indifferently well, and carry great burdens, and

hath also a pace swift and easy enough for their mill and market service'. Some of Carew's countrymen had already experimented with cross-breeding, it seems, though evidently from a position of some ignorance:

not long since it happened that one brought over a he ass from France because of the strangeness of the beast (as everything where it comes first serves for a wonder), who following his kind begat many monsters, viz. mules, and for monsters indeed the country people admired them; yea, some were so wise as to knock on the head or give away this issue of his race, as uncouth mongrels.

Donkeys continued to be used for some purposes. In his *Whole Art of Husbandry*, first published in 1707, John Mortimer gives several testimonies of his admiration for mules which, he found, frequently out-performed the horses of his day,

28 Lord Burghley on his grey jennet in the grounds of Hatfield House. Just as the flowers depicted allude to his manly virtues, the mule was symbolic of his office as Lord Chancellor (although he was the last-recorded holder of that post to favour the mule over the horse). The artist and date are unknown: Burghley, who died in 1598, is shown in old age.

which makes me wonder that they are not more minded in England, than they are, especially considering their Hardiness, and freedom from Distempers, and the length of their Lives, which is almost double that of Horses. In which particular, those that are bred in the cold Countries far exceed them that are bred in the hot.

For those minded to give them a try, Mortimer suggests that for the best breed 'you must take care to get one of the largest and finest He-Asses you can procure'.

Per Kalm records the presence of 'asses' (by which he similarly refers to donkeys) around London in 1748, when he identifies two of their most valued qualities:

These animals are used by several people in this country. They were commonly quite as small as year-old foals. The principal reason why they keep them is said to be that those who have lung disease, or *Hectique*, might have the opportunity of drinking asses' milk, because the *Medici* in this place prescribe it as the surest and best *medicine* for these distressing *passions*. It is also for this reason that troops of donkeys are seen, particularly in the district round about London. Besides that, donkeys are used hereabouts to carry burdens. In particular, bakers, who send round their men to sell bread, use donkeys to carry the bread-baskets, when a large basket commonly hangs on each side of the saddle. The gypsies, who roam about this country, use only donkeys instead of horses to carry their children and baggage.

'Milch asses' continued to find favour in London up to the nineteenth century. They changed hands with great rapidity, generally being disposed of after six months for about one-third of the £7 or £8 for which they had been bought.

The hardiness and sure-footedness of the donkey recommended it for grazing in areas that would scarcely support a horse: Dent notes that in the west of England the march of enclosure and the consequent loss of common land drove owners to graze their donkeys (introduced there, he suggests, by gipsies) on precipitous pastures where no horse would have been safe. The same modest requirements no doubt recommended the donkey for adoption as an urban animal (illus. 29), pulling smaller vehicles such as milk-floats, refuse carts and costers' wagons. By the end of the nineteenth century 3,000 donkeys a year were changing hands at the Friday afternoon market at Islington, the principal donkey exchange for London. (A few ponies from the bottom of the heap were also sold there, according to Gordon 'brought together to show the donkeys to advantage'.) Some came from Wales at that time, but most originated in Ireland, where 200,000 of them were said to be employed in agriculture: Gordon records that herds of perhaps 100 at a time could still occasionally be met with being driven from Milford Haven or Holyhead to London, although most now arrived by rail. They would travel in characteristically heavy shoes which would be changed immediately – evidently no easy task in itself: unlike horses, the donkeys objected so violently to this process that they had to be lashed in a travis or turned on their backs in a manner similar to that adopted for shoeing cattle (p. 446). There was virtually no trade in donkeys from the English countryside by this time, it seems, a situation that Gordon ascribes partly to the difficulties associated with their breeding, which made them economically unattractive.

The same author mentions, however, that a few Spanish donkeys were then in use on the Hatfield

29 'The Milk Boy'. Etching and aquatint with hand colouring by R. & D. Havell after George Walker (fl. 1803–15), from Walker's *Costume of Yorkshire* (1814). The commentary provided by Walker is of interest: 'The land near all the large towns is occupied chiefly by cow-keepers, who supply the inhabitants morning and evening with milk. This is brought in tin pails either in covered carts or upon asses. The boy and ass represented here are portraits. The cropped ears and jagged tail of the poor animal are striking marks of the barbarous taste of the little miscreant who rides him . . .'.

estates of the Marquis of Salisbury, their impressive size making the indigenous animals look like 'mere dwarfs', while George Culley reports that he had seen a 'Spanish ass' at Beverley (Yorkshire) which stood 14 hands 3 inches high and was kept as a stallion, attracting fees of 2 guineas a mare. Tegetmeier and Sutherland mention that the Duke of Beaufort had a team of large mules at Badminton, where they were used for farming and general carting work, as well as drawing the hound-van, and that A. J. Scott of Rotherfield Park, near Alton (Hampshire), also bred a number of large mules (from English cart mares and foreign jacks) which

he employed very satisfactorily for farming and estate work. These few ventures, despite their evident success, stand out as exceptional initiatives that serve only to confirm the continuing rarity of mules and donkeys in the English landscape.

World War One brought about a belated realization at the War Office that the animals that had repeatedly proved their worth in maintaining the peace on the frontiers of the colonies could also make a serious impact on the European front. Such was the dearth of home-bred stock at this time that Army suppliers were forced to look abroad for mules and for jacks required for breeding purposes: tasked with procuring animals with which they were totally unfamiliar, it was inevitable that the suppliers got landed with the very worst examples that could not otherwise be got rid of to more knowledgeable local users. As Tegetmeier and Sutherland record, subsequent experience served only to confirm the worst prejudices of the British soldiers as to the character of the mule, and institutionalized misuse ensured that any flaws with which they were credited duly manifested themselves in abundance. This unhappy relationship remained unresolved by the time the petrol engine was adopted as the Army's principal source of horsepower: no one mourned the passing of the mule, while those animals lucky enough to escape the bloodbath of the Flanders battlefields might well have been happy to turn their backs on British equestrianism and to return to the devil they knew in the arid countryside of Mediterranean Europe.

30 Robert Peake the Elder (fl. 1580–1635), *Henry, Prince of Wales, in the hunting field with Robert Devereux, 3rd Earl of Essex,* *c.* 1605, oil on canvas. The Prince (no more than eleven years old at the time) sheathes his woodknife or 'hanger', having dispatched the buck at his feet. He and his companion are dressed in costumes of hunting green; in the background is glimpsed the palisade of a deer-park.

TWO

The Art of Venery and its Adjuncts

THE HUNT: PRIVILEGE AND EXCLUSION SINCE 1066

> His house was perfectly of the old fashion, in the
> midst of a large park well stock'd with dear, and
> near the house rabbits to serve his kitchen, many
> fish-ponds, and great store of timber . . . He kept
> all manner of sport hounds, that run buck, fox,
> hare, otter, and badger, and hawks long and short
> winged . . . The great hall was strewed with mar-
> rowbones, and full of hawks p[er]ches, hounds,
> spaniels, and terriers. The upper sides of the hall
> were hung with fox skins of this and the last years
> killing, with here and there a polecat intermixed,
> gins, keepers, and huntsmans poles in abundance
> . . . The windows which were very large served for
> places to lay his arrows, crossbows, stonebows, &
> other such little accoutrements . . . His table cost
> him nothing, though very good to eat at; his sports
> supplied all . . . [He] got on horseback without
> help, and until past fourscore he rode to the death
> of a hare as well as any.

Anthony Ashley Cooper's engaging word-picture of Henry Huntington (*c.* 1562–1650), second son of George Hastings, later 4th Earl of Huntingdon, whose 'way of living had the first place amongst us', conjures up an ideal existence to which numbers of the English gentry have aspired for the past thousand years. During the eighteenth and nineteenth centuries in particular, rising prosperity enabled many of those so minded to achieve this state of hunting nirvana, but the longer history of the chase is one in which inherent rights were few and privileged concessions were won only with painful slowness, first by the nobility from a succession of monarchs reluctant to relinquish rights claimed exclusively for the Crown, and later by the growing yeoman class from whose ranks the English squirearchy would evolve and for whom access to hunting privileges became a matter of primary importance in their progress up the social scale. Throughout this period the landless, penniless commoner never lost the conviction that the birds of the air and the beasts of the field were God-given creatures placed on earth for the benefit of all men, but his social superiors consistently conspired to ensure that he was denied almost all access to them, framing elaborate laws that had the effect of turning animals into private property, to which he simply had no entitlement.

The principle was one that had already begun to surface in Anglo-Saxon England, but certainly from the moment of their arrival the Norman monarchs were single-minded in claiming exclusive rights over the principal game animals, and especially deer. The mechanism they employed was to declare huge tracts of land to be *forestae regis* – royal forests whose resources were to be protected by specially drafted laws. 'Afforestation' did not necessarily imply that the Crown claimed ownership of this territory but it did assert rights over the 'vert and venison' – the trees and the game – which it contained. While the presence of woodland within these estates was clearly of some importance, it was by no means a prerequisite: the areas of forest so designated invariably contained a range of habitats, in differing proportions according to their location, including woods, pasture and arable land, moorland and heath; the forest perimeter was deliberately widely drawn so that the game it contained remained under royal jurisdiction even when the animals ventured out of the woods in search of food. The forest might also encompass farms and smallholdings as well as commons, wastes and entire villages, whose inhabitants found themselves willy-nilly subject to the laws of the forest instead of the already onerous civil laws (or in addition to them in cases that were not overridden by forest legislation). The hunting of all animals within the forest was prohibited except under licence; possession of hunting weapons or of traps and snares was similarly outlawed. Even the possession of dogs within the forest was prohibited, unless the animals had been 'lawed' – a seemingly benign term that signified a somewhat brusque treatment. In the words of Manwood's *Treatise of Laws of the Forest* (1665), it involved the animal 'being brought to set one of his forefeet upon a piece of wood eight inches thick and a foot square, then one with a mallet, setting a chissell two inches broad upon the three claws of his forefoot, at one blow doth smite them cleane off'. Lawing may stand as a metaphor for the whole tenor of the forest administration.

The forests were governed by their own courts or 'eyres', administered by officers appointed directly by the king; officially they were convened every seven years, but in practice sat often very irregularly.

On occasion the Normans had no qualms about forcibly depopulating designated forests, and Harrison conjures up a picture of them as they 'daily overthrew towns, villages, and an infinite sort of families for the maintenance of their venery'. While incidents of this kind undoubtedly did take place, it was not an invariable practice: in her excellent survey of the evolution of field sports, Emma Griffin finds a reference (on the veracity of which she is duly cautious) of 1079 to the New Forest, where it was said that 'so great was [William I's] love of hunting . . . that he laid waste more than 60 parishes, forced the peasants to move on to other places, and replaced the men with beasts of the forest that he might hunt to his heart's content'. With or without such methods, by the time of his death William had created a further twenty such royal forests. The *Anglo-Saxon Chronicle* makes the following comment (*sub anno* 1087) on his obsession:

> He set up great game-preserves, and he laid down laws for them, that whosoever killed hart or hind he was to be blinded. He forbade [hunting] the harts, so also the boars; he loved the stags so very much, as if he were their father; also he decreed for the hares that they might go free. His powerful men lamented it, and the wretched men complained of it but he was so severe that he did not care about the emnity of all of them; but they must wholly follow the king's will if they wanted to live or have land or property or his good favour.

Such was William I's authority that he was able to impose his will in these matters, but his successors were soon made aware that the nobility on whom the monarchy depended for its authority took a different view. William Rufus found himself compelled to approve a number of concessions in which certain of his barons received rights of their own, extending either to take deer within specified areas (rights of chase) or lesser game including hares, rabbits and pheasants (rights of warren). Although won from the Crown, these concessions were made also at the expense of lesser tenants of the land concerned, for they found their former rights to take smaller game extinguished by the privileges that now passed to their landlords.

Under Henry I the range of the royal forests was extended to include vast tracts as far north as Yorkshire: Griffin suggests that as much as one-third of England may have been so designated at this time. Measures to protect the king's rights were insisted upon with a new ferocity: William of Newburgh observed that 'from his ardent love of hunting [Henry] used little discrimination in his public punishments between deer killers and murderers'. Under Stephen further grants were made in an attempt to buttress support for the monarchy but when civil war racked the country in the years 1135–54 the game suffered widespread slaughter in the reaction against the king: the *Gesta Stephani* records that 'many thousands of wild animals, which formerly had overflowed the land in numerous herds, were so suddenly exterminated that from such a countless swarm you could soon scarcely have found two together'. Henry II managed to re-establish some royal privileges, forbidding in his Assize of the Forest (1184) 'that anyone shall transgress against him in regard to his hunting-rights or his forests' and willing that 'full justice be exacted from the offender as was done in the time King Henry, his grandfather'. Under Richard I and John, however, the process of disafforestation was extended, resulting in more privileges passing from the monarch to the nobility. The shifting balance of power culminated in

the presentation to King John of *Magna Carta* in 1215, part of which specifically aimed to redress in favour of the barons the tendency of the monarchy to designate increasing tracts as *forestae regis*. Under the terms of a new instrument drawn up in 1217, the *Charta de Foresta*, a relatively more liberal regime began to prevail in the forests, with terms of imprisonment replacing the physical mutilations hitherto exacted on offenders (although the extent to which the full force of the law had always been applied is not clear). Concessions were gained too over the practice of lawing dogs which, although not discontinued, was thereafter limited to those areas where it had been current at the time of the accession of Henry II, while the penalties imposed on offenders were brought into line with common law. The provisions of the *Charta* were implemented only slowly, however, with the monarchy fighting a vigorous rearguard action in defence of its ancient rights for much of the following century. None the less, under Henry III it was reiterated that 'No man henceforth shall lose either life or limb for killing our deer', although the miscreant still faced 'a grievous fine if he hath anything whereof, and if he hath nothing to lose, he shall be imprisoned a year and a day'. The process of disafforestation continued to gather pace, especially under the weak regime of Edward II.

These reforms can scarcely be interpreted as evidence for democratization, however, and for the peasantry they offered few redeeming features: having wrested their respective estates from royal control and subsequently consolidated them into ever-larger private fiefdoms, the barons proved no less assiduous in imposing rigid and exclusive controls over their forests. Additionally, just as the king might have hunting rights over others' lands, he granted rights of 'free warren' to favoured barons, entitling them to hunt over territory belonging to lesser landholders. A glimpse of the keenly felt inequalities under which the poorer folk laboured is provided by a petition presented during the Peasants Revolt in 1381, 'that all warrens, as well in fisheries as in parks and woods, should be common to all; so that throughout the realm, in the waters, ponds, fisheries, woods and forests, poor as well as rich might take the venison and hunt the hare in the field'. It proved a utopian aim that found no answer from the monarchy or the aristocracy; such liberalization of forest laws as took place at this time in no way benefited those at the lower end of the social scale.

From the point of view of game animals, the extension of rights of ownership to a larger constituency of landowners had indeed a seriously deleterious effect, for they found themselves under increased pressure from ever-larger numbers of hunters. The result was that the deer population in particular entered a period of sustained decline, exacerbated by progressive loss of habitat

as increasing numbers of trees were felled to provide timber for building and charcoal to fuel a growing range of smelting activities, particularly in the iron and lead industries. Expanding arable cultivation and grazing of livestock also made inroads into the forest as the farming community consolidated its position. As a result of these twin onslaughts, swaths of territory formerly tree-covered were reduced to barren heath incapable of supporting the deer population that formerly had proliferated there. As a means of protecting the dwindling stocks, those who could afford it turned increasingly to the construction of parks, their perimeters completely empaled in order to preserve the stock within and to exclude those with no right to be there (illus. 31). These moves were to have important effects on the nature and conduct of the hunt (p. 108).

Under Richard II the first Game Law to be administered by the Common Law courts rather than

31 Deer parks in a landscape: the heavily emparked western part of the county of Sussex, a detail from John Speed's *Theatre of the Empire of Great Britaine* (1611).

the eyres of the Forest Courts entered the statute book, a move regarded as a landmark. In 1390 Parliament ordained

> that any kind of artificer or labourer or any other who lacks lands and tenements to the value of 40s a year, or any priest or clerk if he has not preferment worth £10, shall not keep any greyhound, or any other dogs, if they are not fastened up or leashed, or have had their claws cut, on pain of imprisonment for a year. And that every justice of the peace shall have power to enquire and punish every contravention.

This new statute had the effect of excluding all the commonalty from even the few forms of hunting to which they had previously been limited, for the king himself added a clause to this Act prohibiting the lower classes from hunting with 'hounds and ferrets, hays, nets, hair-pipes, cords, and all other devices to take or destroy beasts of the forest, hares or rabbits, or other sport of gentlefolk'. Richard Almond observes that the level set for the property qualification was such as to permit the more prosperous yeomen to engage in certain forms of hunting, but on the other hand they remained excluded by other measures from hunting in the royal or seigneurial forests, which were still subject to Forest Law. These measures left the bulk of the population even worse off than before, for their ancient rights to take game from wastes and commons were abolished in favour of new restrictions that limited all hunting to the upper classes.

The degree to which illicit hunting with nets and other devices was perceived to threaten the very survival of the red and fallow deer populations is alluded to in an 'Act for deer-hays and buck-stalls' introduced by Henry VII in 1503–4, where it was asserted that the greatest destruction hitherto

hath been, and yet is, with nets called deer-hays and buck-stalls, and stalking with beasts . . . so that if the said nets or stalking should unlawfully be used and occupied in time coming . . . the most part of the forests, chases, and parks of this realm should be therewith destroyed.

Henceforth it was forbidden that 'any person or persons, spiritual or temporal, having no park, chase, nor forest of their own, keep, not cause to be kept any nets called Deer-hays, or Buck-stalls'; the stalking of deer 'with any bush or beasts' was similarly outlawed, on pain of forfeiture.

Technological innovation led to the drawing up of legislation by Henry VIII in 1533–4 and in 1541 designed to limit the use of firearms as well as crossbows: although primarily introduced to correct those who 'of late have laid apart the good and laudable exercise of the long-bow', the Bill for Cross-Bows and Hand-Guns (1541) also acknowledged that these had become a source of 'great peril and continual fear and danger' to the keepers of forests, chases and parks, among others, and henceforth outlawed their use against 'any deer, fowl or other thing, except it be only at a butt or bank of earth'.

James I hunted almost as though his life depended upon it, and indeed he saw it literally as essential to his royal well-being, for it was reported of him in 1605 that:

> The King . . . finds such felicity in that hunting life, that he hath written to the Councill that it is the only means to maintain his health, which being the health and welfare of us all, he desires them to take the charge and burden of affairs, and foresee that he be not interrupted or troubled with too much business.

So great were the difficulties raised by this predilection in the execution of state affairs that they were remarked upon by a number of foreign ambassadors, as when a Venetian envoy reported on 4 September 1603 that 'for the next twenty days he [the king] will be without his council, away upon a hunting party, and everything is at a standstill', or on 22 February 1607 when the ambassador confessed to the Doge his inability to communicate with the monarch, knowing that 'the King is very much put out if his own Ministers, and much more foreign Envoys, dare to mention business to him at such a time. He desires to enjoy the chase in the company of very few and with a most private freedom.' On the other hand, it was quickly appreciated in diplomatic circles the king's predilections might be turned to advantage, as revealed by a report by the Venetian secretary to his masters, dated 18 September 1603:

M. de Vitry, Captain of the French Royal Guard has been sent here with, perhaps, thirty hounds as master of the chase, to amuse the king, and is in the highest favour. His presence inspires the Spanish and the Flemish with suspicion, and the English too, perhaps, who are jealous because he has suggested to the king that he should conduct his hunts all through the night.

Yet another Venetian recorded in 1618 that the king and his courtiers would follow the game

often for the space of eight whole days, until it is quite exhausted and dead, and to effect this without killing the horses, relays are posted in various places. Being thus freshly mounted, the sportsmen are enabled to continue the hunt with greater spirit. On his Majesty coming up with the dead game, he

dismounts, cuts its throat and opens it, sating the dogs with its blood, as the reward for their exertions. With his own imbrued hands, moreover, he is wont to regale some of his nobility by touching their faces. This blood it is unlawful to wash off, until it fall of its own accord, and the favoured individual thus bedaubed is considered to be dubbed a keen sportsman and chief of the hunt and to have a certificate of his sovereign's cordial good-will.

Such was the single-mindedness with which the hunt was prosecuted that on occasion the careful arrangements outlined above proved inadequate: on 16 May 1609, for example, the chase was so prolonged that a number of horses died in the headlong pursuit, one under Prince Henry himself. Some years later, in 1616, the King injured his leg in a fall while hunting, 'but in spite of all, he will not lose an hour of his hunting, and as he cannot ride on horseback he either goes in a carriage or has himself carried'.

Charles I inherited his father's love for the hounds and even took them with him on military expeditions. Charles II occasionally distinguished himself in the field but he was perhaps more at home on the turf at Newmarket.

The hounds themselves had traditionally been augmented by animals which reverted to the king on the deaths of certain bishops or abbots who ran packs of their own, while a number of sheriffdoms and serjeanties also carried obligations to contribute towards them: Round notes instances of serjeanties held in return for the training of leash-hounds and for the supply and maintenance of harriers, bratchets and wolfhounds. The king further exercised rights of seizure over other citizens' hounds. Control of the export of hounds was placed in the hands of the Master of the

Buckhounds, in an attempt to regulate the supply. Each pack would additionally have bred its own pups and manuals giving advice on such matters were already being published. Under James I and Charles I the number of hounds in the pack seems to have been stabilized at sixteen couples.

Royal warrants empowered the Masters and Purveyors to provide for the needs of the hunt at the expense of the community in which they found themselves. In 1614 Sir Thomas Tyringham was given authority to take up sixteen beds together with provision for 30 horses and for the king's hounds, in all places adjacent to the court, 'at reasonable prices'. In April 1621 a similar warrant authorized him to take up beds, stables, rooms and so on on his own terms, which must have been a questionable blessing to those who had such places to let.

In his Act for the better Preservation of the Game' of 1670–71 Charles II formally instituted a profession that would have a major impact both for better and for worse as far as the animal kingdom was concerned – the gamekeeper. The Act acknowledged that

divers disorderly persons . . do betake themselves to the stealing, taking and killing of conies, hares, pheasants, partridges and other game intended to be preserved by former laws, with guns, dogs, tramels, lowbels, hays and other nets, snares, hare-pipes and other engines, to the great damage of this realm, and prejudice of noblemen, gentlemen and lords of manors and others, owners of warrens . . .

The Act further decreed

That all lords of manors, or other royalties, not under the degree of an esquire, may from

henceforth by writing under their hands and seals authorize one or more . . . game-keepers within their respective manors or royalties, who . . . may take and seize all such guns, bows, greyhounds, setting-dogs, lurchers, or other dogs to kill hares or conies, ferrets, tramels, lowbels, hays or other nets, hare-pipes, snares or other engines . . . as within the precincts of such respective manors shall be used by any person or persons who by this act are prohibited to keep or use the same.

Gamekeepers or others authorized by any justice of the peace were authorized to 'seize, detain and keep' any offending material, 'or otherwise to cut in pieces or destroy' such things as the Act prohibited. Warrens, even if not enclosed, were given special protection (as were rabbits found on the edges of warrens); offenders had to yield treble damages and costs to the owner as well as facing three months' imprisonment. Similar protection was extended to fish-ponds and moats, the gamekeepers having the right to 'cut in pieces and destroy all and every such angles, spears, hairs, nooses, trolls, wears, pots, fish-hooks, nets and other engines whatsoever' that might be found in the possession of an offender. From this time onwards gamekeepers would form a major impediment to unauthorized hunting: the game animals themselves, of course, were oblivious to the benefits of being killed by one social class rather than another, while many other species would find themselves persecuted literally out of existence as the keepers sought to preserve the creatures in their care so that they could be shot or hunted by their legal lords and masters.

From this brief survey, the unbroken attachment of the monarchy and the privileged classes to the hunt becomes clear. Their single-mindedness reached its peak, perhaps, during the reign of James I, for many of whose nobles hunting had become, according to Robert Burton's *Anatomy of Melancholy* (1621), nothing short of an obsession: 't'is all their study, all their exercise, ordinary businesse, all their talke: and indeed some dote too much after it; they can doe nothing else, discourse of nought else'. The dedicated hunter would remain a familiar figure for centuries to come, but already the nature of hunting was beginning to change: a large proportion of the deer (increasingly fallow rather than red deer) were by now confined within parks and their very status as wild beasts had begun to be called into question. William Harrison was one of those who doubted 'whether our buck or doe are to be reckoned in wild or tame beasts or not', suggesting further that the hunt had become so emasculated that it was now 'more meet for ladies and gentlewomen to exercise . . . than for men of courage to follow'. In the face of continuing scarcity in the following centuries, deer came to be repeatedly chased by the hunt and captured rather than being killed, so that they could be hunted again on another occasion. A wider range of game – including, most notably, foxes – was also hunted as deer became scarcer, but quite quickly these too became so scarce that they began to be specially reared or even imported in order to satisfy the sporting appetites of the hunting community (pp. 112–13). Any pretence that hunting was conducted primarily for the provision of food for the larder or for preservation of livestock was by now beginning to wear decidedly thin: enjoyment of the pursuit for its own sake had almost entirely replaced any utilitarian dimension that might once have driven it, although from its very earliest days the conduct of the hunt had been regulated to ensure it provided pleasure in equal measure to any more prosaic end.

THE CHASE IN THE MEDIEVAL PERIOD

Possession of extensive estates bestowed by the Crown was one of the primary attributes by which the upper strata of the feudal hierarchy distinguished themselves. In a society in which the positions men had carved for themselves were constantly to be insisted upon by assertion of the rights associated with their status, one of the most jealously guarded of these was the exercise of hunting privileges. It was axiomatic, in the words of *Piers Plowman*, that 'lewede men' were placed on earth to labour and lords to hunt. At least in theory, there was a kind of contract between those privileged to exercise control over the wild population and the farmers and smallholders whose stock and crops were constantly at risk from these creatures, but in practice the hunting classes seem seldom to have been motivated in their day-to-day actions by any sense of social conscience. For his part, the country-dweller was doomed to look on with thinly disguised envy at the self-indulgent activities of the rich, or simply to subvert the system as best he might by helping himself to such game as he could lay hands on without being caught.

Hunting was inextricably bound up with the practice of conspicuous consumption that formed a necessary expression of power, with venison in particular representing an unattainable luxury that would almost never legitimately pass the lips of the poor. In keeping with this artificially engendered status, a great deal of stress was placed on the observation of approved protocols for the conduct of the hunt, for the getting of venison was no less a public expression of privilege than its consumption. As an essential skill to be mastered by every nobleman, the art of venery was instilled from youth along with the other essentials of education: Coggins notes that Edward I possessed his own heron hawks by the time he was nine, while

Almond observes that Alexander III of Scotland hunted in the Forest of Galtres (Yorkshire) in 1251 at the age of ten and Henry VI coursed hares at Bury St Edmunds (Suffolk) in 1443–4 aged twelve. Instruction would have included not only the prescribed techniques to be followed in hunting the different animals of the chase but also field-craft, including the many signs that helped the hunter to recognize the species concerned and its location. Principal among these were an ability to identify their individual tracks and (perhaps most importantly) their droppings, termed variously according to species as 'fewmets' or *fumées* (red deer), croties (fallow, roe and hare), lesses (wild boar and wolves) or spraints (otter). Every kind of hunt evolved its own extensive vocabulary of terms that had to be learned, as well as a wide range of signals given with the hunting horn, carried by all the principal personnel so that the various elements of the hunt could stay in touch and could communicate the course of events to each other. Without extensive schooling in all these arts, it was impossible for anyone to participate in any way whatever – or indeed to show himself as socially fitted to occupy the position of privilege implicit in the chase. Those involved in hunting – essentially a large-scale group activity rather than a solitary pursuit – asserted this privilege through insistence on proper observation of all the customary formulae that ruled its conduct. The entire vocabulary of the hunt was constructed in debased and anglicized French in a manner that made it incomprehensible to those unschooled in it and was itself a device that ensured exclusion of the uninitiated. Hunting undertaken without attention to these formalities was liable to be perceived to be – and was indeed likely to be – illicit, so that it was in the interests of privileged landowners to underline their authority by adhering as closely and as visibly as possible to courtly practice.

Perhaps for this very reason, no mention is made in the early written sources of individual activities in which the hunter stalked his prey by stealth, for such an exercise presented no opportunity for display of the virtues bound up with the hunt. As with other aspects of Continental practice discussed below, hunting by stealth seems to have been contrary to the whole spirit in which the formal hunt took place in England. However, there was inevitably a great deal of clandestine hunting which observed none of these niceties. Poaching took place at the highest levels of society – perhaps most infamously when in the early fourteenth century the Earl of Derby was (posthumously) charged in the forest-court of the Duchy of Lancaster with taking 2,000 deer from the royal forest of High Peak over a period of six years – but others arraigned included lesser noblemen, innumerable monks and certain 'clerks and scholars' of Oxford as well as many ordinary folk. Certain senior clergy enjoyed hunting rights which the more ostentatious observed with all ceremony, but the numbers of others convicted of poaching suggest that covert pursuit of game for the pot was widespread in their ranks. Neighbouring landowners seem to have been wilfully casual about straying into estates where they had no right to be and did so with a certain amount of bravado: even when pursuing game with horses and hounds, these transgressors would certainly have dispensed with much of the prescribed ceremonial as described here. Also endemic was trespassing by landless country-dwellers in the parks and estates of their social superiors in order to fill the stomachs of their families and, perhaps, to challenge the authority of unjust legislation. Quite extensive poaching, perhaps by organized urban gangs, has also been conjectured by Naomi Sykes on the basis of frequent finds of skeletal remains of deer in excavations within medieval towns, amongst which any sign of having been dismembered in the formal manner demanded by the hunt is absent. Clearly no ceremony was observed by any of these clandestine forays, or in the equally illicit taking of animals that happened to stray into commons or wastes: any such creatures were run down, shot, netted or trapped by whatever means proved most expedient.

Hunting under the Tudors and Stuarts

Although enforcement of the Forest Laws had relaxed in the course of the fifteenth century, particularly during the 30-year disruption occasioned by the Wars of the Roses, they were enthusiastically revived by Henry VII, both through the forest eyres which he reinstated in 1488 and through new legislation. In 1485–6 his Act shewing the Penalty for Hunting in the Night, or with Disguising identified a number of new crimes. It can be no coincidence that the wording of the Act blurs any distinction between poaching and a range of more heinous offences against the person and the state:

> divers persons in great number, some with painted faces, some with visors, and otherwise disguised, to the intent they should not be known, riotously, and in a manner of war arrayed, have oftentimes of late hunted, as well by night as by day, in divers forests, parks and warrens . . . in special in the counties of Kent, Surrey, and Sussex, by colour wherof have ensued in times past great and heinous rebellions, insurrections, riots, robberies, murders, and other inconveniences . . . which offences could not be punished . . . because the said mis-doers, by reason of their painted

faces, visors, and other disguisings could not be known . . .

Henceforth, it was decreed, offenders in this fashion would be guilty of felonies and punished accordingly. Griffin notes that at the first forest eyre held during Henry's reign, in 1488, the lists of miscreants were lengthy and the offenders brought to trial included several royal officers implicated in abuses of the trust placed in them.

Henry was an avid hunter, to be found regularly in the field almost to the end of his 24-year reign. All his enthusiasm was inherited by his successor Henry VIII, who passed entire days at a time in the saddle and was notorious as an unforgiving rider inclined to treat his horses as entirely expendable, exhausting several animals in a single day. Of several enlargements made to the royal forest during his reign – and especially at the time of the Dissolution – the most important was the creation of an extensive hunting ground stretching between his palaces at Nonsuch and Hampton Court (both in Surrey), the latter coerced from Cardinal Wolsey in 1529. The areas partially surviving today as Hyde Park, St James's Park and Regent's Park were all afforested at this date. At the same time, the continuing process of attrition of the natural resources mentioned above led to the total loss of some of the richest reserves in the country – most notably the former royal forest of High Peak (Derbyshire) where the combination of consumption of the timber by local industries and illicit grazing by flocks (exacerbated by a succession of severe winters – and, of course, the activities of the Earl of Derby mentioned above) resulted in total loss of habitat and ultimately of deer. Many of the noblemen favoured with former monastic estates at the time of the Dissolution lost no time in liquidating the forests they had inherited, accelerating the changes taking place in the landscape.

Under Edward VI the capital offences established by Henry in the Acts of 1539–40 were repealed in 1547, although they were later revived for a period of three years during a period of rebellion and instability. A further act of Elizabeth in 1549–50 proved more pragmatic to offences against the hunting legislation, classifying them as misdemeanours, punishable by three months' imprisonment, treble damages and a seven-year surety.

James I yielded to no one in his enthusiasm for hunting and reasserted his rights as monarch to hunt anywhere in England. He too instituted a revival of all the legislative measures already in place to protect the game in the royal forests that remained to him. A game warden's warrant issued in 1620 and reproduced by Griffin gives a flavour of the sustained competition for resources coming from the disenfranchised:

> Persons of meane qualitie in our counties of Northampton, Huntingdon, and Rutland do usually commit many disorders in hunting, tracing and poaching with beagles, hounds and mongrills, coursing with greyhounds, using setting-doggs, engines and netts, shooting with crossbows or gunnes . . . to the great decay and spoil of the several games of hares, pheasants, partridges, ducks and other fowls.

James's son Prince Henry (illus. 30) showed every sign of proving even more dedicated than his father until his premature death, when the mantle was inherited by his brother, the future Charles I, who proved also a dedicated hunter. During the period of his personal rule when he dispensed with Parliament, Charles sought to revive many of the medieval boundaries and rights within the royal forests, including those that had since been disafforested. In 1632 he revived the forest eyres, first in the Forest of Dean and Windsor Forest and later extending to Essex and Northamptonshire. Griffin finds that in the Forest of Dean 800 crimes were uncovered at that time, stretching back over 40 years. Eventually, when he was forced to recall Parliament in 1640, Charles came under attack for his use of the eyres and was forced to relinquish all the gains the Crown had made since the beginning of the reign of James I.

The regime change of the Civil War and the Commonwealth era brought no respite to the pressures on the deer, either directly in the form of widespread poaching or indirectly through further depredation of their essential habitat. The royal estates in particular came to be targeted by vengeful and hungry citizens – soldiers as well as civilians – for whom the end of monarchical control held out, however briefly, the prospect of access to the stocks of deer that hitherto had been denied them. Incursions into the former royal parks were widespread. Those at Windsor were particularly targeted: firstly they were overrun by local residents who had been forced to witness the flaunting of royal power there for centuries past, and when Parliament sent in the military in 1642 to restore order, the soldiers proved even more destructive: 'My Lord General [Essex] his soldiers destroyed all the Deer of the said [Little] Park, being above five hundred, and burnt up all the Pales'. It was a picture repeated in many other forests, private as well as royal, for they formed equally potent symbols of the system of privilege that now seemed on the verge of extinction. The Parliamentary sympathies of Sir Robert Harley, for example, proved insufficient protection for the 500 deer in his park in Herefordshire, all of which were lost at this time; on the other hand, the Parliamentarian Sir Bulstrode Whitelocke managed to maintain a pack of harriers for his own use at Windsor, although by now the game must have been thin on the ground.

Other threats to the great parks manifested themselves at this time, as graziers' flocks began to find their way into the woodlands from which they had for so long been excluded; elsewhere parks and estates, broken up and sold off as old fortunes crumbled, were turned over to the plough. Those deer that had escaped with their lives must have found themselves competing ever more desperately for available grazing

Being naturally anxious that the resources of the royal estates which now fell to them should not heedlessly be dissipated, Parliament gradually re-imposed control. After a decade of confusion and near chaos, the Council of State began to consider measures for the more effective management of surviving forests and (in accordance with its handling of other royal resources) for the sale of assets that might form a source of revenue, but by the time of the Restoration, little had been achieved in this respect.

It should not be thought that under the Tudors and Stuarts, at least, the deer had ever been regarded purely as a passive resource, for it is clear that they were by now managed on a considerable scale. Large numbers of animals were regularly transported over hundreds of miles in efforts to improve the game in one royal park or another or to meet the short-term requirements of the monarch – a practice described elsewhere in some detail by the present author. The technique evidently had been applied to fallow deer since their first introduction under the Normans and evidence is now gathering for its continued use in the following centuries: Anne Rowe has produced documentation for several such movements between parks in Hertfordshire, the earliest of which involved six does and two bucks sent by Henry III to stock a new park at Great Gaddesdon in 1241 and 30 does contributed to Queen Eleanor's park at Langley in 1276. From the early years of the

sixteenth century numerous records survive of red deer being brought from as far away as the western isles for the benefit of the Scottish court at Stirling and Falkland, where they were confined in a deer-fold (evidently with a wattle fence) before their fate was decided. Expenditure is recorded for nets and for 'six score and four fathoms' of ropes 'to draw the deer with', as well as for their transport: repeated journeys were made by one Robert Matheson, often accompanied by four assistants, between the two royal palaces in the years 1504–6, with horses and litters bearing the deer. The same practices were well established too at the English court: in 1538, for example, Sir Francis Bryan, Master of the Toils, received payment for taking no fewer than 1,000 deer in a variety of parks in order to replenish stocks at Henry VIII's palace at Nonsuch, and in subsequent years large consignments of several hundred deer at a time are recorded as being decanted from royal forests widely distributed in counties from Nottinghamshire to Sussex into a variety of parks. Litters may also have been widely used for these deer, although incidental references to 'carriages' and wagon wheels imply that wheeled transport was also used when appropriate. At other times the deer seem to have been herded (presumably roped together): a letter of 1538 from the Bishop of Chester to Thomas Cromwell reports that 'On Wednesday last I set forth my deer to be conveyed to the King's Grace to the number of 26; there never was such a drove seen.'

These removals evidently became a matter of routine under James I and Charles I, whose horizons even extended to the Continent: animals were introduced to royal parks from Denmark, Germany, France and Ireland at this time, while others were exported as gifts to the royal houses of Austria and France. More detailed French sources from the mid-seventeenth century give descriptions of carts mounted with cages with sliding doors and (apart from sawing-off their antlers to avoid damage or injury) the general consideration with which the deer were to be treated; it was none the less a stressful process for them and the English sources mention the expectation that numbers of them might be expected to die in transit.

Following the Restoration, in order to encourage indigenous regeneration Charles II declared a closed period of from three to five years to be observed in all royal forests, during which time no fallow deer or red deer were to be killed. Other landowners helped build up the royal stocks, to judge by a sum of £75 'paid to several keepers for their fees at 5s. a head for 300 deer, presented to his Majesty by several noblemen and others, and delivered into Windsor Forest, Waltham Forest and Enfield chase'. Replenishing with foreign deer began in the first winter following his coronation, when £148 1s. was paid out 'for taking 33 Jermayne Deere out of a shipp at Tower Hill and Conveying them in five waggons to Waltham fforest'; the master of the ship *Angel Gabriel* received £44 for 'freight of the stags that came from the Duke of Oldenburgh'; Sir Richard Ford was paid £176 8s. 8d. for freight and other disbursements in Hamburg 'for a parcel of deer that were sent to H[is] M[ajesty] by the Duke of Brandenburgh' in 1661. During James II's reign further large-scale movements of deer are recorded, including one consignment of 108 animals from Germany, for which a detailed costing survives.

Responsibility for these onerous arrangements fell to the Master of the Toils, with his staff of serjeants and yeomen. It was arduous and demanding work, with much of the movement of stock taking place during the worst weather in the winter months. Wagons transported both the deer and the heavy 'toils' of canvas and netting with which the animals were caught and which gave

their name to the office. Something of the pattern of life in this department emerges from a warrant of 1 October 1686 for £152 7s. 2d., to be paid:

> To Thomas Howard, yeoman of the tents and toyles, for his charge in removing the toyles and waggons from Whaddon Chace in Buckinghamshire to Haddam Hall Park in Hertfordshire, and taking and removing the redd deere there to Epping Forest and to Bagshot Parke, and for removing the said waggons and toyles from Bagshott Parke to Lord Aylesbury's parke in Wilts, called Tottenham Parke, and taking and removing 192 fallow deer to the forrest of Alice Holt in Hampshire.

During his brief reign, James II proved equally well disposed to hunting and William III maintained efforts to restock the royal parks. Even in her advanced years, Queen Anne proved a dedicated hunter, driving headlong in a one-horse chariot through the parks and open countryside around Windsor: on one occasion she was reported to have pursued a stag for 45 miles. With the advent of the Hanoverian line, however, interest fell away. George I did maintain the royal staghounds (now called buckhounds) but had little real interest in hunting. The whole conduct of the royal hunt by now had been reduced to a shadow of its former self: George II hunted primarily carted deer (pp. 132–3), a pursuit rendered even more bizarre by the substitution in 1728 of an elk for the normal quarry. The elk, released at Windsor, was said to have given a 'brilliant run', though an account by a Windsor huntsman of a similar chase, in 1829, quoted by Jane Roberts, has a distinctly more convincing air: 'he wobbled away – I could not call it running – for half an hour, and I took him at Bagshot. The hounds would not hunt him.'

By this time, beyond the confines of the parks owned by the king and the major noblemen, the fox and the hare had replaced the deer as the primary quarry of the hunt in all but some far-flung areas in the south-west and in Scotland. In the process of this major shift of interest, a much wider sector of country society had come to enjoy the formalities of the hunt in a landscape now greatly impoverished in terms of its deer population: since foxes in particular were classed as vermin and universally detested for the damage they wrought, there was little to inhibit enthusiasm for the growth of this hunting community – at least not until foxes themselves began to grow scarce, as described below. Large numbers of landowners and other country-dwellers were now hunting in a collaborative manner, in pursuit of quarry that was not in itself socially divisive.

Early Hunting Literature

Reconstruction of the early practice of hunting is dependent partly on pictorial records – most often incidental illustrations to medieval manuscripts – and partly on textual sources. Even the few texts that survive take somewhat different perspectives on the importance of various aspects, but all have in common that they were written exclusively for an aristocratic audience. Otherwise, records of legal proceedings prove most useful in adding detail to both established practice and its abuse.

At the head of the English sources stands the *Art of Hunting* (1327) by William Twiti, huntsman to Edward II; strictly speaking, Twiti's text was written in Norman French and 'Englished' by another (supposed) royal huntsman by the name of Gifford. This brief prose work takes the form of a dialogue between master and pupil, a device that (along with the basis of the text) may

already have been borrowed from other sources and would remain popular with authors in this field until the eighteenth and nineteenth centuries. Twiti lists the principal 'beasts of venery' – hare, hart, wolf and boar – and those of the chase – fallow and roe buck, fox and marten. He makes no mention of female deer: on the Continent, at least, these were considered inferior – appropriate for driving into nets and harvesting for the table but not worthy animals for the hunt – and it may be that Twiti's silence on the subject indicates that here too they simply did not register amongst the game appropriate for the attentions of the aristocratic hunter.

More extensive and informative is the *Master of Game*, compiled between 1406 and 1413 by Edward, 2nd Duke of York (*c.* 1373–1415), grandson of King Edward III and cousin of Henry IV, at whose court Edward occupied, somewhat uneasily, the office that gave the book its title. (Never wholly free of suspicion of treachery, Edward was also favoured by Henry with other more substantial offices, but the *Master of Game* was compiled to while away the time he spent in prison for treason at Pevensey Castle.) The text is in large part a translation of the *Livre de Chasse* of Gaston Phébus, Comte de Foix, a kinsman of the Plantagenets, to which Edward added a number of interpolations and several additional chapters of his own authorship that reflect English as opposed to French practice – with which Edward would have become personally familiar during a period when he held office as governor of Aquitaine. The whole therefore presents an accurate reflection of the conventions observed in English hunting at the turn of the fifteenth century – deeply indebted to Continental practice, including the preservation of an arcane vocabulary in debased French and a series of highly formalized rituals, but often with something of a twist introduced by centuries of insular development. Whereas Gaston's text is extensively illustrated and forms the single richest source of imagery of the French hunt to have survived, the earliest edition of Edward's text has no such illustrations to show its English equivalent, although several later copyists added their own. To some extent it is permissible to extrapolate from one to the other, but caution must be exercised since detailed practice clearly varied between the two countries. While much importance is rightly attached to the *Master of Game*, it is significant that (as noted by Griffin) Henry v purchased no fewer than twelve hunting books in a single year, 1421, indicating that the number of sources in circulation must have been considerably wider than surviving examples tend to indicate.

Of a similar date (*c.* 1400–70) is a short tract titled *The Tretyse of Huntyng*, which remained unpublished until 1987. Unlike most of the others it is an independent work, not reliant on a pre-existing text; as observed by its editor Anne Rooney, however, it shares with them the characteristic of being 'virtually useless' as a practical handbook, concentrating instead on terminology, horn signals, and characterizations of the animals themselves. In her words, 'Hunting to support life does not need the details with which the hunting manuals concern themselves; these are instead the features of the medieval chase which made it courtly and non-utilitarian.'

The *Boke of St Albans* was the first hunting treatise to be printed in England, although it continues a tradition of extensive plagiarization, namely of Twiti and Edward of York. Strikingly, it made its first appearance only a decade after Caxton introduced the printing press and thereafter it was reissued no fewer than 22 times in the following century and a half – more frequently, in fact, than any book other than the Bible. Its public included not only the newly upwardly mobile yeomanry,

eager for access to the arcane customs of their social superiors but also, perhaps, the hunt servants of the great households who by now might be expected to follow the more rigorous etiquette of the manual rather than merely absorbing what they could from their fellows.

The successor volume on hunting practice is presented in much the same way as the earlier texts with the title *The Noble Art of Venerie* (1575): traditionally it is attributed to George Turberville, to whose authorship it is assigned here although some authorities give it to George Gascoigne. While aimed at a readership perhaps drawn more widely from the new class of minor gentry, the text remains heavily dependent on the treatises of Gaston Phébus and others, notably Jacques du Fouilloux's *La Vénerie* of 1573.

Sir Thomas Cockaine, who enters the lists with his *Short Treatise of Hunting* (1591) describes himself as 'a professional Hunter, and not a scholler'. He recommends hunting of the hare in the winter, then roe from beginning of March to Whitsuntide, stag thereafter and buck from midsummer. James Cleland, in his *Institution of a Young Nobleman* (1607) recommends that his readers should

know the nature of beastes which you are to hunt, their wiles, the time and season when they should be hunted, the places where they remain in winter, and where in sommer, the winds which they feare and flie from, to finde them out, to knowe their courses, and whether they be for land or water.

None of the above English sources gives any detailed description of the less 'noble' methods by which deer or other game might be taken – even when the information is included in the same French texts on which they draw so heavily. Phébus, for example, writes that as well as being pursued with hounds, some deer were taken 'with nets and with cords, and with other harness, with pits and with shot and with other gins'; in his translation, however, the Duke of York interjects that 'in England they are not slain except with hounds or with shot or with strength of running hounds'. It is striking too that in Edward's translation no mention is made of the stalking horses that seem to have been an accepted part of the French hunter's equipment, or of the lightly built stalking carts in which Phébus suggests the hunter, decked with leaves for camouflage, could approach the game at close range unobserved.

These less formal methods would undoubtedly have been adopted by the hunt servants required to fulfil the demands of the kitchens when the lord was unavailable for hunting, or to provide for the exceptional requirements of feast days. Cummins finds a number of references to huntsmen being dispatched in this way, including an order from Edward II to the Sheriff of Southampton

> to pay to the King's yeoman John Lovel, whom the King is sending with twenty-four running hounds, six greyhounds, two berners and a fewtwerer to take the King's fat venison in the said county . . . He is also to deliver to [Lovel] salt for the said venison and carriage for the same to London.

Frequently a lardener would accompany the huntsmen to take charge of salting the carcasses in barrels. For one exceptional Christmas dinner in 1251, Henry III ordered 430 red deer, 200 fallow, 200 roe, 200 wild swine, 1,300 hares and 450 rabbits, as well as partridges, pheasants, swans, cranes, salmon and so on – clearly not a demand that could be met if the huntsmen were to observe all the niceties of the chase or without the involvement of specialists to take charge of the logistics of preservation and transportation. Phébus describes these techniques so that the lord might be familiar with them when dealing with poachers and the like, but from Edward of York's perspective these lesser activities simply had no relevance to the noble art of venery and hence they found no place in his text.

OF HOUNDS AND HORSES

As the court progressed around the royal castles and favoured successive lords with its onerous presence, the whole establishment of men and animals from the hunt, the kennels and the stables accompanied the royal presence so that sport could be made instantly available at the king's command. The nomenclature applied to the dogs is complex, overlapping and sometimes contradictory, but may be broadly summarized as follows for the medieval period and to some degree extended to more recent times.

The hounds (illus. 32) constituted the most important element of the kennels and formed the core of the hunt as it developed in its classic form. The varying nomenclature applied to them reflects the mixed character of the breeds (or rather strains) comprising each type of hound, together with the characteristics of their respective methods of hunting and the specialized tasks allotted to them. There were those that hunted primarily by scent – 'scenting-hounds' or bratchets, which might operate on the leash – lymers, also called leash-hounds or liam-hounds – or as 'running hounds', also referred to as raches or harriers. Others were less proficient at following a scent but relied on their sense of sight – gaze-hounds – and could be relied on at the conclusion of the hunt to outstrip the scenting hounds and ultimately the quarry. Most hunting involved a variety of hounds to be deployed at different stages as the chase progressed.

Lymers were in character close to what would now be termed bloodhounds – the latter effectively being their descendants. Their scenting abilities made them indispensable in the early stages of the hunt when the specific deer identified by the huntsman was being unharboured from his covert (p. 129) this led to them being referred to occasionally as staghounds, although the term was not species-specific. Twiti held that 'all the beasts which are chased' (hart, hare, boar, wolf) were dislodged with a lymer, while all those that were hunted up (buck, doe, fox and vermin) were to be found by the bratchets or scenting hounds. With the rise of park-hunting, less of a premium was placed on scenting ability but the bloodhound's effectiveness at tracking down poachers as easily as deer gradually led to its reputation as a tracking hound for the pursuit of men rather than beasts.

Greyhounds were the supreme dogs of the medieval hunt and were generally bigger-framed, more muscular and rougher-coated than their present-day counterparts, although Round finds evidence that they were, in fact, varied both in size and character: 'some are of a greater size and some lesser; some are smooth-skinned, and some are curled. The bigger therefore are appointed to hunt the bigger beasts, and the smaller serve to hunt the smaller accordingly.'

The large element of cross-breeding brought to bear on greyhounds in the search for both speed and strength is reflected in the term applied to them in some early texts – bastards. They had a principal role under their handlers (known as fewterers) in deer hunting, either in bringing down the deer in the chase *par force* or immobilizing those that had been wounded by arrows fired at the tryst (p. 128) so that they could be dispatched by the hunters. Greyhounds were essentially classed as gaze-hounds, coming into their own after the scenting hounds had located the quarry and set it

32 'How a man should enter his yong houndes to hunte the Harte'. From G. Turberville, *The Noble Art of Venerie* (1611).

running: they had no facility for finding a trail on their own. They were also deployed against smaller game such as hares, and no other breed could match them for speed and agility. Their refined, present-day form was not achieved before the eighteenth century, however, by which time their days as hunting dogs were effectively over and all the breeders' efforts went into improving their performance in hare-coursing (p. 229).

On the Continent a burlier hound of the greyhound variety was favoured for the biggest game, including boar: termed the alaunt (or alant), they seem not to have been favoured in Britain, where their role was performed by mastiffs. These heavy and unrefined dogs 'that men call curs' were principally valued here as guard dogs, but some were drafted in to boar hunting, being deployed after the hounds had done their work in tracking the boar to a standstill. They also functioned as bercelets – dogs to drive and retrieve game for the marksman. Although judged to be 'of a churlish nature and an ugly shape', their courage and loyalty made them valuable companions in dangerous situations.

Lurchers, according to the *Sporting Dictionary*, were originally produced from a cross between the traditional sheepdog and the greyhound, which, 'from breeding in and in with the latter, has so refined upon the original cross, that very little of the shepherd's dog is retained in its stock, its docility and fidelity excepted'. In addition to serving as useful hunting dogs, they were also favoured by small farmers, for whom they would work the livestock and also chase the odd hare if it presented itself. The lurcher was also the dog of choice for the poacher, to whom it recommended itself by its discretion in running mute.

A variety of lesser dogs also found places on the hunt. Terriers (as we shall see) cropped up in a variety of roles and proved especially useful when the game went to ground. (The Revd Bingley derives its name, *terrarius*, from its customary 'subterraneous employment'.) Spaniels – it would seem originally from Spain (as their name implies) but already well established in the medieval period – were judged to be limited in their usefulness, but to be ideal for partridge and quail hunting with the hawk (p. 186), although they could also be trained as 'couchers' or setters and were considered good in the water in pursuit of wildfowl. On the other hand, Phébus judged them to have 'many bad qualities like the country that they come from', causing mayhem amongst the other hounds by running about barking: 'unless I had a goshawk or falcon . . . I would never have any', he writes, to which the Duke of York adds 'especially there where I would hunt'.

The running hounds that formed the majority of the pack (under their keeper, the berner) are perhaps the most difficult to characterize. An insertion in the *Master of Game* recognizes that in England there were 'many kinds of running hounds, some small and some big . . . and these hounds run well to all manner of game, and they [that] serve for all game men call them harriers'. The implication is that packs were still quite miscellaneous in character and it would be mistaken to try to identify any of the dogs in question too closely with present-day breeds of hounds, many of which began to take on their individual characters as late as the eighteenth and early nineteenth centuries. Cummins suggests that in general medieval hounds were somewhat similar to modern foxhounds but burlier, less leggy, and of a wide range of colours. Any hound with a suitably bold nature could, with close training, be turned into a useful harrier (whose role was unspecialized at this time, but included the clearing of lesser game from the forest in order to allow the hart to be hunted without distraction). Rough-coated Welsh hounds achieved an early reputation for themselves, and several further broad groupings are identified by Markham as lying behind the foxhounds which make up today's most characteristic population – the so-called slow hound, a tall and heavy animal, bred in the west and north-west of England; the middle-sized dog, 'which is more fit for the Chase, being of a more nimble composure, and are bred in Worcestershire, Bedfordshire, and many other well mixt soyls, where the Champain and Covert are of equal largeness'; and the 'light, nimble, swift, slender Dog, which is bred in the North parts of this Land, as Yorkshire, Cumberland, Northumberland [etc]'. Markham also mentions the beagle, 'which may be carried in a man's glove, and are bred in many countries for delight only'. The term beagle originally signified such a small-sized and rather slow-paced hound which might be used to hunt a variety of lesser game, whereas talbots were originally larger-sized hounds, which Cummins suggests were probably bred down to a smaller size from the Norman period onwards, possibly by means of greyhound crosses. To this list Longrigg adds the 'lemon-pie' hound as being principally employed as a staghound, while the *Sporting Dictionary* (1903) mentions that fallow deer were customarily hunted with 'a dwarf kind of stag-hound (called buck-hounds) . . . kept for the purpose'. Most staghounds (or hart-hounds) and buck hounds would originally have formed the larger end of a continuous spectrum of types and the term designates a role rather than a breed.

In the early 1700s the small Northern and larger Southern hounds still existed as separate populations, although commonly crossed to give middle-sized dogs well suited to fox-hunting (though still very mixed in character); from the mid-eighteenth century, however, these crosses were in turn bred to produce what came to be a more standardized form of foxhound with more speed and stamina (p. 155), which by 1800 had been adopted by all hunts except those in the north that continued to hunt on foot, where Northern hounds retained their popularity in the form of fell-hounds. By the turn of the nineteenth century, the most highly developed hounds had literally left the traditional beagles behind; this term then became limited to the slower hounds that could easily be followed on foot, associated especially with hare hunting.

Hunting hounds were generally weaned at two months, Turberville suggests, and sent 'abroad into Vyllages to keepe in some fayre place which is neare unto some water, and farre from any Warren of Coneys, for . . . if they should be neare unto warrennes, they might breake out and be drawne to hunting amysse after coneys'. In a practice recalling the customary arrangement for rearing fighting cocks (p. 235), it was not unknown by the eighteenth century for landlords to include in leases a stipulation that country tenants should put up such hounds as might be required. Once they were old enough to join the pack, it was recognized that hounds were much improved by their keepers taking them often to the fields and woods and generally accustoming them to their company, as well as by rewarding them after the hunt with curées (pp. 129–30) when they had done well. This seemingly benign attitude was tempered with advice that when the hounds had 'done amiss' they should be soundly beaten, and especially they were to be 'chastized surely from sheepe and other cattell'; the hounds, after all, 'are beasts, and therefore they need to learn that which men will they should do'. Extreme measures were resorted to with hounds that persisted in chasing sheep: Peter Beckford mentions that 'some will couple them to a ram, but that is breaking them with a vengeance: you had better hang them'. The hounds would, however, have to work yoked together in pairs, with couples spun from horsehair, while under the huntsman's direct control.

Extensive advice is given for the benefit of 'any yong Gentleman, who will breed Hounds to hunt the Foxe', by Sir Thomas Cockaine in his *Short Treatise of Hunting* of 1591. Such a pack, he thought, should comprise some fourteen or fifteen couple of 'small Ribble hounds, low and swift', along with two couples of terriers. (Beckford would later estimate 40 couples as an appropriate size for a mature pack.) The aspirant pack owner was encouraged to borrow a couple of experienced foxhounds to set good examples to the youngsters; training would begin when they were 'full twelve moneth and a quarter olde', with the benefit of some fox cubs to be recovered by the terriers. These would be set free one at a time, with the older hounds released to hunt them by scent and with the young ones following on their heels. Once the technique had been mastered, two couples within the pack would henceforth be designated as trailers, whose task it was to pick up the initial scent; once they had met with success, the rest of the pack would be cast off in pursuit of the game.

Terriers, whose primary task was to help extricate foxes and otters when they went to ground (though they might sometimes run with the hounds), had their own training regime:

You must make a Trench of seven yards long, two foote broade within, and then make a crosse Trench over the same of five yards long, and so little Crosse Trenches in the same of an ell long so conveyed, that one run into another, cover all your Trenches with Clods or Turffes, and leave four holes open at the ends thereof for ayre. Then put in your Foxe Cub, and at the same hole put in one of your Terriars, and when the same hath found the Cubbe, you may helpe him with another, and if you find those too weake you may put in the other couple also: but you must make sure that your Terriars at the first be well eased and kill the Cubb. By that time your Terriars have kild half a dozen Cubbes in this sort in the earth, they will fight very boldly.

The methodology favoured here recalls that by which other terriers were introduced to the sport of badger-baiting (pp. 225–6).

Whatever the quarry they were destined to hunt, much emphasis was placed on disciplining the hounds and ensuring that they remained focused on their quarry. They were to respond instantly to the huntsman's voice, be he on foot or on horseback. For those destined to deer hunting, with the approach of their first entry to the field it was advised that 'you must feed your young hounds with chippings of bread upon the top of an old Buckes head' and exercise the pack against the hare. Thereafter, when they entered the park for the first time it was to be in the company of a number of horsemen equipped with long rods to ensure that

the hounds stayed close to the stirrup; deviants were to be beaten into place, but then 'cherished' and encouraged with a piece of bread, 'in which beating you make your hounds so obedient of the voyce of man, that they will at every worde come in to the stirrup'. As they improved, larger parks and open forest would be visited and they might be tried against a stag or two, but if so the hunters had to be on hand to dispatch it quickly with their swords before it wrought havoc on the dogs with its antlers. For his part the huntsman was expected to comb his hounds regularly to remove fleas and to rub them down with a haircloth after an outing in order to make them 'fine and smooth'.

Markham recommended training hounds with 'the chace of a traine scent . . . drawn either across ploughed lands, or athwart green fields, leaping ditches, hedges, payles, rails, fences, or running through a warren'. In order to avoid confusing the young hounds, later authorities recommended that in their instruction they should be taught to concentrate on a single quarry, although it seems clear that early packs were not (or not always) so specialized. Round, for example, finds one William Fitz Walkelin paying the king £40 in 1200 for leave to have his hounds hunt for hare, fox, wildcat and otter in Derbyshire, while in 1315 the king's own pack of deer hounds was dispatched to Northamptonshire to pursue foxes, wildcats and badgers. Gardiner later observed in 1750 with reference to hare hunting that

a Dog generally prefers that Game he was first used to, and blooded with. This few Sportsmen attend to, but on the contrary, if they can bring their young Hounds to Stoop and challenge a Cat, Coney, or Red Herring dragged by a string, think themselves well off with a fine promising Breed.

The surprising inclusion here of fish as well as fur finds support at the turn of the nineteenth century in the *Sporting Dictionary*, which suggests that the train (by now more commonly called a drag) might be made from 'the skin of a hare or fox, newly killed; a slice of bacon, and a red herring firmly united; or either, plentifully impregnated with oil of aniseed.'

THE PERSONNEL OF THE HUNT

As ever, for the privileged to enjoy their destined way of life, an extensive cast of supporting personnel was necessary – invariably most numerous in the royal household but replicated with varying degrees of elaboration throughout the aristocracy according to the wealth and status of the individual. The *Constitutio Domus Regis* of 1135–6, conveniently analysed by G. H. White, provides a glimpse of the specialized retinue employed within the Household and associated with the hunt, including knight-huntsmen, huntsmen (*catatores*), specialized wolf hunters (*luparii*), bow-bearers and other archers, horn-blowers, and keepers of several kinds of hounds – velterers, berners, braconiers and lymerers. Another snapshot is presented in May 1212, when King John (illus. 33) is recorded as being accompanied on his progress by no fewer than 167 greyhounds, 70 other hunting dogs and 52 handlers; later in September of the same year, presumably in response to different opportunities on offer, an astonishing 300 greyhounds accompanied the king, along with 16 boarhounds, 9 bercelets and 64 handlers.

The *Constitutio* gives a reasonably well-rounded picture of the variety and status of the hunting specialists maintained on the royal establishment:

Each one of the horn-blowers shall have 3 pence a day. And there are twenty servants each of whom receives 1 penny a day. Each keeper of the greyhounds shall have 3 pence a day, and 2 pence for his men, and a half-penny a day for each greyhound. The keeper of the kennels shall have 8 pence a day. The knights-huntsmen shall each receive 8 pence a day. The hunt-servants shall each receive 5 pence. The leader of the bloodhound shall receive 1 penny a day and 1 halfpenny for the bloodhound. The keeper of the running hounds shall receive 3 pence a day. The huntsmen of the stag-hunt shall each receive 3 pence a day; and there shall be 1 penny for each four of the greater staghounds, and 1 penny for each six of the lesser staghounds. Two men each receiving 1 penny a day shall attend to the greater staghounds, and two men each receiving 1 penny a day shall attend to the lesser staghounds. Each one of the keepers of the small hounds shall receive 3 pence a day. The huntsmen of the wolf-hunt shall have 20 pence a day for horses and men and hounds, and they are required to have 24 running hounds and 8 greyhounds; and they shall have 6 pounds a year wherewith to buy horses; though they themselves say it ought to be 8 pounds. The bowman who carries the king's bow shall have 5 pence a day, and the other bowmen likewise . . .

Further officers appearing at later dates and in other positions are mentioned as they make their appearance below.

Some hunting officials were indeed of gentle birth. William Twiti himself evidently was not nobly born, but his position of chief huntsman to Edward II was one of some prestige: his position and wage of 9d. a day in 1326 may be compared to

33 Hunting the hart with hounds: a 14th-century illustration purporting to show King John (1166–1216) hunting *par force*.

that of Edward, Duke of York, author of the *Master of the Game*, who in 1401 received 12d. a day as master of the royal harthounds. Almond comments on the manner in which hunt servants, mixing frequently with their social superiors and being of necessity fluent in the arcane language of the hunt, were well placed to benefit from social advancement when the opportunity presented itself.

WEAPONS OF THE HUNT

In pursuit of the game, much of the skill and effort was contributed by the hounds up to and sometimes including the kill itself, although depending on the species and the type of hunt being prosecuted, the *coup de grâce* might fall to the hunter to deliver. The full range of weaponry associated with the hunt is discussed in Howard Blackmore's encyclopaedic *Hunting Weapons*.

For the dispatch of larger game, a thrusting sword was carried by the principal hunters, capable of finishing off deer or other game brought down by the hounds. From the later medieval period single-edged swords called woodknives became the general-purpose weapons of choice: designed for hacking rather than thrusting, they were frequently presented in scabbards which housed also a knife and/or a set of other useful implements forming a 'trousse', like the 'wodeknyffe shethe fowl of toweles' owned by Henry VIII. In a form that came to be known later as the hanger, the woodknife survived into the seventeenth century, when one of its functions was recorded by Richard Blome:

> The Huntsman presents the Person that took the Essay with a drawn Hanger, to have a Chop at his Head, and after him, every one hath a Chop if it is not cut off; and generally the Huntsman, or Keeper is provided with such a Hanger, that is not over Sharp, that there may be the more Chops for the gaining more Fees, every one giving him a Shilling at least.

The most formidable opponent the hunter was ever likely to confront face-to-face was the wild boar, whose sheer weight and power would test not only the man but also his weapon. Earlier swords for this purpose had a single-edged 4-foot blade with reinforced guards and a hilt that allowed it to be used two-handed. By the fifteenth century these had evolved an even stronger form of blade, which was solidly triangular, square or octagonal along most of its length, with only a short, leaf-shaped edged section towards the tip, an arrangement also applied to boar spears (see below), the

two weapons almost merging in this form. The development of this type of sword had taken place on the Continent, and indeed boar hunting in England was an extinct sport by this time; nevertheless, at the time of his death Henry VIII had several examples of this type of weapon (known as an *estoc*, or in English as a tuck) in the custody of his 'hunter Armerer' at Westminster: Henry's post-mortem inventory lists two 'iij Edged Tockes' and six 'bore spere swordes', all with 'vell[v]et skaberdes'; five other weapons of this sort (capable of being used in battle as well as in the hunt) were kept in the removing wardrobe, one 'a longe Tocke gilte with gonnes having a locke and a skaberde of blak vellut the crosse and pommel guilte'. Combination arms of this sort were also popular prestige weapons on the Continent. A more everyday (and probably more effective) refinement was for the blade to be fitted with a cross-bar to stop it penetrating too deeply and becoming embedded in the victim's flesh; rotating or spring-loaded cross-bars were developed to allow these barbed blades to be accommodated in the scabbard.

The knives carried by lesser functionaries came into play in 'undoing' the deer after its slaughter. On the Continent it was customary for the noble hunters to undertake this task and elaborate trousses of finely crafted implements were produced to this end, often grouped in the scabbard of a heavy chopping knife to be worn on the belt, but in England it seems to have been customary for the duty to be delegated once the process had been symbolically initiated by the master of game: an illustration survives of Queen Elizabeth being presented with a knife in order to make the first cut (illus. 34).

Spears in a variety of weights were carried according to the game being sought – from heavy boar-spears guaranteed not to shatter under the onslaught of a wild boar to light javelins to be launched at wildcat if they took to the trees. Black-more finds a reference to the use of boar-spears in England at the end of the fourteenth century: these came to be produced with 2-foot-long heads made in the same manner as the specialized swords mentioned above, with a thickened blade and with a cross-bar to limit penetration. Some of Henry VIII's many boar-spears had 'asshen staves', some 'trymed with Crymesyn velvet and fringed with redde silke' and others 'knotted and lethered', some with 'heddes parcell graven and guilte'. Nicholas Cox's advice in 1674 that the boar-spear should be 'very sharp and broad, branching forth into certain forks, so that the boar may not break through them upon the huntsman', indicates that the basic form, with some sort of cross-bar, had survived up to his day.

Henry VIII's proficiency with the throwing javelin impressed Erasmus who recorded in 1529 that the king 'had such natural dexterity, that in the ordinary accomplishments of riding and throwing the dart he outstripped everyone'. There are no records of his success with this weapon in the field.

Otter-spears traditionally had trident heads, or occasionally had double blades, as illustrated by Richard Blome (see illus. 45): the alternative term, otter-grains, implies just such a bladed head, whether forked or not. Henry VIII owned 'Thre grayned staves trymed with crymsyn' and others 'partlie gilt'. The form remained little changed until the nineteenth century, when spring-loaded heads began to find some favour.

Bows and arrows were among the classic weapons of the hunt. The lone hunter might stalk his prey with them, but more commonly they were used to pick off deer driven towards the huntsman by beaters (p. 130). For the purist, this was always a less noble activity than hot pursuit of the quarry with hounds. Sir Thomas Elyot, in *The Boke named the Governour* (1546) wrote:

34 Queen Elizabeth presented with a hunting knife by a huntsman, so that she may make the first cut in 'undoing' the hart; other huntsmen in the background summon the hounds with their hunting-horns for the curée. From G. Turberville, *The Noble Art of Venerie* (1611).

'Killyng of dere with bowes or greyhoundes, serv-eth well for the potte . . . But it conteyneth therein no commendable solace or exercise, in comparison to the other fourme of huntynge'.

At the opening of the medieval period, bows were somewhat shorter than they became in their classic form, a length of about 4 feet being favoured. Giraldus Cambrensis mentions that those used by Welsh archers at the end of the twelfth century had staves of 'wild elm'. In the course of the following century the 5-foot-long English longbow evolved, for which yew was the favoured material: these were effective over a distance of some 300 to 400 paces. A number of contemporary authors such as Walter de Mile-mete illustrate such bows in use (illus. 35), show-ing them commonly to be shaped only in a perfunctory fashion, with many knots showing in the stave. Blackmore observes that even a royal hunter illustrated in the Douce Apocalypse, from the third quarter of the thirteenth century, uses a similarly rough-hewn bow; they are, furthermore, commonplace in the Holkham Bible Picture Book of the following century. Although range must have been a major consideration, it was always limited by the strength of the individual archer and too powerful a bow would have been self-defeating for the less muscular hunter. Even the most able-bodied were advised to use weak bows during drive hunting (p. 130), when multiple targets presented themselves in quick succession, in order to avoid wearing themselves out. So wholeheartedly was the bow adopted on this side of the Channel that while admitting he had little personal knowledge of the weapon, Phébus advised that 'he who wants to know all about them must go to England, for there it is their real craft'. There is some evidence for the use of composite bows in medieval England, but they were never widespread.

For a standard arrow a shaft length of some 2½ to 3 feet was favoured; in his *Toxophilus* of 1545, Roger Ascham lists fifteen varieties of wood that might be used for this purpose. The fletching of the arrow was more closely specified, with flights cut from the quill-feathers of geese being favoured over those of other birds. Typical arrowheads for the hunt had wide, flat barbs (termed broadheads); more often than not these would disable the deer or other game rather than killing it outright, at which point the greyhounds would be released to drag it down so the hunter could finish it off. Other forms of game called for arrowheads of different design – some broad arrows extend to form swallow-tails; others with crescentic or forked heads were deployed against large game birds as well as animals, said to have been aimed at the latter with the intention of hamstringing rather

than killing them outright. Arrows with expanded, blunted heads (*bougons*) that might stun rather than kill outright were used against squirrels, rabbits and other small fur-bearing animals, the value of whose pelts would have been diminished by unsightly incisions, and also for birds (see illus. 35). Blackmore mentions that these were recommended as back-up weapons for ladies out hawking.

A rapid decline in the use of the bow set in from the later sixteenth century, to the point where John Evelyn could write in his *Sylva* (1664) that 'the use of Bows is laid aside amongst us' – a development, incidentally, that led also to a decline in the cultivation of yew trees.

Crossbows firing bolts with great force were also used as highly effective hunting weapons and had the advantage that they could be fired by women and by elderly persons who lacked the strength to span a longbow. Their range and power greatly exceeded that of the self-bow, although their rate of fire was very much lower. On the evidence of illustrations in Queen Mary's Psalter, fourteenth-century hunting crossbows had simple wooden bows mounted on a stave, but they still required a cumbersome 'hook and stirrup' system to span them, the archer securing the bowstring to his belt and pushing down with his foot on a loop mounted on the end of the stave until the string could be engaged with the release mechanism. With the adoption of composite bows and ultimately (from the late fourteenth century) of steel bows, spanning mechanisms involving levers were introduced which could cope with the increased strength of the bow but which were scarcely (if any) faster in operation than the manual method. The bolts fired by crossbows were shorter than traditional arrows and of heavier construction, but the range of heads with which they were fitted for hunting mirrored those used with the longbow.

35 Duck shooting with a roughly hewn bow and a blunt arrowhead, from Walter de Milemete, *De Nobilitatibus, Sapientiis et Prudentiis Regum* (1326–7).

By the turn of the sixteenth century, at least, use of the hunting crossbow was by no means confined to the disadvantaged: Jane Roberts finds a reference to Henry VII inviting Philip of Castile to hunt in the Little Park at Windsor, 'where Every eyche of the kyngs kylled certene deare, their owne hands, with their Crosbowes'. From 1531 comes a record of one Giles Churchill, occupying the post of Yeoman of the Crossbows at the court of Henry VIII; he was also responsible for the royal stalking horse, pointing to the rise of a new kind of hunting at close quarters. The ageing Queen Elizabeth is recorded as shooting deer in a paddock at Cowdray Park (Sussex) with the aid of a crossbow, while in the succeeding reign Anne of Denmark had the misfortune accidentally to kill one of James I's favourite hounds with one of these weapons at Theobalds (Essex).

A variant of the crossbow, termed the stone-bow or bullet-bow, fired pebbles or lead pellets and was exclusively a hunting (or indeed poaching) weapon, for use against birds or small mammals.

Developed on the Continent by the early fourteenth century, they remained popular up to the 1800s.

By the time of his death, Henry VIII owned several sporting firearms. Perhaps the earliest-recorded casualty to fall to the new fangled weapons was that noted by Blackmore, of a water-hen, 'kylled with the gun' in 1531. Even in their earliest, cumbersome form, there were undoubted advantages to firearms, although some sportsmen foresaw in them the death of traditional sport. The same author quotes a letter of 1548 from Sir Edmund Bedingfield to the Earl of Bath, complaining of

such persons as dayly do shoote in hand-gonnes, and beat at the fowles in ryvers and pyttes so as ther is no fowle that do remayne in the countrye; a man disposed to have a flight wt hawkes may seeke tenn myles ere he fynde one coople of fowles to fly at, wheare in all yeres past ther shulde have been founde in the same places [500] coople of fowles . . . If this be not reamyded, you wt all the rest of the nobilitie may put foorth your hawkes to breede and to keep no more.

These same concerns led to the introduction of a licensing system that sought to limit the range of species that could be pursued. Henry VIII's Bill for Cross-Bows and Hand-Guns of 1541 included the stipulation that if anyone obtained a licence 'to shoot any cross-bow, hand-gun, hagbut or demi-hake' then the said licence should include details of 'what beasts, fowls or other things the said person . . . shall shoot'. A surviving Elizabethan draft gun licence quoted by Blackmore includes the provision that the weapon was not to be used within five miles of any of the Queen's houses nor 'at any Brooke waters ryvers or plasshes mete or convenyent for hawkinge'; in Scotland hunting with firearms was outlawed altogether in the sixteenth century, but the advance of shooting for sport proved irresistible. Ultimately such a person as Henry Mackwilliam, a Gentleman-Pensioner and hence an upholder of traditional values amongst the equestrian class, was issued with a gun licence in 1567 with permission to shoot a wide variety of game including (with the permission of the owner) deer.

BEASTS OF THE FOREST, THE CHASE AND THE WARREN

Although the nomenclature changed during different reigns, the principal animal of the forest remained invariably the red deer (*Cervus elaphus*) – especially the male, designated the hart. Undoubtedly the female hind was also hunted for its food value, but the hunting texts speak only of the hart as an appropriate object for the chase. Boar and wolf also feature in all the literature as beasts of the forest, though most hunters probably never encountered them. Bear hunting is also included in most of these texts, but bears were never present in the wild in Britain during the period under review: the precise date when they became extinct is obscure, but they had certainly disappeared by the time the earliest hunting manuals were compiled and their presence there indicates no more than the indebtedness of the authors of these tracts to Continental precursors. The hare was also esteemed as a first-rate quarry for the hunter, evidently for the quality of the sport it provided rather than for its flesh.

Forming a second division were the 'Beasts of the chase'. These included the fallow deer (*Dama dama*) and roe deer (*Capreolus capreolus*), which later would rise to greater prominence as the red deer population declined; the otter, which attracted several centuries of attention from the hunting community; the fox, whose status rose from little more than vermin to the most widely celebrated animal of the hunt; the wildcat, marten and polecat, all of which would be hunted to near-extinction. More occasionally included is the badger, though it was never highly regarded as a game animal on account of its ponderous and nocturnal nature – the *Master of Game* comments that its pursuit 'hardly needed any great mastery'; it was, nonetheless subject to continuing persecution by methods that scarcely merit inclusion under the heading of hunting, but which are described on pp. 217–22. Beasts of the warren – notably the rabbit – were never deemed worthy of the hunter's attentions, although they were extended protection from poachers by the law.

These hierarchies may not have been based simply on estimation of the hunting qualities of the beasts concerned, but were linked very precisely to hunting rights.

HART AND BUCK

In its conduct, the hunt for the hart (known from the sixteenth century as the stag), six years old at the least and with a full head of antlers – was formalized and hedged about with ritual to an extraordinary degree – principally, it would seem, to reinforce its exclusive status, being ultimately royal game to be enjoyed only by those to whom the monarch had granted specific rights. The *Master of Game* identifies the hart as the most challenging of quarries, fleet of foot and 'of marvellous great cunning'. Neither was its strength and boldness to be underestimated – especially at rutting time, when male deer could prove 'wonderfully perilous beasts' and potentially deadly: 'with great pain shall a man recover that is hurt by a hart, and therefore men say in old saws: "after the boar the leech and after the hart the bier"'. Hounds and horses as well as men were at risk of their lives from its wounds.

Two principal methods of pursuit coexisted throughout the medieval period: hunting 'at strength' with hounds, usually rendered in its original French as *par force* [*de chiens*], was the classic method observed in England throughout the medieval centuries. Being necessarily labour-intensive and hence suited to the resources of a considerable household, it answered all the requirements of hunting etiquette outlined above, while affording the principal participants an opportunity to display and to hone their equestrian skills in lengthy and sometimes quite demanding pursuit of the deer. In the alternative arrangement, termed drive hunting or the 'bow-and-stable' method, the principals waited at a preordained place, termed the tryst, while the deer were driven towards them so that they could be shot with the longbow or the crossbow. Apart from being a more efficient method of killing large numbers of deer if required, for example, for a particular feast, this had the

advantage that it could be practised by those too old or infirm to contemplate a lengthy day in the saddle; although there appear to be no medieval records of women taking an active part in this activity, it certainly provided opportunities for close spectating and the elderly Queen Elizabeth, at least, regularly took an active part in this form of hunt, armed with a crossbow (see below). As noted by Cummins, in the description of a bow-and-stable hunt given in the fourteenth-century poem *Sir Gawain and the Green Knight* the harts and bucks are allowed to go free (the hunt taking place in the closed season) while the hinds and does are killed, suggesting a further explanation for the coexistence of this rather prosaic method of harvesting deer alongside the *par force* hunt focused exclusively on the stag. It may also be noted that fallow deer were singularly unsuited to *par force* hunting, since their natural tendency was to stay grouped in the herd and they also lacked the stamina required for a satisfyingly extended chase; the majority of them probably were culled by the bow-and-stable method.

The convention for *par force* hunting was set out by Edward, Duke of York in his *Master of Game*, in which the chapter on 'How the hart should be moved with the lymer and run to and slain with strength' is entirely his original contribution, not being included in the tract by Gaston Phébus on which so much of the text depends. The process would start with one or more of the huntsmen going out on the evening before the hunt in order to establish the location of a specimen worthy of the hunters' attentions; these would normally be the lymerers who, with their scenting hounds on the leash, would use all their craft to identify a suitable animal and to pinpoint the precise thicket in which it had taken refuge for the night. The hunt would assemble early the next morning, when the lymerers would report to the lord on their findings, backing up their observations with specimens of the fewmets which indicated to them the size and condition of the target. (Common custom had the lymerer gathering these up in the field and carrying them home within the wide end of his horn, stopped with grass, for scrutiny by the lord.) The hounds were then divided into a number of relays, to be posted at strategic points in the landscape where the chase would take place in order that its course could be controlled as far as possible. The lymerers would then be dispatched to the covert where the chosen deer was 'harboured' and from which it would be 'cast off' by the first group of hounds, designated the finders (later 'tufters').

After it was on the move, each time the hart (with the body of hounds in pursuit) passed by one of the relays, those hounds too would be released in order to reinforce and refresh the pack. The chase might well continue for a large part of the day, with the deer using all its strength to outrun the hounds and its guile to outwit them by doubling back and, where possible, taking to the water in order to confuse the scent. For their part, the pursuers would attempt to guide the hunt into open landscape where they could begin to build up speed and to gain on the hart. Eventually, having been exhausted by the chase, the hart would generally turn at bay towards the hounds – the climax of the hunt but also the most dangerous time for the dogs and for the lord, whose task it was to approach the deer from behind and to dispatch it with his sword: a common method involved first immobilizing it by severing the sinews of one of its hind legs, and thereafter piercing it through the spinal column at the shoulders or through the heart. At this point the hounds were generally permitted briefly to tear at the carcass in order to give them some immediate gratification for their efforts.

After the kill the deer would be 'undone' on the spot according to fastidiously prescribed rules (although with some variation on these between different sources). The carcass would be turned on its back, the hide slit from end to end and separated from the flesh so that it could be laid flat on the ground. Various parts of the body were assigned to selected recipients according to custom and the generosity of the lord, while the internal organs were removed for the hounds. In a departure from French custom, where it was invariably the lord who carried out this ritual, Edward of York anticipates that in England the task was more likely to be delegated to one of the huntsmen, asserting that 'it belongeth more to woodmanscraft than to hunters' and omitting all further detail. It was important, none the less, that the aristocratic participants were all well versed in the procedures and in their symbolic significance in drawing the hunt to a seemly conclusion.

An important step followed in which the hounds received their customary reward in what was termed the 'curée'. The paunch and 'small gut' of the deer were washed and cut up, mixed with blood and bread and laid out for the pack to eat: originally they were placed on the hide of the deer, hair-side up, but Edward of York places them on the grass under the skin, to which the head and antlers remain attached; after a celebratory blowing of horns (and baying by the hounds at the head of the stag) the hounds were uncoupled and allowed to rush towards their treat, which in Edward's procedure was uncovered to them by the skin being pulled away by means of the antlers. After the running hounds had been given their fill, the lymers were then to be allowed to feed. (The *Tretyse of Huntyng* suggests that the lymers should already have been rewarded with 'brede & chese' at the site of the bed from which they had first successfully moved the hart.) The whole process was seen as of integral importance in developing application of the hounds to their task: it was invariably to take place at the conclusion of the hunt so that the hounds associated the reward with their success in the field. (To impress the point further, they might have been fed only bread during the previous days.)

At the conclusion of the hunt, Twiti prescribes that the hunters should 'carry the head home before the Lord; and the heart, tail, and gullet should be carried home on a forked branch, and you should blow the menée at the door of the hall'.

As an alternative to the *par force* hunting of individual deer, drive hunting or (as it was termed by the later medieval period) bow-and-stable hunting was deployed when larger numbers of deer were required for the larder or when the lord himself was unable or unwilling to spend hours in pursuit of a single animal, perhaps due to infirmity (or in the event of his being, in fact, a lady: although images of ladies hunting are not uncommon in medieval manuscripts, they are thought likely to be mischievous commentaries on the nature of women rather than representations of reality). In contrast to *par force* hunting, in which the end-point of the hunt was unknown, in this form of hunting the lord had the deer driven towards a prearranged vantage point known as the tryst, from which he and his guests (all on foot) could shoot them with the bow or crossbow as they passed. As described in the *Master of Game*, this method required, if anything, larger numbers of ancillary helpers to act as beaters and to help contain the numerous animals likely to be put up during the driving, so a primary duty of the Master was to liaise with the sheriff of the shire and with the local foresters to ensure that sufficient personnel were supplied to form a cordon – the stable – around the area to be hunted. In addition, the fewterers (in charge of the greyhounds that

would be stationed with the lord) were required 'to make fair lodges of green boughs at the tryste to keep the King and Queen and ladies, and gentlewomen and also the greyhounds from the sun and bad weather'; at such royal occasions the king's Yeoman of the Bows would also be positioned there, equipped with a suitable array of armament.

Having unharboured the deer with hounds from their respective resting places, the huntsmen thereafter kept them on the move with the aid of the beaters, some of whom might be mounted; any immature or lesser deer (termed 'rascals' and 'follies') – and in view of the focus on female deer in some bow-and-stable hunts as mentioned above (p. 128), possibly also mature stags – that came up against the outer cordon would be allowed to pass through, while the principal quarry would be turned back towards the tryst. Arrows or bolts released by the lord and his shooting party were more likely to wound the deer than to kill them outright, at which point the greyhounds would be released to pull them down.

In order to cope with the much larger gamebags to be expected on these occasions, carts were provided 'to bring the deer that should be slain to the place where the curées at huntings have been usually held', and for as long as the hunt was prosecuted, it was anticipated that these carts would 'go about from place to place for to bring the deer to the curée'. Here the carcasses would be laid out in rows, any great harts killed separated from the hinds or younger deer slain, 'all the heads one way – and every deer's feet to the other's back'. When he had surveyed the day's kill, apportioned any deer selected to go to particular beneficiaries and selected those for his own table, the lord would normally retire from the hunt leaving the Master of Game to officiate over the further sharing out of game amongst the participants and to oversee the baying of the hounds and the curée as described above (though with somewhat less ceremony), making use of the best head and skin recovered in the course of the day. Thereafter the hunt servants would be left to complete the butchering by themselves.

Emma Griffin has noted that frequent references to deer-hedges as early as the eleventh century may indicate that animals were already being channelled into organized killing zones at this time. If this were indeed to be the purpose of these hedges, they would represent a strikingly early insular development (perhaps even a pre-Norman initiative), for as she also points out, drive hunting finds no place in Phébus's text and the discussion provided by Edward, Duke of York, is his own contribution. It is further suggested by Richard Almond that the greater detail offered on drive hunting by Edward (compared, for example, to Twiti) may reflect the increasing favour it found in the later centuries of the medieval period, culminating in the *grand battus* favoured by Continental princes in which the forest setting was dispensed with altogether, the animals being herded into courtyards or city squares to be slaughtered *en masse*. While these spectacles were never reproduced in England, Henry VIII certainly took to drive hunting with some enthusiasm after his career in the hunting saddle was brought to a premature end by injury: on one notable occasion at Hatfield (Hertfordshire) in 1541, some 200 deer are said to have been slain in a single day in what seems to have been a deliberate demonstration of nonchalance designed to impress his arch-rival, François I, whose ambassador was in attendance. Hampton Court was provided during his reign with a paddock where captive deer could be held in readiness for such an exercise. Queen Elizabeth too, being denied the opportunity to join in the pursuit, was partial to picking off the odd deer as they were driven past her by the hounds, favouring

the crossbow for the purpose rather than the long-bow. At Clarendon Park in 1574 some 340 bucks were killed in a single drive-hunt, while in 1584 the Earl of Leicester organized an event at Windsor at which 60 to 80 great harts were confined within a paddock: they ran up and down for a time in front of the Queen, who shot several with a crossbow (the wounded being pulled down by greyhounds) before she withdrew to a hide on a hillock where the stags, having been let out of the toils in batches, were coursed by greyhounds in order to give her further target practice. Outside the immediate circle of the monarchy, however, drive hunting had largely disappeared by this time, the stocks of deer having dwindled beyond the point where they could sustain exploitation of this kind. None the less, it was at just this time that John Coke (quoted by Cummins) wrote that 'we have also small parkes made onely for the pleasure of ladyes and gentylwomen, to shote with the longe bowe, and kyll the sayd beastes': perhaps it may be surmised that this activity was more closely related to the coursing of single deer by the hounds (as described on pp. 127–8), and that this may to some extent have compensated for the loss of the more profligate form of entertainment. Natural features of the landscape (particularly narrow valleys) were made use of in early forms of this kind of hunt in order to channel the deer towards the tryst, to be augmented later by earthen banks, hedges, and ultimately with nets or with canvas 'toils'.

Little of the former glories of the chase survived in these debased spectacles, but even within the field of conventional hunting far-reaching changes had overtaken its practice as a result of the progressive enclosure of deer. While some parks (at several thousand acres in extent) remained large enough to accommodate the hunt in something approaching its traditional form, with bodies of hunters ranging over a variety of landscapes, most were more modest in scale. The stock within such a park effectively became isolated from the deer population at large, although some owners took care to include in their circuits special deer leaps (*saltatoria*) – lower stretches of fencing which provided an inviting prospect to deer on the outside but which gave on to a steep bank sloping down to a dry ditch on the inner face which made it impossible for the deer to return the way they had come. (Parks granted by the king – and especially those within the precincts of the royal forest – were absolutely prohibited from including deer leaps in their circuits, or any other means by which deer could be siphoned off from the royal reservoir of game.) None the less, they proved an attractive means by which the emparked population could be topped up without further effort or expense on the part of the owner, although he might find it expedient to provide browsewood or hay for the deer during winter and seasonally to exclude other grazing animals that competed for the finite amount of natural fodder within the pale. In the course of the Middle Ages almost 2,000 such parks are estimated by Cantor to have been constructed.

Increasingly the deer within such parks were likely to be fallow rather than red deer, and bucks rather than harts became the everyday object of the hunter's attentions. A royal pack of buckhounds had existed since the Tudor age – two, in fact, one with a hereditary master based at Rockingham Forest (Northamptonshire) and the other a Household or privy pack, founded by Henry VIII in 1528. Immediately on the accession of James I, the Privy pack experienced a striking change of fortune, having endured something of a lean time under Elizabeth: at the close of her reign, the Master of the Privy Buckhounds disposed of a staff comprising one serjeant, three

yeoman prickers (who rode with the pack) and five grooms (who did not), but under James the establishment was immediately expanded while the pack acquired a wagoner or 'keeper of the hound van'. The hereditary branch evidently failed to satisfy the needs of such a demanding huntsman as James I and within the first year of his reign he initiated attempts to annexe the hereditary kennel to the Privy pack, so as to gain direct access to its hounds; it was only in 1613, however, that he succeeded in reforming part of the hereditary pack (together with a portion of the Privy pack) into a separate kennel for Charles, Duke of York.

Under Charles II the salary of the Master of the Buckhounds was increased and the budget for the pack rose in 1662 to £2,378, although much of it remained unpaid. Later attempts to discontinue some liveries and allowances were abandoned in the face of renewed protests from the servants, but extracting payment from the Crown proved no easier. James II got little opportunity to enjoy the Buckhounds although as Duke of York he had been a passionate huntsman, having a separate pack with a budget of £1,341 5s. a year.

In keeping with the numbers of animals available, later buck hunting evidently was accompanied by little of the formality that had accompanied the pursuit of the hart, and without the need for so extensive a body of servants. In 1703 the two royal packs were at last formally combined to form a 'United pack', which was abandoned as an economy measure only in 1901, shortly after the accession of Edward VII.

A continuing decline in the deer population in the later eighteenth century led ultimately to the introduction of carted deer – specimens selected from the park, carried in a closed van to a pre-arranged spot where they would be released for the hunt to pursue across the countryside. In this distant and emasculated echo of the medieval *par force* hunt, the deer would be run to a standstill but then rescued from the attentions of the hounds and carted back to its park in order to recover and to provide sport on another occasion. In a manner reminiscent of the bears and bulls who featured with almost monotonous regularity in public baitings (pp. 208, 212), some of these deer became so well known as to be given familiar names – Moonshine, Starlight, and so on – and to have their exploits reported individually in the press. The hunting of carted deer by the Royal Buckhounds seems to have provided an impetus for its wider adoption: within a decade, most of the packs dedicated to deer hunting were operated in this way. Only in Devon and Somerset were there hunts still pursuing exclusively wild red deer at this time, the Acland family maintaining a pack of 40 couples of 'yellow-pie' hounds of the same type as the royal buckhounds: Longrigg observes that these perpetuated one of the principal failings of the old packs in that they lacked the stamina for a prolonged chase, a characteristic that was by now beginning to be bred out of contemporary foxhounds. The Tiverton staghounds were founded as late as 1896, and the Quantock hunt in 1902.

BOAR

Hunting the wild boar (*Sus scrofa*) was subject to restriction from the eleventh century onwards, when it was designated as one of the beasts of the forest. Boar formed the most formidable opponent the hunter was ever likely to face in the British Isles, in terms of its strength, ferocity and stamina.

It is the beast of this world that is strongest armed and can sooner slay a man than any other . . . the wild boar slayeth a man with one stroke as with a knife, and therefore he

can slay any other beast sooner than they could slay him. It is a proud beast and fierce and perilous, for many times have men seen much harm that he hath done. For some men have seen him slit a man from knee up to the breast and slay him all stark dead at one stroke so that he never spake thereafter.

Although the above account of the boar in the *Master of Game* opens with the formula that it is 'a common beast enough', the words are those of the original French author and scarcely applicable to England where true wild swine are thought to have disappeared by the late 1200s – a century and a half before Edward, Duke of York came to compile his translation. The fact that Edward translated only one of the eleven chapters on the boar prepared by Phébus may be a recognition of the unlikelihood that his readers would ever encounter such a beast. Even later, the fifteenth-century *Boke of Huntyng* continues to maintain the fiction that the valiant hunter might yet be called upon to face such an enemy (as his Continental cousins continued to do) and that he would be called upon not only to kill it but to know how to 'undo' it in the prescribed manner. Twiti had earlier prescribed that if properly undone the carcass should end up in 32 'dainty morsels'; 'and you should give your hounds the bowels broiled with bread, and this is called the reward'. Unlike the approved practice in the curée, the reward was to be eaten 'on the earth'.

The etiquette of the chase gave the hunter no protection here. After it had been tracked by the hounds, during which time it was likely to turn and confront them several times before tiring and making its final stand, custom demanded that the boar be tackled at close quarters by the hunter with the spear and if necessary dispatched with a sword (illus. 36). Some evidently approached it on horseback – Phébus recommends a cautious gait at the trot rather than an outright gallop and with the spear shaft held in the hand around the middle and not couched as a jousting lance – while others evidently felt safer on foot. The fact that specially reinforced versions of both spears and swords were developed for boar hunting (p. 123) speaks eloquently of the sheer physicality of the encounter and no doubt testifies to a great many engagements when the hunter's weapons had proved inadequate, probably with fatal results. Harting notes that tenure of certain lands might come with a duty to participate in the boar hunt, citing Thomas de Musgrave who, in 1339, held one carucate of land in Oxfordshire of the King 'by the service of carrying one boar-spear, price twopence, to the King, whenever he should hunt in the park at Cornbury; and do the same as often as the King should so hunt, during his stay at his manor of Woodstock'.

Turberville excludes the boar from the 'beasts of venery' as being unsuitable for chasing with hounds,

for he is the proper prey of a Mastif and such like dogges, for as much as he is a heavie beast, and of great force, trusting and assying himself in his Tuskes and his strength, and therefore will not so lightly flee nor make chase before houndes . . . I thinke it a greate pitie to hunte (with a good kenell of houndes) at such chases: and that for such reasons and considerations as followe:

First, he is the onely beast which can dis-patch a hounde at one blow, for though other beastes do bite, snatch, teare, or rende your houndes, yet there is hope of remedie if they be well attended; but if a Bore do once strike your hounde, and light betweene the foure quarters of him, you shall hardly see him escape; and therewithall this subtiltie he hath, that if he be runne with a good kenell

of houndes, which he perceveth holde in rounde and followe him harde, he will flee into the strongest thicket that he can finde, to the ende he may kill them at his leysure one after another, the whiche I have seene by experience oftentimes . . .

Agayne, if a kennell of houndes be once used to hunte a Bore, they will become lyther, and will never willingly hunte fleeing chases agayne . . . [so] who soever meaneth to have good houndes for an Hart, Hare, or Row-deare, let him not use them to hunte the Bore . . .

After further details of the nature of the wild bore, Turberville turns to the mode of its hunting:

if he do stande at Baye, the huntesmen must ryde in unto him as secreetly as they can without muche noyse, and when they be neare him, let them cast rounde about the place where he standeth, and runne upon him all at once, and it shall be harde if they give him not one skotch with a sworde or some wounde with a Borespeare: and let them not stryke lowe, for then they shall commonly hit him on the snoute, bycause he watcheth to take all blowes on his Tuskes or there aboutes. But let them lift up their handes hygh and stryke right downe; and let them beware that they stryke not towardes their horses but that other waye; For on that side that a Bore feeleth him selfe hurte, he turneth heade strayght waies, whereby he might the sooner hurt or kyll their horses, if they stroke towards them. And if they be in the playne, then let [them] cast a cloake about their horses, and they maye the better ryde about the Bore, and stryke at hym as they passe; but staye not long in a place . . .

He has one final word of advice : 'It is a certayne thing experimented and founde true, that if you hang belles upon collers about your houndes necks, a Bore will not so soone stryke at them, but flee endwayes before them, and seldome stand at Bay'.

Even in the heyday of boar hunting, however, there is evidence that valour was sometimes tempered with prudence in seeking out the boar, for in the Exchequer Roll for 1198, references are found by White to payments for nets for catching them. Later, in 1210, payments were made to one Thomas Porcherez (or Porkerez), a boar hunter and presumably a member of the Household, who had in his possession 23 hounds *ad porcos* – for hunting boar.

Estimates of the date of the extinction of the wild population in Britain centre around the turn of the fourteenth century; certainly by the time it was adopted as the evocative emblem of Richard III, the boar had disappeared from England. Thereafter several monarchs attempted to reintroduce wild populations with animals brought from the Continent, but success was always limited: Charles I is said by Thomas Pennant to have procured numbers of them and to have turned them loose in the New Forest, where they were annihilated during the Civil War. Private citizens too tried and failed to turn the clock back: Gilbert White records in his *Natural History of Selborne* that General Howe released some wild swine imported from Germany into the forests of Woolmer and Alice Holt (Hampshire) which he held by a grant from the Crown, but 'the country rose upon them and destroyed them'. Harting records too that 'the late Earl of Fife, who tried many experiments in introducing different animals into the Forest of Mar, turned out some Wild Boars by the advice of the Margrave of Anspach . . . but the experiment in this case did not answer, for want of acorns,

their principal food'. Amongst other abortive attempts, the same author mentions a nineteenth-century reintroduction by a Mr Drax at Charborough Park (Dorset), involving boar from France and from Russia:

They were not hunted but caught in nets or shot. Writing to a mutual friend in September, 1879, Mr Drax says: 'I fenced them in with a wood paling in the wood where I built the present tower, and used to shoot them . . . They were savage and troublesome, however, to keep within bounds, and I therefore killed them.

WOLF

Wolves (*Canis lupus*) were one of the few animals that could generally be destroyed by anyone without incurring a penalty, for the danger they presented to livestock (and even *in extremis* to human life) rendered them fair game for all – except within the precincts of the royal forest, perhaps on the basis that the hunters might too easily be seduced by other quarry. On the other hand, the fact that a prescribed season emerged for hunting the wolf – from Christmas to 25 March – indicates a degree of ambivalence on the part of the landholding class towards what was evidently seen as a challenging source of sport, though it seems doubtful that any such nice feelings could have survived the imposition of bounties for the killing of wolves by any means whatever.

Only a century before the Norman Conquest, King Edgar (959–75) is said to have demanded tribute from Wales in the form of 300 wolf carcasses a year, a figure that had quickly to be modified as it proved unsustainable. Although the population was evidently on a more modest scale, wolves continued to form a significant presence

36 A fully armoured Guy de Warwick delivers the *coup de grâce* to a wild boar with his sword. From the Taymouth Hours (*c.* 1325–50).

and to form a real threat: Harting notes, for example, that by the thirteenth century the monks of Melrose in the Scottish borders were specifically allowed to set traps for wolves when they were denied any such rights over other animals. So significant was the danger posed by wolves that grants of land were commonly made on condition that the landholder should be responsible for their destruction within his domain, while others were obliged 'to hunt the Wolf whensoever the king should command'. These measures occurred country-wide, indicating the scale of the endemic population: Harting cites the example of William de Limeres, for example, who held land as far south as Southampton 'by the service of hunting the Wolf with the king's dogs', while in Scotland the duty to hunt them was enshrined in statutes of the fifteenth and sixteenth century, as follows:

> ilk baron within his barony in gangand time of the year sall chase and seek the quhelpes of Wolves and gar slay them. And the baron sall give to the man that slays the Woolfe in

his barony and brings the baron the head, twa shillings. And when the baron ordains to hunt and chase the Woolfe, the tenants sall rise with the baron. And that the barons hunt in their baronies and chase the Woolfes four times a year, and als oft as onie Woolfe beis seen within the barony . . .

In his account of the *Constitutio Domus Regis* – the Establishment of the King's Household – drawn up soon after the death of Henry I on 1 December 1135 and mentioned above, White notes the presence of a considerable separate establishment for the wolf hunt: the huntsmen were to have 20d. a day for horses and men and hounds, the latter numbering 24 running hounds and eight greyhounds, in addition to £6 a year with which to buy horses (though they evidently thought £8 more appropriate). Neither the number of huntsmen is mentioned nor their individual rates of pay. The hounds, although clearly specialized in their quarry, are not referred to specifically as wolf-hounds: it may be that these were bred in time from the more powerful specimens of greyhounds – already under King John references emerge to the 'keepers of the wolf-hounds' (*canes luvereticos*). Annual payments to wolf hunters in Worcestershire are noted from the reigns of Henry II, Richard I and John. White also records that when Conan, Duke of Brittany and Earl of Richmond, visited Jervaulx Abbey (Yorkshire) in 1156 he had been aghast at the numbers of wolves roaming the district and later granted the Abbey the right to keep mastiffs in order to control them. Several references are found to payments made in 1206 to one Walter the wolf-hunter, for making snares to take them, a stratagem that would not have been tolerated for valued game animals, and in the same vein John le Wolfhonte and another were required to set snares for wolves in March and September; in June when the wolves gave birth to their whelps, John was required to enter the forest with a specially trained mastiff in order to destroy the young.

Edward I mounted a campaign in the counties towards the Welsh Marches with a view to ridding them of wolves altogether: Peter Corbet was employed with the specific task of taking and destroying all the wolves in Gloucestershire, Worcestershire, Herefordshire, Shropshire and Staffordshire – evidently with some degree of success, although the deer in Macclesfield Park in nearby Cheshire were still being targeted by wolves in 1302–3.

The *Master of Game* says of the wolf that 'Men take them [and here Edward, Duke of York inserts 'beyond the sea'] with hounds and greyhounds with nets and with cords', as well as with snares, 'hausse-pieds' – traps designed to hoist the quarry into the air – and with 'venomous powders'. The suggestion of Edward's interpolation is that they were already something of a rarity in England at the turn of the fourteenth century. Records confirm the presence of wolves at Marske near Richmond (Yorkshire) until 1369, while John of Gaunt (1340–1399) is said to have hunted the area between Wensleydale and Stainmoor which abounded with them: he is one of several candidates credited with slaying the last wolf in England, near Leeds. The latest documentary evidence for their presence dates between 1394 and 1396, when the monks of Whitby were recorded as having been paid 10s. 9d. 'for tawing 14 wolf skins' – perhaps the product of an all-out assault on a declining population. Isolated specimens may well have survived after that time, but by the fifteenth century the wolf was effectively extinct within England. Richard Almond notes that wolf tenures associated with certain estates survived probably longer than the wolf population itself – in 1370 Thomas Engaine held lands in Pitchley (Northamptonshire) on condition he provided dogs to be used in hunting wolves, while in 1427 Robert Plumpton held wolf-hunt land in Nottinghamshire and wolf chasing in Sherwood Forest.

In Scotland wolves were said to be so numerous as to have overrun the country and destroyed many flocks in the mid-fifteenth century. An account survives of an epic drive hunt arranged for the diversion of Mary, Queen of Scots, in 1563 by the Earl of Athol, employing 2,000 Highlanders as beaters: in addition to some 360 red deer and some roe, the bag included no fewer than five wolves. A bounty of £6 13s. 4d. was offered for a wolf to be killed in Sutherland in 1621, and the last wolf in Scotland is said by Pennant to have been slain in 1680 by Sir Ewen Cameron of Lochiel. (Harting finds other claims for this honour, the latest from 1743.)

In Ireland Turberville believed there to be 'great store' of wolves remaining, and 'because many noblemen and gentlemen have a desire to bring that countrie to be inhabited and civilly governed' he takes the trouble to set out what he believes to be an effective (though not very elegant) method of hunting them, taken largely from Jacques de Fouilloux's *Traité de Vénerie*. It involved setting up an ambush with the aid of two or more wolf-hounds (a breed with which Ireland was particularly blessed – large and powerful creatures bred from rough-haired greyhound stock): these would be concealed at the chosen spot, which would be at some distance from the coverts where the wolves had their lairs; the site would be baited with the carcass of a horse, whose forequarters had been hacked off and trailed through the surrounding pathways leading to the site of the trap. In the course of the following night the wolves would find their way to the carcass to feed, and each time one arrived first one pair of hounds and then the other would be released to overwhelm it from all sides. There seemed to Turberville to be little point in trying to hunt the wolf *par force*, for, he says, 'A Wolfe will stand up a whole day before a good kennel of houndes unless ye Greyoundes course him', and even then, he adds, 'I have seene a Wolfe . . . out runne four or five brace of the best Greyhoundes that might be founde'. So critical did these specialized hounds become in the control of the wolf population that in order to preserve the stock Cromwell issued in 1652 a 'Declaration against transporting of Wolfe Dogges':

Forasmuch as we are credibly informed that Wolves doe much increase and destroy many cattle in several partes of this Dominion, and that some of the enemie's party, who have laid down armes, and have liberty to go beyond sea and others, do attempt to carry away such great dogges as are commonly called Wolfe dogges, whereby the breed of them which are useful for destroying of Wolves would (if not prevented) speedily decay. These are therefore to prohibit all

persons whatsoever from exporting any of the said dogges out of this Dominion; and searchers and other officers of the Customs . . . are hereby strictly required to seize and make stopp of all such dogges, and deliver them either to the common huntsman, appointed for the precinct where they are seized upon, or to the governor of the said precinct.

In spite of such tactics, wolves survived in Ireland in some numbers beyond the middle of the seventeenth century, when an Order in Council of 1653 is found to specify bounties of £6 for a bitch, £5 a dog, £2 'for every cubb which preyeth for himself' and 10s. for every suckling. They were not eliminated in the far west until the opening years of the following century: the last record of them in Co. Cork comes from about 1710. Wolf cubs were generally considered untameable, although the Revd Bingley records that Sir Ashton Lever (d. 1788) had one 'which, by proper education, was entirely divested of the ferocious character of its species'.

While wolf fur was considered wonderfully warm and suitable for making luxurious cuffs, the *Master of Game* warns that the skin, if inadequately cured, 'stinketh ever'.

BEAVER

While there is a wealth of evidence for the former presence of beaver (*Castor fiber*) in the British Isles (other than in Ireland, where they seem never to have established themselves), the manner of their going is only imprecisely documented. Their numbers were already limited by the medieval period and the latter centuries of their existence appear to have been lived out in what Bryony Coles, in a useful survey, has termed a 'cloak of invisibility': by contriving to avoid contact with the human population, she suggests, the declining years of the beaver population were extended as late as the eighteenth century – much later than their final appearance in the conventionally accepted historical record. All the details that can be reconstructed from their earlier history confirm that such a strategy of self-effacement would have been well chosen, for beavers got nothing but grief from encounters with mankind.

Their thick pelts proved a prime attraction: the presence of a beaver-skin bag in the Sutton Hoo (Suffolk) princely grave – the richest ever found in Anglo-Saxon England – demonstrates that the animal had an established prestige value long before the Norman conquest. Wulfstan, the pious Anglo-Saxon bishop of Worcester who continued to hold office under William I, is on record as having been chided for his custom of wearing humble lambskins rather than the sable, fox or beaver fur considered appropriate to his rank in society. Amulets incorporating beaver teeth had been numerous in the graves of less exalted pagan Saxons, implying that they were attributed special powers; these largely failed to survive the impact of Christianity, and although there evidently was a later awareness of a classical tradition that attributed a particular virtue to 'castoreum', a musky substance secreted by the beaver, these beliefs seem to have survived in medieval Britain essentially in literary and symbolic form, though perhaps also in the field of medicine. Finally, the beaver's flesh, while evidently devoid of outstanding culinary qualities, was prized by some purely for its rarity and prestige value and by others on the basis of a peculiar sophistry as a form of fish, suitable for eating on fasting days.

An oblique and somewhat speculative indication of the former distribution of the population is provided by place-name evidence. Since the days of John Leland's *Itinerary* of the 1540s, Beverley (Yorkshire) – 'beaver stream' – has been acknowledged as the best known of about twenty such place names alluding with a greater or lesser degree of certainty to a former localized presence of the animal; the common seal of the town, recorded from 1345, includes the figure of a beaver, confirming that there was already a corporate consciousness of the association at this early date. While the number of other potential beaver place names is considerable, Aybes and Yalden point out that they are at the same time strikingly less common than, for example, names associated with wolves (almost 330): in addition to the difficulties of interpretation in dealing with place names, they observe pertinently that cultural factors may have had some influence on this disparity – the slaying of a single wolf, for example, being an event that might be memorialized in this way while the killing of a beaver would scarcely merit such a record. By themselves, place-names can inform us only tentatively about the former beaver population.

Legal sources

In setting tariffs for the furs of ermines, martens and beavers for which the monarch was to have the value wherever they were killed ('because from them the borders of the King's garments are made'), the laws of Hywel Dda of *c.*940 provide early documentary evidence for the presence of the animal in Wales. Here beaver pelts are valued at 120d., compared to only 24d. for a marten skin – a considerable differential but one that Coles observes is mitigated by considerations of size (a beaver pelt being approximately six times the size of a marten fur) and hence may not necessarily imply significantly greater prestige or extreme rarity. Incidentally, Charles Wilson noted earlier, in 1858, that in this same law code the entire carcass of the beaver was valued at the same rate as the pelt, suggesting that in this context, at least, no value whatever was placed on the beaver's flesh, nor on the castoreum which it produced.

Other early laws also prove valuable here: in England an early twelfth-century Act from the reign of Henry I, also noted by Wilson, established a scale of tolls to be levied on exports – including beaver pelts – through the port of Newcastle upon Tyne. Scotland followed a few years later when, in the reign of King David I (1124–53), a similar law was formulated on the basis of the legislation concerning Newcastle; further evidence comes from the era of Robert the Bruce (1306–29) when the Scottish parliament, meeting at Ayr, passed a revised series of export duties to be paid on fur-bearing animals, in which the beaver once again features. A number of earlier authors have considered the significance of this legislation, including the possibility that there was an element of re-export of foreign-sourced furs involved in the trade, but the weight of evidence points persuasively to the exploitation of local beaver populations which otherwise scarcely register in the record. On the other hand, the absence of any mention in corresponding laws of later date seems to imply by the same token that the supply quickly dwindled to negligible proportions.

First-hand observation

Direct reference to the former presence of beavers in Wales, specifically on the River Teifi, is provided by Giraldus Cambrensis in a key passage taken from his *Itinerary*, compiled before 1188:

The Teivi has [a] singular peculiarity, being the only river in Wales, or even in England, which has beavers; in Scotland they are said to be found in one river, but are very scarce ... The beavers, in order to construct their castles in the middle of rivers, make use of the animals of their own species instead of carts, who, by a wonderful mode of carriage, convey the timber from the woods to the rivers. Some of them, obeying the dictates of nature, receive on their bellies the logs of wood cut off by their associates, which they hold tight with their feet, and thus with transverse pieces placed in their mouths, are drawn along backwards with their cargo, by other beavers, who fasten themselves with their teeth to the raft. The moles use a similar artifice in clearing out the dirt from the cavities they form by scraping. In some deep and still corner of the river, the beavers use such skill in the construction of their habitations, that not a drop of water can penetrate, or the force of storms shake them; nor do they fear any violence but that of mankind, nor even that, unless well armed. They entwine the branches of willows with other wood, and different kinds of leaves, to the usual height of the water, and having made within-side a communication from floor to floor, they elevate a kind of stage, or scaffold, from which they may observe and watch the rising of the waters. In the course of time, their habitations bear the appearance of a grove of willow trees, rude and natural without, but artfully constructed within ... [They] ... live indifferently under the water, or in the air, and have short legs, broad bodies, stubbed tails, and resemble the mole in their corporal shape. It is worthy of remark, that the beaver has but four teeth, two above, and two below, which being broad and sharp, cut like a carpenter's axe, and as such he uses them. They make excavations and dry hiding places in the banks near their dwelling, and when they hear the stroke of the hunter, who with sharp poles endeavours to penetrate them, they fly as soon as possible to the defence of their castle, having first blown out the water from the entrance of the hole, and rendered it foul and muddy by scraping the earth, in order thus artfully to elude the stratagems of the well-armed hunter, who is watching them from the opposite banks of the river . . .

Giraldus's account of the Welsh beavers forms a remarkable example of early field observation, including what appears to be original material infused with the authentic ring of first-hand experience. It also incorporates elements of entirely spurious received wisdom that have been taken to undermine his authority, however, but it is perhaps more appropriate to see these two streams of information as parallel (and supposedly complementary) in nature, rather than as a demonstration of undiscriminating credulity. His assertion as to the way the beavers (and moles) use one another's bodies to transport materials, for example, is a myth noted by Pliny and thereafter widely diffused in bestiaries, where it is applied variously to alpine marmots and also to badgers (see p. 218). The scholarly Giraldus had studied in Paris and had travelled as far as Rome: this fanciful passage – together with that concerning the beaver's stratagem of self-castration (see further below) – may have been absorbed in the course of his Continental travels; its presence here is a sign of the book-learning that would have drawn admiration from his contemporaries, rather than the more dubious reaction it elicits today. His detailed anatomy is also a bit shaky – beavers have cheek-teeth with which to masticate their food in addition to their prominent incisors – but his descriptions of their lodge-building techniques have no classical precedent and seem to demonstrate a genuine

familiarity. Incidentally, he makes no mention of dam building by beavers, and Coles points out that given sufficiently deep water they feel no need to resort to building artificial barriers; these would undoubtedly have betrayed their presence very quickly to the local human population, whereas their lodges, suitably camouflaged with living willows and other plant life, would more easily have allowed them to escape notice. The populations may already have been thinned out by these means, with only the less visible inhabitants of deeper waters surviving by this time.

Giraldus's observations represent the only eyewitness account (if such it be) of beavers in Britain. From later centuries there are hearsay testaments to their former presence in various places, but better evidence can be supplied from other sources.

Consumption of beavers

Although never a major food source, there are some indications that beaver flesh was counted among the prestige products to be found on the tables of the early medieval aristocracy. While the evidence (summarized by Coles) remains thinly distributed, it is none the less persuasive. At Castle Acre (Norfolk), for example, two beaver mandibles were found in association with other food refuse in a context tentatively dated to the period 1066–1140: the fact that the bones of rabbit and fallow deer – both Norman introductions – came from the same layer, places the beavers (perhaps taken in the Fens) amongst a range of prestige foods that graced the table of the de Warenne family – one of the most powerful in Norman England. Discoveries tending to support this special status have been made at two other medieval sites: at Wolvesey Palace, residence of the bishops of Winchester, a beaver cranium came from a context likely to be medieval and including what could be interpreted as butchery refuse, while a humerus and ulna from twelfth- to fourteenth-century layers at Jarrow (Durham) have been interpreted as the remains of perhaps a high-status gift to the long-established monastery there. Although still tentative, these remains collectively suggest a trend that may well be confirmed by further excavated finds.

There was another context in which the beaver featured in the diet of certain privileged persons in the medieval period, as alluded to in a later passage from Giraldus's account:

> The beavers have broad, short tails, thick, like the palm of a hand, which they use as a rudder in swimming; and although the rest of their body is hairy, this part, like that of seals, is without hair and smooth; upon which account, in Germany and the arctic regions, where beavers abound, great and religious persons, in times of fasting, eat the tails of this fish-like animal, as having both the taste and the colour of fish.

Britain seems here to be specifically excluded from the practice as a religious observation, although some evidence of its currency is suggested from a single later source. In his *Book of Nurture*, compiled in the mid-fifteenth century and described by Coles as a treatise on how to manage the household of a great lord, John Marshall includes beaver tail as an appropriate titbit and lists it as an alternative to salt porpoise or seal. While there is no specific reference here to any religious significance, the fact that all these mammals are grouped by Marshall amongst the fish dishes implies that they would indeed have been considered as appropriate fare for fleshless days. (Martin Martin noted in 1703 that the seal occupied a similarly ambivalent position amongst the Hebridean islanders, some of whom maintained that it was appropriate for consumption during Lent.)

Castoreum

Giraldus's discourse on the beaver, quoted above, continues with the following passage:

> When the beaver finds he cannot save himself from the pursuit of the dogs who follow him, that he may ransom his body by the sacrifice of a part, he throws away that, which by natural instinct he knows to be the object sought for, and in the sight of the hunter castrates himself, from which circumstance he has gained the name of Castor, and if by chance the dogs should chase an animal which has previously been castrated, he has the sagacity to run to an elevated spot, and there lifting up his leg, shews the hunter that the object of his pursuit is gone. Cicero speaking of them says, 'They ransom themselves by that part of the body, for which they are chiefly sought.'

By mentioning Cicero (and later Juvenal and St Bernard) as his sources for this passage, Giraldus conveniently signals to us that he has here left the realms of personal observation and is drawing instead on literary tradition. (Other moralizing tracts are similarly inserted here and there in his text and are not to be confused with his topographical descriptions.) The wide circulation enjoyed by this belief in the medieval period was perhaps due less to direct classical scholarship than to the fact that it was taken up by the Church and endowed with a new, Christian message. It was also marked by multiple misunderstandings.

Castoreum is a pungent secretion generated in the beaver's abdominal castor sacs and exuded to function as a territorial marker. Its musky smell led to castoreum being sought out as an ingredient for perfumes – in a manner similar to civet – and already in the classical world it had gained a further reputation as an alexipharmic defence against poison and as a component of the *materia medica*, used in the treatment of an astonishing range of complaints from insomnia to hiccups, and for easing childbirth: the full range of its virtues is given by classical authorities such as Pliny and Dioscorides. Writing in the middle of the nineteenth century, Dr Charles Wilson observed that castoreum was still held in high regard in pharmacy right up to his own day amongst German apothecaries, but that its use was now all but abandoned in Britain – although only within comparatively recent times. By virtue of these beliefs, castoreum came to rival in value the pelt of the animal itself: the sacs, carried internally, were excised when the animal was skinned, dried to prevent putrefaction, and sold on to manufacturers. Wilson, incidentally, mentions that other body parts of the beaver had also been held in high estimation for medicinal purposes.

By the time the beaver emerges from the pharmacopoeia to enjoy an independent literary and later iconographical tradition of its own, the sacs, carried by the animal internally, had become hopelessly confused with its testicles. By a further misunderstanding, the testicles, which also form part of the beaver's internal anatomy, had (in the popular imagination) become relocated to an external position – essentially so, in order for the beaver to be able to perform its supposed act of self-emasculation. As presented by Cicero, the beaver's actions were prompted by a very rational desire to save its own skin, but its supposed actions were quickly reinterpreted in an aphorism coined by Æsop, to the effect that 'a prudent man will thus always be ready to sacrifice his wealth for his safety'

and subsequently were taken up as a parable by the Church, endowed with a new, moral dimension, as expounded in a bestiary compiled from earlier sources but surviving in a copy of *c.* 1220–50 (illus. 37):

There is an animal called the beaver, which is quite tame, whose testicles are excellent as medicine. The naturalists say of it that when it realises that hunters are pursuing it, it bites off its testicles and throws them down in front of the hunters, and thus takes flight and escapes. If it so happens that another hunter follows it, it stands up on its hind legs and shows its sexual organs. When the second hunter sees that it has no testicles, he goes away. In like fashion everyone who reforms his life and wants to live chastely in accordance with God's commandments should cut off all vices and shameless deeds and throw them in the devil's face. Then the devil will see that that man has nothing belonging to him and will leave him, ashamed.

In addition to the bestiary image reproduced here, two further representations are found by Coles to show the currency of this theme in the English church: a Norman tympanum over the entrance to the church at Ribbesford (Worcestershire) – in an area close to the Severn with a concentration of beaver-related place names – appears to show a beaver displaying its lack of testicles to an archer intent on shooting it, while a choir stall in Winchester Cathedral is ornamented with what is interpreted as the figure of a beaver which may once have held its amputated testicles in its mouth. It seems highly likely there were more people in England schooled in the spurious details of beaver anatomy than had ever seen one in the flesh. Certainly most manuscript illustrators were at a loss

37 A highly stylized beaver (lower right) in the act of biting off its own testicles in order to escape the attentions of a hunter; a second beaver, still intact, flees behind. From a bestiary compiled in England *c.* 1220–50 but drawing on a variety of earlier (Continental) sources.

as to what sort of creature it was: a noteworthy exception is formed by two beavers represented in the Lambeth Apocalypse, thought to have been compiled in London *c.* 1260–75, where anatomical correctness is marred only by the inclusion of prominent testicles, carried externally (illus. 38).

The end of the beaver

The attentions of hunters undoubtedly hastened the disappearance of the beaver from the British landscape. In some regions, environmental factors may also have played a role in its demise: at an increasing pace from the sixteenth century onwards, drainage schemes in the wetlands and the increasing canalization of river courses for water-borne transport and for the powering of mills would have reduced its potential habitat; the same period saw the rise of agricultural interference

with river courses for the floating of meadows (pp. 466–7), and all of these initiatives would have had a negative impact any on surviving beavers.

In the 1566 Act for the Preservation of Grayne, the status of the beaver had tumbled to the point where it was included amongst the vermin that found themselves with bounties on their heads. Had the populace needed further encouragement to persecute the beaver, here they had it. Only a decade later, William Harrison, in his *Description of England* (1577), was to revert to the opinion that they survived by that time only in far west: 'to saie the truth we have not manie bevers, but only in the Teifi in Wales'; a map compiled by Harrison's contemporary Humphrey Lhuyd and published by Ortelius in 1573, bears an inscription over the lower reaches of the same river to the effect that 'hic fluvius solus in Britannia castores habet', seemingly confirming Harrison's view – if both of them are not merely relying on Giraldus' account from several centuries earlier. Even here, the evidence of decline piles up: a later map maker, John Speed, wrote in 1627 that none had been seen on the Teifi for some years and in the following century Thomas Pennant too was able to refer only to 'the former existence of those animals in our country'. A similar picture emerges in Scotland (summarized by Harting and by White): in 1526 Hector Boece asserted in his *Chronicles of Scotland* that they were still common in the region of Loch Ness, but within 150 years Sir Robert Sibbald knew of no survivors there or elsewhere in Scotland.

Based on all these sources, opinion became widespread that beavers had in fact died out by the early decades of the seventeenth century, but Bryony Coles crowns her survey with a fascinating discovery that fully justifies her contention of a somewhat longer survival for the species under the historical radar. The Act for the Preservation of Grayne, which had contributed to the troubles of the beaver as outlined above, was also responsible for a dramatically later record of their presence than had hitherto been acknowledged: under the terms of the Act, churchwardens had been

made responsible for payment of bounties on slaughtered animals and in the churchwardens' accounts for the parish of Bolton Percy (Yorkshire) for 1789 we find one of their number, John Swail, disbursing the sum of 2d. for the head of a beaver – a paltry sum but a most valuable record showing the survival of the native species up to the closing decades of the eighteenth century.

Within a tantalizingly short time, efforts were already being made to re-establish the beaver, sometimes with European stock and occasionally with animals imported from Canada (*Castor canadensis*). Kitchener records that in 1870 a number of transatlantic beavers which had been kept at Sotterley Park (Suffolk) escaped from their enclosure and for two years survived and bred in the wild; after a time they seem to have died out – according to Harting at the hands of an unsympathetic human population. In the north the 3rd Marquis of Bute seems for a time to have had remarkable success with a colony planted on the Isle of Bute: a first consignment of four animals in 1874 was followed by a further batch of seven in the following year: they quickly built dams and lodges which drew admiration from all who

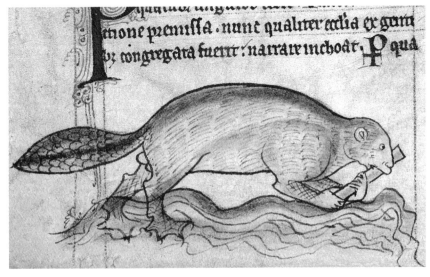

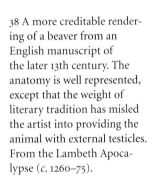

38 A more creditable rendering of a beaver from an English manuscript of the later 13th century. The anatomy is well represented, except that the weight of literary tradition has misled the artist into providing the animal with external testicles. From the Lambeth Apocalypse (*c.* 1260–75).

experienced them. Conroy et al. identify them as of Scandinavian origin, while Kitchener claims that the second and more successful batch only were North American. Either way, the colony had, for unspecified reasons, died out by 1887. Soon afterwards, in 1902–3, the 9th Duke of Argyll similarly experimented at Inveraray Castle with Canadian beavers, of which a total of twelve were released into the wild; they too soon died out. A more successful colony, introduced at just the same time by Sir Edmund Loder at Leonardslee (Sussex), survived (with the addition – according to Kitchener – of only two more animals in 1917) until the eve of World War Two. Today, tentative efforts to reintroduce the beaver continue.

but by the end of the eighteenth century they had disappeared too from northern England and were already rare in Wales and the Marches. Thomas Pennant evidently was familiar with them there, describing them as some three or four times the size of a domestic cat and very muscular. In his day they were taken, he says, 'in traps, or by shooting; in the latter case it is very dangerous only to wound them, for they will attack the person who injured them, and have strength enough to be no despicable enemy.' By the mid-1800s they had been exterminated from much of Scotland apart from the Grampians and the north-west, from which residual population some resurgence has recently been seen.

WILD CAT

The wild cat (*Felis silvestris*) features only infrequently in the hunting annals, although King John's household included three wildcat hunters. In the *Master of Game*, although recognized as a fearsome opponent for the hounds, the wild cat is judged to provide poor sport because he either 'soon putteth him to his defence or he runneth up a tree'. To this opinion, deriving from Gaston Phébus, the Duke of York adds:

> Of common wild cats I need not speak much, for every hunter in England knoweth them, and their falseness and malice are well known. But one thing I dare well say that if any beast hath the devil's spirit in him, without doubt it is the cat, both wild and tame.

By the sixteenth century they seem to have become extinct in much of southern England, apart from the far south-west. They survived rather longer in the north, with 141 of them being killed at Corbridge (Northumberland) between 1677 and 1724,

PINE MARTEN AND POLECAT

Another of Edward of York's insertions in the *Master of Game* continues: 'As of all other vermin I speak not, that is to say of martens and pole cats, for no good hunter goeth to the wood with his hounds intending to hunt them, nor for the wild cat either.' All these 'vermin' remained of secondary interest until declining deer populations from the sixteenth century onwards led to a new interest on the part of hunters in species that previously had been held in some disdain, and since their favoured diet is of poultry and other birds (including game birds and their eggs), they were much persecuted by farmers and later by gamekeepers. A variety of traps for polecats (*Mustela putorius*), martens (*Martes martes*) and other vermin is discussed and illustrated in Mascall's *Booke of Engines and Trappes* (1590).

None the less, there were those who found these two members of the Mustelid family a worthwhile quarry. Cockaine describes the 'marterne' (also referred to – like the polecat – as the foumart) in 1591 as 'the sweetest vermine that is hunted';

indeed, so alluring was their scent to the dogs that, once encountered, 'you will mervaile what it is your hounds finde of'. When the pack detected its presence, 'the crie is mervailous strong and great for halfe an houre: for she will runne rounde about you in the thickets. When she groweth wearie she will take a tree, from whence you must put her . . . so secretly as none of your hounds espie her, and then will she make you fresh sporte againe for a quarter of an houre'. Peter Beckford was one of those who thought them worthy of pursuit, although with certain caveats:

> If you have martin-cats within your reach, as all hounds are fond of their scent, you will do well to enter your young hounds in the covers they frequent. The martin-cat, being a small animal, by running the thickest brakes it can find, teaches hounds to run cover, and is therefore of the greatest use. I do not much approve of hunting them with the old hounds: they show but little sport; are continually climbing trees; and as the cover they run seldom fails to scratch and tear the hounds considerably, I think you might be sorry to see your whole pack disfigured by it. The agility of this little animal is really wonderful; and though it frequently falls from a tree in the midst of a whole pack of hounds all intent on catching it, there are but few instances, I believe, of a martin's being caught by them in that situation.

The climbing abilities mentioned by these authors proved the marten's best method of defence (illus. 39). An inhabitant of woods and bushy coverts, it was characterized by the *Sporting Dictionary* as 'nearly as expert in climbing trees, and leaping from one to another, as a squirrel'. The fur of the marten brought it to prominence (and

placed it in danger from hunters and trappers) from an early date; it was adopted, for example, as the customary lining for the robes of magistrates. A duty was placed on the export of its skins from Scotland as early as the fourteenth century and the wearing of its fur was restricted by Scottish sumptuary legislation in 1457; by the late sixteenth century it was said to be as scarce as the beaver and by 1800 it was extinct or rare in many counties throughout the British Isles. Langley and Yalden trace its continuing decline thereafter, with only isolated stragglers surviving in some remote areas – incidentally, often on barren and rocky ground, a long way from the pine forests that were its natural habitat.

Far from numbering among the 'sweetest vermine', the most striking characteristic of the polecat (otherwise also known as the foumart, as well as the fitchet) was, according to the *Sporting Dictionary*, the fact that 'The effluvia, or rather stench, arising from their bodies is so truly offensive, that it has long since laid the foundation of the well-known proverbial expression of "stinking like a pole-cat"'. Given that its diet included (when it could get them) eggs, poultry and the nestlings from dove-houses, the polecat was as unpopular as the pine marten. One of its few positive traits was, according to Pennant, that it 'will mix with the ferret, and that [warreners] are sometimes obliged to procure an intercourse between these animals, to improve the breed of the latter, which by long confinement will abate its savage nature, and become less eager after rabbets'.

Despite its malodorous nature, the polecat's fur was sought after to some degree, for in the fur market in Dumfries, for example, some hundreds of skins were sold annually: the surviving records peak at 600 in 1831, but within 25 years the price had tripled from 12s. to 36s. a dozen as the population declined. Their preferred habitat in lowland areas and valley bottoms brought them into direct conflict with farmers and later with gamekeepers, who persecuted them mercilessly. Having been formerly widespread in Britain, their progressive disappearance from successive counties in the second half of nineteenth century is recorded by Langley and Yalden, a decline which they relate particularly to the evolution of the sporting estate and the gamekeeping profession, as well as to the development of more efficient sporting guns. Harvie Brown noted that many were taken in steel traps set for rabbits, and that their survival rate was highest in those areas where rabbits were not systematically trapped. Changes in habitat were probably also a potent factor: the process of defor- estation which seems to have reached its greatest extent in the eighteenth century was especially destructive, after which deliberate planting pro- grammes instituted around 1750 and extended over the following century, began to reverse this trend.

Given its almost complete disappearance by the late 1800s, an article from that time by J. E. Hart- ing documenting the methods by which it had been hunted within living memory, is of special value and interest. After a brief county-by-county survey in which he notes, for example, that in the parish of Corbridge (Northumberland) the church- wardens' accounts note payments for no fewer than 653 foumarts' heads between 1677 and 1724, much of his attention is focused on neighbouring Cumberland, Westmorland and Lancashire, where they had been (and were still, to a small extent) hunted with hounds. Of five packs formerly kept in Cumberland specifically for the polecat, only one, at Aspatria, survived by the 1880s; it was com- posed of otter hounds, together with a quartet of terriers. Given the difficulties of unearthing them once they had gone to ground, the Aspatria hunt often worked by moonlight when the foumart was abroad hunting and hence more vulnerable to the hounds; the season started in February, with March and April being the busiest months (some packs, at least, took up foumart hunting at the end of the season for hares). Nocturnal hunts tended to start about 10 p.m.; alternatively, 3 or 4 a.m. was favoured for early morning outings. A distance of 3 to 5 miles was an average chase, but 10 was not uncommon. Older polecats seldom

39 *Hunting the marten*, an illustration from Henry Alken's *National Sports of Great Britain*, first published 1820.

died without managing to inflict injuries on some of the hounds.

One of Harting's correspondents from the neighbourhood of Rochdale (Lancashire) recalled a more artificial form of hunt, in which the animal would be caught live in a trap and released the night before it was intended that it should be hunted. It was evidently an uncertain form of exercise, which might end at the first fence or carry the hunt for miles; on one occasion the same animal was hunted for a whole week on successive mornings before finally being taken.

The most noted practitioner was one Captain Hopwood of Hopwood (Lancashire) who possessed an outstanding pack of otter-hounds trained to follow no other scent but the foumart and who hunted regularly, not only in the counties of north-west England but also in Merioneth and Montgomeryshire, where the terrain allowed the hunters to go on horseback. Hopwood generally began hunting at daybreak and recorded runs above twenty miles over the wildest country; sometimes the hunt would run the quarry to ground one day, mark the spot and return the following morning so that the hounds could resume where they had left off. Demonstrating the range of approaches that might be brought to the hunting of the polecat, Harting's correspondent concludes his account of Hopwood's exploits:

Capt. Hopwood never hunted at night – a course which is only taken for the purpose of killing the Foulmart, by hunting up to him while still travelling, giving him little or no chance of escape. Nor were the Foulmarts ever caught in traps, or turned out to hunt. The Captain only hunted on the strictest principles of wild and fair sport, and his pack will long be remembered in the counties over which he hunted.

By World War One polecats had effectively been eliminated from all but a few remote spots in Scotland, with the only substantive population in the south surviving in the region of Aberystwyth in the far west of Wales.

HARE

Therefore he was a pricasour aright;
Grehoundes he hadde, as swift as fowel in flight;
of pricking and of hunting for the hare
was al his lust, for no cost would he spare.

The high estimation given to the hare (*Lepus europaeus*) in Chaucer's word-picture of the hunting monk was one shared by hunters at large, for the hare was invariably included amongst the principal beasts of venery. Twiti, for example, was enthusiastic, considering the hare 'the most marvellous beast that is in this land', while one of the more strikingly original contributions of Edward of York to the text of the *Master of Game* (in which he gives the chapter 'Of the hare and of her nature' pride of place at the beginning of his tract) is his addition of an entirely new chapter which explains 'How an hunter should seek and find the hare with running hounds and slay her with strength'. Whereas Gaston Phébus himself had gone so far as to concede that 'much good sport and liking is the hunting of her, more than that of any other beast . . . if he were not so little', Edward opens with an assertion that 'it is to be known that the hare is king of all venery', an assertion repeated by later texts such as the *Boke of St Albans*. For Sir Thomas Elyot,

Hunting of the hare with grehoundes, is a ryght good solace for men that be studiouse, or theym to whome nature hathe not gyven personage, or courage apte for the warres. And also for gentilwomen, which feare nether sonne nor wynde for appayryng theyr beautie.

The sheer sport offered by the hare was one of its principal virtues, for it could be relied on to provide a challenge by running in a bewildering succession of tangents and zigzags, frequently doubling back and crossing its own trail to produce a real trial for the scenting hounds. The *Sporting Dictionary* describes the hare's propensity to pull ahead of the hounds until, when out of sight, 'she throws herself to the right or left, and returns in a parallel line to the track she went before; getting into which, she is said to run the foil', by which technique she frequently managed to make her escape. (Females, incidentally, were judged generally to stay closer to their home territory – where they might have several young deposited – with much doubling and circling, while males were more likely to make a headlong, high-speed dash.) The hare also had the advantage (to the hunter) that it could be pursued in all weathers, at any time of day and during all seasons: it breeds, in fact, for nine months out of twelve, producing some twenty leverets in the process (the gestation period is one month). None the less, a new legislative measure introduced in 1522–3 by Henry VIII signalled that the hare was now coming under pressure: whereas the king and his nobles had hitherto 'exercised the game of hunting of the hare for their disport and pleasure', it appeared that the said game was 'now decayed, and almost utterly destroyed, for that divers persons in divers parts of this realm, by reason of the tracing in snow, have killed and destroyed . . . the same hares, by x, xij, or xvi, upon one day'; accordingly, it was henceforth forbidden for anyone to 'trace, destroy, and kill any hare in the snow' by any means whatever. By this time, however, hunting the hare was, in the words of the *Noble*

Art of Venerie, 'not a privilege confined, like that of the buck, to great noblemen, but a sport easilie and equalie distributed, as well to the wealthie farmer as to the great gentleman'. It was also deemed an appropriate sport for ladies – perhaps even more so than men, in the opinions of Elyot (quoted above) and of William Harrison, who declared that 'the hunting of that seely [defenceless] beast . . . are pastimes more meet for ladies and gentlewomen to exercise'.

Even amongst the self-conscious nobility, the hare had the advantage that it could be hunted with less formality than the deer (illus. 40). None the less, Edward of York gives a wide range of calls and instructions to be given by the hunter to the hounds, again in arcane French or with a variety of blasts on the horn: the bulk of his text is indeed given over to appropriate calls and blasts to cover every eventuality, while the hunt itself is treated in less detail. A number of hunters were expected to be involved, however, and in the most formally constituted hunts the etiquette to be observed indicates that the pageant of the hunt far outweighed in importance the value placed on the quarry. Hence if one of the hunters came across the hare crouching in the grass or could see its location from his elevated viewpoint on horseback, there was no question of him attacking it himself but rather he would draw the attention of the hounds and their handlers to its position with cries and with appropriate blasts of the horn and, when they had all drawn close, start the hare running again. For their parts the hounds were to remain strictly coordinated and any tendency to be distracted by sheep or other animals was to be corrected by the horsemen lashing them back into place with long rods which they carried for the purpose.

The best hunting was judged to take place in open 'champaigne' country but it was practised

40 Hare hunting provided an opportunity for spontaneous sport without the full panoply involved in the pursuit of deer. From the early 14th-century Queen Mary's Psalter.

everywhere with a variety of hounds to suit the terrain: beagles performed best in hilly country unsuitable for horses, while the large Southern hound was favoured for low-lying land (illus. 41); the hounds now called harriers, originally a cross between the Southern hound and the dwarf fox-hound, were favoured for open country where the hare might run for five or six miles without a turn. Cockaine's advice was that the huntsman should 'keepe himselfe eight skore yardes behind the hounds at the least, that they may have roome to undo a double'; if they still failed, then the hunters should take to beating the area in case the hare had squatted down, in order to set it running again. The hare had a variety of other tricks up its

sleeve, a favourite being that it might 'take [refuge in] a flocke of sheepe, or . . . a heard of Swine or of beasts'.

Having been 'well chased and well retrieved' by the hounds, the carcass of the hare was to be held aloft and the death announced with the horn; when it had been skinned the carcass was to be chopped into small pieces 'so that it hang together', and again held up by one of the berners to a second bout of horn blowing during which 'every man help and holloa' while the hounds bayed at the hare, which was then torn asunder by the berner and a piece thrown to every hound in turn. Variations are recorded at this stage as at every other: Twiti holds that the 'hallow', comprising the neck, head, shoulders and sides of the animal were to be given to the hounds while the loins 'should remain for the kitchen'. As an alternative method of rewarding the hounds, Cockaine advises that 'A good Huntsman ought to . . . carry with him a peece of bread in his sleeve to wet in the bloude of the hare for the reliefe of his whelps', which should be further indulged with a good meal on their return to the kennels.

Judging by the appearance of hares in images of 'the world turned upside down', the fact that they are commonly shown hunting men with crossbows (as in the Flemish *Romance of Alexander the Great* of 1344 in the Bodleian Library) suggests that in everyday life it was they who were likely to suffer death in this way at the hands of the solitary hunter.

Hare hunting with hounds remained popular during the 1800s: even prosperous urban tradesmen could by that time take advantage of the harrier packs associated with a number of cities. Griffin estimates that there were about 90 packs at the turn of the twentieth century, though she observes that many by that time were using dwarf foxhounds that were too fast for the quarry: some subsequently adjusted their speed by switching to slower basset hounds, while others converted to fox-hunting. Beagle packs, hunting on foot, also saw a rise at this time. Beckford mentions the employment of countrymen with local knowledge as 'hare-finders', to ensure that sport could be had at every outing, and also (with less enthusiasm) the use of 'trap hares', caught in their breeding grounds to be released before the pack or a pair of greyhounds.

In the fourteenth century Phébus had mentioned that hares were also taken with nets and snares and hare-pipes, but Edward interjects that no self-respecting hunter in England would stoop to such practices – which is not to deny that there

were many in the country who were perfectly content to get their dinner in this way. Much later the *Sporting Dictionary* describes hare-pipes as a form of lure, mentioning that 'instruments so curiously constructed, to imitate the whining whimper of the hare . . . being formerly found a very destructive nocturnal engine in attracting the attention of hares, and bringing them within the certain possession of the poacher, their use was prohibited (by particular specification) in every Act of Parliament for the preservation of game, from the reign of Richard the Second to the present time'. By the time the *Dictionary* was being compiled at the turn of the nineteenth century, however, the editor judged that 'there is not now such an article to be seen, or found in the kingdom'. It may be suggested that he was, in fact, completely misled by the unfamiliarity of the type of object in question, for quite a different device with the same name is described and illustrated by Mascall (illus. 42), for whom the hare-pipe was a form of snare, constructed of a hollow cylinder of elder, worked into two points at one end and with a noose passing through it: once the quarry entered the noose, 'the more they plucke and drawe, the more it strikes in and pierce the flesh of the beast'. All the references to hare-pipes quoted above from early legislation, where they are invariably grouped with nets and snares – and also below in relation to otters, which Turberville says may be taken 'in traps and in snares, as you may take a Hare with Harepypes, or such like gynnes' – corroborate this identification and indicate that the wind-blown instrument envisaged by the (otherwise quite reliable) editor – who may well have been familiar with birdcalls acting on the principle he describes – never existed.

Another part of the stock-in-trade of the expert poacher was the 'gate-net', considered by the same manual to be 'the most destructive nocturnal

41 *Hunting ye Hare with deep-mouthed Hounds*. Engraving commissioned by Richard Blome for his *Gentleman's Recreation* (1686).

instrument that can be bought into use': when the net had been fixed to the lower bar of the gate to a field of young corn or clover, and pegged to the ground, a lurcher was sent to scour the field in a circuitous manner, startling the hares towards the gate by which they had gained access to the field and driving them into the net.

FOX-HUNTING

Originally classed as mere vermin, the fox (*Vulpes vulpes*) makes only an occasional appearance as a beast of the medieval chase. In Edward I's wardrobe accounts, for example, are references to six couple of foxhounds which had their own master – 'William de Foxhunte, the king's huntsman of foxes in divers forests and parks'. The *Master of Game* anathematizes the fox as 'a false beast and

The Hare pipe,

This Engine is called a Hare pipe, becaufe it is made hollow, they are commonly made for the hare, of pipes of Elder, of fire or feuen inches long, and for the Foxes and dogges, they are made of pane plate, nie ten or eleuen inches long, with two fharpe pikes in the mouth thereof, and the more they plucke and drawe, the more it ftrikes in and peirce the flefh of the beaft. And alfo for the Fore or other fuch, it fhall be good to arme the ftring or line with red wiar for wearing. Which line, the one end is put in at a hole made in the pipe fide, as ye may fee, and fo drawne double

42 The hare-pipe (a form of snare), from Leonard Mascall's *Booke of . . . Sundrie Engines and Trappes to take Polcats . . . and all other Kindes of Vermine and Beasts whatsoever* (1590).

as malicious as a wolf', asserting too that 'she has a venomous biting like a wolf'. The intention here may have been less to portray the fox as a dangerous adversary than to consign it to the category of verminous animals appropriate for extermination by any means possible and in any season.

So far as may be judged from the texts, it was customary at this period (around 1400) for the fox to be pursued with hounds until it went to earth, 'and then men may dig him out and take him'; alternatively it might be taken 'with hounds, with greyhounds, with hayes and with purse-nets' – although it was necessary to get to the captive fox quickly in order to avoid having the nets gnawed through. Doubtless many more foxes died in traps and snares than were pursued by hounds in the medieval centuries.

By the later medieval period a fox-hunting season had begun to be observed that ran from Christmas to the Feast of the Annunciation (25 March), implying that polite society had begun to hunt the fox with its customary formality; the fact that only inedible game was generally hunted during Lent

may have added to its appeal. The populace at large, meanwhile, no doubt got on with the task of exterminating the fox as best it could, given its reputation as a resourceful predator on poultry. By the sixteenth century, animals were being spied out in advance and their earths stopped on the eve of the hunt in order to ensure a good run for the hounds.

Over the next hundred years, and increasingly after the Restoration, the declining returns from deer hunting drew further attention to the fox as the only fast-paced alternative quarry offering a good run across the countryside (though not so fast that it could not also be hunted on foot in certain areas – notably by the so-called fell-packs in the north). James II kept a pack of foxhounds, seemingly a royal revival from Plantagenet era, which cost him £700 a year. His enthusiasm for the chase is revealed in a request made while he was in exile at Brussels, when he asked for his hounds and huntsman to be sent over: 'I now begin to have plenty of stag-hunting', he says, 'and the country looks as if the fox-hunting would be very good.' Both Turberville and Cockaine considered it possible to have 'good pastime at this vermin', while Arthur Stringer in his *Experienc'd Huntsman* (1714) considered it 'a brave, noble Chace for such who keep good Horses and Hounds'. Stringer was one of those dedicated hunters who recognized that the pace of the hunt needed to be improved, urging his readers to use 'fleet hounds, for slow hounds signify little for that pastime'. Longrigg observes that the quarry could outrun these slow hounds all day – a form of hunting described as 'walking the fox to death' – and that the hunt still ended as often as not with the fox having to be dug out of its earth.

Although the belief that the packs were too slow for their quarry evidently was widely shared during the early decades of the eighteenth century, much credit for galvanizing fox-hunting into its modern form is attributed to one man, Hugo Meynell, who inherited an estate at the Leicestershire village of Quorn in the 1750s. Having bought an old aristocratic pack at the age of eighteen, Meynell set about breeding hounds for stamina and speed as much as a keen nose. At first he is judged to have hunted with more enthusiasm than science – in his youth Meynell had the reputation of never going out with fewer than 100 couple of hounds – but during the 1760s and 1770s he made solid progress and others followed: the Pelham family's Brocklesby hounds in North Lincolnshire, for example, are singled out for setting new standards of uniformity as well as performance, by close application of the principles of inbreeding – means that were beginning to show remarkable results at just this time in livestock breeding in the area (p. 428). Incidentally, in 1730 Sir Robert Walpole suggested to the 11th Earl of Carlisle that he might take up an appointment as Master of the Royal Foxhounds and Harriers, with a salary of £2,000 for himself, a deputy and all expenses; the Earl declined the offer, however, and a formal royal pack of foxhounds was never founded.

As the hounds speeded up, the quality of the horses turning out in the field was also found to be in need of improvement: almost everyone in the hard-riding Quorn is said to have ridden a thoroughbred. The *Sporting Magazine* observed in 1799 that: 'Meynell's hunt is . . . at present so truly refined to a degree of perfection, by the speed of the hounds, the excellence of the horses, and the emulative and determined resolution of the riders, that the scene has certainly never before been equalled in this Kingdom.' This height of perfection was reached after a century or so during which improvements had been wrought on hunting mounts to the extent that they began to be matched against each other in cross-country steeplechases and their

influence spread even to the racetrack: Nicholas Russell observes that Markham earlier considered that horses inadequate for the rigours of the hunt might still prove useful on the racetrack – 'a reversal of modern practice where second-rate Thoroughbreds often wind up as hunters, steeplechasers and show jumpers'. Jane Roberts further notes that as early as 1711, when the 'round Heat' at Ascot was first laid out for racing, a precondition applied to many of the races was that all runners should be 'Horses that have stag-hunted in Epping or Windsor Forests with the King's hounds'. By the final decades of eighteenth century, most of mounts were being bred with a considerable infusion of thoroughbred blood (nowadays three-quarters or seven-eighths thoroughbred is seen as desirable for a hunter). Many sires of the most vaunted racehorses are thought likely to have spent a greater part of their energies on improving the quality of the hunting stock at this time.

The faster pace also imposed the need for more attention to be paid to condition – Longrigg notes that until the mid-1800s many owners used to the gentler pace of the traditional hunt entered their horses for the season seriously ill-prepared for a demanding run, with the result that many were strained or even killed before they had time to get into form. (Stringer astutely pointed out that the hunter needed to be in as good condition as a racehorse.) Also in response to the headlong pace of the faster hunt, many riders began to rely on the curb bit rather than the snaffle, which hitherto had been standard equipment for the fox-hunt. The practice of having a second horse emerged, so that the hunt could be prosecuted without loss of pace, and some would arrive riding a 'covert hack' and leading their hunter in a manner reminiscent of the medieval knight, saving his charger's energies for the field (p. 39). All this speed was too much for some people: Gardiner, writing in 1750, already found the headlong pursuit of the fox so demanding that 'but for the Name of Foxhunting, a Man might as well mount at his Stable-Door, and determine to gallop twenty Miles an End into another County'.

So much emphasis on equestrianism wrought changes on the character of the field. Much larger numbers of participants were now likely to turn out (illus. 43) – 'immense ungovernable fields' in the words of one observer – all dedicated to chasing the fox at full tilt but without necessarily much insight into the niceties of the hunt. Longrigg notes that the earliest handlist of the Belvoir hunt, dating from 1757, indicates 290 horses hunting with the hounds, and similar fields remained common at the turn of the nineteenth century. Rising costs changed the make-up of the membership, with privately owned and financed hunts giving way to subscription packs in which there was inevitably a wider range of experience and expertise, while the character of the hunting terrain was also affected by contemporary trends towards greater numbers of enclosures, with hedges and ditches intersecting the landscape and forming more obstacles in the landscape for the field to negotiate: hunting now seldom took place on the flat but took on the character of a steeplechase.

The work of the hounds, which formerly had been at the centre of the chase, was now understood by fewer in the field, with many embarrassing transgressions being committed by those who misread (or ignored) the signals coming from the Master and his huntsmen. The training of the hounds, which hitherto had formed a major preoccupation of writers (and readers) on the subject of hunting, was now increasingly a matter for the professional huntsman rather than the membership at large.

With such dispatch were proceedings now concluded that the timing of the hunt often slipped from its former early morning start (designed to intercept the fox at his most sluggish, after a night's foraging and with his stomach full) to mid-morning, and to the point where most foxes were killed in afternoon. From the mid-1800s it became possible for enthusiasts to participate in more distant hunts, as railway companies provided services that could whisk the dedicated urban hunter into the countryside or provide horseboxes that could be uncoupled at convenient rural halts.

A striking phenomenon associated with fox-hunting is the way in which it gradually took over some of the ritual formerly associated with deer hunting – especially that surrounding the kill. The fox was now elaborately honoured by the hunters and by the pack in a way unknown to his medieval ancestors (illus. 44): novices were introduced by 'blooding' at their first kill in a manner reminiscent of James I's practice on the stag hunt (p. 106), while various 'trophies' were cut from the fox's anatomy and presented to those who had distinguished themselves in the hunt. In an interesting reprise of the entry of a wider community into deer hunting, handbooks were compiled to guide the tyro hunter through the minefield of arcane vocabulary and ritual. In such a self-conscious social milieu, dress attained a new importance as riding coats gave way to frock-coats and ultimately to tight-fitting tail coats, with hunting 'pink' emerging as the colour of choice for the leading figures and with other forms of clothing deemed appropriate for less exalted participants.

All this increased attention inevitably had an adverse effect on the fox population, so that in order to preserve their sport hunters found themselves in the curious position of having to encourage and protect the very animals they purported to control. It was not entirely a new dilemma, for others have noted that as early as 1587 William Harrison had expressed the belief that foxes would

43 Something of the concentrated mayhem of hunting with a large field is conveyed in *The First Ten Minutes. The Leicestershires*, 1825, coloured engraving, by Henry Alken (1785–1851) after John Dean Paul.

already have been 'utterly destroyed by many years agone' had they not been 'preserved by gentlemen to hunt and have pastime withal'. With the new attention directed at foxes in the eighteenth century, numbers began to fall more dramatically. Artificial earths were constructed and coverts planted in order to shelter the wild population. The hand-rearing of cubs was experimented with, and the capturing of young in some well-stocked areas for transportation to others where there was less sport became common, a practice that led to the rise of much illicit trapping and trading. An international trade in cubs developed by the early nineteenth century, with many Continental foxes passing through Leadenhall Market in particular, where they changed hands for 10s. to 15s. a piece; by mid-century 1,000 foxes a year were being imported from Holland, Germany and France, as well as from Scotland.

Hunting practice also had to be modified in some areas, to the point where the fox would be rescued from the hounds at the end of the hunt in order to run another day: Griffin refers to one well-known fox in Devon that was caught and released

no fewer than 36 times by hounds trained to avoid killing or injuring the quarry. Alternatively, a captive fox would be carried in a bag to a prearranged release point and set loose, with the pack heading off in pursuit after a suitable delay. These 'bagmen' had already become common by the end of eighteenth century and remained so for the next hundred years, although many traditionalists were scathing of the poor sport they offered: confinement made them, in Beckford's words, 'stink extravagantly', so that the scent was 'too good' for the hounds and made them idle; they were also likely to be stiff-limbed and broken in spirit, while their unfamiliarity with the countryside in which they were released made them more tentative in their flight as they sought out possible hiding places and escape routes.

Other difficulties arose as hunters intent on increasing the fox population came into conflict with farmers anxious to protect their poultry and with the growing numbers of gamekeepers assiduously trying to breed pheasants and partridges for the shooting estates. Hunts found themselves further embroiled over rights of access which they

44 The fox is duly honoured in *The Death*, by John Frederick Herring Snr (1795–1865). Coloured engraving by Huffman & Mackrill.

claimed in their increasingly questionable mission to control 'vermin', but once the courts had established the principle that landowners and farmers could sue for damage caused by the hunt, new and more mutually respectful patterns of behaviour emerged that allowed fox-hunting to take a more equable place in the pattern of country living.

OTTER

That the otter (*Lutra lutra*) has been persecuted for a thousand years and more is perhaps scarcely surprising, since its taste for fish and its skill as a hunter inevitably led into conflict with fishermen (and later with fish farmers). The *Master of Game* asserts that 'a couple of otters without more shall well destroy the fish of a great pond or stank, and therefore men hunt them', and a similar assessment is made in the *Noble Arte of Venerie*: 'even as a Foxe, Polcat, wildcat, or Badgerd will destroye a Warren, so will the Otter destroy all the fishe in

your pondes, if he once have found the waye to them'. The profligacy with which the otter is wont to treat its prey only served to alienate it further: Oliver Goldsmith was typical in deprecating the fact that 'it destroys much more than it devours', and its 'killing for its own amusement, and infecting the edges of the lake with quantities of dead fish' – a reference to the otter's alleged habit of taking no more than a bite or two out of its catch before plunging back to seek new sport. River fishermen too were greatly vexed by the destruction wrought by otters on their traps and nets: Goldsmith continues that 'the damage they do by destroying fish is not so great as their tearing in pieces the nets of the fishers, which they infallibly do whenever they happen to be entangled. The instant they find themselves caught, they go to work with their teeth, and in a few minutes destroy nets of a very considerable value.' It remains only to say that the occasional depredations they might make during severe weather amongst lambs, rabbits and poultry only added to the numbers of the enemies ranged against them.

More recent apologists for the otter have sought to redeem this unenviable reputation by stressing that trout and salmon by no means form the exclusive basis of the otter's diet: slower-swimming coarse fish, eels, crayfish and frogs are now known to form a more regular source of nourishment, as well as the occasional coot or moorhen – all of them, incidentally, great destroyers of fish spawn and of the larvae of mayfly and other forms of fish food. A balanced population of otters is presented by such authors – several of them admittedly having formed the backbone of the sporting otter-hunting population – as positively beneficial to a well-stocked river; they further observe that the otter can seldom out-swim salmon, trout or pike and that they serve to improve the stock by thinning out the weaker specimens. (The rats, voles, insects, bark and weeds which commonly supplement the otter's winter diet play no part in these arguments.) Fish-ponds are undeniably vulnerable to their attentions, although given the otter's reluctance to dig, these are easily protected by fencing.

One factor which worked in its favour, at least, was that the otter was scarcely ever estimated as worthy of pursuit for food. Thomas Pennant comments on the 'excessively rank and fishy' nature of otter flesh, a characteristic that might have led to its being approved for eating on meatless days by the 'Romish church'. Pennant himself had seen an otter prepared for the table in the kitchens of a convent at Dijon belonging to the Carthusians, 'who by their rules, are prohibited during their whole lives, the eating of flesh'. This kind of speciousness may account for a wider uncertainty that surrounded the status of the otter, even amongst the likes of Izaak Walton's hunter who, in response to a question as to whether it was a beast or a fish, responded:

Sir, It is not in my power to resolve you, I leave it to be resolved by the Colledg of Carthusians, who have made vowes never to eat flesh. But I have heard, the question hath been debated among many great Clerks, and they seem to differ about it; yet most agree that his tail is Fish: and if his body be Fish too, then I may say, that a fish will walk upon land (for an Otter does so) sometimes five or six miles in a night.

Thomas Fairfax, writing in 1765, was of the opinion that otter flesh was 'both cold and filthy . . . and therefore not fit to be eaten', although he acknowledged that 'there are those in England, who lately have highly valued an otter-pie, much good may do them with it'. The Revd William Daniel in his *Rural Sports* records an occasion at Bridgnorth (Shropshire) in 1796 when four otters were killed: 'the Hearts &c were dressed, and eaten by many respectable people who attended the hunt, and allowed to be very delicious; the carcasses were also eaten by the men employed, and found to be excellent'. Amongst later writers, Captain L.C.R. Cameron also admits to having eaten on occasion the hearts of otters roasted with butter and herbs, which again proved quite palatable, but it seems doubtful that this could ever have been a widespread practice.

The otter in his element

The natural distribution of the otter in Britain is widespread, from the northern isles to the south coast, but by nature the population has always been diffuse. Although they are said to favour rivers with a stony bed and with plenty of cover in the form of fallen trees and root systems extending into the water, in fact they are highly tolerant and take readily to the sluggish channels of the

Fenlands and the chalk streams of the Downs. The species also occurs in estuaries and around the coast, and exists equally happily on sea fish or on freshwater varieties.

By nature they are nocturnal, working the waters by night and lying up during the day. The individual territory they may occupy is extensive: average distances of some six to twelve miles overland have been calculated as typical for the wanderings a single otter might undertake in a night, keeping close to river courses here, cutting off a loop in the stream there and on occasion striking out into the countryside – all in search of a day's food. (Other estimates would extend this range even further: the Earl of Coventry records one occasion when his hounds followed the scent of an otter for 21 miles.) After resting in one or other of its established holts or shelters, scattered over the river banks, rocks and drains of his territory (all of which are likely to be visited on a regular basis but will not be distinguished by any nest or structure – not even to the extent of having been dug out), the otter will be off again on a new quest the following night. During the summer months it will sometimes 'lie rough' at some distance from the water, or may take its ease in sheltered reed and osier beds.

The season at which the females give birth has been widely discussed: claims are made by some authors that most of the cubs are born in winter while others insist on summer as the more common season (and this would have the advantage of an optimum diet being available for the lactating mother), but the evidence seems to favour the conclusion that they can appear at any time of the year. The bitch normally withdraws to a particular holt to give birth: some authorities reserve the term 'couch' for this nursery holt; others use this word merely to indicate a lair on the ground surface, as opposed to a semi-subterranean 'holt',

often in a hollowed-out river bank and with a discreet underwater entrance. Up to five cubs may be born in a single litter, with two or three being the most common number. The bitch will stay with them for up to a year; dog otters, on the other hand, lead essentially solitary lives – especially so as they get older.

Otter-hunting

Although anathematized by some – Izaak Walton, for example, judged the otter to be 'villainous vermin' – yet there have long been organized hunts dedicated to the pursuit of the otter for sport. It proves, indeed, to be one of the oldest organized sports involving packs of hounds hunting by scent, pursued at established times of the year from the reign of Henry II onwards. Although there was an element of self-interest for the monarch in protecting his valuable fisheries, it is clear that the otter was also hunted for sheer enjoyment.

An early reference found by Cameron is for the appointment of one Roger Follo as 'King's Otter Hunter' in 1175. A generation later, King John signed letters patent at Dunstable on 7 June 1216 in favour of Ralph and Geoffry (or Godfrey), appointed jointly 'King's Otterhunters', and on at least one occasion the same monarch dispatched his pack of hounds to the sheriff of Bristol with the command that he was to hunt them for the space of two months at his own charge. 'John le Oterhunte' became huntsman to Edward I, and the fact that Edward III forbade the killing of otters except by packs of hounds provides the clearest evidence that the exercise was seen in the light of pleasurable recreation rather than merely as vermin control.

Under Richard II the first of an entire dynasty of otter hunters makes an appearance with the appointment in 1385 of John de Milbourne as

Master of the King's Otter-Hounds in Essex. In the following year, a writ directed the sheriffs of the counties of Essex and Hertford to pay the said John 2d. a day and his assistant or deputy Geoffrey Brown 1½d. a day for the space of a year in wages; they were further to receive ¾d. a day each on account of the eight dogs that each maintained in their respective packs. It is to this very person that Edward of York, compiler of the *Master of Game* (1387–91) defers when he breaks off his brief account of the otter with the words 'Of the remnant of his nature I refer to Milbourne the king's otter hunter' – clearly in the expectation that his courtly readership could supplement any of the author's shortcomings by direct access to the officer concerned. On 18 February 1422 William Milborne became 'Valet of our Otter-hounds', and later John Milborne (a brother) was assigned to 'the office of keeping the King's Dogs for Otterhunting'. When Edward IV succeeded he made Thomas Hardegrove 'holder of the office called Otterhunte' by letters patent dated 18 July 1461. On his accession, Henry VII granted 'the office of Otterhunt to Edward Bensted and Philip Boterley, squiers'.

While the establishment of the royal pack of otter-hounds was evidently of considerable antiquity, a new development occurs during the reign of Mary Tudor when the Corporation of Norwich was ordered to maintain a pack of hounds to hunt the rivers of Norfolk. In the course of the following reign, otters had become so abundant on the River Yare that in 1577 the Norwich Assembly passed a declaration that fishermen operating between Conisford and Hardley Cross should be bound to keep a dog to hunt the otter and that a general hunt should henceforth be organized twice or three times a year. The extent to which other packs were maintained beyond the royal prerogative is unknown at this time, although Cameron notes that in the early years of the seventeenth

century one of the meetings of conspirators involved in the Gunpowder Plot was said to have taken place during an otter hunt in Staffordshire.

While the later Tudors had all maintained the tradition of the royal pack, under James I otter-hunting (like every other field sport) was more vigorously pursued. In 1616 the Master of the Otter-Hounds was granted a licence 'to take hounds, beagles, spaniels and mongrels for His Majesty's disport. Also to seize such hounds &c as may be offensive to the King's game', and James also issued an ordinance commanding millers to stay their watercourses when the hounds were out. In the course of the seventeenth century (perhaps increasingly after the Civil War), the role of private citizens becomes increasingly visible. Under the Commonwealth, Izaak Walton enjoyed sport on the River Lea between Hoddesdon and Ware with Ralph Sadler, described as a 'Gentleman-Huntsman', and certainly there were other packs by this time – witness, for example, Walton's assertion that 'all men that keep otter-dogs ought to have pensions', to be provided, he suggested in the first edition of *The Compleat Angler,* by 'the Commonwealth' and substituting 'the King' in subsequent editions published after the Restoration. At this time the royal pack was quickly re-established by Charles II, with John Cott appointed as Serjeant of the Otter-hounds. James II also maintained a pack, but the sport evidently languished under the later Stuarts and with the succession of the Hanoverian dynasty the royal pack vanishes from the record.

The method of hunting in these earlier centuries is generally characterized by the use of comparatively few hounds, and although they might be referred to as 'otter-hounds', little is known of the actual varieties concerned. Turberville later advises the use of four 'servants or varlets with bloudhounds or such houndes as will draw in the lyame' (that is, leash-hounds capable of following a scent), although as a preliminary he recommends forming an assembly of residents from the area in order to gather local intelligence on where otters are most likely to be found. Sir Thomas Cockaine recommended in 1591 that it was a prudent measure for a huntsman to be sent to the river early in the morning in order to 'note the tracks and movements of the otter before the hounds are brought'; once its general whereabouts on the previous night had been established, then the hunter was advised to take his pack to the spot 'and cast your traylors off upon the trayle you thinke best.' The otter's habit of fishing up-stream, so that the water 'bringeth him sent of the fishes that are above him' was well appreciated, as was its tendency to abandon one lodge or holt for another possibly some miles away if the fishing should prove unrewarding.

As the pack closed in, the 'varlets of the kennels' were to be disposed in pairs on either side of the water, one pair up-river from the hunters and the other down-river, to investigate the various holts and resting places which the hounds might identify, to beat the banks of the stream and beds of bullrushes and ultimately to flush out the otter so that 'eyther the houndes shall light upon him, or els some of the huntesmen shall strike him, and thus you may have excellent sporte and pastime in hunting'.

In the event of the water levels being high and the otter being likely to make a break down-river, Turberville suggests that it might be useful

> to have a lyne throwen overthwart the River, the whiche two of the huntesmen shall holde by eche ende, one on the one side of the River, and the other on that other: and let them holde the line so slacke that it may always be underneath the water, and so go on with it: and if ye Otter come diving under

ye water, he shall of necessitie touche their line, and so they shall feele and know which way he is passed, the which shall make him be taken sooner.

As mentioned, the kill might be effected by the hounds or the hunters might get some sport with their spears. Illustrations in several versions of the *Livre de Chasse* of Gaston Phébus indicate that hunters might make use not only of conventional hunting spears but also of multi-pronged tridents, a custom also reflected in the practice of later centuries (see illus. 45). After the otter had been put down into the water by the hounds, the sportsmen would position themselves at convenient shallows both above and below the spot and would use their spears in order to 'pound' or contain the otter and to turn him back should he try to pass, harrying him each time he vented in the intervening water (and taking care to avoid injuring the hounds in the process); ultimately the quarry would be exhausted by the combined onslaught of hounds and spears until 'he is at length impaled upon the spear of one of the hunters and borne aloft in triumph'. Writing in 1591, Cockaine regarded this as the normal method of killing the dislodged otter: 'Then must be on either side of the water two men with Otter speares to strike him, if it be a great water'; if water levels were low, however, 'you must forbeare to strike him, for the better making of your houndes'. Nicholas Cox, in his *Gentleman's Recreation* (1677), on the other hand, advised an attempt at spearing at the first opportunity and only if it failed to bring in the hounds. Fairfax too considered in 1765 that the normal accoutrements of the hunt would include 'a sort of instruments, called otter-spears'. William Somervile, in his epic poem in celebration of hunting titled 'The Chace' (1735), captures the climax of such an otter hunt with his lines: 'Pierc'd thro' and thro' / On pointed spears they lift him high in air; / Wriggling he hangs, and grins, and bites in vain . . .', and in visual terms Landseer's image of *The Otter Speared* (illus. 46), brings as much drama to the occasion as Somervile's verse. Although otter-spears evidently survived in everyday use up to the eve of the nineteenth century, by the mid-1800s they had come to be considered unsporting and were no longer used by the hunting gentry. Lomax, the doyen of otter hunters, was praised by *Fores's Guide* for using 'neither net, spear, nor any warlike engine, save horn and hound in pursuit of his game'. For those of a more prosaic turn of mind such as Stringer, if deep water threatened to frustrate the success of the spear-men, then 'guns are the only instruments'.

Otter-hunting of this variety, with the aid of a few hounds or terriers and with spears with which the hunters could finish off the quarry, lingered in some places after the more self-consciously 'refined' form of pack hunting described below had become widespread. Lydekker asserts that spears had been entirely laid aside by 1896, although it is noteworthy that less than a decade earlier the encyclopaedic *British Rural Sports* carried an account of formal otter-hunting in which spears remained as standard implements (although acknowledgement is made that some hunts had already eschewed this practice). All indications are that the practice was considered archaic by this time, but the details given are useful: spears are characterized as not only useful in killing the otter but also in enabling the sportsman to leap over brooks – clearly indicating the origin of the long pole which had by now become standard equipment in most hunts. Its characterization by 'Stonehenge' as 'an ashen staff about twelve feet long' indicates that the pole later shrank as well as losing its spear point, which he describes in the following terms:

It should have an iron head, either fixed on or screwed into a socket fixed on the pole; but the permanent head answers al the purposes required, and is very much cheaper. It can also be made by the village blacksmith, and if lost in the ardour of the chase, may be easily and cheaply replaced. If the head is made to screw on and off, it is usual to have a concealed barb, which comes out of a mortice on the animal being transfixed, and thus holds him firmly fixed on the spear; but the slightly barbed spear-head is quite sufficient to secure him firmly if fairly through him, and even the concealed barb will not do this unless it also pierces the body of the animal. Where the spear is used, each sportsman should have one, and a spare one or two may be carried by an attendant, in case of accident.

The rather primitive form of hunting described above gave way in the course of the nineteenth century to a more self-consciously formalized sporting pursuit, strongly influenced in its *mores* by fox-hunting and beagling. Hence the typical make-up of these later packs, with a designated Master of Otter-Hounds (who might well also be the principal financial backer), a prescribed 'country' over which they hunted, fixed kennels with a kennel man, huntsman and whipper-in (these offices often being combined), an organizing committee with an appointed secretary, fee-paying subscribers and a following of enthusiasts ('the field') would all have been familiar to fox-hunting men (and, increasingly, women). Very often, indeed, the same packs with the same Masters might pursue otter in the summer and fox in the winter, although in general otter-hunting was a more socially accessible and less expensive pursuit, since it required no horse in order to participate;

HUNTING ỹ OTTER

45 *Hunting ye Otter*, engraving commissioned by Richard Blome for his *Gentleman's Recreation* (1686): two- or three-pronged spears were favoured in the otter hunt.

it could also accommodate those for whom a hard day's riding no longer held the same appeal. While a degree of informality of dress was tolerated, many packs adopted hunt uniforms, although who might wear them (subscribers only, officers only, and so on) varied from pack to pack: a coat of red or blue (but on occasion green or grey) with various trimmings and with the hunt's own buttons, was commonly combined with a pair of white serge trousers or knickerbockers. The huntsman was also likely to be provided with a uniform, which added to his authority in negotiating access for the hunt over private estates. The thigh boots favoured by earlier hunters were abandoned at this time for

46 Edwin Landseer, *The Otter Speared, Portrait of the Earl of Aberdeen's Otter-hounds*, 1844, oil on canvas. The hunter hoists the carcass on his spear, while the typical rough-coated otter-hounds bay at it in the climax to the hunt.

a more genteel pair of brogues with 'plenty of eyelet holes pierced in the lower part of the uppers' in order to let the water run out quickly, or for serviceable boots and gaiters.

Otherwise, the only equipment needed was a horn for the Master (often fitted with a reed in the nineteenth century for the musically challenged) and a pole or stave for the hunt members. This would typically be about 6 feet long with the ends shod with steel, one of them taking the form of a v-shaped prong and the other a ferrule, recalling the socket into which in former times a spearhead could have been fitted. These poles were not themselves intended as weapons (and indeed striking the otter with one was considered very bad form); rather they served in probing the banks and they helped steady the hunters while wading through the water; they also played a role in thwarting the otter's attempts to escape underwater. They did, however, have a ritual function in recording the kills in which its owner had participated, either by means of transverse notches cut with a knife or by brass tacks driven into it; convention allowed kills to be transferred by the owner to any new pole he might acquire, but for those who bought them rather than simply cutting a suitable ash stave Cameron advised that 'it is not considered the thing to have a selection of brass tacks inserted by the shopman when buying a pole'. (Another relic noted as surviving into the twentieth century on some poles in the West Country was a small screwed-in ring, to which one end of a net might be attached to prevent the otter's escape under water, a practice that survived in Devon long after the stickle – see below – had been adopted elsewhere.)

Various members of the kennel staff would be expected to carry couples by which the hounds could be restrained when appropriate, and one of them might be provided with the means of digging out the quarry – sometimes in the form of a handy multiple tool (illus. 47) – if it went to ground.

Some packs were composed of members sufficiently well heeled to allow them to travel for extended periods to further-away venues: already in the 1830s James Lomax, a noted hunter, set the fashion of travelling with his otter-hounds from one county to another – he hunted widely from the Scottish borders to Land's End, and also in Ireland. Waldron Hill led a similarly itinerant life, travelling with a horse-drawn hound-van on the mainland and as far as 'the Emerald Isle, the natives of which went almost wild with delight at the sport he was wont to show'. (Although some spasmodic hunting by native as well as visiting packs developed, otter-hunting was never markedly popular in Ireland: Cameron concluded that 'there being no horses connected with the sport . . . it seems never to have appealed to the majority of Irish sportsmen'.) The Bristol Wagon Co. produced an enclosed wagonette-style vehicle at the end of the nineteenth century at prices ranging from £45, while the ever-resourceful Captain Cameron (author of *The Book of the Caravan* as well as *Otters and Otter-Hunting*) developed a design for a 'home from home' which accommodated the hounds, two men, a boiler and all the feeding troughs and necessities for 'lying out'.

But it was the spread of the railways that impacted most noticeably on the conduct of the hunt, to the benefit of both the hunters and the hounds. More distant hunting grounds were now brought within easy reach: Davies, for example, recorded that his hounds had formerly had to cover up to 60 miles in a day and were then no good for anything for the whole of the following week, but with the advent of travel by railway they could now hunt three or four days out of seven. By the turn of the twentieth century, under the

Railway Coaching Arrangements Regulations, members of otter hunts in uniform could travel at a discounted fare provided they returned on the same day: one aficionado is recorded as having taken advantage of this arrangement by travelling on the midnight train from Euston to Carlisle in order to enjoy a day's hunting before making his way home again in the evening.

The pack

Even up to the time of the formalized packs of the late 1800s, it is clear that most hounds maintained for hunting the otter had other functions to fulfil according to the season and the alternative prey at hand. *Fores's Guide* for 1850, for example, reports of the Caernarvonshire Foxhounds that 'they follow the good old fashion of hunting martin-cat, fox, foumart, and otter', while the harriers belonging to Mr Williams of The Glôg in Dorset 'hunt fox, otter, and hare, indiscriminately'. Elsewhere, the author seems less than happy at the promiscuous use of hounds by some Devonshire harriers

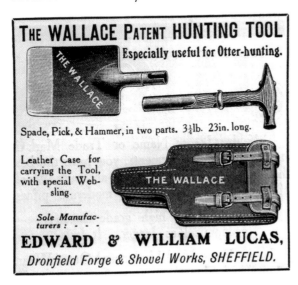

THE WALLACE PATENT HUNTING TOOL

Especially useful for Otter-hunting.

THE WALLACE

Spade, Pick, & Hammer, in two parts. 3¼lb. 23in. long.

Leather Case for carrying the Tool, with special Web-sling.

THE WALLACE

Sole Manufac-turers : - - -

EDWARD & WILLIAM LUCAS, *Dronfield Forge & Shovel Works*, SHEFFIELD.

47 Advertisement, *c.* 1908, for 'The Wallace Patent Hunting Tool' – especially recommended for otter-hunting.

and otter hunters, however, declaring that 'we hold that the foxhound for the fox, and the harrier for the hare, is the right thing the world over'.

One factor in favour of this kind of specialization was that the hounds at least were clear about what they were supposed to be hunting: no end of confusion must have been caused by the expectation that they would suddenly switch from one sort of game to another. One useful stratagem to remind the hounds of their quarry for the day, as suggested by Stringer, was to let them smell the skin of the appropriate species before they set out.

It was entirely normal to find a variety of breeds combined in packs nominally described as 'otter-hounds'. In broad terms, two basic kinds of hounds might be encountered – rough and smooth. The rough varieties might be either true otter-hounds or rough-coated Welsh hounds, while the smooth varieties included staghounds, foxhounds and harriers; various cross-breeds might also be encountered. The rough coat of the true otter-hound was invaluable for protection in face-to-face contact with the otter; strong legs for swimming were also considered essential attributes. True otter-hounds became more widely distributed in the nineteenth century, although only two hunts are recorded as being composed exclusively of this breed – the Kendal & District and the Dumfries-shire, the latter becoming especially famous for breeding the finest specimens, which became quite widely distributed. The head of such a hound resembled that of a bloodhound but was flatter, with large, pendulous and hairy ears; its coat was hard, dense and wiry (see illus. 46); an appropriate height was above 22 inches, with some reaching 26 inches and over. A quality much prized was its fine voice, many accounts of chases noting with approval the 'music' or the 'chorus' provided by the hounds. For all their classic status, some authors thought the superiority of otter-hounds over foxhounds to be overstated: in nine cases out of ten, according to Clapham, the pack would be made up primarily of foxhounds together with 'a very few rough-coated otterhounds... and unless they are hopeless physical wrecks they are put into the pack to keep up the theory that they are a pack of *otterhounds*'.

Many of the foxhounds which constituted the most common alternative were cast-offs from kennels – so-called gift hounds, received at little or no cost having been deemed to be too old or too big for fox-hunting. Not all foxhounds took to otter-hunting – one authority put the chances of successful conversion at 10:1 against – and (compared to true otter-hounds) foxhounds had a tendency to be distracted by the scents of other animals, notably foxes but also deer and Muscovy ducks, and to be easily deflected from their quarry (termed 'rioting'). They were, none the less, useful in following a drag and 'marking' a holt harbouring an otter.

Stringer recommended that a water spaniel 'is very requisite and useful in otter-hunting... and is a very great encouragement to hounds in taking [to] the water, seeing the spaniel before them, and will cry the otter when he vents, as fluently as a hound'. His advice seems not to have been widely followed.

Conflicting claims for and against each variety abound in the literature, with some slight advantage seeming to emerge in favour of a pragmatic mixture. Whatever the case, the huntsman was expected to know not only the qualities of every hound in his pack but also its voice and what it sought to communicate. Up to fifteen couples might be found in a good-sized pack, although the numbers fielded would be matched to the size of the water and some hounds might be kept in reserve to replace others that had become exhausted by the chase.

However the main pack was constituted, one or two couples of terriers formed a normal (even essential) adjunct. Their duty was not to track the quarry but to dislodge it from its lair once the hounds had cornered it: 'the process of ejectment, generally a bloody one in close quarters, it is their duty to serve', as Davies put it. Even more so than foxhounds, many terriers – the majority of them – did not take to otter-hunting, and those that did were at considerable risk from their close-quarter encounters with the otter and even from the hounds. If introduced from the mouth of the holt the terrier would be brought face-to-face with the otter and would be lucky to survive its claws and teeth; the alternative method, which would be followed if possible, was for the hunters to dig into the rear of the chamber and for the terrier to drive out the otter with its barking from behind, although there was always a danger that the hounds would become confused in the mêlée and to attack the terrier as well when it emerged, sometimes with fatal results. Given their excitable nature, the terriers were seldom run with the pack in case their whining and barking distracted the hounds from following the drag; instead they would be placed in the care of some junior member of the hunt, whose task it was to bring them up on a leash when required and to retrieve them again as soon as the dislodgement was complete.

Lengthy treatises survive on the care of hounds and on the planning, construction and administration of kennels. Even their siting within the country covered by the pack was carefully pondered: writing in 1908, Cameron expressed the opinion that it was essential for the kennel to be sited close to a strategic railway junction so that the hounds could easily be carried to the more distant parts of their territory by early-morning trains without wearing themselves out in getting there, and the dense national network of lines presented possibilities for longer-distance travel as alluded to above. This arrangement also reduced the expense of 'lying out' away from home – not to mention the disruption this caused to the routine of the hounds.

The field

More than other forms of hunting, the pursuit of the otter provided opportunities for 'the field' – the body of supporters and interested onlookers who turned out to follow the hunt – to play an active part in the chase: at times, their presence and positive engagement could be critical to success. Cameron asserts that

> While the Master is engaged in hunting his hounds in the water, and his whippers-in are assisting him by putting hounds to his horn or to a holloa, it is the members of the Field, posted up and down both banks of the stream, who alone are able to keep him informed from time to time as to the movements of the hunted Otter.

It was therefore incumbent on the Master to engage them in the proceedings and to discourage them from simply running up and down trying to catch the action. Many of them became skilled and useful participants, taking their cue at all times from the Master and staying out of the way of the hounds, although sometimes they would be more trouble than they were worth, whether through ignorance of the conventions being followed, sheer empty-headedness or over-enthusiasm. The primary duties of the field were to keep well behind hounds; to remain quiet so as not to disturb the hounds at their work; and at a mark to stand still on the bank and watch for the otter when it escaped into the water. The latter was largely a matter of watching for the 'chain' of air bubbles or the v-shaped ripple that might give away its presence; if spotted the field would 'tally' the otter by shouting 'Tally-ho!' or the more ancient and proper 'Heu gaze!', at the same time pointing to the spot.

No duty engaged the field more directly than the formation of a stickle – a human barrier formed across the shallows at the direction of the Master if the quarry was in danger of escaping downstream. 'If the Master calls for a stickle', explains Cameron,

> it is the duty and privilege of the Field to respond and form one by entering the water and standing in it, leg to leg, from one bank to another as close together as possible, moving their poles gently to and fro in the water so that they may have a chance of ascertaining whether the Otter succeeds in . . . getting below them or not.

Once the otter had been killed by the hounds, the field might 'join in the chorus of "Whoo, whoop!" wherewith rejoicing is made at the happy consummation of the day's business', and then help to keep the crowd off by forming a hollow square around it while it was weighed and the 'trophies' – the head (known as the mask), tail and paws – were cut off. If they had distinguished themselves sufficiently on the day, members of the field might be lucky enough to be rewarded with a trophy. At the conclusion of the hunt Stringer recommends that the carcass be held up on a pole, quarter-staff, otter-spear, or pitchfork so that the hounds may bay at it while the hunters clap them and show their appreciation, 'then throw him down among them and let them bite at their pleasure'.

Various assertions are made as to the extent of the hunting season: the *Master of Game* places it from 22 February to 24 June. Later a convention arose that the otter season ran from some point between Shrove Tuesday and the middle of April until mid-September (and even during that time high water in the rivers might further curtail hunting opportunities), but amongst those who regarded the otter primarily as vermin there were no such niceties to be observed. In 1780, for example, Arthur Stringer wrote that 'The Season for otter-hunting is said to be in winter, but he may as well be hunted in summer as in winter . . . though the most satisfactory time for it is in frost and snow, because you then see his seal [paw prints] and trail in the snow, and so be satisfied you do not hunt counter' – that is to say, that the hounds are following the trail in the right direction. Other passages in Stringer's text confirm that he was no fair-weather hunter: 'I once in frost and snow hunted and traced an otter into a large long root in a bog . . . yet . . . the old otter . . . went in at another root, and went in under the ice near twenty paces'; although Stringer failed to catch the otter (a female) on that occasion, he did dig out and kill both her cubs. Elsewhere he muses that

> an otter upon ice, will fight more stoutly, and make a much longer battle, than on any sort of rough ground, the reason for it being (in my opinion) is, he having sharp claws, stands very firm upon ice . . . I have seen an otter upon ice, run, or rather walk half a mile, and four couple of hounds baying at him, as if he had been a bull or a stag, and would not, or durst not touch him, till I came up to encourage them . . .

By the modern era, however, such behaviour would have been considered eccentric amongst sporting hunters: Davies, for example, avers in 1885 that 'the chase of the otter, owing to floods and cold water, is necessarily suspended for seven months in the year', while 'Stonehenge' writes in 1888 that 'No other season but the summer will suit this sport, because the cold water of early spring, winter, or autumn, will chill and cramp hounds and men to a dangerous degree.' Amongst this community, it was normally fox-hunting that occupied the winter months.

For the benefit of the wider constituency now drawn into otter-hunting, a variety of handbooks offered advice. A chapter on 'The otter and his ways', heavy with anecdote, was contributed by the Revd E.W.L. Davies to the Badminton Library volume on *Hunting* (1885), but for a full-length monograph giving a rounded assessment of the character of the hunt and its elaborate conventions we have to wait for the publication in 1908 of L.C.R. Cameron's *Otters and Otter-Hunting* – a wonderfully comprehensive survey, both retrospective in character and full of expert tips for the tyro huntsman. Richard Clapham's *Book of the Otter: A Manual for Sportsmen and Naturalists* appeared in 1922, and Cameron contributed several chapters to the Lonsdale Library volume on *Deer, Hare and Otter Hunting* in 1936; this was followed by Robert Colville's *Beagling and Otter-Hunting* in 1940, and together these constitute virtually the whole of the modern practical literature on the subject. The present survey of the conduct of the otter hunt since the 1800s is based largely on these sources.

Cameron's convenient characterization of an ideal hunt – even if such a thing were a rarity – helps us to form a picture of what might be involved:

> A two or three mile drag, gradually improving – a solid mark at a holt not absolutely impregnable – a prompt ejectment of the quarry by the terriers without recourse to a spade, crowbar, or shaking the bank by

jumping upon it – a good 'view' when the Otter is put down [enters the water] ... a two hours' swim in a deep pool or long stretch of quiet water, with hounds speaking to the wash and the Otter frequently 'gazed' and 'tallied' – a possible land excursion when the game gets tired of the water and runs a ring back to the stream with the hounds close on his rudder – finally a handsome kill by hounds and terriers, unassisted, on a shallow in full view of most of the Field.

While control of the otter population was still nominally the primary purpose of the hunt, it is clear that there was also by now an awareness that over-zealous hunting could be self-defeating and ruin the sport. Accordingly, while dog otters were pursued mercilessly, there was widespread agreement that bitches with cubs were not to be pursued. Occasionally both would accidentally fall foul of the hounds, when elaborate expressions of remorse were common. Davies, for example, quotes a correspondent as saying 'I regret to say that last year, 1883 ... I had the great misfortune accidentally to kill four cubs', and records another instance when 'as bad luck would have it [five cubs] were lying in a dry hollow bank near some shallow water, so the hounds and terriers killed them all instantly'.

The 'blank days' drawn by some hunts were not always to be taken as an adverse comment on the skills of the Master but might reflect a real absence of game. While this might have been welcome news to the fishermen, it was problematic for the subscription hunts. James Lomax, one of the most resourceful of Masters, resorted on occasion to capturing otters in one place, 'sacking' them and moving them to other waters where the sport was in need of improvement. Later, writing of the success of certain artificial drains in encouraging

the otter population by providing safe havens (and even giving a description of how to construct them so that they would appeal to the otters), Davies comments that 'their whereabouts should be kept secret, or be well looked after; otherwise the trapper might turn them to dangerous account'.

By the same token, if the hunt discovered an otter on a small stretch of water offering little sport, it might be driven back to the river or be given a quarter of an hour's grace to make good its escape before the hounds were once more set loose on it. Other instances are recorded (notably in Lomax's hunting diary) of otters being spared after being driven to a standstill by the hounds or being captured at the end of the day and released later in the night – all in the interests of better sport on a subsequent day.

The normal fate of the otter, however, was to be worried to death by the hounds. The hunters made a point of standing aside during this process; the only time when they might normally touch the otter was in 'tailing' it – grasping it by the tail and pulling in order to precipitate a quicker end if a seemingly unbreakable stand-off had developed between the hounds and their quarry. Although the inevitably bloody end of the chase is the part that squeamish modern minds find most difficult to deal with, the hunters regarded it as the climax of the day and were quite unapologetic about it. The language used by Lomax in his diary (later published but written for his own amusement) is revealing:

We worried him in grand style ... we worried him with all the honours . . . we worried him gallantly, amid the shouts, the splashings, and whoops of an excellent field of sportsmen ... we worried her in the middle of the river, to the astonishment and delight of nearly a thousand spectators . . .

[the huntsman] tailed it close to Mr Lloyd's carriage full of ladies, and there he was worried, to the delight of a very numerous and select field.

The otter is accorded due status as the hero of the day, as though he were a willing participant in the pageant, and indeed the denial of a 'good end' to any such animal was seen as reprehensible: the activities of trappers and poachers were certainly frowned upon, and on one occasion Lomax deprecates the actions of an innkeeper on the River Calder who 'waited the day we left till six o'clock when the factory stopped, and when the bed of the river became nearly dry, he, with some hundred blackguards armed with sticks, stones, and pitchforks, murdered the poor otter'. There is no reason to doubt his genuine sense of outrage.

Otter trapping

As with other species, the hunting of otter with hounds was carried on alongside the more prosaic practices of trapping. Certainly until the nineteenth century, nearly all such traps were constructed of organic materials and have left little physical trace, but some mention of them can be found in written sources. The *Master of Game*, for example, records that 'men take them . . . with small cords as men do the fox with nets and other gins'. Turberville observes that 'it is possible to take them under the water, and by the ryvers side, both in traps and in snares, as you may take a Hare with Harepypes, or such like gynnes', although, 'if they be taken in snares, if they abyde long, they will sone sheare themselves out with their teeth'. The fullest account of the method used to take otters in basket traps or 'weels' (illus. 48) is given by Leonard Mascall in his *Booke of Fishing* (1590). These were stronger and more elaborate than the

basket-traps used for taking fish which, it was found, the otter could easily penetrate in order to make off with the contents:

They take the Otter or water Wolfe, in a wele made and devised for the nonce . . . made with a double teme or tonuell, and against the utmost teme within is set an yeirne [iron] like *a gredyeirne* with foure hooles staying and sliding upon two round stickes, which must be set upright in the wele before the teme, to holde up the yeirne: which two stickes must be fast bound to the wele, both above and beneath, then must ye have a good stiffe rod, the one ende shall be set over the wele to hold up the gredyeirne or grate, and the other ende of the rodde, must reach over the inner teme, and a small oziar tied at that end of the rodde, which small Oziar must be made with a round knot, and so put downe upon the ende of the nethermost Oziar in the midst of the inner teme, but a very litle way put on [so] that when the Otter is in the first teme, he comes to the second where the fish is, and there he puts off the Oziar, and the rodde flirtes up, and the gredyerne falles and stoppes the utmost teme where he came in, and as soone as he heares it fall, he will turn backe, without touching any fish, gnawing at the grefyerne where hee came in, and so is drowned.

From the time of the 1566 Acte for the Preservation of Grayne, which introduced the payment of bounties for heads of vermin, the trapping of otters adopted a more purposeful aspect as churchwardens took over responsibility for remuneration of those who killed pests of various types within the parish boundaries. By 1731 as much as 7s. 6d. a head was being offered at Prestbury (Cheshire), although the fact that this initiative produced only eight otters in the three years following the decree seems to indicate that populations were not as numerous as might have been expected.

By the nineteenth century, metal gin-traps with sprung jaws were also deployed against otters, usually buried in the mud at a recognized landing place: on springing the trap the otter would plunge into the river, but ultimately would be drowned by the action of the trap dragging it down, after which it remained only for the hunter unceremoniously to retrieve it with a grappling iron. St John recommends that any such trap should have a specially powerful spring and should be firmly attached to a peg by means of a chain incorporating swivels, so that it could not be broken by twisting.

The fur trade

References in the Pipe Rolls indicate that otter fur was estimated of a quality to merit inclusion in the wardrobe of King John, where it keeps company with sable, ermine and squirrel; none the less, although Veale finds sufficient occurrences in the documentation of late medieval England it seems generally to have enjoyed no more than average popularity. Quantities of skins appear amongst both imports and exports, and in rather specialized circumstances they even provided an alternative to hard cash: the Pipe Roll of Henry IV for 1408 contains a record from Ireland that one John, son of Dermod, was charged '2 Otters' skins for his year's rent of Radon, 5 Otters' skins for the 2½ years preceding, and 162 Otters' skins for arrears of rent for many years then past', making a total of 169 skins. Izaak Walton's fisherman, in conversation with his companion the hunter, asserts of an otter's skin that 'it is worth ten shillings to make gloves; the gloves of an Otter

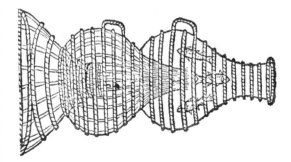

This figure vnder shewes the setting of the gredyerne, before the teme of the wele, and when he falles, to rest on two stiffe ojiars on the lower part of the sayde teme, as ye make see aboue: but when ye shall set ior tyle the saide gredyerne, it must be pluckt vppe aboue the mouth of the

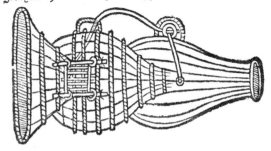

48 Basket trap for otters, from Leonard Mascall's *Booke of Fishing* (1590). Having been lured into the first chamber in an attempt to get at the fish beyond, the otter would be trapped by the iron grill falling into place behind it.

are the best fortification for your hands that can be thought on against wet weather'.

Pennant asserts that the best skins came from animals killed in the winter – a general rule for furs, in fact – and indeed in his day most of the pelts came from otters trapped in the sub-arctic territories of Europe and of North America, where the intense cold produced much thicker furs than those found on British animals. In those countries, he says, the skins were used for lining clothes, but in England their use was by his day largely directed to the production of covers for pistol furniture (preference being given again to the larger skins of varieties from northern latitudes).

Their use in clothing seems never to have died out completely, however, for Fairfax in 1863 observes that well-dressed skins made 'a valuable addition to a lady's winter wardrobe, the under fur being peculiarly soft, silky and of a rich brown colour'.

Fishing with otters

The idea that the otter might be trained to catch fish on behalf of a human master has a surprisingly long history. Gudger notes the late fifteenth-century Vincent de Beauvais as recording in his *Speculum Naturale* that otters were occasionally trained by fishermen to drive fish into their nets, a statement repeated by a number of sixteenth- and seventeenth-century authors, including the Englishman Edward Topsell in his *Historie of Foure-Footed Beastes* (1658). Gudger was of the opinion that all these later writers may simply have been repeating de Beauvais' suggestion, for corroboration is otherwise hard to find.

Persuasive evidence, however, manifests itself in the form of Robert Wood, referred to in the State Papers for 1618 by the title of Keeper of His Majesty's Cormorants, Ospreys and Otters: the grouping is an understandable one, bringing together these otherwise disparate creatures under a single master for the royal pursuit of fishing (line-fishing being as yet little practised as a sport). Shortly afterwards, in his *Compleat Angler* (first published 1653), Izaak Walton presents a scene in which a family of otter cubs is discovered and is about to be killed by the hunter when the fisherman intervenes:

No: I pray, Sir, save me one, and I'll try if I can make her tame, as I know an ingenious gentleman in Leicestershire, Mr Nich. Seagrave, has done; who hath not only made her tame, but to catch fish, and do many other things of much pleasure.

The fullest account of the capturing and training of otters is that given by Oliver Goldsmith, who is so matter-of-fact in his account as to suggest that the practice was quite a widespread one and scarcely worthy of special note. Adult animals, he suggests, could never be tamed and would take every opportunity to escape, but the young ones might more easily be taken and 'converted to useful purposes'. His account is worth quoting at length:

if under the protection of the dam, she teaches them instantly to plunge, like herself, into the deep, and escape among the rushes or weeds that fringe the stream . . . It is only when the dam is absent that they can be taken . . . [for] if the old one is absent, they continue terrified, and will not venture forth but under her guidance and protection. In this manner they are secured and taken home alive, where they are carefully fed with small fish and water . . . The manner of training them up to hunt for fish requires not only assiduity but patience; however, their activity and use, when taught, greatly repays the trouble of teaching; and, perhaps, no other animal is more beneficial to its master. The usual way is, first to learn them to fetch as dogs are instructed; but as they have not the same docility, so it requires more art and experience to teach them. It is usually performed by accustoming them to take a truss stuffed with wool, of the shape of a fish, and made of leather, in their mouths, and to drop it at the word of command; to run after it when thrown forward, and to bring it to their master. From this they proceed to real fish, which are thrown dead into the water, and which they are taught to fetch from thence. From the dead they proceed to the live, until at last the animal is perfectly in-structed in the whole art of fishing. An otter thus taught is a very valuable animal, and will catch fish enough to sustain not only itself but a whole family. I have seen one of these go to a gentleman's pond at the word of command, drive up the fish into a corner, and, seizing up the largest of the whole, bringing it off, in its mouth, to its master.

Other writers confirm the comparative ease with which they might be trained: St John, for example, asserts that 'when caught young, no animal is more easily tamed than the otter; and it will soon learn to fish for its master'. He sug-gests that it should be kept in the almost constant company of its trainer, so as to become perfectly familiarized with his voice and his presence. The literature contains many anecdotes of individu-als who formed successful relationships of this kind with otters. St John mentions a sportsman from Altyre (Morayshire) who caught and tamed a half-grown otter 'and in a short time taught him to catch trout, taking sometimes above a dozen in a forenoon out of the small stream near the house'. Bewick knew of two such persons, one whose otters ran with his dogs and the other, a resident of Inverness, whose otter followed him everywhere. The Revd W. Bingley in his *Animal Biography* (1813) gives further examples of otters being taught to fish, including one that would drive trout into a net held by its master.

By the later nineteenth century, according to Salvin, otters were 'frequently trained for fish-ing, both in this country and in the East', and indeed in the 1840s he had trained one himself. His suggestion was that they should be taken young and confined in a yard, secured over the top and sides with wire; it should contain a pond, a hollow tree-trunk into which the otter could

creep after swimming and a sunny, south-facing shed filled with dry straw for his bed. Their use-fulness depended to some degree on the fact that they could do no more than grasp a fish under water and could not swallow it. When it surfaced, Salvin's custom was to hold the animal with one hand and remove the fish with the other, giving the otter a piece of fish as a reward; following this, it was ready to go straight back into the water to continue fishing.

HAWKS AND FALCONS

No less than *par force* hunting with hounds, the practice of falconry was imbued with an aristo-cratic character throughout the medieval period (illus. 49); other than the Crown and the nobility, the records show increasing numbers of non-noble practitioners taking the field before falconry was taken up more widely by the emergent yeo-manry as a badge of their new-found affluence. Subsequently it entered a long decline from the period of the Civil War onwards – partly due to changes of fashion and to the rise of firearms, ex-acerbated, perhaps, by loss of habitat due to the spread of enclosures, elimination of wastes and drainage of fenland – when its practices and con-ventions were maintained only by a small coterie of dedicated followers for whom the preservation of the sport was of greater importance than any return from the hawks in the form of game, and for whom the advantages of the increasingly efficient shotgun held no allure.

Present-day authorities divide the population into two broad groups, namely the long-winged falcons of the family *Falconidae* and the short-winged hawks of the *Accipitridae*. (Harting further categorizes the first group as being dark-eyed and the second as yellow-eyed.) The division is one of long standing, corresponding broadly with that made on practical grounds by medieval writers and practitioners who termed them respectively hawks of the tower and hawks of the fist – epithets alluding to the ways in which, respectively, they were deployed in the field, but reflecting the same anatomically determined division. Essentially, the falcons (hawks of the tower) comprised those species that were carried into the field unhooded and were cast off to rise freely on their long wings on the thermals until they had gained a suitably high viewpoint where they 'waited on'; when the prey was put up by the hunter's dogs, the falcon made its customary spectacular attack, hurtling down on its chosen target in a headlong dive (or 'stoop') and often killing the game outright with its tremendous impact (their closing speed has been calculated at over 200 mph). In order to re-cover the falcon to his fist, the falconer had to resort to use of the lure (pp. 182–3). The princi-pal birds in this category were the peregrines, gyr-falcons, sakers and lanners, as well as the smaller merlins and hobbies.

The short-winged hawks of the fist, on the other hand, remained hooded until shortly before they were cast off, flying directly at the game when it rose into view, binding to it in mid-air and bringing it to the ground; after their target had been secured, hawks were trained to return to the fist without use of the lure. The principal members of this group were the goshawks and sparrowhawks.

Other distinctions are encountered from time to time in the early literature, based on the game for which the bird was to be used and taking less account of the hawk itself. 'Hawks of the river' were those deployed against waterfowl (illus. 50). The game in this sport, termed 'flying at the brook', was generally put up by spaniels: the *Master of Game* asserts that spaniels were particularly useful

49 Badge, late 14th century, of lead alloy, representing a fashionably dressed falconer riding out; his falcon is carried on the left hand, which is protected by a hawking-glove with a tassel at the wrist.

in this role if taught to swim – a sentiment no doubt echoed by generations of falconers for whom an ability to swim was similarly an asset at any job interview. The quarry was characteristically ducks, but the hawks might also be trained to take larger birds (see below).

Peregrines (*Falco peregrinus*) were the supreme native birds of the hunt in Britain. The term falcon denoted in its strictest sense the female peregrine only, although throughout recorded history it has been more widely applied to the other mem-bers of the *Falconidae* (just as the word hawk has come to refer indiscriminately to members of both families). Male peregrines were designated tiercels (or variations thereof), in acknowledge-ment of the general rule that they tend to be one-third (*tierce*) smaller than their female coun-terparts (and consequently were less highly val-ued), but once again the term came to be applied promiscuously to males of other species, whether or not they displayed the same size differential: Turberville, for example, was one of those who paid scant attention to etymology, advising that 'Tyrcelles . . . are the male byrdes and cockes of everie sort and gender', while Harting adds that in his day the females of any species were called falcons. The superior size and fierce character of the female peregrine made it the most highly estimated of the falcons. Ducks, pheasant and partridge fell easily to it, but even larger game-birds like geese, herons, cranes and bustard were no match for it. These larger birds played no part in the natural diet of the peregrine, which had to be taught to engage with them and to hunt collaboratively with the hounds. Generally peregrines would stoop on their prey from above, but as mentioned by Cummins they could also be taught to pursue herons as they spiralled upwards, following in similar fashion until they

had gained enough of a height advantage to strike downwards.

Other falcons rivalling the peregrine were all imported to Britain. Gyrfalcons (*Falco rusticolus*), even larger and more deadly than the peregrine, were particularly highly rated: most hunting birds were brought at considerable expense from Scandinavia and ultimately from Iceland (including, it is thought, stragglers normally resident in Greenland), so that they were more rarely seen in the field. King John favoured these for taking cranes and herons, and in 1204–5 is recorded as having 'ordered the bailiffs of several ports to secure all the hawks and gerfalcons which should be brought beyond the sea till [the king's falconers] should choose what they thought fit for the king's use'. White birds were most highly valued, followed by greys. They were regarded as the most effective of all falcons in pursuit of cranes.

50 A lady flying her falcon at a duck. From the Taymouth Hours (*c.* 1325–50).

Sakers (*Falco cherrug*) came either from eastern Europe or the Middle East, while the popular lanner (*Falco biarmicus*), now restricted in the wild to south-east Europe, formerly had a distribution that included France and Spain as well as the British Isles: a resident population certainly existed on the English mainland up to the thirteenth century, but by the 1400s some, at least, were being imported from Ireland. Being less prone to flying off, the lanner was believed to be capable of exerting a restraining influence on the peregrine and consequently the two were often flown together; for its part, the lanner might learn to wait on at height for the game – a technique it never adopted in the wild. Cummins characterizes it as hardier and less choosey than the peregrine (though humbler in appearance). Turberville makes special mention also of the 'Tunician falcon' favoured in England, which he characterizes as 'muche of the nature of a Laner, yet somewhat lesse'; James I and Charles I were among those who acquired falcons from as far away as the Barbary coast.

The remaining falcons employed in Britain were all of smaller size and of native origin – the merlin (*Falco columbarius*), with a reputation for amenability, and the hobby (*Falco subbuteo*), attractive in appearance, but less highly esteemed; both were trained to take small game like larks.

The principal short-winged hawks that make an appearance in the records are the goshawk (*Accipiter gentilis*) and the sparrowhawk (*Accipiter nisus*). These never achieved the prestige of the falcons: their keepers were distinguished from (and disdained by) the falconers by their own titles – the austringer being a trainer of goshawks and the sparviter specializing in sparrowhawks. Goshawks (the best of which were imported from Scandinavia) had a reputation for being difficult to train but for being highly effective against

partridge and pheasant. Cummins mentions that they were also flown against much larger game such as bustard as well as hares, which were too large for the goshawk to kill them outright: it would instead be taught to bind itself to the prey with its talons and bring it to ground, encumbering it until a hound could be dispatched to finish the deed. Sparrowhawks, especially favoured by ladies, would similarly take partridge and pheasant, but were more commonly flown against blackbird, thrush and larks.

During the Norman period ownership of hawks was restricted to the upper echelons of society, but under the Forest Charter of 1215 every free man was granted the right to have an eyrie in his own woods from which he could lawfully harvest the nestlings in order to train or to sell them. Both the birds and their eggs were protected by legislation that could bring a year in prison, or worse: a thief was summarily excommunicated by the Bishop of Ely for stealing a hawk from the Bishop's cloisters at Bermondsey. Under Henry VII's Game Act of 1485 stealing eggs or fledglings from the king's manors was outlawed, reiterated in an Act of Henry VIII in 1539–40, where it was stated that 'It shall be a felony to take, in the King's ground, any egg or bird of any faulcon, goshawk or laner, out of the nest.'

Leases issued by landowners would on occasion reserve the right not only for hunting but also for gathering the young of all the hawks' nests on their territory. Many trained hawks started their lives in the native countryside, where nests once discovered were carefully watched and shielded as far as possible from poachers. Nestlings might be taken from the eyrie once they had reached a level of independence where they could survive on their own, in which case they were termed 'eyasses'; more mature birds, captured in the wild (perhaps with the use of a decoy pigeon and a net) after their plumage had developed, were termed 'passage hawks' if they had not yet reached their first moult or 'haggards' following their first migration. With much patience and time, both were capable of being trained, though eyasses required a great deal more attention: haggards would already have learned how to hunt independently, but eyasses had to be taught everything and had a reputation for more neurotic behaviour that was likely to last their whole lives; generally the more mature they were before being captured, the better.

Numbers of serjeanties held of the Crown came with duties to provide hawks for the king's use. In 1251 and in subsequent years John Fitz Bernard, 'king's yeoman, marshal in fee of the king's goshawks' is mentioned by Round as being sent 'to buy and take such birds at the king's market throughout England'. A flourishing trade developed which saw hawks obtained in the wild passed on to middle men, who might arrange for their training – a process that would add considerably to their value – or sold directly to those with established mews and with appropriate personnel to school the hawks in their role. James IV of Scotland is recorded as acquiring hawks from numerous places within his kingdom, from the northern and western isles to Berwick-upon-Tweed and Galloway.

Falcons from the Continent might arrive as royal or diplomatic gifts or in the normal course of a lucrative trade with supply routes stretching from the Baltic to North Africa. King John is recorded as receiving a cast of gyrfalcons from the King of Norway and the practice peaked under Edward I, when numerous such gifts were received: Coggins notes two white and six grey gyrfalcons sent to him by Magnus VI of Norway in 1276 and 1279, with another three white and six grey following in 1280; a total of over 100 birds were received by Edward from various quarters in the course of his reign, including thirteen white and 31 grey gyrfalcons, 38 other gyrfalcons, thirteen peregrines and seven goshawks. The port of King's Lynn emerged as a regular point of arrival for Norwegian falcons: Cummins notes that the royal mews were commonly supplied via King's Lynn in a trade that was so regular that the keeper of the king's gyrfalcons acquired the rights to taxes on certain shipping. The port of Boston (Lincolnshire) also features in the records, as when Henry de Hauville held certain lands of the king in 1271 'by serjeanty of receiving at Boston the gerfalcons sent to the king'; the same Hugh held similar rights 'by serjeanty of falconry' at King's Lynn, Yarmouth and Ipswich. Round further records that:

> It is to Boston fair that the King's falconer goes to buy the birds that come, probably, from Norway or from Iceland. For under Lincolnshire [in the Pipe Rolls] we meet not only with Norway hawks, but with an Iceland gerfalcon, and in that county the birds appear to have been treated almost as currency.

Birds arriving from more southerly points of origin frequently passed through Flanders, where they might pause to be trained by local falconers (especially those of Brabant) who enjoyed a high reputation for their skills. Birds that had already been trained (and which had mewed or moulted) had significant value added to their resale price.

Transporting these sensitive creatures was clearly a challenging task which could all too easily result in their succumbing to stress. When a consignment of several birds was involved, they might be carried on a specially made framework termed a cadge; the weight was taken by straps passing over the shoulders of the falconer, who stood in the centre of the framework surrounded by up to twenty birds, all secured to the bars which were suitably padded in order to improve the grip of the falcons and to protect their feet. Alternatively, Round cites a reference to the king's goshawk men and falconers undertaking a Channel crossing through Dover in 1181 when 31s. was spent on 'hutches' for the birds. Whatever the method, rather than wearing hoods to keep them calm, the birds would have their eyelids 'seeled', which is to say they were closed by having a thread passed through the lower eyelids and tied over the top of the head – a process they might also have to undergo during training (see below).

Characteristically, the English constructed an elaborate hierarchy by which particular hawks were designated as appropriate to persons of rank on a finely graduated social scale. Even contemporaries seem to have found something bizarre and comic in this piece of social engineering. A more detailed list in the *Boke of St Albans*, carrying these distinctions to remarkable limits, is now judged to have been compiled in a spirit of irony rather than an excess of zeal, although doubtless it reflects some elements of a hierarchy that would have been recognizable to contemporaries. In this list, the allotting of the gyrfalcon to a king, the peregrine to a prince and so on through dukes, earls, barons, knights, squires, ladies and young men certainly seems too rigid to have been sustainable in reality, while the inclusion at the bottom end of the scale of priestly falconers has been taken to stray into satire. Certainly by the reign of Elizabeth all attempt at regulating ownership of hawks had been abandoned. Almond suggests that the sport probably reached its zenith at this time, paralleling the emergence of a burgeoning class of minor gentry from the ranks of the former yeomanry.

The early literature relating to the hawks was first reviewed in two still-useful works edited by J. E. Harting, firstly in the notes to *A Perfect Booke for Kepinge of Sparhawkes or Goshawkes, written about 1575* (1886) and later in his impressive *Bibliotheca Accipitraria. A Catalogue of Books Ancient and Modern relating to Falconry* (1891).

TRAINING AND EQUIPMENT

Whether native or imported birds, hawks were expensive to buy and carried a high risk that they might simply fly off when released in the field, so a great deal of effort was invested in careful and time-consuming training regimes designed to establish a bond (based on dependence rather than emotion) between the bird and its handler. The following is again extensively indebted to Cummins for its detail.

Before being installed with the other hawks in the mews, eyasses generally spent a period in a 'hack house' – an outbuilding in a withdrawn area where they would be disturbed as little as possible and where they would mature on an elevated platform lined with straw, being fed three times a day on lean beef. In time they would be allowed to fly free in order to gain strength and exercise their muscles, before their training began; inevitably, some would abscond at this point and had to be recaptured. When the time had come to begin their training they would be taken from the hack house at night, with their eyes seeled, in order to be introduced to the equipment that henceforth would form part of their everyday lives (illus. 51), principally their jesses and bells. The jesses were a pair of soft leather thongs, generally either of calf-skin or dog-skin, knotted around the legs at one end and with a metal ring at the other; for a sparrowhawk the jesses were generally about 6 inches long, and for a goshawk 10 inches. The jesses with their terminal rings, termed vervels, were primarily anchor points, allowing the attachment either of short 'lunes' or lines, by which the falconer could keep hold of the bird perched on his hand, or a longer leather strap with a button at one end, termed a leash, used to secure the bird to its perch or block. The vervels could also be both decorative and informative: examples in gold and in silver are well known, some of them engraved with the owner's name or with his arms (illus. 52), so that wandering hawks could be identified and returned to their masters. By the aforementioned Act of 1539–40 Henry VIII declared it a felony if anyone should

> find or take up any faulcon, jerfaulcon, jerkin, sacer or sacerit, goshawk, laner or lanerite, of the King's, and having on it the King's arms and verviles, and do not within twelve days bring or send the same to the master of the King's hawks, or to one of his faulconers, or to the chief of the shire.

In time vervels were displaced by figure-of-eight swivels or 'tyrets'. The diminutive spherical bells, of a size appropriate to that of the hawk itself, were tied to one of the hawk's legs with leather straps named 'bewits'; according to Harting, goshawks also had bells attached to their tails. In early life the bells would warn the falconer if the hawk had 'bated' or fallen from its perch, while out in the field it would allow him to retrieve the hawk if it had disappeared from view with its prey. Milan was the most favoured centre for their production, although the *Boke of St Albans* mentions that bells made in Dordrecht in the Netherlands were also 'passing goode'; others were evidently cheaply produced, like those noted by Cummins as part of a cargo passing through Wolfreton (Yorkshire), rated as '13 [dozen] de

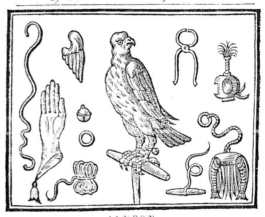

51 Title-page from Edmund Bert's *Approved Treatise of Hawkes and Hawking* (1619), illustrating items of hawking equipment.

haukes bellys . . . 13d', which may be compared with the 6s. to 8s. a dozen normally paid by James IV of Scotland.

When it ventured out, the hawk would be fitted with a hood in order to encourage it to sit calmly on the falconer's fist. According to Harting, hoods were unknown in Europe before the Crusades and were introduced from the Saracens. Accustoming the bird to the hood took a great deal of patience, beginning with a loosely fitting training hood known as a rufter, which at first would repeatedly be fitted and taken off in the dark and which had a sufficiently large opening for the beak for the bird to be fed with chicken legs and the like while hooded, in order to make it feel at ease. Feeding always took place on the fist, in order to further accustom the hawk to handling. Hoods for trained hawks were normally of leather, velvet-covered, braided and embroidered in the case of superior examples and almost invariably topped with a plume of feathers or a tassel by which the falconer could grasp it; they were slit at the back to allow the hood to be passed easily over the bird's head before being closed with a draw-string. Turberville advised in 1575 that a hawk 'muste have a hood of good leather, well made and fashioned, well raysed and bossed agaynst hir eyes, deep and yet streyght ynough beneath, that it may better abyde on hir heade and yet never hurt hir'. Some hoods were further padded to protect the hawk:

52 Vervel of silver found in 2004 in Hertfordshire, with an escutcheon bearing the Tudor rose on one side and the royal arms on the other. It corresponds closely to the description of 'ix vervells of silver with the kinges Armes' found in the Secret Jewel House at Westminster by the compilers of Henry VIII's inventory, although the Tudor arms are those current in the reign of Elizabeth I.

Henry VIII was supplied with '2 calf skins to make stockes for halkes hoddes . . . and 2lb of wool to stuff the same'.

Other hawking equipment was assigned to the falconer rather than the falcon. Principal among these necessities was a glove; hawking gloves were customarily made in pairs, but all the wear and tear would normally be suffered by only one glove, normally that on the left hand. Surviving gloves at the Ashmolean Museum and in the Burrell Collection associated with Henry VIII and James I respectively, serve to illustrate the general characteristics; Robert Cheseman, falconer to Henry VIII, wears such a glove in his splendid portrait by Holbein (illus. 53). Soft doeskin was favoured for the fingers and hand area, sometimes reinforced with dog- or buckskin to protect the hand from the talons of the bird; the Ashmolean glove is lined with doeskin, that in the Burrell Collection with silk. Both are embroidered, the Burrell glove more especially so; it also has a deep fringe extending to a tassel. Both are strictly gauntlets rather than gloves, with deep, flaring cuffs at the wrist. While the cuff would have given protection to the wrist area, this was sometimes extended by means of a bracer, presumably separately strapped to the wrist.

The falconer would also carry a pouch or bag in which he might keep titbits with which to tempt his hawk back to the fist or to attach to a lure; the hawking set in the Burrell includes a bag to match the glove (illus. 54).

The lure was a device necessary for use with certain hawks, designed to attract them back to their falconer after they had dispatched their prey – or had failed to make contact with it. Feeding young birds with titbits placed on the lure helped instil the mental association. Traditionally, the lure, which was weighted and swung around the falconer's head on a cord in order to attract the bird's attention, incorporated a pair of wings, often taken from the normal prey of the hawk, and had attached to it a morsel of meat which would form the hawk's reward when it responded. (Bert suggests that formality could be dispensed with on occasion, when a dead pigeon whirled on a piece of string would prove equally effective.) Continental falconers, it seems, customarily operated the lure while remaining on horseback while in England, according to the tract *De Arte Venandi* by Emperor Frederick II, they invariably dismounted and, he writes, customarily threw the lure repeatedly into the air instead of whirling it about their heads; they also spurned the cries and calls uttered by their Continental counterparts – partly, it is suggested, because the cranes and herons most commonly sought in England were raised by cries from the hunters which were likely to lead to confusion if directed also at the falcons. To judge from the descriptions given below, the lures used by royal falconers invariably incorporated a leather or textile 'body' which was richly embroidered.

The descriptions in question are taken from the inventory drawn up at the death of Henry VIII, which show numerous caches of hawking equipment held at several residences. Some are for multiple items, such as 'lewers of Crymsen Satten embrawedered with vennes gould . . . haukes hoddes embrawedered with vennys gould two brasers embraudered lykewise one paire of weringe gloves garnysshed with embraudery and smale perles & two hawkes gloves embraudered one with vennes goulde thother with silke'; elsewhere, the contents of 'a litell coffer of prynted Lether' at Westminster included 'xxxvj paire of Belles of silver . . . Foure paire of belles of golde . . . ix vervells of silver with the kinges Armes . . . xij Andelettes [small rings] of silver . . . ij hawkesgloves embroidered'. Others illuminate single cat-

egories of material. Hoods, for example, occurred in large quantities but in plain form at Greenwich, including, in a closet next the king's privy chamber 'Cx hawkes whoddes embrawdered hanging uppon the wall' and in another chamber close by 'Cxxxviij hawkes whoddes of leather', while amongst the more elaborate versions one might expect to find were noted in the king's 'secrete studie' at Westmister 'xviij hawkeshoodes embraudered with gold and silver' and further 'hauke hoddes embraudered withe gold and peerle'. The jesses listed include 'one paire of Jesses for haukes with two ringes of metall guilte' and the vervels 'iiij vervelles of Silver for hawkes', while amongst the bells were 'foure haukes belles of damaskyn worke' and 'xij payer of hawkes belles small and greate'. Gloves were well represented, including 'viij fawkoners gloves vij with embraudery and Tasselles of gould Silver and Silke', while bags included 'twoo Double hawking bagges with ringes Silver gilte enameled blacke', 'vij hawkinge bagges wherof one velvet crimson one crymson Satten one white velvet striped with golde and iiij of bustyan' and 'a Hawking Pouche of chaungeable silke'. Lures included 'a Lewer of clothe of golde embrawdered with roses', 'xviij lures embrawdered and xvj other lures playne', 'foure lewers whereof two of them be of cloth of golde & ij of crimson satten embraudered', and 'vij lewers of Nedell worke and embrauderye and one of Crymsen vellet'. The whole document forms the most remarkable inventory of hawking equipment – among very much more.

Having graduated from the hack-house to the mews, the hawk would now find itself in the company of the whole panoply of other hawks, to which it would have to become accustomed. It would be assigned its own perch, solidly constructed and of a diameter that would be comfortable for its feet; the perch might also be padded. It

· ROBERTVS CHESEMAN ·
ANNO · D M

ETATIS · SVÆ · XLVIII ·
· M · D · XXXIII ·

53 Hans Holbein, *Robert Cheseman*, falconer to Henry VIII, with a falcon on his gloved hand, 1533, oil on panel.

would also be familiarized with the outside world by spending time 'weathering' while secured to a block in the form of a truncated cone with a ring on the top or to a bow-perch – a curving withy, the ends of which were pushed into the ground to provide a stable support. At this stage, to avoid the hawk being overwhelmed by too many new experiences at once, its eyelids might be seeled once again, the threads gradually being slackened off to allow its sight to be progressively restored over a period of time. Now it had not only the other hawks to get used to, but also the sight and sound of men, horses and dogs (a process of familiarization termed 'manning'), all of which it would have to become accustomed before it could function in the field.

54 Hawking bag, illustrated in the *Archaeological Journal* (1861), at which time it was in the possession of Lady North.

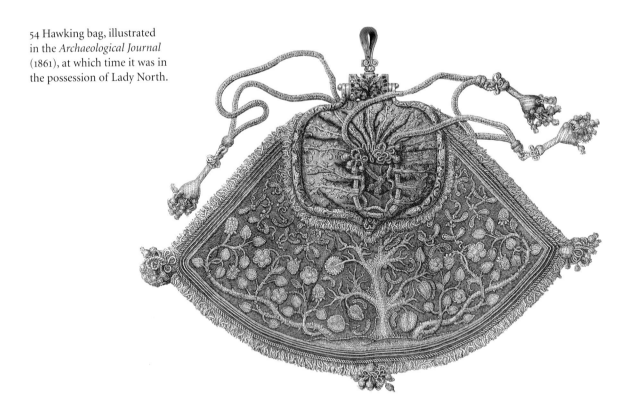

Coggins makes some interesting observations on the royal mews at Charing, adjacent to White-hall Palace, begun under Edward I in 1274 and completed six years later at a cost of over £500. The mews prove during that reign to have been used almost exclusively for keeping falcons, the king's hawks being generally boarded-out either with those occupying serjeanties associated with hawk-ing duties or with others recompensed in cash. The falconers of the royal household outnum-bered those assigned to the hawks by a factor of up to five times during Edward's reign, although there was some variation in the numbers con-cerned, perhaps reflecting the king's own changing tastes: for example, in the year 1305–6 sparrow-hawks evidently were being experimented with and made up nearly a quarter of all the hawks flown. Together with the ancillary officers such as the keepers of dogs associated with falconry, the

establishment associated with the falcons charac-teristically numbered from 75 to 100 personnel.

Having been accustomed to feeding on the fal-coner's fist before graduating to killing for itself captive chickens or pigeons, the hawk's training out of doors progressed by encouraging the bird to fly to the hand from a short distance on a long line (the creance), attached to the jesses by means of a swivel; it would then fly at the lure in the same way, rewarded repeatedly with morsels of meat, and within a month it would be flying freely in this way. Training continued in the field, with the young bird flying at wild game in the company of a more experienced falcon: partridge or snipe net-ted by wildfowlers might play a role here, and also hares, released alive or their carcasses pulled along in a 'train'. In this way, trainees were exposed to a carefully graduated range of experiences: Cum-mins mentions that those destined to fly at crane or heron, for example, might similarly be introduced to their intended quarry in the form of a train, perhaps with a morsel of meat tied to the corpse, then to weak or emasculated birds, before graduating to flying in the company of a more experienced bird and being allowed to join it just at the moment when the quarry was about to be overwhelmed; it would then be allowed to eat the heart of the heron or crane together with some other titbits, arranged on the corpse. This process also allowed individual birds to be assessed to see if they had the (highly desirable) propensity to fly in a 'cast' with another falcon: their effectiveness was greatly increased by hunting them in pairs. This was also the point at which they would be taught to 'wait on', circling above the falconer's head until the game had been raised for them to begin their attack.

Flying the falcon

A seasonal rhythm was imposed on hawking by the fact that nothing could be achieved while the hawks went through their annual moult (mewing); during this period they would be kept in the mews in order to minimize the possibility of damage to their developing plumage. As Edward, Duke of York points out, the season 'lasteth seldom at the most more than half a year. For though men find from May unto Lammas [1 August] game enough to hawk at, no one will find hawks to hawk with.' In practice the season commonly ran through the winter until March for hawks and April for falcons.

A striking characteristic of the hawking expedition was the likelihood that it would include (or might be composed entirely of) women. There are many images of female participants (see illus. 50), and unlike those of ladies hunting (or indeed jousting with each other wearing fine robes rather than

armour) the hawking images are judged to form accurate representations of everyday reality. Some ladies might prefer to concentrate on smaller game such as blackbirds and thrushes, but images are just as likely to show wildfowl, crane or heron being pursued. The hawking expedition carried with it no requirement for hard riding, physical exertion or even too personal an involvement with the death of the prey. Hawking parties at court were occasions when guests might be treated to something of the ostentation that formerly had marked the royal hunt – hence the lavish character of so many of the accoutrements mentioned above. In the case of royal expeditions, care might have been taken in advance to ensure that rivers to be hunted were well stocked with wildfowl and also to ensure that bridges were in good repair (or should be built anew) so that parties could cross from one bank to the other as the sport demanded; alternatively, a local guide might be provided to lead the party safely through the river at points where it could be forded.

A variety of hawks might be carried into the field by one of the falconers, arranged on a cadge and awaiting their turn to be unhooded and cast off. As the party progressed, dogs (or occasionally beaters) would flush up the game from the undergrowth or the river bank. Spaniels are commonly associated with this work, and indeed they were thought well suited to the task, whether on land or water: not every reference is to be trusted, however, for the early *Treatise of English Dogges* mentions that there are varieties suitable for individual types of game, but that 'the Common sort of people call them by one generall word, namely Spaniells'.

CORMORANTS

While the history of the human encounter with cormorants (*Phalacracorax carbo*) is largely one of persecution and extermination (p. 308), there were occasionally more enlightened episodes in which the natural skills of the birds were turned to human advantage. A familiarity with the practice of fishing with cormorants – an ancient custom in China and Japan – was progressively introduced to Europe by travellers, by missionaries and by servants of the Dutch and later the British East India Company. In the Orient it had been a lowly trade forming part of the subsistence economy, but when it came to be taken up in Europe it was initially in courtly circles in early the early seventeenth century that it was practised. In England, after a period of popularity under the early Stuart monarchs, it fell into abeyance for almost two centuries until it was revived briefly in the 1800s by a small number of sporting enthusiasts in search of alternative forms of diversion, before effectively disappearing altogether.

EARLY LITERARY FAMILIARITY

As early as 1926 E. W. Gudger drew attention to the fact that long before formal diplomatic contact was established at the turn of the seventeenth century, there had been accounts by individual travellers to China which brought some knowledge of the practice to a certain select readership. (The following accounts are conveniently transcribed by Gudger.) Cormorant fishing is first mentioned in an account of Odoric of Pordenone's three-year sojourn in China during the 1320s, which was published in Italian in 1513, in French in 1529 and ultimately in English by Richard Hakluyt in 1599. The following passage is from a more recent and more accessible translation by Sir Henry Yule:

And mine host, wishing to gratify me, said: 'If thou wouldst like to see good fishing, come with me.' And so he led me upon the bridge, and I looked, and saw in some boats of his that were there, certain water-fowl tied upon perches. And these he now tied with a cord round the throat that they might not be able to swallow the fish which they caught. Next he proceeded to put three great baskets into a boat, one at each end and the third in the middle, and then he let the water-fowl loose. Straightway they began to dive into the water, catching great numbers of fish, and ever as they caught them putting them of their own accord into the baskets, so that before long all three baskets were full. And mine host then took the cord off their necks and let them dive again to catch fish for their own food. And when they had thus fed they returned to their perches and were tied up as before. And some of those fish I had for dinner.

In this way the essential outlines of the practice were made known in the West, supplemented by passages by other authors. Galeotto Pereira's account, translated into English by Richard Willes as *Certaine Reportes of the Province of China* and published in Richard Eden's *History of Travayle in the West and East Indies* (1577) mentions the practice of tying cords under the birds' wings to prevent them flying away, though this never seems to have been adopted in the West, while a further account by Juan de Mendoza, published in English by Richard Parke as *The Historie of the Great & Mightie Kingdome of China* (1588) includes a description of a well within the fishing boat for storage of the live fish – another innovation not followed here.

CORMORANT FISHING IN THE SEVENTEENTH CENTURY

For the adoption of the technique into England we have to thank that inveterate sportsman King James I. By 1610 the royal cormorants were already sufficiently expert to be shown off to a visiting German prince, Louis Frederick of Württemberg, who recorded that 'at a sign given by the master who has trained them [the birds] plunge under the water to catch eels and other fish, and which at another signal are made to give up and disgorge them alive'. The name of the master concerned is not recorded, but he is likely to have been one John Wood who, in the following year, was paid the sum of £30 'in respect he hath been at extraordinary charge in the bringing up and training of certain fowls called cormorants, and making them fit for the use of fishing'. In 1612 Wood, by now named in the state papers as Keeper of His Majesty's Cormorants, was paid a further £30 'to travel into some of the furthest parts of this realm for young cormorants, which afterwards are to be made fit for his Majesty's sport and recreation'. Their presence is recorded at various times at the King's hunting lodges at Thetford (Norfolk), where Louis Frederick saw them, and at Theobalds (Essex); on occasion they were brought to London, as indicated by an account of the king's dedication to these birds transmitted to Venice on 10 July 1618:

Then there is another most extravagant hunt or rather fishery, effected by a large bird called a cormorant, the site of whose exploits belongs to the king. His Majesty constantly has a pair of them hooded at his Court. This very day he was to fish with them in the Thames from a boat. They have a very wide craw, and being well trained, dive in the ponds or streams, and after remaining some while under water, come to the surface with the prey in their mouth, or even in their craw, as they are unable to swallow because their throat is bound with a lacet.

The report is of particular interest in mentioning that the king deployed his birds from a boat: no other instance of this is known from the West. In the same year a certain Robert Wood (perhaps a son of John?), named as Keeper of His Majesty's Cormorants, Ospreys and Otters, was allowed the sum of £286 on 10 October for constructions within the vineyards at Westminster, on which ground

for the better bringing up and keeping of the said cormorants, &c., for his Majesty's disport, he hath taken a lease of for four years of the Lord Da[n]vers, wherein he hath undertaken to make the said fish-ponds, the same to be paled, and stored with sundry sorts of fish, with a sluice to bring water out of the Thames to the said ponds; and also for building a house, which he hath likewise undertaken to build there, to keep the said ospreys, cormorants and others in . . .

Interest was also aroused in France where, it seems, the court had established a colony of its own, for in February 1619 Wood received instructions 'to attend the French ambassador with the cormorants sent by his Majesty's good brother the French King', while on 14 October a payment of £60 was made to Robert 'whom his Majesty intendeth to send with divers cormorants to his good cousin the Duke of Lorraine'. In the same year further sums were paid to John and Robert Wood towards their 'services and expenses in procuring haggard cormorants for the King' (the term haggard – applied also to hawks – designated a bird caught in the wild after reaching its adult plumage) and later that year the Keeper again enters the records in a dispute over his right to fish with the birds in privately owned streams. Three years later John and Robert received a further £84 'for their charges in yearly journies to the North, in providing haggards and cormorants, for the King's disport in fishing'. In 1624 certain royal cormorants were caught up in a diplomatic incident when another member of the Wood family named Luke had to be recompensed for expenses sustained 'in his late travels, with three cormorants, to Venice, having been stayed in his passage thither, and his cormorants taken from him, by the Duke of Savoy, to his great loss and hindrance'.

By now the cormorants evidently formed a well-established component of the royal household, with several servants assigned to their care. Indeed, by the year of James's death the expenses were evidently thought to be getting out of hand: a Royal Commission appointed to consider 're-trenchment of His Majesty's charges' recommended that the office of Keeper of the Cormorants be abolished, with an annual saving to the Household of £84.

From just this time there survives an extensive account of cormorant fishing in England, later reproduced in the first great survey of birds in English, the *Ornithology* of Francis Willughby, edited for publication by John Ray in 1678. The description itself is far from first-hand in nature, for the passage in question is a quotation from a Latin text by Johannes Faber, recounting the experiences of Cassiano dal Pozzo when the latter travelled to the French court at Fontainebleau in 1625–6 with his patron Cardinal Franceso Barberini. The passage published by Willughby is none the less of interest in the English context, not least for confirmation of the fact that James was by now sufficiently well provided with cormorants to bestow them as gifts to the French monarch:

They are wont (saith Joh. Faber) in England to train up Cormorants to fishing. When they carry them out of the rooms where they are kept to the fish-pools, they hood-wink them, that they be not frightened by the way. When they are come to the Rivers they take off their hoods, and, having tied a leather thong round the lower part of their Necks that they may not swallow down the fish they catch, they throw them into the River. They presently dive under water, and there for a long time with wonderful swiftness pursue the fish, and when they have caught them they arise presently to the top of the water, and pressing the fish lightly with their Bills they swallow them; till each Bird hath after this manner devoured five or six fishes. Then their Keepers call them to the fist, to which they readily fly, and little by little one after another vomit up all their fish a little bruised with the nip they gave them with their Bills. When they have done fishing, setting the birds on some high place they loose the string from their Necks, leaving the passage to the stomach free and open, and for their reward they throw them part of their prey they have caught, to each perchance one or two fishes, which they by the way as they are falling in the air will catch most dextrously in their mouths.

Cassiano continues (in a passage not included in Willughby's translation but reproduced in the original Latin by Harting) that the birds he saw fishing at Fontainebleau had been presented to the French monarch by the king of England – clearly James I – who had sent with them a man as their keeper and trainer. An alternative account of these birds, published by Baron Dunoyer de Noirmont in 1857 and followed by other writers including

Zeuner, derives them from the Netherlands: given the exceptional nature of Faber's evidence (and the absence of corroboration in Noirmont's account), there seems little reason to doubt the veracity of the testament transmitted by the eyewitness Cassiano – one of the most trustworthy observers of his day. Indeed, in a recent Europe-wide survey of the subject, Christine Jackson finds no evidence that cormorants had been introduced to the Netherlands in the seventeenth century.

Although direct evidence from the reign of Charles I is lacking, it seems that he failed to heed the advice of his father's commissioners, for the antiquary Sir Thomas Browne (1605–82) has left a description of a colony of cormorants at Reedham (Norfolk), from whence, he writes, 'King Charles the First was wont to be supplied'. No record survives of what became of the royal birds during the Commonwealth, beyond an oblique reference in Thomas Pennant's *British Zoology* which mentions that 'Whitelock tells us, that he had a cast of them *manned* like hawks and which would come to hand . . . the best he had was one presented to him by Mr Wood, *Master of the Cormorants* to Charles I'.

Surprisingly, the office of Keeper of His Majesty's Cormorants was re-established at an early stage in the reign of Charles II, for already in 1665 the annual payment (still £85) due to this officer was said to be two years in arrears. Thereafter it seems to have been extinguished in Britain, though in France its popularity was maintained well into the eighteenth century: Dunoyer de Noirmont cites a report in the *Mercure de France* of October 1713 of the magnificent cavalcades attracted to Fontainebleau to witness the royal cormorants at work, and he notes that the office of keeper of the cormorants survived there until at least 1736.

NINETEENTH-CENTURY REVIVAL

Although cormorant fishing evidently fell into abeyance in England by the later seventeenth century, public familiarity with oriental practice would have been maintained, first of all by a series of publications mentioning (and in some instances illustrating) the custom. The most notable of these were the widely read accounts of a series of embassies to China, the first by Johan Nieuhof, published in translation in 1669 and the next (which appeared only in Dutch and German) in 1670 by Olfert Dapper – both of them employees of the Dutch East India Company. Dapper's account had the advantage of an illustration detailing the various activities of the birds and their handlers. English readers were informed directly through the extensive account by Sir George Staunton of his experiences on the famous embassy by Lord McCartney in 1792–4, published as *An Authentic Account of an Embassy . . .* in 1798. But it is from the 1840s that the practice was revived in England and from that time the most detailed first-hand accounts by exponents survive. Principal among these was Captain F. H. Salvin, an accomplished falconer whose book (co-authored with G. E. Freeman) *Falconry. Its Claims, History and Practice* (1859) contains some 'added remarks on training the Otter and Cormorant' by Salvin himself. He records that a certain E. C. Newcombe of Feltwell Hall, Norfolk, had brought from Holland in 1846 a cormorant already trained to fish by a member of the Loo Hawking Club; despite Newcombe's initiative, it seems that the Norfolk countryside proved uncongenial to the bird and the experiment was deemed a failure. The following year a member of the same club brought an untrained and immature cormorant for Salvin, who applied his skills in falconry to its training with consummate success: so adept did his new charge become as to earn the name Isaac Walton.

Salvin's notes, compiled on the basis of his experience with this and other successfully trained cormorants, are full of invaluable insights into their husbandry and use in the field, in which some aspects come directly from familiarity with the sources already mentioned while others are clearly extemporized in order to answer problems as they arose. The particular value of the birds, he suggests, came in the heat of summer, 'when fishing with the rod is impossible' and when most rural sports are at a standstill. His perspective is very much that of the pragmatic English sportsman, applying personal experience gained in other fields to the solution of practical issues encountered on a daily basis. His notes are presented in the clear expectation that they will be taken up and followed by other like-minded individuals, and take the form of a practical handbook rather than an account of a sporting curiosity.

The ideal stage at which to capture the birds, he suggests, is while still young but sufficiently covered with feathers as to be nearly fit to fly, although wild adults were also found to be susceptible to training, just as mature hawks could be tamed. For their quarters he recommends a long, south-facing shed provided with nesting materials of short straw placed within a circle of rocks on which the birds can perch. A second rockery is recommended for the surrounding yard, so that the birds could also perch outside in the commanding position which they favour. The ideal yard would also be provided with a pond or with a plank-built tank in which the birds could bathe and keep themselves clean. The yard itself would be strewn with sand.

The appetites of the young birds are described as voracious, although over-feeding brought the danger of apoplexy. If a bird should appear out of sorts, the chances are it would prove to be suffering from indigestion, for which Salvin prescribes powdered rhubarb. Clearly he paid close attention to their eating habits:

> You must fix your cormorants' dinner-hour so that it shall not be too late in the day; for as they always take their bath after dinner, there would not be time for them to get dry before going to roost were the meal late.

Even such an enthusiast as Salvin had to admit that their table manners were not of the best: commenting on the clean and odour-free nature of his trained otter (p. 175), he observes that the same 'cannot be said of Isaac Walton & Co., who indulge so much in musk, and are not very nice feeders'.

Training the birds for the field and stream also required a great deal of patience and dedication:

> You must now begin to 'carry' them for two or three hours every day for nearly a week, just as you do hawks, with this difference, that in the one case you are constantly hooding and unhooding the bird, whilst here you have to be hooded *yourself*; that is, you must wear a *fencing mask*; otherwise the bird will take out your eye for a certainty, to say nothing of biting your face.

Other authors comment on an additional hazard at this stage, for it was customary for all the primary feathers on the left wing to be trimmed within two inches of the bone, to prevent the birds from flying off. The left wing was invariably chosen for trimming in this way, since it was anticipated that the bird would be carried on the left fist and it was deemed judicious that the cut feathers were kept as far as possible from the face of the handler.

Having accustomed the birds to being handled under continual attention in this way, and to being rewarded for good conduct by occasional scraps of raw fish (for the affections of the bird are said to 'lie more in the stomach than in the heart'), the time had arrived to let them enter the tank, filled for the occasion with specially netted fish. After allowing them to take their fill on two or three occasions, the cormorants would then have straps fitted around the bottom of the neck and be taught in the yard to hold the fish in their gullets; any birds that regurgitated them too quickly would find that the others would quickly rob them of their fish, and by further rewards from the handler for good behaviour the birds would gradually come to accept the benefits of the relationship and be ready for the river. A moor-side stream was deemed the most desirable starting point, plentifully supplied with trout: their natural sliminess made them ideal for the birds to get used to, whereas spiny fish like perch could easily irritate their throats. If a trained cormorant (a 'make bird') was at hand, it would greatly facilitate the learning process by demonstrating the *modus operandi* to the others. Those that proved reluctant to dive were encouraged with the crack of a whip over their heads, or with clods of soft earth thrown at them. Training was continued until the birds were well fatigued.

Once these trips to the countryside had become routine, single cormorants might be carried on the fist with jesses on the feet attached to a leash, while the handler walked or rode on horseback. When several birds were being exercised together they would travel in a 'palanquin', a rectangular construction of light wood and canvas divided into compartments, one for each bird to avoid fights breaking out (illus. 55); these would be closed with canvas flaps fitted with buckles to either side. Two men were required to carry it on padded poles, which could be made to fold up for ease of storage; in acknowledgement of the origin of the idea, Salvin recommends that it be painted in the Chinese style. Once the river had been reached the palanquin would form an operational base for the birds being used in pairs in rotation, with some working and some drying out their wings perched on top. The routine was physically demanding on the handler too, who was expected to spend a considerable amount of time thigh-deep in the water, encouraging the birds in their task (illus. 56), on occasion lifting them on to the bank and helping them to disgorge by pressing gently on their throats just below the fish, and from time to time rewarding them with small fish. The day's activity might involve a descent of the stream by several miles, with the handler dressed in heavy protective clothing and carrying a creel on his back for the catch. Salvin records one expedition he made to the northern counties with four cormorants, in which 28 days of fishing yielded 1,200 good-sized fish. The cormorants seem to have been a match for anything from minnows up to small pike, and were equally happy taking sea-fish in the brackish waters of estuaries. Eels proved a favourite food with the birds, but their tendency to slither away as soon as they were regurgitated tended to reduce the otherwise orderly routine of the expedition to chaos and Salvin thought they were best avoided.

Salvin was witnessed in action with his cormorants in 1867 by Harting, who confirms every aspect of the skills demonstrated both by the birds and their handler. On that occasion the expedition was to a large pond at Midhurst (Sussex) where several birds were put through their paces (three individuals are named as being in Salvin's ownership in this account, in addition to the above-mentioned Isaak Walton). Their efficiency in probing every crevice in the bank is vividly described, along with their speed in overtaking and seizing any trout put up 'as a greyhound would a hare'; any that were too big to be swallowed instantly were brought to the surface in the bird's beak and with a twist of its head turned in an instant to vanish head-first into its gullet (some indeed were so large that the tail remained protruding until the bird was relieved of its catch and rewarded with a piece of chopped fish). The trout were washed to relieve them of the cormorant's acrid saliva and proved none the worse when served up at dinner the same evening.

The ornithological artist Jemima Blackburn had heard of these birds, although they all died before she could record them. 'They are now beautifully stuffed, and set up in the Hancock Museum at Newcastle' she writes, 'with little collars around their necks to prevent their swallowing the fish they caught'. Pursuing these birds in the 'Catalogue of Birds in the Hancock Collection' of 1899, Jackson found the following entry:

Cormorant, Phalacrocorax Carbo (Linn.) Female, mature, winter . . . Stuffed to represent a trained bird taking a fish, by John Hancock, 1884. Remark. – This bird was trained by Capt. Salvin and was named 'Isaak Walton'

by the donor, who used it for catching fish for some time. It died in 1880, when it came into my possession. On dissection it was proved to be a female.

Salvin did not have a complete monopoly on cormorant fishing in England, for Harting mentions a Mr T. Evans of Sawston (Cambridgeshire) who owned several, all trained for him by his falconer, John Barr. He describes these as travelling to the river not in a palanquin but following their master across the fields like a pack of hounds before diving into the water at a crack from his whip. According to Harting the birds showed every sign of pleasure at this arrangement, although when after a day's fishing they had their neck straps removed and were allowed to fish on their own account their enthusiasm was such that 'a good deal of "whipping in" was required to get them home'.

Harting's first-hand observations of these various birds and their respective trainers provide further valuable insights into their management. He found, for example, that 'cormorants are by no means difficult to train, and do not require half the care and attention which has to be bestowed

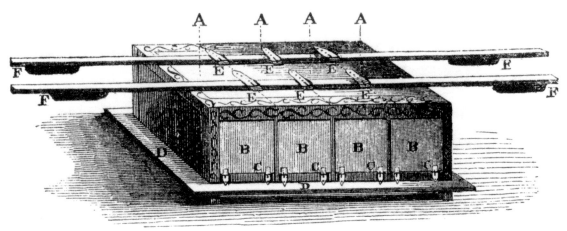

55 A palanquin for transporting cormorants: A cabins; B doors; C strap-hinges; D floor; E straps for poles; F padded poles for carrying. From G. E. Freeman and F. H. Salvin, *Falconry* (1859).

56 Hands-on cormorant fishing in an English stream: from G. E. Freeman and F. H. Salvin, *Falconry* (1859).

upon Hawks for example'. Although they might be taken from the nest just as they are ready to fly, he thought it preferable to catch them later in the year when they are fully feathered and have already gained some experience in fishing. Catching them is presented as a simple matter, with a series of gin-traps with the teeth bound to prevent them damaging the birds being set on top of the posts marking the river channel of an estuary, each gin to be attached to the post by a line with a float.

It is easy to arrange with a fisherman to keep watch in a boat at a little distance; and as soon as a Cormorant alights and is trapped, it will come off at once into the water, and should be taken up as soon as possible, a cloth thrown over the back and wings, two corners being tied securely under the chin, and the other two corners under the tail behind the legs. The bird may then be tethered by the legs . . .

On getting ashore with two or three captures, the flight feathers of the left wing should be cut neatly with a large pair of scissors, and the birds turned into a loose box, or any outhouse from which they cannot escape, care being taken to lay down straw, tan, or sawdust, to prevent the breakage of the tail feathers, which are so useful to them as rudders when in the water. Here they may be fed on fish until such time as they can be forwarded to their ultimate destination.

The wider public was for a time in 1883 treated to daily exhibitions of the birds at work at the International Fisheries Exhibition, brought from Berlin to London in that year. A *Special Catalogue of the Chinese Collection of Exhibits* mentions the presence of a full-sized model of a cormorant boat, accommodating both cormorants and fisherman. The displays proved hugely popular, not least – according to Gudger – with the Prince of Wales, who was so impressed that he was said to have bought the birds at the end of the show. Neither Gudger's efforts nor my own have succeeded in tracking down any corroborative evidence for this claim, however, and nothing is known of the fate of the birds thereafter.

57 Interior of the Cock-Pit Royal at Birdcage Walk, on the south side of St James's Park, London. Etching by Augustus Pugin, published by Rudolph Ackermann, 1808.

THREE

Urban and Rural Sports and Pastimes

PERSECUTION AND PROTECTION OF URBAN AND RURAL ANIMALS

If some kind of contract, however unequal, can be said to have existed between landowners or farmers and their animals, any such claim for the other representatives of the animal world with which rural and urban society was brought into contact on an organized basis is more difficult to sustain. It is true that some kind of practical justification was applied, for example, to the baiting of bulls destined for the butcher's shop, in the mistaken belief that when killed in a state of agitation their flesh was rendered more palatable; more than a mere old wives' tale, this prescription was indeed enshrined in the bylaws of a number of towns or cities where slaughter was prohibited without first submitting bulls to the dogs. In the case of other animals such as bears and badgers that were similarly tormented, the exercise was never claimed to have any higher purpose than to test the mettle of the dogs, whether mastiffs or terriers, that were pitted against them by their owners: the subjects of the baiting were here given little consideration, although strange to say, among the bulls and bears regularly baited at Bankside in London (and no doubt elsewhere), some emerged to command a personal following amongst the regular crowds and were given pet names in an almost affectionate manner.

Early authors on cockfighting were at pains to stress its respectable and indeed virtuous nature, not shirking from identifying it with the aristocratic field sports that included also hunting and hawking. George Wilson, writing in 1607, asserted that 'in this pleasant exercise there is no collusion, fraude, or cozening tolerated, nor any used . . . neither is there any brawlings, or quarrels suffered in those places: but all men must there use civile and good behaviour, what degree or calling soever he be of' – the very antithesis, as it happens, of the reputation generally given to the cockpit. Markham opens his chapter 'Of the Fighting Cock' with similar sentiments, declaring that he has been moved to compile his text 'since many of the best Wisdomes of our Nation have been pleased to participate with the delights therein', being convinced that the subject 'is (for our pleasure sake) as worthy of generall Knowledge as any delight whatsoever'.

Similarly specious arguments were made in relation to badger-baiting, whose proponents confidently predicted that any attempt at prohibiting their sport would lead to the badger's total extermination. There is perhaps a grain of reason in this way of thinking, as demonstrated in the case of swans (p. 326), where it was only when they ceased to be reared in a controlled manner in order to be eaten by the rich that they were exposed to the very real danger of extinction, while foxes too have been simultaneously hunted and preserved in such a way as to ensure the survival of the population (pp. 156–8); as a justification for the badger's persecution, however, it scarcely holds water.

With the rise of a growing (but by no means universal) revulsion at the needless tormenting of animals, a succession of legal measures found their way on to the statute book. In 1835 these were formalized in an Act to Consolidate and Amend the several Laws relating to the Cruel and Improper Treatment of Animals, which decreed amongst other things that any person keeping premises for the purposes of baiting animals or for cockfighting should be liable to a penalty of up to £5 10s., while under the provisions of a later amendment in the same year, defaulters could be sentenced to two months' hard labour.

Further legislation in the form of the Act for the more Effectual Prevention of Cruelty to Animals (1849) saw baiting in all its forms extinguished from the metropolis as a public spectacle, although it took some years further to be stamped out in the provinces. The wording of the relevant passage of the Act reads as follows:

That every Person who shall keep or use or act in the Management of any Place for the purpose of fighting or baiting any Bull, Bear, Badger, Dog, Cock, or other Kind of Animal, whether of domestic or wild Nature, or shall permit or suffer any Place to be so used, shall be liable to a Penalty not exceeding Five Pounds for every Day he shall so keep or use or act in the Management of any such Place, or permit or suffer any Place to be used as aforesaid; provided always, that every Person who shall receive Money for the admission of any other Person to any Place kept or used for any of the purposes aforesaid shall be deemed to be the Keeper

thereof; and every person who shall in any Manner encourage, aid, or assist at the fighting or baiting of any Bull, Bear, Badger, Dog, Cock, or other Animal as aforesaid shall forfeit and pay a Penalty not exceeding Five Pounds for every such offence.

In a formal sense, our present-day attitudes to animal cruelty may be said to have been shaped by this Act, although in the case of the badger, at least, further measures would be required to reinforce its protection (see below).

With the exception of the fighting cock, the bird species considered here (and similarly fish) were initially at greater risk from economic considerations than from the attentions of sportsmen, although from at least the sixteenth century the latter would become increasingly important in setting the agenda for both their exploitation and protection. (The same had been true for those species classified as game for many centuries before that time, as dealt with in the previous chapter.) Scarcely a single species of bird avoided the attentions of our ancestors, occasionally as in the case of nightingales and linnets to be caught, tamed and brought within a domestic setting, some like the hawks to enter a working relationship; uniquely, swans were brought within a system of ownership that none the less left them with a degree of independence. For the most part, however, encounters with the human race by those species that avoided becoming the object of sporting attention, whether fish, flesh or fowl, led nowhere but the pot.

THE BAITING OF BULLS, BEARS AND OTHER ANIMALS

The tormenting of certain animals – all of them demonized to some degree in consequence of the displays of savagery they were forced to mount in attempts at self preservation – formed a popular pastime amongst both urban and rural populations from all ranks of society, from the time of the Conquest in 1066 until formally outlawed by the Cruel and Improper Treatment of Animals Act (1835). In a society where contests of physical prowess between men were popular (whether, for example, in armed combat, in wrestling matches or later in boxing matches), it was perhaps inevitable that curiosity – to put it at its most neutral – would result in various disparate species being pitted against each other: for instance, a seemingly endless stream of unfortunate creatures found themselves thrown to the lions in the menagerie at the Tower of London for the amusement of the monarch (or perhaps to flatter his ego with demonstrations of the invulnerability of the king of the beasts), while in the backyards of the less salubrious taverns horses, donkeys or any other species that might come to hand were regularly sacrificed in what can only have been very unequal contests. Even such an aristocratic visitor as the Duke of Nájera was entertained in 1544 with the spectacle of 'a pony with an ape fastened on its back, and to see the animal kicking among the dogs, with the screams of the ape, beholding the curs hanging from the ears and neck of the pony, is very laughable'. In the following century, one of the entertainments laid on in 1682 for Mohammed Ohadu, the Moroccan ambassador, was the baiting to death of 'a fine but vicious horse' that was said to have killed a number of men and other horses; in the event the dogs failed to overcome the horse, which was instead put to the sword in front of the visitors.

If later sensibilities consigned such 'sports' to the more furtive end of the social spectrum, for much of the time-span examined here they formed part of the fabric of everyday life and,

being frequently associated with wakes and fairs, may even be said to have been celebratory in nature. As early as 1174 William fitz Stephen records that in London on the forenoon of most feast days during winter, 'either foaming boars with lightning tusks, fight for their lives to "save their bacon" or stout bulls with butting horns or huge bears do battle with the hounds let loose upon them'. In the course of the following centuries these spectacles remained a regular part of the provincial calendar, while in the capital and the growing cities they developed into weekly or even daily events organized for profit, with bulls and bears emerging as the victims of choice.

While the different species were accorded some degree of individual treatment, as discussed below, much of their experience was shared and they would frequently find themselves on the same programme of entertainment. Dogs formed the common element in most such encounters: while some of these were effectively kept on a 'professional' basis and were provided for the purpose of staging the spectacle, others were privately owned and baitings provided owners with opportunities to show off their prowess (and no doubt to make a little money through betting on the side). In early eyewitness accounts by foreign visitors to London, the dogs are often the first thing to catch their eye. Two such accounts are of particular interest in setting the scene for much of what follows, the first left by Alessandro Magno, a Venetian whose ship brought him to London in 1562, as translated by Giles Dawson:

Across the river in a certain place [in Southwark] they have perhaps two hundred dogs, each separated from the other in certain small boxes made of boards. The dogs are of the kind we use in Venice for bull-baiting. They also have, in another pen many bears and in another some wild bulls . . . To enter below one pays a penny . . . and two to go up into the stands. The amusement lasts from the vesper hour until evening, and they put on very fine baitings. First they lead into this space, which is closed about, and there is no way out unless they open certain doors, and they bring in, I say, a worthless horse with all its trappings, and a monkey in the saddle, then four to six of the younger dogs, with which they make an attack. Then these are replaced by leading in more experienced ones, in which baiting it is a fine sight to see the horse run, kicking and biting, and the monkey grip the saddle tightly and scream, many times being bitten, in which baiting, after the attendants have intervened a while, with frequently the death of the horse, and it is removed from the scene, they bring in some bears, either one by one or several together, but this baiting is not very fine to see. Finally they bring in a wild bull, and they tie it with a rope about two paces long to a stake that is fixed in the middle of the enclosure. This baiting is finer to see than the others and is more dangerous for the dogs than the others, many of which are wounded and die, and it lasts until evening.

In a further report, produced by the secretary of the Duke of Württemberg when his master visited London in 1592, it is again the dogs that form the principal focus:

On the 1st of September his Highness was shown in London the English dogs, of which there were about 120, all kept in the same enclosure, but each in a separate kennel. In order to gratify his Highness, and at his desire, two bears and a bull were baited; at such

times you can see the breed and the mettle of the dogs, for although they receive serious injuries from the bears, and are caught by the horns of the bull and tossed in the air so as frequently to fall down again upon the horns, they do not give in . . .

Evidently the numbers of dogs fluctuated from time to time, and indeed this whole area of London was in a state of flux for much of the latter part of the sixteenth century, as outlined below: in 1599 Thomas Platter, a visiting Swiss traveller, similarly puts the numbers of dogs present at 120, while at the time of a visit by Philip Julius, Duke of Stettin-Pomerania, in 1602 they were estimated (as they had been earlier by Magno) at 'more than 200'. A near-contemporary bill among the papers of Edward Alleyn, actor and some-time proprietor with his father-in-law Philip Henslowe of the Bear Garden in Southwark (see below), advertises a challenge match open to all, of the kind favoured by cockfighters of the day (p. 249), in which participants were invited to bring their own dogs:

Tomorrowe beinge Thursdaie shalbe seen at the Beargardin on the banckside a greate mach plaid by the gamstirs of Essex who hath chalenged all comers what soever to plaie v dogges at the single beare for v pounds, and also to wearie a bull dead at the stake and for your better content shall have plasant sport with the horse and ape and whiping of the blind beare. *Vivat Rex.*

Orazio Busino, chaplain to the Venetian embassy in London, left the following account in his *Anglipotrida* of 1618, in which the tenacity of the dogs is again acknowledged:

the result of our observations after various assaults was that both the bull and the bear overpower the courage of the dog, who although he occasionally makes some good hits, yet in the end is frequently killed on the spot, either from being tossed by the one or hugged, torn or bitten by the other . . . the dogs . . . are detached from the bear, by inserting between the teeth . . . certain iron spattles with a wooden handle, whilst they take them off the bull, keeping at a greater distance, with certain flat iron hooks which they apply to the thighs or even to the neck of the dog, whose tail is simultaneously dextrously seized by another of these rufflers.

From the reign of Elizabeth onwards, attempts were made to curb these spectacles, largely as a result of Puritan sensibilities which were offended partly by the cruelty inflicted on the animals and partly because they seduced the populace from their proper occupations and into reprehensible activities. By the reign of Charles I baiting was officially banned on the Sabbath (which had become the customary day for it to be held in London) but evidently it continued to be widely practised: in 1633 the King declared that while various wholesome games might be indulged in after divine service others remained prohibited, including 'bear and bull baitings, interludes . . . and bowling'. Baiting itself attracted no particular condemnation from the monarchy, however, and Charles and his queen patronized bull- and bear-baitings at Whitehall and at Greenwich on a regular annual basis (mostly at Whitsuntide).

The Puritan parliament, however, took a disapproving view of these low sports, perhaps as much for the opportunities they offered for potentially seditious gatherings as for their moral degeneracy. In 1642 an attempt was made – evidently with limited success – to prohibit animal baiting altogether. On one occasion troops from Cromwell's forces chanced upon a bear-baiting when they entered the town of Uppingham (Rutland): the bears, though the innocent parties in the entertainment, were promptly seized, tied to a tree and shot. The same fate befell other animals in London at the hands of Colonel Pride's troops (below).

None the less, these establishments survived into the Restoration period. Samuel Pepys was an infrequent visitor to the bear garden: while he considered it 'a very rude and nasty pleasure' he records one visit on 14 August 1666 when he and his company 'saw some good sport of the bull's tossing the dogs – one into the very boxes'. John Evelyn noted a variety of such entertainments presented to the public on 16 June 1670:

> I went with some friends to the bear-garden, where was cock-fighting, dog-fighting, beare and bull baiting, it being a famous day for all these butcherly sports, or rather barbarous cruelties. The bulls did exceedingly well, but the Irish wolfe-dog exceeded, which was a tall greyhound, a stately creature indeede, who beat a cruell mastiff. One of the bulls tossed a dog full into a lady's lap, as she sat in one of the boxes at a considerable height from the arena. Two poore dogs were killed, and so all ended with the ape on horseback, and I most heartily weary of the rude and dirty pastime, which I had not seene, I think, in twenty years before.

These spectacles seem always to have drawn their most dedicated audiences from the nobility and the mob, and certainly by the seventeenth century any support they had enjoyed from respectable middling folk ebbed away. Despite falling from favour with polite audiences, the public baiting of animals survived up to the early years of the nineteenth century, although by 1819 Rees's *Encyclopædia* concluded that by then it was 'rarely practised'. Repeated attempts to introduce legislation prohibiting bull-baiting in 1800, 1802 and 1809 were defeated on the grounds that such a move would represent an interference with personal liberties. Eventually, under William IV penalties were attached and 'places in and about the Metropolis . . . kept and used for the purpose of fighting or baiting of bears and other animals' were henceforth banned; furthermore, 'any person who shall within five miles of Temple Bar keep or use, or shall act in the management or conducting of, any premises or place whatsoever for the purpose of fighting or baiting of bears, cock-fighting, baiting or fighting of badgers or other animals' was open to a fine of £5 or in default to two months' imprisonment with hard labour.

BANKSIDE, THE PARIS GARDEN AND OTHER LONDON VENUES

In the royal warrants issued to the officers mentioned below, frequent reference is made to 'the Game of Paris Garden' and to 'the Master of Her Majesty's Game' there. The property in question lay within the area of Southwark bordering the Thames and known more generally as Bankside. (Despite repeated reference to the Paris Garden as the site of animal baiting, it seems that only the landing stairs used by visitors arriving by river from the City and from Westminster lay within the curtilage of the manor of that name, while the baiting took place further to the east.) It was here in Bankside that some of London's most influential theatres were located by the end of the sixteenth century – most notably the Globe, the Rose and the Swan – and the early history of the theatre and of bull- and bear-baiting are closely bound up

together. When permanent homes for these spectacles first emerge they are identical in form, and in some theatres plays and animal baiting would indeed alternate on different days within the same premises and with the same promoters. A letter to Lord Cottington dated 1639 conjures up the animated atmosphere of the area with a description of the Paris Garden, where:

> you may hear the shouting of men, the barking of dogs, the growling of bears, and the bellowing of bulls, mixed in a wild but natural harmony. This appears to the writer a picture of the world, for 'All the world is but a bear-baiting'. There are some who do not endure to see the bears, but they are generally rustics, and of little judgment, who do not know how to regard this business, nor do they approve of recreation.

The earliest establishments seem to have been little more than open areas of ground with rudimentary grandstands thrown up around them: John Stow in his *Survey of London* (1598) mentions particularly the Bear Garden, in which 'were kept, beares, bulls, and other beasts to be bayted, as also mastives in several kennels, nourished to bayt them. These bears and other beasts are kept in plots of ground scaffolded about for the beholders to stand safe'. By mid-century these arrangements had begun to take on the appearance of more permanent theatre-like buildings, as recorded in the pictorial maps prepared by Braun and Hogenberg in the years 1554–8, by Ralph Agas in 1574 (illus. 58) and by William Smith in his manuscript 'Description of England' of *c*. 1580. Two tiers of sitting or standing room are indicated within the adjacent theatres, one designated for 'The bolle bayting' and the other for 'The Bearebayting'. In a supposed contemporary *View of London about*

58 The twin arenas for 'The bolle bayting' and 'The Bearebayting' at Southwark. Detail from a woodcut map of London of the 1550s attributed (wrongly) to Ralph Agas. The dog kennels are shown schematically to either side of the yard enclosing each of the theatres (the rectangular shaded areas are stews or fishponds, seemingly associated with the 'Pike Garden' lying immediately to the west).

the Year 1560, the performance is announced by pennants flown from the open roof, in a manner widely adopted by the theatre; Alessandro Magno's description from just this time mentions that the stands were provided with awnings to shelter the audience from the sun and rain; the dogs were tied up in slips nearby. In 1583 the collapse of the viewing platform at one of these establishments led to a major calamity, as reported by Stowe:

> The same thirteenth day of January, being Sunday, about four of the clock in the afternoon, the old and underpropped scaffold round about the Bear Garden commonly called Paris Garden . . . overcharged with people, fell suddenly down, whereby to the number of eight persons, men and women, were slain, and many others sore hurt and bruised to the shortening of their lives.

The crush of people attending on that occasion is underscored by Philip Stubbes in his *Anatomie of Abuses* (1583) where he adds that 'either two or three hundred men, wemen, and children (by estimation)' were involved:

> some had their braines dasht out, some their heades all to quasht, some their legges broken, some their armes, some their backes . . . This wofull spectacle and heavie judgement . . . the Lorde sent downe from Heaven, to shew unto the whole world how greevously he is offended with those that spend the Sabboath in such wicked exercises.

The Revd John Field added of the 'old and rotten' structure that 'not a stick was left so high as the bear was fastened to'. New scaffolding structures were built straight away, but were soon replaced by a purpose-built theatre styled the New Bear Garden of an open octagonal form.

In 1598 the German traveller Paul Hentzner saw the various sports on offer at the Bear Garden:

There is still another place, built in the form of a theatre, which serves for the baiting of bulls and bears; they are fastened behind, and then worried by great English bull-dogs, but not without great risk to the dogs, from the horns of the one, and the teeth of the other; and it sometimes happens they are killed upon the spot; fresh ones are immediately supplied in the places of those that are wounded or tired.

In 1613 the Bear Garden was in turn demolished and replaced by a new theatre, to be called the Hope, whose specification, drawn up by Henslowe, is revealing for the twin functions it was intended to serve. The builder was required to

newly erect, builde and sett upp one other Same Place or Plaiehouse fitt & convenient in all thinges, bothe for players to playe In, And for the game of Beares and Bulls to be bayted in the same . . . And to builde the same of suche large compasse, fforme, widenes, and height as the Plaie house Called the Swan . .
.

Three galleries were to be built within, and as well as specifying details of the stage there are requirements for the building of a bull-house for six bulls and three horses. A later notice reproduced by Bentley adds a further interesting detail:

The Hope on the Banks side in Southwarke, commonly called the Beare Garden. A Play House for Stage Playes. On Mundayes, Wedensdayes, Fridayes and Saterdayes. And for the Baiting of the Beares on Tuesdayes and Thursdayes. the Stage being made to take up and downe when they please.

Having had their genesis in such close relation to the theatre, establishments like the Hope shared its fate when in 1642 Parliament first banned all 'publike Stage-Playes' and later ordered that 'the Masters of the Bear-Garden, and all other persons who have interest there, be enjoined and required . . . that for the future they do not permit to be used the game of bear-baiting in these times of great distraction until this House do give further orders herein'. In the event, baiting continued in defiance of Parliament and despite repeated banning orders until the mid-1650s, when a notorious incident seems to have turned public opinion in a significant manner: a child had inadvertently been locked into the bears' enclosure where it was devoured. Damaging as this incident was for the image of the Bear Garden, it was made worse when the bearwards, having offered the child's mother half the proceeds from the next baiting by way of compensation, were found to have given her just £3 out of £60 of income. There seems to have been little outcry when a few months later, Colonel Pride turned up with a body of troops and slew all the bears (some or all of them reputedly with his own hand); the dogs are said by some reports to have been shipped to the West Indies, and after that baiting disappeared altogether from Southwark.

Other bear gardens had already sprung up north of the river to take the place of these establishments, notably at Tothill Fields, Saffron Hill and Islington, as well as at Hockley-in-the-Hole in the Smithfield area, whose name became a byword for beastly pursuits up to the nineteenth century.

THE ROYAL OFFICERS

From the time of the earliest records of animal baiting the monarchy played a prominent role in promoting diversions of this kind. In the reign of Richard III the office of Royal Bearwarden was first created. In 1484 John Browne was appointed 'Maister Guyder and Ruler of all our Beres and Apes'. A patent of 2 June 1573 to Ralph Bowes describes him as 'Cheif Master Overseer and Ruler of all and singular our game pastymes and sportes, that is to saie of all and everie our beares bulles and mastyve dogges' and allows him to 'take up' or press animals for the royal service. A number of subordinate officers titled Keepers of the Bears and Mastiffs also appear in the records, generally not salaried but paid a fee whenever the bears were baited in the royal presence. The animals in question were normally brought to the particular palace in which the court found itself in residence at the time (often Whitehall or Greenwich). In May 1559, for example, after dinner the Queen entertained the French ambassador 'to bear and bull bayting, and the Quens grace and the embassadurs stod in the galere lokying at the pastime tyll vi at nyght'. Neither Henry VIII nor Elizabeth I were averse to visiting the public baitings of bulls and bears in Southwark, and indeed the royal bearwards were accustomed to exposing the monarch's animals to public baiting there when they were not required at court. Hence a strong community of interest developed, and if sufficient animals were lacking for a royal performance, others could easily be drafted in from the public domain for the occasion.

In 1598 John Dorrington was made Keeper of the Bandogs and Mastiffs with a fee of 10d. a day for the exercising of this office and the keeping of twenty mastiff bitches, while another keepership, that of the bears, was held in 1599 by Jacob Meade, also involved in running the Bear Garden along with Henslowe and Alleyne. Together these two, members of the Globe company, purchased the post and are recorded as being paid £30 partly for attendances with the 'game' at Greenwich during

a visit by Christian IV of Denmark, at Whitehall at a reception for the Prince de Joinville, and for occasional baiting of the lions in the Tower. It scarcely comes as a surprise that James I, obsessed with sporting pastimes, should be credited with introducing this new dimension to baiting when he first pitted a bear against one of the lions at the Tower menagerie, an encounter deemed so successful as to warrant the construction thereafter of 'an especial place' where the lions could be baited with 'dogges, beares, bulles, bores etc'. Stow records such events from the years 1604, 1605, 1609 and 1610.

Under Charles I, when the king's barber, Thomas Caldwell, was appointed 'chief master of his Majesty's games and pastimes, that is to say, of his bears, bulls and mastiffs', he was again specifically empowered 'to take up for the king's service any bear or bull upon such price as he can agree with the owner'; if no such agreement could be reached then it was pronounced lawful for 'two justices of the Peace near the place to set an indifferent price upon the same, whom his Majesty requires to be assisting Caldwell, and that the owner of such a bear or bull shall not refuse the price so imposed'.

BEAR-BAITING

Few precise details of the bears themselves survive. They had appeared in England as occasional imports since before the arrival of the Normans: Kiser notes a pre-Conquest record from Norwich stating that the city was required to provide the king with a bear and six dogs for his amusement, while the majority of the population – if they ever encountered one at all – would have seen them in the company of their travelling handlers or bearwards (illus. 59) at seasonal fairs, where the local population might have been invited to try the courage of their dogs in combat, unless

59 Bear-baiting depicted in the Luttrell Psalter (*c.* 1340). The bear, fitted with a (?metal) bridle but with its claws clearly intact, is chained to a stake and is urged on by the bearward with a stave and cudgel, while the dogs are similarly encouraged by their handlers.

the bear had been trained to perform in other ways. If the prospect of bear dancing seems momentarily more benign than bear-baiting, one has only to read the opinion of the Revd William Bingley. The bear, he says, may indeed be taught to walk upright, to dance and to perform various tricks in response to an instrument or to the voice of its leader:

But to give the Bear this kind of education, it is necessary to have it taken young, and to accustom it early to restraint and discipline . . . The excessive cruelties practised on this poor animal in teaching it to walk erect, and to regulate its motions to the sound of the pipe, are such as to make sensibility shudder. Its eyes are frequently put out; and an iron ring being passed through the cartilage of its nose, to lead it by, it is kept from food, and

beaten till it yields obedience to the will of its savage tutors. Some of them are taught to perform, by setting their feet upon heated iron plates, and then playing to them whilst in this uneasy situation. It is truly shocking to every feeling mind to reflect that such cruelties should be exercised upon any part of the brute creation by our fellow-men. That they should be rewarded by numbers of un-thinking people who crowd around to see the animal's rude attempts to imitate human actions, is not to be wondered at: but it is much to be wished that the timely interfer-ence of the magistrate would prevent every exhibition of the kind.

Almost a millennium of mistreatment in this way would have passed before the law finally came to the rescue of the bear, while the population at large remained for the most part oblivious to the iniquities inflicted on it.

According to Brunner, the creatures involved were mostly smaller brown and black bears (although it may be noted that some contemporary descriptions mention individuals as 'of great size'); all were imported from central and eastern Europe, especially Russia. Brunner further asserts that the bears' canine teeth and claws were normally removed in order to make for a more balanced contest, though none of the early accounts make any mention of such a practice and several directly contradict it. Also absent from these eyewitness statements is any mention that the bears were led by a ring through the nose, although this remains the practice today with dancing bears in south-east Europe and the Middle East; on the other hand, the evidence from John Johnston's *Description of the Nature of Four-Footed Beasts* (1678) suggests that this may indeed have been true (although Johnston spent much of his life on the Continent, where his book was first published in Latin (1657) and the image he includes is almost certainly derivative). More conclusive, perhaps, is the testimony of the series of jugs produced in Nottingham stoneware in the form of bears with just such a feature (illus. 60), dating from the turn of the eighteenth century and seeming to show that some of them (in whatever role) were indeed controlled in this way. It seems likely, in fact, that practices changed over the centuries.

Occasional references suggest that amongst the royal bears in particular, polar bears were to be seen in London from time to time. In the mid-thirteenth century there was already one in the Tower menagerie which was allowed occasionally to fish in the Thames, while Foxe's *Book of Martyrs* records one occasion on the Thames *c.* 1539 when Henry VIII 'was then in his barge with a great number of barges and boats about him, then baiting

60 Jug, of Nottingham salt-glazed stoneware, *c.* 1750, in the form of a bear with a collar, clasping in its paws a dog with which it has been baited. The bear's head forms a removable cup.

of bears in the water, over against the Bank'. Again under Edward VI it is recorded that on 29 May 1550 that 'The [French] Ambassadors . . . went into the Thames, and saw both the bear hunted in the River, and also Wildfire cast out of Boats, and many pretty Conceits', while in 1623 an evening's entertainment for the Spanish ambassador reached its climax when James I's bearwards 'turned a white bear into the Thames, where the dogs baited him swimming, which was the best sport of all'. Even in the provinces, bears were occasionally baited in the water: a series of documents published by Hodson refer to bear-baiting taking place in 1668 'in the River of Wye near the [Wye] Bridge' in Hereford: whether a polar bear was involved is unrecorded, but presumably any such must have been immature animals, fully grown polar bears being of a size that would make them impossible to handle in this way. In a record of the bears in residence at the Bear Garden appended by John Taylor to his poem *Bull, Beare, and Horse* (1638) two of them, Mad Besse and Will Tookey, are described as 'white beares'.

A number of noble families as well as civic corporations had their own bears and bearwards to attend them. These would have been precious assets to be preserved, and care would have been taken to ensure that any damage suffered by the bears was limited and not lethal.

The essentials of the conventional spectacle offered at early bear-baitings were recorded by a member of the retinue of the Duke of Nájera, at his visit to London in 1544:

In another part of the city we saw seven bears, some of them of great size. They were led out every day to an enclosure, where being tied with a long rope, large and intrepid dogs are thrown to them, in order that they may bite and make them furious. It is no bad sport to see them fight, and the assaults they give each other. To each of the large bears are matched three or four dogs, which sometimes get the better and sometimes are worsted, for besides the fierceness and great strength of the bears to defend themselves with their teeth, they hug the dogs with their paws so tightly, that, unless the masters come to assist them, they would be strangled by such soft embraces.

Robert Laneham, in his description of an entertainment arranged for Queen Elizabeth at Kenilworth in 1575, spares his reader none of the gory reality of a bear-baiting while by no means disapproving of it. The contest proceeded, he writes,

with plucking & tugging, skratting & byting, by plain tooth & nayll to [one] side & toother such exspress of blood & leather waz thear between them, az a months licking I wæn wyl not recoover . . .

It was a sport very pleazaunt of theez beastz: to see the bear with hiz pink nyez leering after hiz enemiez approch, the nimbleness & wayt of ye dog too take hiz avauntage, and the fors & experiens of the bear agayn to avoyd the assauts: if he wear bitten in one place, hoow he woold pynch in an oother to get free: that if he wear taken onez, then what shyft, with byting, with clawyng with roring tossing & tumbling he woold woork too wynde hym self from them; and when he waz lose, to shake hiz earz twyse or thryse wyth the blud & the slaver aboout hiz fiznamy, waz a matter of goodly releef.

As already indicated, most animals might expect to be repeatedly baited over a matter of years and some bears of exceptional courage became long-term favourites of the sporting public: from the sixteenth and seventeenth centuries the names survive of some that became widely and almost affectionately familiar to the public – Harry Hunks, George Stone, Besse of Ipswich, Moll Cutpurse and Sackerson – although the 'goodlye beare' George Stone was killed in a baiting before the King of Denmark in 1606 and Harry Hunks finished his days old, blinded and regularly whipped. Gratuitous as this treatment may seem, it evidently formed a regular part of the show, as we learn from the conclusion to Hentzner's description referred to above:

> To this entertainment there often follows that of whipping a blinded bear, which is performed by five or six men standing circularly with whips, which they exercise upon him without any mercy, as he cannot escape from them because of his chain; he defends himself with all his force and skill, throwing down all who come within his reach, and are not active enough to get out of it, and tearing the whips out of their hands and breaking them.

Given that some of the bears may have been deliberately blinded at an earlier stage in their life (as the Revd Bingley has informed us), there would probably have been a fairly regular supply of old and sightless animals who ended their days in this way.

Neither were men and dogs the only adversaries that the bear might have to face. In addition to the rigours of the lion's den at the Tower as mentioned above, the following account of the bear from Topsell's *Historie of Foure-Footed Beastes* (1607) has all the hallmarks of eyewitness experience:

> Beares, they will fight with Buls, Dogges, and horses: when they fight with bulles, they take them by their hornes, and so with the weight of their bodie, they wearie and presse the beast, until they may easilie slaie him: and this fight is for the most part on his backe . . . There is also a mortal hatred betwixt a horse and a beare, for they know one another at first sight; and prepare to combat, which they rather act by policie then by strength: The beare falling flat on his backe, the horsse leaping over the beare, which pulleth at his guts with her forefeet-nailes, and is by the heeles of the horsse wounded to death, if he strike the beare upon his head.

Bear-baiting never recovered its popularity with polite society following the Civil War, but survived as an increasingly furtive pursuit in the yards of disreputable drinking houses up to the nineteenth century (illus. 61).

61 By the 19th century bear-baiting had been reduced to a backyard pursuit devoid even of the theatrical setting that had had attracted earlier enthusiasts. From Henry Alken's *National Sports of Great Britain*, first published 1820.

BULL-BAITING AND BULL RUNNING

In bull-baiting as practised in the professionally organized world in London, the bulls – like the bears just discussed – represented assets which were by no means to be lightly destroyed by their tormentors: certainly they were expected to put up a spirited fight, but ultimately the aim was to preserve them to fight another day. If anything, it was the dogs that were the more expendable, although the bull was constrained to some degree in his ability to attack them. In his eyewitness account of 1618 quoted above, Orazio Busino continues:

The bull can hardly get at anybody, as he wears a collar round his neck with only fifteen feet of rope, which is fastened to a stake deeply planted in the middle of the theatre. [Men] are at hand with long poles to put under the dog so as to break his fall after he has been tossed by the bull; the tips of these poles are covered with thick leather to prevent them from disembowelling the dogs. The most spirited stroke is considered to be that of the dog who seizes the bull's lip, clinging to it and pinning the animal for some time; the second best hit is to seize the eyebrows; the third, but far inferior, consists in seizing the bull's ear.

These conventions are confirmed in a more detailed description of the conduct of a bull-baiting left by the Frenchman Henri Misson, who visited England in 1697:

They tie a Rope to the Root of the Horns of the Ox or Bull, and fasten the other End of the Cord to an Iron Ring fix'd to a Stake driven into the Ground; so that this Cord being about 15 Foot long; the Bull is confin'd to a Sphere of about 30 Foot Diameter.

Several Butchers, or other Gentlemen, that are desirous to exercise their Dogs, stand round about, each holding his own by the Ears; and when the Sport begins they let loose one of the Dogs: The Dog runs at the Bull; the Bull, immoveable, looks down upon the Dog with an Eye of Scorn, and only turns a Horn to him to hinder him from coming near: The Dog is not daunted at this, he runs round him, and tries to get beneath his Belly, in order to seize him by the Muzzle, or the Dewlap, or the pendant Glands, which are so necessary for the great work of Generation: The Bull then puts himself into a Posture of Defence; he beats the Ground with his Feet, which he joins together, as close as possible, and his chief Aim is not to gore the Dog with the point of his Horn but to slide one of them under the Dog's Belly, (who creeps close to the Ground to hinder it) and to throw him so high in the Air that he may break his Neck in the Fall. This often happens: When the Dog thinks he is sure of fixing his Teeth, a Turn of the Horn, which seems to be done with all the Negligence in the World, gives him a Sprawl thirty Foot high, and puts him in Danger of a damnable squelch when he comes down. This Danger would be unavoidable, if the Dog's Friends were not ready beneath him, some with their Backs to give him a soft Reception, and others with long Poles, which they offer him slant-ways, to the Intent that, sliding down them, it may break the Force of his Fall . . . Sometimes a second Frisk into the Air disables him for ever from playing his old Tricks: But sometimes too he fastens upon his Enemy, and when once he has seiz'd him with his Eye-teeth, he sticks to him like a Leech, and would sooner die than leave his

Hold. Then the Bull bellows, and bounds and kicks about to shake off the Dog; by his Leaping the Dog seems to be no Manner of Weight to him, tho' in all Appearance he puts him to great Pain. In the End, either the Dog tears out the Piece he has laid Hold on and falls, or else remains fix'd to him, with an Obstinacy that would never end, if they did not pull him off. To call him away would be in vain; to give him a hundred Blows would be as much so; you might cut him to Pieces Joint by Joint before he would let him loose. What is to be done then? While some hold the Bull, others thrust Staves into the Dog's Mouth, and open it by main Force. This is the only way to part them.

Misson notes that if the bull had particularly sharp horns these were enclosed by wooden sheaths, to preserve the dogs from immediate evisceration. He also mentions that, in contrast to the mastiffs favoured in earlier centuries, the dogs he saw were 'of moderate size' only, but this was not the experience of his contemporary John Houghton, who writes in his *Collection for Improvement of Husbandry and Trade* (1681):

> The bull takes great care to watch his enemy, which is a mastiff dog (commonly used to the sport) with a short nose that his teeth may take the better hold; this dog, if right, will creep upon his belly that he may, if possible, get the bull by the nose; which the bull as carefully strives to defend by laying it close to the ground, where his horns are also ready to do what in them lies to toss the dog; and this is the true sport. But if more dogs than one come at once, or they are cowardly and come under his legs, he will, if he can, stamp their guts out . . . and when they

are tossed, either higher or lower, the men above strive to catch them on their shoulders, lest the fall might mischief the dogs. They commonly lay sand about that if they fall upon the ground it may be the easier. Notwithstanding this care a great many dogs are killed, more have their limbs broke, and some hold so fast that, by the bull's swinging them, their teeth are often broken out . . . This is a sport the English much delight in; and not only the baser sort, but the greatest lords and ladies.

The role of the bulldog proper in these activities seems barely to be registered. Mastiffs feature more generally in the early accounts, whereas the *Sporting Dictionary* of 1803 describes bulldogs as already scarce:

> The breed is by no means so numerous as formerly, in consequence of the gradual decline of bull-baiting, and the great number taken abroad, for many of which great prices were obtained. The natural ferocity, strength, and thirst for blood, in this animal, rendered them a formidable nuisance in their unrestrained state, and they are now seldom seen at their full liberty, either in town or country; the owners, from a proper fear of the law, finding it more prudent to keep them properly confined.

While the bull generally was capable of giving as good as he got, then, and might have a lengthy career in the ring, the wear and tear (in the all-too-literal sense) from repeated baitings must have been considerable and death provided the only means of escape from the torment. Edward Alleyn's papers contain the following letter from William Fawnte, a potential supplier:

I understoode bey a man which came with too Beares from the Gardeyne, that you have a deseyre to bey one of mey Boles. I have three westorn boles at thes tyme, but I have had veery ell loeck with them, for one of them hath lost his horne to the queyck, that I think that hee will never bee able to feyght agayne; that is mey old star of the west: hee was a verey eesy bol; and my Bol Bevis, he hath lost one of hes eyes, but I think if you hed him he would do you more hurt then good, for I protest I think hee would [either] throw up your [dogs] in to the loftes, or eles ding out theare braynes ageanst the grates.

The naming of individual bulls in the manner witnessed by Fawnte was widespread and some indeed became household names, either fanciful – Goldilocks was one such – or more prosaic, like Ned Whiting; even some of the mastiffs which tormented them attracted a following of their own.

Some doubt has been expressed over the tradition that in certain towns bulls intended for butchering had by law to be baited before slaughter.

While the conventional wisdom was that the exercising of the bull immediately prior to its death would render the beef more tender, others maintaining that the reverse is the case have claimed that the word baiting in this instance might refer to feeding rather than worrying with dogs. Unfortunately, this more benign interpretation is supported by neither concrete evidence nor the weight of the historical record: boars were meted out similar treatment on occasion, Moffet recording the opinions of some that for preparation of the best carcases one should 'thrust a knife into one of his flanks and let him run with it till he dye', while 'others gently bait him with muzzled dogs'.

In these same provincial towns, bulls and other animals certainly fought each other to the death in the manner already described (illus. 62), although, in keeping with the festive origins of these customs, the final encounter with the hounds was frequently preceded by a general mêlée in which the animal in question was chased through the streets by the populace at large (and occasionally exacted its revenge on them). The most famous ritual of this kind, taking place annually in

62 A country bull-baiting: A dog has been tossed in the air by the bull, while two participants attempt to break the dog's fall by interposing themselves below, in the manner recorded in metropolitan baiting arenas. From Henry Alken's *National Sports of Great Britain*, first published 1820.

Tutbury, as recorded by Robert Plot in his *Natural History of Staffordshire* (1686), evidently had its origins in the annual renewal of tenurial agreements, in which the formalities were followed by a general engagement of the populace in a custom that served the purpose of publicly acknowledging the conclusion of the business at hand. After the legal niceties had been completed, Plot describes how

the Minstrells went anciently to the Abbey gate, now to a little barn by the Town side, in expectance of the Bull to be turned forth to them, which was formerly done . . . by the Prior of Tutbury, now by the Earle of Devonshire: which Bull, as soon as his horns are cut off, his ears cropt, his tail cut by the stumple, all his body smeared over with Soap, and his nose blown full of beaten pepper; in short being made as mad as 'tis possible for him to be; after Solemn Proclamation made by the Steward, that all manner of persons give way to the Bull, none being to come near him by forty foot, any way to hinder the Minstrells, but to attend his, or their own safeties, every one at his perill: He is then forthwith turned out to them . . . to be taken by them and by none other, within the County of Stafford, between the time of his being turned out to them, and the setting of the Sun the same day; which if he cannot doe, but the Bull escapes from them untaken, and gets over the river into Darbyshire, he remains still my lord Devonshire's bull: but if the said Minstrells can take him, and hold him so long, as to cutt off but some small matter of his hair, and bring the same to the Mercat cross in token they have taken him, the said bull is then brought to the Bayliff's house in Tutbury, and there coller'd and

roap't, and so brought to the Bull-ring in the high-street, and there baited with doggs: the first course being allotted for the King, the second for the Honor of the Towne, and the third for the King of the Minstrells. Which after it is done, the said Minstrells are to have him for their owne, and may fell, or kill and divide him amongst them, according as they shall think good.

And this Rustic-sport, which they call the Bull-running, should be annually performed by the Minstrells only, but now a days they are assisted by the promiscuous multitude, that flock hither in great numbers, &c.

While the Tutbury bull running was suppressed in 1778, another such festival, held every 13 November, survived at Stamford (Lincolnshire) into the nineteenth century. Eyewitness accounts (assembled by Malcolmson) describe an occasion reminiscent of those still observed in Pamplona and elsewhere in northern Spain, with side streets, shops and houses barricaded in anticipation of the boisterous crowds of people (though in this instance pursued by or in pursuit of only a single bull) that would surge through the streets for a large part of the day. Here there was no mutilation or greasing of the bull beforehand, for one witness describes how it would eventually be 'loaded' by the bullards – the participants: 'some have hold of his horns, and others his ears, some are beating his sides with bludgeons, and others are hanging at his tail'. Having begun at 11 o'clock and paused for lunch, they would then drive the bull towards the crossing of the River Welland, where the bullards would surround him and try to throw him over the parapet of the bridge and into the water, a ritual known as 'brigging the bull'. This was followed by a spell of baiting with dogs on the adjacent bank (during which the bull was not tethered), and later he would be driven back to town and slaughtered, the meat being sold to the poor or served up in the public houses.

Celebration of the foiling of the Gunpowder Plot formed a common occasion for festivities involving bull-baiting, a tradition observed at Lincoln up to the 1820s, while elsewhere parliamentary or local elections might provide the motive. At Beverley (Yorkshire), up to the eighteenth century, it was said to have been

> the custom, from time immemorial, for every Mayor of this town on his election, to give a bull to the populace, for the purpose of being baited, on the day of his being sworn into office; and which was always done either in the market-place, or at the door of the donor – several of the Aldermen of those days having rings fixed in the pavement, opposite their houses, for that purpose.

Smaller towns and villages observed somewhat similar customs, not necessarily having any symbolic meaning but merely in celebration of a feast day or holiday. Writing in the early years of the nineteenth century, Samuel Pegge mentions how, 'on occasions of rendezvous and public meetings of merriment . . . the landlord of the alehouse will give a tup (so they call a ram) or a pig well soaped, with the tail, and the horns, and the ears, respectively cut off. He that catches the tup is to have him; but if he is not taken, he returns to the landlord.' By way of example he mentions that in Kidlington (Oxfordshire), 'on Monday after Whitsun week, a fat lamb is turned out, and the maids of the town, having their thumbs tied behind them, run after it; and she that with her mouth takes and holds the lamb, is declared Lady of the Lamb'. Elsewhere it might be a goose that formed the object of the contest, suspended by its legs

from a convenient branch so that horsemen could take it in turns to try to seize it by its well-greased neck as they rode underneath.

Although contests involving bulls were much more widespread than bear-baiting, no purpose-built theatres for these entertainments were constructed beyond the capital; instead they would often take place in the local market-place or, as public appetite for this kind of spectacle waned, in a publican's yard. Following the Gunpowder Plot celebrations at Leominster (Herefordshire) in 1794, an entry in the chamberlain's accounts records the payment of 1s. 6d. to a labourer 'for cleansing the Corn Market after bull-baiting'. A number of towns retain a 'bull-ring' element among their street names, but there seems no reason to think that this signifies more than the former presence of a captive wrought-iron ring, either fixed to a post or embedded in the paving, to which the beast would be tethered. Malcolmson notes place-name evidence of this sort in Darlington (Durham) and in Harewood and Hornsea (Yorkshire), and occasionally more tangible evidence can be found. Such a post was excavated *in situ* at the turn of the last century in Totnes (Devon), 3 feet 1 inch in length and 2 feet 9½ inches in circumference at the base where it was packed with stones, and with a D-shaped ring at the top, passing through the thickness of the post. In Newcastle in 1821 building works on the Sandhill uncovered a large stone set with an iron ring which apparently had served this purpose but which had been abandoned or buried when bull-baiting, which had customarily taken place at that site, was prohibited in the town in 1768. It was again uncovered at the beginning of the twentieth century, when it was found that a former millstone had been utilized for the purpose, showing signs of several replacements of the iron shackle over years of use.

The *Sporting Dictionary* mentions in 1803 that the towns of Wokingham (Berkshire) and Stamford were 'the only places of note' where then survived the practice of bull-baiting – described as 'formerly not merely a pleasing pursuit, but an extatic diversion, of the most unfeeling, and least humane, part of the very lowest, and most abandoned, orders of the people'. By this point the anti-baiting lobby had such a head of steam behind it that in a short time it triumphed and bull-baiting was no more.

BADGER-DIGGING AND
BADGER-BAITING

Badger: To tease or to annoy by superior numbers.
In allusion to the ancient custom of Badger-baiting.
Brewer, *Dictionary of Phrase and Fable*

How perverse, that a creature by nature so inoffensive should have given its name to a form of aggression and persecution. Rather, its name like its character should be a byword for discreet self-effacement and quiet contentment, yet these characteristics failed to stop the species being pursued almost to extinction. While it would later receive some benefit from legislation designed to protect it, the badger's early experience of the law was anything but conducive to its well-being. Having been targeted (along with the wolf and the fox) in a number of proclamations in the fourteenth and fifteenth centuries which gave 'leave and licence' to anyone to 'hunt and take without any penalty' any of these species, the badger appeared in a further list of 'noyfull fowles and vermyn' named in the Elizabethan Acte for the Preservation of Grayne (1566) which made provision for a bounty to be paid for their destruction. Of all the mammals named in this list (including otters, pine martens, polecats, stoats, weasels and rats), foxes and badgers were singled out for a special rate of 12d. a head – three times that for any other animals and six times as much as otters: clearly they were viewed in a very poor light indeed. Lovegrove has made a valuable analysis of the evidence for subsequent payments from parish records up and down the country, recording wide fluctuations from different areas and from different times, but concluding that an average of about three badgers a year were removed from each parish by this means. This figure takes no account of animals killed in the course of the hunt or taken to be baited, which attracted no recompense from the churchwardens, and it also conceals much higher levels of mortality in some areas: the Revd Macpherson puts the average for Kendal at nine a year, augmented by others grouped together with foxes in the records.

Some degree of protection was extended to the badger by the terms of the Act for the more Effectual Prevention of Cruelty to Animals (1849), but in reality it seems to have made little impact in preventing the continuing attrition of the badger population over the following century.

THE BADGER IN THE WILD

Left to their own devices, badgers will choose to establish themselves on some secluded, well-drained and wooded slope, giving plenty of cover while remaining open to the warming rays of the sun. Their immensely strong front limbs, which make them such formidable assailants, have as their primary purpose the excavation of their set (or sett), a ramifying series of tunnels or pipes, some of them enlarged into chambers at the intersections to serve as living and sleeping quarters (sometimes termed kennels or ovens). Starting modestly, the set will be extended and elaborated

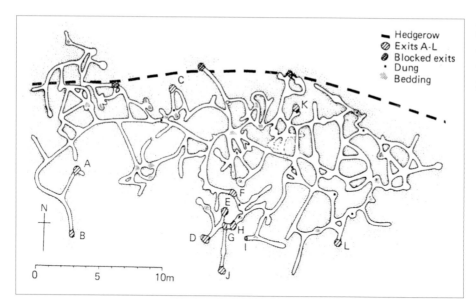

63 Plan of an extensive badger set in Gloucestershire, with 94 tunnels totalling 310 metres in length.

Legend:
- Hedgerow
- Exits A-L
- Blocked exits
- Dung
- Bedding

with each season (illus. 63): some are estimated to have been in continuous occupation for perhaps a hundred years and a number of them for several centuries, with tunnels on three or four levels and extending to a depth of 20 feet or more. A single family might excavate several subsidiary sets within easy reach of their primary residence, serving principally as boltholes.

For greater comfort, the various chambers in which they sleep the days away – for, as Turberville says, 'The Badgerd battles much with slepe, and is a verie fat beast' – and in which the young are born, are furnished with a carpet of soft leaves, assiduously collected every summer from June to August and equally rigorously cleaned out every spring. Pease describes how the badger might be seen going about the process of collection, 'bumping along backwards a heap of bracken and of grass or old straw . . . under his belly and encircled by his forefeet . . . [to] disappear tail first down his hole, still hugging and tugging his burden', a process later recorded in greater detail (and with accompanying photographs) by Eric Neal; Millais records seeing on one occasion as much as three

cartloads of old bedding of this kind being ejected again in the spring from a set in West Sussex. Badgers are prone to infestation by lice and ticks, and doubtless this fastidious routine helps keep the problem in check. Further scruple is displayed in the way they dig small, conical latrine pits at some distance outside the entrance to the set, in which they deposit their faeces. In Britain they have no natural enemies beyond men and their dogs. Both the accumulation of waste and the presence of latrine pits at the entrance provide all-too-visible clues for hunters that a particular set is in current occupation.

So accommodating are the badgers that many instances are recorded of other animals taking up residence in some part of the set, apparently without attracting the badgers' ire: although rabbits and rats have been found in dual occupancy (normally creating their own burrows within the complex), the most common interloper is the fox. The interaction between foxes and badgers is discussed at greater length below, but it will be enough to mention here that foxes have even been found bringing up their families within one or other of the blind tunnels in a set (though there are also instances of fox cubs being killed by ill-tempered badger sows, anxious for the well-being of their own young).

By way of diet they regularly forage for roots, bulbs, nuts and berries, as well as beetles, frogs, worms and snails. If the opportunity presents itself they will gladly make a meal of moles or hedgehogs, a nest of young rabbits or the eggs of partridge, pheasant and other ground-laying birds. Wasps' or bees' nests attract them both on account of the grubs and (in the case of bees) for the honey – Linnaeus's name for the species was *Meles ursus*, the honey-eating bear, but the name fell from use when it was established that the badger belongs with the Mustelidae and is not a member of the bear family (though some memory of the Linnaean nomenclature is perpetuated in the current name, *Meles meles*).

Badgers are monogamous by nature, but a well-established set may contain an extended family of several individuals; they are also gregarious and may regularly visit other sets within the neighbourhood without provoking adverse reaction (except, perhaps, in the presence of recently born cubs or females in oestrus). Cubs are said mostly to be born in March, no matter when conception might have taken place over the previous year, but young have been noted at all times of the spring and summer; up to four form a standard litter.

OBSERVING, HUNTING AND DIGGING THE BADGER

It is a reflection of the badger's elusiveness (and its comparative lack of impact on other, more highly valued natural resources) that it features relatively little in the early literature. Indeed, until the advent of keepered estates and of a growing general interest in natural history in the nineteenth century,

many country-dwellers not actively involved in pursuing them might well have gone through life with little consciousness of the existence of badgers in their midst and without ever catching sight of one.

Early notices

Never a beast of the chase, the badger (or 'grey' as it was called at the time) was dismissed by Edward, Duke of York, in his *Master of Game* as 'not a beast that needeth any great mastery to devise of how to hunt him, or to hunt him with strength, for a grey can fly but a little way before he is overcome with hounds, or else he goes to bay and then he is slain anon'. Later writers were prepared to acknowledge that the badger might still offer 'greate dysporte' in its pursuit, and there is plenty of evidence to suggest that organized hunting of the species has a long history.

Turberville in his *Booke of Huntyng* (1576) repeats the ancient belief (committed to print by Gessner amongst others) that there were two sorts of badgers to be found in Europe, one with paws like a dog and the other with cloven hooves. By introducing this information into a passage that otherwise confirms his genuine familiarity with the species, both in captivity and in the wild, he effectively blurs the distinction between fact and fable, no doubt confounding generations of his readers in the process:

For the better understandyng of the diversitie, let us coyne a worde, and call the one Badgerd-pigges, and the other Badgerdwhelpes . . . Bothe sortes . . . do greate hurte in Warreynes and Connigrees, especially when they be full of little rabbets . . . They pray also upon all Pullen, as Geese, Duckes, Hennes, and such lyke. I can speake by experience, for I have brought up some tame untill they were foure yeares olde, and being so brought up, they are verie gentle, and will playe with yong whelpes, and never hurt them . . . Those which I have brought up, would come to me at a call, and followe me like whelpes of houndes . . . It is a pleasure to beholde them when they gather stuffe for their nest or for their couch, as straw, leaves, mosse, and such other things: and with their forefeete and their heade, they will wrappe up as much together, as a man would carie under one arme, and will make shifte to get it into their holes and couches.

The provision of bedding in this way attracted the attention of Topsell in his *Historie of Foure-footed Beastes* (1607), where a curious belief is recorded:

This beast diggeth her a den or cave in the earth, and there liveth; never coming forth but for meat and easement, which it maketh out of his den: when they dig their den, after they have entred a good depth for avoiding the earth out, one of them falleth on the back, and the other layeth all the earth on his belly, and so taking his hinder feet in his mouth, draweth the belly-laden Badger out of the cave, which disburdneth her cariage, and goeth in for more till all be finished and emptied . . .

Evidently this was a widely held view, repeated by Nicholas Cox in his *Gentleman's Recreation* (1677) along with the assertion that 'his Legs are longer on the right side than the left, and therefore he runneth best when he gets on the side of an Hill, or a Cart-road-way'. Richard Blome further perpetuated many of these fantasies, but they had cold water poured on them by Arthur Stringer in

his *Experienced Huntsman*, first published in 1714, who wrote dismissively of the idea that one badger might use another as a 'sledge or drag' that 'I believe it to be the conceit or imagination of some unsolid projector who had no experience in the matter'. More usefully, Turberville, augmented by Cox, indicate between them that by the sixteenth and seventeenth centuries badger hunting and digging in the form later encountered was already a well-established practice. There were two options: either to go in pursuit at night when the badgers were out in search of food and to trap them as they were driven back into the burrow, or, having first ensured that they were indeed inside the set, to dig them out. For the first of these options a moonlit night would generally be chosen for the convenience of the hunters, whose first task was to locate the set (and all the subsidiary sets in the neighbourhood) and to block up the majority of the burrows. Within the remaining entrances sacks would be placed, each with its mouth held open by a 'bender' (a green switch or withy) or by an old barrel hoop. The dogs were then released to scour the area and to track the badger, driving it back to the set, while men beat the undergrowth to dislodge any animals that might be secreted there. Too early a find might put them in danger, for, as Turberville writes, 'if ye hounds chance to encounter him, or to undertake ye chase before he be gotten into his earth . . . then wil he stand at bay like a Bore, and make you good pastime'. Elsewhere Cox writes of the badger hunt:

If she be hunted abroad with Hounds, she biteth them most grievously where-ever she lays hold on them. For the prevention thereof, the careful Huntsmen put great broad Collars made of Grays Skins about their Dogs Necks. Her manner is to fight on her Back, using thereby both her Teeth and her Nails, and by blowing up her Skin after a strange and wonderful manner, she defendeth her self against any blow and Teeth of Dogs, onely a small stroke on her Nose will dispatch her presently; you may thrash your heart weary on her Back, which she values as a matter of nothing.

These statements were identified by Stringer amongst the many 'errors and gross mistakes' in Cox's work:

as to his fighting on his back, it is clean contrary, for while the badger keeps his feet hounds cannot kill him, he being so broad over the back and rough withall that the mouth of a hound can do him no harm; but when he comes to be thrown on his back, the least bite by the breast kills him dead . . . As to blowing up his skin, it is as true as the other . . . I have been at the death of several badgers and never saw any such thing.

Those badgers that escaped being cornered in the open and which made their way back to the set would instantly be trapped in one of the sacks placed in the entrance burrow. Turberville comments:

and as soone as the Badgerd is in the poke and streyneth it, the poke slippeth off the hoope and followeth him into the earth, and so he lieth, tumbling therein untill he be taken, and these men are of opinion, that as soone as ye Badgerds head is once within the Sacke or [poke], hee will lie still and wil not turne backe againe for any thing.

A man would be detailed to stand nearby to see that the badger did indeed remain in the sack, and

draw-strings or running loops were sometimes fitted to the neck to further contain the prisoner.

If, on the other hand, the badger was already in its set and had to be forcibly extracted, the dogs – specifically terriers – once more had a primary role, with one being sent down the burrow to attempt either to make the badger bolt or to keep it penned up in one spot, barking incessantly in order to pre-occupy the badger while the diggers made their way towards the noise. Even though its task was to keep the badger rooted to the spot rather than to attempt to overwhelm it, the role of the terrier was a tremendously challenging one to which very few dogs proved equal: if the pressure were not kept up the badger was likely to try to rush the terrier in order to escape down another of its burrows, so a fresh terrier would be sent in at regular intervals over however many hours or days the operation might take. Alternatively, the badger might try to dig itself in where it stood, so placing itself beyond the reach of the terrier and of the diggers. These tactics were already well understood in Turberville's time:

This subtletie they have, that when they perceive the Terryers beginne to yearne [bark at] them, and to lye at them, they will stoppe the hole betweene the Terryers and them, least the Terryers should followe them any further: and then if the Terryers baye still, they will remove their baggage with them, and go into another chamber or angle in their Burrowe.

Cox too, though extensively plagiarizing Turberville, has a good description of the badgers' technique of 'barricadoing the way as they go' – an effective subterfuge well attested by later diggers. As the *Sporting Dictionary* has it, 'in a light or sandy soil, badgers can make way as fast from their pursuers, as the latter erroneously conceive they are gaining ground upon them, and to this perhaps it is owing that there are so many drawn battles between the pursuers and the pursued'.

Turberville was also the first to advise the use of a number of 'good and arrant Terriers, garnished with collers full of belles, to make the . . . Badgerd start the soner', observing that these collars 'wil be some defence to save them from hurting', and although these recommendations were repeated by later writers into the eighteenth century they were rejected thereafter on the grounds that the bells were in fact totally ineffectual and collars more likely to strangle the terrier by getting snagged on roots rather than affording it any protection. Meanwhile a whole panoply of tools would be deployed in order to reach the badger. Turberville recommends the following:

> The instruments to digge withal must be these, sharpe poynted Spades, round hollowed Spades, and flatte broade Spades, Howes, or Mattocks, and Pickaxes, a Colerake and a payre of Clampes or Holdfasts, Shovells both shodde and bare, an Axe and a sharpe paring Spade, the sharp pointed Spade serveth to begin ye trench first, where the ground is hardest and broader tooles would not so wel enter: the round hollowed Spade serveth to digge amongst Rootes, and may be so made with such sharpe edges, that it will cut the rootes also: the flat broade Spade, to digge withall when the trench is better opened and the ground softer: the Howes, Mattocks, and Pickaxes to digge with in harder grounde where a Spade will make no riddance of the worke: the Colerake to clense the hole and to keepe it from stopping up: the clampes or holdfasts to take a Foxe or Badgerd out alive, wherewith

you may make pastime afterwards, or to help the terriers when they are aferd to bite a vermine: ye Shovels both shod and bare, serve to cast out ye earth which the Spades or Mattocks have digged, according to ye hardnesse or softnesse of ye grounde wherein you digge: the paring Spade to keepe the trench in fashion: and the Axe to cut the rootes or any other thing withall . . . And wt these instruments and such like necessary implements a Lord or Gentleman may fill a prettie little Cart or Wagon made for ye purpose, ye which he may cause to be carried on field with him, always provided that when the sayd cariage is loded, he forget not to cause his Cooke and Butler to hang good store of bags and bottels about the raves and pinnes thereof.

So generously provided, Turberville anticipated that while the hired hands got on with the task of digging out the quarry, the 'Lord or Gentleman' would take his ease on the greensward – or, more appropriately, on what was clearly a remarkably early form of airbed:

> a Lord or Gentleman whiche will follow this pastime, should have halfe a dozen Mattes to lie uppon the ground on, as they hearken to the Terriers: some use to carrie a windbed whiche is made of leather strongly sowed on all the foure sides, and having a Pype at one of the corners to blow it as you woulde blowe a Baggepype, and when it is blowen full of wind to stoppe it up and lie upon it on the grounde: but this were too great curiositie: and yet a Lord or Gentleman cannot take too great heede of the colde and moysture of the earthe, for he may thereby take sundrie diseases and infirmities.

These comforts aside, the language in which Turberville describes the dig evokes the excitement and the attraction it held for the dedicated hunter, who saw himself committed to an epic struggle with his enemy: 'In this order of battell, a noble man or gentleman may march to besiege the Foxe and Badgerd, in their strongest holes and castles. And may breake their Casmates, Platformes, Parapets, and worke to them with Mynes, and countermines, untill they get their skynnes, to make furres and myttens.' The inevitable conclusion of the struggle lacked much in the way of glamour, however, usually ending in the use of 'clampes or holdfasts to take a Foxe or Badgerd out alive, wherewith you may make pastime afterwards' (illus. 64), or by the simple (though lhazardous) expedient of hauling it up by the tail and dropping it into a sack. Although holdfasts continued to form part of the badger-digger's standard equipment up to the twentieth century (see below), an alternative suggested by Arthur Stringer in the eighteenth century bore

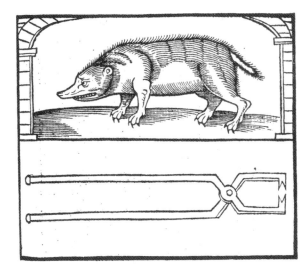

64 The badger, from Turberville's *Booke of Huntyng*; prominent below the (hopelessly generalized) beast are the all-too-believable iron tongs or holdfasts with which he was to be drawn from his set.

more resemblance to a shepherd's crook. While discussing it first in terms of fox-hunting, he goes on to say that it is 'full as necessary for pulling out a badger':

the best and easiest method of getting out a fox when earthed, is to carry a little crook in your pocket about eight inches long with a socket and a hole for a nail. When you happen to earth a fox, cut a stick . . . and put it into the socket of the crook and nail it on, and if within reach of him you shall very rarely (if ever) fail to pull him out . . . This crook that I have mentioned is a much better way than the clamps or pincers which I find all our former writers speak of. For I cannot find it possible to take a vermin out of the earth with them, unless you were within four or five foot of it; but I have with a crook pulled out several foxes and badgers, nine or ten foot further than my hand could reach. Beside, the crook is carried in your pocket without trouble.

Although most badger hunts had no motivation other than sport – or at least vermin control – there might be some economic dimension to the chase. Already in the *Master of Game* the badger is acknowledged as

the beast of the world that gathereth most grease within and that is because of the long sleeping that he sleepeth. And his grease bears medicine as does that of a fox, and yet more, and men say that if a child that hath never worn shoes is first shod with those made of the skin of the grey that child will heal a horse of farcy if he should ride upon him, but thereof I make no affirmation.

Turberville repeats much of the Duke of York's estimate of the inherent virtues of the badger and as late as 1800 the *Sporting Magazine* is found extolling an astonishing range of properties supposedly inherent in a variety of badger products:

> The flesh, blood, and grease of the badger are very useful for oils, ointments, salves, and powders, for shortness of breath, the cough of the lungs, for the stone, sprained sinews, coll-achs, etc. The skin, being well dressed, is very warm and comfortable for ancient people who are troubled with paralytic disorders.

The fur was not very highly esteemed: according to Turberville 'The skynne of a Badgerd, is not so good as the Foxes, for it serveth for no use, unlesse it be to make myttens, or to dress horsecollers withall.'

Contrary to the assertion in the *Master of Game* that it was inedible, some people found badger meat highly acceptable. Cox reports that it was eaten in Italy and Germany, but that while 'some have eaten it here in England, [they] like it not, being of a sweet rankish taste'. (Turberville had earlier described it as 'wallowish sweet and rammish': 'I my selfe have eaten of it', he continues, 'and digested it well, and without any maner of annoyance'.) Others were even more positive – for example in his *Notitia Venatica*, first published in the 1840s, Robert Vyner writes:

> The author of these observations has both cured and eaten the hams of badgers himself, and can answer for their excellence. They should be cured by the receipt for doing pig's hams, in which he used a little garlic and sugar and treacle, which render them much more mellow. They should be smoked and grated like tongue or dried beef, which they far excell in flavour.

Later encounters

By the nineteenth century, badger digging had been embraced by many of the sporting gentry whose aim was not always the extermination of the quarry but more often the sheer enjoyment of the pursuit, perhaps prompted by other considerations such as the unwitting interference of a badger with local fox-hunting. Combined with an increasing aversion to the wilful persecution of the badger, there was by now also a growing sense that its numbers were in serious decline and even that its continuing survival was imperilled: as early as 1846 Charles St John had judged it 'likely soon to be extirpated'; Harvie Brown felt that populations had been diminished, although he knew too that in some areas it had fared better than in others, partly due to measures for its protection put in place by some landowners; James Ritchie was inclined to attribute some part of its decline to the rapid spread of cultivation and of the destruction of forests seen from the mid-1800s.

By the end of the nineteenth century, according to H. A. Bryden, one or two dedicated Badger Clubs had been formed, operating according to strict rules. By this time a reasonable stock of foxes was actively sought after so that regular sport could be provided for the hunt – even to the extent of encouraging them to take up residence by digging artificial earths, roofed over with timber or thorn bushes. If it should happen that a badger decided to capitalize on this initiative and to extend the earth for his own quarters, he was likely to find himself 'banished' by the hunt and subjected to digging. Vyner, in his *Notitia Venatica*, observes: 'Badgers are a sad nuisance when they take to an artificial earth, and should be immediately caught, or they will in a short time pull down and destroy the whole of the interior.' The process of removing them became a welcome extension of the chase for some of the stouter devotees who would relish a day spent out in the woods as a pleasure in itself. Fairfax Blakeborough mentions one such in the Exmoor and West Somerset area who claimed to have dug out ten to twenty brace each season over a twenty-year period, most of which were removed to new quarters rather than being killed.

The actual process of digging was back-breaking work, usually delegated to a few workmen and to volunteers who seem never to have been in short supply: Fairfax Blakeborough makes reference to 'that little band of men one discovers in every locality, who rarely miss an otter hunt, the digging out of a fox, the drawing of a badger, or the many expeditions with hound, terrier, gun and spade, which every now and then punctuate rural life'. The little band would come (if permitted) with their own dogs, eager to test their courage in the field, and armed with a considerable array of tools considered essential for the process of dislodging the occupant (illus. 65), these bearing a remarkable resemblance to those described by Turberville three centuries earlier. The shovels would now be of sheet metal rather than having iron-shod wooden blades as in the sixteenth century, but otherwise the tongs or holdfasts for grasping the badger in the final moments are the only items to show much development. For these, Pease suggests:

the handles should be made of wood, as steel and iron 'give' under pressure of a man's strength at one end and the badger at the other. With wooden handles and steel fittings there is enough spring to work the guard, which is put on to secure the animal.

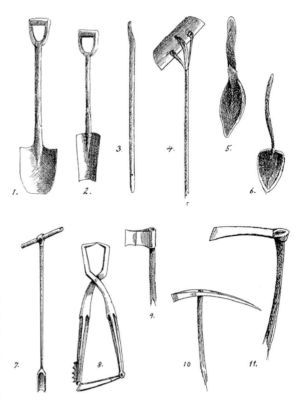

65 Implements for badger-digging, adapted from Sir Alfred Pease, *The Badger* (1898). 1 'ordinary gardening or rabbiting spade'; 2 'drainer's long narrow [spade]'; 3 crowbar; 4 scraper or coal-rake; 5-6 hand-shovels 'for opening the holes to let in air to the dogs'; 7 auger or 'earth piercer, in order to locate the fight'; 8 holdfasts with which to seize the badger; 9 hatchet; 10 pick; 11 mattock.

Descriptions of these excavations (several of them from around the turn of the twentieth century) provide some of the best early accounts of the extent and complexity of sets (as well as evidence for multiple occupancy by other species encountered along the way). Fairfax Blakeborough, for example, recalls one occasion when such a dig ended up with a trench 22 yards long and 22 feet deep before reaching the quarry. These pursuits had no aim beyond the capture or extermination of the occupants, however, and it is only with the more scientific investigation of set construction in recent years that their full extent and complexity has come to be appreciated (see illus. 63).

By way of out-of-season occupation for the foxhounds, some sportsmen took to hunting badgers *par force*, with the intention of running them down in the manner of a fox, with the hounds confronting them above ground and before they had an opportunity to go to earth. Given the nocturnal habits of the badger, these hunts necessarily took place at night, as reported by Bryden in 1904:

> A season or two back a pack of hounds, the Axe Vale, were got together in the West of England to hunt badgers at night. Ten and a half couples [of hounds] were used, and very good sport was shown. At first moonlight nights were chosen, but it was found that the hounds ran just as keenly in black darkness as by light of the moon. On these occasions the master and whippers-in wore belts and carried policemen's lanterns. This may be classed as a legitimate sport . . .

In the spring of 1902, he reports, the Axe Vale killed seven badgers and ran two to ground. Most nineteenth-century writers, however, were eager to stress the non-lethal nature of the sport they followed and to distance themselves from the badger baiters (and indeed from the gamekeepers who brought about many badger deaths in the cause of preserving their stocks of game-birds). While vigorously defending badger digging, H. H. King – a confirmed terrier man – conceded that it might sound like dull sport:

> but to those who love good terriers and make and work their own, who have studied woodcraft and have learnt to interpret some at least of the signs and sounds of wild animals

and birds, a day spent in the woods or on the hillside badger-digging in the company of gamekeepers, woodmen and others of that ilk is a good day.

Enthusiasts like King certainly saw themselves as playing no role in persecuting the badger but rather championed it against those interested merely in its extermination or persecution by baiting. Even the gamekeepers whose fellowship he enjoyed must have been of an enlightened kind, for many of them would gladly have cleared badgers completely from the estates they oversaw. The spring traps favoured by many of their number against 'vermin' were, incidentally, largely ineffectual against badgers: they would almost invariably smell them out if laid in the entrance to the set and would either simply go round them or would set them off by rolling over them. Often a tuft of hair from the badger's heavily clad skin was as much as the trapper was likely to retrieve.

The *Field Book* mentions that in the 1830s badger skin was still favoured for pistol furniture and the hair for painters' brushes of the finest quality. (Until recently, shaving brushes were commonly of badger hair.) A new market for badger products arose with the increasing popularity of elaborate Highland dress amongst the Scots (see, for example, the portrait of *The MacNab* by Sir Henry Raeburn, *c.* 1810, in the Kelvingrove Art Gallery, Glasgow), including the wearing of sporrans made from the facial mask of the badger. This tendency received a tremendous boost following the first visit of Queen Victoria to Scotland in 1842 – described by Harvie Brown as 'a sad year for the poor Badgers' – and more particularly when certain Scottish regiments adopted badger sporrans: officers and senior NCOs of the 93rd Regiment of Foot, the Sutherland Highlanders, were so equipped and the tradition continued after their amalgamation in 1881 to form the Argyll and Sutherland Highlanders.

BADGER-BAITING

Few creatures defend themselves better, or bite with greater keenness, than the badger: on that account it is frequently baited with dogs trained for that purpose, and defends itself from their attacks with astonishing agility and success . . . this singular creature is able to resist repeated attacks both of men and dogs, from all quarters, till, being overpowered with numbers, and enfeebled by many desperate wounds, it is at last obliged to yield.

In this matter-of-fact account from the *Field Book* of 1833, the badger's natural courage – invariably deployed in its own defence rather than used aggressively – can be seen to have sealed its fate at the hands of those with no more thought than to try the courage of their dogs or merely to enjoy the spectacle of what was, despite the qualities displayed by the badger, an uneven combat: if not killed outright where it stood, the only other outcome might be that it was preserved to be baited another day, until ultimately it succumbed.

The odds were further stacked against the badger by various measures designed either to extend the combat or to save the dogs from an early death. Turberville provides suggestions as to the manner in which the badger, having been captured alive and placed in a sack, 'you may . . . hunt with Terryers in your gardens or close courts, at your pleasure'. He further gives chilling hints as to how the badger may be emasculated so that the dogs might gain familiarity with their quarry and so improve their performance on their next expedition into the field:

Take them and cut away the nether Jawe . . . and never touche the upper Jawe, but let it stand to shewe the furie of the Beast, although it can do no hurte therwith: then make an earth in some of your closes and make it large inough, because that the Terryers may fight and turne therein the better, and that they may go in two together: then cover the borowe or earth with bordes and turves, and put the Foxe or Badgerd therein: then put in al your Terryers both yong and old, and encourage them with wordes . . . as the Arte requyreth. And when they have yearned [barked] sufficiently, then begin to dig with spades and mattockes to encorage them agaynst such tyme as you must use to digge over them: then take out the Foxe or Badgerde with the clampes or pinchers, killyng it before them, or lette a Greyhounde kill it in their sight and make them reward thereof . . . If you will not cut the Jawe of the Foxe or Badgerd, then break out al his teeth that he bite not the Terryers, and it shall suffyze as well.

Writing in the early 1700s, Stringer continues to stress the usefulness of these encounters with a captive badger in familiarizing the terriers with their potential opponents: 'the greatest use he is for, is to kill him with hounds or mastiffs, or if you have young terriers that you would enter, the best way is to cope or muzzle him so that he cannot bite, and put him into an earth made on purpose, and encourage your terriers to him'. By the late eighteenth century the practice had been refined only to the extent that new methods had been found to increase the badger's torment. The *Sporting Magazine* for 1788 reports:

They dig a place in the earth about a yard long, so that one end is four feet deep. At this

66 Badger-baiting, from Henry Alken's *National Sports of Great Britain*, first published 1820. The figure on the right sits astride a box-like structure, which typically would have turned in a right-angle just out of the picture; the badger was introduced at one end, the terrier at the other. The angle replicated a feature commonly found in badger sets, offering a degree of cover from which a defence could be mounted against an intruder.

end a strong stake is driven down. Then the badger's tail is split, a chain put through it, and fastened to the stake with such ability that the badger can come up to the other end of the place. The dogs are brought and set upon the poor animal, who sometimes destroys several dogs before it is killed.

While Pease voiced his disapproval of the practice in 1898, he none the less conceded that 'there are degrees of wickedness' and gave instead details of the 'correct' form of an L-shaped box-like structure to be used in baiting (illus. 66), observing that 'when a badger is placed in a properly constructed badger-box there are few terriers that would not be vanquished in the encounter'. An alternative form, lacking the right-angled bend, had been described a few years earlier by Macpherson:

> The contest took place in a wooden structure something like an old-fashioned clock-case in appearance. It measured in length from 7 to 8 feet. The depth and height about 3 feet. One extremity of the case was partitioned off for the Badger's den. This recess was entered by a hole, either round or square, through which the dog had to seize the Badger and drag it forth. The case was of necessity strongly built, and barred above.

While these arrangements had the advantage of providing terriers with experience of the badger, which (if they survived) they might in future carry into the field, none of them provided much in the way of viewing opportunities (though the grille on top of the structure described by Macpherson provided some means of following the course of events within). No doubt the public baitings that took place and which attracted some dozens of spectators at a time were conducted in full view of the crowd and with no thought for recreating any semblance of a natural habitat for the badger. Henry Alken mentions as an 'illustrious example' of the prowess of some terriers, that 'within these few years the dog of a ge[ntle]man . . . drew a fresh, strong, and game badger, 74 times in ten minutes'.

Even after the worst excesses of treatment in this way were rendered illegal under the terms of the Act relating to the Cruel and Improper Treatment of Animals (1835), it is clear that there remained a community that liked nothing better than seeing a badger worried to death by dogs. By the later decades of the nineteenth century the hunting community was at pains to distance itself from this practice, which was presented as an attribute of the lower social classes. Thus H. A. Bryden, in his *Nature and Sport in Great Britain* writes:

> Country people and dog fanciers have a rather senseless predilection for digging out badgers and killing them. This is, probably, a relic of the barbarous 'badgering' craze of our rude ancestors. There is little of sport or pleasure in the business. The badger is much worried but seldom killed by the dogs employed. He is usually slain by a blow with a heavy bludgeon . . .

Rather curiously, Alfred Pease in what he justly claimed as the first monograph dedicated to the badger (1898) and in which he condemned baiting unreservedly, thought that the end of the practice (at least in the eyes of the law) would have unhappy consequences for the creature: 'Badger-baiting, it seems, was the price the race had to pay for its existence', he wrote, 'and with the happy disuse of a brutal sport the harmless badger has been doomed to extinction'. Fortunately his assessment that 'the only method by which any British wild animal can be preserved from extinction in this age of what is termed progress, is to hunt it' proved unnecessarily pessimistic, and in any case illicit badger digging and baiting remained widespread in Britain.

DEER AND HARE COURSING

With the rise of the drive hunt (pp. 130–31) the chase was in some sense brought within the realm of spectator sports, a development that was taken one step further with the advent of deer coursing. In coursing the possibility of chance survival for the quarry was further diminished: here deer which previously had been trapped with nets and held in a paddock were released one at a time to be pursued by greyhounds from one end to the other of a delimited stretch of track, the principal element of interest being to see which hound would outrun the other. Often these were effectively two-hound races, but from the sixteenth century it became customary for some low-grade dog (the 'teazer') to drive the captured deer over the first 150 yards to what was known as the law-post, at which point the greyhounds would be released in order to course it over the last mile or so towards the spectators; bets would be placed on which hound would outrun the deer.

To either side of the course, spectators would be stationed to take their entertainment from the spectacle; the siting of such courses within the parks of the aristocracy ensured that audiences were limited to those of suitable status. Griffin mentions examples at Ravensdale (Derbyshire), where the course, 80 yards wide and a mile in length, was marked out with hedges in an arrangement that may have originated as early as the fourteenth century; at Clarendon Park (Wiltshire) fences took the place of the hedges, while elsewhere temporary courses were established with no more than posts and ropes. In the Little Park at Windsor a course was laid out probably in the mid-fifteenth century: in the reign of Elizabeth it was described by John Stow as a 'lawnde or coursynge place, rennynge all ye lengthe of ye parke, and all ye hill servynge as a continuall standynge to beholde and judge of ye course wt ease'. John Norden's survey of the park notes the position of another 'standing', evidently constructed especially to provide a viewpoint, and yet others were constructed on a temporary basis: Jane Roberts finds in the Lord Chamberlain's accounts for the visit of the Duc de Brion in 1601 payments 'for makeing readie a standinge in the little P[ar]ke at Windsor against ye huntinge there, for two daies'. Deer coursing continued at Windsor into the seventeenth century.

The best-preserved coursing installation is that at Lodge Park (Gloucestershire), which has been the subject of a recent survey by Katie Fretwell. The course was laid out by John 'Crump' Dutton, who acquired in 1618 the Sherborne estate on which the park lies. Sixteen years later, a visitor left an impression not only of the course but also of the handsome lodge that Dutton had constructed, from whose balcony and roof-terrace spectators could view the whole course:

> This stately Lodge was lately built at the great Cost and Charges of a noble true hearted gentleman, more for the pleasure of his worthy friends, than to his own profit; It is richly furnished to entertaine them to see the kingly sport, and pleasure, admirably performed, in the rare Paddock course of a Mile in length, and wall'd on either side. There I spent a full houre, with the good favour of the Keeper, in viewing that neat, rare Building, the rich furnish'd rooms, the hansome contriv'd Pens and Places, where the Deere are kept, and turn'd out for the Course; all the manner, and order of the Paddock Sport.

The course, still visible on the ground, narrows progressively along its mile length, from some 220 yards to just under 100 yards, exactly in the manner specified in the later *Sportsman's Dictionary*.

Fretwell reproduces 'The Articles and Orders of the Paddock Course at Shireborn in Gloucestershire', a document in eighteenth-century hand which, she observes, depends heavily on contemporary printed sources such as the *Dictionary* and ultimately on Richard Blome's *Gentleman's Recreation* of 1686, but which includes references to a number of local features that contribute towards a reconstruction of the course of events. Two types of spectacle were on offer: a 'breathing course' primarily for the exercise of the hounds, in which the deer (usually fallow) was intended to be preserved, and a 'fleshing course' which culminated with its destruction; fees were charged to gentlemen wishing to enter hounds, varying according to the type of course required and the level of the betting. The keeper was to be given a day's warning so that suitable deer could be put up in the holding pen at the start of the course, while the hounds were to be brought to the slips at an agreed hour before the course. Once the deer had been set running had passed the law-post, the keeper would slip the hounds 'with a falling collar, which is slipt thro' the rings'. Further down the course was a second marker, termed the pinching-post: if the deer turned back before the pinching-post, the course was declared invalid, while if one or other of the hounds 'pinched' the deer before it reached the pinching post, it would be declared the winner. The end of the course was marked with a transverse ditch: a deer that managed to outrun the hounds and leap the ditch was to regain its freedom (or rather it would be confined to a second paddock, no doubt to be coursed another day), while the hound that first followed it across the ditch would be declared the winner. Judges were to be stationed at the pinching post and at the ditch, in order to ensure proper conduct.

Deer coursing seems to have fallen from general favour at the turn of the eighteenth century, giving way, perhaps, to racing on the one hand and to fox-hunting on the other.

Alongside this new form of trial for the deer, hare coursing increased in popularity, not least as a vehicle for heavy betting. Two hounds were released together in pursuit of one hare, the winner being the one that killed the hare. Early references to the practice are lacking, but by the sixteenth century at the latest elaborate rules had been developed – according to the *Sporting Dictionary* by the Duke of Norfolk in the reign of Queen Elizabeth. Early coursing had taken place in a country setting without need for elaborate preparation: beaters searched out the hare, which was coursed wherever it was found. The rules as recorded in the *Sporting Dictionary* refer to this 'free range' era, in which the hare was found and coursed in its natural habitat: the two greyhounds to be coursed were placed in the charge of a handler who would be responsible for releasing them from their slips or thongs, and who would follow the hare finder into the field, with the spectators some 40 yards behind; if the terrain permitted, the hare was to have 'twelve score yards law' when it was put up before the greyhounds were released, after which the hounds acquired points for a variety of manoeuvres – turn, cote, slip, wrench, tripping, jerkin, go-by, bearing – as well as for the death.

By the time this account was published, however, the common form of hare coursing had already changed. By 1776 Lord Orford of Houghton Hall (Norfolk) and 25 gentlemen had formed the Swaffham Coursing Society, sponsoring meetings in November and February. Other clubs soon followed, composed in the words of the *Sporting Dictionary* of 'the most opulent and respectable members, meeting two or three times a year and holding inter-county matches with crowds of several 100s and betting.' Notable groups were those at Bradwell and Tillingham (Essex), Flixton (Yorkshire), and at Ashdown Park (Berkshire)

and Epsom (Surrey). Hares were now trapped in advance and released into an enclosed arena – more visible to the spectators but leaving the hare no chance of escape. If the experience offered less excitement, it had certain compensations, for the *Sportsman's Dictionary* commented with some candour in 1778 that:

Coursing with Grey-Hounds, is a recreation in great esteem with many gentlemen. It affords greater pleasure than hunting in some respects. As, First, because it is sooner ended. Secondly, it does not require so much toil. Thirdly, the game is for the most part always in sight. Fourthly, in regard to the delicate qualities and shape greyhound.

COCKS AND COCKFIGHTING

Every year on the day called Carnival . . . scholars from the different schools bring fighting-cocks to their masters, and the whole morning is set apart to watch their cocks do battle in the schools, for the boys are given a holiday that day.

The custom of Shrove Tuesday cockfighting in London, as recorded *c.* 1170–1183 in the prologue to fitz Stephen's *Life of Thomas Becket*, forms the earliest reference to the sport in the English language and conjures up a world remote from the highly charged atmosphere in which the sport was conducted on the eve of its ultimate proscription by statute in 1849. Its progress from festive schoolboy pastime to highly regulated public contest, in which large sums of money – not to mention personal or civic pride – were staked, spans a great swath of English social history. Royal patronage was extended under the Tudors and Stuarts; treatises on the subject were published for the benefit of seventeenth-century gentlemen; aristocrats and industrial workers vied with each other in the breeding of all-conquering specimens in the era of industrial expansion; and finally, rising public revulsion at the slaughter regularly enacted in the cockpit led to its being outlawed under the Act for the More Effectual Prevention of Cruelty to Animals.

FORMATIVE YEARS

The juvenile milieu alluded to in fitz Stephen's account may have been characteristic rather than exceptional in the early years of the sport, and its popularity (and indeed active encouragement) in the scholarly context – especially on annual feast-days – would continue up to the nineteenth century, often with an appropriate fee (the cock-penny) being paid to the master. Not until the 1200s do we find the first mention of adult interest in England, but given the acknowledged antiquity of the sport in the classical world (see below) it would not be surprising if some form of such amusement had not long preceded its entry into the historical record. By 1365 Edward III was moved to call on the authorities in the City of London to issue a proclamation forbidding a number of pastimes, including cockfighting, and to compel able-bodied men 'at leisure times on holidays to . . . learn and exercise the art of shooting' with the bow. No aversion to cockfighting itself seems to be implied in Edward's command, beyond the distraction of the citizenry from their martial training, and indeed the practice was later hallowed by royal approval under Henry VIII. The iconic building Henry constructed at Whitehall in 1533–4 to house the first purpose-built cockpit in England is easily recognizable in contemporary topographical views, its tall pitched roof with a lantern on top standing out among the lower

ranges of the palace. The *History of the King's Works* reproduces the expenditure on a variety of details which hint at its sumptuous appearance, adorned with 'beasts of stone' and fitted out with 'seatts, borders, pendans, chappitrells, armys, badgys and dyvers other thyngs', many of the details gilded for maximum effect. An account of a visit by the Spanish physician and scholar Andrés de Laguna only five years later sets the scene for the cockpit itself and for much of what follows. The following is from a translation of the document of 1599 by René Graziani:

In London in the year 1539 I observed the extraordinary virtues and courage of these cocks. King Henry the Eighth of that name had had a sumptuous amphitheatre of fine workmanship built, designed like a colosseum and intended exclusively for fights and matches between these little animals. Round about the circumference of the enclosure there were innumerable coops, belonging to many princes and lords of the kingdom. In the centre of this colosseum, if I remember correctly, stood a sort of short, upright, truncated column about a span and a half from the ground in height and so thick that a man could scarcely get his hands around it. Very heavy bets on the mettle and valour of the cocks were customarily made by the noblemen. The cocks were brought out from the cages already mentioned where they were tended and pampered with the greatest diligence. They are placed two at a time on the column in full view of the great numbers of spectators. The jewels and valuables which were bet on them were placed in the middle. These are taken by whoever's cock wins . . . As soon as they are placed in their positions by their handlers, they start confronting each other with the boldness and resolution of two martial captains, beating their wings and erecting their coxcombs [*crestas* – more properly hackles] to join battle. Then after each has watchfully stepped round the circle, they as it were twine themselves together so bloodily and cruelly that they do not disengage until one or the other of them is left stretched out on the earth. The other is so badly mauled and covered with wounds that it too dies within a few hours. This latter one, as soon as it sees itself the victor, notwithstanding its great loss of blood and that it lacks breath and strength, flies over its conquered adversary and begins to crow with a feeble, worn-out voice as its signal of victory. They summoned for its cure many expert surgeons – for there are special salaried ones in London just for wounded cocks – but no remedy or medicine is of any use against the Fates. After its death, the owner of the cock will swear that he would not have taken a thousand ducats for him.

Writing two or three generations after that, at which time the cockpit was still in intensive use, George Wilson records not only the delight taken by 'our late Prince of famous memory' but also the influence exerted by the structure he had built at Whitehall,

> wherein his Majestie might disport himselfe with Cocke-fighting, among his most noble and loving subjects, who in like manner did affect that pastime so well, and conceived so good an opinion of it, not onely because the King was so addicted to it, but also in regard of the great valor and incomparable courage that the Cockes shewed in their battels, the which did inflame their hearts, that

they caused Cocke-pits to be made in many Citties, Boroughes, and Townes throughout the whole Realme. To which Cocke-pits resorted, both Dukes, Earles, Lords, Knights, Gentlemen, and Yeomen, there to recreate and delight themselves, with Cocke-fighting.

A reference from 1604 (the year after James I's accession) to the need to replace the matting with which it was covered, now 'broken and torne with Cockes fighting there', indicates that the Whitehall cockpit remained in regular use up to his reign.

James granted to George Colmer the office of Cockmaster, to be held for life and to have the authority to decide on disputes over wagers concerning cockfighting. Later in the same reign 100 marks per annum were paid to William Gateacre for 'breeding, feeding, &c. the King's Game Cocks' during the lifetime of Colmer, on whose death his office would fall to Gateacre. By now the sport had acquired a demonstrable country-wide following, with inter-county matches regularly being arranged.

During the Commonwealth, cockfighting was (along with other sports) singled out for official disapproval, not on moral grounds but on the basis that it provided a cover for potentially seditious gatherings. On 11 March 1651 the Council of State wrote to the 'Militia Commissioners of the several Counties' in the following terms:

> We have many informations that the enemies of this commonwealth are still driving on their designs to raise new troubles amongst us, and holding many dangerous meetings . . . for contriving and disposing of their plots, under colour and pretence of cockfighting, horse racing, hunting, and other meetings for recreation.

Henceforth the Militia was to attend and to prevent or disperse any such meetings.

Not surprisingly, with the Restoration these measures were thrown into reverse by a monarch who delighted in sports. The following account of Charles II comes from the memoirs of Sir John Reresby:

> The King was soe much pleased in the country, and soe great a lover of the diversions which that place did afford, that he lett himself down from Majesty to the very degree of a country gentleman. He mixed himselfe amongst the croud, allowed every man to speak to him that pleased, went a-hawkeing in mornings, to cock matches in afternoons (if ther were noe hors races), and to plays in the evenings.

The continuing development and spread of cockfighting in the eighteenth century and beyond is discussed below. In the meantime, a series of tracts produced in the 1600s establishes the basis of later understanding of the sport, although it is clear that the texts constitute little more than a literary formalization of long-established conventions already hallowed by centuries of everyday practice. They also mark the definitive acknowledgement of cockfighting as a polite pastime: while it had benefited from the support of two monarchs – both of them, admittedly, passionate for field sports beyond all normal bounds – the authors of these works took pains to emphasize the patronage that cockfighting now received from the generality of the aristocracy and from gentlemen of respectable character – the very audience whom they sought to address. By the time Robert Howlett published his contribution to this output in the opening years of the eighteenth century, the title of his work confirmed the status of the sport

as fitting for the highest in the land – *The Royal Pastime of Cock-Fighting*. Using these tracts as a framework, something of the practice of cockfighting can be reconstructed and the qualities sought in the birds themselves can be identified.

THE 'OLD ENGLISH GAME FOWL'

While belonging to the same genus as the domestic fowl, *Gallus gallus*, by dint of rigorous selective breeding fighting cocks (also called game-cocks, match-cocks or battle-cocks) were isolated over the centuries as a distinctive strain, characterized by medium-sized but muscular build; broad-shouldered with an elongated cone-shaped body and with powerful legs, their heads were armed with a formidable beak. In his *Commendation of Cockes* (1607) George Wilson is fulsome in his peroration in praise of true fighting cocks and dismissive in equal measure of their cousins, the 'Dung-hill, or craven Cockes', of which he writes that 'the best and chiefest pastime that they will or can make you is, when they are well boyled, or stewed, and layed in a platter with good store of plumbes about them'. All writers agree on the peerless standing of these birds among the fowls. The following is from Thomas Bewick:

> The appearance of the Gamecock, when in his full plumage, and not mutilated for the purpose of fighting, is strikingly beautiful and animated; his head, which is small, is adorned with a beautiful red comb, and his chin and throat with wattles; his eyes sparkle with fire, and his whole demeanour bespeaks boldness and freedom. The feathers on his neck are long, slender and pointed, and fall gracefully down upon his body, which is thick, muscular and compact; his tail is long, and the flexile feathers which fall over it form a

beautiful arch behind, which gives a grace to all his motions; his legs are strong, and armed with sharp spurs, with which he defends himself, and attacks his adversary; he lays hold with his beak, and strikes with the feet and wings. When surrounded by his females, his whole aspect is full of animation . . .

A number of varieties of these noble birds are distinguished by their plumage (illus. 67), with the Black-breasted Red acknowledged as the classic type. Amongst numerous other varieties may be mentioned some whose descriptive names are self-explanatory – the Silver Duckwing, Black, White, Dun, and, by virtue of certain feminine traits in its appearance, Henny – and others of more obscure origin, for example Pole Cats, Tassels and Muffs. Early writers, notably Gervase Markham in his *Pleasures of Princes* (1614) – reproduced thereafter in his *Country Contentments* (issued in thirteen editions between 1615 and 1676 and representing in that form the most influential tract of its kind), place considerable importance on colouring as an indicator of the character of the cock – 'If he be Red about the head, like scarlet, it is a sign of lust, strength and courage; but if he be pale, it is a sign of sickness and faintness'. Later opinion, supported by extended experience in the cockpit, denies that colour is of the least significance, and even decidedly henny cocks are sometimes recorded as having triumphed over more classically coloured opponents. (The author of an entry on game-cocks in Abraham Rees's *Cyclopædia* suggests that on occasion these henny cocks were able to deliver a killer blow before their opponents had even woken up to their masculinity.)

Finding themselves in fortunate possession of a successful bird, owners were at pains to capitalize on its good points by careful breeding. Doubtless the ideal breeding pair would each be outstanding in their own right, but while some placed predominant importance on the father's role, Markham and his followers were persuaded that the mother was key:

And it is a Note amongst the best breeders, That the perfect Hen from a Dunghill Cock, will bring a good Chicken, but the best Cock from a Dunghill Hen can never get a good bird; and I have known in mine own experience, that the two famousest Cocks that ever fought in these dayes, the one called Noble, the other Grissel, begot on many ill Hens very bad Cocks; but the most famous Hen Jinks, never brought forth ill Bird, how bad soever her Cock were.

Influenced, perhaps, by the elaborate lore surrounding horse-breeding (p. 40), Markham laid importance too on the season and the phase of the Moon at the time of conception: 'the best season of the year to breed in, is from the encrease of the Moon in February, to the encrease of the Moon in March: for one March Bird is ever better worth than three at any other season'. Howlett favoured much the same season for the breeding of 'great cocks' and also stressed the necessity that chickens should be hatched by the same hen that laid the eggs, 'lest they take on the personality of the sitter'.

When the young cocks in the brood reached the age when they started to behave aggressively towards each other (that is to say, at some time between the ages of three and nine months), the time was deemed right to submit them to dubbing – the removal of their combs and wattles. Without the benefit of this procedure the bird would have been seriously disadvantaged in the cockpit, the comb providing an ideal grip for its opponent and being especially sensitive to injury. Some care was necessary in the timing and execution of this

67 A pair of strikingly proud fighting cocks, dubbed, cut-out and spurred for the match, by Hilton Pratt, *c.* 1860, oil on canvas.

operation – which might (if the cock was lucky) be carried out with surgical scissors – not only to avoid injury but also to preserve the bird's handsome looks. Carried out in timely fashion, the procedure, according to Markham, endowed the bird with a 'fine small, slender and smooth head', whereas, 'to suffer the Comb to grow to his bigness, and then cut it away, it will make him a gouty thick head, with great lumps'.

Following a spell caged up in a pen to recuperate, during which butter might be rubbed into the wound to help it heal, the young cock was ready to begin a new life in preparation for the contest. Only the most promising of the brood would be selected for the privileged but gruelling training regime to which the young cock would ultimately be submitted. Rigorous assessment would ensure that he displayed all the most desirable physical traits, combined with a quick eye and a naturally combative temperament which could be observed, according to Markham, 'in his walk, by his treading [copulating], and in the pride of his going, and in his pen by his oft crowing'.

THE COCK-WALK

In order that the young fighting cock might develop his full potential, it was deemed essential to remove him entirely from his family environment and to isolate him in the carefully controlled but austere environment of a 'walk', where he would remain until old enough to fight – ideally at two years of age, 'at which time he is perfect and compleat in every member; for to suffer him to fight when his spurres are but warts, you may well know his courage, but never his goodnesse'. The

234

specification for the ideal cock-walk was remarkably stringent, and a long way from the hurly-burly of the farmyard. Markham's advice was that

> that walk is best for a Fighting Cock which is farthest from resort, as at Wind-Mills or Water-Mills, Grange-houses and such like, where he may live with his Hens without the offence or company of other cocks. Lodges in Parks are also good, and so are Cony-Warrens, only they are a little too much haunted with vermine, and that is dangerous.

For owners with large estates it became customary for leases to include a requirement that tenants of suitable properties would provide facilities for walks. In addition to being withdrawn from the world, the company of a great many hens was to be avoided at the walk, for fear that too much treading might enfeeble the potential champion: three hens for each cock was deemed a sufficient number.

Once the cock entered his training regime, during the six weeks before he was due to fight, the closest attention was paid to his diet and exercise, in order to bring him to the peak of physical fitness. At that point he would be removed from the company of his hens and would spend much of his time within the confines of his own pen, to be 3 feet high and 2 feet square, built from solid planks above, below and on three sides, and with a door at the front in the form of a grate, the bars some 2 inches apart; in front of the grate were to be two troughs of soft wood, 'one for his meat, the other for his water'. Several such pens might be arranged in a row or one above the other, but if so they were to be provided with 'over-shadowing boards' so that one cock might not see another.

A perch (or series of perches) was to be provided in the pen, of sufficiently large diameter to allow the cock a good grip but short enough to ensure that he perched in a 'close-heeled' manner that would serve him well when he came to be turned out into the cockpit, for a poor posture could be the ruination of a good cock. Markham's advice was that

> the best way is to have in your roost a row of little Perches, not above seven or eight inches in length, and not a foot from the ground, so that your Cock may with ease go up to them, and being set, must of force have his legs stand neer together. It is a rule, that he which is a close sitter, is ever a narrow striker . . . Let the footstool of the Perch be round & smooth, and about the bigness of a mans arm . . . for the Perch is the making and spoyling of any Cock whatsoever . . . Again, you must be careful, that when your Cock doth leap from his Perch, that the ground be soft whereon he lighteth, for if it be hard or rough, it will make your Cock grow gowty, and put forth knots on his feet.

His text continues with lengthy and detailed advice on every aspect of the following weeks' preparations.

> When your Cock, as aforesaid, is put up into his Penne, you shall for three or four dayes feed him only with old manchet [fine white bread], the crust pared away, and cut into little square bits, and you shall give him to the quantity of a good handfull at a time, and you shall feed him three times in a day . . . You shall ever let him have before him the finest, coldest, and sweetest Spring-water that you can get.
>
> After he hath been thus fed four days, and his Corn, Worms, Gravel, and other course feeding gone from him, in the Morning take

him out of the Pen, and another Cock also, and putting a pair of Hots upon each of their heels, (which hots are soft bumbasted rolls of Leather, covering their spurs, so that they cannot hurt or bruise one another,) and so setting them down on the green grass, let them fight and buffet one another a good space, as long as in their teaching they do not wound or draw blood one upon another; and this is called sparring of Cocks; it heateth and chaseth their bodies, and it breaketh the fat and glut which is within them, and maketh it apt to cleanse and come away.

After your Cocks have sparred sufficiently, and that you see them pant, and grow weary, you shall take them up, and taking off their Hots, you must have deep straw baskets made for the purpose, with sweet soft straw to the middle, and then put in your Cock, cover him with sweet straw up to the top, and then lay on the lid close, and there let your Cock stove and sweat till the Evening.

But yet before you put him into the stove, you shall take Butter and Rosemary finely chopt, and white Sugar-candy, all mixt together, and give him a lump thereof, as much as your thumb, and then let him sweat; for the nature of this scouring is to bring away his grease, and to breed breath and strength . . .

After four of the clock in the Evening, you may take your Cock out of the stove, and licking his head and eyes all over with your tongue, put him into his Pen, and then taking a good handful of bread, small cut, put it into his trough, and then pissing into the trough also give it him to eat, so as he may take his bread out of the warm Urine, for this will make his scouring work, and cleanse both his head and his body wonderfully.

By now the manchet was replaced in the cock's diet with specially made 'cock bread', for which the following is Markham's recipe:

You shall take of Wheat-meal half a peck, and of fine Oat-meal flower as much, and mixing them together, knead them into a stiff paste with Ale, the white of a dozen Eggs, and half a pound of Butter, and having wrought the dowe exceeding well, make it into broad thin cakes, and being three or four dayes old, and the blisterings of the outside cut away, cut it into little square bits, and give it to the Cock.

There be some others that in this bread will mixe Licoras, Anniseeds, and other hot Spices, and will also in the Cock-water steep slices of Licoras, but it is not commendable, for it is both unnatural and unwholesome, and maketh a cock so hot at the heart, that when he comes to the later end of a battle, he is suffocated and overcome by his own heat . . .

Following a day of rest with only ordinary bread and water, the cock was put through his paces once again:

you shall take him into a fair even green Close, and there setting him down, having some Dung-hill Cock in your arms, you shall shew it him, and so run from him, and entice him to follow you, and so chase him up and down for half an hour at least, suffering him now and then to have a stroke at the Dung-hill Cock. And when you see he is well heated and panteth, you shall take him up and bear him into your Cock-house, and there first give him his scouring . . . and then stove him in a basket, as is before said, till Evening, and then feed him as was formerly declared.

Thereafter days of rest alternated with sparring or chasing followed by scouring and stoving for a fortnight; in the course of a further two weeks exercise was to be taken only two or three times a week. During the third fortnight of the six-week programme the exertions were to be less violent, with only some moderate chasing up and down 'to maintain his wind', after which, 'finding your Cock in lust and breath, you may fight him at your pleasure, observing that he have at least three dayes rest before he fight, and well emptied of his meat before you bring him into the Pit'.

LATER LITERATURE ON THE COCKFIGHT

If we pursue the subject of cockfighting through its later literature a number of developments can be detected which refine, extend or overtake the conventions established during its earlier phases. As ever, these notices no doubt reflected rather than originated changes in everyday practice, although it seems likely that the growing volume of writings would at least have promoted a degree of harmonization of sporting practice over the country at large, where regional variations on metropolitan conventions in the cockpit itself had been widespread. On the other hand, raising and training the birds remained very much an art rather than a science, and on the few occasions when the opinions of ordinary practitioners appeared in print – for example in *The Life and Letters of John Harris, the Cornish Cocker* (1910) – they tend to be dismissive of armchair experts. Undoubtedly there was much rehashing (or plain plagiarization) of the classic texts, especially by the authors of compendia such as Thomas Fairfax's *Compleat Sportsman* (1762) or William Baldiston's *British Sportsman* (1792), but a few sources stand out.

Robert Howlett's *Royal Pastime of Cock-Fighting* (1709) is one of the works that builds on earlier literature rather than recycling it, although many now-familiar sentiments reappear in more self-consciously elegant form. Howlett's basic requirements for the cock remain largely unchanged: he must have outstanding courage, and 'must never fail to strike, or peck whilst he has either Blood or breath left in him'. Ill nature is not to be tolerated, however, and 'you had better commit such a Cock to the Pot, than to the Pit'; a similar fate is recommended for the cock who is not a close-heeler, 'and more profit you will find in stewing him for the Table, than in stiving him for the Battle, when once you discover him to be a Bird defective in his Heeling'. Much emphasis is put in good shape and size, but in contrast to Markham and his followers, Howlett declares colour to be immaterial. The little type of cock he favours provokes eulogies on its qualities:

> when he comes to the Fight he affords you most Pleasure and Delight, no sooner is he set down, but like Lightning he falls upon his Enemy, Dances a Bloody round, and in his sparring Capers higher than your head, then links and never looses 'till his hold breaks, or his Adversary dies. They rise and fall together, still striving to the last which shall strike most, and hardest blows, Stabing each other without intermission, till Death conclude the Combat. – O rare Birds: what Pleasure upon Earth can equal this?

Howlett is the first author to advise on the desirability and the complexities of in-breeding, designed to capture the qualities of a particular line. The hen, he advises, 'must either be a mother or a sister of some admirable Cocks, who have been known to signalize their valour in the Field of Honour'. An old cock should be matched with a young hen, or vice-versa, but not a father with a daughter or a brother with a sister. (The advantages of in-and-in breeding, p. 428, had not yet been identified). February, March and April are recommended as the best breeding months for larger cocks, but for small cocks 'June, July, or any time indeed serves for them'. Later writers, including Sketchley, advised that three years of age was the maximum at which a cock should be used for breeding.

It may be mentioned here that certain game-cocks of Indian breed were introduced perhaps as early as the reign of Charles II and thereafter in increasing numbers. A fight between English and Indian game is said to have been recorded in a painting (unlocated) by John Harris Reid, animal painter to George II, and records survive of a similar match at Market Drayton (Shropshire) in 1760, when a number of Asil cocks were vanquished by the home team. (English cocks were later transported to India, where, however, they failed to live up to expectation.) Malay fighting cocks were also widely imported and on occasion interbred with English fowl; Atkinson is dismissive of the flaccid results of these unions.

Howlett takes his reader through the various stages of preparing a cock for the pit, with many asides illustrating long personal experience. On dubbing, for example, he writes that if it is carried out too early, 'there will be no Comb remaining either to grace or guard the Head, and he'll look so Capon like, that you will hate to see him when turned into the pit. But if you leave it too long, they will be heavy headed'. He has advice to give too on the most desirable formation:

in cutting, if you observe this for a rule, to leave the comb round like a Half-moon, it will make the Cock appear as it were Roman-nos'd or Hawk-bill'd, and will not only be a good guard to his Head, but will render him much handsomer to look upon: Whereas close

cutting makes them appear sneaking and also much weakens the Beak of a Cock, and by that means many times looses the Battle.

Dubbing continued as a standard practice for as long as the sport survived. Writing in the later nineteenth century W. B. Tegetmeier recommended that it should be carried out with curved scissors 'made for trimming the feet of horses'. He maintained that it caused the cocks minimal discomfort and that they recovered almost immediately from the operation.

Howlett's specification for the walk to which the young bird would be consigned after his head had healed was no less prescriptive than Markham's, and there the cock would, 'like an absolute Monarch . . . reign without controul and be beyond the hearing of the hourly challenges of neighbouring cocks'.

You are always to choose a Walk that is grac'd with solitude, having green fields, or pleasant Meadows on one hand, with Mountainous, Hilly dry ground on the other, and a murmuring brook or twatling Rivelet, or in their stead some pleasant Pools, or Ponds of clear sweet Water . . .

The crucial importance of the walk continued to be recognized into the nineteenth century, when Sketchley, for example, would write that even 'half-bred fowls in a well-furnished walk will beat the best game when starved or pined'. Clay-bound areas were to be avoided, he suggests, for the cock's glossy plumage would easily be defaced. He continues:

Gentlemen who command any number of walks have infinitely the advantage of those whose walks are few and limited; the advantages over the latter are pre-eminently great, for many are so beautifully situated that even the crow or the sight of a cock seldom comes across them; they are neither fretted nor teazed, which ever causes them to lose much of their flesh and destroys that martial fire and spirit . . . [and] makes him tardy and slow to action.

The fitting out of the walk was also attended to in detail. Howlett placed particular importance on a good perch for the cock, suggesting that it might be 'wraped round, and close with well twisted Thum-ropes of Hay, into which he may set his claws, and by that means hold himself fast without stradling, or lying wide with his legs'. Reiterating earlier opinion, he advises that a bad perch 'spoils a good Cock, and makes him not worth a Groat, that might otherwise have been a jewel of impreciable Value'. The floor below the perch was not to be so hard that the cock might risk bruising his feet or breaking his claws when descending from the perch.

Against the general run of advice, Howlett recommends the regular sparring of young cocks fitted with 'hutts' or hots (later termed muffs), but only to the point where they begin to close with each other. Do this once or twice a quarter, he advises, and 'they will grow both skilful and cunning in Fight; their wind will be lengthened, their Sinews grow stronger, and their Joints more elegant, and flexible'. In training, the familiar round of scouring and stoving was applied in order to bring the cock to perfection, with bread soaked in urine providing the staple diet. Two kinds are specified: ordinary bread, for which some used baker's bread and others insisted on the addition of oats, peas, beans, liquorice, sack or strong ale (for which white wine was to be substituted in hot weather), sugar candy, aniseed, caraway seed, the whites of ten or

twenty eggs and one or two yolks; and best bread, which would include all of the above plus 'syrup of clove-gilliflowers', dates, eringo, wood sorrel, ground ivy, feverfew, dandelion, borage and lemon juice. Either sort would be made into little flat loaves, left for two days and then served up with the crusts removed.

When it came to matching the cock for its battle, Howlett continues to favour hand and eye over weighing, although the qualifications for the task were stringent: 'there is both a Lady's Hand, and a Hawk's Eye, a Fox's Head, and a Lion's Heart, to be found in every skilful Handler, and he that is wanting in any one of these, is a Person very unfit to have the management of a Cock when turned into a pit to fight'. Matching in this way was clearly a finely judged process, and it was perhaps characteristic of the age of growing rationalism that more objective methods should have been sought: Robert Plot, in his *Natural History of Stafford-shire* (1686) illustrates a device invented by Sir Richard Astley and designed to introduce a degree of scientific objectivity by accurately gauging the length and girth of the cocks (illus. 68), but few owners are likely to have been persuaded to submit their prize fowls to such an indignity. Ultimately, the simple expedient was adopted of matching by weight (see below).

Howlett's rather enjoyable volume had been preceded into print by another insightful tract, addressed particularly to 'the Nobility and Gentry of Scotland' and again underlining the refined audience it sought by its title – *An Essay upon the Royal Recreation and Art of Cocking* – by William Machrie. Indeed, in his opening salvo Machrie goes so far as to deny any populist following whatever for the sport:

'Tis as much an Art, as managing of Horses for Races, or for the Field of Battle: And tho' it has been in Vogue over all Europe, yet 'twas never Esteem'd nor Practis'd, but by the Nobility and Gentry; it was kept up only by People of Rank, and never sunk down to the hands of the Commonality, where the Art of managing this Fierce and Warlike Bird, had been either lost or slighted.

However effective this may have been in massaging the ego of the reader of his work (Machrie further declares that 'I shall be very indifferent, about what Reception it may meet with from the common Herd of Mankind'), his claim is clearly nonsense. Some of his observations on the qualities to be sought in a fighting cock are perhaps of more enduring interest to those removed from first-hand experience of the battle. His preference above all is for a cock 'that riseth well and carries the bloody heel':

First, a well rising Cock no sooner catcheth hold with his Beik, but he riseth with a blow and sometimes two or three . . . And then 2dly, If he direct his stroaks chiefly at the Head, Neck and throat of his Adversary, it is a clear and sure Mark of a prime, high-metall'd and

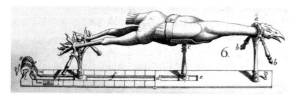

68 Device 'to match game-Cocks', as illustrated in Robert Plot's *Natural History of Stafford-shire* (1686). It is shown 'with a Cock put in it at full stretch' and is designed to 'give an exact measure of the length of the Cock to the eighth part of an inch'; further, 'for the Size of its body, it is measured by the girth, either by the brass ring . . . which may be taken in, or let out . . . or else by a Girdle and buckle, as may be seen upon the cock; all which have been approved by the best Masters.'

well rising Cock . . . Wherefore I conclude that a Cock that doth strike more at the Head and Throat, than at the Body, is certainly the best; by reason on[e] blow or two to these parts are more dangerous, and some times kill outright; whereas in any other part it taketh many, even to disable.

Much of Machrie's advice on the regulation of the walk follows that already familiar from the literature above, differing only in detail. The specification for the pen follows that favoured by older writers until it comes to the door, which instead of being made with a grating is evidently to be solid, 'with a hole cut in the middle thereof, through which your Cock is to receive his light in time of Feeding; for which hole you may have a darkening Board to obstruct the Light, if the same occasion him to fret, crow, or struggle in the Pen; as also for keeping him warm in the Night or Day, especially after his Stove and Purging.' Clearly, Machrie's cocks spent much of their training in obscurity. Instead of a wooden feeding trough which might threaten the cock's beak, he recommends a bowl of soft material: 'in my opinion, the crown of an Hat, or a piece of soft Leather, or strong Cloth made for the purpose, is more fit than anything made of Wood'.

Machrie's recipe for cock-bread is less extravagant than some of those quoted above, but includes also 'a little Salt-peter well pulverised . . . which is both cooling and cleaning'. He has his own preferences for the method in which the bread should be baked, recommending that it should be formed 'into Loaves, and not into broad thin cakes . . . which takes away very much of the Substance of the Bread', and is more particular too in the source of the urine with which it should be mixed in feeding it to the cock, specifying that it should be 'presently past by a Boy or Girl'.

A major variation is the recommendation that cocks should be sent to fight as yearlings (termed 'stags' in the cockfighting world): 'Altho' it is a received opinion that a Cock never comes to his full vigour, strength and courage, untill he be two years old', he suggests, 'yet in the month of June and July a Stagg makes a better Battle than a Cock of two, three or four years old'. (The season is significant, since the older cocks will be in moult at this time, and off their best performance.) On the whole, a less intensive training regime had by this time replaced the incredibly stressful round of sparring and stoving that had been characteristic in Markham's day, and no doubt the less intervention there was the better it was for the cock: in the mid-nineteenth century Atkinson would comment that he had 'nearly as often seen condition forced out of a main of cocks as [he had] seen it forced in'. In his day a mere nine days' preparation was deemed adequate, with a combination of light sparring, gentle handling, and physicing only for those cocks that needed it.

In the matter of preparing the bird for the fight, cockpit practice had evidently been tightened up since Markham's day. In particular, the trimming of the cock's hackle was now controlled, as outlined by Machrie:

When you Poll your Cock, leave a little mane or small Ridg of short cut Feathers from the root of his Comb, along the hinder part of his Head, for a Cock to hold by. As for the rest of the Feathers of his Neck (called his Heckle) they ought to be much longer than the Ridg: All which is reckoned a Fair Heckle: But if otherwise cut so bare, that there's no hold to rise by, a Foul Heckle.

. . . then cut his Tail pretty short; which done, cut the upper part of his wings. If he be a small Cock and riseth too high, an Inch and a quarter shorter than his Body; but if a large Cock, not so short, for the latter needs a longer Wing than the former, in respect of his weight. As for the under part of the Wing, six or seven of the foremeost Feathers thereof, must be cut sloping, and a great deal shorter than the rest . . . and notice that the upper part of your Cock's Beik be but a little longer than the lower; otherwise in Fighting he'll neither Mouth nor hold well.

In relation to the time necessary to prepare the cock fully for battle, Machrie mentions that strength and wind are less critical if the cock is to fight with artificial spurs: for, he says, 'untill a Cock arrive at the Age of two years and a half, or two at the least, his own Weapons will do but little hurt or execution, and to fight him without gantlets would be an impardonable piece of Folly'. For a narrow-heeled cock, he suggests, 'give him such as will kill, which will be an Inch long or thereabouts; but to a wide Heel'd one, a little longer'. He goes on:

Before you set on your Weapons, cut of your Cocks natural ones, as short as the socket of those you put on; and lest they blood, sear them a little with an hot Iron or Tobacco Pipe, two or three days before Battle . . . Altho' Silver or Mix'd-Mettal-Weapons, are generally made use of, yet Steel ones are preferable; because they receive a better point than any other, and make not so great a Contusion of the parts they cut; which makes the Wounds sooner and easier cured.

Metal spurs of Roman date are said to have been found in Cornwall, at Silchester (Hampshire) and in Southwark, but the dating of all of them remains suspect. Their adoption in the modern period is thought to date from around the time of the Restoration: Charles II is said to have presented a pair to Nell Gwynn, *c.* 1660. Cosimo III, Grand Duke of Tuscany, gives an account of their use, 'of silver or steel, very long and sharp', during his visit to England in 1669. Further references come from the reign of William and Mary when, on 6 April 1698, an employee of the Duke of Rutland claimed expenses for having paid to a Mr Sherburne on the Duke's behalf 'for 6 pairs of cocks' spurs at Newmarkett, 3li.'. (Another bill for the previous day reveals the considerable preparations that attended the outing: 'charges for 28 days gathering up the cocks for Newmarkett meeting, my selfe, a boy and 2 horses, at 8*s.* per day, 11li. 4s.')

Early spurs took the form of conical caps, usually made of silver, designed to reinforce the cock's natural spurs. An early set of 'Rules for Cocking', which Atkinson conjectures may date back to the time of Charles I, decrees that all battles over £5 were to be fought 'in fair reputed silver spurs'. By the early eighteenth century, the conical cap form had been replaced by spurs in the form of an elongated spike, with a socketed base to be located over the trimmed base of the cock's own spurs; a pad of chamois leather within the socket would ensure a comfortable fit. Both types are perforated by fixing-holes, by which means the spurs were sewn with flax thread to fixings of pigskin or some other form of strap. The best of these spiked spurs were also made of silver, but given the enormous stresses to which they were subjected the metal had to be tempered – an art said to have been lost today. Atkinson asserts that the silver was alloyed with copper, rendering them 'more elastic and finely tempered than the finest steel, and . . . of an extreme lightness'. He gives details of a number of eighteenth-century makers (Cockspur Street at the north end of Whitehall had a particular concentration of them, as

its name implies); he describes too their makers' marks and the finely made boxes in which sets of such spurs were often sold.

It might be thought that the life of any cock fighting in metal spurs was bound to be a short one, but Gilbey mentions one bird, named Old Duckwing, who fought four years in succession at the Lincoln race meetings and who 'in his eighth year, almost blind and gouty footed, beat a fine fresh cock in a few blows. He never fought without breaking or bending his spurs almost double.'

The more impecunious would spur their cocks in steel – less prestigious but capable of producing points that were thinner and more deadly. For this reason the use of steel spurs was generally prohibited at closely regulated pits such as the Cock-Pit Royal:

> It is understood on all occasions, that battles for 5l. and upwards must be fought in silver spurs, unless the contrary is expressly agreed upon, for this reason, that the battle is not so soon ended in silver, and the fowl has more opportunity of displaying his powers than in steel spurs.

All facets of the match were indeed now subject to more formal regulation (and it is significant that the seventeenth-century texts had been silent on the matter of artificial spurs).

CONDUCT OF THE COCKFIGHT

In the conduct of the classic cockfight, there was nothing random in the choice of adversaries. Each cock had to be carefully matched by its owner or cock-master with a bird of similar stature, 'for what availeth it to feed never so well', asks Markham, 'if in the matching you give that advantage which overthroweth your former labour?'. Length and strength are the characteristics which are to be most carefully assessed, 'for if your Adversary's Cock be too long, yours shall hardly catch his head, and then he can never endanger eye nor life: and if he be the stronger, he will overbear your Cock, and not suffer him to rise, and strike with any advantage'. The combatants were therefore submitted to close scrutiny with the eye and assessment with the hand in order to reach agreement on a particular match.

Owners or their feeders would attend the cockpit first for 'showing' and matching of the pairs to be pitted against each other. The feeder had been a crucial figure in the management of the fighting cock since the seventeenth century, but the first extensive description of his duties and those of the others involved in the administration of the match comes from the opening years of the 1800s. By this time the final introduction of the cocks into the pit had fallen to a separate individual, the setter-to. Their respective duties, as characterized by William Taplin, are worth quoting at length, beginning as follows with an account of the feeder:

a person whose occupation is to collect, handle and feed a pen of cocks, to fight such main or match as may be made or agreed on, by those who deposit the battle money, and are called the Masters of the Match. These find or procure the cocks, of which the feeder takes charge; and to his judgment is submitted the entire management of selecting, rejecting, feeding, physicing, sweating, sparring, weighing, cutting out (alias trimming,) and bringing his bag and cock to the pit; where, upon delivering to the setter-to, his function ceases in respect to that particular cock . . .

The cocks so agreed to be matches, are under the management of their different feeders till the day specified in the article for their being shewn and weighed; which day is upon most occasions the day but one preceding the day on which the main begins to be fought. This ceremony is attended to with the most scrupulous nicety on each side; every cock is weighed to a quarter of an ounce; his colour described almost to a feather; his marks . . . taken down in writing with the same accuracy as the weight; the whole being entered in the match-bills to be produced, read, and compared with the cocks as they are brought to pit at the commencement of every battle.

The number of cocks having been shewn and weighed on each side, the match-bills containing their weights are compared; and all those who are either dead weights, or within an ounce of each other, are said to fall in, and are called main battles; in contradistinction to those who do not come within the ounce of each other, and are thrown into the byes; which are generally fought for a trifling sum, and have no affinity whatever to the main.

The introduction of accurate weighing intensified the task of the feeder, whose primary object now was to have his cock weighed in at the lightest weight he could achieve (by judicious dieting and by purging) and then to feed it intensively before the match to help it gain as much of a weight advantage over its opponent as possible. As the author in Rees's *Cyclopædia* has it, 'those which, proportionately to their bulk, had been previously most reduced, or brought down, now have the opportunity of being fed and brought up again, thereby gaining upon the weight of their opponents'. The most skilled feeders commanded a status equivalent to today's racehorse trainers; Gilbey records that in the reign of George III it was more usual for the feeder's name to appear on the programme than that of the owner.

In Taplin's day the feeders generally reached an agreement with the Masters of the Match that they would receive the whole of the door money, in compensation for the fortnight or three weeks in which they would have been engaged in preparing the cocks. The birds would be carried to the arena in specially made cock-bags stuffed with a little straw (or with a flannel lining in cold weather); the generality of these would be of canvas but aristocratic owners would have bags of velvet or silk, often embroidered with a representation of a cock and with their own arms. By the nineteenth century the arms of the appropriate city or county were added to the bags of cocks representing them in matches organized with one team of owners against another.

An equal pairing having been reached, the cock was submitted to its final preparation for the match:

> first, with a pair of fine Cock shears, you shall cut all his main off, close unto his neck, even from his head, unto the setting of his shoulders; then you shall clip off all the feathers from his tail, close unto his Rump . . . Then you shall take his wings, and spreading them forth by the length of the first feather of his rising wing clip the rest slope wise with sharp points, that in his rising he may therewith endanger the eye of his adversary: then with a sharp knife you shall scrape smooth and sharpen his spurs . . . Lastly, you shall see there be no feathers about the crown of his head for his foe to take hold on, and then with your spittle, moistening his head all over, turn him into the Pit to move his fortune.

Thus far all the regulations and conventions alluded to have related to single combat between two cocks, and although references to multiple birds being entered in a single mêlée go back at least to the reign of James I (see below) the one-to-one battle remained the classic form. At the start of the individual match the cocks would each be taken from their bags and 'scrupulously compared in feather and marks with the original description entered in the match-bill on the day of weighing'. (The 'marks' mentioned here refer not only to plumage but to those applied by the owner himself: in the early nineteenth century Rees's *Cyclopædia* reported that 'The marks are generally made in the eyelid, nostril, or connecting membrane of the toes by cutting a notch in one or more of them, and are described as right, left, or both eyes or nostrils cut, or in right or left feet'.) Half a century earlier, in the 'Rules and Orders for Cocking' published in 1751 by Reginald Heber, it had been pronounced 'That every cock matched, shall fight as he is first showed in the Pit, without sheering or cutting any feathers afterwards to a disadvantage, without the Consent of both Parties that made the Match'; if any deviation were to be discovered the match would be suspended. Clearly, the old custom of matching cocks by hand and eye (not to mention last-minute cutting out) had fallen into abeyance. (All these remarks relate to the most highly regulated matches only: Gilbey makes it clear that in many 'subscription mains' held around the turn of the nineteenth century, birds were matched by the simple expedient of drawing lots.)

Then, with the cocks in the hands of the setters-to, the match would begin 'amidst clamours indescribable, and offers of bets innumerable'. The battle commenced with the cocks being introduced to each other head-to-head by their feeders. When they were released, each would attempt to rise above the other, trying to get a grip with its beak on its opponent's head and thereafter slashing at the head and neck with its spurs and beak; the eyes were particularly vulnerable, while body blows were likely to be less decisive. All writers at whatever age marvel at the total commitment of best cocks to fight literally to their last gasp; runaways were few and their fate would have been sealed no less conclusively, ending their days forthwith in the pot rather than cockpit. The match, according to Taplin,

> invariably consists of an odd number of Battles; as twenty-one, thirty-one, or forty-one; which match once made, and the cocks weighed, is then called a main of cocks: when fought, and finished, the winner of the odd battle (or more a-head) is the winner of the main.

Within the ring all the advantages of careful selection and assiduous training came to bear. Cocks with a high-bearing posture were at an immediate advantage, being generally able to rise above low-bearing opponents. From this vantage point they were in a position to seize their opponents from above and to drive down at them with their spurs, although Rees's *Cyclopædia* makes it clear that going for instant domination was not always the best stratagem:

> Action in fighting, to be excellent, should be rapid, but without hurrying; quick, but cautious; to break well with their adversary, that is, on the first onset to throw off, or parry the blow and then to hit; for if they strike and hit together at the onset, it is not unusual to see the thigh or wing broken, or the spur pass through the body of one or both. It is of consequence also, that in the early part of the battle, they should strike without laying hold, and keep a distance, as laying hold in the beginning of the battle is almost useless, but not so when the first efforts are past, and they become a little weary.
>
> It is usual for the cock to aim at the head with the beak, but this stroke is known to be more fatal when he lays hold of the point of the wing, as in this case the spur enters some part of the body or the wing, and disables the fowl more certainly.

The references here are to cocks fighting with metal spurs – almost standard by the nineteenth century – but in earlier years, if fighting 'with their own weapons', an advantage was gained by the cock with the sharpest spurs: such a bird, in Markham's words, was said to be sharp-heeled or narrow-heeled when 'every time he riseth hitteth, and draweth bloud of his adversary, gilding (as they term it) his spurs in bloud, and threatning at every blow an end to that Battail'. Such a sharp-heeled cock, he continues, 'though he be a little false, is much better than the truest Cock which hath a dull heel, for though the one fight long, yet he seldome wounds, and the other though he will not endure the uttermost hewing, yet he makes a very suddain and quick dispatch of his business, for every blow puts his adversary in danger'. Machrie's estimation of the advantages of 'a prime, high-metall'd and well rising cock', as quoted above, concur with this estimation.

By a complex system of 'telling the law', in which a referee would count out birds which, through blindness or other injury, were unable to continue in the match or which refused to fight, matches which had not already been decided by the death of one or other of the opponents would be brought to a conclusion. Rees's *Cyclopædia* recounts in some detail the application of these rules, all designed to ensure that every match ended up with an undisputed winner.

Betting provided the whole impetus of cock fight. The largest purse recorded in the earlier centuries of the sport, placed at the Old Red Lion near Gray's Inn, was for 10 guineas the match and for 500 guineas the main. As with all forms of gaming, some were led to wager more than they could deliver: at the cockpit is was customary for those who could not pay to be hoisted in a basket over the pit and to remain there until the end of the main, a practice that continued up to the early nineteenth century (see illus. 69). Gilbey points out that of the nineteen regulations forming the earliest surviving set of rules for cocking (1751) only six apply to the conduct of the fight while the others relate to betting and the resolution of disputes.

If fortunate enough to survive the battle, the cock was then subjected to a further bout of intensive personal attention from his feeder:

> When the battail is ended, the first thing you do, you shall search his wounds, and as many as you can find, you shall with your mouth suck the blood out of them, then wash them very well with warm urine, to keep them from ranckling, and then presently give him a roul or two of your best scouring, and so stove him up as hot as you can, both with sweet straw and blanketing, in a close basket for all that night; and then in the morning take him forth, and if his head be much swell'd, you shall suck his wounds again, and bath them with warm Urine, then having in a fine bag the powder of the herb Robert, well dryed, and finely feirlt, pounce all the sore places therewith, and then give the Cock a good handful of bread to eat, out of warm urine, and so put him in the stove again . . . and by no means let him feel the air untill all the swelling be gone, but twice a day suck his wounds, dresse him and feed him, as is aforesaid

Severed blood vessels were to be given particular attention, the reader being enjoined to 'bind thereunto the fine soft down of a Hare, and it will both staunch and cure it'. Any injuries to the eye were to be treated with similarly close attention: ground ivy was to be sought out at the foot of a hedge and well masticated by the handler: 'and having chewed it very well in your mouth, and suckt out the juyce, spit it in the eye of the Cock, and it will not only cure it of any wound, or any blow in the eye, where the sight is not pierced, but also defend it from the breeding of Films, Hawes, Warts, or any such infirmities which quite destroy the sight'. After the cock had been returned to its walk further close inspections of his wounds were to continue in the following weeks, any 'unsound bunches' being cut with a knife and pressed out with the thumbs, 'then with your mouth suck out all the corruption, and then fill the holes full of fresh Butter, and it will cure them'. Sir Walter Gilbey comments on these closely prescribed attentions that there would be nothing comparable to them for several generations, but in fact the parallels with the care lavished upon hawks (pp. 180–82) are striking, and practice in one sport seems to have influenced the other.

SHAKE-BAGS

All the highly regulated battles of the type described above would have taken place between pure-bred or half-bred game-cocks fighting at around the approved weight. Clearly there would have been many opportunities for birds falling outside these stringent specifications at more informal cockfights up and down the country, but even in the more closely regulated pits there were occasions when overweight birds (generally those above 4 lb 8 oz.) would fight in ancillary contests where their less glamorous appeal was matched by their designation as 'shake-bags' (or shag-bags). This term, like the earlier variants it replaced – turn-outs or turn-pokes – alludes to the more informal means by which these birds were introduced into the battle, the feeder being required to do nothing more than to 'take the Bag by the bottom, and shake the Cock out at the Mouth upon the Pit, and so let him go against his adversary, from which Custom they are called Shake-bags here in England'. Betting and potential winnings were generally much lower for these less closely regulated encounters.

The shake-bag tended to lack many of the finer points of breeding of the 'little Battle Cock', required more feeding and still took two years to reach fighting condition, whereas by Howlett's day the little cocks were deemed ready for the pit at one year old. The bigger birds also fought in a more wary manner and without the fierce commitment of their cousins: 'after twenty turns and hovers, perhaps he strikes a blow, then stands again, and either pecks, or may be scraps the Earth, as if he meant to fight no more. Then drag back and forth, to see if he may safely rise'. Clearly the author had little time for these ungainly creatures.

Gilbey refers to fighting with shake-bags as a Dutch custom and characterizes their usual arena less as the cockpit than the ale-house, where patrons favoured size rather than refined technique and where prizes might as often be in the form of a fat pig rather than hard cash. An advertisement (typical of many) in the *Daily Courant* of 29 April 1710 shows, however, that they were by no means restricted to lesser venues:

> At the Cockpit Royal in Cartwright Street the south side of St James's Park, this present Saturday . . . will be seen the Royal Sport of Cock-fighting for 2 Guineas a Battle, a pair of Shagbags fight for 5l. and a Battle Royal. Beginning at exactly 4 a Clock.

Gilbey mentions that shake-bags often fought wearing lancet-shaped spurs (also called sickles), the more conventional bodkin-like form being less appropriate for these heavier birds. An advertisement from the reign of Queen Anne, quoted by Ashton, shows that both types of spur and both types of cock might feature in a single main in the early years of the eighteenth century – a time when conventional practices were not yet set in stone; it also suggests an origin for the new fashion in spurs:

> Note that on Wednesday there will be a single battle fought with Sickles after the East India manner. And on Thursday there will be a Battle Royal, one Cock with a Sickle, and 4 Cocks with fair Spurs. On Friday there will be a pair of Shake bags fight for 5l. And on Saturday there will be a Battle Royal between a Shake bag with fair Spurs, and 4 Matchable Cocks which are to fight with Sickles, Launcet-Spurs, and Penknife Spurs, the like never yet seen. For the Entertainment of the Foreign Ambassadors and Gentlemen.

WELSH MAIN, DEVONSHIRE MAIN AND BATTLE ROYAL

Conventional mains of cocks were generally described as 'short' or 'long'. By the early nineteenth century at least, short mains were generally characterized as those lasting a day or two, while long mains might stretch over a week. Further variations on these conventions occurred when the individual victors in a main were denied the benefit a spell of rest and recuperation following one-to-one combat but were obliged instead to continue fighting one another until only one bird was left standing. Several forms of (quite literal) sudden-death playoffs can be identified, which must have contributed in no small measure to the emergence of public opposition to the sport.

The first type of main, the 'battle royal', involved the introduction of a number of cocks – the more the better seems to have been the rule – into the cockpit together; the last bird on its feet after the ensuing free-for-all was the winner. The practice may well have derived its name from the fondness of James I for displays of this kind: when he visited Lincoln in 1617, for example, 'he appointed four cocks to be put on the pit together, which made his Majesty very merry'. The term makes an early appearance in a report from the reign of William III, carried in the *Postman* of 20/22 April 1699:

> On 18th April, His Majesty hunted and in the afternoon went to the cock-pit where a Battle Royal of 9 cocks together at once upon the pit was fought: most of them were killed and two brothers carried the victory after fighting as long as both could stand by the other.

In the Welsh main, victors in conventional one-to-one contests (involving perhaps eight or sixteen cocks of similar weights, around 4 lb 4 oz.) were repeatedly matched against each other until, at the end of the series, a single cock emerged as victor of the main. All the birds on either side might belong to a single owner, or be the property of a number of subscribers. This is said to have been the most popular type of contest in the northern counties. Victors in individual matches would collect winnings on each of those, while the champion at the end of the day would win a purse, a gold cup, a fat hog or some other prize.

The Devonshire main evidently was more common in the south-west. It followed the conventions of the Welsh main, except that a wider range of weights might be encountered, the lightest pair fighting first, and so on.

METROPOLITAN AND PROVINCIAL COCKPITS

By the turn of the seventeenth century the Whitehall cockpit remained the most important in the capital although evidently there were others of some pretension, for in his *Survey of London* (1603) John Stow records that 'Cockes of the game are yet cherished by divers men for their pleasures, much money being laid on their heads, when they fight in pits, whereof some be costly, made for that purpose.' The less well heeled were catered for in back rooms and yards at inns and also, not infrequently, at theatres, where cockfights might alternate with dramatic performances – a convention memorialized in the present day designation of the theatrical 'pit'. (Given this practice, it may have seemed almost conventional that in 1629–30 Henry VIII's great octagon at Whitehall, in which plays as well as cockfights had been presented under James I, should have been converted by Inigo Jones to serve as a theatre for the more cultured court of Charles I; it was demolished in 1675.)

Greenwich Palace had possessed an earlier cockpit, built in 1533 for Henry VIII. The *History of the King's Works* records that it was constructed complete with 'a cocke cope ffor the kyng's cocks with vi roumes in the same'; it also had 'iiii ryngs ffor men to sytt upon' and 'a place in the gallarye over the bowlying allaye ffor the quene to syte to see the cocks ffyghtyng'. The presence of the queen and her ladies in waiting must have had an impact on the wider involvement of women during the Tudor period, but the reference remains a rarity. A later monarch, James I, who preferred the setting of his private retreat and hunting lodge at Royston (Hertfordshire) to the formalities of courtly life, had a 30-foot diameter cockpit built there in brick for the entertainment of himself and his entourage.

A new 'Cock-Pit Royal' emerged on what is now Birdcage Walk to the south of St James's Park, its location still marked by Cockpit Steps. This establishment seems to have been 'royal' only in name, for unlike the others so far mentioned it was a public amenity. An advertisement in the *Daily Courant* (20 March 1710) shows it in full swing:

At the Cockpit Royal on the South-Side of St. James's Park, this day will begin a great Match of cock-Fighting, which will continue all the week, for 6 Guineas a Battle and 10 Guineas the odd Battle, between the Gentlemen of Essex and the Gentlemen of Sussex.

By the early nineteenth century this had become the only place in London where 'long mains' were fought: William Taplin tells us that in some of these the cocks were furnished by 'opulent individuals' while others were subscription matches involving multiple owners 'who bred their cocks in distant counties, but fight them only in town' – generally speaking in the spring. Taplin also gives a more detailed description of the interior at St James's, which agrees closely with an etching (see illus. 57) prepared for the *Sporting Magazine*:

The cockpit is circular, and completely surrounded with seats six tier deep; exclusive of a rail, with standing room all around the summit of the uppermost seats; forming,

in the whole, a perfect amphitheatre. The concentrical circle on which the cocks fight is a raised mound of earth (surrounded with boarding,) about twenty feet in diameter, and should, according to the technical term of the sport, be covered with a fine green turf, denominated sod . . . but as it is an article difficult to obtain in the Metropolis, and would be inconvenient and inapplicable during hard frosty weather. when many matches are fought, matting upon the surface is substituted in its stead.

On each side of the circular mound, at its extremity, and exactly opposite to each other, are two small seats for the setters-to; who retire to those seats during long fighting, or when ordered by the betters and spectators so to do. Directly over the centre is suspended from the dome, by a chain, a very large circular branch, containing a great number of candles, affording a profusion of light; for nearly all the matches fought there are very unnaturally decided by night, the company going to pit at six o'clock in the evening.

The Cock-Pit Royal enjoyed something of a boom at the turn of the nineteenth century, when more mains are said to have been fought there than for many years previously, but it was pulled down in 1816 after the freeholders, the governors of Christ's Hospital, who collectively disapproved of the sport, refused to renew the lease. A ground plan was published in *Country Life*, CXI (1952), showing it to be a circular structure with an internal diameter of 30 feet and with 'pen rooms' to either side of an entrance staircase.

After this a third establishment, designated the 'Royal Cock-Pit', was built in nearby Tufton Street, again not by the Crown but by subscription; it survived in use until cockfighting was banned in 1833.

(This would appear to be identical with the 'New Royal Cock-pit' recorded by Gilbey and mentioned in 1831 as having been built in Little Grosvenor Street, Millbank.)

Samuel Pepys had earlier paid two visits to the 'new Cocke-pitt . . . in Holborne'. On the first occasion (30 March 1668) he was put off by the 'great deal of rabble' thronging the pit, but a week later (6 April 1668) he penetrated to the interior, though he remained unimpressed:

> to the new Cocke pitt by the King's gate, and there saw the manner of it and the mixed rabble of people that came thither; and saw two battles of cocks, wherein is no great sport, but only to consider how these creatures without any provocation do fight and kill one another – and aim only at one another's heads, and by their good wills will not leave till one of them be killed.

At Newmarket public matches were held on a regular basis at the royal cockpit, owners being invited to enter by submitting their birds to the Masters of the Match. The *London Gazette* (5–9 February 1679) announced:

> The Masters of His Majesty's Cock-pit do desire all gentlemen that love the game to send in their cocks to the pit at Newmarket in such seasonable time as they may be fit to fight, they intending to begin the said Cock match on the 15th day of March: and there shall be feeders ready to take care of their cocks.

William III and his household seem to have shared Charles II's enthusiasm: Gilbey quotes a report that during his reign on rainy days at Newmarket the cockpit was 'enclosed by stars and blue ribands', alluding to the orders of chivalry displayed by the press of enthusiasts. At ordinary meetings the clientele might embrace the entire spectrum of society, as captured in a representation by William Hogarth (illus. 69); when this was reproduced in the *Sporting Magazine* for 1797, the accompanying text accurately identified the setting as Newmarket, and not Westminster as often claimed.

With the growth of horse-racing as a national sport (a development in which Newmarket had again played a leading role: see p. 85), it became commonplace for cockfights to be organized in order to coincide with the races both there and at other courses – presumably involving little more than demarcating the fighting platform on the ground – or rather the 'sod' as distinct from the 'turf', respectively synonymous with cocking and racing. The cockfight by no means provided a mere side-show to the racing and occasionally took precedence in the timing of events. Not the least remarkable feature of this partnership was that Edward Stanley, 12th Earl of Derby and founder of the Jockey Club itself, emerged also as the most avid breeder of fighting cocks in his day, sending up to 3,000 birds a year out to walk and building a reputation for them of near invincibility.

Wrestling matches also regularly featured in combination with cockfighting. At Newlyn and at Gwennap (near Redruth), both in Cornwall, are arenas where each of these sports was followed with equal ardour. A great antiquity has been claimed for the Gwennap theatre in particular, the largest of its kind in England, with twelve concentric tiers of earth-cut seats faced with stone, the whole enclosed by a stone wall. Popular opinion, as recorded by John Harris, the 'Cornish Cocker', was that it was 'undoubtedly pre-Roman and probably made by the Phoenicians', but in truth its origins are obscure; Pevsner suggests that it may owe its origin to mining subsidence

69 Interior of the Cock-Pit Royal at Newmarket, by William Hogarth. The lengthy commentary accompanying a reproduction in the *Sporting Magazine* (1797) mentions that Hogarth's original plates had by then been 'worn to a useless state by the numerous impressions taken from them' and goes on to provide details of the tableau represented: 'The scene of the cock-pit is supposed to be laid at Newmarket: and in this motley group of peers, pickpockets, jockies, butchers, and gamblers of every denomination, Lord Albemarle Bertie, a lover and promoter of the diversion, is entitled to precedence. His lordship was totally blind, and therefore his passion for amusements of this nature was thought extremely singular ... The shadow on the cock-pit is the reflection of a man drawn up to the ceiling in a basket, and there suspended as a punishment for having betted more money than he can pay. For theatrical decoration, we have the King's arms, and a portrait of Nan Rawlins ... a famous cock-feeder, well known in Newmarket ...'.

and goes only so far as to note that the present form of the structure is early nineteenth century. Its beginnings certainly lie considerably earlier than that, for John Wesley preached there in 1743 – having had to bide his turn until a cockfight had finished. By Harris's day the Chapel had triumphed and the place had become 'the scene of Methodist tea-fights and orgies of fanaticism and psalm-singing'. At 130 feet in diameter and with seven tiers of seats, Newlyn was smaller, but still more formally structured than the more rudimentary venues that characterized the rest of the country.

Machrie mentions the recent establishment of a cockpit on the Links of Leith, at a prudent distance from the disapproving eye of the burgesses of Edinburgh. (The Leith cockpit seems to have been founded in 1683, two years after cockfighting is said to have been introduced to Scotland during a visit by the Duke of York, later King James II.)

Needless to say, in barns and inns – or even out of doors – up and down the country, cockfighting was practised in a variety of more informal surroundings and with a minimum of special equipment, although numerous towns and villages possessed a formal (if not necessarily elaborate) pit. Perhaps the earliest reference to such a designated place comes from Winwick (Lancashire) in 1514: Henry Fishwick published an account of an armed clash that took place there around the site of the cockpit where weekly fights were staged, adjacent to the church. Other records from the seventeenth century and later confirm that churchyards not uncommonly formed the setting for regular cockfights and even the church itself might be pressed into use, as at Hemmingborough (Yorkshire) where the parish register records that on 2 February 1661 four men had fought with cocks within the church. From 1619 comes a record of the 6th Earl of Derby forming a cockpit within a garden at Chester, while the presence of others are recorded by Borsay at Bath by 1694, Whitehaven by 1706, York by 1736 and Manchester by the early 1750s, the latter forming part of a veritable leisure complex, with upwards of 200 pens and two feeding rooms. Writing in 1873, W. B. Tegetmeier recalled witnessing an illicit match in his youth, staged in a back room over a shop with no more preparation than a piece of matting laid out for the benefit of the cocks: many contests no

doubt were held in an equally ephemeral setting. Gilbey records that one of the last mains fought in London took place in 1840 at Battersea Fields – beyond the five-mile radius of Temple Bar within which cockfighting was proscribed by an Act passed five years earlier (p. 202).

With the introduction of the 1849 Act for the More Effectual Prevention of Cruelty to Animals, cockfighting began to disappear from the public stage. The wording of the relevant passage of the Act (p. 198), targeting as it does those who promoted, staged and profited from public spectacles rather than the practices they encouraged, had the effect of stimulating growth in the staging of cockfights at private houses, often as after-dinner entertainments. John Harris (p. 237) was one of those who made a tidy income travelling the country in order to stage these events for well-heeled private clients. The effect on public matches held in the countryside was not immediate, but gradually took hold: at Easter 1850, perhaps as a last grand gesture, a main between Norfolk and Suffolk took place that was described as 'the greatest meeting ever held in England', while a ten-day meeting took place at the same time at Gallowgate Pit at Newcastle, mostly sixteen-cock Welsh mains at 50 guineas each. The last such open match in England is said to have taken place at Gallowgate, following which cockfighting survived only in a clandestine and largely unrecorded manner.

ADVOCACY FOR AND AGAINST THE COCKFIGHT

From the early appearance of texts vouching for the antiquity and probity of the practice of cockfighting, it seems clear that opposition to the sport was already beginning to be manifested in England by the sixteenth century at the latest, coinciding with a rise in sensibilities among the Puritan community, at least, which was offended by all forms of inhuman practice. Recourse by numerous authors to Greek and Roman sources in order to buttress the respectable (if not heroic) pedigree of cockfighting implies a perceived need to rebut its critics.

The fact that cockfighting had a Classical origin (whether or not the tradition was an unbroken one) was a factor used in its promotion from an early date. When Andrés de Laguna protested of the scene he had witnessed in the cockpit at Whitehall in 1539 (p. 230) that it seemed to him a 'great childishness and rather vulgar to esteem such a thing so highly', the response delivered to him was in the form of an adaptation of a speech by the Athenian politician Themistocles, who used the example of the single-minded pursuit of victory driving the combatants in a cockfight to motivate his army against that of Xerxes, then threatening the extinction of Athens. Repeated appeal was made to the same Classical sources, and to the unswerving courage of the fighting cock as an exemplar for the youth and soldiery of England, for centuries to follow. Although evidently a military man by background (he claims to have coached many of his potential readers in the arts of swordsmanship), Machrie chose to stress the capacity of the sport to render human conflict obsolete, by engaging men 'untill all the Wars in Europe, wherein so much Christian Blood is spilt, be turned into that of the Innocent pastime of Cocking'.

George Wilson opened his *Commendation of Cockes* of 1607 with a direct appeal to the Old Testament:

It is written in the first Chapter of the first Booke of Moses, called Genesis, that God gave unto man, soveraigntie, Rule & Dominion over the fishes in the sea; over the fowles of the aire; and over every living thing that

he had made: and behold it was exceeding good, and was appointed unto man for to doe him homage, and to serve him in all places, and times, in his severall and necessary uses, and not only for clothing and sustenance for his bodie; but also for recreation and pastime, to delight his minde: as with Cocke-fighting, Hawking, Hunting, and such like. For honest recreation is not prohibited by the word of God: but rather tolerated and allowed.

Others would have none of this interpretation. William Perkins, in his *Cases of Conscience* (1632) writes:

The bayting of the Beare, and Cock-fights, are no meete recreations. The bayting of the Bull hath his use, and therefore it is commanded by civil authority; and so have not these. And the Antipathy and cruelty, which one beast sheweth to another, is the fruit of our rebellion against God, and should rather moove us to mourne, than to rejoyce.

Equal contradictions can be found between those who argued for cockfighting on polite grounds and those who were diametrically opposed to it. Philip Stubbes, in his *Anatomy of Abuses* (1583) mentions that the people who flocked 'thick and three-fold' to the cockfights held on Sundays were plunged into a milieu where

nothyng is used, but swearing, forswearyng, deceit, fraud, collusion, cosenage, skolding, railyng . . . fightyng, brawlyng, quarrelyng, drinkyng, whoryng; and whiche is worst of all, robbyng of one an other of their goodes.

Attempts to limit the evils of gambling (referred to latterly by Stubbes) came in the reign of Charles

II with an Act against Deceitful, Disorderly, and Excessive Gaming (1664), which decreed that any person who 'by unlawful device, or ill practice' should win money from a variety of named sports (including cocking, horse-racing and dog-fighting) should forfeit three times the amount so gained.

Undoubtedly cockfighting was predominantly a male pursuit. César de Saussure commented on a visit to England in the 1720s that 'Ladies never assist at these sports', but a casual reference in a letter of April 1687 from Bridget Noel to her sister the Countess of Rutland provides a rare hint that they too might occasionally be drawn into the craze: Bridget excuses herself from visiting her sister in the immediate future for 'hear is a co[c]king and hors[e] matches which we have promesed to be at'.

Many nineteenth-century fans were genuinely mystified by the inclusion of cockfighting amongst the sports banned by the Act for the More Effectual Prevention of Cruelty to Animals (1849) (see p. 198) while other pursuits such as hunting and fishing escaped. Herbert Atkinson summed up their position rather well:

When we know the facts, it seems illogical that the sport was classed with the baiting of bulls and bears tied to stakes to be worried by dogs, and racing, hunting, coursing, shooting and fishing (all of which are infinitely more cruel) to be allowed and encouraged.

The Game cock is reared in luxury and allowed every liberty for two years, then taken over by the feeder and as much care bestowed on his diet and training as any other Athlete. When in perfect condition he is matched with an equal adversary equally equipped. He dies totally gratified. Death is often more sudden than an electric shock.

Similar sentiments from several founder members of the SPCA are adduced in support of this view, including one statement to the effect that 'cockfighting is attended with the least cruelty of all our diversions'. It was to fighting alone, Atkinson claimed, that we owe 'the production and preservation of the finest breed of Fowls in existence'. Laying great stress on the natural combativeness of the birds, Atkinson defends even the use of metal spurs as a form of kindness:

It is a mistake that can be entertained only by the ignorant, to suppose that the use of silver and steel spurs are an additional cruelty. If left together in a natural state, it will be a work of some hours, whereas a battle with two cocks in good condition rarely lasts five minutes, and a great many are struck dead much quicker than if their heads were cut off clean.

LATTER DAYS OF THE GAME-COCK

The survival of the breed beyond the point at which cockfighting was banned was due largely to the emergence of poultry shows in the mid-nineteenth century. Scott describes the continuing popularity there of fighting cocks and the fact that it remained customary for many years to show cocks dubbed in the traditional manner, although even an enthusiast like Tegetmeier was forced to acknowledge that, robbed of its primary *raison d'être*, those who maintained the breed in this way 'have succeeded in producing from the Game fowl (the most useful of all) a bird, which beyond laying an average number of eggs in spring and summer, is about as useless as a bird can be'. This was strong condemnation of a society that had deprived it of what Tegetmeier saw as its natural function, rather than a criticism of the bird itself, for he was at one with Atkinson who judged the fighting cock 'unequalled in elegance of form, and . . . universally regarded as the highest possible type of gallinaceous beauty'.

COCK-THROWING

Nothing has been said above of the custom – it can scarcely qualify as a sport – of cock-throwing, and indeed it had nothing in common with cock-fighting as described. The cock in this case was of the common dung-hill variety and its opponents were the youths of the particular neighbourhood – or commonly pupils of the grammar schools for whom the practice was widely mounted as a Shrove Tuesday treat: the encounter was made even more unequal by the cock being either tethered to the ground or partially buried so that only its head remained above ground, the diversion taking the form of a barrage of sticks and stones hurled at the unfortunate bird until it succumbed.

HOMING AND RACING PIGEONS

The economic importance of the pigeon is discussed elsewhere (pp. 316–26), but in the course of the 1700s a shift in interest can be detected amongst many owners towards the more 'polite' sphere, so that by the time John Moore published his *Columbarium* in 1734, for example, it was addressed to a new breed of pigeon fanciers rather than to those whose interests lay in the productive value of the dovecote. Pigeons were now kept, he writes,

> even by Persons of the greatest Distinction and the first degrees of Quality, who have held these Birds in so great Esteem, that they have endeavour'd to attain at least an

experimental Knowledge of them, purchasing at great Expence as many of the distinct Sorts as they could hear of and cultivating them in their own Houses.

One of the paragons of this new breed of owners was named as Richard Atherton, who carried his interest to the point of designing his projected new home to shelter the pigeons as well as himself. In short, he was, in Moore's view,

> a Gentleman both of Will and Ability to prosecute his Fancy in this Branch of Natural History, [and] was building a stately House in Lancashire, on the Top of which he design'd to have four Turrets, in which his Pigeons were to be dispos'd according to the nearness of Relation between the different Species, but Death put an end to the Undertaking in the Year 1726 . . . He was a very compleat Judge of a Pigeon and wou'd spare neither Cost nor Trouble to procure the best; he had one powting Cock which he valued at five Pound, and a very choice Collection of many other Kinds.

Moore's advice is directed in his book to those who, like himself, had 'ventur'd . . . to launch forth into this new Science', and the location of this interest within the realms of experimental knowledge and natural history distances him from Markham's rustic economy and identifies him rather as a true product of the Enlightenment. None the less, his practical advice provides insights into contemporary practice in the dove-house or in the loft. Either one ought to be built facing the south or south-west, for example, 'or, you may make a Hole in the Roof of your House, and there lay your Plat-form' where the pigeons could sun themselves – always remembering to construct it so as to be inaccessible to cats. The more ambitious pigeon-fancier by this time would have gone for a more sophisticated means of entry to his loft, and one which served a number of purposes – not all of them entirely honourable:

> As for your Trap or Airy, it is always built on a Plat-form or Floor of Deals, on the outside of your House, that your Pigeons may have free Passage into it . . . Some build these very small, with three Doors, one on each side, which all draw up together by pulling a single String, intending chiefly to catch stray Pigeons, whom they decoy into it, by strewing Hemp-Seed or Rape and Canary, which all Pigeons are fond of. Others build them very wide and lofty, so that four or five Persons may conveniently stand in them together, with a Shelf or two on either Side, designing them to give Room and Air to Pigeons of the homing Sort, which they are obliged to keep confin'd; this Practice is of very great Use, by keeping such Prisoners in a good state of Health.

Almost a century later, W. B. Tegetmeier's advice on the building of the 'airy' or area corresponds in large part with that of Moore, introducing only some clever devices for allowing ingress of birds which have accidentally been shut out without giving them the opportunity to leave again. Moore's advice on the internal arrangements provides a warning against necessarily equating the number of nesting-boxes in any dovecote with the population that might have been expected within it, for he recommends that owners should allow 'at least two Holes or Breeding-Places for every Pair; for the more Room they have, the more quiet they will sit, and breed the better'. Overcrowding was also liable to lead to the accidental destruction of both

eggs and young if the adult birds began to fight with each other. Moore's advice on the nesting-boxes themselves is detailed and worthy of reproduction at length:

> To make your breeding Places, you may erect Shelves of about fourteen Inches broad; allowing eighteen Inches betwixt Shelf and Shelf; for otherwise your tall Powters, by being forc'd to crouch for want of Height, will get a habit of playing low, and spoil their Carriage: In these Shelves erect Partitions at about the Distance of three Feet, fixing a Blind by a Board nail'd against the Front, on each Side of the every Partition; by this means you will have two Nests in the Length of every three Feet, and your Pigeons will sit dark and private. You may if you please, fix a Partition between each Nest, to prevent the young ones from running to the Hen, when sitting on the other End, and cooling her Eggs; for in breeding Time, when the young ones are about three Weeks old, the Hen, if a good Breeder, will lay again, and leave the Cock to take care of, and bring up the young ones.

In every nest he specifies that a straw basket or an earthenware pan should be placed, 'both which are made and adapted to this very purpose'. The *Complete Pigeon & Rabbit Fancier* suggests that 'a pan proper for a tumbler or any other small pigeon ought to be three inches high, and about eight inches over the top, sloping like a wash-hand bason towards the bottom; and these should be varied in proportion to the size of the pigeons'. Tegetmeier counsels the use of simple bowls, 'made heavy, so that they are not likely to be overset', which could be recessed into the shelf to avoid the danger of the young falling out and being unable to regain the nest. These pans, which 'can be made by any brick, tile, or coarse earthenware maker', had the dual purpose of preventing the eggs from rolling out of the nest and of minimizing any disturbance to the chicks which, 'if you have a Mind to look on them', as Moore says, 'often puts them into a scouring'.

There is advice too on the best means of delivering food and drink – the first in a hopper-like structure from which the grain descends into a trough, suitably shielded so that the birds cannot scatter and waste the contents, and the second by means of a bulbous glass bottle of 3 or 4 gallons capacity with a long neck, inverted in a stand so that it feeds on demand into a bowl below. A wide variety of grains and seeds, beans and peas is recommended by way of food, with the addition of a 'salt cat', an adjunct of the dovecote first recorded in the sixteenth century (see also p. 323) and now described by Moore in some detail:

Being thus enter'd on the Head of Diet, it necessarily leads us to consider a certain useful Composition call'd by the Fanciers a Salt Cat, so named, I suppose, from a certain fabulous oral Tradition of baking a Cat in the Time of her Salaciousness, with Cummin-seed, and some other Ingredients as a Decoy for your Neighbour's Pigeons . . . Take Gravel or Drift-Sand, Loom, such as the Brick-Makers use, and the Rubbish of an old Wall, or, for want of this a less quantity of Lime, let there be a Gallon of each; add to these a Pound of Cummin Seed, a Handful of Bay-Salt or Salt-Petre, and beat them all up together into a kind of Mortar, mixing 'em up with stale Urine, and your Pigeons will take great Delight in it.

The gravel and sand in this recipe is estimated to be beneficial to the pigeon's craw, the lime to

hardening its eggshells, the salt and urine to encourage them to drink, while the cumin seed, 'in which Pigeons delight . . . will keep your own Pigeons at home, and allure others that are straying abroad, and at a Loss where to fix upon a Habitation'. The mixture should be placed in lidded jars with holes formed in the sides so that, he suggests, the pigeons can peck it out. By the mid-nineteenth century, however, Tegetmeier – one of the most respected authorities of his day on pigeons as well as poultry in general – would judge the salt cat 'a nauseous and filthy compound', offering no advantage over a straightforward supplement of salt and calcium.

Tegetmeier also advises that amongst 'the more artificial and delicate high-class varieties' of pigeons it is advisable to separate the sexes during the winter months when, in contrast to the ordinary domestic pigeon, they are unlikely to mate. Accordingly, segregated accommodation had to be provided in the specialist loft, with separate entrances allowing the cocks and hens to be let out separately and on different days. In due course, appropriate pairs of birds would be placed together in a special mating cage for a few days, after which time they could generally be regarded as stable partners.

Among the most exalted names of those associated with the breeding of pigeons in the nineteenth century is that of Charles Darwin, who was attracted to the study of pigeons for three principal reasons:

because the evidence that all the domestic races have descended from one known source is far clearer than with any other anciently domesticated animal . . . because many treatises in several languages, some of them old, have been written on the pigeon, so that we are enabled to trace the history of several breeds . . . and lastly, because, from causes which we can partly understand, the amount of variation has been extraordinarily great.

His researches proved absorbing, leading him to join two of the London pigeon clubs and to engage the interest of 'many of the most eminent amateurs'. In the course of these researches he minutely characterized all the known varieties, concluding that 'nearly all the chief domestic races existed before the year 1600'. When Darwin's work in elucidating the principles of evolutionary development came to be recognized in the British Museum (Natural History) in London, a case containing a rock dove and a selection of its domestic descendents was chosen to illustrate these principles (illus. 70).

HOMING AND CARRIER PIGEONS

The highly developed homing instinct of the pigeon was thought by early writers to be driven purely by the strong bonds existing between paired doves. More recently, the actual mechanisms involved in their finding their way back to their lofts have attracted more attention: these are now seen to be complex in the extreme and (despite considerable research) are still imperfectly understood. A recent survey by Hans Wallraff of the factors involved identifies the position of the sun, geomagnetic forces, smell and responses to wind direction as significant factors, in addition to the use of visual landscape features which form the basis of traditional understanding of this facility and hence the training methods applied by owners to the pigeons in their care. A great deal of work remains to be done.

This special way-finding facility of the pigeon (although no doubt dependent on capacities shared to a greater or lesser extent with a much

70 Early exhibit (1887) from the British Museum (Natural History) – today the Natural History Museum – illustrating the differentiation of different breeds of pigeons from a common ancestor, the rock dove, according to Darwinian principles.

larger number of migratory and other birds) had been first appreciated in the classical world but evidently was made little use of in message-carrying in England before the 1700s; Francis Willughby, for example, while he knew that 'They make use of these birds to convey Letters to and fro, chiefly in the Turkish Empire', had seen carrier pigeons himself only in the 'King's Aviary' in St James's Park and in one privately owned loft in London. A certain confusion had, perhaps, already arisen between what are now known as carrier pigeons – a term restricted to a number of varieties of 'a very artificial and high-class breed', characterized by warty excrescences of the membrane around the nostrils and the eyes – and the quite distinct homing pigeons of more conventional appearance which have been much cultivated since the eighteenth century and which form the basis of present-day pigeon racing. Moore writes of the homing pigeon as follows:

Such is the admirable Cunning, or Sagacity of this Bird, that tho' you carry 'em Hoodwinkt, twenty or thirty Miles, nay I have known 'em to be carried three-score or a hundred, and there turn'd loose, they will immediately hasten to the Place where they were bred.

The implication that this facility is entirely natural is misleading, for the young birds have to be led through a period of training by their owners, without which most of them would be unlikely to be able to perform this feat; their natural abilities vary widely, however, with some performing much better than others in distant and unfamiliar territory. What is true is that they can all be improved to some degree by means of progressively increasing the distances over which they are required to travel homewards. According to Tegetmeier:

As soon as the young birds can fly strongly their training commences. They are taken day after day to gradually increasing distances from home, and then liberated. In this manner both their observation and power of flight are exercised, until at last they know

their way accurately, and can fly back long journeys without loss of time.

Barker suggests that for two nights prior to their first flight the birds should sleep in their travelling baskets to accustom them to enclosure, and that thereafter an ever-increasing range of 1, 2, 3, 5, 8, 13, 23, 31, 40 and 60 miles would be appropriate, up to a maximum of 150 miles in their first year. He further mentions that some trainers test them on all four points of the compass before introducing them to long-range flights.

During the early days of the railway in which Tegetmeier wrote (and he recalled that in the earliest pigeon races in which he participated the birds were often taken by steamer downriver from London to Gravesend for release), the custom during racing was for the pigeons to be taken to some distant place, 'either previously fixed on, or the direction of which may be decided by lot on the morning of the race', and there released. The best birds were confidently expected to return typical journey times from, for example, Southampton to London (a distance of some 70 miles), in under an hour. On landing in one of the traps or in the 'area' of its home loft, it would be captured and conveyed to the agreed finishing point (usually a public house), frequently by relays of runners to ensure the earliest possible arrival. Today the same principles apply, although the timing of the return of the bird to its loft is now recorded mechanically, without the need for last-minute athleticism on the part of the owner.

More than any other factor, the coming of the railways boosted opportunities for competitions of this sort and a thriving practice soon developed in transporting hampers full of homing pigeons up and down the country in order for the birds to race each other back to their respective lofts. These baskets came in various forms and materials: W. E. Barker, for example, favoured those of willow, given additional rigidity by the addition of canes to stop them (and their precious contents) being crushed if luggage was inattentively piled on top of them in the guard's van; a small door in the side or on top allowed the birds to be loaded individually into the basket, while a drop-front permitted them all to be released simultaneously. The release was generally entrusted to the railway staff at the chosen destination – ideally a small, quiet station on elevated ground manned by sympathetic pigeon fanciers, although no doubt every such exercise involved a degree of compromise. (A recording held in the oral history archive of the National Railway Museum, NAROH 2000–53, mentions that later in the twentieth century it became common for 'convoyers' to accompany larger consignments of pigeons, sleeping with their charges overnight and orchestrating their simultaneous release – literally at the drop of a hat – in the morning.) While the birds made their way home in the shortest time possible, the basket would be returned by rail to the sender. The arrangement seemed to work perfectly well on most occasions and the railways evidently were well adapted to what was expected of them (illus. 71); the Hansells record that Marylebone station in London even had a designated 'columbadrome' to care for the pigeons in transit. With the advent of improved roads and large-scale pantechnicons, further opportunities arose to test the prowess of the birds and compensated to some degree for the decline of the railway network in the later twentieth century.

If the use of pigeons in carrying messages had been slow to take root in Britain, it became well established for specialized purposes alongside the developing networks of the railways and the electric telegraph. Lofts were established by the press at Folkestone and Dover from which news

of financial movements and current affairs (perhaps previously transmitted by pigeon to ports on the Continental mainland) could be carried quickly on to London. Towards the end of the nineteenth century the *Daily Graphic* still relied on pigeons to carry the results of the Derby from Epsom to London: times of 20 to 25 minutes for the dash to Fleet Street were recorded. Wider public appreciation of the capabilities of the pigeon post arose during the period of the Franco-Prussian War, when contact was maintained with the besieged city of Paris in 1870–71 only by this means: the GPO organized the collection of suitably succinct messages in Britain which were forwarded to Tours, where some 200 of them might be photographed on to a postage-stamp-sized sheet to be carried into Paris by pigeon. Later, during the Boer War, an entire military communications network was established within a 500-mile radius of Cape Town: a War Office 'Sketch Map of Cape Colony shewing Military Pigeon Post Stations' dated 1902 survives in the British Library (Maps MOD IDWO 1669).

When World War One broke out, therefore, it was perhaps inevitable that the potential of the pigeon post for both good and evil was quickly appreciated. An early awareness of its possible use for seditious purposes – Lord Kitchener seems to have regarded them with particular disfavour – led to owners being ordered by the government to confine their pigeons to their lofts and to clip their wings, but quite soon their potential to contribute to the war effort began to be exploited more positively and ultimately some 100,000 birds entered military service – all of them donated voluntarily by owners. The army was fortunate in appointing as the begetter of its new Carrier Pigeon Service the owner of the periodical *Racing Pigeon*, A. H. Osman, who combined a lifetime's knowledge of his subject with a natural organizing

71 Advertisement, 1913, for a drop-front basket designed for the transport and release of pigeons on the railway system.

minesweeping duties at the time: most of these had no radio whatever, and when they got into difficulties the pigeons they carried with them were their only hope of rescue. Operating up to 150 miles off the coast, they were well within the capabilities of good pigeons and many citations attest to the effectiveness of the birds in saving the lives of trawler crews (as well as airmen on dangerous sea patrols far from help). Osman's own unit within the Army grew from an initial 60 men enlisted for the Carrier Pigeon Service to the point where every assault would be accompanied by a contingent of pigeons carried in baskets by their specialist handlers to the front line. On one single day on the Somme alone, he records, over 400 operational messages were sent back by infantry units and also by tanks (which carried their own pigeons) – 'not a bad record for the pigeons', he quotes one commentator as saying, 'and a good mark for the stout lads who had to take them up with them over the barbed wire, trenches, and shell craters, and so on into the unknown'. By the end of the war Osman's personnel numbered over 400, the mobile lofts in which their charges were transported 150 (illus. 72) and the pigeons some 22,000.

A further remarkable role was performed by the birds in the Intelligence Pigeon Service, whose activities sound rather quaint but which evidently proved effective. Osman describes the manner in which his charges were deployed:

A small balloon was constructed with a metal band worked by clockwork. To this band was attached a small basket containing a single pigeon with a message holder on its leg, and to each basket was attached a small parachute. The balloons were liberated in favourable conditions of wind and at intervals automatically released from the special ring a single

ability. At his instigation, racing (and all-important training) of birds was soon reinstated under permit from the authorities: some idea of the popularity of the sport can be gained from the number of 500,000 such permits that were issued by the end of the war. Although wireless radio was beginning to become more widely used, there remained many circumstances under which the pigeons proved of vital use – indeed Osman declared confidently that 'for espionage, scout service work and many important duties pigeons will never be replaced'.

An early assignment was with the fleet of trawlers on which the Royal Navy depended for

72 Motorized mobile pigeon-loft on service in World War One on the reserve line for the Ypres salient at Dickebusch (West Flanders).

basket with a bird. These were dropped into Belgian and French territory . . . and . . . a request was made to the finder to supply intelligence information that was needed, at the same time giving the finder hopefulness and cheer as to the ultimate success of the allies' cause and promising reward for the information supplied . . . Much valuable information was obtained in this manner.

Most homing pigeons never saw war service, however, and from the second half of the nineteenth century their natural instincts were channelled instead into competitive racing. Although the sport continues to attract a small aristocratic following (Queen Elizabeth II is an enthusiast), it has long been marked by a democratic spirit and has attracted a large working-class following in the mining and industrial areas. The typical racing pigeon's quarters are as likely to be a snugly built wooden shed as an architect-designed dovecote, although the birds themselves change hands for enormous amounts of money and are treated with every indulgence by their owners. As well as the devices necessary to record the time of arrival of any given bird in a particular competition, automated drinking and feeding equipment is now comparatively widespread.

PIGEONS AS SITTING DUCKS

Throughout the eighteenth century, some parts of the pigeon population, at least, remained protected from the growing menace of sporting hunters: in 1751 shooting pigeons attracted a fine of 20s. or three months' imprisonment for each bird killed. At just this time, however, a novel sporting craze exposed the pigeon to a new hazard as pigeon-shooting clubs began to appear – the precursors of today's sport in which clay pigeons form the targets. It was common practice in the early days of this sport to tie the pigeon's feet together, or to clip its wings, so that the sportsman with his heavy and inefficient firearm had a better chance of success. Over the course of the next century these clubs became increasingly popular: in the London area, Battersea and Ealing became particularly noteworthy and with the founding of the Hurlingham Club in Fulham (in its early days exclusively dedicated to pigeon shooting) the sport entered the height of fashion as a recreational pursuit (illus. 73). As targets for the marksmen, live adult pigeons were released into the air, having been held until that moment under a hat – later replaced by a box with a sliding lid and a draw-string, or by a spring-loaded trap. Firing from a distance of 20 yards, the competitors (generally arranged in teams) were not allowed to advance the gun to their shoulder until the bird was on the wing; it had to fall within 100 yards of the release point to be counted as a hit. At the end of the day, the team having killed the most birds were declared the winners and in the event of money having been wagered on the outcome were entitled to the stakes.

The fortunes of those pigeons kept in the comparative safety of the dovecote became increasingly and precariously bound up with those of their species who were targeted in the shooting clubs, for the organizers of competitions often had difficulty in finding adequate supplies of adult birds. In competitions in London the pigeons were by now valued at 2s. 6d., for which in some matches the contestants had to pay. A thriving black market in stolen pigeons developed to service these needs, and the owners of dovecotes found themselves having to reinforce their security measures against thieves who – even if they might find themselves unable to break into the dovecote – would come in the night and attempt to frighten the birds into nets which had been placed over the exits. Accordingly, some dovecotes of the period were fitted with strongly reinforced doors – one at West Thurrock (Essex), built in the eighteenth century, has a double door, the inner one of iron with three bolts – while the windows were at times fitted with iron spikes designed to foil the nets of the thieves. The Hansells recount how the enthusiast Charles Waterton, around the turn of the twentieth century, had a dovecote built specifically to counteract this threat, with the reinforced entrance 20 feet above ground level.

Along with other forms of acknowledged cruelty, pigeon-shooting matches attracted increasing opposition in the later 1800s and eventually, in 1905, they were banned altogether.

WILDFOWLING AND BIRD-CATCHING

The varieties constituting what we should now call game birds in the sense that they were pursued for food were enormously wider even a century ago compared with today: Annie Grant counts some 75 species 'from swans and cranes to pipits and

73 *Members of the Red House Club, shooting for the Gold Cup,* 1828, drawn and etched by Henry Alken, aquatinted by R. G. Reeve. The pigeons are here released from collapsible traps.

larks' amongst the bones recovered from medieval settlements, drawn from coastal areas to high moorland and from woods to marshes. As a proportion of the total diet consumed the numbers were never very high, however; legislation recognized at an early stage that certain species were especially desirable in this respect and rights over them were reserved to landowners, who in turn were quick to protect their privileges, to husband these resources and to promote their increase.

In the following descriptions of various methods employed in taking birds, many of the accounts relied on come from the seventeenth and eighteenth centuries, when interested observers began to note down effective practices. Some of these will reflect traditions going back to earlier centuries, while it is clear that others – notably the use of duck decoys – were of more recent introduction. They will, in any case, represent only a few of the methods that were in reality employed, which in turn were a tithe of earlier techniques developed by generations of countrymen in response to their particular myriad environments: the mechanics of fowling may be easily described, but success depended on intimate familiarity with local topography and with the habits and preferences of the bird life that inhabited it. Even the audiences for whom those very tracts were written were already likely to be separated from those country-dwellers who had grown up almost as partners with the wild populations and who approached the task of extracting a living from them with a knowledge that was gleaned from daily interaction rather than texts. No one technique was used exclusively by any one fowler and, in addition to the few described below, birds were also taken, in the words of George Markham (whose *Hungers Prevention* of 1621 will be of particular use in the following survey), 'with other particular Engines of which there are divers kindes, and doe carry divers shapes, according to the seasons of the yeare when they are used, and the manner of the place in which they must be used'. The particular quarry sought was, of course, another factor of fundamental importance.

The birds themselves were pursued primarily for consumption, although Markham acknowledges that some had other values. He divides them into three groups:

the first such as are fit for foode, as Pidgeons of al kindes, Rookes, Pheasants, Partridge, Quailes, Rayles, Blackbyrds, Fellfares, Sparrowes, and a world of others.

Secondly, such as are preserved for voyce, and are called singing Byrds, as the Nightingall, Throstell, Linnet, Larks, Bulfinch, Spynke and divers of the same, all which are good in the dishe also.

Thirdly . . . all such as are for pleasure onely, as Hawks of all kindes, Castrells, Ringtailes, Buzards, Kites, and generally Birdes of Prey.

These categories were, of course, fluid and not mutually exclusive. Whether treasured for their song or merely for their appearance, birds of almost any species were always liable to end up on the dinner table: Markham extols both the beauty of the pheasant, for example, 'as rare as any Byrde that flies', but also its eating properties, 'when shee is in the dish, & well cookt by a skillfull and ingenious workeman'. Even the skylarks mentioned above would be lucky to escape the pot, for in his *History of Birds* William Yarrell reminds us of a time before they came to epitomize freedom of spirit in a way that renders them today completely untouchable in the wild:

From the number of male Skylarks sold for cage birds and the high price which the best songsters among them command, various means are used to entrap them, yet it is rather the excellence of the species for the table, its abundance and the ease with which it is taken that form the great incentive to the lark-catcher. Out of the vast flocks which . . . assemble in autumn, thousands are caught by dragging nets over the stubbles and fallows at night, and by day even more are enticed by a call-bird within the reach of clap-nets. Hundreds are also snared in time of snow; while during the 'flight', scores are uselessly shot, attracted by a piece of wood beset with bits of looking-glass . . .

In a note, the same author adds that 'Brighton enjoys the credit for consuming more Larks than any other place in England, except London. Dr Wynter in 1854 estimated those entering the metropolitan markets alone at 400,000'. Poulterers could generally be relied on to supply not only larks but also blackbirds and thrushes with as much ease as other wildfowl.

SOME LOST SPECIES

Amongst the larger game birds, one of the most spectacular is the crane, *Megalornis grus* (illus. 74), formerly widespread in England (Yalden and Albarella find 225 place names with a 'crane' element) but extinct as a breeding species in Britain, probably since the late sixteenth century. The same authors note how crane bones are comparatively numerous from early medieval and earlier excavated sites, but that during the final phase of their decline they are rarely found outside high-status residences. By this time, it seems, aristocratic landowners with rights over game had become eager to preserve cranes for their own sport in falconry as much as for their value on the table, although the two necessarily went hand-in-hand as an expression of privilege. (Creighton characterizes the crane as bony, awkward to eat and not valued for its taste, but the difficulty in obtaining it made it none the less highly valued at medieval feasts.) Henry VIII extended his protection to their eggs in 1534 by instituting a fine of 20d. for every egg taken by miscreants, though naturally prompted purely by self interest: Samuel Pegge finds references to him entertaining the French ambassadors in 1527 to a banquet of (amongst many other things) twelve swans and twelve cranes. Although hunting undoubtedly took a heavy toll on the crane, it seems likely that its end was hastened by progressive drainage of its natural habitat in the Fens, after which occasional winter visitors from Scandinavia were all that might be expected. William Turner, writing in 1544, was unequivocal about there being a surviving breeding population at that time: cranes, he said, 'breed in England in marshy places. I myself have very often seen their pipers [their young], though some people born away from England urge that this is false.' While they remained flightless the young birds were, it seems, easily caught and were amenable to being brought up in captivity, where they could be force-fed for the pot. A century or so later, in his edition of Willughby's *Ornithology* (1678), John Ray mentions that 'in the Fen-Countries in Lincolnshire and Cambridgeshire there are great flocks of them, but whether or no they breed in England . . . I cannot certainly determine'. Opinion now is that these were already likely to have been winter migrants rather than

74 'Grus, The Crane', from John Ray, *The Ornithology of Francis Willughby* (1678).

resident birds and by 1766 Pennant writes that 'at present the inhabitants of those counties seem unacquainted with them'. More than a century later, Tegetmeier could add to Edward Blyth's *Natural History of Cranes* (1881) the fact that four had been shot in Norfolk in 1869, but these are judged to have been casual visitors: the resident population was by now definitively extinct.

The fate of another casualty amongst British game birds – the largest of recent times, the great bustard, *Otis tarda* (illus. 75) – is similarly thought to have been determined by a range of factors. Like the crane, it was consumed in quantity at festive banquets in the medieval period, but its ultimate decline may have been due as much to the progressive enclosure of the open landscape it favoured as to its persecution by fowlers. Yalden and Albarello suggest that the bustard may not indeed have established itself in England until the open, treeless landscape that typified medieval agriculture in East Anglia, the Wolds and the Downs had evolved in the first place; it may be noted in this context that there is no Anglo-Saxon word denoting the bustard. Thomas Moffet, writing at the end of the sixteenth century, recalled encountering them in some numbers: 'I have seen a dozen of them lie in a wheat field, fattening themselves . . . with ease and eating; whereupon they grow to such bigness, that one of them weigheth almost fourteen pounds.' In 1766 Pennant could still write that they were to be found in the autumn in Wiltshire, 'in large turnep fields near the Downs, and in flocks of fifty or more'; he also asserts that they could weigh up to 25–7 pounds and achieve a wingspan of 9 feet. His is the last eyewitness account of them, however, before they disappeared. In addition to the environmental factors that may have hastened their decline, they would have made a particularly easy target for fowlers shooting them with sporting guns on the wing, for although they could run at some speed their take-off and progress in flight was slow and cumbersome. Bingley adds that the young ones were sometimes coursed and taken by greyhounds.

The capercaillie (*Tetrao urogallus*), on the other hand, disappeared from all but the northern counties of England during the medieval period but remained well established in the pine forests of Scotland until extensive deforestation in the eighteenth century drove it out. The crucial role of habitat in the history of all these birds is reflected in the history since that time of this large woodland grouse: it was successfully reintroduced in 1835 following a period of extensive reforestation, but in recent years has found itself under pressure once again, with native pine forests proving scarcely extensive enough to maintain the population and with their commercial equivalents representing hazardous and unpredictable substitutes.

BIRD-LIME

Perhaps the simplest way of taking small birds, without the need for any of the sensitive and intricate devices that skilled trappers deployed in great variety, involved the use of a glutinous adhesive which the trapper would deploy around the target zone: any contact with it by the bird – whether beak or foot or feather – was enough to stick it fast, so encumbering its escape. The preparation of bird-lime was a somewhat painstaking matter, as made clear in the closely specified discourse 'Of the making of the best Lyme' committed to print by Markham in 1621 (and expanding on a similar recipe given in *Jewell for Gentrie* a few years earlier):

To make then the best and most excellentest Bird-lime, you shall take at Midsomer the Barke of Holly and pill it from the Tree, so much as will fill a reasonable bigge vessell, then put to it running water, and set it on the fire, and boyle it till the grey and white Barke rise from the greene, which will take for the most part, a whole day or better in boyling, then take it from the fire and seperate the Barkes after the water is very well drained from it, which done, take all the greene Barke and lay it on the ground in a close place, and a moist floare, as in some low Vault or Cellar, and then with all manner of green

75 The great bustard (*Otis tarda*). Preparatory drawing in ink and water-colour, 1791, by Thomas Bewick for his *British Birds* (1797).

weedes, as Docks, Hemlock, Thystels and the like, cover it quite over a good thicknesse, and so let it lye for the space of tenne or twelve daies, in which time it will rot and turne to a filthie and slymie matter, then take it up from the ground and put it into a lardge morter and there beate and grinde it exceedingly till it be comed to one universall paste or toughnesse, without the discerning of any part of the Barke or other substance, which as soone as you see, you shall take it out of the morter, and carry it to a quicke and swift running streame, and there wash it exceedingly, not leaving any mote or foulnesse within it, then put it up in a very close earthen pot, and let it stand and purge for divers daies together, not omitting but to skum it and clense it as any foulnesse rises, for at least three or four dayes together, and then perceiving no more skum will arise, you shall then take it out of that pot and put it another cleane earthen vessel and cover it close, and so keepe it.

Applying the resulting substance to the twigs, branches and strings used to enmesh the birds required further preparation:

you shall take of it such a quantitite as you shall thinke fit, and putting it into an earthen pipkin, with a third part of Hogges-grease, Capons-grease or Goose-grease, finely clarified . . . and set it one a very gentle fire and there let them melt together, and that you cannot discerne any separation of the bodies, but all one entire and perfit substance, then take it from the fire and coole it, stirring it still till it be cold.

If the weather was frosty (when the basic mixture was apt to lose its adhesive power), the addition of 'oyle of Peter (which the Pothecaries call Petrolium)' ensured that it remained fully functional. The best quality was also necessary if it was to remain effective in damp or wet conditions: amongst the additives to improve waterproofing and resistance to frost suggested by Mascall in 1590 were 'rosome' [rosin?] and white turpentine.

Having been suitably prepared, the lime was then applied to the twigs or rods in front of a fire to keep it malleable; the sticks were to be repeatedly rubbed against one another until each was smoothly coated. Strings were treated in similar fashion, 'the knots only excepted, which must be a little better lymed then any other part of the corde; both because of their weight and that they may fasten a great deal the sooner'. So equipped, the fowler was ready to go in search of birds both large and small, for the sticking power of the lime was such that it could be used in taking a wide range of species.

Typically, for larger birds such as geese, a live decoy of the same species would be tethered in one of their usual haunts, while the area round about it was staked out with row after row of limed rods, placed at an angle and spaced about a foot apart, 'till you have covered the haunt all over, and left no place for any Fowle to fall besides them'.

The majority of the rods – *Jewell for Gentrie* recommends that the most supple are to be cut from the trunk of the tree rather than from its branches – would incline into the wind, but occasional rows were be set at right angles to intercept birds trying to follow the line of the sticks. For smaller waterfowl the rods might be set at the water's edge where the birds would come ashore; in this case the rods had to incline away from the shore, while other rods could be set overhanging the water itself in the hope of besmearing birds swimming near the shore. Limed strings could be interspersed with the rods in either setting, those over the water being held clear on forked sticks. Variations for birds such as pheasants involved binding bundles of limed twigs together to form 'bushes', to be set in the ground or amongst the undergrowth where they habitually ran, while in stubble fields limed straws would be used; frequently when one bird was limed in this way the others in its covey would be attracted by the commotion and would themselves become caught up – 'by reason that they come flocking and close together, like so many Chickins, they wil so besmeare and daube one another, that if there be twenty in the Coovey hardly any one will escape'. The author of the *Jewell for Gentrie* writes that he has little to say on the use of the lime-bush, 'for it is commonly knowne and practised of all both Winter and Sommer'.

Plovers were targeted with limed strings draped across their landing areas, while for smaller species a little dome of limed twigs constructed over a tempting deposit of grain would suffice. Larger birds such as geese, heron and crane could also be taken with limed twigs; only the spacing of the rows needed to be increased, to induce the birds to walk between them.

Leonard Mascall offers the following method for taking 'sea-pies and crows': two small oziers are

Y Y Y Y Y Y Y Y Y Y Y Y Y Y Y Y Y Y Y Y Y Y Y Y

bent together crosswise near the end and bait is tied to the twigs with a short thread; the twigs are then limed and placed on some water weed or rushes with the intention that the birds will 'flie away with it in their bylles, and soon they shall be lymed therewyth . . . for the twigs will turne and touch her wings, and then the pye will fall'. Such a stratagem worked only for certain varieties of birds: 'you will hardly catch the Kyte, because he takes the bayte in his feete, and the other takes it in their billes'. An alternative 'Pretie way to Take a Pye' is given as follows:

Ye shall lime a small threede, a foote long or more, and then tie one end about a piece of flesh so big as shee may flie away withall: and at the other end of the thread, tie a shoe buckle and lay the flesh on a poste, and let the threede hang downe, and when she flies away with it the threede with the buckle will wrappe round her, and then she will fal, so ye may take them.

Such was the efficacy of the lime that the fowler had no need to stay permanently on the spot, but could visit periodically to check on results, although he might beat a few of the alternative haunts nearby before retiring in order to encourage the fowl into the area he had prepared. If on his return any of the twigs or strings were missing, his dog would be sent into the bushes to flush out any birds that had taken cover on finding they were unable to fly, or into the water in pursuit of those attempting to escape by swimming. In time the birds might become wary and desert a site where trapping of this sort was carried out repeatedly, but a month's rest was generally enough to bring them back again.

STUPEFACTION, OR 'PRETIE WAYS TO MAKE BIRDS DRUNKE'

Several methods are given in *Jewell for Gentrie* by which birds could be rendered incapable of escape by tempting them with food laced with drugs or alcohol. The first, titled 'A rare secret to catch Fowle, as Geese, Duckes, or Birds', involved the use of *Nux vomica*, 'otherwaies called in English the Spring Nut': a quantity was mixed with grain and strewn on a spot habituated by wild geese and so on, 'and as soone as they eate of this, they will sound, and you may take them with your hand'. An alternative means of administration was to insert the powdered nut into a piece of meat, 'and so soone as any fowle eates of this, they will be overcome, and they will flie, boult upright, and fall downe to the ground straight againe, and so you may take them'. Powdered *Nux vomica* was also recommended for the destruction of kites, ravens and other 'carronous fowle'.

Grain steeped in lees of wine or in the juice of hemlock might also be scattered for unwary birds, 'and if they eat thereof, straightwaies they will be so giddie that you may take them with your hand'. The following recipe is also provided in *Jewell for Gentrie*:

Take the seede of Belenge, and the rootes also, and steepe them in water the space of a day and a night: then seeth the said seeds in the water that they were steeped in, so that the seeds may well drinke and soke up the water, then lay the said seeds or graine in the places where wilde Duckes and wilde Geese are wont to resort, and they will eate this graine or seede so prepared, and thereupon will sleepe as they were drunke, and in the meane time you may take them with your hands; but there must be a pretie quantitie of this, especially for wilde Geese. This may also serve to take all manner of Fowle that goe together in sholes or companies. If you seeth this graine in Brimstone, and lay it in the places where Birds and Fowles are wont to feede, and all that eate of it will fall downe and die: but to keepe them that they die not, you must give them to drinke Oyle Olive, and shortly after they will revive againe. This is approved.

Enterprising hunters armed with no more than a bow and arrow had reaped a steady – if elusive – harvest of wildfowl for thousands of years before the advent of gunpowder transformed the potential reward for individual initiative. Hawking too provided an effective means of targeting individual birds (pp. 175–86), but trapping had always offered a far higher success rate and the prospect of a more dependable food supply – ever a more important consideration than the mere display of skill, at least until the advent of the feudal aristocracy. Many large estates may have emulated the example of Richard de Swinfield, a thirteenth-century Bishop of Hereford, who is recorded as employing a fowler to set nets in the autumn to catch partridges and other birds for the episcopal kitchen. Twines and strings, snares and nets were more effective than weapons – even after the development of efficient shotguns that brought sportsmen into an arena that hitherto had been the preserve of less glamorous skills, slowly evolved and handed down form one generation of countrymen to the next. The fowler interrogated in Aelfric's *Colloquy* shows that in Anglo-Saxon England on the eve of the Norman conquest a wide range of techniques was in use, including the use of nets, snares, lime, decoys and traps, and a glance at a survey such as the Revd H. A. MacPherson's *History of Fowling*

provides confirmation that many of these techniques were observed (with local variations) over much of the Old World, often having developed independently in response to common needs.

Some of the methods used depended on active pursuit of the birds (usually while they were in roosting mode) and some involved traps to which the quarry was attracted. A judicious scattering of grain might be all that was required to bring them within reach, or it might be that they were lured by some eye-catching device. These included the 'gig', made from quill-feathers in the manner of a shuttlecock, which danced and bobbed in the wind; in the absence of wind, one author asserts that a fox-tail, 'pulled up within the compass of your net will make the larks strike at it as if it were a weasel'. Larks, which were a particular target of English fowlers, might also be attracted by use of a 'larkmirror', a rotating device set with shards of broken looking-glass that flashed in the sunshine in an appealing manner: the *Jewell for Gentrie* recommended it for use 'at the latter end of the yeare, when Birds are least apt to play'. Birdcalls – whistles in various materials which imitated the call of the particular game – were widely commended. These would be quite species-specific: a quail-call illustrated by Rowley is made from a goose leg-bone in which two lateral holes are drilled and to one end of which is attached a segmented tube of leather that, when compressed in the manner of a bicycle pump, forces air through the holes. A less usual form developed to mimic the rasping call of the land rail (or corn-crake) took the form of a rattle in which a toothed cog-wheel was rotated against a wooden tongue.

For certain species, live decoys in the form of birds that had already been trapped were also effective, whether in cages or in the wild more generally tethered to a stake within the trapping area where they could flutter about, attracting other birds – particularly those of similar species – within its compass. Sometimes the opposite strategy was adopted and a bird inimical to those being targeted might be used to catch their attention: the *Jewell for Gentrie* recommends the use of a tethered owl to attract smaller birds that could be trapped as they swooped on it (see illus. 76). It was a standard practice among fowlers that some proportion of the live catch on any particular day would be saved for use as decoys on the next. How that catch might be effected depended on local conditions and on the particular species being targeted.

Snares, frequently made from plaited horse-hair, constituted a form of trap easily available to all, by which birds with particular behaviour patterns on the ground could be taken. Willughby and Ray tell us that the shepherds in Sussex, for example, caught large numbers of wheatears by this method:

They dig long turves of earth, and lay them across the holes whereout they were digged, and about the middle of them hang snares

made of horse-hair. The Birds, being naturally very timorous, if a Hawk happen to appear, or but a cloud pass over and intercept the Sun-beams, hastily run to hide themselves in the holes under the Turves, and are caught by the neck in the Snares.

MacPherson quotes the testimony of one such shepherd who claimed to catch three or four dozen birds on a good day by this method, and to have had a personal best of thirteen dozen in a single day, sold to a poulterer in Brighton who took all that could be caught at 18d. a dozen. The same source mentions an even greater number being taken in one day by a fellow shepherd at East Dean in the same county:

I think they said he took nearly a hundred dozen, so many that they could not thread them on crow-quills, in the usual manner; but he took off his round frock and made a sack of it to put them into, and his wife did the same with her petticoat. This must have

76 'Owling', by Henry Alken, 1821. The captive owl is agitated by pulling on a string attached to it; the other birds swoop in with the intention of mobbing the owl and become smeared with bird lime which has been spread on the nearby perches.

happened when there was a great flight. Their numbers are now so decreased that some shepherds do not set up any coops, as it does not pay for the trouble.

On occasion the snares formed part of traps known as 'springes' or 'sprints', in which the noose was attached to a supple wand that sprang straight when it was tripped, tightening the noose around the quarry and hoisting it into the air. Snipe and woodcock were taken in this way: Pennant describes their use in Westmorland, where they were 'Laid between tufts of heather with avenues of small stones one each side' to guide the birds into the traps, 'for they will not hop over the pebbles'.

Heron were among the other species specifically targeted with special traps. Robert Howlett, in his *School of Recreation* (1684) writes of 'the most approved way' of taking the great Fish-devouring Herne':

> Get three or four small Roaches, or Dace, take a strong Hook, (not too rank) with Wyre to it, and draw the wire just within the skin, from the side of the Gills, to the Taile of the said Fish, and he will live four or five days, (if dead, the Herne will not touch it.) Then having a strong Line, of a dark-Green-Silk, twisted with Wyre, about three yards long, tye a round stone or a Pound to it, and lay three or four such hooks, but not too deep in the Water, out of the Herne's wading; and two or three Nights will answer your Expectation.

The use of nets of various kinds provided trappers with the potential to scale up their activities, with luck taking large numbers of birds at a time. Amongst the principal varieties recorded are flight-nets, in which the birds became entangled on the wing, passive nets to take them on the ground and clap-nets which were thrown over the quarry by various methods; smaller hand-nets, mounted on poles, might also be used at close quarters to trap individual birds. Materials and mesh sizes were chosen according to the game being pursued: to take plover, for example, Markham recommended 'the strongest & best twind Packthred, with great and large mashes, at least two Inches from poynt to poynt, or from knot to knot', the net to be 'verged on each side with very strong Corde'.

Some netting took place at night, when certain species at least were roosting and more easily taken. Fire was often used to take those hunted with clap-nets, while some flight-nets, especially in the coastal regions, intercepted night-flying birds.

Flight-nets and other static nets

At their simplest, flight-nets might simply be strung up on poles in locations where they could be expected to intercept unwary birds. Coastal settings were especially productive and waders of all sorts were especially vulnerable to being taken, but nets could also be placed in the flight path of birds taking off from enclosed ponds and lakes. Stevenson records that they were brought out for two seasons in the year, at Michaelmas (September to October) and at Lady Day (March to April). He provides an excellent account of their use on dark, still nights in late nineteenth-century Norfolk:

> On the flat shores of the Wash, at the mouth of the estuary, long nets, some six or seven feet deep, are stretched upright on poles, somewhere about high water mark; and the birds, in their nocturnal flight, strike the nets, and, becoming entangled in the meshes, are taken alive in the morning . . .

The meshes are large, so that various gulls and wildfowl are caught by them. But the smaller *Tringae*, and even larks, are taken in some quantities, being entangled by their struggles. I have heard of as many as sixty dunlins having been secured at one haul – and on one occasion as many as 140 head, principally seagulls.

At nearby King's Lynn, Rowley records that 'about 2,000 yards of net are set, not all in one length but mostly four or five breadths together, and in angles or curves, with guies at the extremities to keep it well extended'. These extreme lengths seem to be characteristic of later use, and were employed, for example, by bird-catchers on the Sussex Downs in the late nineteenth century. Orientation might to some extent be determined by the quarry sought: Stevenson observes that lapwings prefer to fly with the wind while ruffs and reeves fly against it from choice, so that the nets needed to be arranged accordingly.

The same technique might be used to trap woodcock and similar inland birds. Richard Blome in his *Gentleman's Recreation* describes the method of clearing 'cock-roads' or 'through-fares' some 30–40 feet in width through the woods, along which birds might be driven into nets hoisted on pulleys in the trees. Alternatively, the birds could be driven at ground level by parties of beaters, into nets arranged at a slope to intercept the birds, which were cornered underneath them. Other species prone to creeping away from danger by running along the ground rather than instantly taking flight, could also be taken by this method. Pheasant were similarly pursued – there was even a special sort of rake or 'driver' made from osiers whose scratching was thought to be particularly effective in herding them. Driving the birds along the ground was a delicate operation, in which careful judgement was essential if they were not to be panicked into flight. Markham suggested that camouflage might help: 'it shall not be amisse if you wear over all your face a hood of some light green stuffe as sutable as you can to the leaves of the trees, having onely loope-holes for your eyes and nostrills', preferably with a wreath around the head and leafy branches attached to the clothing.

Other flight nets evidently were manipulated in use. Some echo of what may have been a widespread practice can be found in the account by Andrew Heaton of a technique used in Essex in the nineteenth century for trapping pochard – diving ducks that proved too elusive for the more conventional decoys described below: in the ponds they frequented, he tells us, pairs of trappers would work together, with one man putting up the birds while another released a net carried on weighted poles into their flight path; those caught by the net would fall to the bottom where a pocket was provided to hold them fast.

Passive nets

In his *Gentleman's Recreation* (1686) Richard Blome (drawing on earlier sources) mentions two methods by which partridges could be taken on the ground. The first relied on the tendency of partridge to remove themselves from danger by creeping along the ground rather than taking off instantly, a habit that allowed them to be driven gently into a tunnel-net, its catchment area increased by extending further stake-nets to either side of the mouth (illus. 77). Alternatively, during the 'wooing season' a hen partridge could be confined in a cage within a net (termed a hallier-net), pegged flat on the ground round about, in which any males attracted to the scene would become entangled.

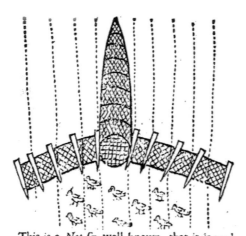

This is a *Net* so well known, that it is needless to give any further description of it.

77 Tunnel-net for taking partridges, from Richard Blome, *The Gentleman's Recreation* (1686).

Clap-nets

These involved the active participation of the fowler in securing the catch, frequently by enticing the fowl with decoy birds of some sort and then throwing the net over them while on the ground (illus. 78). Markham outlines the method, advising the fowler to 'spread his net plaine and flatte upon the ground, staking the two lower ends firm unto the ground', with poles inserted at either side and braced by cords staked out in line. The fowler would then attach a long cord to the top of the net which he should lead to a hide constructed at a distance, from where he could observe the fowl on their arrival, having taken care 'that his Net lye so tickle and yare that upon the least pull or twich it will rise from the earth and fly over'. Ideal spots included those where threshing or winnowing had recently taken place, so that there was plenty of grain to attract the birds.

Quaint though Markham's description sounds, the technique was highly effective and survived in use to the latter part of the nineteenth century. The testament of a contemporary fowler with 50 years' experience, recorded by G. D. Rowley in 1877, is worth quoting at length. In this instance it was deployed on the meres of East Anglia and on occasion would produce a catch of three or four dozen plovers at a time:

We place the net on a hill surrounded by water about five inches deep, and use stuffed decoy birds, about ten in number, and one living bird . . . The net is 25 yards long and 8 yards deep, and the mesh 2¾ inches square. This is for land work. For water it is 10 yards long and 4 yards deep. We place ourselves 140 yards from the net, sheltered with

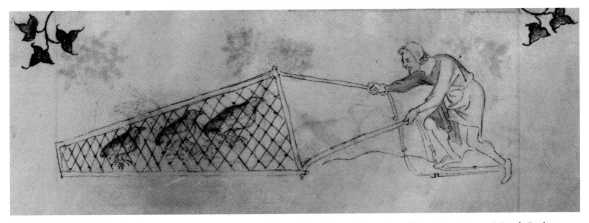

78 A peasant uses a simple clap-net to capture a covey of partridges. From the early 14th-century Queen Mary's Psalter.

reeds tied on to rods to hide us. When the plovers come down upon the hill we pull the net over them . . . We catch from Sunrise to sunset . . .

We always set to pull against the wind. The decoy birds sit on hills 1 foot across and 2 inches above the water at the head of the net. When we see any plover a quarter of a mile off, or perhaps more, if the sun shines on the decoy bird, we pull the string which is fastened to his leg, and the bird opens its wings. The plovers then come direct to the net, and fly very low over it. When they are all passed and clear, the string is pulled again, and, the decoy opening its wings, the plovers think some of the party behind have begun to settle. Then they turn back, meeting the wind which they always do, and try to drop near the decoy-bird; but finding the water too deep, they draw onto the hill and are covered with the net. When the water-nets are set, everything is under water except the decoy-birds standing on their little hills; but with the land-nets all is visible.

Stevenson presents a similar description of the technique in action, and mentions that in certain of the now-drained areas of fenland, controlled flooding to a depth of about 6 inches would be arranged by means of a sluice specifically for this purpose, the fowler, if necessary, creating artificial island refuges to attract the birds. Later developments of this technique included means of firing the nets over the birds (including the use of rockets), but they were described by Rowley in 1877 as 'clumsy and not much used'.

A development of this technique was the 'day-net', which employed two opposed nets staked out and braced in the manner already described with lines drawn in between them so that, when thrown over, the edges of the nets just touched (illus. 79). A stale or decoy tethered in the middle helped to attract the birds: although the species was no doubt adjusted according to the birds being sought, *Jewell for Gentrie* suggests that a lark is best of all for this purpose and that the process involved 'fixing her fast to a long stick mortessed in a stake, which you must fasten in the ground, yet so as the sticke may move up and downe, and at every motion the Larke may flutter with her wings'. Gigs provided further visual attraction: 'you shall have a long Pole, hung about with shittle cocks of feathers, which you shall place within thirtie or fortie paces of your Nets, so directly in the mouth of the Winde, that they may wherle and turne about with a ceaselesse motion: this will gather about you abundance of Larckes, and all sorts of Birds'. A birdcall might be also be used maximize the attraction of the trapping area.

In 1681 Thomas Baskerville mentions Dunstable (Hertfordshire) as having 'large fields about it, where in the season they catch good larks,

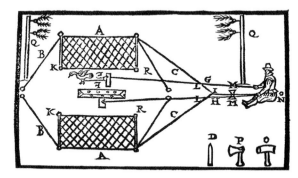

79 The 'Day-net' for trapping larks, bunting and so on, from Markham's *Hungers Prevention* (1621). Details shown include the nets A laid on the ground and braced at either side by the tail-lines B-C; the fowler holds the single line M with which he pulls the nets over and two further lines G-H with which he activates the live 'stale' or decoy E and the mechanical lure set with fragments of looking-glass F respectively; further lures or 'gigs' made of feathers are attached to flanking upright poles Q.

which have the greatest esteem for birds of that kind in London', and from Thomas Pennant we learn that the principal technique used at Dunstable from mid-November onwards involved the use of a clap-net deployed at night:

> This Nette, when you come into the place where the haunt of Birds are, which rest upon the earth . . . you shall then spread it upon the ground and let the neather or furthest end thereof (being plummed with small plummets of lead) lye loose on the ground, and then bearing up the former ende, by the strength of men at the two formost endes, onely trail it along the ground, not suffering that ende which is borne up to come neere the ground by a full yard or more. Then one each side the Nette shal bee carried great blazing lights of fire . . . and by the lightes others with long poales to beate up the birds as they goe, and as they rise under the Netts so to take them.

Jewell for Gentrie adds the observation that the birds, 'when they heare you tread, then will they flutter up into your net, which you shall quickly heare, then let down your net to the ground, and gripe them, and take them from under your net'.

A striking development of this nocturnal technique – widely used on the Continent as well as in England, testifying to its efficacy – was that known as low-belling, in which the use of a light (the 'low') and a hand-bell was combined with nets (illus. 80). Full advice on the deployment of this method is given in the *Jewell for Gentrie*:

> go with a great light of Cressets, or ragges of linen dipt in Tallow that will make a good light, and you must have a panne of plate, made like a Lanterne, to carrie your

light in . . . and carrie it before you on your brest, with a Bell in your other hand of a great bignesse, made in manner like to a Cowbell, but of greater bignes, and you must ring it allwayes after one order, with two to goe with Nets one of each side of him that carries the Bell, and what with the light that so doth amase them, and the Bell that so doth astonish them, they will, when you come neere them, turn up their white bellies, which you shall quickely perceive, then lay your Nets on them and take them; but the Bell must not stint going: for if it cease, then the Birds will flye up if there be any more nigh. This is a good way to catch Larckes, Woodcockes, and Partriches, and all other land-Birdes.

More detailed advice is provided by Markham in *Hungers Prevention*:

> After the night hath covered the face of the earth . . . the Ayre being mild, and the Moon not shining, you shall take your Low-Bell, which is a Bell of such a reasonable size as a man may well carry in one hand, and having a deep, hollow, and sad sound, for the more quick and shrill it is the worse it is, and the more sad and solemne the better: and with this Bell you shall have a net (of a small mesh) at least twenty yards deep, and so broad that it may cover five or six ordinary Lands and more, according as you have company to carry it (for the more ground it cover, the more is your sport, and the richer the prey that is taken); with these instruments you shall go into some stubble field, either Wheat, Rye, or Barley, but the Wheat is the best, and he which carrieth the Bell shall goe the formost, and toll the Bell as hee

goeth along, so solemnly as may be, letting it but now and then knock on both sides; then shall follow the net, being borne up at each corner and one each side by sundry persons; then another man shall carry an old yron Cresset, or some other vessel of stone or yron in which you shall good store of sinders or burning coales (but not blazing), and at these you shall light bundles of dry Straw . . . and then having spread and pitcht youre Nette where you thinke any Game is (having all your lights blazing), with noyses and poles beat up all that are under the Net, and then presently, as they flicker up, you shall see them intangled in the Net, so as you may take them at your pleasure: as Partriges, Rayles, Larkes, Quailes, or any other small Birdes of what kind soever may lodge upon the ground, which done, you shall suddenly extinguish your lights, and then proceede forward and lay your Net in another place.

The mesmerizing effect of the bell (which was to be the only sound heard during the advance) followed by the sudden blaze of the torches was crucial to its effectiveness. According to Markham 'the sound of the Bell makes the Byrdes to lye closse, so as they dare not stirre or offer to remoove away, whilest you are pitching and laying your net, for the sound thereof is dreadfull to them'. The exercise could continue all night, he suggests, so long as there is no moon.

Hand-nets and batfowling

A well developed type of hand-net, called by Markham the sparrow-net, was again specifically for night-time use – preferably in late evening or just before dawn. To the top of a long pole was attached a cross-bar 'like unto the head of an ordinary hay-rake', suitably braced; a shorter pole with similar cross-bar was anchored to the first in a socket and secured with a thong which allowed it to pivot so that the two heads could readily be brought together by pulling on a pair of cords, secured to the extremities of one head and running through corresponding holes on the other; the mouth of a wide purse-net was then secured to the cross-bars so that it could be opened and closed at will, while its closed end was tied to the pivot already mentioned. Armed with this device a lone fowler could make his way around the thatched eves of houses or other promising sites ('Barnes, Stables, Stackes, Hovels, Out Houses, Dovecoates'), knocking the heads together in order to frighten the birds out of their nesting places and into the waiting mouth of the net, which was quickly closed by pulling on the cord. It was particularly recommended for sparrows, robins, wrens, starlings, and 'extravagant Pygions that lye out of the Dove-Coate', and the quarry was recommended especially to sustain mewing hawks in need of fresh morsels.

Batfowling (see illus. 80) was a group activity suited to bushy or wooded country or for use along hedgerows where varieties of birds might perch for the night. Markham gives the personnel as one to carry a cresset or lamp and others with torches mounted on poles; a third company will be armed with long poles with bushy ends: willow, birch or hazel are recommended.

Kindle some of the torches while those with bushy poles beat the trees etc. Which done you shall see the Birds which are raysed, to fly and play about the lights and flames of the fier, for it is their nature through their amazednesse, and affright at the strangenes of the lightt and at the extreme darknesse round about it, not to depart from it, but as

80 'Taking birds with a Low-Bell and Bat Fowling', commissioned by Richard Blome for his *Gentleman's Recreation* (1686).

it were to scorch their wings in the same; so that those which have the rough bushye poales, may . . . beat them down with the same & so take them.

Nets might be used to supplement the poles, and other authors recommend the use of limed boughs to entangle the birds. The 'folding net' recommended at the turn of the nineteenth century by the *Sporting Dictionary* was evidently much like Markham's sparrow-net:

Upon the net being spread, by separating the side rods to their utmost extent, before the corn-rick, out-houses, eaves of stable thatch, yew hedge, or whatever spot it is intended to try . . . the assistants begin to beat . . . with their poles; when the birds

279

being thus suddenly alarmed from their resting-place, make instantly for the light, when the net being directly closed (if by a skilful practitioner) the success is beyond description; it being a common thing, in large remote farms, and in severe winters, to take twenty or thirty dozen of sparrows, and other small birds, in one evening's diversion.

DUCKS AND OTHER WATERFOWL

Writers on the Fens and marshes, to a man or woman, invoke a Golden Age before the advent of widespread drainage, when water covered much of the landscape and the skies were seasonally dark with clouds of migrating birds. Thus Wentworth-Day:

> those were the days when Fen skies were thunderous with the wings of wildfowl. Great teams of mallard and shoveller etched their way against the high skies. Vast gaggles of geese and herds of white trumpeting swans made the starlit silences clamorous . . .

Some 300 square miles of present-day farmland stretching from northern Lincolnshire to Huntingdon and out to the Norfolk coast were seasonally or permanently inundated to such a degree that they formed one great watery waste land, up to the period of the first large-scale attempts to tame it in the seventeenth century. Lord Burleigh's General Drainage Act (1601) set the agenda, but it was the import by James I of the Dutch engineer Cornelius Vermuyden in 1621 that gave a major impetus to the project that eventually would run for some two and a half centuries before it could be declared substantially complete. Whatever the bounty in terms of wildfowl, the human inhabitants of this region tended to be regarded by their contemporaries with – at best – pity throughout this period, but the fact is that they adapted themselves perfectly well to this evolving landscape of meres and bogs and reeds, balanced between open water and dry land but offering singular resources which they learned to exploit with commendable efficiency. In fact, the very process of change benefited some of the fowling techniques described here by concentrating the wildfowl on to smaller and more accessible areas of water, enabling the development of new methods of trapping that were ineffectual on wide stretches of water.

Duck drives

Patterns of activity in the fens were governed every bit as much by the seasons as they were in the fields. The summer months, when the birds were in moult and at their most vulnerable, provided particular opportunities and if the wildfowl were in less than peak condition at this time considerations of sheer accessibility none the less took precedence. Doubtless many stratagems that have left no trace were developed to exploit this annual bounty, but from the medieval period we may begin to glimpse some of the techniques developed over centuries or perhaps millennia of close observation and careful planning and which survived into the modern era where they could be recorded.

In his advice to wildfowlers, Markham mentions that while the birds are in moult, dogs can be used to drive them out of their cover and into nets, for in their flightless state 'sheepe will not drive more easily than those Fowle at this time'. The custom no doubt had a long tradition amongst individuals or small groups of fowlers, but on the Fens it was transformed into a community activity that brought together large numbers of people to drive entire flocks of grounded fowl into an extensive array of nets. Men, women and children would assemble in massed boats to sweep across the marshes, beating the birds out of the reeds and inexorably towards the nets, arranged at a suitably constricted part of the mere, where they could be systematically slaughtered. By staking out the nets along a narrowing stretch of shoreline, the beaters concentrated the birds in an ever more confined space and ultimately into tunnels of netting, from which there was no escape. The harvest from these drives could be impressive and almost inevitably became a source of envy amongst those who found themselves excluded from the benefits: from 1280 and from 1415 there are records of disaffected countrymen invading the property of the Abbot of Crowland (Lincolnshire) in order to drive his wildfowl and from 1432 a more fully documented incident in which an armed mob seized the Abbot's nets and carried off with them 600 birds. That even this may have been a modest catch is indicated by a more extensive notice of the practice in Francis Willughby's *Ornithology* of 1676, published in English translation two years later, with both editions edited by and extensively enhanced by John Ray. In both versions the passage in question (almost certainly interpolated by Ray) gives useful details of actual practice, showing the process to be more complex than the above summary might suggest, and is accompanied by an explanatory diagram:

> In the Fens of the Isle of Ely, Norfolk and Lincolnshire, about Crowland, and elsewhere, Ducks, Wigeons, Teal, and other birds of this kind, at what time they moult their feathers and cannot fly, are taken yearly in great number in Nets, placed after this manner.

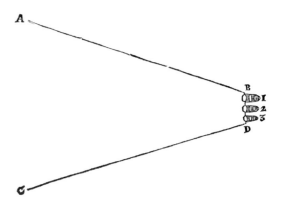

AB, CD are Nets extending a great length in form of a wall or hedge, inclining one to another, at the further end of which, before they concur in an angle are placed 1, 2, 3, or more conoideal Nets, like tunnelling Nets for Partridges. Which things being so prepared, and the day of fowling set, there is a great concourse of men and boats. These drive the Birds, now unable to fly, into the grounds enclosed in the Nets with long Staves and Poles, and so by degrees into those Conoideal Tunnels, 1, 2, 3, disposed, as we said in the angle. By the way many are knocked down by the Boatmen and other Rabble with their Poles, others and more are driven upon the side Nets, AB, CD. These belong to them who own the Nets (for the Nets for the most part have several owners) those fall to their shares that killed them. Those which are cooped up, and driven into the end-tunnels, 1, 2, 3, belong to the Lord of the Soil. To one Fowling sometimes you shall have four hundred Boats meet. We have heard that there have been four thousand Mallards taken at one Driving in Deeping Fen.

Cook and Pilcher further reproduce a document in the possession of the Spalding Gentlemen's Club in which 155 dozen birds are mentioned as having been caught 'at One Push into the Netts' in 1728 in the same Deeping Fen; daily totals of 394, 387 and 305 dozen birds are recorded in this source. The document is also instructive as to both the make-up of the catch and the rights of ownership:

> That is, the country People have Right of Common, Enclosing hundreds of acres with large Nets having pipes at their Ends and driving the Moulted Mallards or Male Wild-fowles into those Nets. N.B. There are very few female or Ducks when they being with their Young feeding out at Sea, but the Drakes being sick or unable to fly their Wing Feath-ers being gone with casting their Feathers stay amongst the Reeds and Rushes in the broad fresh Waters.

The scale and the indiscriminate nature of these catches inevitably gave rise to concern among the owners of rights and eventually legislation was produced in an attempt to limit a perceived decline amongst the bird populations. In an Act introduced in 1534, 'The Cause of the Decay in Wildfowl' was attributed to 'the taking them in Summer Time and in their Moulting Season' and henceforth the taking of fowl between 31 May and 31 August was to be prohibited. However, the dissolution of the monasteries that hitherto had played an important role in administering control in the Fens – the smaller ones suppressed in 1536 and larger establishments such as Crowland, Thor-ney and Peterborough, in 1539 – threw the rhy-thms of life into disarray and the poorer folk in particular were left destitute and short of food. In 1550 the Act was repealed, allowing continuation of the former practice.

It had, indeed, some persuasive advocates. Markham, for example, acknowledged that some

decried the driving of fowl, but to him it provided the opportunity of turning poor-quality fowl into much better specimens, by taking them alive and fattening them in captivity: if such critics, he suggested,

> please to consider the great infinits of these Fowle which cannot decrease & the excel-lency of the time for feeding and cram-ming them, whereby one is made more excellent than twenty, they cannot chuse but both allow it and practise it, for who know-eth not that any Fowle which preyeth for itself abroad, except it be the Mallard, Teyle and Plover, but is a great deale less sweet and pleasant than the crambed Fowle, some tasting of Fishe, some of mudde, and some of grasse.

Only in 1710 was the practice of driving water-fowl in this way finally declared illegal.

Duck decoys

In the same source in which he described driving in such useful detail, Ray also referred to 'a new artifice' which ultimately would transform the method of trapping ducks from the blunt instru-ment it had always been to an ingenious pursuit in which a single man could be expected to pro-duce annual catches of 5,000–10,000 birds, far exceeding the wildest dreams of the massed ranks of his ancestors.

Duck decoys, whose numbers had reached almost 200 when recorded by Payne-Gallwey in 1886 (with a further twenty in Ireland), made their first appearance in England by the early decades of the seventeenth century at the latest. Primacy is generally given to that erected at Waxham (Nor-folk) around 1620 by Sir William Woodhouse; it was he, according to Sir Henry Spelman (d. 1641), who 'made among us the first device for catching Ducks, known by the foreign name of a *koye*'. The term betrays the origin of the idea in Holland (*endekooy* in Dutch means a duck cage), although the medieval traps referred to above were already known as decoys – from the same origin – evidently indicating a longer familiarity amongst the fenmen with practices across the North Sea.

Conventionally, responsibility for the next well-documented decoy is given to the otherwise unknown Sydrach Hilcus, conjectured to have been brought from Holland on purpose at the initiative of King Charles II: his installation, built at a cost of £30, was placed in the unlikely setting of an island in the lake of St James's Park, where it could never have achieved the levels of success claimed by some of its rustic contemporaries, although it had the advantage of attracting the attentions of John Evelyn, who alludes to it several times in his diary between 1665 and 1681 and who had earlier seen decoys in operation in Holland in 1641. The Dutch origin of the idea, at least, finds further support in a passage – again almost certainly one interpolated by Ray – in the 1678 edition of Willughby's *Ornithology*:

> Our Country-men (imitating, as I suppose, the Low Dutch, who were Authors of the invention) in maritime and fenny places, in Pools prepared by a new Artifice and fitted with their Channels and Nets, and stored with Coy-Ducks, take yearly in the Winter-time Duck and Mallard, Wigeon and Teal, and other birds of the Duck-kind in great numbers.

The passage goes on to describe every detail of the conventions and practices that continued to be observed up to the demise of the decoy in the later nineteenth and twentieth centuries, surely indicating that the use of decoys had been adopted in the fens some generations earlier than those recorded in polite literature. The pace of change observed by those whose livelihood depended on the predictable functioning of the 'new Artifice' would never have allowed for their widespread adoption in such a short space of time and it seems clear that the countrymen had no need of royal example in seizing the benefits offered by the device which had already proved so effective among the Dutch. For confirmation of this thesis it may be noted that an estate map from Suffolk dated 1652 and showing an entire complex of decoys (see below, illus. 84), recently published by Tom Williamson, indicates that rural East Anglia was getting on with the business of trapping ducks in the Dutch manner long before London society was charmed by Charles II's souvenir of his sojourn in Holland. Writing on the process of 'Imbanking' ten years later, William Dugdale observed that 'Decoys are now planted upon many drayned Levels, whereby greater numbers of Fowl are caught, than by any other Engines formerly used; which could not at all be made there, did the waters, as formerly, overspread the whole Countrey'.

These fens and coastal marshes – 'far remote from common High-ways, and all the noise of people' – were indeed a more appropriate setting than St James's Park for such decoys, and their characteristically withdrawn locations no doubt contributed to the scarcity of information on their beginnings. Even within the countryside their operators developed a reputation for reclusiveness: the character given them by the Revd Richard Lubbock was that 'they hide away their manœuvres against the wildfowl in as much mystery as the Rosycrucians threw around their search after the philosophers stone'. Eager writers on natural history were no more welcome than any-one else within the decoy, so that inevitably mis-conceptions are not infrequently encountered: even Thomas Bewick goes notably adrift in his description of their operation. An air of undis-turbed calm was assiduously cultivated within the precincts of the decoy: any necessary repairs or alterations would be carried out at night, and ice-breaking, if required, would be completed before the arrival of the ducks at dawn; even the decoy-man's cottage was planted around with trees and made as inconspicuous as possible, in order that nothing should upset the birds.

A sheltered expanse of water some few acres in extent would generally be sought, although some decoys would be built on the margins of more extensive lakes, on river banks and even on tidal inlets. More than any of the other techniques used to trap fowl, decoys positively benefited from the drainage of the Fens (as confirmed by Dugdale's observations, reproduced above), that resulted in the formation of smaller, more sheltered and more accessible stretches of water.

Their characteristic features and method of operation were surveyed in the later nineteenth century by Sir Ralph Payne-Gallwey, whose *Book of Duck Decoys* has never been surpassed: it expands on the account given in Willughby and Ray's volume, but nowhere contradicts these early observations. Typically, from the water's edge a number of ditches some 60 to 70 yards in length would be dug, initially at right angles to the shore but curving and tapering as they proceeded – pref-erably into scrub and low trees that would screen their extremities from the water; in this way, only half the length of the ditch would be visible from its mouth. Over the whole length of the ditch netting would be stretched over a series of hoops, initially of poles or withies but by the nineteenth century commonly of iron; the largest hoop, at

the mouth, would be an expansive 18 to 20 feet in width and 12 to 15 feet high, but successive hoops would diminish in height and width to a mere 2 by 1½ feet at the extreme end. The water in the ditch was held by most experts to need a maximum depth of only about 6 inches: Lubbock suggested variously that depths of 16 to 24 inches were more appropriate, but he was taken to task by later authors, who were of the opinion that pochard in particular would always escape in such a depth of water by diving and doubling back to the entrance. The whole installation together formed what was termed a pipe.

To one side of the pipe a series of ten to twelve reed screens, each about 12 feet long and 6 feet high, were erected in echelon fashion some 3 feet apart, their ends overlapping so that the operator, the decoyman, could pass up and down the length of the pipe unseen by birds on the water. Lower screens, termed dog-jumps, joined the inner end of one screen to the next, the entire installation being withdrawn a little from the water's edge to form a narrow passageway that doubled as a land-ing place for the birds. To the ducks on the water the whole formed a tranquil and inviting vista (illus. 81), and the wild birds were further put at their ease by the presence of a small flock of tame ducks – some 20 to 30 were thought ideal – kept on site specifically for that purpose.

Either one of two methods was used by the decoyman to attract the ducks into his trap – 'allur-ing', as opposed to the traditional 'driving' – the simplest of which, termed feeding, involved the decoyman in catching the attention of the tame ducks with a low whistle which they would rec-ognize as a signal that food would be forthcom-ing in the form of handfuls of grain thrown from the cover of the screens; as they were drawn in, the decoyman would retreat up the pipe, distrib-uting more grain, with the tame birds following

81 'Entrance to a decoy pipe with dog at work and wild fowl following him up the pipe'. From Sir Ralph Payne-Gallwey, *The Book of Duck Decoys* (1886).

and the bolder spirits among the wild ducks following them in turn, eager to join in the feasting. Once a good number of birds had penetrated well into the pipe, the decoyman would double back towards the mouth where, at the appropriately named 'head-shew place', he would reveal himself to the ducks inside while still being screened from those outside the pipe. The appearance of the human figure would send the wild birds flying for their lives down the pipe and into its closed end, while the tame ducks, not alarmed by the familiar sight of the decoyman, would simply swim back amongst the unsuspecting fowl left on the water. The man's task was now a simple one: unhitching the terminal tunnel-net – which would normally

be on dry land – from the fixed pipe, he would dispatch his catch by breaking their necks with a quiet efficiency that did not disturb the peace on the lake. So discreet was the whole operation that, with luck, it might be repeated two or three times in succession, gradually thinning out the population but always leaving a few birds on the water at the end of the day that they might return in future with others in tow.

The widely used alternative to enticement by feeding was 'dogging', in which a closely trained dog provided the lure that drew the ducks into the pipe. The ruse depended on the observation that when they catch sight of a predator such as a fox on the edge of the water, ducks will swim towards it, quacking loudly and making a show of aggression – just as long as the offender does not turn to confront them, in which case they scatter in disarray. At a silent gesture, the decoyman's dog (commonly called Piper with reference to his workplace) would be set off from the mouth of the pipe, clearing the dog-jump between the first and second screens and showing himself briefly to the ducks on the narrow landing at the water's edge before vanishing again, to reappear at the next screen down the tunnel, and so on (illus. 82). Once the ducks were drawn in, the procedure for frightening them down the pipe to their fate was as before. John Ray's text (quoted above) indicates

that the duties of the dog were already fully established in the mid-seventeenth century and no doubt had been adopted from Holland along with the other features of the decoy:

The Whelp in compassing the hedges ought always to keep his tail directed towards the Pool, his head toward the Pipe . . . Those [ducks] behind he allures and tolls forward, they following him to gaze at him as a new and strange object.

(In this passage Ray also says of the dog that 'he terrifies the Birds before him, and drives them

82 'Decoyman enticing wild ducks up the decoy pipe by the use of a dog'. From Sir Ralph Payne-Gallwey, *The Book of Duck Decoys* (1886).

286

forward', but in this detail he is mistaken, for the dog's sole role was strictly to entice the birds forwards, after which he would lie down out of sight.)

Whichever of these two methods was used, calm deliberation and rhythm was invariably required, if necessary allowing the process to extend over a number of days in order to preserve the quiet attraction of the pond.

Payne-Gallwey is encyclopaedic on the finer details of every aspect of the above. The lake itself was better smaller than larger – 2 to 3 acres was all that was required: larger than that and some of the ducks were too remote to be allured, the shelter was inadequate and the surface was prone to icing up (for, unlike the earlier mass drives which were timed to coincide with the annual moult, decoying was a winter activity, with a season extending from October to March); a modest depth for the lake of 2–3 feet was ideal, shelving towards the margins. If the pond could be fitted with dams and sluices to maintain a fixed water level, so much the better. Steep banks had the advantage that they made the lower entrance to the pipes, with their conveniently placed ledges to the side (often conveniently strewn with feed), all the more inviting; in the absence of natural banks, additional reed screens or dense planting could be used to limit the convenient roosting places, although too much intervention of this sort inhibited the desirable possibility that the pond might develop its own breeding population. The pipes on such a lake could vary in number from one to eight, although four or five was considered optimum: radiating in a variety of directions (illus. 83), they gave the decoyman the option of always choosing one leading into the wind, some operators preferring a breeze at a slight angle to the pipe rather than directly down it. Ducks, in any case, prefer swimming into a light headwind rather than having it behind them, and they invariably take off against

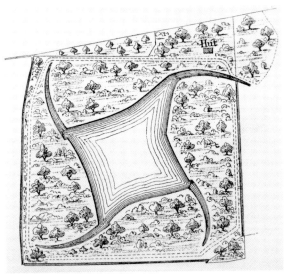

83 Ashby (Lincolnshire) decoy, a modestly sized four-pipe decoy producing an average of some 3,000 wildfowl annually in the mid-19th century. From Sir Ralph Payne-Gallwey, *The Book of Duck Decoys* (1886).

the airstream, so that they were in this way further drawn to their fate. They also prefer swimming into a gentle current, so that a flow of water from the pipe, induced by the further use of sluices at some later decoys, would again enhance its appeal – as well as helping to keep it ice free in cold weather.

These considerations might all be regarded as ideal, but in practice decoys were established in a wide range of disparate settings. Those in Norfolk, for example, developed on much larger stretches of water than were strictly necessary or desirable, although the populace there had no sense of their shortcomings until a Lincolnshire man, George Skelton (d. 1840) was brought in by a local landowner to set up a new decoy: Payne-Gallwey records that when he asked for a mere 2–2½ acre pond he was laughed at by the Norfolk decoymen until he started turning in much bigger catches than they were able to achieve – 1,100 teal fell to his nets in seven days during the decoy's second year of operation. Even these smaller lakes inevitably failed to conform to the schematized ground plans drawn up by Payne-Gallwey and owners naturally adapted the disposition of the pipes to suit the local topography: the estate map of 1652 from Flixton already mentioned (illus. 84) shows (in perhaps the earliest representation of such an installation) no fewer than twelve pipes arranged to take every advantage of the site. Pennant expands on the desirability of a number of them:

It is necessary to have a pipe or ditch for almost every wind that can blow, as upon this circumstance it depends which pipe the wild fowl will take to; and the decoy-man always keeps on the leeward side of the ducks, to prevent his effluvia reaching their sagacious nostrils.

At Fritton Lake on the borders of Suffolk and Norfolk, perhaps as many as 23 pipes were in use together at the turn of the nineteenth century.

Diamond-mesh netting of hemp was to be preferred in their construction; treated with tar it would last up to 25 years. A larger mesh might be used at the mouth of the pipe, decreasing progressively along its length. In the course of the nineteenth century wire netting became more prevalent, but it tended to whistle in the wind in a potentially alarming manner and the ducks that flew into it in their mad dash down the pipe were frequently cut and spoiled. Some pipes incorporated nets that could be lowered to prevent the birds flying back out again: Richard Blome, in his *Gentleman's Recreation* of 1686 suggests they were common in early decoys but evidently they lost favour (although a late decoy at Berkeley Castle (Gloucestershire) had one of these). At Iken (Suffolk) this idea was developed into a holding cage placed between the end of the pipe and the detachable tunnel-net so that large catches could be retrieved in batches.

As decoy ducks, crosses between wild and small brown farmyard birds were preferred as suitably biddable and not so noisy that they alarmed the wild birds. Ray expands on their duties: 'Of the Coy-ducks some fly forth and bring home with them wild ones to the Pool, others have the outmost joynt or pinion of their Wings cut off, so that they cannot fly, but abide always in the Pool.' Later authors confirm this distinction, although pinioning was generally thought unnecessary except, perhaps, at coastal sites where a few pinioned widgeon might be added, so that their characteristic whistle would attract others of their kind. Folkard was of the opinion that early decoys were served only by 'wandering decoy-ducks' which

84 Decoy pipes at Flixton Water (Suffolk), extract from the 'Survey of the Island of Lothingland'. Interestingly, the pipes curve both to left and right: Folkard thought it important that the pipes should all be on the same axis to avoid confusing the decoyman and his dog in their work.

could be expected to bring back wild stock in their wake, suggesting that resident populations were a development of the period when the rise of shooting increased the risk of losing the entire tame stock of the pond. A surviving lease for Skellingthorpe decoy (Lincolnshire) indicates that they were regarded as part of the installation, for it stipulates that on expiry the lessee was to relinquish the decoy 'well and sufficiently repaired . . . together with twenty drakes and fourscore tame ducks'. In Payne-Gallwey's day a decoy owner at Ivythorne (Somerset) experimented with placing a dummy teal of painted wood in the pipe, but inanimate decoy birds of this kind were not normally used. The tame birds were to be fed in the evening after the wild population had flown off to feed – always in one or other of the pipes so that they became completely accustomed to them, with the decoyman occasionally softly whistling to them in his characteristically low note, so that they might always associate it with feeding. During alluring by feeding, a judicious amount of grain or hemp-seed was to be offered to them – just enough to keep them interested without causing a rush that might alarm the wild birds. Some early authors such as Blome attribute a degree of 'subtilty' to the tame ducks, suggesting that they were in some sense complicit in the fatal deceit of their wild kin, but it was no more than the prospect of food that set them swimming into the decoy, while daily familiarity with the decoyman and his dog made them immune to the periodic stampedes of panicking wild fowl down the dwindling bore of the pipe. Feeding times of 8, 12 and 4 o'clock were thought to be most propitious, while 3 o'clock worked best for dogging.

Even the best kind of dog was specified – preferably fox-like in appearance, with a bushy tail. Some decoymen resorted to tying fox pelts on to their dogs, but the practical effects of these measures were disputed. Of prime importance was the ability of the dog to respond instantly to the silent signals of its master, to maintain a steady pace as it made its way over the successive dog-jumps (or was sent round one of them again if the decoyman judged that the attention of the ducks had not been sufficiently engaged), and never to turn back on them in a way that would instantly send them scrambling for open water. Dogging was the method favoured at most inland decoys, while feeding proved more effective at coastal sites, particularly those frequented by teal and those where the intertidal areas were under water for extended periods: hungry birds always reacted better to feeding, while those with full stomachs were more likely to respond to the dog's eye-catching performance. Even then, Pennant records, they might need special arousal: 'Sometimes the dog will not attract their attention, if a red handkerchief, or something very singular, is not put about him.' Finally, some species reacted more strongly to one method than the other, with wild duck and teal reportedly responding best to the dog and widgeon to feeding.

These, then, were the characteristics of the classic decoys that came to be built in considerable numbers, notably from the early eighteenth century up to the mid-1800s. They predominated in the eastern counties, from the Holderness peninsula in Yorkshire to the Essex marshes – the latter specializing particularly in teal. South Lincolnshire alone had about 30 decoys. They were to be found as far south as Abbotsbury (Dorset) – see illus. 100 – where three pipes led off the inland lake and a fourth opened on to the adjacent tidal channel of the West Fleet. They were numerous in the Somerset Levels and occured with decreasing frequency as far north as Cumbria.

Their effectiveness was quite astonishing: Pennant, for example, records that 31,200 ducks were taken in one season by ten decoys around Wain-fleet (Lincolnshire), and as two teal or widgeon conventionally were counted as one duck, the number of individuals would have been many more. At Ashby in the same county, the records for a single four-pipe decoy on a 2-acre pond reveal 100,000 ducks taken over the space of 34 seasons, while Steeple decoy (Essex) took 7,364 ducks in a single season in 1714. Daniel Defoe was informed of similarly lucrative decoys:

> it is incredible what quantities of wild-fowl of all sorts, duck, mallard, teal, widgeon, &c. they take in those duckoys every week, during the season; it may indeed be guessed at a little by this, that there is a duckoy not far from Ely, which pays to the landlord, Sir Tho. Hare 500l. a year rent, besides the charge of maintaining a great number of servants for the management; and from which duckoy alone they assured me at St Ives (a town on the Ouse, where the fowl they took was always brought to be sent to London;) that they generally sent up three thousand couple a week.

Payne-Gallwey observes that collectively they contributed to the markets 'the enormous total of half a million birds, of a purely wild and valuable nature, and this too without firing a shot'. Records preserved for some decoys indicate that mallard formed the bulk of the catch, followed by teal; pintail, shoveller and widgeon were caught in lesser numbers.

Other forms of decoy – in effect passive traps without the need for human interaction as outlined above – also appeared in some areas; their form is likely to have pre-dated that of the pipe-decoy. At their simplest these were large cages of netting into which the ducks might wander through a tunnel leading into the centre, but from which they seemed incapable of finding their way out again. Writing in 1918, Joseph Whitaker mentions that he had heard of as many as 71 birds being taken in a single night by this method, which he judged particularly useful for teal.

An alternative form of cage had a drop-door at one end, raised and lowered on a pulley operated with a windlass by an observer hidden in a nearby sighting-house. Once the birds had been tempted in by bait in the form of food and by the reassuring presence of some tame ducks, the observer would carefully lower the door and remove the hapless birds at his leisure. Among the earliest examples of this type, which was favoured in the West Midlands over the decoys of the eastern marshes, is that recorded from Haughton (Nottinghamshire) – its foundation date unknown but judged by Payne-Gallwey to be 'of considerable antiquity' – while the type reached perhaps its most sophisticated form at Hardwick Hall (Derbyshire), where two sliding doors were used. Once trapped inside the ducks had to be left there until the remainder of the flock had taken off for the night, so as not to discourage their return; needless to say, this placed a severe limit on the numbers that could be taken – 300 to 400 a year was the best that could be expected.

Whatever their form, they clearly exerted an appeal to the gentry as well as to the working fowler: to Folkard, writing in the later nineteenth century, 'A decoy is one of the most ornamental acquisitions to a private landed estate that can well be imagined, and at all times presents an object of amusement and attraction.' Clearly they also had considerable commercial value and were accorded appropriate protection: they were considered private preserves and hence were protected from trespass by common law. Greater difficulties arose over the respective rights of rival decoy owners and punt-gunners over the reservoir of wild game, but principles were gradually established by which birds already within the area of a decoy might be protected from disturbance from competing wild-fowlers. Long-established decoys were recognized as privileged places, near which shooting might be controlled, but not all were protected in this way: the rise of sporting shooting in the nineteenth century brought more and more guns into prox-imity with the decoys, and the fate of that at Berk-eley, said to have been ruined by incessant firing following passage of the Ground Game Act in 1880, will not have been unique.

More insidious and ultimately devastating to the functioning of the decoys was the progres-sive drainage that – having helped to create ideal conditions for decoys in the first instance, as out-lined above – eliminated more and more of the expanses of water that formerly had characterized the fenland landscape, for with them went many of the migratory birds. On Thorne Moor (Lincoln-shire) half a dozen decoys were overwhelmed in the process of warping – the laying down of estu-arine silt in order to improve the soil. The advent of the railways also took its toll: one owner at New-port (Monmouthshire) was compensated £500 for his loss of amenity when the Great Western Railway was led within half a mile of his decoys, although elsewhere the ducks seemingly were less discom-moded: at Orwell Park (Suffolk), for example, Payne-Gallwey records that the Great Eastern line to Felixstowe ran within 30 yards of the decoy but had little effect on its operation.

By the eve of World War Two only eleven decoys remained in working order and today none are in commercial operation: the last one to close was that at Orwell, which was taken over by the Wild-fowl Trust for a period to facilitate ringing. In recent years, all the surviving or restored decoys have been operated purely for this purpose.

SHOOTING FLYING

The introduction of firearms to England preceded their general adoption for shooting birds on the wing by a matter of 100 years or so, for it was not until the early decades of the seventeenth century that ignition systems on guns reached a degree of sophistication that offered the gunner a more-or-less instantaneous response to his pressing the trigger and it took another generation for the practice of taking pot-shots at sitting birds to be replaced by the more demanding exercise of tak-ing them in flight. Early matchlock guns, in which pulling the trigger resulted in a lighted fuse or taper being brought into contact with powder in an ignition-pan, were far too slow and cumber-some for such a task, and the noisy wheel locks that superseded them, in which a spring-loaded and serrated wheel brought into contact with a flint generated a shower of sparks to the same end, were only marginally better. By the 1620s flint-lock weapons, in which a single spark was struck from the flint, were being imported into England and began to enter the sporting armoury – although still likely to be used in conjunction with a crutch-like rest to support the muzzle of the long barrel while the marksman set up his musket as discreetly as possible before taking aim and shooting at the birds where they sat. Well before this time, how-ever, guns were beginning to be deployed against slow-moving targets on the ground: J. H. Gurney reproduces a number of records from Norfolk dat-ing between 1519 and 1538 of crane and bustard 'kylled with ye crossbowe', as might be expected, but also notes three birds in the same list 'kylled wt. ye gunne'.

By the later sixteenth century handbooks were being produced to aid those taken by the new sport, but as Blackmore points out the rudimen-tary level of understanding contained in works such as Cyprian Lucas's *Three Bookes of Colloquies*

(1588) would have contributed little or nothing to the effectiveness of the hunter. Apart from the difficulties of unwieldiness and uncertain ignition, the early sporting marksman had to cope with the fact that his weapon fired only one lead ball at a time, and it was only with the development of 'hail shot' that his chances considerably improved. Initially the balls for this small shot continued to be made individually, but in the course of the seventeenth century the technique was introduced of passing molten lead through a sieve and allowing the droplets to fall into water, producing small shot approaching in size the coarser varieties of the present day.

In his *Hungers Prevention* (1621), Markham unequivocally counsels the fowler that in using one of these firearms (for which he recommends a barrel length of 5½–6 feet), the fowler will be

> at no time striving to shoote at a single Fowle, if he can by any meanes compass more with his levell . . . but rather the longest and largest Rancke and File of Fowle you can finde, for . . . one shoote is as much as you can get at one time and in one place.

He already advises the use of 'round haile-shot or drop-shot . . . [of a] bignesse according to the game you shoote at'. To enable the fowler to get within range, he anticipates that he will approach the target under cover of a stalking horse, either a live animal (illus. 85) – 'any old Jade trayned up for that use' – or one that has been constructed artificially. For this purpose 'any pieces of oulde Canvasse' could be used, being fashioned into 'the shape or proportion of a Horse with the head bending downeward, as if he grazed, stuffed and painted like a horse'; indeed, the device was not necessarily species-specific, and could take the form of a cow (designated the 'oxe-engine') or a

deer, perhaps embellished with a set of real antlers. Whatever the form, the device would be mounted on a spiked stave, allowing the fowler to approach the target birds (with all due caution and with such oblique flanking movements as might be desirable to avoid alarming them) with the device held before him, before planting it in the ground and freeing both hands for the aim.

An alternative to the stalking horse suggested by Nathaniel Baily in his *Dictionarium Rusticum* (1740) is the 'cocking cloth', little more than a square of canvas with leather-bound corners which the fowler would throw over himself, with the muzzle of the gun protruding through a hole: with this, he suggests, 'the Pheasants will let you come near them, and the Cocks will be so bold as to fly at it'.

Robert Howlett's *School of Recreation*, published more than 60 years after Markham in 1684, still advocates shooting at sitting targets, but the frontispiece to his volume includes an image of sportsmen shooting birds in flight. Two years later, the text of Richard Blome's *Gentleman's Recreation* more formally marks the arrival of the method that added a new technique to the wildfowler's armoury and which would spawn generations of sportsmen in the centuries to come:

> It is now the Mode to shoot flying, as by Experience found the best and surest Way; for when your Game is on the Wing, it is more exposed to Danger; for if but one Shot hits any Part of its Wings so expanded, it will occasion its Fall, altho' not to kill it; so that your Spaniel will soon be its Victor, and, if well disciplined to the Sport, will bring it to you.

The technique clearly still had some way to go, however, to judge from the remarks of George

85 'Stalking', with the aid of a stalking-horse. Commissioned by Richard Blome for his *Gentleman's Recreation* (1686).

STALKING

Markland in his *Pteryplegia; or, The Art of Shooting Flying*: at the time of its publication (1727), Markland judged the standards of shooting in England abysmal compared to those already being achieved in France, commenting that 'It's as rare for a profess'd Marksman of that Nation to miss a Bird, as for one of Ours to Kill'. The use of hides or stalking horses continued to play an important part in bringing the shooter within striking distance of his target.

Thereafter an entire genre of writing emerged to cater for this new constituency, generating an extensive literature that has recently been reviewed by Robin Chute in his *Shooting Flying* (2001). Here we again find quoted Baily from his *Dictionarium Rusticum* of 1740, acknowledging that by now, in terms of the guns in his armoury, the serious fowler ought to have them 'of several sorts and sizes, sutable to the Game he designs to kill', but recommending that 'The Gun, most proper for the sport, should be of four Foot and a half long in the Barrell, and of a pretty wide bore, something under a Musket'. More manageable weapons were already being recommended by other writers: Giles Jacob in his *Compleat Sportsman* (1718) thought 3½ feet appropriate for 'land-fowl' while Thomas Page in *The Art of Shooting Flying* (1766) thought 3–3½ feet adequate for the purpose.

Authors gave due attention too to the education of the uninitiated in the techniques, as well as the hardware, of shooting for sport. Jacob was the first to advise the need to offset the aim to take account of the movement of the birds and the time delay before the shot intercepted them: 'And if the Birds be out of reach, fire at a mark about six yards before, and then the shot will take them as they are passing.' In the anonymous *Essay on Shooting* (1789), derived from Magné de Marolles' *La chasse au fusil* and generally attributed to John Acton, the author gave hints on improving technique by assiduous target practice, his favoured method being to tie small pieces of white paper round the necks of sparrows and have them thrown into the air so that the tyro could blast them with increasing consistency: 'it affords excellent diversion in seasons when game cannot be pursued', he writes, 'or in wet weather, from underneath the shelter of a shed, or a barn door'.

As the fowler's armoury became more sophisticated (notably with the introduction of breech-loading guns in the later 1700s, percussion caps in the 1820s and centre-fire cartridges in the 1850s) there came a parallel development in the format adopted by sporting shoots: from being a comparatively solitary pursuit, involving no more than a couple of dogs to point and retrieve, the practice of the 'battue' was introduced from France in the later 1700s. Acton's translation of Magné de Marolles, published in 1789, provided an early guide:

Eight men go in a company; four of them are equipped with fowling-pieces, and four with sticks only, for the purpose of beating the bushes, furzes, &c. This band then range in a straight line, the beaters being placed in the intervals between the shooters, at the distance of ten or twelve paces, the whole forming a front of eighty or an hundred paces, so that in advancing, they sweep a great tract of country . . . it is in general a very bloody sport . . . more particularly adapted for places where the game is not in great abundance.

The cumbersome process of reloading came to be handled by an accompanying loader: the percussion ignition detonating lock of 1807 began the slow business of replacing the flintlock, cutting loading times by a quarter; breech-loading guns with a much higher rate of fire, having been experimented with since the sixteenth century, began to make an appearance on the moors from the 1850s. A fully reliable bolt-action breech-loading system was finally developed only in the second quarter of the nineteenth century, although there were still some hunters who preferred to cling to their muzzle-loaders; no doubt they formed the same constituency that had disapproved of the new-fangled double-barrelled guns that began to make their appearance in the 1700s and indeed there were many who disapproved of battue hunting altogether, branding it indiscriminate, unsportsmanlike and – worst of all – un-British.

The later nineteenth-century 'drive' was a close relation of the battue. As mentioned above, battue shooters had moved forward in a line through covert, with the birds shot low and flying away;

in the drive which came to replace it, the shooters remained stationary while the birds were driven towards them by beaters – flying forward, high and fast. Despite presenting more difficult targets, the numbers of birds bagged climbed steadily through the 1800s – several thousand birds from a single shoot became common: in 1896 a record for the nineteenth century of 3,113 pheasants killed in one day was set at Sandringham.

What is incontestable is that participants no longer required the least knowledge of or sympathy with the countryside in which they took their sport. Furthermore, so devastating was the effect on game stocks of this new form of mass slaughter that the numbers of game birds quickly became locally depleted, so that an entire new economy had to be invented to ensure that hunters could be confident of returning home with full game-bags. Partridges and pheasants began to be reared by hand for release at the appropriate time: eggs were collected from the wild (or even were imported) and hatched under broody hens before being turned over to keepers for rearing, sometimes in specialized pheasantries. Only by intensive breeding and the employment of professional gamekeepers could such an economy be sustained; vast areas of heath and moorland which had been lost to any economic activity beyond the grazing of sheep now found a new lease of life as grouse moors at the service of sportsmen, increasingly likely to be urban dwellers, whisked to every remote corner of the country by a railway system at the height of its development.

For their part the keepers, in order to protect their vulnerable charges, adopted an intensive regime of extermination directed at those 'vermin' most likely to pose a threat to eggs or chicks – whether polecats, weasels and stoats, or magpies, crows or kites. The population of game birds soared seasonally before being culled by the

guns, but many other species came under year-round pressure from which their numbers would never recover.

The beginnings of the practice of punt-gunning – the stalking of wildfowl with a large-bore scatter-gun mounted on a lightly built flat-bottomed punt – may be conjectured to go back to the 1600s; certainly it was well established in the course of the eighteenth century. With the increasing availability of firearms, punt-gunning took its place in a natural way amongst the range of practical methods embraced by fen-dwellers as part of their mixed economy of fishing, fowling and reed-cutting, all practised on a seasonal basis, but by the nineteenth century it had also attracted sporting adherents. A manual, produced by Lieutenant-Colonel Peter Hawker with the title *Instructions to Young Sportsmen*, imparted the rudiments of punt-gunning (amongst other forms of shooting) to an audience that had no access to traditional knowledge handed down from father to son: first published in 1814, it ran ultimately to ten editions during his lifetime, with a further one prepared after his death. Writing of punt-gunning, Hawker commented that

This method of shooting wildfowl is the best calculated for the amusement of a gentleman, as he may go out between breakfast and dinner; and, in frosty weather, perhaps kill his twenty or thirty couple in a day, followed by his companions, who may keep at a distance, to enjoy a sight of the sport; and afterward join in the 'cripple chace'.

He was dismissive of its detractors, who condemned it as an occupation merely for rustics, and H. C. Folkard too might write of it that 'there is no sport more captivating and exciting'. For the countrymen who depended on it for a living, however, it was a hard, solitary and frequently uncomfortable profession, conducted in dangerous conditions and in the full face of the elements.

While he might scull his craft into the general area occupied by the target wildfowl, the punt-gunner had to manoeuvre himself within range while lying face-down and out of sight, so that a primary requirement of the punt was that it should have a low profile and should be as lightly built as possible (illus. 86); a narrow beam was also essential, so that the gunner could control the punt from the prone position, but fine judgement was necessary in order to avoid making a craft that was unstable. Typical dimensions were from 16 to 22 feet in length, with a beam of just under 3 feet. Fir could be used throughout in the construction, or elm might be substituted for the lower strakes only; oak was simply too heavy for this purpose. A flat bottom was a necessary feature, or at the least a rounded bottom with a flat floor within; either way, it should have a spring in it fore and aft, so that the fore end could be pushed as far as possible on to the mud banks within which it characteristically operated. The fore part might be kept wide in order to support the weight of the punt-gun which rested on it, although many punts were narrowed at either end, so they could be the more easily manoeuvred in either direction; strong cross-pieces or thwarts gave the craft rigidity, one of them commonly perforated by a crotch-headed bolt (or simply provided with a notched timber support) on which the gun was cradled. Regional variations were many, and indeed gunners frequently built their own punts. Those of the east coast, notably around Maldon (Essex), were virtually coffin-like, no more than 2 feet 10 inches wide, with near-vertical sides

composed of two broad strakes only: they were considered particularly well suited to the final, cautious approach to the birds, when the punter could easily reach over the sides with his paddles or setting-sticks (poles with which he pushed against the bottom), but they required very careful handling to avoid capsizing.

No varnish was applied to such a craft, merely tar for waterproofing, although nineteenth-century gunners at least were advised to apply a coat of matt paint of a dusky-white hue. It was also recommended that they should wear white clothing, but it may be doubted that this was a custom much observed by the professionals.

Punt-guns were formidable weapons, with typical barrel lengths of 8, 9 or even 10 feet and a bore of 1¼ to 1½ inches, firing around ½ to 1 pound of shot; a big one might weigh 150 pounds. Their genesis lay in the period of muzzle-loading and flintlock ignition systems; many of this kind survived in use well into the nineteenth century, although breech-loading and cap-firing percussion guns introduced at this time greatly eased the wildfowler's lot. Reloading a muzzle-loader was a particularly hazardous operation in an unstable punt, and the whole process took about 10 minutes – ten times as long as a breech-loader. Whichever type of gun was used, the firing mechanism had to be kept dry by means of a waterproof cover, which could easily be thrown off as the gunner homed in on his target.

Needless to say, the recoil from such a weapon was considerable. Some gunners carried a padded cushion of straw and sacking to protect their shoulder; most preferred to hold the butt under their armpit so that the recoil was never passed directly to their body. Even so, it was inadvisable to brace the feet against anything but the sides of the boat if broken bones were to be avoided (and the knees too had to be kept clear of fixtures), for

86 William Henry Pyne, drawing of 1817, showing wildfowlers at work with (above) a gun mounted on a sledge for use in the winter months and (below) a similar punt-mounted gun for use in open water.

both gun and gunner were thrown back violently by the discharge. For the same reason no trigger guard was fitted, and the gunner was advised to squeeze the trigger with all his fingers rather than one. In order to minimize these difficulties, various recoil-absorbing devices came to be incorporated in later guns, the simplest being a breeching formed of rope and anchored to the stem of the boat, but the value of the rope was questioned by some: it was liable to break from time to time, exposing the fowler to real danger, and even in normal use it had a tendency to stretch a couple of inches under the recoil before springing forward again by as much as a foot, easily injuring the un-

wary. Even more frowned upon under normal use was the employment of any form of metal swivel fixed to the fore-end cross-piece of the boat, since these seriously threatened the whole integrity of the craft, although a more stable alternative introduced in the nineteenth century, in which the swivel was mounted directly on to a stanchion or strong knee-piece, bolted directly to a strong bottom plank of elm, mitigated this problem to some degree and allowed even bigger guns to be used. Steel coil-springs were also fitted to the mountings of many such guns at this time. Gunsmiths such as Holland & Holland produced refined versions of breech-loading guns for this new clientele, though generally of more modest proportions than those favoured by the countrymen.

At all times, the weight of the gun (especially the later stanchion-guns) and the lightness of the punt were in delicate balance which all too easily could be upset, resulting in the craft capsizing. Reloading – especially of muzzle-loaders – added to these hazards: the inexperienced were advised to beach the punt before even attempting it. Rough weather added to the danger: Duncan and Thorne give advice on drawing the gun within the boat and lashing it (and everything else) down; *in extremis*, they counsel two-man crews to jettison the gun, sliding it carefully over the stern with a float attached so that it could be retrieved in calmer conditions.

A further essential part of the gunner's equipment was a waterproof ammunition box, to be mounted at the stern of the punt to help counteract the weight of the gun. Here would be stowed the cartridges for a breech-loader, or the black powder, shot and oakum (used in preference to conventional wadding) for a muzzle-loader, as well as loading and cleaning equipment. The shot was commonly cast by the fowler himself in a hand-mould producing six to a dozen pellets at a time, at an average of about 240 to the pound of lead; charges could be prepared in advance by placing the shot in a cylindrical mould and setting it in tallow, so as to minimize reloading times.

The practical advice given by Hawker, based on long experience and familiarity with professional fowlers (whose *modus operandi* was seldom committed to paper) provides an idea of the general principles involved in stalking the birds: 'When you see a flock of birds, bear up to windward, and then skull or drift down among them. If they fly up, your labour is lost, but, if not, you may make a most unmerciful havoc; and, at the same time, you and your boat will be kicked back for some yards.' The task of manoeuvring within range of the target demanded just as much skill as the shooting and no doubt took much longer to learn. Maximum use had to be made of whatever cover was provided by mudflats and due account had to be taken of the tide as the gunner picked his way through the creeks that threaded between the banks in order to make progress without detection. There were other hazards to contend with: Hawker advised that 'the gunner's principal enemy is the curlew, which often springs up from the edges of the creeks, alarms the whole place, and, sometimes, prevents their earning four or five pounds'.

A vivid description of the punt-gunner at work with all this equipment is provided by J. Wentworth-Day in his *History of the Fens*:

Lying flat in the bottom of the punt, his legs stretched out behind on each side to steady it, a small stalking stick in either hand, he gradually and noiselessly approaches the unconscious fowl, which go on feeding, little aware of the enemy that is drifting down upon them. As long as they keep their position all is right, but as soon as one rises on the water and shakes his wings, and the rest of the birds draw together, it is plain they suspect danger. If the gunner is not yet within shot, now is the time for his greatest caution; however he quietly drifts down to within about a hundred yards – the cover is thrown off the lock of the gun, a bright flash, a loud report, the boat flies back many yards through the water, and two pair of half-birds (as they call pochards here) and a pair of ducks are lying breast upwards on the water. The dead birds are collected, the punt is drawn up on to a bank, the big gun is sponged out and loaded, and, after scanning the horizon with his eagle-eye, he proceeds in search of another trip of fowl.

Considering the rudeness of the tackle, it is wonderful with what accuracy these fellows shot. The guns were always of the rudest description, and I never saw a swivel of any kind used in this fen. The gun just lay flat in the boat, the muzzle protruding a few inches, and the line of aim was regulated by the man reclining to the right or the left of the boat, according to the distance that the fowl are from him. The end of the butt was padded, and when it went off, the shooter let it fly under his right arm, and woe to his shoulder if by chance it resisted the recoil. The powder in use was common blasting powder, the shot No. 2, the wadding oakum or coarse fen grass; charge, about three ounces of powder to one pound of shot.

Perhaps the only thing lacking in Wentworth-Day's account is a sense of the scale of destruction that could be wrought with such a weapon. The bag he describes was, perhaps, fairly typical, but H. C. Folkard conveys something more of the killing power at the punt-gunner's disposal:

On the smoke clearing off he beholds, as it were, a pathway of dead and dying ducks, extending a long distance in a line with the position of his gun . . . one by one there emerges from the dead and dying, some less severely struck, winged or wounded birds, which make off as best they can, fluttering and struggling in the water; and thus the imaginary pathway soon becomes a broken and scattered extent of dead, dying, and disabled victims.

A shoulder-gun might be included amongst the fowler's equipment to finish off those injured birds ('cripples') left on the water, while his setting-stick might be fitted with a forked terminal to pin down wounded birds on the mud banks. Hawker recommends his young followers to 'paddle in among your prisoners, and belabour, with a stick, all that have life remaining, or you will, probably, be capsized in trying to catch them'. Recovering wounded birds from the ooze could be the most hazardous part of the whole operation: wooden pattens or 'splashers' helped stop the fowler sinking up to his knees (or worse) most of the time, but 'rotten' holes could easily swallow a man with no chance of struggling free. Given these difficulties, the gunner was advised that he might be forced to return home with no more than half the birds he had wounded.

Typically the punt-gun would eliminate everything in line with the muzzle from about 60 to 100 yards in range. The closeness of the point of aim to the water level was important in bringing about this mass slaughter: Hawker recommended a height of around only 6 inches. The elevation of the barrel was already to be adjusted to the desired range – about 80 yards – before the punt closed on the birds, for there would be no time for last-minute adjustments of aim other than those brought about by the gunner gently shifting the weight of his body. Ideally the firing mechanism would already be cocked, with only a piece of leather or cork inserted in front of the hammer for safety, to be withdrawn before the trigger was pulled.

The punts of the Hampshire estuaries were considered by Hawker to have been very poorly evolved, so that the unfortunate fowlers there were considered to be 'always the worst equipped of "big gunners"'. By Hawker's day, there had indeed been so many fatal accidents with them that many fowlers took to paddling to a convenient mud bank and closing on the birds on their hands and knees, pushing the punt before them into an appropriate position and discharging the gun remotely. Craft were developed specifically for this purpose, with room for the gun only, while on the coast of Sussex certain 'mud-sledges', which abandoned all pretence of being boats, took the place of punts. The fowler needed to be provided with thigh boots for this purpose, and also pattens to support his hands and feet. 'This is perhaps the most laborious, and the most filthy work in all the department of wildfowl shooting', Hawker wrote.

Other big guns encountered in the fens of the eighteenth and nineteenth centuries were designed to be operated from hides on the embankments enclosing waterways and hence were called bank-guns. They were similar in character to punt-guns but likely to be mounted on a swivel and hence capable of being of even bigger dimensions; their killing power was mitigated by the higher elevation at which they were used, however, since they did not sweep the surface of the water with the same deadly effect as the punt-gun.

ICE-GUNNING

Much of the punt-gunner's trade was carried on in extreme discomfort during the winter when the threat of ice was never far away. Making discreet progress was difficult when thin sheet ice crackled under the prow of the punt and the fowler was always in danger of being frozen in or having his punt crushed by broken ice being swept about on the fen. When severe frosts locked the whole stretch of water in ice, making punting impossible – which it commonly did for weeks on end – the gunner was forced to exchange his punt for a sledge, on which he could venture out in a manner that drew on many of the skills he had acquired in more clement conditions. The sledge took the form of a rudimentary platform mounted on bone

runners – normally the long bones of horses or cattle, pegged directly to the bottom of the sledge (see illus. 86). Progress was made by means of the gunner kneeling on the sledge and pushing himself along with the aid of two spiked sticks, before adopting a prone position and closing on the birds in much the same way as he would in his punt, with the aid of setting-poles. (Skating had been practised in a similar manner, using bone runners and a spiked pole with which to gain momentum, for millennia before the introduction of steel skates.)

Sledge-guns differed little in appearance or operation from those used on the punts, and no doubt were normally the same weapons. The effect of the recoil was, if anything, even more dramatic on the ice, with the gunner and his sledge being thrown backwards by several yards at the discharge. An awareness of solid obstacles (or thin ice) to the rear clearly was necessary if the gunner was to avoid injury, or worse.

FISHING WITH TRAP AND LINE

Long before fishing became a polite pursuit for the leisured classes, the harvesting of fish was a matter of applying the most effective means possible to retrieve them in bulk. In addition to inshore (and, as time went by, deep-sea) fishing, regular catches were taken on the foreshore with the aid of stake-nets set out in the sand or with passive weirs or sea-hedges – enclosures of hurdles, brushwood or dry-stone construction, that were simply covered by the sea at high tide and which trapped unwary fish within their perimeter as the tide receded. Jenkins mentions that shoreline traps of this sort could extend continuously for a distance of 2 or 3 miles. By the time of the Conquest it seems that Bath Abbey already had an estate at Tidenham

(Gloucestershire) with no fewer than 104 weirs, 30 of which were described as *cytweras* (basket-weirs) on the tidal reaches of the Severn; the provision of rods for building and repairing the weirs frequently was a condition of later tenancy agreements. The precision with which such agreements were drawn up and the attention that had to be paid to the established rights of others is well illustrated by the lease for an estuarine fishery at the mouth of the River Tees, granted in 1229 by one Peter de Brus to the Abbot of Fountains Abbey (Yorkshire):

> Peter grants the Abbott . . . may make and hold two fisheries in the sand that lies between the whole (common) field of Estun and the mid-stream of Teyse, as far as the sand remains at low tide . . . and removable . . . wheresoever they will throughout the whole sand-bed . . . And the Abbot . . . shall fish with seines and nets and boats . . . as far as the mid-stream of Teyse . . . the fishermen of Cotom [Coatham] may take . . . outside the said fisheries, bait [haschias] for their fish-hooks, as they have been wont; and saving the fishing-right of the men who have been wont to fish there without fixing stake [pale] or making weir [sepe] . . .

McDonnell, who first published this agreement, observes that the area in question was exclusive of the mid-stream channel, and indeed no one could claim rights that would interfere with the navigable channel in tidal rivers or in those open to traffic.

The origins of basket-weirs lie in the period before the Conquest: they are mentioned in the early tenth-century Laws of Hywel Dda and Bond reproduces the terms and conditions applied to Tidenham:

At every weir within the thirty hides (of the whole estate) every alternate fish belongs to the lord of the manor [Bath Abbey] and every rare fish of value, sturgeon, porpoise, herring or sea-fish; and no one has the right of selling any fish for money when the lord is on the estate without informing him about it.

The seashore was also the source of shellfish gathered in large quantities from at least the tenth century. Oysters, cockles, mussels and winkles are mentioned by Aelfric and continued to be exploited in areas such as the Boston Deeps up to modern times. Oysters were particularly favoured, not only for their eating qualities but also, in the era before refrigeration, for their capacity to survive dormant for months in water-filled casks kept in appropriate conditions.

RIVER FISHING

Although fishing with a hook and line was a familiar pursuit in medieval England, it produced nothing like the numbers of fish caught by trapping. By far the majority of the fish caught on the rivers were taken with nets and with traps of various sorts, frequently deployed in association with fish-weirs like those in use on the foreshore, as above; clearly they represent a well-established phenomenon, and evidence for their use goes back well into prehistory. The wedge-shaped structures for deflecting the fish into the trap commonly were little more than fences or screens of hurdles or reeds and were never of masonry. Rights in many of the 'fisheries' recorded in the *Domesday* survey are thought to have been exercised by constructing weirs of this sort, some of them with their catchments extended by stake-nets. In some areas, at least, most of the fisheries were in ecclesiastical or monastic ownership rather than on secular estates: the Cistercians of Tintern Abbey (Monmouthshire) were typical in holding numerous weirs by the twelfth century on the Wye, the Severn and the Usk, for example. In other areas weirs might be held in common by freeholders, in the same way that they held rights of pasture. McDonnell suggests that this may have been particularly true in the territories of the former Danelaw, where (in contrast to Anglo-Saxon Wessex) they survived in some numbers for several centuries beyond the Conquest: at Rossington near Doncaster (Yorkshire), for example, he notes a grant of 'all the right in the common fishery of the great vivary . . . on the east side; saving to William [de Rosinton] his common of fishery on the west side, where the monks of Kirkstall and the men of Besacre and Hegales have their common'. Darby observes that some fisheries were subject to grants and leases even more complex than those for *terra firma*, with rights over certain stretches of water being divided into half-fisheries and quarter-fisheries in terms of territory, but also periodically into half-nights and even eighths of a night.

The former widespread distribution of weirs (and a consciousness of the need to limit their potentially destructive effect on fish populations) is confirmed by a passage in Pennant's *Tour in Scotland* (1769), in which he notes the presence on the River Don at Aberdeen of a number of '*cruives*, or wears, to take salmon in. The owners are obliged by law to make the rails of the *cruives* of a certain width, to permit fish of a certain size to pass up the river.' Other ancient laws recorded by the same author obliged the owners of weirs to leave a free passage for all fish from Saturday night to Monday morning.

TRAPS

The Pembrokeshire traps mentioned by George Owen (pp. 303–4) may have been of the kind described by Jenkins as surviving more recently on the River Conway and on the Menai Straits, which relied primarily on the force of the water to retain the fish within a lattice or grating. Daniel Defoe left a vivid account of the operation of such a trap at the head of the estuary of the River Dart at Totnes (Devon):

Here we had the diversion of seeing them catch fish, with the assistance of a dog. The case is this, on the south side of the river, and on a slip, or narrow cut or channel made on purpose for a mill, there stands a corn mill; the mill tayl, or floor for the water below the wheels is wharft up on either side with stone, above high-water mark, and for above 20 or 30 foot in length below it, on that part of the river towards the sea; at the end of this wharfing is a grating of wood, the crossbars of which stand bearing inward, sharp at the end, and pointing inward towards one another, as the wyers of a mouse-trap.

When the tide flows up, the fish can with ease go in between the points of these crossbars, but the mill being shut down they can go no further upwards; and when the water ebbs again, they are left behind, not being able to pass the points of the grating . . . which like a mouse-trap keeps them in, so that they are left with about a foot, or a foot and a half water . . . the person who went with us . . . put in a net on a hoop, which we call in this country a shove net: the net being fix'd at one end of the place they put in a dog, who was taught his trade before hand, at the other end of the place, and he drives all the fish into the net, so that only holding the net still in its place, the man took up two or three and thirty salmon peal at the first time.

More usually, however, the funnel-shaped traps associated with weirs were made from green willow or osiers, with internal baffles that prevented the fish from escaping once they had entered. The Severn provides some of the best evidence for early practice (supplemented by a series of sixteen medieval basket traps, stake alignments and hurdling uncovered by exceptional tides in January 2007), many of the routines having survived in use within living memory.

Perhaps the most characteristic feature of the Severn salmon fishery – and one that formerly was widespread in England – is the use of wicker traps deployed in weirs consisting of lines of stakes driven into the river-bed, with or without additional hedges or leaders placed so as to guide the fish into the traps. In the most extensive weirs, several hundred conical traps termed 'putchers', loosely woven from osiers, may be mounted three or four deep, generally with their mouths facing upstream to catch the fish returning to open water on the ebb tide although occasionally reversed to take them swimming upstream. Characteristically, the putchers are 5 or 6 feet in length and 2 feet in diameter at the mouth, tapering to about 6 inches at the tip.

In the alternative form (exclusive to the Severn) termed 'putts' (illus. 87), the trap is scaled up to measure 5 or 6 feet across the loosely woven mouth, which joins smoothly with a more closely woven middle section, tapering to 6 inches or so; a third, removable section (termed the forewheel) at the end, tapering to about 2 inches and stopped with a bung of straw or wood, was supported in use on a forked stick. These impressive constructions, measuring some 12 to 14 feet in length, were

deployed in single rows of up to 120 traps, all invariably arranged with their mouths upstream. They were too cumbersome to remove during the closed season, at which time the forewheels were removed allowing the fish to pass through unmolested. Jenkins mentions that over 11,000 of them were in use in the 1860s.

Although uncertainty over the terminology makes it difficult to tell when one type of trap or the other is being referred to in the literature, some form or another was certainly in use from the time of the Conquest and beyond. No doubt other variants came into use from time to time: Jenkins draws attention to a rare form of basket trap from Wales, noteworthy for having a timber framework at its mouth and for having the osiers held in position by a spirally knotted rope.

Weirs appear with regularity in the historical record when, contrary to law, they were found to have encroached on the navigable waters, forming hazards or obstructions to river traffic: in 1224–5 it was decreed that 'wears shall be utterly put down . . . through all England, except by the sea coast', but evidently this measure had little lasting effect, for in the following century an Act Remedying Annoyances in the Four Great Rivers of England, Thames, Severn, Ouse and Trent (1346–7) was followed five years later by another order requiring the destruction of weirs, which in turn had to be reiterated no fewer than nine times. None the less, the practice persisted, with some weirs being far from slight in their construction, if we may judge from George Owen's *Description of Penbrokshire* (1603), where he describes 'the greatest weare of all Wales', built on the River Teifi at Cilgerran:

built of strong tymber frames and artificially wrought therein with stones, crossing the whole river from side to side, having

87 Working salmon putts being tended near Berkeley (Gloucestershire) on the River Severn, 1963. Their three-part structure is clearly visible.

six slaughter places, wherein fish entering remaine enclosed, and are therein killed, with an iron crooke, proper for that use.

In navigable rivers, weirs extending across the entire width of the tideway in this manner were entirely inimical to river traffic; having attracted the displeasure of the authorities for centuries, definitive legislation was introduced in the nineteenth century in the form of the Salmon and Freshwater Fisheries Act (1865), which allowed the continuation of weirs with 'immemorial rights' but banned others from extending more than halfway across the river and those leaving less than 40 feet of clear water or one tenth of the width. From this point onwards the spread

of further weirs was prevented, but some of the most ancient survived in use until after World War Two.

NETS

On the lower reaches of the river hand-held nets were deployed against individual fish in the shallows while 'stop nets', each about 30 feet long, were deployed from rowing boats anchored offshore across the fast-flowing shallows. Taylor describes the head-line of the latter nets as being strung from long arms projecting to the fore and aft quarters of the boat and balanced on the gunwale so that the assembly could be lowered into the water by one man; when a fish was detected the support that had kept the net in place was kicked away so that the net could be heaved out of the water with the fish trapped in its terminal bag. A third variant, the long net, required one man stationed on the shore anchoring one end of the net and two more to row out into the stream, paying out the net as they progressed; having reached their limit they circled back to the bank where a fourth man seized the other end of the net, which was then hauled in along with any fish (again mostly salmon) which happened to be caught up in it.

In the absence of a great many vigorous water channels of the kind particularly associated with traps, it may have been that netting lay behind a good deal of the fishing carried out in the Fens that came to supply a considerable proportion of the London market's needs. Writing of the Fens, Daniel Defoe writes of the fishing industry as follows:

> Here is a particular Trade carried on with London, which is no-where else practised in the whole Kingdom . . . For carrying Fish alive by Land-Carriage; this they do by carrying great Buts filled with Water in Waggons, as the carriers draw other Goods: The Buts have a little square Flap, instead of a Bung, about ten, twelve, or fourteen Inches square, which, being opened, gives air to the Fish; and every Night, when they come to the Inn, they draw off the Water, and let more fresh and sweet Water run into them again: In these Carriages they chiefly carry Tench and Pike, Pearch and Eels, but especially the former, of which here are some of the largest in England.

Doubtless these found their way to the stews of Bankside (see illus. 58) to be kept alive at the end of their journey until finally sold for the pot.

EARLY ANGLING AND ITS LITERATURE

The earliest surviving texts dealing with angling already display such a wealth of detailed knowledge as to imply a lengthy foregoing period when the arcane conventions of fishing with rod and line had been elaborated but when there was clearly no imperative to commit them to paper. One of the earliest manuscript sources, dated *c*.1420 and ascribed to one Piers of Fulham (Trinity College, Cambridge), is quick to establish its non-utilitarian agenda by describing itself as 'a gentlymanly tretyse full convenyent for contemplatiff lovers to rede and understonde', implying that there was already a following, sophisticated to some degree, for the arts of fishing. Of a similar age is a two-page tract entitled 'De arte Piscandi', in Sloane MS 1698 (British Library), which includes an astonishing array of recommendations for bait (twelve kinds of worms and a range of flies and insects) considered appropriate to the pursuit of different kinds of fish at various times of the year.

The full flowering of this genre is marked by the appearance in 1496 of the *Treatyse of Fysshynge wyth an Angle* – effectively the *ur*-text on the topic and printed a mere twenty years after Caxton's introduction in 1477 of the letter-press. It was produced by Wynkin de Worde as an extra chapter in his second printed edition of the *Boke of St Albans*. Earlier versions of the text on fishing appear in manuscript form from the early to mid-1400s and its publication bound up with the other tracts is claimed as a matter of deliberate policy by de Worde, who feared that a simple pamphlet might fall into the hands of 'ydle persones whych sholde have but lytyll mesure in the sayd dysporte of fysshyng' and who, with access to the advice he gives, might 'by this means utterly dystroye it' for his true audience. Formerly attributed to a certain Lady Juliana Berners, Prioress of Sopwell, it is now considered a compilation of earlier anonymous sources and not an original work; de Worde, indeed, makes no claim to originality, mentioning that some of the information it conveys had been 'founde wryten in bokes of credence'.

Scholarship applied in recent years to the subject of early angling finds that the English experience was – as might indeed have been expected – little different from that of virtually the whole of continental Europe. The work of W. L. Braekman and of Richard Hoffmann, for example, has helped to demolish the misguided claims of earlier writers on the supposed uniqueness of the English contribution, but it leaves us with a picture of greater rather than less interest, for clearly much of the wisdom committed to print in 1496 had in fact been in wide circulation at a (possibly considerably) earlier date, hence extending the practice of fishing for pleasure by several generations.

The *Treatyse* makes clear from the beginning its recreational and aristocratic credentials by placing fishing firmly on a par with the other 'disports' of hunting, hawking and fowling (which formed the sole concerns of the first edition of the *Boke of St Albans*), and offering the 'vertuous: gentyll: and free borne' reader the consolation that even should he never succeed in catching anything his life will have been enriched by the experience; fishing for material gain formed no part of the author's interests.

Every page of the treatise is full of practical advice: rods, lines, hooks, sinkers, floats (illus. 88); how to handle the equipment; how to choose where and when to fish; and suitable bait for eighteen varieties of fish. Each aspect of the angler's equipment is dealt with in a way that attracts approval from present-day aficionados. The rod was to be of tripartite construction: for the butt a sturdy length of hazel, aspen or willow was recommended, socketed at one end and rein-

forced with a ferrule; into this was fitted the middle section, of hazel, to which was spliced a supple tip section formed of 'a fair shoot of blackthorn, crab-tree, meddler or juniper'. The materials were to be cut in the winter, set straight in an oven and seasoned before use, by which means the angler was promised a rod that would be 'light and full nymbyll to fish with'. Reels were not yet in use: instead, a length of line was secured to the splice and carried down to the tip, where it formed a loop, to which the main line was attached. This arrangement provided an extra degree of security, for if the tip of the rod were to be broken while the fish was being played, the extra loop would ensure that the catch (and all the tackle) remained attached to the rod.

For the line itself, horsehair was recommended, plucked from the animal's tail; a later writer, John Dennys, in his *Secrets of Angling* (1613) counselled that for the best quality it should be carefully chosen from the tail of some lusty stallion. While a single hair might suffice to take a minnow, multiple strands were plaited together to make lines appropriate for a variety of fish – up to a maximum of sixteen for salmon and with the addition of wire to protect it when fishing for pike or similar predatory fish. Recipes follow in the treatise for dying the horsehair in various shades, later elaborated by Mascall into a range of five essential hues – yellow, green, tawny brown, russet and dusk-coloured – appropriate to different waters and different seasons; the angler would achieve these tints using alum, marigolds, coperas, walnut leaves and old ale, as appropriate. Other sources mention alternatively the use of hemp, bast or pack-thread for lines.

It was already common practice to deploy a long line to which were attached a number of hooks on by-lines, deployed either with the aid of a rod or fed into the water from a hand frame. The treatise anticipates that the angler would not only tie his own flies but would also make his own hooks. As a starting point for these the text recomnds a variety of needles – appropriate to embroiderers, tailors and shoemakers – and instructions are given for annealing and cutting them, forming the barb, expanding the end to be bound to the line and subsequently re-tempering them. A range of flies is described, for use in pursuit of different varieties in different months of the year. In April, for example, the text recommends 'The Stonefly, the bodye of blacke wull: and yellowe under the wynge, and under the tayle and the wynges of the drake', while at the beginning of May 'a good flye' is described as having 'the body of roddyd wull and lappid aboute wyth blacke sylke: the wynges of the drake and of the redde capons hakyll'.

Floats of cork are recommended, pierced by a quill to stand upright in the water, and a variety of weights of lead, regulated in size according to the line in use, round and smooth to avoid snagging. Bottom fishing (with weights), middle water (with float) and surface fishing with flies are all discussed (illus. 88). Broadly contemporary examples of all

such items are known from archaeological sources, giving form to these descriptions.

Despite its primarily recreational agenda, the *Treatyse* does include some less sporting ways of taking fish by rendering them senseless in the water, including feeding them with seeds of henbane, valerian or mallow crushed with alcohol. Despite the author's protestations, there seems little reason to imagine that all practitioners were in it merely for the sport: in many cases, their motives for pursuing the fish would have been every bit as mundane as those who resorted instead to the decidedly unsportsmanlike fish trap.

Leonard Mascall's *Booke of Fishing* (1590) draws heavily on the *Boke of St Albans* while providing many useful supplementary observations. He advises on the best places to fish, the most propitious times of the day and the ideal weather conditions. He lists a variety of fishing flies and a range of baits, including 'the Grasshopper with his legs cut off . . . the whites of hard egges steeped in tarte ale . . . young frogges, the feete cut off by the body or by the knee . . . or . . . young Myse not haired'. Vegetarian options include (for roach) one based

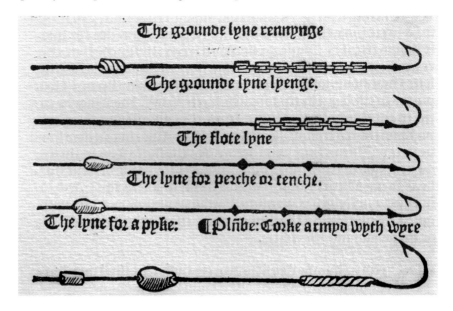

88 Lines furnished with a variety of floats (of cork) and sinkers (mostly of lead – the last of 'Corke armyd wyth wyre'). From the *Treatyse of Fysshynge wyth an Angle* (1496).

on wheat: 'seeth it like furmantie; then take it out of the water and drie it, then frie it with hony, and good store of saffron, and then put it on your hooke'. As well as advice on the taking of fish in rivers and streams, he provides numerous methods by which the angler can protect the stock for his own exploitation by exterminating competitors from the natural world – trapping otters in basket traps, taking herons with baited hooks, setting limed twigs for kingfishers and limed strings with floats to mire coots and moorhens, shooting cormorants and ospreys with crossbow or gun.

While Mascall's work remains essentially a practical handbook, though aimed at a gentle audience, with the appearance of Izaac Walton's *Compleat Angler* fishing was presented as equally a philosophical as much as a physical pursuit. Walton's first edition appeared in 1653 and was followed by three further editions before a 'Part II: . . . being instructions how to angle for a Trout or Grayling, in a clear stream', was added by Charles Cotton in 1676. Since Walton's death in 1683, his text has remained the single most influential work of its kind in any language and, it has been suggested, was responsible almost single-handedly for establishing the perception that England had in some way a pre-eminence in the historical development of angling. While insular custom followed (or at least was in line with) Continental practice throughout the medieval centuries and up to the mid-seventeenth century, from that period it came to be viewed as in some sense privileged and its practitioners began to see themselves as participating in an art form. Something of this sense survives to the present day, when trout streams and salmon rivers can command rents that place them beyond the reach of all but the most affluent.

FISH

The species pursued by river fishermen included all those mentioned below in the context of fish-ponds (pp. 363–7): bream, pike, perch, roach, tench and trout feature most prominently; less commonly encountered are chub, dace, gudgeon, ruff, barbel, burbot and even minnows.

Following their introduction by the mid-fifteenth century as a pond fish (p. 364), carp also begin to feature as river fish as escapees made their way into the natural waterways: the later editions of Gervase Markham's *Country Contentments* refer to them in this way, indicating that a feral population was well established by the end of the first half of the seventeenth century, and within two decades Walton would refer to carp as 'the queen of rivers . . . that was not at first bred, nor hath been long in England, but is now naturalized'.

Otherwise, the fish most sought after in the rivers it frequented was the salmon, which habitually ascends the rivers in the summer months to gain its spawning grounds between September and February; after two seasons the young migrate to the ocean and return to spawn as adult fish. The migratory habits of the salmon were little understood before the early modern period, although Walton reveals that insights into its life-cycle had begun to emerge under the seventeenth-century spirit of enquiry:

And as I have told you that Sir Francis Bacon observes, the age of a Salmon exceeds not ten years; so let me tell you, that his growth is very sudden, it is said, that after he is got into the sea, he becomes, from a Samlet not so big as a Gudgeon, to be a Salmon, in as short a time as a gosling becomes a goose. Much of this has been observed, by tying a ribband, or some known tape or thread, in the tail of some young Salmons which have been taken in weirs as they have swimmed towards the salt water; and then by taking a part of them again, with the known mark, at the same place, at their return from the sea, which is usually about six months after.

Now the supreme sporting fish of Britain's rivers, the salmon was formerly trapped and netted as described above, with maximum efficiency and minimal ceremony, to form a major food source. So efficient were these methods that already in 1284–5 Edward I felt compelled to introduce 'A Penalty for taking Salmons at certain Times of the Year' in the major rivers: no fish were to be taken from 8 September to 11 November, and additionally it was decreed that 'young Salmons shall not be taken nor destroyed by Nets, nor by other Engines at Millpools, from the midst of April unto the Nativity of St John the Baptist [24 June].'

Berwick-upon-Tweed was formerly the site of a highly evolved and extensively regulated salmon fishery, already sufficiently well regarded in the reign of Elizabeth I for the Queen to claim one barrel of fish in every twelve and supporting by the mid-nineteenth century (according to Sheldon) some 75 to 80 boats working a season from 15 February (formerly 10 January) to 10 October. The same author describes how, from low water, lookouts would be posted along the estuary in order to pinpoint shoals of salmon making their way up-river; at the first sign of the fish, the cobles would push off, each crewed by half a dozen men and carrying a long sweep-net carefully arranged on the stern, its upper margin fitted with cork floats and the bottom with stone sinkers. Paying out the net as it went, the coble would describe a wide circle in the tideway before returning the end of the net to the shore, where the crew would now haul it in, manhandling the living salmon from the narrowing circuit of the net into a tank

formed within the stern of the boat. This process would be repeated several times until the flood tide ended the day, when the entire catch would be rowed down to the town quay for counting and weighing. Apart from the sweep-net (still employed on the Tweed in a small way today), various other forms – the stell, the bob and the hanging net – were made use of according to conditions on the river.

Pennant recorded there a record single catch of over 700 fish, but 50 or 60 were more common in his day. Defoe too visited Berwick in 1727, when he was surprised to find that 'that which we call Newcastle Salmon' was in reality 'taken as far off as the Tweed, which is three score miles, and is brought by land on horses to Shields, where it is cured, pickled and sent to London'. Guild regulations in Berwick (and indeed an Act of Parliament) had sought to ensure that the whole curing process should be carried on in the town, but clearly they were being widely ignored. Scott records that prior to the late eighteenth century the salmon were generally boiled in salt water in large boilers and pickled in vinegar, after which they were packed in barrels to be sent all over the country and as far afield as Spain and Italy; alternatively, some fish were transported live in tanks in ships' holds. Salting was also used but was abandoned in Berwick around 1770; in the course of the next decade pickling too was overtaken by the practice of packing the fish in ice, stored from the winter months in ice-houses in the town; the advent of the railways consolidated this practice, but by that time the industry was already in severe decline. Sheldon records that the volume of fish caught had fallen by four-fifths over the 30 years before mid-century; some blamed the advent of steam-driven boats, but the true reasons for the loss of the fish stocks are unclear and are likely to be complex.

Basket traps were deployed against the lamprey, of which two species are most commonly found – the sea lamprey (*Petromyzon marinus*), which appears seasonally in the freshwater river systems, and the river lamprey (*Lampetra fluviatilis*), which occurs over a longer period of the year. Formerly the lamprey was amongst the most esteemed of fish – Henry I is said to have died of a surfeit of them, while Henry III maintained several weirs on the Severn specifically targeted at them. Lamprey pies were sent regularly as gifts by the corporation of the city of Gloucester to persons of influence in London and live fish were commonly transported over long distances packed into bottle-shaped baskets submerged in water. Unaccountably, their popularity dwindled to the point that in the eighteenth and nineteenth century their major consumer was the North Sea cod fishery, which used them as bait; these too travelled in large baskets in which, Taylor tells us, the fish periodically had to be stirred in order to prevent them suffocating.

An important piece of legislation, the Act for Preservation of Spawn and Fry of Fish of 1558–9, is noteworthy not only for the range of species it alludes to, constituting those most commonly pursued in the rivers of England and Wales, but also for the range of devices it mentions as being commonly deployed against them. The Act was prompted by growing awareness that the 'spawn, fry and young breed' of a variety of fish 'heretofore hath been much destroyed in rivers, and streams salt and fresh within this realm, insomuch that in divers places they feed swine and dogs with the fry and spawn of fish, and otherwise, lamentable and horrible to be reported, destroy the same, to the great hindrance and decay of the commonwealth.' Henceforth, it was decreed, no person, using

any manner of net, weele, but, taining, kepper, lime, crele, raw, fagnet, trolnet, trimenet, trimboat, stalboat, weblifter, feur, lammet, or with any device or engine made of hair, wool, line or canvas; or shall use any heling-net or trimboat, or by any other device, cawtel, ways or means whatsoever heretofore made or devised, or hereafter to be made or devised, shall take and kill any young brood, spawn or fry of eels, salmon, pike or pikerel, or of any other fish, in any flood gate pipe, at the tail of any mill, wear, or in any straits, streams, brooks, rivers fresh or salt within the realm of England, Wales, Berwick, or the marches thereof; nor shall from and after the first day of June, next coming, by any of the ways and means aforesaid, or otherwise in any river or place above specified, take and kill any salmons or trouts, not being in season, being kepper-salmons or kepper-trouts, shedder-salmons or shedder-trouts.

Thereafter no pike or pikerel under 10 inches were to be taken or killed, no salmon under 16 inches, no trout under 8 inches, nor any barbel under 12 inches. Furthermore, after 1 June following, no one was to 'fish or take fish with any manner of net, tramel, kepe, wore, hivie, crele, or by any other engine, device, ways or means whatsoever, in any river or other place above-mentioned, but only with net or tramel whereof every mesh or mask shall be two inches and a half broad; angling excepted'. Provision was made, however, 'That in all such places where smelts, loches, minnies, bulheads, gudgions and eels, have been used to be taken and killed', it should remain lawful, only for the taking of these species, to continue to use such devices within the limitations allowed by the new law.

EELS

As mentioned below (p. 366), common or fresh-water eels regularly colonized artificial fish-ponds – whether welcome or not – but they were harvested in much greater numbers from rivers and meres. They formed a particular speciality of the Somerset Levels and of the Fens, but were otherwise widely distributed. They were a major staple of the medieval diet: indeed so fundamental were they to the economy that fisheries in *Domesday* were commonly valued in terms of the numbers of eels produced annually and rents for such fisheries were often to be paid in eels. In 1086 the fishermen of Wisbech (Cambridgeshire), for example, paid rent at the rate of 33,266 eels per annum; Ely Abbey's charter of 970 includes the annual gift of 10,000 eels from the parishes of Outwell and Upwell, which formerly they had rendered to the king, while Ramsey Abbey paid for its building stone with an annual render of 4,000 eels to Peterborough. Thorney Abbey (Cambridgeshire) is said to have taken 16,000 of them annually.

Elvers were considered a particular delicacy in the region of the Severn estuary where they were netted by the ton on the spring tides of March and April. Taylor illustrates the minimal equipment required – no more than a large, hand-held bow-net to scoop them out and a bucket to hold them in. The practice normally took place at night, with the net held under water with its mouth facing downstream; after a few minutes the net was withdrawn, its contents emptied into the bucket and the process repeated. From time to time the law was invoked to protect the young eels: an Act of 1533 prohibited elver fishing for ten years, the ban being made permanent by in 1588 and reiterated in 1677; it was relaxed under George III in 1778 to allow them to be taken for home consumption, later re-imposed and in 1873 replaced with an Elver Fishing Act (1876) which created a closed

season in the Severn each year, before finally being repealed in 1935.

The eel's means of procreation remained – quite understandably – very imperfectly understood amongst early writers. John Taverner contributed the following in 1600: 'I know that some hold opinion that they breede of the May dew, for proof whereof they say if you cut up two turfes of grass in a May morning, and clap the grassie sides of those turfes together, and so lay them in a river, you shall the next day find small young Eeles betweene the sayd turfes.' He points out, however, that if a small bale of hay or straw on which no dew has fallen is put in the water, eels will still be found there, for the reason that 'at that time of the yeare that river being full of such young Eeles, they will creepe into every thing that is sweete and pleasant'. This habit was successfully exploited as an easy way of catching elvers. North observed that 'no Person ever saw in an Eel the least Token of Propagation, either by Melt or Spawn in them; so that whether they breed at all, and how they are produc'd, are Questions equally mysterious'. Walton cites various theories – 'that they breed, as some worms do, out of mud . . . or out of the putrefaction of the earth', or that growing old, 'they breed other eels out of the corruption of their old age'. (Interestingly, he suggests that the possibility of their being generated from the earth 'seems to be made more probable by the barnacles and young goslings bred by the sun's heat and the rotten planks of an old ship, and hatched of trees', a reference to the widely held belief that barnacle geese were generated in this way.) Only in 1922 was the discovery made that eels are migratory at the beginning and end of their lives and that their breeding grounds lie, rather improbably, 2,000 miles away in the depths of the western Atlantic.

Adult eels were readily to be seen in the summer congregating at any mill leat, or trying to force their way through the 'chinckes and holes in the floud-gates'. Most were taken in basket traps somewhat like those described above but specifically modified in design for taking eels. Two sizes were in common use on the Severn, again called the 'putcheon', about 3½ feet long and 14 inches in diameter at the mouth, and the 'weel', about a foot longer and slightly wider. Both are expanded at the mouth, swelling slightly in the centre and tapering to a narrow opening with a removable plug at the base; within were one or two constrictions formed by the cut ends of canes which allowed ease of ingress to eels but no way back. The traps, baited within with some tempting morsel, were tethered to the bank or weighted down in the water with stones. Similar traps were effectively put to use in mill leets (see illus. 103).

Long, tubular nets were also deployed to catch eels, with several one-way traps within and with a pouch at the end, which could be detached on the larger nets.

They were also hunted with multi-bladed spears called glaives, armed with a series of flat, serrated tines riveted edge-to-edge and designed not to penetrate the eel but to grasp it between the tines. Two sorts are identified – one with a short handle and with as many as nine tines for work on 'hard bottom', and another for use in deep water with 'no bottom' featuring longer, narrower and less flattened prongs and a correspondingly long handle – lengths of up to 30 feet are recorded on the Severn by Jenkins. The glaives themselves (illus. 89) show wide regional variations, which Green has reduced to four broad regional types. Not all spearing took place from boats: eels were also pursued on foot along the river banks and mudflats, where they might be discovered buried in the mud. Glaives were certainly in common use by the end of the medieval period and continued to be made up to the twentieth century: an Act of

89 Eel-spear or 'glaive' with typical flat, serrated tines; 19th century, from Minsterworth (Gloucestershire).

1923 prohibited the use of spears for catching freshwater fish but specifically excluded eels from its protection.

An alternative way of taking them, as described by Mascall, was with the 'proching hook' or gorge, attached to a strong line of pack-thread, baited with a worm and mounted directly on to a rod which was inserted into holes where the eels might be lurking; when the hook was taken the rod was withdrawn, leaving the eel to be gently extracted by means of the line. The technique survived until recent times, as described by Taylor, who calls it 'sniggling'.

However they were caught, eels had the advantage of being able to be stored for some time in a perforated wooden box submerged in running water, from which they could be retrieved as needed for the pot. Numbers of these survive in the collections of folk museums.

90 Interior of the dovecote at Willington (Bedfordshire), built *c.* 1541 by Sir John Gostwick to accommodate some 1,400 to 1,500 birds. The louvred roof provides notably free access for the large number of occupants. The interior is divided by a cross-wall into two chambers, one of which retains a two-stage potence.

FOUR

The Living Larder

PROVISIONING THE LARDER

No man need ever have an ill-provisioned house if there be but attached to it a dovecote, a warren and a fishpond wherein meat may be found as readily at hand as if it were stored in a larder.

Olivier de Serres, 1600

While farm animals, discussed elsewhere, provided the well-to-do household with its staple fare, a number of alternative food sources served to separate even further the haves from the have-nots amongst our ancestors. To a greater degree than the domestic animals, access to these other resources was to a large extent limited (at least in the earlier centuries) to the landholding families and to the monastic estates which vied with them in terms of territory and productive efficiency. In addition to considerations of wealth and status, the law was in many instances invoked in order to maintain the exclusive rights of privileged owners, to protect their assets from being plundered and to punish those tempted into transgression.

Access to these assets could transform the quality of life within the privileged household, but they also came to be inscribed in the manorial landscape in such a way that possession of the animal resources themselves became a badge of status and privilege. In this way the dovecote,

for example, evolved into a visible signal of the owner's social standing, migrating in the process from a common location within the buildings of the demesne farm to a more eloquent position closer to the manor itself, or on the approaches from the gatehouse. In the same way, the rabbit warren, which in the early medieval period was typically to be found in the obscurity of the deer-park or on some withdrawn tract of waste ground, came to be re-sited in the seventeenth century in proximity to the house as a further advertisement of the owner's privileged status. An expansive lake carried much more than ornamental significance when it was teeming with carp to supplement the household's larder and to contribute to the elaborate process of gift giving through which mutual debts of fealty were cemented. At times evidence can be found to suggest that concerted programmes might be instituted to accommodate more than one of these resources, as at Higham Ferrers (Northamptonshire), for example, where upcast from the excavation of the fishpond evidently was used to form a pillow-mound for the rabbits.

The varieties in question could scarcely be more disparate – feather, fur, fish and insects (in the form of bees) – and in each case the trajectory of their history followed a course that was peculiar to the particular creature concerned. Each is therefore treated here in turn.

DOVES OR PIGEONS

In an age when fresh meat was available principally in the summer and when winter root crops remained unknown, pigeons (also termed indiscriminately doves) formed an important source of protein for the privileged landowning class, the dovecote acting (along with the fish-pond and the rabbit warren) as a living larder. Initially the keeping of a dovecote may have been an exclusive privilege of the barons, but lesser lords of the manor quickly gained similar rights and (especially after the Black Death) were increasingly inclined to allow their more prosperous tenant farmers to build dovecotes of their own. To these owners were added the monasteries, which in turn were replaced at the time of the Dissolution by the secular clergy, occupying well-endowed parsonages up and down the country. In the reign of James I we find the Lord Chief Justice, Lord Coke, admonishing the constables of every hundred to enforce existing regulations and to ensure that no dovehouses should be erected or maintained by any but the lord of the manor or the parson of the town. On the evidence of Gervase Markham, in his *English Husbandman* (1613), it had begun to be customary for tenants to be able to build their own pigeon-houses (albeit under licence from the landowner), and in 1640 Parliament debated the possibility of abolishing the existing monopoly: a vigorous rearguard action was mounted, with one commentator arguing that it would be a 'blemish of government that the enferiour sort of people should assume that power and libertye w[hi]ch in reason and policye of state ought to belonge to great estates and persons of qualitye and commission', a view reiterated by Hamon le Strange in the very year of Charles I's execution with the assertion that 'To erect a dove house or dovecote is the right onely & badge of a lordship or signorye'.

By mid-century, however, the economic incentive behind pigeon ownership was already on the verge of decline, although dovecotes were to retain a role – by now as much ornamental and symbolic as practical – in the landscape for another 200 years. The building of a dovecote was never an undertaking that could be contemplated by a poor man, and when racing and fancy breeds of pigeons began to be adopted by enthusiasts of every social class in the nineteenth century (pp. 255–8) they tended to be accommodated in shed-like aviaries rather than the striking structures that by now formed an archaic if still prominent feature of the countryside.

The inhabitants of these specially designed houses were the domesticated descendants of the wild blue rock dove, *Columba livia*, an ancestry ultimately confirmed by no less an authority than Charles Darwin (pp. 257–8) but already mooted in the seventeenth century by Gilbert White, who expressed himself of the opinion that 'house-doves' were derived from 'the small blue rock-pigeon' and not from the woodland species; his view was formed partly on the basis of size and appearance, while the wood-pigeon, *Columba palumbus*, was ruled out on account of its resistance to all attempts at domestication, whether by intensive feeding or by the transfer of their eggs from the wild to the dovecote, for none of the progeny hatched in this way ever lived to maturity. Although a large number of fancy varieties of domestic pigeons would eventually be developed for show by later enthusiasts (and it was these numerous variations under domestication that attracted the interest of Darwin), initial interest in them was directed solely towards consumption. In general, it was found that having enclosed a pair of doves within the dovecote until their first brood had hatched, they would thereafter remain there contentedly without the need for further confinement. Loudon's *Encyclopædia of Agriculture* gives May and August as the optimum times for stocking, and recommends that birds of six months or under (termed 'squeakers') are the most amenable to relocation in this way.

The entire economy of the pigeon-house revolved around the squabs – immature birds which were culled before their flight feathers had developed. Pigeons are amongst the most productive of domestic creatures, producing young – normally two at a time – up to ten times in a year for seven years on end. Until new demands developed from the sporting community in later centuries (p. 263), adult birds were generally spared, as were their eggs, in order to maximize the production of squabs. Pigeons are monogamous by nature and the males play exemplary roles in helping to incubate the eggs and indeed play the major role in tending to the young of one brood (fed with a regurgitated pap of partly digested grain known as pigeon's milk) while the mother bird is already engaged in hatching the next clutch of eggs.

DOVECOTES FROM THE NORMAN ERA TO 1700

As well as providing a welcome supplement of fresh meat to the winter diet, there was a certain strategic value to having such a food-source at hand which may have recommended the keeping of pigeons during the unstable centuries following the Norman conquest. (Culver-house, an alternative name for a dovecote, comes from the Old English *culfre*, a dove, but there is no indication in the *Domesday* survey that dedicated pigeon-houses existed in the late Saxon period.) Numbers of free-standing dovecotes are associated with early castle sites and the presence of additional pigeon holes formed within the ramparts of some medieval castles as at Rochester (Kent) and Conisborough (Lincolnshire), and within a drum

tower at Bodiam (Kent) and a corner turret at Tattershall Castle (Lincolnshire) seems to confirm such a link. With 100 or more nesting places in several of these, they were clearly in a position to provide more than a token contribution to the diet, but in most castle and manorial sites it became customary for a larger-scale dovecote to be constructed, capable of contributing to the economy of the household at a sustained and significant level. By way of example, the Lords Berkeley are said to have gathered in the thirteenth century more than 2,000 pigeons annually from just one of their many dovecotes. As mentioned above, later dovecotes often stood close to the main accommodation or even within the courtyard of the house, 'because the master of the family may keep in awe those who go in or come outt', and in this way they came to assume the nature of a badge of authority proclaiming the status of the incumbent.

The earliest that survive are constructed of rubble masonry and are of massive, tower-like construction with walls up to 4 feet thick; remains of such houses of *c.* twelfth-century date have been found at Waltham Abbey (Essex) and at Raunds (Northamptonshire). Occasional discoveries of foundations of cob (clay) mixed with chopped straw, as at Totnes Priory (Devon), of the thirteenth century, suggest that many examples in this impermanent medium will have been lost, but rare survivors occur at Church Farm, Trent (Dorset) and at Alton Priors (Wiltshire). Later examples are of timber-framed construction and, from the fifteenth century onwards, of brick. Tapering slightly as they rise, the earliest dovecotes may have been no more than 10 feet tall, although within a century or two structures of twice that height had become common. At roof level the walls were corbelled inwards to form a low dome, in which a large central oculus or entrance hole was left open to the sky, through which the pigeons might come and go. In the simplest, low-built forms the oculus formed too the only means of access for those who tended the birds, requiring them to climb a ladder placed against the outer wall and to descend another within, but convenience and the increased height of many dovecotes soon led to the formation of an access door at or a little above ground level. Such doors were strongly made for security and commonly were built facing the manor house for ease of supervision. Some authors mention the possibility of an iron grille being substituted for a solid timber door, but given the constant danger to the occupants from 'vermin' of various sorts and from cats, they seem more likely to have been fitted in addition to (rather than instead of) a solid wooden door. A further deterrent to predators was formed by projecting string-courses built into the outer wall, designed to prevent them from crawling up to the roof-top access. Dovecotes raised on stilts or pedestals – common in France, where they attracted tax advantages over those founded on the ground – are only occasionally found in Britain, as at Penpont (Brecknock).

The nesting-boxes built into the internal wall face were generally square in outline and arranged in rows, the alternate courses staggered relative to each other in order to give them structural rigidity. In plan the nesting spaces may either expand radially into the wall thickness, or they may turn at a right angle so that the nest itself is concealed, in which case the angles are arranged to right and left in alternating rows. In keeping with the remainder of the building, the nesting holes may be hewn from stone or chalk, or constructed from stone slabs, clay, or timber and plaster; some are built up from wattles and gypsum plaster, as at Nayland (Suffolk), while later examples are most often in brick. Nesting-places made of basketry

survive nowhere in Britain although they continue to be known on the Continent, while those made in terracotta are limited to a few examples, either cylindrical as at Snape with Thorpe (Yorkshire), or resembling flower-pots on their sides, as at Newtimber Place (Sussex); both types may formerly have been fairly widespread. Before each hole an alighting ledge is sometimes provided, which may be of slate or some other stone and in some pigeon-houses is continuous, providing a promenade at each level (or at least on alternate levels); alternatively, those nesting-boxes of timber and plaster may be provided with perches, as at Tattershall. In general the nesting-boxes start a few feet off the floor level, perhaps to deter predators (further discouraged by overhanging ledges in the interior of some dovecotes) or possibly in recognition of the pigeons' natural reluctance to nest near the ground.

Well-preserved examples of these various types are described and illustrated in Peter and Jean Hansell's exemplary *Doves and Dovecotes* (1988) and *A Dovecote Heritage* (1992). Here a few instances will suffice. At Penrice Castle (Gower), for example, is a well-preserved example probably of late thirteenth- or early fourteenth-century date: it has an internal diameter of 10 feet, has stone-built walls 4 feet thick at the base and stands 20 feet high; the domed roof is pierced by an opening 2 feet in diameter. Later dove-houses were built (or were modified) to incorporate a cupola or lantern (also known as a glover) at roof level, affording shelter to the birds and keeping out the rain from the interior where it would have been liable to damage the fittings described below. Ledges, perches or louvres incorporated into the lantern eased the pigeons' access to the interior. Windows or portals might also be incorporated in some later dovecotes, initially with iron grilles and wooden shutters; from the sixteenth

91 Sectional drawing of a typical dovecote, with central potence. Other features shown include a dormer window for light and ventilation and a cupola for access and egress by the birds, except when closed off by a trapdoor.

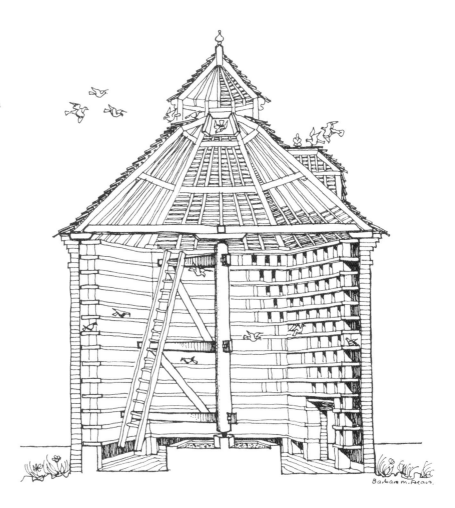

century onwards, window-glass became more readily available.

In smaller, stone-built pigeon-houses, access to the upper levels of nesting-boxes might be gained simply by climbing on the lower courses, but in larger and more sophisticated houses of circular plan a central gantry known as a potence (from the French, meaning a gallows) was included, which brought all the nesting-boxes within easy reach (illus. 91). A strong upright beam (the tree) pivoted in a socket in the centre of the floor and was held upright by a second socket at roof level; a series of horizontal members projected at right angles from the upright, arranged in spiral fashion

so that a ladder, attached to their extremities, was held at a convenient slope. By means of this ladder the attendant could not only reach the upper levels with ease but, by pushing himself along on the nesting-boxes, could rotate the potence around the entire circumference of the wall. Some large dovecotes in France have double potences, allowing two people to work simultaneously in diametrically opposite positions, but so far these are unrecorded in England. Round dove-houses were still being built in some areas up to the eighteenth century, usually by this time of brick or in timber-framed construction and often with nesting-boxes too of brick, plaster or wood, for whose preservation from damage the presence of the potence would have been important. A number of examples still survive: that at Dunster (Somerset) is thought to be some four centuries old.

Rectangular dove-houses appear alongside those of circular form at an early stage in the medieval period, initially of stone or cob and later timber-framed. Amongst the earliest of these is a cruck-framed pigeon-house at Hill Croome (Worcestershire), of the early fifteenth century (illus. 92). Apart from their ground-plan and generally less massive structure, they share many of the features already described. They were more likely to be provided with windows, either set in the wall or formed as dormers in the roof; initially these tended to be closed only by grilles, but from the sixteenth century glass was introduced to some of the better endowed examples: at Queens' College Cambridge, for example, an impressive 13 feet of glass 'for the windows of the pigeon-house' was purchased in 1537–8, while Jesus College bought a remarkable 44 feet 'for glasing ye dove-howsse' in 1575–6. The birds might gain access through pigeon-holes or louvres formed in one or more of the (usually hipped) gable ends or, from the fifteenth century, through a glover. Some of these square or rectangular dove-houses also have potences, although clearly they were ill suited to accessing nesting-boxes in the corners: a square-plan dovecote surviving at Penmon (Anglesey) has instead a central stone pillar about 12 feet high with a series of corbelled stones projecting in spiral fashion to form steps to the top; although all the nesting-boxes here can be reached in this way, in other rectangular buildings with potences the corners were straddled by beams, bringing the least accessible nesting-boxes within reach. Better suited to this type was the form of scaffolding recorded in some dovecotes, with walkways at various levels accessed by ladders: a good example

92 Cruck-framed pigeon-house of the early 15th century at Hill Croome (Worcestershire).

survives at Hawley Manor (Kent). The numbers of nesting-boxes in these rectangular buildings could be increased by incorporating one or more partition walls, fitted out on either side in the same manner as the perimeter.

An interesting regional variation occurs almost exclusively in Scotland and the northernmost English counties: designated the 'lectern' type, these square dovecotes have a single-pitched roof with its taller end turned towards the prevailing wind to provide shelter (sometimes enhanced by the addition of a parapet). Access for the doves is via dormers or louvres formed in the roof. A good example survives within the defences at Tantallon Castle (East Lothian). From here they are densely distributed northwards to Aberdeenshire, but their closest parallels lie in northern Spain and the south of France, and it is from here that the inspiration for the Scottish series is thought to have been drawn.

Some larger dovecotes were of more elaborate design. The most spectacular example recorded from a monastic context was formerly attached to the priory of St Pancras at Southover (Sussex); it was demolished around 1800, but was described and illustrated (illus. 93) in a paper by Gideon Mantell in 1846:

> Fifty years since there remained . . . a dovecote or pigeon house built in the form of a cross, the cells or recesses of which were ingeniously constructed of hewn chalk. These pigeon-holes . . . were in number between three and four thousand, and were arranged in parallel rows, extending over the inner face of each wall of the building. The entrances for the pigeons were four in number, one under the roof at each extremity of the cross, as may be seen in the representation here given. The building measured in length, from east to west, ninety feet; from north to south the same; the height of the walls to the roof was thirty feet. This structure was pulled down within my memory for the sake of the materials.

A close rival in terms of scale survives at Culham Manor (Oxfordshire), dated to 1685, built of brick and containing some 3,000 niches of brick ranged round the walls and partitions; another of similar size survives at Ashby St Ledgers (Northamptonshire). A dovecote with about 2,000 nesting-places and dating from the sixteenth century survives at Newton le Willows (Northamptonshire), while at Willington (Bedfordshire) an impressive structure, almost industrial in character and scale, was built by Sir John Gostwick c. 1541: here the birds access the building via a louvred clerestory to a long gallery, from which the main nesting area is entered (illus. 90).

In later dovecotes the style of architecture adopted reflects with increasing self-consciousness that of the particular manor house or mansion which they served, often forming decorative features in a landscaped setting rather than practical

93 Pigeon-house of the priory of St Pancras at Southover (Sussex), demolished c. 1800. The precise number of nesting-boxes it contained must remain conjectural: it is variously reported as 2,500 and as 3,228.

resources. Polygonal ground plans became more popular from the late seventeenth and eighteenth centuries, but a whole gamut of fashionable styles – Neoclassical, Gothic revival, Chinese, Egyptian – proliferated up to the end of the Victorian period. Few practical innovations were introduced at this time, although the *Complete Pigeon and Rabbit Fancier* of 1823 mentions a new method of repelling rats, weasels and pole-cats intent on scaling the outside walls: 'The external wall should be sheathed with plates of tin, for about two feet in height, and project out three or four inches at the top; which should be pointed with sharp wire, to prevent their clambering any higher.' A few courses of glazed or polished tiles are recorded as being incorporated into some Continental dovecotes in order to achieve the same ends.

Lower down the social scale, less imposing dovecotes became increasingly common features of the domestic landscape. The same work reports that

> There are pigeon-houses of different forms and sizes, built of various materials, but mostly of wood, to be seen in farm-yards, the yards of inns, and gentlemen's courtyards; chiefly inhabited by pigeons kept for the table, which walk about the yard picking up the scattered grains of corn, and feeding among the fowls.

Inns had long appreciated the advantage of being able to harvest a few handy squabs if unexpected guests should turn up, and it was in this context, perhaps, that dovecotes continued longest to serve the prosaic function for which they had originally been conceived, as an ever-ready source of food. Smaller pigeon-houses or lockers of timber, suspended on a tree or against a wall, or mounted on a pedestal, served the needs of smaller, domestic establishments, but no matter how picturesque they were universally disapproved of by the experts as being too cramped, too cold in winter, too hot in summer and subject to rain damage – all to the detriment of the occupants.

OTHER ARRANGEMENTS FOR KEEPING PIGEONS

As mentioned above, it was not uncommon for some of the major castles to have supplementary accommodation for pigeons within the fabric of the walls themselves, and this arrangement can be seen to have become more widely adopted. Tewkesbury Abbey (Gloucestershire) incorporates nesting-boxes above the Norman north porch, while many other monasteries probably were served also by dovecotes on their respective granges. As early as 1375 there is a record that the vicar of Kingston upon Thames (Surrey) 'should have the pigeons or other birds in the church or chapels' and the presence of nesting-boxes in several other churches shows that these birds were by no means expected to be casual interlopers. To give only two examples, at St Mary, Sarnesfield (Herefordshire) 100 nesting-places are formed in the middle stage of the west tower, below the belfry level, while at St Faith, Overbury (Worcestershire) 200 nests are accommodated in a loft under the roof of the chapel. Perhaps the majority of parsons made do with a few pigeon holes in the tower of the church, although wealthier incumbents built detached dove-houses on a grander scale.

Secular manor houses and farm buildings were also commonly adapted in this way, either with an internal loft in some building undisturbed by excessive noise or with blind holes in the external gable in which the doves were encouraged to build their nests in the open air.

THE REGIME OF THE DOVECOTE

A major contribution to the diet of a well-provided household could be made by the produce of the dovecote. Dame Alice de Breyn records in her daybook in 1413 that the daily provisions for her household included a quarter of bacon, one capon, two chickens and no fewer than twenty pigeons, while at a feast given by the Earl of Warwick in 1470 a total of 4,000 pigeons was said to have been consumed. On an everyday basis they must have been particularly welcomed in monastic communities – especially those for which the flesh of four-footed beasts was prohibited – and even in wealthy households where other fresh meat was likely to be freely available only between midsummer and Michaelmas the contribution of the pigeon would have been especially noteworthy. As mentioned above, these would all have been squabs, generally culled at about four weeks, for the adult birds and their eggs were judged too valuable to sacrifice: the Hansells quote one eighteenth-century source as saying that 'though Hennes are more fruitful in laying of eggs, yet pigeons are more profitable by often bringing forth young', the chicks hatching in about seventeen days.

The importance of a well-ordered regime to the population in the dove-house was entirely clear to Gervase Markham when he compiled his *Cheape and Good Husbandry* in 1614: 'They must have their roomes and boxes made cleane once a weeke', he wrote, 'for they delight much in neatnesse'. (In this context the purchase in 1546–7 of 4 gallons of wort by Peterhouse, Cambridge, for washing out the nesting-boxes is noteworthy.) Markham also endorsed the widely held belief that the outside should be as pristine as the interior: 'if the walles be outwardly whited or painted they love it better, for they delight much in faire buildings'. The practice of white-washing the exterior was not entirely altruistic, for owners were ever eager

to attract other pigeons to take up residence in their dove-houses in order to increase the stock. Markham was evidently closely familiar with the way life proceeded within the dovecote, although elements of his knowledge derive from texts stretching back as far as Aristotle:

They will bring forth their young ones once a moneth, if they be well fed, and after they are once paired they will never be divided . . . The Cocke will sit the Egges whilest the Henne feedeth, as the Henne sits whilest he feedeth. He will also feed the young with as much painefulnesse as the Dame doth, and is best pleased when he is brooding them. These kinde of Pidgeons you shall feede with white Pease, and good store of cleane water. In the roome where they lodge you shall ever have a salt-cat for them to pecke on [see p. 257], and that which is gathered from Salt-peter is the best: also they would have good store of drie Sand, Gravell and pybble, to bathe and clense themselves withall, and above all things great care taken, that no vermine, or other Birds, come into their boxes, especially Sterlings, and such like, which are great Egge-suckers.

While some prudent owners followed the regime recommended by Markham and fed their pigeons on a daily basis (which not only kept them in good shape for breeding but also encouraged them not to stray from home), others fed only during the hardest winter weather and yet others not at all. The latter had always attracted the ire of surrounding farmers, for there had long been complaints that flocks of pigeons from such houses looked to their own welfare by decamping to neighbouring farmland where they could devastate crops in the blink of an eye; the well-being of these dovecote owners, the farmers complained, was subsidized to an intolerable degree by their agricultural neighbours. Throughout the medieval period these farmers would generally have been tenants of the lord of the manor himself, so that little improvement was ever registered. Some attempts were made to mitigate this problem by siting dovecotes on remote wastelands, while in Scotland legal measures were later taken to ensure that they were positioned well within any owner's property boundary so that he would bear the brunt of any such promiscuous feeding. When the influential Samuel Hartlib came to record his thoughts on pigeon-keeping in 1655 he chose to concentrate not on its benefits but rather on the unacceptably high demand he believed it imposed on society at large. In an essay titled 'An Estimate . . . of the great destruction of corn by the multitude of Pidgeon-houses', published in his *Legacy of Husbandry* in 1655, Hartlib extrapolates from the situation he found in Cambridgeshire to estimate that there might have been within the kingdom (by which he probably meant England and Wales) some 28,599 dovecotes; by further estimating the population contained in these houses and their average daily consumption of corn, Hartlib computed that the pigeons might 'eat, devour, and spoil' some £1,717,940 worth of corn during the six weeks of harvest alone. Many owners of dovehouses planted no corn themselves, he observed, and there were many parishes containing two or three dove-houses which boasted not one acre of cultivable land; some settlements of 50 or 60 families boasted ten or twelve dove-houses. The product of all these dove-houses, he conjectured, was not worth to their owners one-fortieth part of the cost they inflicted on society at large. Many thousands of families could be maintained on the corn consumed by the pigeons and, indeed, he notes that 'Judge Crook at an Assize was of

opinion, that it was neither fitting nor lawfull for any man to have a Dove-house when so many poor people and their families may be maintained with the Corn that the Doves doe eat, spoyl, and devour'. Adopting an alternative method of calculation, he concluded that some 6 million quarters of corn were lost in this way – 64 million if the potential from seed-corn were to be included – all caused 'by our own wilfull preserving and multiplying so great an enemy in our very bosoms – besides damage they do in unthatching ricks and beating down crops'. (The Hansells express a degree of scepticism at Hartlib's statistics, not least because his estimates of the pigeons' annual consumption were based on the contents of the birds' crops at harvest time and take no account of their more varied diet – including the seeds of weeds harmful to the crops they were said to threaten – at other seasons of the year; they also note the inability of the domesticated species to feed on standing corn, much of their diet coming from grains which have been shed into the stubble at harvest.)

Whether the prolongation of the Commonwealth would have brought about a more general adoption of Hartlib's viewpoint is hard to say. Certainly the ethics of pigeon-keeping were still being discussed in 1689 when John Selden first published his *Table Talk*:

Some men make it a case of conscience whether a man may have a pigeon-house, because his pigeons eat folks corn; but there is no such thing as conscience in the business; the matter is whether he be a man of such quality that the State allows him to have a dove-house; if so, there's an end of the business; his pigeons have a right to eat where they please themselves.

Since that time, doubt has been cast on whether the offending pigeons really were invariably domesticated doves and not wood-pigeons, but in any case a general falling off of interest in pigeon-keeping as an economic activity can be detected from the late seventeenth century. Many of the Cambridge colleges, for example, amongst which almost every one had kept a pigeon house in the fifteenth and sixteenth centuries and maintained them into the early seventeenth, came to abandon them in the later 1600s; by the end of the century only three remained, the remainder having been demolished. Throughout Britain there followed in the eighteenth century a more widespread collapse of interest as new sources of fodder allowed larger numbers of domestic animals to be over-wintered on the farm and hence reduced dependence on pigeon meat. As A. O. Cooke has it:

It will be neither jest nor paradox to say that dovecotes were in a great measure doomed when the first turnip and the swede were introduced to British agriculture early in the eighteenth century. For these useful vegetables, with assistance later from oil-cake and other feeding stuffs, solved a problem which had long baffled the British farmer; that of maintaining sheep and cattle through the winter months.

On the evidence of Gilbert White, it seems that as well as removing some part of the economic imperative for maintaining tame pigeons, the introduction of the turnip also led to a downturn in the demand for wild wood-pigeons when these too began to feast on root crops: 'of late years', he writes, 'that vegetable has furnished a great part of their support in hard weather; and the holes they pick in these roots greatly damage the crop. From this food their flesh has contracted a rancidness which occasions them to be rejected by nicer judges of eating, who thought them before a delicate dish'.

Pigeon-keeping had also produced some secondary benefits to society at large. The feathers, for example, were utilized in stuffing pillows and mattresses. An eighteenth-century poem eulogizes the 'fruitful dung' of the pigeon, and John Moore in his *Columbarium* of 1735 spends considerable time in highlighting its virtues in improving barren soil:

The Dung . . . of Pigeons challengeth the Priority, not only of the Dung of Fowls, but of all other Creatures whatsoever, on the Account of its Usefulness in human Life . . . Its Benefit in Agriculture is so well known to some Farmers, that Plat gives an Account of those that have fetch'd it sixteen Miles, and given a Load of Coals in lieu of it.

One load of it, he says, is worth ten of any other kind. Tanners also made use of pigeon dung in tanning the uppers of shoe-leathers, 'and if you pick and sift it, will give you eight Pence a Bushel for it . . . so that this Article, and the young Squabs will nearly, if not quite maintain your Pigeons in Food'. (It may be suggested here that it was in the preliminary processes of preparing the hide that pigeon dung would have been used, rather than in tanning as such, but the economic benefit remains undisputed.)

The saltpetre (potassium nitrate) that contributed the fertilizing qualities of the dung was also a vital component of gunpowder, which added to the demand from the end of the medieval period: Moore notes that 'Till the days of Oliver Cromwell we had no Salt Petre brought from Abroad, but it was made at home, from a Mixture of Pigeons Dung, Fowls Dung, Hogs Dung, fat Earth, and Lime'. Although capable of being produced from the dung of other animals, by 1604 pigeon-houses were described as 'the chiefest nurses of saltpetre of the kingdom', and agreements were reached by some owners with powder contractors which allowed them access to the dovecote for half an hour a day for the purposes of extraction – an arrangement extended to two hours a day under Charles I, which must have been a cause of considerable disturbance within the pigeon-house. By a proclamation of 1625, owners were obliged to floor their dovecotes only with 'good mellow earth' and not to make use of brick or flagstones. Having formerly been known to occur naturally in Persia and the Far East, saltpetre was also discovered in its natural mineral form in South America in the eighteenth century, after which the process of recovering it from pigeon dung, requiring precipitation in specially constructed pits, became uneconomical.

HUSBANDRY AND EXPLOITATION OF SWANS

One of the few endemic species to have survived the depredations of earlier centuries but to have fallen in the meantime from a favoured place on the national dining table is the mute swan (*Cygnus olor*) (illus. 94). For centuries in England (but in no other country) mute swans were controlled and husbanded for consumption within a remarkably elaborate system of administration centred ultimately on the Crown, which claimed jurisdiction over the entire population in the wild and exercised its control by means of a highly evolved bureaucracy. Nowhere else were swans considered to be royal birds – a freedom from control that simply meant they were left to take their chances along with the other wildfowl. In a real sense, we reap a continuing benefit from the centuries of

careful husbandry that certainly supported conspicuous consumption of the swan on a grand scale but which protected at the same time the breeding stock and ensured a stable and above all an enduring population. (It may be noted that neither of the winter migrant swan populations, Bewick's (*Cygnus bewickii*) or Whooper swans (*Cygnus cygnus*), played any part in this relationship).

Janet Kear has suggested that the unusual willingness of mute swans in England to nest in close proximity to the human population distinguishes them to some degree from their Continental counterparts. The large numbers of swans to be found near London certainly were a source of astonishment to Francesco Capello, the Venetian ambassador, in 1496/7: 'it is truly a beautiful thing to behold one or two thousand tame swans upon the river Thames', he wrote, 'which are eaten by the English like ducks and geese'. This tendency to gregariousness may have encouraged the development of the relationship examined here, although the birds always retained a high degree of territoriality; furthermore, their changing seasonal habits (flocking only as non-breeders or in winter) mark them out from almost all domesticated animals, which are amenable to being herded throughout the year.

Pinioning was no doubt the principal means by which the swan's semi-domesticated status was first engineered and by which birds were induced to remain on a particular stretch of water. Cutting the main flight feathers would ensure that they remained in the same area until the next moult, while removal of the outer section of one wing rendered the birds permanently flightless. The practice of keeping captured swans on ponds and moats by these means is of lengthy but unknown antiquity, but the mutually aggressive nature of swans meant that large numbers of them could never be farmed in close proximity, while their

 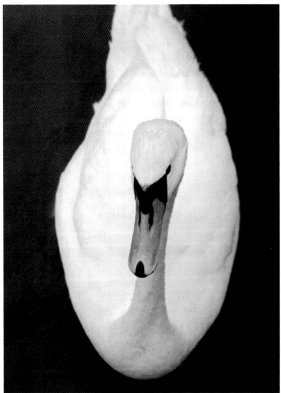

94 Mute swan (*Cygnus olor*). Note the cusped 'nail' at the tip of the beak and the nostrils towards the base, and the knob at the base of the beak: these are characteristic for the species and are reproduced schematically on many of the swan-rolls referred to below.

need for access to open water also placed limits on the numbers that could be kept in captivity. For this reason it became customary to keep captive only such young birds as were needed to see the household through the winter months. It is sometimes suggested that pinioning allowed the adult birds to be recaptured at will, but the essential feature of swan husbandry was that selected cygnets would be removed to captivity for fattening and consumption in the coming year while the remainder of the population would be turned loose until upping during the moulting season in the following year. Most of what follows will be concerned with this breeding population of swans, classed as private property but spending their entire lives on

the open water, mixing (and inevitably interbreeding) with those belonging to separate owners: it was for these birds that administrative measures had to be developed, originating in the twelfth century, surviving in declining usage up to the eighteenth and nineteenth centuries and in vestigial form up to the present day. In the meantime, it may be noted that swans also feature among the species associated with artificial fishponds on some extensive estates (notably those of the bishops of Winchester) where they would have fallen outside this system: Stone notes one of the largest concentrations, of some 200 birds, had been formed at Downton (Wiltshire) by the late fourteenth century.

Behind the prestige and the ritual associated with the ownership of swans lay the all-important fact that they were there to be eaten and formed a source of profit, selling at much higher prices than any other bird. (Capello records that in 1572 the price of a fat swan was fixed by statute at 6s. 8d. while a fat goose merited only 1s. and chickens 4d. each.) Only cygnets in their first year were considered worthy of consumption and then only for a brief season, for after Christmas they quickly lost quality and were judged 'by no means good for the table'. Even in prime condition, swan was not to everyone's taste: Thomas Moffet, in his *Health's Improvement* (1655), found the flesh very dark, although 'for being young they are not the worst of meats', and, 'if they be kept in a little pond, and well fed with Corn, their flesh will not onely alter the blackness, but also be freed of . . . unwholesomness'. In his *Ornithology* of 1678, Francis Willughby was equally grudging in his praise, asserting that 'for its rarity [the swan] serves as a dish to adorn great mens Tables at Feasts and entertainments, being else in my opinion no desirable dainty'. None the less, the swan was the supreme bird of the feast and was consumed in huge numbers by those with privileged access to it. Several requisitions for the supply of swans to the Court at Christmas survive from the reign of Henry III, the largest of them for 125 birds; at a feast celebrating the installation of George Nevell as Archbishop of York in 1466 some 400 swans were consumed, while for the regular feasts held by the Serjeants of Inner Temple in the mid-sixteenth century, Dugdale records annual totals of up to 168 individuals. It seems extraordinary that the swan population could have withstood these depredations, yet in a real sense it was the elaborate machinery set up to exploit the swan on a systematic basis that saved it from following into extinction from England the crane, the bustard and other ungainly species that fell prey all too easily to the indiscriminate attentions of hunters and hawkers.

LEGISLATIVE MEASURES: THE ADMINISTRATION AND PROTECTION OF SWANS

By the time Henry de Bracton compiled his treatise *De legibus et consuetudinibus Anglie* in the mid-thirteenth century, ownership of the swan and its offspring had already become the subject of regulation and, inevitably, of dispute: Bracton records, for example, that swans escaping from private waters might be brought back by the owner, but if they regained their natural liberty they could be seized for the king on the open water, for if the ownership of any swan was unknown it was deemed to belong to the Crown, 'being in its nature a royal fowl'. Several contemporary references show that flocks of swans throughout the length of the country were regularly acknowledged as being in the ownership of various individuals, one such reference mentioning the use of a swan-mark as early as 1230: here, in an agreement between the priors of Coxford and Thetford over fishing rights on the River Thet (Norfolk), the former specifically reserves to himself the use of the swan mark of his own manor. An entry in the Patent Rolls of 1276 further relates to the theft of swans in Norfolk, in which the mark of the owner had been removed by the culprits: tampering with a swan-mark later attracted severe punishment, as seen, for example, in the Order for Swannes (1584–5) where it is ordained that if anyone 'do raze out, counterfait or alter the marke of any swan to the hindryng or losse of any mans game . . . any such offender duely proved before the Queenes Maiesties Commissioners of Swannes, shall suffer one whole yeeres imprisonment and pay iij*li*. vj*s*. viij*d*. to the Queene'. In 1282 mention is made of other miscreants 'who came by night to the water of la Riviere, co. Kent, and carried away eight swans of Stephen de Pencestre and assaulted Roger le Swonhirde, his man' – the first record of a professional swan keeper.

Ownership of a mark (Latin *cigninota*) was necessarily synonymous with ownership of the swans which bore it and, although a decree of 1405/6 reiterated the principle that no one could own a swan-mark unless it be by grant of the king, formal registration of owners and marks began only at the end of the fifteenth century. Until this time property in 'games of swans' remained protected purely by customary laws which, although as yet uncodified, were sufficiently effective to be regularly invoked against poachers. Formal weight was first given to these provisions in the reign of Edward IV by the Act concerning Swans, which came into effect in 1482–3. According to the preamble to this Act, illegal keeping of swans had seen a marked increase in the preceding years: 'our said Sovereign Lord the King, as other Lords, Knights, Esquires, and other noble men . . . heretofore greatly stored of Marks and Games of Swans' had found to their cost that

> divers Keepers of Swans have bought or made to them Marks and Games in the Fens and Marshes, and other Places and under Colour of the same; and of Surveying and Search for Swans and Cygnets for their Lords and Masters, have stolen Cygnets, and put upon them their own Mark, by which unlawful Means the Substance of Swans be in the Hands and Possession of Yeomen and Husbandmen, and other persons of little Reputation.

Accordingly, the Act established formal limits on ownership, decreeing that thenceforward 'no person . . . shall have or possess any such Mark or Game of his own . . . except he have Lands and Tenements of the estate of Freehold to the yearly value of Five Marks above all yearly charges'. Henceforth it was to be lawful for properly qualified persons to seize the said swans as forfeit, 'whereof the King shall have one Half, and he that shall seize the other Half'.

Even after the adoption of the new Act, additional codes of ordinances continued to be developed at a local level. One of the most extensive to survive is that relating to the River Witham and its tributaries, drawn up at Lincoln in 1524 and published by Sir Joseph Banks. Variations in local regulations must have been considerable, although they were never allowed to conflict with the national legislation; accordingly, periodic steps were taken by higher authority to consolidate these local ordinances and to make them applicable to ever-larger areas. In the reign of Edward VI, for example, a set of orders was issued (undated) by proclamation of the Privy Council to apply to the whole of the Fenland area. These orders form the basis for all subsequent proclamations and represent a considerable advance on all those that preceded them. In 1584–5 a further step was taken towards unifying the ordinances and enlarging their scope with a new proclamation which applied to the whole of England. This was later reissued, early in the reign of James I, with six additional clauses added, and a further version appeared in the years 1615–20. At or soon after the accession of Charles I a new edition was formulated; the text, reproduced from a copy of 1629, was published by Bowyer. A further set of orders appeared in 1632 as an eight-page pamphlet entitled *The Orders Lawes and Ancient Customes of Swanns*, 'caused to be printed by John Witherings Esquire, Master and Governour of the Royall Game of Swans and Signets, throughout England'; the introduction makes it clear, however, that these were not new regulations but were derived from others dating from the reign of Elizabeth I or earlier. Thereafter, only a few locally applicable ordinances are known.

The drawing up and enforcement of local legislation was a matter for the Courts of Swan-mote. These were similar in function and procedure to ancient Forest Courts and with a jurisdiction confined to certain swan-bearing areas – sometimes even to a particular river. They were set up under commissioners, often local justices, to deal with transgressions against swan law and to settle disputes between individual owners and between private gamesters and the Crown. The earliest appointment of Commissioners is found in the Patent Rolls for 1463. A manuscript in the Bodleian Library (MS Tanner 91) gives a full account of the 'true forme of keepeing a session of ye swanmote'.

The officer charged by the crown with protecting its rights and implementing legislation, whether national or local, and with bringing malefactors before the courts of Swan-mote was the Master of the King's Game of Swans, also referred to as the Royal Swan-herd or Swan-master. The office is first recorded in 1361, when Thomas de Russham was charged by the king with 'the supervision and custody of all our swans as well in the water of the Thames as elsewhere within our Kingdom'. Although the Swan-master's primary responsibility was for the care of the royal swans, this necessarily involved him also in supervision of birds under private ownership. In the fifteenth century it was a salaried appointment, but the office of Swan-master later became a post of profit under the Crown, its status rising to become one of those posts reserved for some courtly favourite or high official. That the office survived under the Interregnum (1649–60) is shown by a certificate published by Peacock, which validates a Lincolnshire swan-mark dated 30 January 1651 and is endorsed by one George Hill, who signs himself 'Swannerd to ye Comonwealth'. No doubt the swans found themselves under particular pressure at this time, as did the deer and other species which hitherto had enjoyed royal protection from a hungry populace. Former practice was resumed at the Restoration with the appointment as Swan-master of Edward Montague, Earl of Sandwich, to be followed by his kinsman the Earl of Manchester. Thereafter, in the course of the eighteenth century, the prestige (and profitability) of the office declined. The Duchy of Lancaster had its own Swan-master, who ranked equally with the royal appointee, although he was not allowed to take up any swans even within his own jurisdiction except in the presence of the royal official.

The Swan-master exercised his authority at a local level through deputies, from whom he drew his profits from rentals. Five such deputies exercising functions in defined areas are mentioned in the Act of Resumption of 1 Henry VII (1485), but later they became more numerous and were appointed to supervise single counties or single rivers. The deputies derived their income from the fees of their office, most of which came from the registration of marks and for upping, while summary fines also provided a useful source of income. In the earlier codes, rights over stray swans, swans belonging to outlaws or felons and so on were assigned to the Crown: the Orders, Lawes & Customes for 1632, for example, contain a provision that 'all stray Swannes which no man can challenge by his Marke, these are the King's onely. And they are to be seazed for the King, and marked on the legge, but are not to be carried away the first yeare.' In later years the fines and confiscated birds came to be counted among the perquisites of the Swan-master and his deputies.

There were strong protectionist dimensions to the Swan-master's duties, extending beyond the birds themselves to the environment in which they lived. Needless to say, there was nothing altruistic in these measures, which were designed rather to maximize returns to the owners or 'gamesters'. A proclamation of 1547–53, for example, is prefaced with the statement that it was drawn up 'for the conservation and kepyng of the Kynges Swanes and Sygnetes . . . And for the co[n]servation of fish and foule . . . wythin the sayde counties and liberties'. During the nesting season no landowner could 'mow, shear, or cut any thackets, reed, or grass, within 40 feet of the swan's nest, or within 40 feet of the stream'. Stealing eggs was judged a particularly heinous crime: under Henry VII it was punishable by a year and a day in prison plus a fine; later the punishment became less draconian, so that by the time of Edward VI anyone who should 'wilfully put any swans away from their nests . . . or else take up and destroy, or bear away their eggs' was to be fined, for every offence, 13s. 4d., but under James I three months' imprisonment or a fine of 20s. became customary. Hazards to the young birds were banished from the river, with strictures like one of 1632 that 'If there be any Weares upon the Rivers not hauing grates before them, whereby the Swanes and Cignets may be defended from drowning: the owner of such Weare shall forfeit to the King thirteen shillings foure pence'; elsewhere the owners, their swan-herds or the Swan-master himself were given authority to demolish any such weirs. The ordinances also regulated the construction of fish garths and the setting of nets, while the steeping of hemp or flax was prohibited in any running water and within 40 feet of the waterway; there was also a ban on 'any other filthy thing be[ing] thrown in the running waters, whereby the waters may be corrupt'. The setting of 'engines, or any manner of snares, to take bitter[n]s, or swans, between the Feast of Easter, and Lammas' was

banned and was punishable by fines, as was the use of hooks, nets or 'lymestrynges' (see pp. 267–70). For eight weeks following Easter the hunting of 'ducks or any other chase in the water or neere the haunt of Swannes . . . with any dogges or spaniels' was forbidden. Hawking and later the shooting of wildfowl with handguns was banned from the beginning of May until early August. All breaches were punishable by fines or by forfeiture of swans to the Crown.

In seasons of extreme weather the Swan-master had a duty of care towards all the birds in his territory. In times of drought he had to remove them to a well-watered place and during periods of severe frost had to ensure that they were fed and that the ice was broken to provide open water for them. Needless to say, there was a cost, the convention being that the officer should 'have recompense for his paines, in makinge wakes [channels] & the owners therby who have their Swanns p[re]served shall beare p[ro]portionable charges in that behalfe'. In this context, the Dyers' Company records for 1509 contain the following record: 'Payd, in the grete frost, to James the under Swanherd, for upping of the maister's swannes iiijs.' and 'For bote hyr iiijd.', while an early account book in the Vintners' possession includes an entry 'for 31 swans taken up in the Frost for their taking up and their meat 4d. a piece, 10s. 4d.' For these and for all his claims against individual owners, the Swan-master had the ultimate sanction of seizure of birds against payment.

His primary duties, however, were concerned with the establishment of ownership and with its manifestation by marking the birds and maintaining a record of all the marks in his territory. The period of most concentrated activity fell during the annual upping, when all the swans were in turn lifted from the water and the new broods of cygnets were parcelled out among the gamesters. The rules for conduct of the upping were elaborate and precisely defined. They established first of all the period during which the upping and marking of swans was to take place, normally immediately following the feast of St John the Baptist (25 June–1 July); the timing coincides with the period when the adults are in wing-moult and when the cygnets have not yet fledged, factors which have implications for the ease with which they can be caught. The Swan-master or his deputy was responsible for seeing that proclamations to this effect were read in all the market towns in the area. The Master had a duty to attend the upping himself, the regulations decreeing that he should 'yearely come at the usual dayes of marking Swannes in that streame (on pain of losing his Fees during his absence)'. The presence of all the gamesters with swans in the given area was also required; they were allowed to send deputies, each to be provided with a written deputation which was read aloud to the assembled company before marking started. The deputies had to be approved by the Swan-master, and if in due course he became dissatisfied with their conduct, he had the power to dismiss the deputy and to appoint another in his place. Neither the gamesters nor their deputies were allowed to leave the field at the end of the day without express permission from the Swan-master. Rowers and waders had to be assembled by the master and were paid by him: he had the power to command them to attend. He also had to arrange at the start of the day for supper to be provided for the entire company when they had finished. All of the charges involved were recovered in proportion from the gamesters.

SWAN-UPPING: THE MARKING, RECORDING AND DISPOSAL OF SWANS

So assembled, the party would set off on the water, systematically surrounding with their boats each family of swans in turn, securing them with their swan-hooks and lifting them from the water in order to establish the ownership of the parent birds and to mark the offspring accordingly. Those who attended without a swan-hook were liable to be fined: according to the *Orders, Lawes and Ancient Customes* of 1632, 'upon the Upping dayes every Gamster that caryeth not a Hooke (except such Gentlemen as for pleasure goe to see their owne game) shall forfeit eight pence a day'. To be found carrying a swan-hook at any time other than the upping could also be punishable: the *Order for Swans* (1629) states that 'If any person, or persons, be found carrying any Swan-hooke, and the same person being no Swan-herd, nor accompanied with two Swan-herds; every such person shall pay to the King thirteene shillings foure pence (that is to say), three shillings foure pence to him that will informe, and the rest to the King.'

No swan could be upped or marked except in the presence of the Swan-master. Much of the practice is shown in a Victorian engraving of swan-upping on the Thames (illus. 95): the legs of the captive swans are tied behind their backs until they are put ashore with their companions for marking (and in this instance for pinioning). When the entire family had been marked and recorded, the Swan-master would authorize its release; before the birds were returned to the water a tuft of feathers was pulled from the back of the head of the parent birds by their owners, so that those already treated would not needlessly be pursued a second time.

Despite the large body of knowledge that survives concerning the appearance of the marks, surprisingly little is recorded concerning the method of their application, although most were undoubtedly inscribed with a knife, as recorded by Sir Joseph Banks:

> In the autumn of 1820 Mr Chapman of Marshchapel [Lincolnshire] informed me that in his youth, about forty years ago, the custom of marking Swans was still kept up in the Marsh Towns in his neighbourhood and that he had attended when the persons employed by the owners met together and marked the birds. He showed me the manner of marking, which he did by cutting with a sharp penknife a double line through the skin that covers the beak and stripping off the skin between.

Many of the additional nicks in the edge of the beak mentioned below were also certainly formed in this way as remained the practice of the present-day Vintners' and Dyers' Companies until recent years on the Thames. One nineteenth-century warden of the Dyers' Company records that the marks needed renewing every three years. But not all were made with the knife: Henry Best of Elmswell in Yorkshire recorded in 1641 that 'Our marke is three holes boared with an hotte-swipple in the right side of the nebbe, and a gagge cutte betwixt the two uppermost holes'. A further reference to a mark being applied by branding rather than cutting occurs in the Water Bailiff's record of marks in use on River Arun in the 1630s is recorded by Fowler: 'John Apsley of Pulborough Esq.r his swanns are butted on the left wing, and burned with a boate key (in this sort I/I) on the left side of the beake neare to the eye'.

Similar practice is implied by mention of swans belonging to David Cecil, appointed bailiff of Whittlesey Mere in 1507, which were, according to Minet, 'marked on both sides of the bill with the print of a key'. Branding was perhaps quite widely used, particularly for the more elaborate marks, but only a single branding iron has so far come to light and was recorded by N. F. Ticehurst.

95 Swan-upping on the Thames. In this 19th-century illustration the skiffs belonging to the Queen, the Dyers' Company and the Vintners' Company are identified by their respective standards. The crews, sporting swan feathers in their hats, catch the birds by the neck with their swan-hooks and immobilize them in the boats by tying their feet behind their backs; marking or pinioning is carried out on the bank.

It was found in 1925 at Heydon Hall (Norfolk), together with documentation relating to the mark itself and had been used for impressing the crowfoot mark of the Richers family: it is described as a thin iron rod, mounted with a wooden handle and with the crowfoot device at the other end, the whole some 12 to 18 in long. It accompanied a deed of sale by Henry Richers to Erasmus Earle in 1637, relating to the mark and to the game of swans identified with it.

Most such marks belonged to private owners and were their absolute property: an owner could not only sell his mark, as just instanced, but could alienate it by deed of gift or he could lease the mark (including, of course, all the swans which bore it) in return for rent; like other property, marks were heritable by the owners' heirs. Registration fees were, of course, payable to the Swan-master on inheritance. In granting new marks the Swan-master had a particular duty to 'look that the mark shall not hurt no other mark in the book'.

It was less common (but not unknown) for marks to be associated with certain manors, from which they were inalienable. A number of corporate bodies and institutions also owned marks: these included religious houses, colleges and hospitals, all of whose chief officers might also hold marks in their own right. Certain chantries and parish churches also came to be owners, generally by bequest from those seeking to have their memories perpetuated: the will of Thomas Hippe of the parish of Sutton St James (Lincolnshire), dated 25 April 1527, for example, reads 'I bequeth my marke of Swanes to the chapell of St James for to kepe an obit yerly upon the Fryday bifore Care Sonday . . . for my soule and all my good frendes soules', while four parish churches in Norfolk (Acle, Billockby, Caister and Hickling) possessed rights through endowments for maintenance of lights before the image of the Virgin; their marks were recorded as belonging to 'Our Lady's light of . . .'. A few towns and guilds were also owners, including the two City of London livery companies who are the only owners to retain their rights on a stretch of the Thames to the present day – the Dyers and the Vintners.

The convention today is that all unmarked birds belong to the monarch, but formerly the Crown had its own mark (or rather several marks) as well as laying claim to unmarked adult birds and to cygnets whose parentage was not established. There was always a presumption that if ownership was in doubt or if an owner became disqualified for any reason, the game reverted to the Crown. The most dramatic instance of this nature took place with the Dissolution: many monastic marks survive in the rolls long after this time, evidently passing first to the Crown and later being granted to private owners, although the marks themselves continue to be referred to as 'the mark of the abbot of . . .'. In time, other smaller-scale forfeitures, including those of miscreants, became the perquisite of the Swan-master rather than the monarch.

It was during the upping that the Swan-master's skill as record keeper was put to the test, for all depended on meticulous notation of every detail. A prime requirement of the office was that 'the King's Swannerd, or his Deputy, shall keep one swan book, with all the marks of the swans, in the same book'. This book or roll formed a reference source on which the whole operation depended. As a running record the Swan-master had to maintain also 'a book of the name of every Swannerd, and his masters, and so shall inroll in the same book every swan that is marked, and of what mark, and who is the owner of the swan mark'. This 'upping book' or journal was renewed each year; in it was recorded the location of each brood of swans found, the number of cygnets in each brood, the mark and the name of the owner of each parent bird and in what manner and to whom the cygnets were allocated. Other particulars that had to be recorded such as the sale of cygnets, the names of the buyers and sellers and the prices paid, the capture of unpinioned, unmarked or doubtfully marked birds, the determination of their ownership, and their disposal, were also probably entered in the upping book but may (together with other records of fines, receipts, etc) have been recorded in a third book. A number of extracts from upping books are reproduced by Ticehurst.

If both parent birds bore the mark of the same gamester, all the progeny would be similarly marked. In this respect swans are said to be unlike other creatures, where the normal custom is that all the progeny belong to the mother. Coke gives the following explanation – romantic in concept but not wholly accurate in points of fact:

> the cock swan is an emblem or representation of an affectionate and true husband to his wife above all other fowls; for the cock swan holdeth himself to one female only, and for this cause nature hath conferred on him a gift beyond all others; that is, to die so joyfully, that he sings sweetly when he dies . . . [and] therefore this case of the swan doth differ from the case of kine, or other brute beasts.

Rules regarding the apportioning of cygnets between respective owners of differently marked birds were strict, although variations are recorded at different times and in different places. Equal division of the brood was the general aim, with the owner of the male parent having the first pick: typical is the rule that 'when Cignets are taken up, the owner of the Cob must chuse the first Cignet, and the Pen the next, and so in order'. Alternatively, ownership could be decided by lots. If three or more cygnets were produced, then the owner

of the land on which the nest had been built was entitled to one of them 'for the spoyle of his Grass'; he paid a fee of 1s. to the Crown for this privilege. If only one parent survived of the original pair then half the cygnets were marked for the Crown, though they were left with the family. Birds of ambivalent status which were seized by the Swan-master had to be made available for inspection by possible claimants and to this end it was ordained of 'every Swannerd, intending to keep any swans or signets, that they shall keep them in a p[e]n, or a pit, within twenty foot of the King's highway, so that the King's subjects passing by, may have the sight of the said swans, upon pain of 40s.'

The Swan-master's authority did not end with the open water, for he was empowered to enter any rivers, ponds or moats in pursuit of his duty. It was deemed that

> if any Gamester or other person whatsoever having swans to feed doe feed them in any vault, celler or privy corner, close, yard or otherwhere th[a]n in open place where gamesters may come to see, & vew them: that in such cases it shalbee lawfull for any suspecting the same . . . to search the place wthout contradiction of the owners thereof.

Neither were his duties entirely seasonal, for he had year-round control of all transactions involving swans. Gamesters might gather up cygnets destined for fattening and eating that year at the time of the upping (in which case they were not marked), but if at any other time a gamester wished to remove swans from the open water he could do so only under supervision of the Swan-master and in the presence of two or three neighbouring gamesters or their swan-herds. When marks and birds changed hands, it was essential that the transaction was attended by the Swan-master and entered in his roll, otherwise it had no validity. When an entire game of swans was transferred it required no more than registration of the fact that the mark was in new ownership (and, of course, payment of a fee to the Swan-master). In this way, several marks might come to be owned by a single gamester. If they changed hands by inheritance, again the records had to be amended for the new owner's title to be validated.

SWAN MARKS AND ROLLS: THE ICONOGRAPHY OF OWNERSHIP

The marks applied to the beaks of swans were varied in nature. A number of groupings or families of marks have been distinguished, but the choice of one kind of mark or another seems to have been entirely arbitrary. The simplest were composed of linear devices, transverse or diagonal lines, triangles, squares, circles and the like. Some were clearly stylized representations of objects – often weapons, including swords (illus. 96: 1), spears, bows and arrows, and crossbows, or implements, including forks (illus. 96: 2), spades (illus. 96: 3), hammers, masons' squares and combs. The latter types were particularly popular in the Fens but almost totally absent from the Thames, whereas the adoption by monastic houses of the abbot's or prior's staff as their device (later transferred to secular ownership: illus. 96: 4) is found equally in either area. Others resemble merchants' marks, but although Ticehurst traces several sixteenth-century owners who were wealthy merchants, he is able to establish links with a known merchant's mark in only one instance. The same author detects occasionally canting allusions to the owner's name: one certain example is that of William Rippling in the Fens who adopted as his device a 'rippling comb', used in the carding or rippling of hemp, and mentions

two other candidates – the fleur-de-lis of Richard Flower of Ely and the two bows of Sir William Bowes. Some marks are overtly heraldic in character, although there seem to be few connections between the devices represented and those belonging to armigerous gamesters: shields are common, as are chevrons, annulets, crosses, trefoils, lozenges and other charges. Letter-marks are occasionally found (illus. 96: 11), but all are comparatively late in date.

Marks could be 'differenced', in the heraldic sense, by various means – for example by changing their orientation on the bill or by adding to or omitting components. An important means of distinction involved cutting lateral nicks of various shapes to either side of the upper mandible (illus. 96: 2, 5–6, 11; illus. 97: 1.3), in which case they were termed 'gaps', or to the lower mandible, known as 'ticks'. In the earlier period ticks were depicted in the rolls as triangles or semicircles projecting from the outline of the bill, but later it was more common to indicate them by a written surcharge on or beside the bill. The Trafford manuscript includes several marks in which the ticks are indicated by both methods as well as a number with written surcharges only (illus. 96: 1, 7, 8).

Further variations could be introduced by pinioning one wing or the other or by marking the legs or feet of the swan. The legs could be marked by cutting or branding on the flattened outer surfaces; such a mark could be used as a secondary distinguishing feature, for example, for identifying birds, already beak-marked, that had been forfeited to the Crown. Leg-marks were normally described on the rolls by a written surcharge, sometimes with a drawing of the appropriate symbol. In the Trafford manuscript one mark is illustrated on a beak outline but is indicated as being on the leg (illus. 96: 9); on another the leg-mark is recorded alongside the conventionally placed

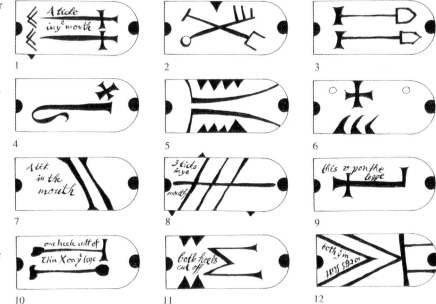

96 Beak-marks 1–8 and other marks from the Trafford manuscript, *c.* 1637, redrawn from the author's photographs by the late Harry Lange. 1 Swords and ticks (Baldwer); 2 fork and [?] key (Wensley); 3 spades (Some); 4 crozier (Worletch); 5–6 gaps (Shadd, Odome); 7–8 ticks (Crisby, Crane); 9 leg-mark (Cockett); 10 leg- and heel-mark (Medly); 11 heel-mark (Marshall); 12 web-mark (Edwards). This form of schematic representation of the beak is adopted by the majority of the surviving manuscript rolls.

beak-mark (illus. 96: 10). A representation in the Everard Roll of a leg and foot together with a leg-mark, drawn alongside the beak, is exceptional.

The feet were not marked on the surface but were cut or notched in a distinctive manner. They presented two possibilities: one involved the cutting off of one or both of the hind toes (referred to in the documents as the 'heels': see illus. 96: 10–11) or one or more of the claws; the other involved cutting notches into the edges of the webs, punching holes out of them or cutting parallel slits to form what was termed a tongue, free on its long edges but attached at either end (illus. 96: 12). An illustration from the mid-fourteenth century, which Gurney and Ticehurst both illustrate as a swan having a mark punched on its foot, is to be interpreted rather as a jocular image of a goose being shod to go to market (see also p. 347 and illus. 101). The majority of foot-marks were used in association with beak-marks; in the Fens they were used as a method of differencing, while in Yorkshire every owner had a leg- or foot-mark

which was placed upon the cygnets at the midsummer upping, while the beak-mark was added at a second upping at Michaelmas only on those birds selected to remain on the water to increase the stock, the remainder being penned up for fattening. Best, for example, records that

> The swanners gette up the younge swannes about Midsummer, and footemarke them for the owners; and then doe they allsoe pinnion them, cuttinge a joynte of theire right winges; and then att Michaelmasse doe they bring them hoame, or else bringe hoame some, and leave the rest att some of the mills, and wee sende for them . . .

The same author notes that 'our footmarke is to cutte or slitte them on both the in-webbes, and to cutte rounde holes in the out-webbes'. Elsewhere foot- and leg-marks might be applied when swans changed hands, for a registered owner acquiring already-marked birds was not allowed simply to add his own device: double-marked birds were liable to be declared forfeit to the Crown. Footmarks are again recorded by means of superscripts accompanying the beak markings (illus. 96: 10–12). The 'Orders and paynes of the Court of the manor of Hempholm (Yorkshire) to be observed by the Swanners' (*c.* 1679–1708), reproduced by Poulson, decree that 'Every person shall enter into the swanning book his foot mark, as well as his beak mark, in pain of forfeiting all such swans to the King'.

All the illustrations of marks referred to so far have been from rolls of the simplest and most common sort, in which a plan view of the beak is given with the marks inscribed in the appropriate places. Most of the 70 or so surviving books and rolls comprise tabular grids showing outline bills of this sort, generally including a representation of the curving 'nail' at the tip and often showing the knob at the base of the bill (see illus. 94). Some variety of anatomical elaboration is also

encountered. A few examples include the nostrils, while some show the eyes and the forward part of the head, represented in plan view like the beak and varying both in completeness and in realism (illus. 97). More elaborate are those in which a side elevation of the head is combined with a plan view of the beak, turned through 90 degrees in order to display the markings to their full advantage, a form peculiarly associated with Norfolk rolls. Among the illustrated examples (illus. 98–9) is one from a privately owned roll, seemingly drawn up for Sir Arthur Caple in the period 1588–1632. This curious anatomical convention was misinterpreted by an early author on the subject, W. H. Yarrell in his *History of British Birds*, who mistook the plan views of these beaks for side elevations and in redrawing them for publication doubled up the nicks on the margins to form lozenges in the centre – an understandable error but one that attracted Ticehurst's particular scorn. Others occur with an even more idiosyncratic perspective in

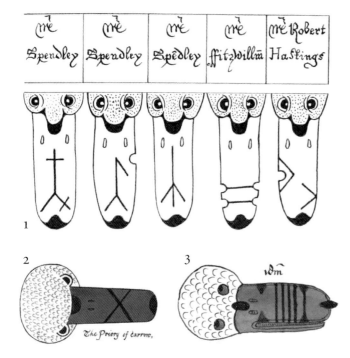

97 Beakmarks from: 1 Fulford Hall roll, 1650; 2 Hornor roll, post-1671; 3 Everard roll, 1566. Here the heads and upper surfaces of the beaks are shown from above, but in the Everard roll a distorted side-view of the lower mandible is also included.

which the lower element of the bill is represented along one edge of the beak, viewed either from the top or from the side. Even in some realistic-looking representations the representation of the nail on the tip of the beak draws our attention to the fact that they are distorted in order to show the whole extent of the mark. Most accomplished but uncommon are views in which the head and the upper neck are shown in elevation while the beak with its markings is shown almost naturalistically in a three-quarter view. Some quite realistic heads are shown on a roll of marks said to have been in use on the River Yare in 1661 but in fact including marks of all ages and drawn up only in 1846; it owes little in terms of style to the earlier series beyond the curious perspective of the beaks, which the artist has seriously misinterpreted.

The grids or frameworks within which the marks are shown also vary in elaboration. Some rolls have no grids at all but most have simple linear boxes, each box enclosing one marked beak with the name of the owner written over it, generally arranged horizontally but occasionally vertically. A few have more decorative treatments of the borders: the fleurs-de-lis inserted between the beaks on the Cooper roll of c. 1590 are further elaborated in a British Library manuscript with dots and hatching to give it a whimsically arcaded appearance. One example in the Wisbech Museum has decorative green, yellow and blue bands forming borders. In two instances, the Colvile Roll in the Wisbech Museum and the Cutts Roll in the Bodleian Library (illus. 98: 7–8), the frame is divided into squares, each containing a drawing of a swan's head and upper neck in profile, with the bills coloured red in one instance and pink in the other; only in half a dozen other books, mostly from Norfolk, are the bills coloured. In the roll formerly at Hanford Hall near Blandford (Dorset) and described by Mayo, the frame as well as the

heads and bills on each page have been printed by hand from a single, rather irregular wood-block, providing a labour-saving boon to the scribe. Colouring, beyond occasional reddish tints on the bill, is unusual: an incomplete book of marks from Elsing Hall, Norfolk, has a blue wash on the first membrane and a green tint thereafter.

In the course of repeated copying and recopying of marks there was ample opportunity for error or variation. In order to promote uniformity, orders were issued periodically to the effect that all swan-rolls in private possession were to be compared with the official one and made to agree with it, both in respect of the marks recorded and of the owners' names. At other times the keeping of rolls by private swan-herds was specifically forbidden: the Witham Ordinances, for example, decreed that 'there shall no Swannerd keep, or carry any swan book, but the King's Swannerd or his Deputy', possessing such a book or showing it to another person attracting a 40s. fine.

None of the surviving rolls is thought to antedate the statute of 1482: the oldest known example, now in the National Archives, dates from the decade following the passing of that Act, but many of the names are written over earlier erasures. Of 61 examined by Ticehurst only 12 can be dated with any accuracy and 7 of these belong to the late seventeenth and early eighteenth centuries. Many are copies of earlier documents: it seems to have been of frequent occurrence that, on his appointment, a new deputy did not necessarily succeed to his predecessor's roll, but had a copy made which would include any additions or amendments made during the latter's term of office. They rarely present an accurate picture of any one moment in time: names are to be found on rolls of a date long after the owner recorded had died, while other marks continued to be referred to as those of former owners. Ancient monastic marks are a

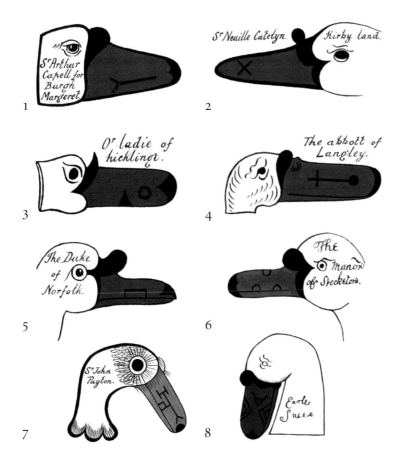

98 Beakmarks from: 1 Caple roll, *c.* 1620; 2 British Library: Add. MS 23732, *c.* 1670; 3 Society of Antiquaries roll, *c.* 1630; 4 Emeris roll, *c.* 1620; 5 Wentworth roll, 1649; 6 Windham roll, 1673; 7 Cutts roll; 8 Colvile roll. Here the heads are broadly in profile; in 1 and 2 the beaks have the appearance of being orthographic but the position of the nail at the tip indicates a degree of distortion; to a greater or lesser extent, the other beaks are all twisted to give a top view.

OPPOSITE: 99 The Broadland swan roll, late 15th century. Forming an early record of ownership throughout the Broadland area, the entire roll is comprised of five membranes measuring 13 feet in length; it records 99 marks in total, many of which can be traced in later rolls from the area. The heads are given as side views, the beaks as plan views.

constant feature of late sixteenth- and seventeenth-century rolls and are almost always referred to by the names of their original owners. Of those examined by Ticehurst, two belonged to the years just before 1500, three to the years 1535–58, twelve were Elizabethan, 25 to the first half of the seventeenth century, eleven to the second half, and eight were later. To these can be added a swan-roll of the late fifteenth century measuring over 13 feet in length, recently acquired by the Norfolk Record Office (illus. 99).

By the mid-eighteenth century the custom of swan keeping had become much reduced both as to numbers of gamesters and to stock, with only a few of the largest landowners maintaining the practice. The increasing popularity of the turkey on account of its taste, its cheapness and the ease with which it could be reared eventually made the keeping of swans wholly uneconomic. The account by Sir Joseph Banks quoted above makes it clear that the practice had survived in Lincolnshire up to the previous generation but that it had then died out. In Norfolk it endured very much longer: a roll of *c.* 1820 shows a number of marks then in use on the River Wensum; 'the mark now in use for breeding swans left on the river' is mentioned by Southwell in 1897 and, according to Ticehurst, as recently as 1928 nine owners still exercised their rights on the Yare and the Wensum. Today, most people are aware of the practice (if at all) through press reports of the annual voyage carried out by the Swan-Masters of The Queen, the

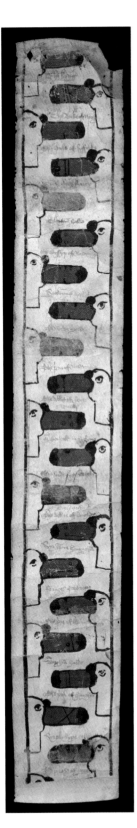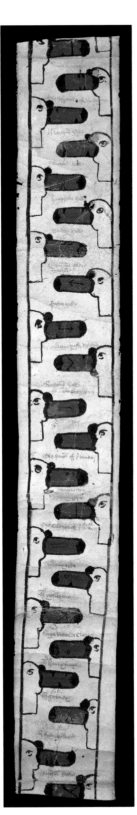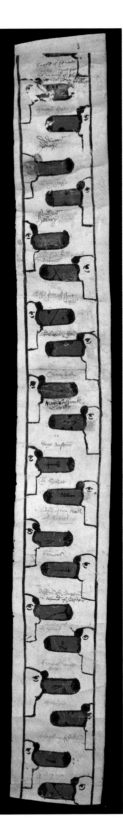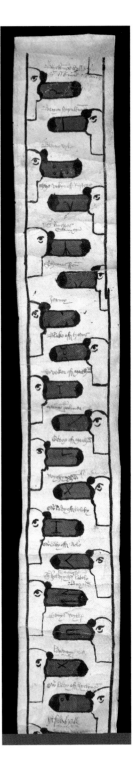

100 The swannery at Abbotsbury (Dorset). The picture encapsulates the integral position that swan husbandry can occupy in such a landscape, where reeds may be harvested for thatch as well as for making hurdles, baskets and so on. The arched structure in the middle ground is a duck decoy (see pp. 282–91).

Vintners' Company and the Dyers' Company on the Thames between Walton and Whitchurch: formerly, marking took place between London Bridge and Henley, but in recent years it has been curtailed in view of the fact that swans no longer breed on the tideway. The Dyers seem to have exercised their right with sober propriety since the early sixteenth century but a more hedonistic streak formerly marked the swan-voyage of the Vintners, whose right to mark is first recorded in 1510; in addition to those who did the marking, it was the custom in the eighteenth century for the liverymen and their guests to lend convivial support by following on behind in the Company's barge, appropriately named *The Bacchus*, carved and painted with festoons of grapes and with gilded bacchic figures on the prow.

An alternative location where much can be learned of present and past practices in swan husbandry is the swannery at Abbotsbury (Dorset) (illus. 100), acquired by the Earl of Ilchester at the Dissolution and perpetuating what seems always to have been one of the largest colonies in England. In 'The Case of Swans', Coke cites an inquisition of 1592 in which it was established that in the estuary from Abbotsbury to the sea there were 500 swans of which 410 were adults and that the greater part of them were unmarked; 400 birds had been seized by the sheriff, upon which the persons claiming the swans, Lady Joan Young and Thomas Saunger, pleaded that they derived their title from the abbot of Abbotsbury who 'had always had and enjoyed the swans without using any mark'; the Crown admitted the facts but denied the alleged right of the defendants; judgment was given in favour of the Crown, which held that swans unmarked in a public river are the king's. Nowadays, however, the swans at Abbotsbury are entirely at liberty.

A number of distinct swan-bearing areas provide vnarily comprehensive system of regulations described above. To a large extent these areas can be defined in terms of their respective river systems, and in several instances they coincide with the territories historically assigned to particular officials, further reinforcing their validity. Norfolk, for example, is generally divided into an eastern sector referred to as Broadland and a western region forming, together with Cambridge, Huntingdon, Northampton and Lincolnshire, the area known as the Fenland. Lincolnshire was certainly prolifically stocked, and as far north as Holderness in Yorkshire swan-rearing was widely practised. Bedfordshire is represented in the ownership rolls; otherwise the River Thames features most prominently, a jurisdiction stretching originally from the estuary up to Oxford but later extended to Cirencester and commonly designated as including 'all other creeks and rivers running into it'. To the south, ownership on the River Arun is well documented, while the practice is recorded as far west as Dorset.

In time, stocks of swans – like many domesticated or semi-domesticated species in England – were expanded by the introduction of new blood from the Continent. Ticehurst notes that swans were kept on the Scarpe in Belgium and at Saint-Omer in northern France, but the highly structured system of ownership reviewed here seems to have been an English peculiarity. It is a striking fact that in a surviving list of customs dues payable to the King's Bailiff at Sandwich (Kent) in the mid-fifteenth century, live swans attracted duty at the rate of half a mark per bird – twice their value on the market as food and double the duty paid on the next highest taxed item. Despite these punitive rates, imports were occasionally made, as witnessed by an entry for two pairs of swans in the Chamberlain's accounts for Canterbury under the year 1529–30. It seems unlikely that importation was ever on a large scale, but even local trading brought together swans from a variety of habitats.

PHYSICAL REMAINS: THE ARCHAEOLOGICAL RECORD

By its nature, swan keeping has left little trace in the archaeological record. Even when cygnets were removed from the open water to be fattened for the table, a hurdled enclosure around a pond or pit was all that was needed to contain the pinioned birds. In the mid-sixteenth century the city of Oxford customarily placed its annual quota of cygnets for fattening with private citizens who had appropriate facilities, supplying them with bread, oats and barley at the city's expense; later the city's game of swans was placed on lease in return for four fattened cygnets a year. Those with larger numbers of swans who regularly fattened them for the table found a need for more permanent swan-houses and swan-pits of their own. Two Cambridge colleges certainly had swan-houses, although little is known of their details. The corporation of Norwich acquired from the Crown the property of the suppressed Blackfriars and in 1544 gave approval 'for castyng a mote next the ryver, to kepe in sygnettes, where some tyme was the friers jakes aforesaid; and for makyng a fense-wall out of the grownd, from the north end of the dortor to the water-gate, to fense in the mote'. Also in Norwich is the only preserved swan-pit, belonging to St Helen's Hospital, founded in 1547 on the site of the dissolved hospital of St Giles and succeeding to the latter's swan-rights. The present swan-pit was constructed in 1793 on the site of an earlier one. The pit itself is a rectangular brick structure some 74 feet by 32 feet in extent and 2 feet deep at the shallow end, with a ramp for ease of access.

Water from the river was fed through a sluice and regulated to an average depth of 4 feet; Southwell records that floating troughs for holding food were formerly anchored along three sides and filled through spouts. From early in nineteenth century private owners were allowed to send their cygnets there for fattening; a fixed charge of 1 guinea was levied, or alternatively the owner could bring two lean birds on condition of receiving one fat one in return; others were bought by the hospital at upping time to be fattened and sold later, at a profit, to anyone requiring them. Up to the 1880s as many as 100 cygnets are said to have occupied the pit between Michaelmas and Christmas, but thereafter public taste for the birds seems to have gone into terminal decline.

THE END OF A CUSTOM

With the loss of public appetite for the swan came the gradual abandonment of its associated rituals and regulations of ownership. No legal device marked the end of these customs: they simply became irrelevant. In 1878 the SPCA brought a private prosecution at Slough (Berkshire) against the three Swan-herds who continued to mark – those of the Dyers' and Vintners' Companies and the Royal Swan-master himself, alleging that the practice inflicted unnecessary suffering on the birds. The case failed, but thereafter the current royal mark was simplified in order to minimize discomfort to the swans and later, at the behest of Queen Alexandra, the royal swans ceased to be marked. Pinioning was abandoned in 1978 and all beak-marking was abandoned in 1997 in favour of numbered leg rings. Swan-upping by these three owners continues as a colourful spectacle on the Thames, although today its primary purpose is to monitor the well-being of the swans rather than to prepare them for the table.

POULTRY

Although almost every smallholding must have supported one or two chickens or ducks – and, if they had access to grazing, geese as well – their presence is nowhere recorded in any great detail before the sixteenth century, by which time East Anglia in particular was already beginning to emerge as a major production area. Turkeys were introduced to Europe from Mexico in the second decade of the 1500s and quickly established their popularity, progressively displacing the widespread husbandry of swans and making inroads into the market for geese. Intensive fattening became widely adopted in response to soaring demand from the cities: the *Agrarian History of England* mentions turkeys being fed with barley, oats and bruised acorns, hens with wheat soaked in milk, capons with corn and peas or with malt barley, and geese with grass and malt.

Some other insights are provided by Markham's *Cheape and Good Husbandry*, published in 1614 and later editions – and plagiarized almost word-for-word in the anonymous ('A. S.') *Husbandman, Farmer, and Grasier's Compleat Instructor* of 1697. For the serious poultryman a mixed economy of several species evidently was envisaged, in which a great deal of attention was paid to the poultry house (at least in its ideal form) and its 'scituation':

you shall understand that your Henne-house would be large and spacious, with somewhat a high roofe, the wals strong, both to keepe out theeves and vermine, the windowes upon the Sunne rising, strongly lathed, and close shuts inward, round about the inside of the wals upon the ground would be built large pens of three foot high, for Geese, Duckes, and great fowle to sit in. Near to the eavings of the house would be longe Pearches, reaching from one side of the house to the other, on which should sit your Cockes, Hennes, Capons and Turkies, each on several Pearches, [as] they are disposed: on another side of the house in that part which is darkest, over the ground pens, would be fixed hampers full of straw for nests, in which your Hens shall lay their Egges . . . let there be pins stricken into the Wals, so that your Poultrie may climbe to their Pearches with ease: let the flore by no meanes be paved, but of earth, smooth and easie . . . this house would be placed either near some Kitchin, Brewhouse, or else some Kilne, where it may have ayre of the fire, and be perfumed with Smoake, which to Pullen is delightfull and wholesome.

When it came to matters of breeding, even for chickens the influence of the planets was judged to be important, the best time to start the process being recommended as 'in February, when the Moon is increasing', and thence until October, although it was predicted that the first brood would always be the best. A total of nineteen eggs at the most could be covered by the hen at one time, it is suggested; the prudent poultryman was advised to mark them on their upper sides and to turn them after a few days if the hen had failed to do so herself. Preservation of those eggs destined for eating was clearly a problem, although the recommendation here was that if covered 'in a heap of good old Malt' they would remain sound all the year round.

Once the chicks were hatched, oatmeal and breadcrumbs – later crusts – soaked in milk were recommended for their diet before they progressed to grain. 'If you will have them Cram-fat', as Markham puts it, they were thereafter to be cooped up and force fed as follows:

mix Wheat-flower with Milk, make it up into a Paste, roll little bits somewhat long, big in the middle, and narrow in the ends; dip them in the Milk, and thrust them down their Throats, and in Fourteen days they will be exceeding fat: and thus you may use Capons, Pullets and other Fowle, suitable to be cramb'd, and make them fat.

Evidently it was anticipated that capons, 'the guelt Cocke-chicken', would form a significant element of the flock. The process of spaying cockerels in order to produce capons was clearly a matter of some delicacy: 'the best time to take away the Stones of the Cocks, is when the Dam has left them, and their Stones come down; to do it, you must see it experimented, or else you will never be an artist at it, by private Directions'.

The primary aim of this process was to ensure that they should rapidly put on weight 'for the dish', which might be achieved by feeding them at their liberty in the poultry yard or by confining them in pens in a purpose-built henhouse. Capons might also take on a useful adoptive role about the yard, where they would willingly assume responsibility for

chickens, ducklings, young Turkies, Peahens, Phesants & Partriges, which he will doe altogether, both naturally and kindly, and through largenesse of his body will brood or cover easily thirty or thirty and five; he will lead them forth safely, and defend them against Kites or Buzzards, more better than the Hens . . .

The practice of spaying clearly was a widespread one, and applied to other fowls in addition to chickens, as William Harrison records in his *Description of England*:

The gelding of cocks, whereby capons are made, is an ancient practice brought in of old time by the Romans when they dwelt here in this land; but the gelding of turkeys or Indish peacocks is a newer device and certainly not used amiss, [since] the rankness of that bird is very much abated thereby and the strong taste of the flesh in sundry wise amended.

Geese too recommended themselves as 'profitable to the owner, in their Feathers, Down, Eggs, Flesh and Fat, and are little chargeable in keeping, as contenting themselves with Grass for want of other Food'. Harrison had heard that in the country

their geese are driven to the field like herds of cattle by a gooseherd – and their gooseherd carrieth a rattle of paper or parchment with him when he goeth about in the morning to gather his goslings together, the noise whereof cometh no sooner to their ears than they fall to gaggling and hasten to go with him . . . With us where I dwell they are not kept in this sort nor in many other places, neither are they kept so much for their bodies as their feathers.

Wentworth-Day identifies the goose as 'the most paying bird' for the occupants of the fens: they were to be found in every village, occupying accommodation in ordinary cottages and sometimes sharing it with the occupants, while some of the more prosperous farmers might have flocks of as many as 2,000 fully grown birds in specially fitted-out coops:

The sleeping chambers for geese were fitted with three rows of coarse wicker pens, placed on top of each other. Each bird had its own

nest, which it never left while sitting. A gozzard, or gooseherd, spent the whole of his time looking after his flock. Twice a day he drove the birds to water. When they came home to roost, he gave a leg-up to the geese which dwelt in the top-storey 'without misplacing a single bird.'

Towards the end of the medieval period consumption of immature geese had seen a significant and general increase: Dale Serjeantson notes that by the sixteenth century they account for some 24 per cent of the total, compared with an earlier 2 per cent, in deposits as far apart as Launceston (Cornwall), Winchester and Norwich. The feathers as well as the flesh of the goose proved a useful source of income. Wheeler, in his *History of the Lincolnshire fens*, implies that they were harvested annually for making quill pens during the period of the annual moult, when 'they were quite loose and separated easily, without pain, from the skin, and the practice was justified from the fact that live quills were far superior to those taken from the birds when dead'. Arthur Young indicated that on the contrary 'some wing them every quarter', the quills selling for 5s. a thousand: the process of pulling was undoubtedly an agonizing one, and could result in death from shock if not from the extreme cold of the winter. And it was not only the wing feathers that were harvested: when the 3rd Earl of Orford passed through Deeping Common on the Lincolnshire–Cambridgeshire border on 28 July 1774 he found that 'The inhuman custom of plucking the [geese] for their down prevails, and had just been put into execution, their feathers being mostly bloody, and we found many dead near the road in consequence of this operation.' Markham had been aware of the cruelty resulting from this avaricious treatment a good century and a half earlier:

for the gathering of a Gooses feathers; you shall understand, that howsoever some Writers advise you for a needles profit to pull your Goose twise a yeere, March and August: yet certainly it is very nought and ill: for first, by disabling the flight of the Goose you make her subject to the cruelty of the Foxe, and other ravenous beasts, and by unclothing her in Winter you strike that cold into her which kils her sodainly, therefore it is best to stay till moulting time, or till you kill her, and then you may imploy all her feathers at your pleasure, either for Beds, Fletchers, or Scriveners.

The latter reference serves as a reminder that in addition to the use of the down for stuffing pillows, the flight feathers of the goose were the material of choice for fletchers fitting flights to their arrows, while virtually all writing was undertaken with quill pens – principally derived from geese – up to the widespread adoption of the steel pen in the nineteenth century (see below).

When they had reached maturity (or when the approach of Christmas dictated), geese were driven to market in great flocks in the same way that drovers brought their cattle. As mentioned below, ox-shoes were at times fitted to cattle in order for them to make their long journey, a custom that gave rise to the conceit that geese too were shod for their final journey (illus. 101). Some historians have been misled into taking all too literally this playful allusion: no goose was ever shod in this way, although driving them to market was a regular enough occurrence, as recorded by Defoe:

they have within these few years found it practicable to make the geese travel on foot too, as well as the turkeys; and a prodigious number are brought up to London in droves

101 A goose being shod for market. The substantial travis in which its head is confined (see p. 31) and the horseshoe-shaped shoe are pointers to the whimsical nature of the entire scene. From a misericord of *c.* 1520 in Beverley Minster (Yorkshire).

from the farthest parts of Norfolk; even from the fenn-country . . . as from all the east-side of Norfolk and Suffolk, of whom 'tis frequent now to meet droves, with a thousand, sometimes two thousand in a drove; they begin to drive them generally in August, by which time the harvest is almost over, and the geese may feed in the stubbles as they go. Thus they hold on to the end of October, when the roads begin to be too stiff and deep for their broad feet and short leggs to march in.

Bonser observes that Nottingham goose fair was another major destination for the rearers of geese: the fair lasted three weeks at the height of its success and handled over 20,000 geese. More permanent provision was made in London, initially centred on the area still known as Poultry; the market here was closely administered by the Poulters' Company (chartered *c.* 1504), whose brief was expanded following the Great Fire to include new dedicated markets, notably at Leadenhall.

In East Anglia in particular, turkey raising had already been developed on the scale of a minor industry. The turkey was equally favoured by Markham as 'very profitable for the Eggs, Carcass, and Feathers, and is a good shifter for his Food'. Fattening them was a matter of feeding them for a fortnight with boiled barley or oats, followed by a further two weeks of cramming with paste as directed for chickens. In the early years of the eighteenth century Defoe observed that

Suffolk is particularly famous for furnishing the City of London, and all the counties round, with turkeys; and that 'tis thought there are more turkeys bred in this county, and the part of Norfolk that adjoins to it, than in all the rest of England, especially for sale . . . I receiv'd an account . . . from a person living on the place; That they have counted 300 droves of turkeys (for they drive them all in droves on foot) pass in one season over Stratford-Bridge on the river Stour, which parts Suffolk from Essex, about six miles from Colchester on the road from Ipswich to London. These droves, as they say, generally contain from 300 to 1,000 each drove; so that one may suppose them to contain 500 one with another, which is 150000 in all.

The turkey's habit of roosting overnight rather than nestling on the ground proved particularly trying for drovers on the journey of several days from East Anglia.

Although a measure of seasonality was imposed by these logistical difficulties, it was overcome to

some degree from the eighteenth century when the improved road system was able to support enormous wagons in which the fowls would be packed by the hundred or more: Bonser mentions huge loads of ducks being brought to London from Peterborough and from St Ives by such wagons, each pulled by a team of ten or twelve horses, before these were in turn replaced by 'fast carts' with multi-storeyed accommodation for the birds, as recorded by Defoe:

Besides these methods of driving these creatures on foot, they have of late also invented a new method of carriage, being carts form'd on purpose, with four stories or stages, to put the creatures in, one above another; by which invention one cart will carry a very great number; and for the smoother going, they drive with two horses a-breast, like a coach, so quartering the road for the ease of the poultry, and changing horses, they travel night and day; so that they bring the fowls 70, 80, or 100 miles in two days and one night: the horses in this new-fashion'd voiture go two a-breast, as above, but no perch below, as in a coach, but they are fast-n'd together by a piece of wood lying crosswise upon their necks, by which they are kept even and together, and the driver sits on the top of the cart, like as in the publick carriages for the army, &c . . .

Swans are also included in Markham's text among the 'Domesticke Fowle', doubtless referring to those that had been removed from the open water and pinioned at the previous upping, for consumption during the following winter (p. 327). When their appointed hour approached, it was recommended that for their final seven or eight weeks the proprietor should either coop them up, or put them into a close walk, where they may have a Pond or some other Water to trim themselves in, for nastynes makes them sick, and loath themselves; set them Barly and Water, if abroad, as also dryed Malt, on which they may feed as they list, and then they will sooner be fat.

Ducks are remarkable principally for the miscellaneous nature of the feed with which they were said to be contented: fattening could be achieved with 'any Corn, Chickens guts, and the like', in the space of a fortnight or three weeks. Of interest too is the degree to which wild ducks of various sorts evidently were captured for fattening up:

Several People keep wild Ducks, accounting them better feed than those bred at home; but in this there is trouble; for you must have a convenient place, Wall or Palled in, with a Pond or Spring in it; and covered over, if you give them their Wings, with a strong Net over it high raised, or Archwise bending Poles, with Turfs of Oziar, and Baskets, and other Couvertures for them to shelter and breed in; with secret holes and creeks for their conveniency, to retire; and so delighting and feeding in this imprisonment, they will lay and breed, and want no more attendance, than to be fed twice a day, with Oats, scalded Bran, Fitches, or the like; and in this manner you keep and feed Plover, Widgeon, Sheldrake, and others.

Whether the cramming of wildfowl was a practice of any great antiquity, or one that had developed after its effectiveness in the fattening of domestic poultry had come to be appreciated, is now unknowable.

QUILL PENS

The date at which quill pens began to be widely favoured over those made from reeds is imprecisely identified, but quills seem to have gained widespread favour in the course of the Middle Ages. Despite the introduction of mass-produced steel pen-nibs in the early 1820s, professional clerks and scribes continued to rely on the quill throughout much of the nineteenth century: Michael Finlay finds that London alone consumed an annual average of about 20 million quills in the 1820s and early 1830s. The Stationery Office – perhaps one of the more conservative institutions – was still getting through close on half a million a year in the 1890s, at which time the legal profession continued regularly to engross its documents with quill pens. Many were being imported at this date from as far away as Russia and Canada, but traditionally the geese of the East Anglian and Lincolnshire fens had been the main producers, adding an important dimension to their economic value; swan quills were also utilized, being much more durable than geese, while turkeys and even crows supplied less highly regarded alternatives.

In the case of geese, only the five largest quills from each wing were considered appropriate for this purpose. As supplied by the farmer, they had to go through a process of dressing to rid them of their internal and external membranes, trimming of much of the feathered area, hardening by heating them in charcoal or in hot sand (though traditionalists favoured naturally hard quills, tempered by no more than use) and polishing the barrel with fish-skin or some other abrasive, before the point was formed either by a professional pencutter or by the end user. Quills might be re-cut many times in the course of their lives, which might vary from a day to many years according to usage and quality; hand-cutting the point allowed it to be tailored to individual use, according to the

349

taste of the scribe and the style and breadth of script he aimed to produce. Pens were retailed in bundles of some dozens or hundreds, carefully graded and priced accordingly to quality.

Fish-Ponds

Naturally occurring ponds and lakes had always been fished for their indigenous populations and, like other natural resources, common rights were held over some of them by the medieval period while others were held under licence. By the late eleventh or early twelfth century, however, privileged landowners introduced a new dimension to the exploitation of fish when ponds began to be constructed for their rearing and harvesting. The move was, perhaps, a predictable one in a society in which captive stocks of animals and birds played an increasingly important role in sustaining both aristocratic households and monastic communities, but the necessary investment in capital and in labour placed it beyond the capacities of ordinary folk. An intermediate stage has been posited in which convenient stretches of natural watercourses may have been annexed to form reservations: McDonnell notes one example in the manor of Wakefield in which the channel between an island and the adjacent bank of the River Calder was blocked off, apparently with the intention of using it as a stew for fish caught in the main watercourse. Enterprises of this sort are, however, difficult to detect either in the documentary record or on the ground.

In any case, during the early centuries of their construction any small economic advantage gained in forming a purpose-built pond was certainly outweighed by the element of prestige that was fundamental to the ownership of these resources and to consumption of the fish they produced, for – as

with rabbit warrens and dovecotes – the nobility adopted fish-ponds essentially as badges of privilege. Their produce contributed to an artificially constructed social mechanism in which the importance attributed to certain products of restricted availability took precedence over mere dietary considerations; in other words, pond-bred fish came to form a staple of conspicuous consumption and an important element of currency in the endless round of gift-giving that cemented social cohesion amongst the aristocracy.

McDonnell has drawn a telling contrast between two early works compiled for the instruction of the bailiffs of great households: the first, the mid-eleventh-century *Gerefa*, makes no mention whatever of fisheries, whereas the *Fleta* of *c.* 1290 includes the admonition: 'let each prudent man see to it that his ponds, pools, lakes, reservoirs [*vivaria, stagna, lacus, servoria*] and fisheries of that sort are stocked with bream and perch, but not with pike, tench or eel, which strive to devour a profusion of fish'. In these two works alone, the haphazard exploitation of wild fish stocks can be seen to have given way to carefully regulated husbandry whose principles were already well established and which would survive for several centuries without radical alteration.

In the earlier medieval period some of the better-documented households can be seen to have supplied over half their needs for freshwater fish from their own ponds, but from the fourteenth century the spread of the practice of letting out ponds along with other assets of the demesne brought about changes in social perceptions as well as economy: owners and lessees now bred fish for profit rather than prestige, and the entry of their produce into the market-place altered the dynamic of supply and demand.

Once again the monastic houses played a prominent role, taking many initiatives in the construction and operation of ponds, but earlier suggestions that they had been instrumental in their introduction to England are now discounted: although the abbey at Bury St Edmunds, for example, is recorded in *Domesday* as possessing two 'stews or fishponds', these seem likely to have been natural resources and it was only towards 1200 that ponds began to proliferate on monastic estates. Dyer notes that the Cistercians, who hitherto had played no particularly prominent role in this field, began a period of vigorous construction of ponds and associated mills from the mid-thirteenth century. When they did enter production, however, the monasteries were particularly well placed to take the long-term perspective that was necessary in their planning and financing, and were amongst the most successful operators of freshwater ponds.

CONSTRUCTION

For an understanding of the construction of fishponds, the archaeological record (often difficult to interpret due to the periodic re-digging that was a feature of their operation) is enhanced by two tracts from later centuries that shed a great deal of light on practices which seem essentially to have remained unchanged over 500 years or more: these are the *Certaine Experiments concerning Fish and Fruite* (1600), published by John Taverner, appointed surveyor-general of the King's Woods south of Trent from 1582, and *A Discourse of Fish and Fish-Ponds . . . done by a Person of Honour* (1713), produced by Roger North, a lawyer, politician and writer. Between them, these two authors record many of the practices that can be exemplified in pond construction and, more obliquely, in documentary sources from England in earlier centuries. Taverner also acknowledges a debt to the *New Booke of good Husbandry, very pleasant, and of great Profite both for Gentlemen and Yeomen*

(1599), a text originally written by Janus Dubravius (sometime Bishop of Olmutz) and translated into English by George Churchey, from which it can be seen that English practice was broadly in line with that established on the Continent.

In classic form, a suite of ponds was necessary so that the fish could be ordered and raised in a rational manner: North's recommendations were as follows:

> Your Method must be, to have some great Waters, which are the Head-Quarters of the Fish, from whence you may take, or wherein you may put, any ordinary Quantity of Fish. Then, to have Stews, and other proper auxilliary Waters, so as you lead the Fish from one to the other, whereby you never shall want, and need not abound; and, which is more, lose no Time in the Growth of the Fish, but employ the Water, as you do your Land, to the best Advantage.

As an ideal, North proposes about 15 acres of water arranged in three ponds or, as a minimum, 8 acres in two ponds. Two principal types can be identified – a *vivarium* or breeding pond, and a *servatorium* or holding pond. The *vivarium* was the larger of the two, and was formed most economically by damming a shallow valley or depression fed by a suitable water source. Taverner (following Dubravius quite closely) gives advice on the choice of site and the method of surveying and constructing the 'head' or revetment of the dam, together with its necessary leats and sluices or spillways. The head invariably took the form of a bank of earth or rammed clay – never a masonry wall – which would be given a shallow batter or slope in order to counteract the water pressure. None the less, depending on local topography, some degree of reinforcement with timber piling or framing might be necessary in order to render it stable: Izaak Walton, in his *Compleat Angler*, first published in 1653, follows the Frenchmen Charles Estienne and Jean Liebault, whose *Maison Rustique*, translated into English in 1600, advocates the use of oak or elm piling, fire-hardened in order to maximize its life.

Water had to come from dependable springs or from a stream with a predictable flow and little seasonal variation in water level, since the fish might easily be washed away by floods or the head broken through. According to Edward Roberts, the need for water of quite specific characteristics might go so far as to necessitate separate water sources for the various ponds, since fresh spring-water was deemed best for breeding purposes while the mature fish in store ponds benefited from water draining naturally from the land surface and containing high levels of dissolved nutrients. Matters of acidity and oxygenation affected the suitability of particular waters, as did temperature, since too cold a source might depress the temperature of the pond and discourage feeding and growth among the population.

In order to minimize the risk of flooding, a 'channel of diversion' or bypass might be constructed to lead excess water around the pond in times of flood; this became especially desirable in ponds constructed in the vicinity of larger watercourses. The rate of flow into and through the complex could be controlled by the use of sluices so as to maintain stable conditions. The manufacture of these, for which the heartwood of oak was recommended, required the services of specialist carpenters, who would also produce wooden conduits where necessary, to lead in water from remote sources, and grates, installed at the surface-level spillways at the inflow and outlet of the water in order to stop the fish from escaping, either upstream or down: the fry were especially prone to

being lost in this way unless suitable precautions were taken. Until the eighteenth or nineteenth century such grates were likely to be of wood: North recommends that they be made with struts formed like window bars. Alternatively, simpler screens formed of reeds or wattles, renewed at regular intervals, would suffice.

Stews or holding-ponds were, by comparison, of smaller size and frequently constructed by excavation rather than by damming, although every advantage was taken of natural topography and of any suitably sized ponds that might have formed spontaneously within the neighbourhood. Since a principal function of the *servatorium* was to act as a convenient larder, from which living fish could be taken as required for the kitchen, it would characteristically be sited close to the residence – a garden setting was ideal, since the enclosure wall provided an extra degree of security. This arrangement had several other advantages, as noted by North:

> you may with little Trouble, and at any Time, take out all, or any fish they contain; therefore it is good to place them in some inclos'd Grounds, near the chief Mansion-House, and your Journey to them is short and easy, and your Eye will often be upon them, which will conduce to their being well kept, and they will be an Ornament to the Walks.

Several other purposes might be served by these smaller ponds, and indeed their use sometimes changed with the season, with summer rearing ponds becoming holding ponds in the autumn. It was recommended that for safety these shallower ponds should not be stocked in winter, when they were in danger of freezing solid.

Ponds not immediately associated with the kitchen were designed to hold fish decanted from the *vivarium* in the complex round of husbandry described below. Almost invariably they required some degree of digging out in order to achieve their desired shape and size, and in some porous soils in order to render them watertight they were given a lining of puddled clay (occasionally incorporating a layer of slaked lime to discourage the action of worms). The texts recommend disturbing the natural ground surface as little as possible, however, in order to preserve the natural nutrients for the benefit of the fish; once laid bare, the ground surface was estimated to contribute little or nothing to their nutrition for several years. In view of the regular traffic into and out of these ponds, they frequently shelved towards a shallow access point or 'mouth' at one end or the other, to allow easy use of the nets.

Some such ponds were networked hydrologically into larger water systems, bespeaking a high level of sophistication and understanding. The shortage of oxygenated water in more isolated ponds could be mediated by having the water supply enter by way of a small waterfall, and other non-structural methods of improving the water quality included the introduction of suitable aquatic plants: Roberts identifies watercress as effective in the shallows, lake-wort and water-plantain in the deeper water and marsh marigold around the edges. Ultimately, fish with a particular tolerance to low levels of oxygen might have to be chosen, such as tench, bream, perch or carp. In order to maximize the potential of the pond, however, a round of regular maintenance was recommended.

SEWING AND FALLOWING

All authorities agree that periodic drainage of the ponds was an absolute necessity, preferably followed by an entire season in which they would be left open to the air, a measure that allowed the water to be kept sweet 'by reason it overfloweth such ground as hath taken the sunne and ayre all the summer before'. Taverner's advice on emptying the fish from the pond ('sewing') and exposing the bottom (a process called by some 'fallowing') is as follows:

> About Hollantide [All Hallows] . . . you sew your pond, taking out all your fish; the best and such as you meane to spend that winter, to put into small ponds, or stewes, whereas with a dragge you may take them againe as you neede to spend them: the other store-fish you may put into a like pond . . . It is good to let that pond you last sewed, to lie as drie as you can by any meanes all that winter, and the next sommer until Michelmas: and then to fill it with water of the first floud that happeneth about that time: and sew your other pond betweene Michelmas and Hollantide . . .

Ideally this process would be repeated every three or four years, though in many establishments once in a decade was more realistic. In well-appointed ponds, drainage was facilitated by the use of sluices and leats: one of the Bishop of Winchester's ponds, at Alresford (Hampshire), had no fewer than nine sluices associated with it. Elsewhere it is clear that total drainage was commonly achieved by breaching or 'breaking' the dam. Either way, North recommended removing the stock of fish progressively: 'as the waters fall, you will have Opportunity of fishing with Nets, and so clear the Fish by Degrees; which left to the last, will be too great a Burden to clear, and will not be done without damage'. One benefit of the system of sewing was that it permitted the number of fry to be reduced, which otherwise could 'greatly hinder the growth and goodnesse of your greater fish'; it also allowed a check on the size of the population. At the same time, the operation rendered the fish more than usually accessible to poachers, and for this reason the bishops of Winchester had lodges built adjacent to their pools, so that night watchmen could be left in place during the most vulnerable periods.

Having been so emptied, the pond was best allowed to stand dry for the whole of the following season – longer if necessary, but not too long: North advises that it might be left to stand for two or three years, 'but not longer, unless you delight to see starv'd lean Fish; for such they certainly will be unless you keep an under-stock by three Fourths continuing in the same Water four or five years'.

The performance of the pond could be further improved by the introduction of cattle into the newly drained area: according to Taverner, 'their dung and stale together with the naturall force of the Sunne at the next spring overflowing, will breede an innumerable number of flies, and bod[i]es of diverse kinds . . . of which . . . the fish do feede exceedingly', the 'blowings and seede' of the flies being brought to life by the combination of sun and water. The exposed basin could also be ploughed and planted with summer corn: when Waltham pond (Hampshire) was broken in 1257–8, for example, it was dug with spades before planting with barley, and similarly the Bishop of Winchester's pond at Alresford was sown with 60 acres of barley when it was broken in 1252–3. Otherwise, exposing the pond bottom for a time would at least yield a 'great store of seedes, of weedes, and grasse' that would benefit the future store of fish, provided the rankest weeds were pulled out.

Periodically it might prove necessary to cart away excess mud that had built up in the pond – a process that would vary widely with the local surface geology. At Alresford, 122 men with up to 24 carts worked for three weeks carrying accumulated mud and stone, and when the *vivarium* at East Meon (Hampshire) was broken in 1231–2, some 5 feet of accumulated mud had to be dug out; twenty years later, ten men spent 40 days clearing out the same pond, using stretchers and wheelbarrows to carry away the mud.

The opportunity might be taken to re-cut and repair the banks at this stage, since they had a tendency to become undercut and to collapse into the water. Sluices needed to be tended with the greatest care, a process requiring the services of specialist carpenters and dykers, for their failure could result in flooding of adjacent properties and the loss of all the stock of fish. John Steane records that at Marlborough (Wiltshire), 46 oaks from Savernake Forest were consumed by measures to repair the pond in one season, along with 24 further oaks from elsewhere.

OPERATION AND STOCKING

It will already be clear that the farming of fish was a delicate and labour-intensive pursuit requiring investment and skill in order to turn a profit in much the same way as rearing any other kind of livestock. Casual remarks by the authors cited above show that the parallel was well appreciated: hence North observes that the successful breeder should end up with 'many thousands of bred Fish . . . fed up like Chickens, and in Time turned to great Profit'. It may be noted, however, that the techniques involved did not yet extend to controlled breeding: McDonnell records that it was a French Benedictine monk who, in the fifteenth century, first expressed the eggs and milt from a cock and hen fish into a bowl in order to facilitate fertilization, but the practice was not developed on a commercial scale until at least the mid-eighteenth century. None the less, in the age of rationalism some of the more speculative theories on reproduction which had formerly prevailed were gradually being abandoned: Taverner records that 'I have heard some affirme very constantly that the heate of the Sunne may draw up such spawne of fish before it be quicke, and so the same taking life in the moiste ayre, may afterward fall downe in a shower of raine into a pond', but Taverner preferred the evidence of his own eyes and was dismissive of this or 'any such other monstrous generation'.

Measures might be taken to ensure maximum protection of the naturally fertilized eggs: Leonard Mascall, in his *Booke of Fishing* (1590) mentions that some owners planted willow saplings in the corners of their ponds in order to provide spawning areas impenetrable to predators. Alternatively, he recommended the following strategy:

A chiefe way to save spawne of fish in March, Aprill, and May, is thus:- Ye shall make faggots of wheate, or rie strawe . . . or of reedes. Bind these faggots together with three bondes, and all about thereon sticke of young branches of willowe. Then cast them in the water among the weedes, or by the bankes, and put in each faggot two good long stakes, driven fast to the ground, and let your faggots lie covered in the water halfe a yerde or more. So the fish will come and shed their spawne thereon, and then it will quicken therein, so that no other fish can come to destroy or eate it, and as they waxe quicke they will come forth and save themselves . . .

The process of decanting and sorting, if properly regulated, proved highly beneficial to the fish: 'It is incredible to those who have not seen it as I have done' wrote North, 'how Carps thus ordered by transplanting them every Year or two, will grow'.

Needless to say, it also had its dangers: if the fish were lean and poor from over-stocked waters, for example, he recommends that they should be stocked at double the recommended density at first, 'else the too sudden Plenty of Food at first will surfeit them, and they will die of over-much Blood, as I have found to my great Loss'.

A valuable account of the operation of such a series of fish-ponds is given in the journal of William Moore, Prior of Worcester from 1518 to 1536. In order for the process of redistribution (and stock-checking) to be fully realized, the desirability for the ponds to be emptied completely – 'sewed to ye bottom to be drye', in the words of Moore's journal – was clearly understood, although it is clear that the process was imperfectly accomplished in some instances: at the draining and fishing of 'Park pool' at Battenhall (Worcestershire), for example, it was noted that 'ther is left in the pole moche store of pickerells, gadds peerches Roches & tenches', and similar records appear in relation to other ponds as reminders that that ideals propounded by the authors of manuals sometimes proved impossible to realize. The contents of Prior Moore's ponds are conveniently tabulated in a key essay by Charles Hickling. Mostly the ponds he administered seem to have been refilled immediately after draining, showing that the process was prompted primarily by a desire to stock-check and to redistribute the fish more productively: some 5 cwt of smaller fish were redistributed in this way during the fishing of the 'Nether pool' at Battenhall in 1521. More also made payments to various labourers for periodic ditching, clearing of mud and reeds, and for other work 'abowte ye pooles'; on occasion, he also hired otter-takers, but no expenditure is recorded on feeding the fish.

Feeding was none the less desirable in even the largest *vivaria*, while in smaller ponds it was absolutely essential – particularly in *servatoria* in which fish were being fattened up and brought to peak eating condition – although with colder weather they became less active and less demanding of extra nourishment. It was not to be a random activity, but conducted with regularity: North advises those with a great number of fish being 'kept for an Opportunity' that they should be fed punctually by the butler or a gardener who is always at home, 'for they will expect their Meat as duly as Horses, and Appetite in any Creature, wastes by Disappointment'. Regular feeding had an additional attraction in that it made the fish tame – to the point where pike and bream, for example, would feed from the hand – which made netting them all the easier when their time was up. Carp, bream, tench and other fish 'not of the ravening kind' needed no feeding in the winter, 'but you must not fail to feed all Summer, from March to October again, as constantly as your coop'd up Chickens are fed, and to as good and certain Account'. Boiled grain of any sort, coarse-ground malt or boiled peas were recommended: 2 quarts of grain daily was deemed an appropriate amount to feed 30 carp ready for the table. Bream would thrive on blood mixed in with the grain, by which means 'you may have large breams in six or seven years', while perch and eel 'will feede of the small guts of sheepe being cut, or of any garbage of Chickens, Coneys, or such like, and of bloud of beasts'. Grain might have to be placed in a feeding device sunk in the water, to avoid the attentions of ducks and geese. Taverner calculates that if an acre of pond holds 300 or 400 carp or other fish, 'yet so much feeding you may adde thereunto, that it may keepe three thousand in as good plight as three hundreth or four hundreth without such feeding'.

His recommendation was that new stock should be introduced in January, February or March, 'after which it is not good to carry or handle any fish all the sommer time, until it be October or

November'. Prior Moore similarly stocked in the early spring around Lady Day, just before the growing period for the fish. The colder the weather while the fish were being removed the better, for 'store-fish being taken or handled in hot weather, will be sicke, and not prosper long time after, and perhaps die thereof, although not presently'.

Depending on species, fish took several years to reach maturity and to reproduce. The young had to be separated in order to benefit from the best quality water (see above) and also to protect them from the cannibalistic attentions of their own kind. At other times, pike, perch and eels might be allowed to undertake the thinning-out process as part of their diet: the perch in particular was estimated 'a very great devourer of frie, especially of carpe'.

New stock was transported over quite considerable distances, a factor that has been a source of surprise to more recent authors. They commonly cite the fact that some species (including pike, tench and bream, as well as eels) will survive for a day or so if carried in a basket of wet grass, but from the testament of Roger North in particular, it is clear that by his day the normal mode of transport for breeding fish was in barrels of water. While grass might be useful in keeping fish alive in order to reach the kitchen in a fresh condition, it was useless for stocking purposes:

Some use to put up Fish in Baskets or Hampers for Carriage, stowing them with Grass between; but this is not so good as Water, for the Grass cleaving the Slime of Fish, rubs and cleans it from the Scales; which done, a Carp scarce ever thrives after. And altho' perhaps the Fish may live, they will not grow or thrive, because their natural Slime, scarce recoverable, is rubb'd off; and for the same Reason, it is not good to let

Carps lie at all in Grass, but keep them always in Water, to preserve them from Bruises, and losing their Slime.

He goes into considerable detail on the transport of breeding stock. The process had to take place in winter if any great distance was involved, preferably between the beginning of October and the end of March. Handling of the fish was to be kept to a minimum, and every precaution was to be taken to avoid bruising them. They were gathered together in the water by means of a net, weighted with lead at the bottom and supported at the top with cork floats. From here they were to be taken out 'with Hoop-nets fix'd upon Staves about 10 Foot long, and 10 or 12 Fish at a Time in a Net is sufficient, though but a Foot long, more by their Weight and Struggling, will damage each other insensibly, so as to hinder their Growth and Thrift, and perhaps be the Cause that die'. North's advice in the method of carriage is equally detailed:

The best Vessel for Conveyance, (if you carry above 20 Miles) is, a great Tun that holds five Hogsheads; but if no more than 10, 15, or 20 Miles, ordinary Hogsheads will do well enough. I know by experience you may safely carry 300 Carps, six and seven inches long, in one Hogshead; but from seven to a Foot, not so many by a fourth Part. If they exceed a Foot, then not above 70 or 80 in a Hogshead. Let every Hogshead have 10 or 12 Pails of fresh clean Water, (not Well-Water) every six or seven Miles, if it may be had. There is no need of any great Liberty for the Fish, if their Water be fresh, and often renewed: for one great Use of the Water, is, to bury the Fish, that with mere Weight they might not Crush and destroy one another.

When the 'Place of Discharge' was reached, the fish were to be poured into a hoop-net a few at a time and transferred to their new quarters, 'and with this Care you will scarce lose a Fish'. Merely getting them there was in itself, however, no guarantee of success:

It is not sufficient that fish be alive and swimme away when they are put into a pond, but if they be brused or take heate in the carriage, they will be long before they recover againe and fall to their feeding, and sometime never recover, but after long pining and sicknesse, do in the end die also.

Occasional records from the medieval period suggest that the techniques described by Taverner and North were already several centuries old. Dyer records bream being carried 46 miles from Turweston (Buckinghamshire) to stock the ponds at Knowle (Warwickshire) in 1301–2, while Steane mentions 200 bream being transported to Kennington (Surrey) and 200 to Windsor in order to be released into the royal fish-ponds. Similarly, the sheriff of Cambridgeshire was authorized to buy 3,000 pike from within the county in order to stock the king's fish-ponds at Havering (Essex), while the Constable of Windsor was similarly instructed to acquire 300 pike and 300 dace and roach from within his territories and to transfer them to Windsor. Prior Moore's ponds at Worcester were stocked during two distinct seasons – in the summer with eels, and in the winter and early spring with other fish. Nearly 6,500 eels were placed in the ponds in the space of six years, compared with only some hundreds removed during the whole period covered by the journal; hence no new deposits are recorded after 1524, by which point the population seems to have been deemed to be self-perpetuating. Their supplier (at the rate of 50 for 1d.), could produce 1,400 of them to order; he also made his own 'weles' or wicker traps (see p. 312) – no doubt the means by which he maintained the level of his stocks.

Some species evidently travelled better than others. North observes that 'The Carpe of all pond fish will abide most hardnesse in carriage: next to him the Tench, then the Breame, Pike, and Perch.' He further counsels that 'If you carry any fish in water, let not the Tench or Eele be carried among them, because they cast great store of slime, which will choke and kill your other fish, especially Pike or Perch.'

While the winter was therefore a period of intense activity for the pond keeper, it was also a time of danger for the fish: North records that he lost 3,000 to 4,000 carp in ten years to frost. Having a source of running water within the pond minimized the risk of it freezing solid, and deeper ponds fared better than shallow. In the event of severe frost the keeper was advised to make holes in the ice; in the most intense cold, it might be necessary to remove stock to deeper water. Some species evidently fared better than others: tench, for example, seem to be virtually frost-proof. The soundness of much of this advice is underlined by the record of everyday practice recorded in the journal of Thomas March, written in the early decades of the eighteenth century and abstracted here in an appendix (pp. 367–9)

ROYAL AND MANORIAL PONDS

Royal initiative in this field was first displayed by the Conqueror at York in 1069, when instructions were given that the River Foss should be dammed just above its confluence with the Ouse in order to provide additional protection for the new motte-and-bailey castle: the area so flooded eventually backed up to some 120 acres and its defensive role

was combined with water-supply for one or more mills as well as forming a royal stew. This aspect was clearly of secondary importance during these unstable times, but soon the pool was successfully producing fish – to a maximum of 30 pike and some 45 bream – for bestowal as royal gifts.

By the end of the twelfth century many royal houses and hunting lodges were equipped with ponds: Steane finds ten royal fish-ponds referred to in the twelfth century and as many as 33 in the thirteenth century; the numbers remained high for the next hundred years before going into decline, so that by 1485 only six were still maintained by the crown, most of those within easy reach of London. During reign of Henry III increasing evidence is found for the purchase of freshwater fish to stock the royal ponds and to provide for major feasts: these demands could be considerable, as when on St Edward's Day 1257 the king entertained his guests with 250 bream, 300 pike and 15,000 eels.

The records of the royal fish-ponds provide a window into the methods that might be resorted to in order to amass quantities of fish in a hurry for such occasions. Breaching the dam was evidently a common ploy, recorded at Woodstock (1238), Newcastle under Lyme (1253) and Marlborough (1269), but was specifically forbidden when 100 bream and pike were ordered from Taunton in 1241. Alternatively, the sluice might be opened and whatever was swept out in nets was taken. Such nets – *haias vivarii* – seem to have been a normal part of the equipment of the pond, along with other forms of traps.

During the same reign a royal serjeant known as the King's Fisherman appears in the records. From 1226 the position was occupied by one William, a contemporary of Henry III and possibly specially favoured by the king, for he was still in post 46 years later. Perhaps it was he who initiated many of the improvements and innovations of this period. William can be traced travelling around the king's ponds, both supplying the requirements of the household – as, for example, at Northampton in 1257, where he had instructions to 'take 60 pike and 60 bream in the king's stews . . . put the bream in paste [*pane*] and carry it with the pike to Westminster' – but also bestowing his 'counsel and aid' on the local officials who administered the ponds in the area. Similarly, Robert *Piscator* was sent to Feckenham (Worcestershire) in the 1230s with instructions to take 40 bream and 40 pike. The catches were not necessarily to be eaten directly, for fish retrieved by two other royal fishermen from the Bishop of Winchester's ponds were to be preserved alive by the bailiff in a tank until sent for by the king. The monarchy was notably opportunistic in taking advantage of any dislocations in administration that might occur at times of regime change – particularly among the higher clergy, whose estates reverted to the Crown during any gaps in the succession: Steane records that the Wardens of Winchester gave orders during one such interregnum for 40 female and fat bream, twenty other bream, 40 great pike and 300–400 of other varieties to be taken alive from ponds belonging to the bishopric at Frensham (Surrey) to be transported to Windsor to stock the king's ponds there. On other occasions the fish seized were more certainly destined directly for the table, for their delivery instructions specify that they should be transported in *pane*, as above, or in jelly.

Lesser manors often lacked the elaborate systems of ponds seen in the estates of royalty and the greater aristocracy, but many had the advantage of having mills whose ponds could be exploited, or moats which had long lost their defensive purposes and were now used as convenient stews. Other ponds on manorial estates could equally be pressed into service in the absence of dedicated fish-ponds: Christopher Currie quotes Lord Wharton of Upper Winchendon (Buckinghamshire) in recording that 'The pond in the Wilderness was drawn the 17th Janua[ry] 1686 and all the fish were put in the horse pond which were 75 very Great Carp and 174 lesser Carps and 17 Tench.' Further expedient use of ponds is evidenced in the appendix (below).

Currie concludes that aristocratic fish-ponds before about 1350 exhibit few signs that strenuous attempts were made to realize their full potential in terms of yields; they were, as stated above, primarily seen as conspicuous tokens of luxury. Despite possessing some 400 acres of ponds, the bishops of Winchester, for example, seem to have exhibited remarkably little interest in maximizing their yields, so that the ponds originally functioned at a fraction of their potential. None the less, Roberts has shown that many of the most important ponds associated with the bishopric were founded during the previous century, notably under Henry of Blois (d. 1171), brother of King Stephen and hence at the forefront of aristocratic fashion. Henry built several palatial residences for himself, most notably Wolvesey Palace at Winchester, and the ponds seem to have been established as part of the same initiative. Despite these resources (and it may be noted that the Great Pond at Frensham alone was some 100 acres in extent), quantities of sea fish continued to be bought for the episcopal household, with only the bishop himself benefiting from fresh fish from his own ponds; ultimately, a visit to Winchester by Richard II at the end of 1393 seems to have provided the stimulus for the systematic fishing of the ponds. As with other estates, from the 1400s the bishop's ponds progressively fell into the hands of private lessees, who exploited them for profit.

Following royal practice, many of the pike and other fish recovered thereafter were presented as gifts to nobles living within reach of Winchester. Frequently they were sent live in a bag full of wet grass, so as to arrive fresh for the table, or if intended as breeding stock were transported in canvas-lined barrels. Details of several such transfers into and out of the episcopal ponds are recorded, sometimes involving considerable numbers of fish: when the pond at Alresford was restocked in 1254–5, for example, 115 pike, 229 perch, 603 bream and 1,072 roach were brought from other estates and from the royal pond at Woolmer (Hampshire). The distances involved could also be considerable: one such journey, undertaken in 1231–2 and concerning the transport of live bream from the bishop's pond at Taunton (Somerset) to Winchester, a distance of some 100 miles, took fifteen days to complete, at which point 30 men were hired to carry the fish a further eight miles from Wolvesey Palace to Bishops Waltham. The process involved a great degree of organization, under the eye of the bishop's own fisherman: barrels and canvas had to be acquired and nets too might be transported between estates, as in 1270–71 when nets were carried from Farnham for fishing at Alresford pond and the same nets afterwards were sent on to Bishops Waltham, or in 1312–13 when a cart was hired to take nets from Farnham to Marwell. The requirements are reminiscent of those under which the royal Master of the Toils was expected to operate in relation to stocks of deer (p. 112).

Manorial ponds did not enter the commercial market before the end of the fourteenth century and are little in evidence after that date. Already in the early 1300s many manors were dependent for their fish on commercial sources – mostly, it seems, suppliers living in the vicinity of the large natural fisheries: the household accounts of the Earl of Rutland, for example, show that in 1612 live fish were bought from Paul Robinson, who fished the rivers of Lincolnshire to provide both mature fish for 'present service' and store fish – pike, bream, tench and carp – for the Earl's stew-ponds. The manors that did maintain ponds showed little sign of exploiting them for profit, beyond a growing tendency to rent them out for others to farm, and then never at a very high rate. With the progressive decline of demesne farming in the fourteenth and fifteenth centuries, a great many ponds were farmed out in this way, and more and more ponds fell into the hands of lesser gentry and yeomen farmers: Taverner was to regret that by his day many landowners had turned their backs on fish-rearing, despite the continuing potential of ponds to turn a profit:

I do not thinke that ground would yeeld unto the owner any other way so much benefite, as to be converted into such ponds with heads as afore mentioned, if onely fish were spent uppon the dayes by law ordained for that purpose in this Realme: the which thing if it were observed, no doubt would turn this Realme to incredible benefite, many sundry wayes. But now those that should spend such fish, will rather bestow their money in Rabbets, Capons, or such like.

Following the texts of Dubravius, Taverner and North, a slew of treatises on husbandry published between the late sixteenth century and the mid-eighteenth include sections dealing with fish-ponds – all plagiarizing each other to a large extent but indicating that ponds continued to hold some degree of status. By this time, however, many had been subsumed as garden features and had lost any purposeful programme of maximum exploitation. In this way the elitist dimension of pond

102 A fisherman, with composite rod, line and float; a stave-built tub holds his catch. From the *Treatyse of Fysshynge wyth an Angle* (1496).

ownership became diluted, although freshwater fish, pursued with rod and line from at least the late medieval period (illus. 102), retained something of their former high status up to the nineteenth century, when fishing in streams and rivers for trout and salmon was taken up as a sport by the gentry.

MONASTIC PONDS

The monastic communities were major consumers of fish, not least the Benedictines, who observed a ban on eating the flesh of four-footed beasts up to the end of the twelfth century; each Cistercian house too would have its *magister piscium,* usually a lay brother with a small workforce at his disposal. Earlier claims that the monasteries played a primary role in the introduction and spread of fish-ponds within England are, however, no longer sustainable: it is clear, rather, that it was the secular aristocracy who set up the earliest recorded pools while the earliest monastic records frequently are for pools granted as existing entities by secular patrons: hence Henry I decreed that the Benedictine monks at Selby (Yorkshire) should hold the fishpond 'which existed when the abbey was founded' by William I (1066–87), and it was Henry similarly who granted the Augustinians of Nostell Priory (Yorkshire) their first pond. It is true, none the less, that two of the five *vivaria* mentioned in *Domesday* belonged to abbeys – one at St Albans and one at Bury St Edmunds.

A similar re-evaluation has taken place with regard to the functions performed by many of these monastic fish-ponds, with the concept that they supplied the needs of the community during Lent being particularly undermined. Lent – essentially a period of penance – was almost the least likely occasion when the community's resources in prestige fish would be made available to the monks, for whom salt fish was the normal fare at this time. A number of early grants of ready-made ponds to newly founded religious houses make it a condition that the fish should be reserved for special occasions: thus the Cluniacs at Lewes (Sussex) were given permission by William de Warenne, Earl of Surrey, in a charter dating to the end of the eleventh century, to fish in his ponds specifically 'for the great feasts and for great guests and especially the (memorial) service of my father and mother'.

None the less, some of the most impressive pond complexes are those associated with monasteries. Sulby (Northamptonshire), for example, had a dam right across the River Avon with a leat leading to several ponds and tanks; St Benet's Abbey at Hulme

(Norfolk) had five small ponds in three rows outside the moat, while Kirkstead (Lincolnshire) had seven long ponds arranged parallel to each other, connected by a single channel at right angles and surrounded by banks and ditches.

Many monasteries also incorporated moats that functioned as substitute fishponds, some of them also serving to receive effluent from the reredorter; even today, a modicum of sewage is considered by some fish farmers to be potentially beneficial to the stock.

COMMERCIAL AND DOMESTIC FISHERIES

To the lessees of secular and monastic ponds, the element of prestige was of little or no importance compared to the potential of their resources to provide an income. Fish from these ponds would have found their way to market along with catches made in the wild; their market share increased dramatically from the first half of the fourteenth century (at a period of decline in aristocratic involvement). Later in the century, evidence is found in London along the south bank of the Thames for the trading of fish on a considerable scale: in particular, an area of Southwark known as The Stews (backing on to the Pyke Garden) has been identified as housing extensive holding-ponds (see illus. 58), perhaps with associated leats, operated by professional fishmongers in supplying the open market. (It would appear that the term 'stews' later became transferred to the brothels that flourished in the area during the late Tudor and Stewart period, in much the same way that the meaning of 'mews', initially designating premises for the royal hawks at Charing Cross, later migrated to apply to the coach-houses that replaced them on the site: see p. 185.)

Mill ponds and their associated races provided convenient places for fish rearing and for the taking of eels in traps, and since many of them were owned by manorial estates and by monastic foundations they fell naturally within the kinds of communities that were already alert to their economic potential. At an early date, therefore, such ponds, whether associated with flour mills or fulling mills, are recorded as doubling as stews, with the miller's rent sometimes being calculated in units of fish or eels. It cannot be without significance that the word for a mill-pond, *stagnum*, came in time to be used also to designate a fish-pond. Just how productive they could be is demonstrated by a record quoted by Dyer of two mills on the Avon which yielded 2,000 eels a year between them. The Luttrell Psalter shows basketwork traps of well-established kind in association with such a mill (illus. 103).

A common association of ponds with gardens can be found in medieval England, and from the evidence supplied above it will be clear that many of these will have been utilized as stews, providing a convenient and well-protected means of storing live fish bound for the kitchens. After about 1540 it seems that the ornamental role of such ponds began to predominate, although the supply of fish for food continued to be important. By this time, and increasingly from the mid-seventeenth century, the garden itself became a primary means of expressing social status: in Currie's words: 'It would have been considered more in keeping that the ponds and lakes of the later eighteenth century should be fished by the much less efficient, but more picturesque, rod-and-line angler, rather than that acres of untidy mud should be allowed to spoil the view of an earthly paradise.' The fishpond, therefore, entered into the same dialectic as the dovecote and the rabbit warren, in proclaiming the status of the owner through the landscape he inhabited.

103 Basketwork eel-traps placed in a mill-stream. From the Luttrell Psalter (*c.* 1340).

FISH: SOME PRINCIPAL VARIETIES

With the exception of the carp, whose introduction is discussed below, the range of fishes inhabiting native waters has remained essentially unchanged until the present day, although estimations of their respective qualities have fluctuated with time, as have the prices they commanded. Roach (*Rutilus rutilus*) and dace (*Leuciscus leuciscus*) were amongst the least esteemed freshwater fish, selling for only a ¼d. each on the Severn (the same price as herrings), whereas a mature pike (*Esox lucius*) might fetch 3s. While matters of taste doubtless affected the prices commanded by certain fish, there were also other factors at work: Dyer records that chub (*Leuciscus cephalus*), for example, were 'nowhere caught for food but sold for 7 or 8d. each', purely on the basis of the status attributed to them within aristocratic culture. Perch (*Perca fluviatilis*) were cheap in Prior Moore's accounts at eighteen fish for 1d.: according to North they would 'scarce live

in Stews and small Waters', but none the less he considered them 'one of the best Sorts of freshwater Fish'.

Salmon (*Salmo salar*) was highly favoured on the medieval menu, although its lifestyle generally makes it impossible to know whether the fish in question originated in the sea or in rivers. They were not adapted to rearing in ponds, however, and were invariably harvested from the wild rather than being bred in captivity (see p. 303).

Trout (*Salmo trutta*) – today the principal freshwater fish reared for food – made an early impact: it was difficult to get them to spawn in standing water, although introduced to these conditions they might be expected to 'lie and grow very fat and good, if the pond be of any greatnesse, as some five or six acres of ground, or more, and that he may have good store of small fry to feed on'. According to North, trout also presented difficulties in moving them from pond to pond:

they must be very charily handled in the carriage, and a few of them carried in a great deal of faire and cleane water, and that in cold weather, and may not be handled with the hands, but in a hand-net very charily: and so likewise are all other fish to be used, especially such as you meane to keepe for store.

Bream (*Abramis brama*) were certainly among the more palatable species that were readily available. Among the characteristics that recommended them for ponds was their tolerance of low oxygen levels and their readiness to spawn, although this could lead all too easily to over-stocking. However, in a pond of less than 4 or 5 acres, 'a Breame will be five or six yeares at the least, before it be of any bignesse to eate, as also they will over store any pond with fry, which is a great hindrance to the growth of your bigger fish'. During the process of sewing the pond, therefore, Taverner suggests:

Howbeit if you have any great number of frie, especially of Breame, it were better to preserve but part of them, and the residue to put into some stew or small pond with Pikes: so shall you alwayes have good Pikes, and also your Carpe, Breame, and Tench will be very fat and good.

North shared many of Taverner's perceptions of bream as being slow growing and productive of large numbers of 'such a slimy nasty fry as both robs and fouls the Water, making it unfit for other Fish'. A pond with some 10–12 acres of running water was deemed necessary to maintain them in a healthy condition.

Tench (*Tinca tinca*), which grow to about two-thirds the size of carp, were also less demanding of well-oxygenated water. They formed the most numerous variety – at 2,254 specimens – with

which Prior Moore stocked his fishponds and fed his brethren, and at 1½ to 3d. each they were quite costly, although not universally admired. Taverner advised that 'the Tench of all other fish will best like to be fed, as aforesaid, and will be very good, sweete, and fatte, and next unto him the Carpe'; North too considered them 'when thriven . . . a very good fish'; they had the advantage too of being 'very easilie taken in a Bownet', although this could also lead to problems, and 'whosoever hath them in his ponds, it behooveth him to take great heede that he be not deceived by leud people'. Contrary to all these reports, the tench received so deprecatory an account from Thomas Moffet (1655) that one is caused to wonder whether he had had a particularly unfortunate encounter with them: 'His flesh is stopping, slimy, viscous & very unwholesome; and . . . of a most unclean and damnable nourishment', he wrote: 'they engender palsies, stop the lungs, putrifie in the stomach, and bring a man that eats them to infinite diseases'.

The story of what ultimately became the most popular of pond fish is rather different from the foregoing, for carp (*Cyprinus carpio*) are not native to the British Isles and were certainly introduced, though from where and at what date remains unclear. Early writers looked to the Far East for their origins, speculating that their Latin name implied that Cyprus had formed a staging point on the journey west. Currie has pointed out, however, that they are now known to have been native to certain central European rivers, notably the Danube, and that no more exotic origin need be sought.

The earliest record of their being stocked in England is 1462, when the 4th Duke of Norfolk stored his ponds with them: in the course of the following six years he continued to add further specimens to his own ponds and made gifts of live fish to five of his wealthy neighbours, so that by the 1470s at the latest East Anglia must have been quite well supplied with carp. The *Boke of St Albans* records that 'there be but few in England', although it seems unclear whether this statement relates to the situation at the time the 'Treatyse on Angling' was printed in 1496 or whether it derives from one of the texts circulating earlier in the century in manuscript form. Prior Moore bought some in 1531 and six years later the *Letters and Papers of Henry VIII* record that Thomas Wriothesley received a generous royal gift from the king in order to stock former monastic ponds at Titchfield (Hampshire): 'The bailey [of Guernsey] will give Wriothesley 500 carps to stock the ponds, Mr Huttoft providing the freight, Mr Mylls the tubs, and Mr Wells conveyance of the carps; so that in three or four years time he may sell £20 to £30 worth of them every year'.

By the time Taverner came to write his *Certaine Experiments* in 1600 (relying extensively on Dubravius for his passage on carp), he considered them unquestionably equal to and even better than bream, tench or perch for pond rearing. Roger North recommended them for 'clay country lacking both springs and rivers'. Their hardiness, rapid growth rate, tolerance of poor-quality – even polluted – water, their ease of transport and their excellent eating qualities all recommended carp, as did their tendency to bottom-feed, placing them at low risk from being taken by herons. North records that they were vulnerable to one rather curious enemy in the form of the toad, though how many fish were lost in this way is unclear:

> If you have Carpes in small ditches, in the moneth of March, at what time Todes doe ingender, the Tode will many times covet to fasten himselfe upon the head of the Carpe, and will thereby inuenime the carpe, in such sort that the Carpe will swell as great as he may hold, so that his scales will stand as it

were on edge, and his eyes stand out of his head near half an inch, in very ugly sort: and in the end will for the most part die thereof: and it is very dangerous for any person to eate of any such Carpe so inuenimed.

Otherwise, only a certain reluctance to breed in colder climates counted against them, although the diary of Thomas Marchant shows that considerable success might be expected here too:

> I remember myselfe did once put three spawning Carps into a pond that was some three acres of ground, and with them nine or ten milters about February, and in November next following I did sew the pond, and of those breeders I had 9000 and upwards of Carp frie notwithstanding all the foresaid enemies; and surely a Breame will increase in number much more.

The ponds belonging to the Charterhouse in London are said to have yielded 300 of them a year, and at the Dissolution Henry VIII had 100 carp taken from there 'for the King's store'. By the end of the seventeenth century, however, the carp had lost a good deal of its former esteem. William Nicolson, Bishop of Carlisle, noted that the twelve score of carp he saw recovered from the ponds at Brettenham (Suffolk) in 1703 would formerly have sold for £80 but by his day were not worth above £30. (He also mentions that 'the Carps will carry alive to London, in straw or Grass, without water. Usually conveigh'd in Waggons; four Hoggsheads (of 80 fishes apiece) makeing a load'.)

The pike (*Esox lucius*), for all its ferocious reputation, was also highly esteemed, and was said to be 'very holsome for seke peple'. The young pike (pickerel) assume their adult form when grown to about 3 pounds in weight; larger specimens are referred to in the records as luce. Their principal disadvantage as a pond fish was the damage they caused to the other stock. North warned that 'they are dangerous Guests in the great Waters; for if grown large, they will devour and destroy the best Fish', while Taverner too advised that:

The Pike is in no waie to be admitted into your great ponds, with your other fish, he is so great a devourer, and will grow so fast having his fill of feeding, that being but eight or ten inches in the beginning of Sommer, he may be eighteene or twentie inches before Hollantide.

They were especially fond of carp, but with two ponds it was suggested that an owner should have enough fry 'to feede some good number Pikes withall, wherewith they will be made verie thicke, sweete, and well growne, but not fat'. With good feeding they might be expected to reach 12–14 inches at the end of their first year, and 20–22 inches by the following year. In North's day the pike was 'inferior to no fresh-Water Fish, and now are more esteem'd than ever, being less plentiful upon draining the Fens'.

The majority of eels (*Anguilla anguilla*) were harvested from rivers, natural ponds and those adapted for mills. Numerous properties in *Domesday* are assessed in terms of the numbers of eels they produce: the canons of St John's in Beverley had a fishery yielding as many as 7,000 eels, while several manors were assessed in hundreds – Bottisham and Milton (both Cambridgeshire), for example, yielded 400 and 650 eels respectively. Later it was recognized that well-placed ponds had the advantage that they might be sought out by the eels themselves, moving easily from one water source to another, slithering over the wet grass. Such seems to have been the case at Prior

Moore's Ludbache pool, which, at its fishing in 1634 was found to contain 'dyvers yeles of every sorte', although there had been no stocking of the pond with eels for the previous twelve years and the breeding habits of eels preclude their having bred there.

Moore bought traps which provided a regular supply of table eels throughout the year, with immature specimens being returned to the water unharmed. There were dangers in mixing eels with farmed fish, however, and they were in some senses inimical to carefully controlled farming. As Taverner observes: 'when the Carps, Breams, Tenches, or Roches do lay their spawne in egges in spawning time, you shall many times see five, ten or more small Eeles follow them, and as the spawn falleth from them they eate it, as also Duckes will do the like'. After hatching, the fry of the fish continued to be vulnerable to being eaten by eels until they had grown to a reasonable size. It was, however, difficult to keep them at bay:

And if there run any water from your pond, you shall not possible keepe Eeles out of the same, they will come into the same against the streame. Their manner of breeding is very uncertaine and unknowne, but undoubtedly they are bred in the brackish or sea water: and at the first full Moon in Maie they begin to come into all great rivers, and out of great rivers into lesser rivers . . . all the beginning of Sommer: as likewise with the first floud that cometh about Michelmas, they covet to go downe the streame, and will not stay untill they come into the deepe and brackish waters . . .

The ultimate breeding grounds of the eels had not yet been established (see p. 311), but their life cycle within British waters was at least well observed.

North suggests that while they would not provide a good return in large ponds, 'in Moats which have the Sinks of an House drain into it, is proper enough for them, and they will thrive in it'.

Thomas Marchant (1687–1728) of Little Park, Hurstpierpoint (Sussex), left at his death a diary ranging discontinuously over a fifteen-year period which, in the words of its editor, the Revd Edward Turner, gives 'a faithful representation of the everyday mode of life of a substantial Sussex yeoman'. It casts many interesting sidelights on the everyday application of many of the principles outlined in the foregoing discussion of (often rather grander) fish-ponds and has been abstracted here from Edwards's transcription in *Sussex Archaeological Collections*, 25 (1873).

1714

29 OCTOBER. Went to North Barnes near Homwood gate to see the pond fisht. I bought all the fish of a foot long and upwards at 50s. per C. I am to give Mrs Dabson 200 store fish, over and above the aforesaid bargain; but she is to send to me for them.

30 OCTOBER. We fetched 244 Carps, in three Dung Carts from a stew of Parson Citizen at Street; being brought thither last night out of the above pond. I paid Mrs Dabson £6 for them. We put them all into my new pond; except 5, which we put into the Marldfield stew . . .

31 OCTOBER. Mr Beaumont preached. I could not go to Church, being forced to stay at home to look after, and let down fresh water to the fish; they being – as I supposed – sick, because they lay on the surface of the

pond, and were easily taken out. But towards night they sunk.

9 NOVEMBER. . . . Richard Baldchild, of Wonersh, near Guildford, came hither at night to buy my fish, which I took out when I bought Mrs Dabson's. I sold him 239 for his Master; and 4 or 5 more, which I expect to find in the stew, for £10. He is to fetch them. Put 57 carp and 10 tench into the Marldfield stew, and 3 large fish into the flat stew.

15 NOVEMBER. . . . Thos. Field, and Downer, the miller, were here, to talk with Baldchild. They told me that the pond at Lye would be fisht on Wednesday.

16 NOVEMBER. We took 242 fish out of the stew for Mr Edmead. Recd. £10 of Rich. Baldchild for them. They were, one with another, about 13 inches long.

24 NOVEMBER. May and I fetcht 190 store carp from Thomas Field's, about 4 inches long, and 75 about 6 inches long, for which I gave 2s. 6d. per C. Sent May to Henry Packham to let Mrs Dabson, or Mr Citizen, know that they must be fetcht to-morrow. We brought also the brace of large fish for Stephen Bine. But they proved lean and old.

1716

1 MAY. Fished Mr Whitpaine's pond at Wickham, but the fish were not good. Put 8 of them into the Marldfield stew. They were about 9 inches long . . .

20 NOVEMBER, Gun helpt to fish the new pond. Put 41 of the largest carp into the hovel-field stew, and 511 store carp into the flat stew.

22 NOVEMBER. In the afternoon Gun helpt to fish . . . My cousin Lindfield was here in the morning. Fisht the great pond, and put 220 of the biggest carp into the new pond,

and 18 of the biggest tench. Put also 358 store carp into the flat stew, and 36 tench; and also 550 very small carp into a hole in the lowfield.

23 NOVEMBER. John Harland came to help fish the middle pond, but the water was not out. I gave him 12 . . .

24 NOVEMBER. Fisht the middle pond. Put 66 large carp into the new pond, and 380 store tench into the flat stew, and 12 large carp, 10 large tench, and 57 middle sized tench into the hovel field stew. My wife sent Mrs Beard, Mrs Scutt, and Mrs Courtness a few eels.

25 NOVEMBER . . . T. Challener watcht the New Pond last night.

26 NOVEMBER. May and I went to fish R. Burtenshaw's ponds. That at the green had no fish of any value in it, and of the other we could not get the water above half out. John Westover watched the New Pond last night . . .

27 NOVEMBER. J. Harland and Gun fisht the upper pond. Edwards helpt about two hours. Put 55 sale fish into the new pond, and 25 store carp. Put 56 carp, about 10 inches, into the Hovel-field stew, and 12 tench of about 8 inches. Jno. Wood and R. Gatland mended the grates of the upper pond in the afternoon.

29 NOVEMBER. Gun and May . . . and Edwards moved the fish out of the New pond into the Upper pond – 358. They put (I think) 8 carp and 2 tench into the Marldfield stew for a sample . . .

1 DECEMBER . . . Sold Stephen Carter 300 fish; one half to hold 13 inches one with another, and the other half a foot. Recd. in hand a guinea. I offered him 50 more undersized fish, at 30s., if he liked them when he saw them . . .

4 DECEMBER . . . My wife, Willy, and May went to Lewes this afternoon, and carry'd

two carp of about a foot long, and 13 tench, to my cousin Peter Marchant.

8 DECEMBER. Sharp frost and some snow. Broke the ice, and took the fish out of the Upper Pond, and put them into the fatting close pond . . . . John Box, senr., was here, and bespoke (I think) 60 store carp, and 20 tench.

1717

4 JANUARY. George and May took the fish out of the great pond, and put them into the Marldfield stew – 283. Put 41 culling fish into the flat stew . . . . One Michell's team of Buckwood came for the fish.

5 JANUARY. George and May took the rest of the fish, 34, out of the great pond that could not be found last night, it being dark. Sent 4 carp to Mr Dodson by May. The fish tuns went away this morning. They had a half tun of me, which Richard Michell promis'd to deliver again at Hand-cross next week.

10 JANUARY . . . J. Legeter at the Starr told me he would give me 6d. per lb. for carp a foot long and upwards, and that it was the common price . . .

12 JANUARY. Gave Mrs Beard 3 carp and 2 tench. I weigh'd a carp about 12½ inches long yesterday, indifferently good, and it prov'd 2 lbs. hard weight.

16 JANUARY. Fisht the flat stew. Put 34 carp of about 10 inches into the New Pond, 105 carp into the Horse Pond of about 15 inches, and 210 carp of about 5 or 6 inches into the Great Pond, and about 105 into the ditch in the home field for the middle pond. I broke the screw of the tomkin. Sent 32 carp to Lewes by May, which he sold for 19s. 3d. My cousin Peter Marchant left 3s. to pay for what he took. Mr Courthope had 100 store tench

of about 7 inches, for which I intend to have 7s. 6d. per J. Grey, the coachman.

18 JANUARY. Stephen Bine and his man John drew the tomkin of the flat stew. Pd. my Ld. Treep 6d. for new brazeing a screw.

19 JANUARY. Gave R. Burtenshaw 70 store carp and 30 tench. Put 52 carp and 52 tench into the Edgley Mead pond, 100 tench into the Church field pond, 4 carp 5 inches and 2 tench 6½ inches long into the pond in Tully's Orchard. Those above (all but a few) were of the same size.

22 JANUARY. Recd. 3s. 6d. of J. Box, senr., for 30 carp of about 5 inches, and as many tench of about 7 inches long.

15 FEBRUARY. Recd. 10s. of Mrs Beard for 26 carp of about 10 inches, and 8 tench of about 8 or 9 inches long.

21 FEBRUARY. Recd. 7s. 6d. of Mr Courthope for tench . . .

1720

1 JANUARY. Fisht the new pond.

9 FEBRUARY. Mr Shirley's man here for the tench, and I gave him 20 into the bargain . . .

1727

27 MARCH. Recd. 13s. for 213 store tench of Mr W. Osbourne. They were for his brother. I valued 100 at 10s. 6d., they being about 5 or 6 inches long. The rest at 4s. 6d., they being only about 3 inches in length. Gun and Dancy carried them to Newtimber.

1 NOVEMBER. Went to see Danny sand field pond fished, but they could not get the water out . . .

2 NOVEMBER. Went to see the pond fished . . .

RABBITS

The fecundity of the Rabbit is truly astonishing. It breeds seven times in the year, and generally produces eight young at a time; from which it is calculated, that one pair may increase, in the course of four years, to the amazing number of 1,274,840: so that, if frequent reductions were not made in various ways, there is reason to apprehend they would soon exceed the means of their support, and over-run the face of the country.

Thomas Bewick, *A General History of Quadrupeds* (1790)

Whatever the shortcomings of his arithmetic, the picture conjured up by Thomas Bewick is a striking one and begs the question of why, indeed, the rabbit has not to date inherited the Earth. It will come as no surprise that the species has a number of efficient predators that routinely frustrate this outcome, but what is less widely appreciated is that rabbits owe their entire history throughout the world, except for their endemic place of origin around the western Mediterranean, to human intervention. Introduced to the British Isles from the Continent in the early medieval period and cosseted in captivity throughout the early centuries of their establishment, rabbits came to be bred on an industrial scale for their meat and fur; meanwhile, as bolder individuals escaped in increasing numbers into the countryside, a feral population was established that grew to the point where it threatened the viability of agriculture in some areas – a threat that receded only with the devastating disease that came close to exterminating the species in the mid-twentieth century. At every turn, the boom-and-bust career of the rabbit has been manipulated and exploited by human agency in one of the most remarkable (yet largely forgotten) symbiotic relationships of the historic period.

BEGINNINGS

In the early years of the era when the influence of Norman-French dynasties extended from England though France to southern Italy and beyond, the territory of the European rabbit (*Oryctolagus cuniculus*) was limited to the Mediterranean regions of southern Spain, France and Italy. By the same mechanisms that brought other species to the British Isles at this time (p. 40), numbers of rabbits were transported bodily from their natural habitat, far beyond the northern range of the distribution they had evolved for themselves, as Norman landowners sought to populate their newly won estates in mainland Britain and in Ireland with creatures that graced the parks – and, more importantly, the dining tables – of their Continental cousins. In England these initiatives have long been attributed primarily to the secular aristocracy, but archaeological researches on the Continent clearly show that an important role in expanding the distribution of the rabbit was played there by the monastic movement (for reasons explained below, p. 387), and it seems likely that this would have been the case too in the British Isles. Whatever their special needs, it is clear that many monasteries maintained conventional breeding populations, regulated in the same way as other warrens and producing both food for the community and surpluses which formed the basis of gift giving – as when Prior of Ely sent 60 rabbits to Edward III in 1345.

Multiple difficulties attended the disturbance of the rabbit's natural equilibrium. Most problematic, perhaps, was the adverse climate: untold numbers of the new immigrants were not only discomforted by the cold and wet of the northern winter but sickened and died from its effects. Their new homes had to be chosen with the utmost care – and no doubt a great deal of trial and costly error. The intractability as well as the water-retaining properties of heavy loam and clay soils proved totally inimical to the new arrivals, and the first colonies were successfully established in areas favoured by lighter, well-drained sands. Early records confirm a preference for coastal sites, a notably high number of them on offshore islands. These had the additional advantage of being free from many of the natural predators – foxes, wildcats, weasels, stoats and others – to which the mainland populations were desperately vulnerable, but in order for rabbits to reach their full potential it was necessary for landlords to overcome all of these hazards, and the story of the rabbit's successful establishment owes everything to the ingenuity with which the problems of its management were addressed.

The earliest evidence for their presence appears to come in the form of skeletal remains, but the fine dating of archaeological layers is notoriously difficult and the possibility of later contamination is ever present. At Faccombe Netherton (Hampshire), excavations at a medieval manor site with late Saxon origins produced rabbit bones from two seemingly undisturbed layers, one dated 980–1180 and the other 1070–1204. Further investigations at the Buttermarket in Ipswich (Suffolk) and at Hadleigh and Rayleigh Castle (both Essex) both produced bones from contexts said to date from about 1100. Confirmation of these early dates may emerge from precisely controlled fieldwork in the future.

Indirect physical evidence for an early impact comes too in the form of rabbits carved in stone at two early churches. At Kilpeck (Herefordshire) an *in situ* corbel, dated *c.* 1150, features a long-eared creature which could be a rabbit or a hare, while a more convincing rabbit – possibly of similar date – appears on a detached sculptural fragment (illus. 104) at St Mary's church in Elmley Castle (Worcestershire).

The historical record opens in the early twelfth century – that is to say, within two generations of the Normans establishing their grip on the countryside. Perhaps the earliest mention of rabbits comes in 1135, when Drake's Island in Plymouth Sound was granted to Plympton Priory 'cum cuniculi' – with the rabbits thereon; 40 years later, in 1176, they are recorded on the Scilly Isles. Early associations with island sites are particularly noteworthy – Hayling Island and Lundy are named in early records, while a survey by Matheson of early occurrences in Wales show a remarkable concentration on island sites at the mouth of the Bristol Channel and around the coast, at a time when there was as yet virtually no penetration inland.

In the initial spread of the rabbit, sandy coastal areas played an important role throughout Britain. The Holderness peninsula in East Yorkshire was colonized at an early date and by the thirteenth century rabbits had been established as far north as the Firth of Forth, as at Cramond (Lothian) and at nearby Crail (Fife) – both royal warrens; on the Isle of May a monastic warren was maintained from this time until the Reformation and other monastic warrens are recorded at Arbroath (Angus) in 1325 and at Cupar (Fife) in 1473. They were also established in Ireland, where rights 'in warrenis et cunigaris' were granted over lands in Connaught to Hugh de Lacy in 1204. It is a striking feature of the early distribution of the species, though, that it took the form of deliberately established and largely isolated pockets, with little evidence for many centuries to come of opportunistic colonization by the rabbits themselves.

Their continuing rarity in the thirteenth century is underlined by the fact that in 1235 Henry III seems to have had only one warren, at Guildford (Surrey), which was augmented in that year by a gift of ten live rabbits from the Despencer family. Elspeth Veale notes that five years later

104 Rabbit carved on a detached sculptural fragment at St Mary's church, Elmley Castle (Worcestershire).

the King ordered rabbits for a feast for the first time, when 110 were sent from the estates of the Bishop of Winchester, 200 from the house of the Earl of Warenne, and 200 from a royal escheator. By 1241 the bishopric of Winchester was involved in the stocking of new warrens in other dioceses, as when 100 live rabbits were transferred to Sugwas, a manor of the bishopric of Hereford, and shortly thereafter the Bishop of London transferred live animals from Clacton (Essex) to a property of Peter of Savoy at Cheshunt (Hertfordshire). Soon the King could be found stocking his park at Windsor with animals sent from Guildford by the sheriff of Surrey, from Stamford (Lincolnshire) by the Earl of Derby, and from the Bishop of Chichester.

Before long these tentative beginnings began to bear fruit and rabbits were being produced in thousands by the most successful colonies. The seemingly unstoppable rise of the rabbit had begun.

RABBIT HUSBANDRY: THE WARREN FROM THE TWELFTH CENTURY TO THE NINETEENTH

The key to the establishment of breeding populations on the mainland lay in the setting up of formal reserves or warrens, in which the rabbits could be protected from predation, encouraged in forming burrows, fed through the lean winter months and, of course, could be harvested as required. Early references term these enclosures coneygarths (or coneygars or conigrees); coney was the name applied to all the adult animals, while rabbit (or rabette) was reserved for immature specimens; by the sixteenth century the terminology had evolved to the point where rabbit was the term in almost universal use.

The manor and the warren

For maximum security, the earliest manorial warrens frequently were established within the perimeters of deer parks – already empaled to control the animals, to exclude the human population by force of law and physically to establish a frontier for manorial authority. In 1386, for example, the deer park at Lopham on the borders of Suffolk and Norfolk is recorded as having produced 300 rabbits for the Countess of Norfolk's table.

Protective walls would normally encircle the warren itself. Areas so enclosed were no doubt modest at first but the larger warrens quickly outgrew the confines of the deer park and numbers of them came to occupy many square miles of land. Timber fences enclosed some of the early examples but proved expensive to build and demanding of constant maintenance. Embankments of earth or of cut sods proved more effective, commonly two cut sods in width and laid up to a remarkable 12 feet high. The perimeter bank of the warren at West Dean (Sussex), accompanied by a 12-foot-wide ditch, has been shown by excavation (perhaps exceptionally) to have been lined on its inner face with knapped flints to foil would-be absconders; it was also topped by a fence. Such walls were commonly capped to protect them from the weather, but sometimes were topped with laid reeds, held in place with stones, their cut stems arranged to oversail the inner face of the wall in order to deter potential escapees. Furze or heather might also be thickly planted along the top of the embankment, providing a degree of impermeability and furnishing also green shoots to serve as winter food (see p. 376). In upland counties and in the moorlands of the west, dry-stone walls, again standing up to 12 feet or more in height, replaced those of earth: an excellent example at Woodhall, Carperby (Yorkshire), standing originally up to 8 feet high, is capped with inward-projecting coping stones that would have foiled even the most intrepid of climbers (though deep snowdrifts in winter would have put the effectiveness of even these barriers to the test).

These massive boundary walls are difficult to date and often may belong to the later phases of rabbit keeping: many of those that survive may be no earlier than the nineteenth century. It seems clear that they must have had earlier precursors, however, since it is hard to imagine how the close regulation for which abundant evidence survives could have been achieved without isolating the individual communities to some degree. In warrens dedicated to the production of the more highly prized varieties, whose skins fetched notably higher prices on the market (pp. 387–9), the walls might also preserve the purity of the population by insulating it from opportunist bucks of the more common sort within the feral population that gradually established a foothold in the wild, or from less desirable animals from neighbouring warrens.

Within the walls the principal features were formed by the living quarters of the rabbits themselves, commonly in the form of mounds of light and stone-free earth (illus. 105) – although those on Dartmoor are characterized as 'of piled rocks covered with earth' – artificially heaped up to form what modern researchers designate 'pillow-mounds', a term of no great antiquity, having been coined only in the 1920s. (Early sources refer to them as burys or berreys, from which derives our term burrow – now signifying a single rabbit-hole.) Some of these are indeed pillow-shaped, but others are discoid, elongated, rectangular or L-shaped in plan. In order to further encourage the rabbits to take up residence, artificial burrows were formed within the body of the mound. At their simplest these might be holes driven horizontally into the side of the mound with the aid of an auger. The practice is recorded in a warrant relating to Hampton Court in the reign of Henry VIII, as reproduced by Sheail:

> To Robert Bing, of the Wyke, smythe, for a great long nagre [auger] of irne, to make and bore coney holes within the kynges beries new made for blake conyes in the warren.

In other instances, burrows were formed by digging trenches into the ground surface before covering them with sods, planks or stones and raising the mound over them. Meticulous excavation of such a mound at Y Foel (Powys) has revealed a grid of regular, man-made channels which stand in contrast to the randomly oriented burrows later created by the rabbits themselves, as they adapted the mound to their own requirements – possibly over several generations (illus. 106). In some well-preserved landscapes great numbers of pillow-mounds survive, some of them with a 'segmented' appearance attributed to the presence of regularly dug artificial burrows, now collapsed, which traverse their width at regular intervals.

In the sloping hillsides of the chalk downlands and on the wolds, the mounds tend to be aligned with the incline rather than running across it, probably to facilitate drainage. Evidence of drainage channels within other warrens on flatter ground confirms the importance attached to keeping the

105 A well formed pillow-mound from the Luttrell Psalter (c. 1340).

373

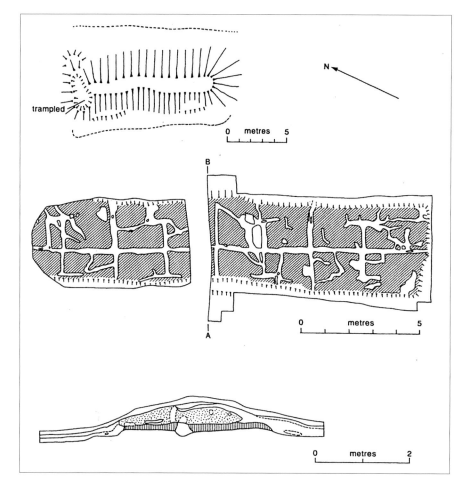

106 Plan and section of a pillow-mound excavated at Y Foel (Powys). The rectilinear pattern formed by artificial burrows cut during construction of the mound forms a contrast with the random alignments of those made later by the rabbits themselves.

population dry. Pre-existing earthworks – Bronze Age barrows, Iron Age ramparts and others – provided in some areas ready-made mounds which were happily adapted by warreners. The rabbits themselves prefer to burrow into a slope, as provided by any such mound, and have more difficulty in making headway on flat ground; drainage of ground-water into burrows dug on the flat, in any case, renders them dangerous, and records of entire nests full of young rabbits being displaced by floodwaters underline the extreme vulnerability of the population to natural disasters of this kind.

Some pillow-mounds occur on light soils that would have been perfectly accommodating to the rabbit population (illus. 107), suggesting that they served a useful function to the warrener in keeping the population within a well-defined area: rabbits are perfectly capable of burrowing through the hardest and heaviest soils by themselves, and the devices described above were designed rather to seduce them into an environment where they could then be more easily controlled. Some mounds are surrounded by ditches, further discouraging the proliferation of burrows beyond their confines; rabbits can swim and will do so *in extremis*, but are rarely tempted into the water if well supplied with food. Further associations with water features have been noted in which the upcast from the excavation of fishponds has been used to form pillow-mounds: a good example can be seen at Higham Ferrers (Northamptonshire).

Apart from the mounds themselves, a prominent feature of the well-appointed manorial warren was the lodge provided for its guardian – the warrener. The warren lodge frequently took the form of a tower-house, in which the ground floor might be used for the storage of animals already culled and awaiting delivery to the kitchen or to market, and for the traps, nets and other equipment appropriate to the post. The warrener's living quarters were on the first floor, allowing him an uninterrupted view of his charges and offering a degree of defensive security against poachers who might turn up from time to time intent on violence as well as larceny. Simple watchtowers are also recorded in some early warrens, as at Lakenheath (Suffolk) in 1365; traces of what may have been a timber tower have been excavated at West Dean (Sussex). The lodge built at Brandon (Suffolk) in the 1380s at a cost of £20 sounds like a substantial defensive structure, with walls 3 feet thick perforated by slit windows. Other good

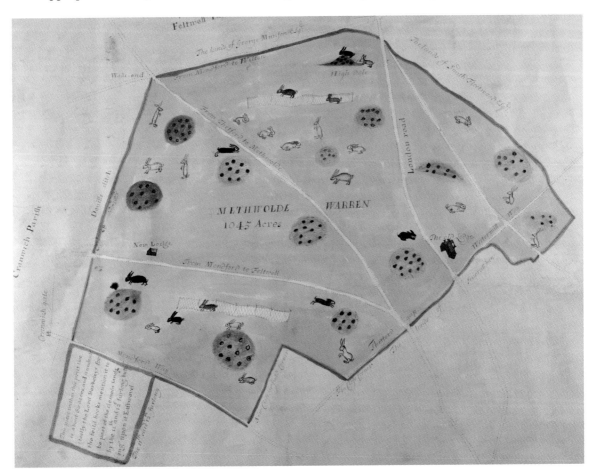

107 Methwold warren (Norfolk), from an estate map of 1699. First published by Tom Williamson, who noted a number of typical features including the incorporation of an Anglo-Saxon earthwork (the Fossditch) as a boundary to the north-west, a warrener's house (the New Lodge), a long net or haye for trapping rabbits, and several pillow-mounds.

examples survive at Thetford and Methwold, both in Norfolk.

Both human and animal predators formed major hazards. Stoats, weasels, polecats and foxes were particularly troublesome, and a great deal of the warrener's time was spent in efforts to exterminate them from the surrounding countryside. Much of the physical evidence for this activity has long since disappeared, but on Dartmoor, where vermin traps were commonly constructed in stone rather than wood, more than 80 examples have been identified, perhaps mostly post-medieval in date; special 'vermin houses' were also built there, in which the warrener could take cover in order to shoot any weasels or stoats that might present themselves. Dogs were also a menace, though the same punitive measures that were introduced to protect larger game during the medieval period (p. 102) also benefited the rabbit. The larger birds of prey, to which the newborn rabbits were particularly vulnerable, were even more difficult to deal with: a common practice was to set up an inviting-looking post that might tempt them to perch while selecting their prey, on which would be set a trap; crows, ravens, buzzards, kites and owls would have been controlled in this way. Preservation of the stock was a principal consideration of the warrener. If a lessee, his lease would invariably include a clause stipulating the minimum population that would had to be left behind at its expiry.

Internal enclosure walls demarcated areas where the warrener could store (and in larger warrens could cultivate) fodder to see the rabbits though the rigours of winter (illus. 108). The natural ground cover of the warren was all too easily grazed to extinction, reducing the surface to an arid, weed-strewn, erosion-prone and unproductive wilderness. In the earlier centuries additional feed took the form of 'browse-wood' from the surrounding forests, frequently stipulated among the perquisites of the warrener whether a member of the manorial household or (more frequently in later centuries) a lessee. Coppices of hazel, elder and ash noted in the vicinity of some warrens indicate alternative sources that could be exploited, and the practice is recorded of laying branches on the mounds in order to provide a degree of winter protection as well as food. Otherwise acorns and bracken might be gathered for the benefit of the rabbits, and in coastal areas sea-holly and rest-harrow is said to have been harvested for their benefit; Thomas Pennant records that one estate on the Flintshire coast was noted 'for the delicacy of the rabbets, by reason of their feeding on the maritime plants'. Seaweed was also fed to them on occasion – but at the expense of tainting the flesh. The green shoots gathered from gorse or juniper bushes or made available through planting within the warren formed a regular supplement to the diet, as did dandelions, thistles and groundsel. In later manifestations of the warren, turnips formed a standard addition to the winter fare. Adequate fodder of whatever sort ensured a contented population with little incentive to escape; conversely, periods of famine caused by drought or hard frost could jeopardize the survival of the whole colony through starvation or mass break-outs.

In the post-medieval period these internal walls also came to provide an important key to population control. The early warrener was generally reliant on nets to capture his animals: initially purse-nets were set up to capture rabbits flushed from their burrows by ferrets or other means. Several medieval manuscript illuminations illustrate the techniques involved: most comprehensive are those from the small-scale Taymouth Horae of c. 1325, which incorporates a lengthy series of images of a lady with a dog trapping rabbits in a warren and in the fourteenth-century Queen Mary's Psalter, in which it is again women who

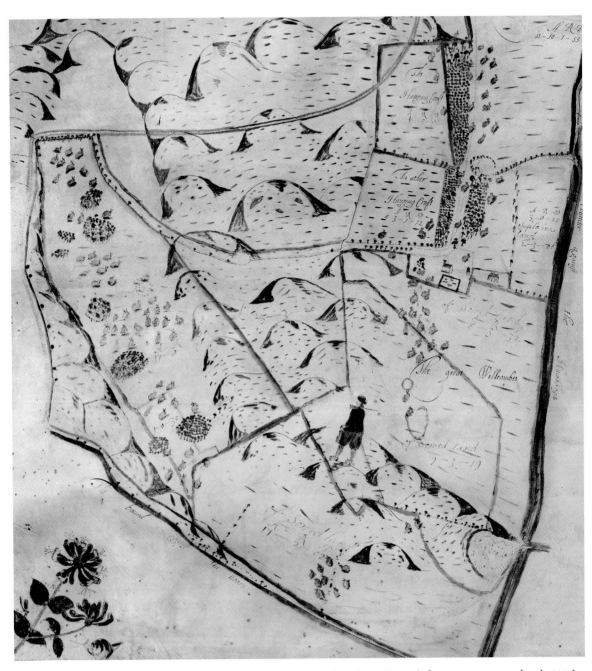

108 A watchful warrener surveys his charges within the warren at Wolstonbury (Sussex), from an estate map dated 1666. In addition to the extensively tunnelled-out mounds, several enclosures in which fodder is being grown are shown, seemingly well fenced to exclude the rabbits.

109 Women using a ferret to flush out rabbits from a burrow into a net. From the early 14th-century Queen Mary's Psalter.

are shown in action, this time introducing a ferret into a burrow and netting the exiting rabbits (illus. 109). Vertically set nets of twine, termed hayes, were later introduced, which allowed larger numbers to be taken. A common practice was to allow the rabbits (which prefer to feed in the early part of the night) to spread out from the warren in search of food; the hayes, which might be up to 150 yards long, would be stretched out to cut off the return of the feeding population to the warren, and so many might be caught that much of the following morning would be spent extricating them. Needless to say, poachers (for which see below) quickly adopted the same methods, so that nets, ferrets and even dogs found in the wrong hands became objects of suspicion. In the West Country crabs and lobsters (termed 'sea-ferrets') were occasionally forced down burrows to the same end; fire and smoke also proved effective in evacuating the warren, though the lingering smell rendered it useless thereafter.

By about the seventeenth century, however, more efficient tip (or type) traps came to transform the culling process. At an opening created at the foot of a wall – commonly that separating the rabbits from their principal food source – an enclosed wooden tunnel termed a muce was created, leading over a pit typically 3 feet wide and 3 feet deep, sometimes with inward-loping stone-lined walls. By opening a shutter in the tunnel the warrener would allow the rabbits to pass freely for a day or two, attracted by the plentiful food available on the other side; subsequently a carefully balanced trapdoor, pivoted centrally, would be released in the floor of the tunnel so that any rabbit that attempted to pass through would find itself tipped into the pit below. So efficient was this process that the warrener was obliged to empty the pit at regular intervals in order to avoid early captives being suffocated by the weight of others on top and their carcasses spoiled. In this way, immature or pregnant animals could be returned to the warren for future selection, while prime specimens were summarily dispatched; their fur, too, suffered less damage by this method of trapping than by the use of ferrets or snares. Numerous examples of type traps survive, notably in several Yorkshire warrens as at Woodhall (Carperby), Whitecliffe Rigg, Dalby, and elsewhere. Some later types are said to have included cog-wheels which allowed the numbers of animals trapped to be counted and the contents of the pit to be regulated.

Yet further enclosures have been identified as shelters (termed 'clappers' – still a commonly found place-name element) where breeding females could be given some respite from the males and where, more importantly, the young could receive some additional protection – not least from the bucks that might easily kill them. (Some clappers appear to have taken the form of timber hutches rather than enclosures). Otherwise the does had to make do with short, blind burrows (called stops) which they hollowed out in zigzag form within the mound at some little distance from the remainder of the colony and disguised with leaves and grass; here the female could give birth to her family and nestle them in a mixture of soft vegetation and fur pulled from her own breast, until, at about six weeks of age, they were old enough to join the rest of the community.

Slightly modifying the figures quoted from Bewick at the head of this chapter, John Sheail in his wonderfully informative *Rabbits and their History* informs us that the does may give birth five or six times a year in a breeding season lasting from February to September. They mate again within hours of giving birth and continue to do so until they once again become pregnant or until the breeding season ends. Their notoriously promiscuous behaviour in the warren contrasts with that in the wild, where they tend to be monogamous.

Recognizing that there were limits to the reproductive capacities of even the rabbit and that resources needed to be husbanded, the Company of Poulters in London imposed (at least from time to time) a closed season on the sale of rabbits in the market. In 1529, for example, the Company ordained that no rabbits should be sold in the City from 22 March until Midsummer, on pain of forfeiture and imprisonment; several offenders were convicted, amongst whom one was to pay a bond of £10 to reinforce an undertaking that he would desist from buying conies from ships originating in Suffolk or Norfolk to sell within the City. The extent of the close season was varied from time to time, as in 1571–2, for example, a cold year of 'snow and moist weather' that depressed the breeding population, when it was prolonged for fear that 'if sparing be not had there will be great lack'. From 1582 to 1589 the extent of the close season was publicly proclaimed each year so that none could claim ignorance of it. Other regulations banned the sale of suckers (unweaned juveniles) within the city before the end of May, again in an attempt to maintain the breeding population.

EXPANSION

Escapes from these highly regulated warrens must have begun almost as soon as they were established, and in spite of the dangers from predators and poachers a feral population gradually established itself. As early as 1347 the owner of an orchard at Petworth (Sussex) had to buy in 2½ gallons of pitch to protect his trees from marauding rabbits. At Elmswell (Suffolk) 16 per cent of the area sown with crops was destroyed by rabbits and in 1391 at Mildenhall (Suffolk) the entire crop was lost. The degree to which some of these depredations may have been made by rabbits from within established warrens is, however, unclear: the animals at Ovingdean (Sussex), for example, where in 1340 was recorded '100 acres arable, lying annihilated by the destruction of the rabbits of the Lord, Earl Warenne', seem likely to have been foraging from the safety of the Earl's warren, rather than merely colonizing his land.

At the same time other warrens underwent a transformation in scale that saw them expanded from exclusive, high-status resources to spread over many miles of landscape, especially on low-quality soils incapable of supporting any other form of productive activity, save the grazing of sheep. In areas such as the Breckland of East Anglia, an expanse of undulating heath noted for its sandy, unstable soils and low rainfall, rabbit-breeding quickly emerged as the most effective use to which the land could be put – especially with the relatively low profitability of grain and the high costs of producing it following the Black Death and throughout the late fourteenth century (when, incidentally, there was also some amelioration of the climate leading to higher rabbit populations). These larger establishments were expensive to run in terms of the labour required to build and maintain the miles of enclosure walls and to tend to their occupants, but the returns were worthwhile. Mark Bailey notes several Suffolk manors on which rabbits formed major contributors to the economy by the late fourteenth century: at Lakenheath in 1384–5 they generated twice the income received from sales of wool, while at Brandon in 1386–7 they contributed 40 per cent of the gross income of the manor. By comparing culling rates over a period of years, however, the same author has detected variations in the region of ten or twenty times, reflecting the continuing vulnerability of populations to cold, wet, famine and murrain – not to mention inbreeding.

As tenant farmers rather than manorial landlords entered the rabbit market, the two activities might go hand-in-hand, with sheep occupying (and manuring) the arable land in winter and being enclosed on the warren while the crops were growing. Warrens appeared on many small farms, some of them supplying no more than the immediate needs of the farmer. Rather than being increased by purchase of breeding stock, the populations of these smaller establishments were generally enhanced by attracting feral rabbits from the surrounding countryside into the warren with fodder; occasionally the farmers were rather more proactive, as witnessed by a case brought before the Star Chamber when the lessee of a warren on Aldbourne Chase (Wiltshire) complained that his neighbour had attempted to entice away his stock by making holes in the surrounding hedges and further that they did 'wickedlie laye ferrets dung and other noisesome and hateful things to Conyes in the holles of the burrowes . . . to th'end to drive away your said subjects Conyes and game and make them forsak his said warren'. Counterclaims of equally heinous behaviour were laid by the defendant against his accuser.

In the marginal uplands, warrening could contribute usefully to the economy of manors and farms, permitting areas too steeply sloping to be easily cultivated to be turned to profit: major investments of this kind were made in Yorkshire where a mixed economy continued to operate until recent times. Some warrens were taken over by leaseholders as independent profit-making concerns: that at Aldbourne, for example, was leased for £40 by the fifteenth century and was capable of supplying on demand 1,000 rabbits for the royal household, while rental of the warren at Clarendon Park in the same county produced an income of £100 for the royal household. By the mid-seventeenth century Thomas Moffet could record that Aldbourne Chase 'affordeth above a hundred thousand couple a year, to the benefit of good housekeeping and the poors maintenance'. These were extraordinary numbers by any standards, gaining for England a European-wide reputation: already by 1555 Conrad Gessner had commented on the 'prodigious numbers' of rabbits occupying mounds in the forests and countryside of England.

Some rentals were paid in rabbits for the table: at the end of the sixteenth century that for the warren at Mildenhall (Wiltshire), for example, was set at 'foure hundred Couple of Conyes', to be rendered to the lord of the manor at any of his properties within 30 miles of Mildenhall; in 1608 rent for a warren at Easton Royal (Wiltshire) belonging to the Earl of Hertford was set at £5 in money and 500 couples of rabbits, to be delivered to the Earl wherever he might choose, while at nearby Durley, a 150-acre warren on the edge of Tottenham Park, the annual levy was 760 couples.

Wider economic pressures naturally impinged on the rabbit population. At the height of the movement for agricultural improvement in the eighteenth century, when corn prices were particularly strong, numbers of warrens were destroyed as landowners sought to turn their sterile acreage into plough-soil by marling (though many of these exercises failed as the improvers over-reached themselves). In some areas of Lincolnshire, for example, tracts of land where improvement had been attempted reverted to warrens when those initiatives failed. Other initiatives that took their toll on warrens included the rise in woad cultivation for the production of dyestuffs in Wiltshire during the early seventeenth century.

Even those populations that coexisted with sheep-rearing found themselves under pressure as more intensive methods of farming proved less accommodating to the rabbits and as new breeds of sheep were introduced which were more discriminating in their choice of fodder and less capable of surviving on ground-cover already closely cropped by rabbits. Many warrens from the Downs to Lincolnshire and the Yorkshire Wolds were ploughed up at this time as, with the aid of intensive manuring and other methods of soil improvement, formerly low-grade land was converted to the production of cereals and winter fodder crops. In other areas warrens were covered over by plantations of young trees, to which the rabbits proved equally inimical.

Other methods of 'improvement', similarly unwelcome to the rabbits, were put to the test within the warren itself. W. B. Daniel records that castration was tried in his day:

A Sussex Gentleman, in the neighbourhood of Chichester, has tried the experiment of cutting Rabbits, which much increases their size, so that at six months old, when prepared for the spit, they have exceeded six pounds and a half in weight. He describes it as a most profitable practice; the operation is performed when six or seven weeks old, and out of three hundred, he never lost one.

By now, however, the status of the rabbit in the wild was becoming distinctly ambivalent. In 1796 Pitt had observed that 'should the commons be pretty generally inclosed' then the rabbits within them 'must be in a great measure exterminated, to make way for a better stock'. He conceded, however, that they were 'yet doubtless deserving considerable attention on impracticable sandy or rocky precipices', on the basis that in supporting them such land would be placed 'in a system of the highest improvement, of which it is capable'. As late as 1881, the Royal Commission on Agriculture concluded that large parts of unprecipitous Norfolk continued to be more viable for the production of rabbits than for any agricultural purposes.

None the less, with their scattering into the countryside – a process that had begun with small-scale escapes throughout the medieval period and had been given a boost by the break-up of numbers of aristocratic estates during the Civil War – the population managed to find a niche for itself and even found itself aided on occasion by positive intervention. The enclosure movement resulted in hundreds of miles of new hedges providing excellent cover and new pathways for colonization.

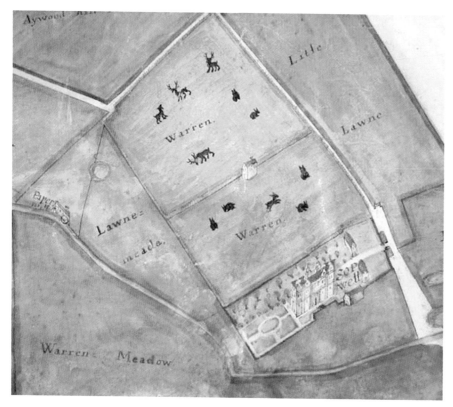

110 Estate map of Sopwell House (Hertfordshire). The house itself is in the foreground with the empaled warren (shared by fallow deer) forming the principal vista from the house; the warren lodge is in the centre of the picture.

In the parklands engineered out of the existing landscape in the late seventeenth and eighteenth centuries the rabbits might find themselves tolerated to some degree as 'useful ornaments' and for a time warrens became fashionable adjuncts to the carefully contrived landscapes in which the gentry now set their houses (illus. 110): Creighton mentions examples at Hopton (Shropshire), where the warren lay immediately beyond a garden laid out around the castle in the late medieval period, and an extremely early one at Castle Bolton (Yorkshire) where a warren was created within the parkland surrounding the house in the late fourteenth century. Perhaps the most elaborate project of this kind for the garden landscape (although extreme doubt must be expressed as to its likely appeal to the rabbits) is that described by Evelyn in his *Elysium Britannicum* (illus. 111):

We might in this place likewise speake of the late subterranean warren by which as our Elysium is situated the Gardiner may reape an underground profit & have the pleasure of a rare & most ingenious invention without prejudice. Especially if the underlayer be sandy & a [bed of] gravel above it, Thus: Dig a pitt 5 or 6 foote deepe 14 Square, & let it be walled or steaned in manner of a Cellar, onely towards the foundation of the wales leave overtures, somewhat resembling large gutter holes, at which the Conies may begin to dig their berrys and draw forth the soyle. To these holes are fitted 4 bords which run in the grooves wrought in as many pieces of timber fixed to the Corners of the Pitt: These boards being drawne up a competent height above the holes hang by lines united to one line which passes over a pully pendant in the middle of the roofe: yet so, as by the slipping of a button, the boards fall suddainely downe & cover the holes like a trap: By this meanes (observing when the Conys come forth to feede) they are caught at pleasure, & are reported to be altogether as sweete fatt & excellent, as any that have the liberty of the upper warren. The pitt thus prepared, you must erect a frame of Timber of a competent height 6. or 7. foote is sufficient above ground, which may be wyred or lathed to defend it from the Vermine; & then making a dore to one side & a ladder to descend into it, tyle it over with a roofe as this segment represents it.

To prevent the occupants of such a fanciful structure from overrunning the garden he advises that some owners 'do chopp off the first joynte of one of their fore feete: this will hinder their digging, but not their breeding'; he also advises that 'the Bucks must be chayned like Beares to a stake, that they do not molest the does whilst they give suck'. In return for these pains, the gardener had the compensation that 'their ordure will be most excellent compost'.

Feral rabbits were further encouraged where they helped to sustain the fox population on which fashionable hunting circles now focused their attentions. The larger warrens had formerly constituted something of a hazard to horsemen as they tended to undermine the ground, but the

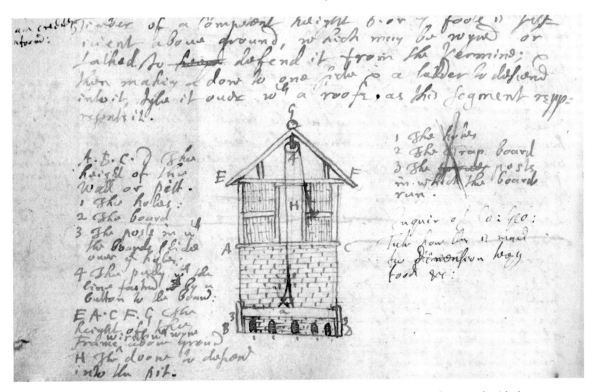

111 John Evelyn's design for a purpose-built rabbit warren. The masonry section ABCD is underground, with the entrances for the rabbits along the lower edge 1; a board 2, running in grooved posts 3, is suspended from a line running over a pulley 4 at roof level. The structure above ground has walls 'wired with wyre' and a tiled roof, and H is 'the doore to descend into the pit'. From *Elysium Britannicum* (compiled *c.* 1650–1700).

112 A lady shooting a rabbit with a blunt-headed arrow. From the Taymouth Hours (*c.* 1325–50).

same constituency could easily tolerate a less dense and more scattered population.

On or off horseback, huntsmen had hitherto largely ignored the rabbit as an object of the chase, although it may be noted that they had always been included among the 'beasts of the warren' (which included also pheasant, partridge and hare) over which rights were extended by means of charters of free warren (see p. 103). The somewhat disdainful tone had been set by the early fifteenth-century *Master of Game*, whose author (Edward, 2nd Duke of York) wrote that 'of conies I do not speak, for no man hunteth them unless it be bish-hunters [low-class fur trappers], and they hunt them with ferrets and with long small hayes'. This poor opinion of their sporting potential continued through the sixteenth century, despite the continuing popularity of the rabbit for the

pot. Occasional images in manuscripts such as the Gorleston Psalter indicate that numbers of them were taken by archers (generally with conventional arrowheads, it seems, although a lady in the Taymouth Hours, illus. 112, takes aim with a blunt-headed arrow of the type more generally reserved for birds – as seen also in the *Livre de Chasse* of Gaston Phébus), but it was with the spread of shooting with firearms that sporting attention began to be more critically focused on them. Although individuals found themselves increasingly under attack in this way, the rabbit population as a whole actually benefited from this new interest as landlords took steps to eliminate many of the predators that now were perceived as a threat to carefully managed reserves of game, whether of birds or mammals: polecats, pine martens and stoats came under new pressures at this time, and several species of birds of prey were poisoned to extinction. Rabbits meanwhile found themselves elevated to the status of game animals, pursued by a growing body of sportsmen for whom the advent of the railways gave further access to the countryside, but by way of compensation many shooting estates took to planting coverts that gave shelter not only to grouse and partridge but also to the rabbit. The growth of scrub was encouraged, with rides cut through them to form shooting alleys. A cycle was introduced in which breeding populations expanded prolifically, only to be slaughtered periodically by the guns on mass shoots.

By the later decades of the nineteenth century the rabbit population had become so widely dispersed that maintaining warrens had become scarcely profitable. The destruction wreaked by feral rabbits was by now so acute that trapping with steel traps (gin traps) was resorted to in attempts to control the population; their deployment was regulated by the Ground Game Act (1880), which limited their use to the mouths of burrows, but it was a restriction that was largely ignored. Farmers sold trapping leases as well as shooting leases, although to some extent the trappers had an interest in maintaining the population (and hence their income) rather than reducing it. Growing public concern for animal welfare led to new provisions in the Protection of Animals Act (1911), which made it compulsory for trappers to visit their traps on a daily basis.

From the period of their earliest introduction, as rabbit populations spread through the countryside so too did the prevalence of poachers, who increasingly came to regard them as common property. Not all poachers confined themselves to the wild population and not all of them were rural low lifes: the canons of Blythburgh (Suffolk) were amongst the most notorious offenders in the fifteenth century, including one mentioned by

Bailey who regularly leased his ferrets to other poachers in the area. While many animals doubtless were taken to eke out the family diet, there are numerous records of larger-scale incursions into the warrens by gangs driven by increasing radicalism rather than hunger and including in their ranks urban tradesmen and craftsmen. Frequently they went heavily armed: in 1444 a pitched battle is recorded between rival gangs from Thetford and from Elvedon (Suffolk). To these men the rabbit posed no threat whatever, but became merely a hapless pawn in a mounting challenge to seigneurial authority that festered for centuries. As late as 1687 a large body of men from Warminster (Wiltshire) invaded the Longleat estate in broad daylight where, in addition to killing many of the rabbits, they threatened violence to the warrener and his wife and broke the windows of their lodge. By the eighteenth century, poaching had reached a considerable scale: in Leicestershire several warrens making £100 a year profit had to be abandoned after they were plundered and extensively damaged.

While the population increased naturally in the countryside, rabbit-keeping also spread from being the exclusively rural pursuit described above to become a common (though necessarily smaller-scale) activity in post-medieval towns and cities. In back yards and gardens rabbits might share the space with a few chickens, or they might even be confined to cellars and pits to be readily at hand when called for by the kitchen. Markham, in his *Cheape and Good Husbandry* of 1614 indicates that this practice was already well established by his day. His recommendation for accommodation of the rabbits which, he writes, 'may as well be kept tame as wilde, and doe above all other Beastes delight in imprisonment and solitariness', are as follows:

The Boxes, in which you shall keepe your tame Conies, would be made of thinne Wainescot boards, some two foote square, and one foot high; and that square must bee devided into two roomes, a greater roome with open windowes of wyar, through which the Coney may feede; and a lesser roome without light, in which the Cony may lodge, and kindle, and before them both a Trough, in which you may put meat, and other necessaries for the Conie,: and thus you make Boxe upon Boxe in divers stories, keeping your Bucks by themselves, and your Does by themselves, except it be such Does as have not bret, and then you may let a Bucke lodge with them: also when your Doe hath kindled one nest, and then kindleth another, you shall take the first from her, and put them together into a severall boxe, amongst Rabbits of their owne age; provided, that the boxe bee not pestred, but that they may have ease and liberty.

As an index of their contentedness with this situation, Markham observes that captive animals 'bring forth mo[r]e Rabbets at one kindling than any wild Cony doth'; besides, 'they are ever ready at Hand for the dish, Winter and Summer, without charge of Nets, Ferrits, or other engins, and give their bodies gratis, for their skinnes will ever pay their masters charge with a most large interest'.

William Ellis, in his *Practical Farmer* of 1738, implies that the keeping of captive rabbits had spread to the countryside too, where he judged that 'Tame Rabbits are great Improvers of a Farm by their Dung', which changed hands at 'sixpence a single Bushel trod in, and is chiefly used to harrow in with Barley and Grass-Seeds'; in his opinion, the rabbits were 'more profit by far in Hutches than in Pits'.

Some of these tame populations, whether in the town or country, comprised the same varieties that populated the warrens, but new breeds were also introduced from the Low Countries, where the keeping of tame rabbits had a longer history. It may have been at this time that the practice of gelding bucks to make them heavier (and apparently sweeter) was introduced: Ellis mentions that he knew of the custom, 'but as I yet never experienc'd the success, I can write no further of it'.

RABBITS FOR THE TABLE

Sentiment had played no part in the introduction of the rabbit, nor in its subsequent husbandry. Until the keeping of pets became fashionable in the sixteenth and seventeenth century, every one of them was destined for the pot. The privileged status of the medieval rabbit and its ultimate fate is confirmed by its regular presence on the menu at royal and aristocratic feasts: by 1270 we have records of the estates of the Archbishop of Canterbury supplying 200 rabbits for the Feast of St Edward at Westminster, and they feature prominently at the coronation feast of Henry IV (1399) and at the installation of the Archbishops of Canterbury in 1443 and York in 1465.

Throughout much of the thirteenth and fourteenth century rabbits sold for four or five times the cost of chickens at 5d. or 6d. each, and as late as 1395 Merton College was paying up to 8d. a couple (plus transport costs of ½d. each) for rabbits brought from Bushey (Hertfordshire) to Oxford for a college feast. By the fifteenth century they were more plentiful, though variations in price reflect continuing unevenness of availability.

In the monastic context the keeping of rabbits went beyond the desirability of regularly putting a cheap and nourishing stew on the refectory table, for following a practice of Roman origin – and one that is difficult for present-day audiences to reconcile with the monks' calling – these communities had a special interest in embryonic or neonatal animals. In the Roman era it had been commonplace for villa estates to include *leporaria*, special gardens in which hares and also rabbits were enclosed for use in the kitchen when required. (Rabbit bones have been found in two Roman contexts in England, at Lynford (Norfolk) and at Beddingham (East Sussex), suggesting that the species may initially have been introduced at this early date, though evidently it did not survive.) A particular delicacy, termed *laurices*, comprised the young cut from their mother's womb or taken new-born from her breast; by the same convenient sophistry that allowed the barnacle goose to be classified as a fish, *laurices* too were stripped of their status as meat so that they could be consumed on the many meatless days that marked the medieval calendar.

In contrast to modern sensibilities that cause many of us to prefer the source of the meat on our plates to be heavily camouflaged, recipes for rabbit pie from the sixteenth and seventeenth centuries frequently specify that the head and ears should be left on. Further anatomical reference was made by fashioning the pie-crust so that it took the form of the body and head of the creature contained within, the ears of which were sometimes threaded through the pastry so that they lay along the surface so as to leave no doubt as to the contents. Otherwise, they were considered by Thomas Moffet 'best roasted, because their nourishing juice is soon soaked out with the least seething, making good broth and bad meat'; his suggestion was that the cook should 'Chuse the Female before the Male, the fat before the lean, and both from a chalky ground and a sweet laire'.

By the seventeenth century rabbit was well established as a staple of the country yeoman's diet.

One contemporary commentator wrote that 'no host could be deemed a good house-keeper that hath not plenty of these at all times to furnish his table'. The expansion of many towns at this time also kept demand for rabbit meat strong. In an action brought against one John Bayley of Reading in 1624, a London poulterer described the accused as 'a buyer of Connyes by whole sale of many persons from theyr grounds', who had sold him in the course of the previous year 'six thousand gray connyes or thereabouts and of blacke connies five hundred or thereabouts'; in evidence another poulterer stated that during the previous year he had made several journeys to Wiltshire each week with two or more horses to fetch rabbits for Bayley, each horse-load comprising 300 rabbits. By the 1700s rabbits sold for 8d. a couple, while the equivalent price for hares was 6d., grouse 3–5d. and partridge 4d.

With the progress of the nineteenth century the rabbit became increasingly a dish for the poor (illus. 113), providing a gamey quality that was otherwise hard for them to experience – and for considerably less than the cost of butcher's meat. Although the consumption of rabbit had moved down the social scale, the volume of demand remained high.

FUR AND FELT

Dominating the populations discussed above were rabbits of the common grey variety, their coats of grey fur with some intermixture of red and with white at the throat. One or two other strains achieved special economic importance on account of their fur, and once a particular population had been so established the warrener had the additional task of ensuring that no common-grey infiltrated the population to dilute the purity of their coats.

113 A 'rabbit man' plying his wares, by Thomas Bewick, 1800. By the 19th century the rabbit had lost all its social cachet and had become a dish for the urban poor.

The earliest sumptuary legislation, introduced in 1337, deemed that the wearing of furs of any kind was a privilege to be restricted to those of gentle birth, but within a generation a stratified hierarchy of furs appropriate to different stations had been introduced that approved the wearing of lamb, fox, cat and coney fur by all but the poorest classes. Records of prices paid are scarce and show wide fluctuations, partly due to the degree of ease with which the major markets could be accessed: skins on Lundy Island, for example, were valued at 5½d. a dozen but were selling for more than twice that price elsewhere in 1310–13. The Countess of Warwick was paying 1s. 4d. a dozen in 1405, but by the middle of the fifteenth century the price obtained by Syon Abbey for its skins was only 4d. a dozen.

Black rabbits formed one of the most successful varieties in the medieval centuries, their coats being judged fit to line or to trim the garments of royalty. While common coney served for the trimming of servants' liveries at the court of King John, the monarch naturally commanded only the best. Henry VII had night-slippers lined with black coney skin while Henry VIII possessed boots of white lamb and black coney skin and a gown of russet velvet lined with black coney. Several garments in the wardrobe of his daughter Princess Mary were 'furred with coney' (all of it black), including a black velvet nightgown, another nightgown of black damask 'furred with 136 black coney skins' and a gown of black satin similarly incorporating 132 skins. At this time black rabbit skins commonly sold for twelve times the price commanded by common greys and frequently were used entire in linings. Markham observed in the early 1600s that 'when another skinne is worth but two pence or three pence at the most [black skins] are worth two shillings or two shillings sixe pence'. Richard Hakluyt noted that the export trade in black coney skins might yet profitably be increased, 'for that we abound in the commoditie and may spare it', and by the turn of the seventeenth century Fynes Moryson could add that England 'hath infinite number of Conies, whereof the skinnes (especially black and silver haired) are much prised, and in great quantity transported, especially into Turkey'.

Silver-greys (also called silver-haired or silver-blue rabbits) were also prized, with populations that were at first especially concentrated in Lincolnshire and Yorkshire but were also raised (along with black rabbits) in East Anglia, notably at Methwold, Wretham and elsewhere along the coast. By the eighteenth century, demand in England for silver-grey skins had declined but a useful export trade to Europe and to the Far East had developed, although this too fell away in the course of the following century. None the less, at this time Thetford continued to produce 20,000 skins a year at 24s. a dozen, sold on the London market. By the 1900s rabbit populations were no longer separated on the basis of their fur, the only demand being for their meat.

Elspeth Veale records that the royal tailor purchased skins from a Lisbon merchant at Winchester fair in 1244, and that shipments of rabbit skins totalling 2,174 were seized in 1228 and 6,000 skins in 1237, the latter from Spanish and Frisian merchants. By the fourteenth century an export trade to the Continent, notably Flanders, had developed: in 1365 a shipment of 12,000 skins to Flanders is recorded, and eighteen years later a further 10,000 skins to Holland. By the mid-fifteenth century this trade had reached considerable proportions: in 1431 one London merchant exported 40,000 skins to Flanders, in 1480–81 a group of Hanseatic merchants jointly exported 138,000 skins and by 1490–91 exports by aliens had topped 286,000 skins. Danzig and the other Baltic ports became major destinations for exports. Lesser numbers of skins were traded in Scotland in the early sixteenth century from a variety of coastal ports stretching from North Berwick to Wick.

Whatever the strain, rabbit fur from does was estimated above that from bucks and its quality was dependent too on the season, with winter pelts fetching a premium. Animals from certain regions were also favoured over others. Those bred on the chalk downlands were especially highly esteemed, both for their fur and their meat: John Aubrey's view was that those from Aldbourne were 'the best, sweetest and fattest of any in England; a short, thick coney, and exceeding fatt'.

The profitability of certain warrens relied more on income from skins than from the sale of meat. Both income streams were highly dependent on access to transport to the towns – and in the case of skins to manufacturing towns in particular.

None the less, such contacts could be maintained over considerable distances: already by the eighteenth century, for example, the warrens of north Yorkshire were sending skins regularly as far as Manchester and London. Demand for fur seems to have fallen sharply following the Napoleonic wars, leading to the closure of some warrens. Others were given a new lease of life a few decades later with the arrival of the railway.

In the early centuries the preparation of skins had been a task that provided some small-scale employment in areas where rabbits flourished, notably in East Anglia, and rural glovers and clothiers also benefited to some degree. For the most part the manufacturing trades were based in London, however, and it was the local carriers and boatmen who benefited mostly from the industry

By now the skins were less frequently used entire, but the hat industry absorbed a great deal of common-grey rabbit (as well the superior black) fur in a process that involved separating the fur from the skin to form it into felt. Once the skin had been dampened, stretched and flattened under pressure for a period, the fur was shaved away with a knife. Sheail estimates that, in season, each rabbit would produce about 1 oz of fur; in 1800 that from the back fetched 20s. a pound, the breach 18s., the belly and throat 16s., the head 14s. and the tail 12s. Waste from this industry went to stuff bedding. The trade survived up until World War One, by which time, however, it was supplied largely from Australia and New Zealand and the native market had been extinguished.

THE SYMBOLIC RABBIT

Rabbits rarely found themselves elevated to the status of heraldic beasts, but an exception is formed by the case of John, 8th Earl of Warenne (1286–1347), a scion of one of the most powerful baronial families in medieval England, for whom the canting reference to the warren proved irresistible. Two of the seals used by John feature warrens populated by rabbits on their reverses, one of them acknowledging his elevation to the title of Count Palatine in 1333. The Warenne arms feature prominently in the decorative schemes of the Gorleston Psalter (mentioned above), an East Anglian manuscript of the early fourteenth century – sometimes in proximity to representations of rabbit warrens in order to underline the connection. The Psalter, which throughout is rich in rabbit imagery, is thought to have been produced under the patronage of the same 8th Earl. Much interplay can be detected here between, on the one hand, the religious symbolism associated with the rabbit (see below) and, on the other, the very practical involvement of the Warennes as one of the major promoters of rabbit warrens on their extensive East Anglian estates, including Methwold, Thetford, Tunstead and Gimingham: the repeated representation of warrens in line-endings and margins and as part of larger representations of rural life goes far beyond anything that can be found in otherwise similar documents of this period.

The heraldic achievements of later and less elevated citizens occasionally include rabbits. The monumental brass of Arthur Strode (d. 1612) at St Aldate's church, Oxford, bears the Strode arms (argent, a chevron between three conies sable): Strode was a Devon man, whose family may have owed its fortunes to rabbit keeping. Another brass at Felbrigg (Norfolk) also features three rabbits: the family of Jane Coningsby (d. 1608) may have adopted this device as a canting reference to their name, evidently being unaware of its true Old Norse origin, deriving from quite another root. In a chapel dedicated to the Cony family at Walpole St Peter (Norfolk), a number of monuments reproduce the family arms incorporating more appropriate coneys (illus. 114).

A symbolic role for the rabbit on an entirely different scale has been explored by David and Margaux Stocker. At its heart is the identification of the rabbit with the human soul – vulnerable and at risk from dangers on all sides; in this trope the church provides a sanctuary for the soul as the burrow does for the rabbit. The theme is said to be made explicit in a wall painting in the parish church at Hailes Abbey (Gloucestershire), where a rabbit is shown sheltering from hunting hounds; once again the possibility that the rabbit is in fact a hare – a more appropriate quarry for the huntsman accompanying the hounds – leaves just a trace of uncertainty. (The same difficulty applies to representations in several manuscript sources – in the Douce Apocalypse, for example – where huntsmen are shown in pursuit of what appear to be rabbits when the historical evidence suggests they might more appropriately be hares.) A further development of this theme equates the

114 Arms of Robert Cony, died 1681, from his memorial slab at Walpole St Peter (Norfolk).

refuge provided by the 'rock' or mountain of Christ's church with the pillow-mound in which the rabbits find safety. The prominent siting of certain pillow-mounds within monastic precincts – sometimes profiled against the skyline – may have been deliberately engineered, the Stockers suggest, in order to draw attention to and to underline this symbolic relationship. In the Douce Apocalypse they find the metaphor made more explicit with rabbits represented as souls facing the Day of Judgement while a Resurrection scene in a stained-glass window at All Saints North Street in York has the dead emerging from burrows rather than graves.

It is within this allusionistic framework that the unique warren lodge at the manor of Rushton (Northamptonshire) finds a place. Unlike the remote and purely functional lodges mentioned above, this richly ornamented building (illus. 115) forms a recreational adjunct to the manor house itself, designed to accommodate parties enjoying excursions from the main building but loaded with purposeful symbolism. Its design was conceived by its founder, Sir Thomas Tresham, a devout Catholic, on his release from imprisonment for his religious beliefs in 1593: references to the number three are found everywhere – in its triangular ground plan, in its three floors, in its three walls each of 33 feet and each with three windows decorated with triangles and trefoils and with three pinnacled gables; a Latin text of 33 letters per wall encircles the building. At a simple level these allusions may be taken to refer to Tresham himself (nicknamed 'Tres' – three) and to his three sons and twice-three daughters, but a more profound reference is to the Holy Trinity, underlining the builder's unshakeable faith. From within the lodge the visitor looks out at the world through the small circular windows which place him in a relationship with the landscape that mirrors that of

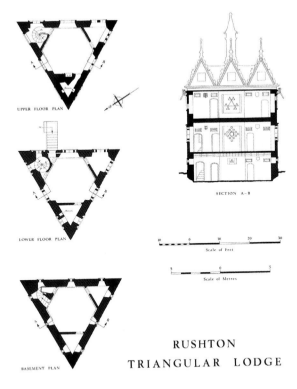

RUSHTON TRIANGULAR LODGE

115 Floor-plans and section of the triangular lodge in the warren at Rushton Manor (Northamptonshire) – the most elaborate monument ever devised with the rabbit in mind.

the rabbits in the adjacent pillow-mounds and call to mind his own vulnerability. Nowhere else is the warren elevated to such a prominent role within a symbolic landscape and nowhere does the rabbit find itself participating so eloquently in the contemplation of divine omnipotence.

LEGISLATIVE MEASURES

References to the rabbit in legal instruments provide a mirror to its progress from exclusive asset to verminous pest. A dramatic measure of its early status is given by a record from the reign of Richard II mentioning that certain poachers had been excommunicated for taking 10,000 rabbits (together with 1,000 pheasants and 2,000 hares) from the manor of North Curry (Somerset) – figures judged likely to be exaggerated, but clearly indicating a plentiful supply. From the same reign, an Act of 1389 prohibited the killing of rabbits and 'other gentlemen's game' except by persons with certain property qualifications; these would remain on the statute book until the late seventeenth century.

In 1671 Parliament passed a new Game Act which relaxed the property qualification but which removed certain animals, notably deer from the list of animals protected in the traditional way; subsequently, in 1692, rabbits too were deprived of this protection. The new measures, however, had the effect of altering rather than abolishing the form of protection offered, since it now became illegal for anyone, with or without qualification, to take animals without permission of the landowner on whose estate they were to be found. Rabbits had become a form of private property and as such enjoyed not less protection under the law but more: as Munsche has it, a poacher of game in the eighteenth century risked no more than a £5 fine or three months' imprisonment, whereas a stealer of rabbits at night risked transportation for seven years or could be imprisoned, fined or whipped. As late as 1765 the Act for the more Effectual Preservation of Fish in Fishponds . . . and Conies in Warrens confirmed these draconian measures.

Despite the punitive nature of these laws and the fact that warren owners were at liberty to protect their property by setting man-traps – two were kept at Ditsworthy warren (Devon) in the eighteenth century – it seems that most offences were dealt with at a lower level. Certain controls could be built into the terms of leases issued by landowners, for example: those issued by a certain Earl of Hertford sought to eradicate poachers from his estates by forbidding that his tenants

should 'keepe any person or servants under them, to walke the . . . warren or grounde which shalbe misliked by the Erle', on pain of dismissal. Generations of such leaseholders none the less saw their profits eaten into in the most literal sense by rabbits foraging outside the warrens or escaping from them into the wild in increasing numbers, and occasionally their plight was formally recognized, as when all those with grazing rights on the downland surrounding Durley warren (Wiltshire) were licensed to kill escapees and to stop up the burrows they had dug in the pasture; similarly, faced with an increasingly uncontrollable feral population at Weeting (Norfolk) the Duchy of Lancaster at first ceased to exercise its right of free warren, charging 10s. for the right to take rabbits from the wild colony from 1414 before abandoning any control six years thereafter. Villagers elsewhere increasingly gained rights over wild rabbits (though not those from the manorial warren). As numbers of rabbits in the wild increased in the eighteenth and early nineteenth century (see below) farmers found themselves in an increasingly invidious position. Tenants were now caught in a double bind as crops came under ever greater pressure, while the rewards to those who had rights to trap and to sell rabbits were undercut as sportsmen glutted the market with cheap meat. Indeed, some tenant farmers lost their rights to sell rabbits at all and found themselves excluded from compensation; others were given limited rights to take rabbits at certain seasons of the year or were allowed to trap them but not to shoot.

Up to the nineteenth century the primary aim of legislation was aimed at controlling the unauthorized taking of rabbits. Following a ban on the buying and selling of game, introduced in 1755, the Night Poaching Act (1828, revised 1844) reformed the earlier laws but failed to tackle the flourishing black market that had developed due to the ban;

under the Game Act (1831), however, trading was allowed by licensed dealers and the black marketeers found themselves undercut. The same Act gave farmers and smallholders complete control of animals on their land, while the Larceny Act (1861) gave further protection to warrens and was reinforced by the Poaching Prevention Act (1862).

An important change of emphasis can be detected in the Ground Game Act (1880), which acknowledged that the rabbit population was becoming increasingly harmful to countrymen and gave the occupiers of land the right 'to protect their crops from injury and loss by ground game'. Pressures increased from within the farming community and calls were heard for the right to compensation from landlords for damage inflicted by rabbits. In 1917 a Rabbit Order was attached to the regulations of the Defence of the Realm Act which empowered authorities to take action to stop damage by rabbits.

The sense of an embattled community under threat from the rabbit as implied by that Act continued throughout the later twentieth century, beyond the scope of this review. The Forestry Act (1920) gave powers to the Forestry Commission to enter land to destroy rabbits on property adjacent to its own plantations where they threatened the very survival of the trees, while the Prevention of Damage by Rabbits Act (1939) permitted local authorities to compel the control of numbers. The Agriculture Act (1947) repealed these provisions, with powers being transferred to the Ministry of Agriculture, which had powers to delegate. Under the Pests Act (1954) certain 'Rabbit Clearance Areas' could be designated, in which the whole population might be exterminated. At this time the national rabbit population was estimated at up to 100 million animals, with some 40 million being killed annually. Legislation had clearly failed to control their increase, but a threat of hitherto unimaginable proportions now hung over the rabbit. With the arrival of the virus *Myxoma*, the seemingly unstoppable career of the rabbit was brought up sharply.

BEES AND BEE-KEEPING

Honey bees (*Apis mellifera*) have been sought out in the wild for their honey and their wax during during untold millennia and by the time of the Roman conquest of Britain they had been widely domesticated (or at least constrained to take up residence in ready-made hives) across much of Europe. During the period of Anglo-Saxon dominance of England there is already evidence, reviewed by H. M. Fraser, of two distinct traditions of bee-keeping which would survive alongside each other well into the period reviewed here: on the one hand was the native British custom of using wicker hives or skeps, which would remain popular in western regions until the mid-nineteenth century, while in the areas more densely settled by the Anglo-Saxons the Germanic practice of making skeps from straw became firmly established. Fraser equates these differences with the use at the start of our period of the terms *vascula* and *vasa apium* respectively in *Domesday*, where, however, their economic significance was considered minor. Little detail is revealed in *Domesday*, incidentally, about Anglo-Saxon bees or their keepers (the *beo-ceorl*), beyond their lowly status in society – equivalent to that of the swine-herd – although in one instance at Suckley (Herefordshire) the *custos apium* is designated the King's Beekeeper, with twelve *vasculae* in his charge.

There is a dearth of detailed information of any kind concerning bee husbandry before the sixteenth century, although the evidence suggests that practices had changed little during the previous 500 years. The tracts that began to appear under the Tudors no doubt capture a good proportion of the earlier traditions, at a period just before bee-keeping, like other forms of husbandry, began to change in response to Enlightenment interest in 'rational' practice. A new breed of theoreticians entered the lists of authors at this time, alongside others of a more philosophical bent for whom bee society exemplified many of the virtues they wished to promote amongst their fellow men – industry, stability, orderliness – as well as a social hierarchy that could be held to demonstrate the benefits of a monarchical administration, as expressed by Gervase Markham in 1614: 'They have a kind of governement amongst themselves, as it were a well ordered common-wealth: every one obaying and following their King or Commander', while for John Evelyn, who had lived through the chaos of the Civil War to enjoy the early optimism of the Restoration, the example they provided was even more acute:

> they institute martialy & live as in a well ordered camp, keeping exact discipline, send out Colonies, march under their leaders at the sound of the Trumpet & are of all the Creatures, the most affected to Monarchy, & the most Loyall, reading a lecture of obedience to Rebells in every mans Garden.

TRADITIONAL BEE HUSBANDRY

While the mid-nineteenth century would prove to be a watershed in the practice of bee-keeping, when experimentation that had begun some three centuries earlier culminated in an entirely new methodology, traditional practices that can be traced back to the period of the Norman Conquest and beyond survived right up to that time and consequently our understanding of earlier

bee-keeping is illuminated by the historical records of later centuries. Although it would be unjustified to assume that no advances were made during this period, there is evidence to suggest that the majority of the routines registered in later centuries can indeed be extrapolated to show a long and largely continuous tradition.

Hives or skeps

Whether wicker or straw hives were in use, the essentials of bee-keeping in skeps varied little, beyond production of the hives themselves. A convenient starting point for their discussion is provided by Robert Plot in his *Natural History of Stafford-shire* of 1686. The beehives in that county, he says, were 'quite different from any used in the South of England' – a statement not altogether true, but his description of them is useful none the less. They were made, he writes,

> of Osier-twiggs interwoven like a basket, and then plaister'd over with a mixture of Clay and Cow-dung, or . . . daub'd over with a composition of Cow-dung and turff-ess, and over that again with Lime which seem only to be the Hives of ancient times, still retained here . . . and not only of Osiers, but of the ferula, withy, &c, and as Mr Butler affirms of privet and hasle . . . Over all this they put a straw hood, as in the Southern Counties, to keep the wax and hony from melting in the Summer, and to cast off the rain and keep the bees warm in winter . . . over which they pegg a square piece of wood at the top . . . which cast of the rain upon the more spreading part of the hood, which must needs otherwise enter in some measure in at the top of it, where the hollow ends of the straw are open to the weather.

Although quite possibly representing the more ancient of the two forms of hives, those of wicker (illus. 116) were by no means seen as inferior to straw skeps. Markham, for example, writes as follows:

> In the Wood-Countries they make them of cloven hassels watteld about broad splints of Ash, and so formed . . . like a sugar-loafe. And these Hives are of all the best, so they be large and smooth within; for the straw Hive is subject to breed Mice, and nothing destroyeth Bees sooner than they, yet you must be governed by your ability, and such things as the soyle affords.

Neither were wicker hives quite as restricted as Plot would have us believe: Edmund Southerne was familiar with both wicker and straw hives when he published his advice on the choice and manufacture of skeps in 1593:

> The best time is to have your hives made about Christmas, for then you may have them better cheape, and straw is best in season,

and the bryers that they bind them withall are then strongest, and will indure the longer: but in any wise let not your Hives be above fifteene or sixteene rolles at the most, both great and smalle: but if your Hives be made of twigges, as in some Countries they use, so they conteine not above half a bushel a piece, it is enough.

Records of hives bought by Oriel College (Oxford) and Syon College (Isleworth) at just this time show an average cost of 3d. each and indicate that hive-makers were already in business at this time. Samuel Cooke writes that the hives used in England in his day (in the later eighteenth century) were 'mostly wicker, made of previt; willow or harl'. Crane and Walker note also the recent use in Belgium of purple moorgrass (*Molinia caerulea*), and since it is plentiful in parts of the British Isles it may once have been used here too in the manufacture of hives.

Most writers agree that the warmest and best hives were those made of straw. The coils of the best-quality skeps would be of even diameter,

116 Wicker skeps – the last recorded in Britain – each with a straw hackle, at Upton Mill (Herefordshire), in the 1880s.

achieved by feeding the straw (wheat was often considered ideal) through a funnel made of horn or leather; the coils were neatly bound in position with briers (bramble vines), stripped of their thorns and fed through the tightly packed coils with the aid of an awl. Broad rather than high, they were typically of some 5 to 7 gallons in capacity, although a variety of sizes would be necessary to suit the size of a particular swarm. Too small a skep would promote a further swarm at an early point while, as Southerne tells us, providing the bees with too large a hive could also prove counter-productive:

> You are to note that when the Hive is bigge, it will aske long time and great labour for the bees to fill, so that the first yeare they cannot have enough to doe it as they may the little Hives: and the next yeare when they should breede Bees, they are busied about filling up their Hives.

In order to support the conical structure of the hive (which was open at the bottom), Cooke recommends the insertion of a 'crown tree' and basal supports:

> Take a stick of Sallow or Hasell about the bignesse of a man's thumbe, let it be a foote long or somewhat more, then cleave it crosse wayes from one end untill you come within a handfull or thereabouts of the other end, and no farther: then bend every quarter severall ways, cutting off the sharpe edge in the midst of every of them. Then must you put the end that is not cleft to the crown of the Hive, and bending every of the parts a severall way, sticke them into the sides of the Hive, that they may force the upper uncleft end hard to the crowne of the Hive. But if the Hive have a little hole in the crowne (as the

most straw hives have) then cut the upper end of your said crowne tree where it is not cleft small enough to go thorow it a little way, leaving a shoulder on the inside to stay it and this is good to keep the crowne of Hives from sagging downewards . . . Then take a smaller stick, and cleave it cleane through in the midst, cutting both the parts flat and smooth, and put them crosswise into the hive, within four fingers of the board they shall stand upon.

Moore favours the use of four splints at the base but suggests they should be driven up into the skirts of the skep to keep it from sinking when loaded with honey: '2 of them are the two door Posts, the other two are hind-Posts set at equal distances'.

For all their rustic appearance, the business of preparing a hive so that it would prove congenial to a swarm demanded careful attention to a great deal of detail. Southerne provides the following advice for dressing a hive before the bees are introduced to it, exhorting the keeper to 'cut away all the little superfluous tickling strawes within side of the Hive, and let it be as smooth as possible . . . for that they cannot abide such strawes'; the natural inclination of the bees was to divert their efforts to tidying up all these loose ends before settling down to their principal task, so that 'they might have filled halfe the Hive with Waxe and honey in that space'. Once trimmed in this way, 'you may then take Sallowe, Willow, or Hasell stickes, which being cleft in the middle and cleane shaven, you may put six parcels into a Hive': these had the dual function of supporting the structure and providing a scaffolding from which the bees might suspend their combs.

The custom of 'clooming' wicker hives with a mixture of cow-dung and lime was quite widespread in the western parts of the British Isles, as was the provision of a straw hood or hackle in an attempt to render them weatherproof. Markham describes the process in some more detail:

> you shall first make up a stiffe morter of Lime, and Cow-dung, mixed together; and then having cross-barred the Hive within, dawbe the outside of the Hive with the morter, at least three inches thicke, downe close unto the stone [base], so that not the least ayre may come in: then taking a Rye-sheaf, or Wheat-sheaf that is new thresh't, and binding the eares together in one lumpe, put it over the hive, and so as it were thach it all over, and fixe it close to the Hive with an old Hoope, or garth, and this will keepe the Hive inwardly as warme as may be.

Writing in 1634, John Levett – who asserted that he had seen bees do equally well in hives of wicker or straw (illus. 117), though straw was warmer – described the method of constructing a 'coat' or hackle with which to surmount the skep in greater detail:

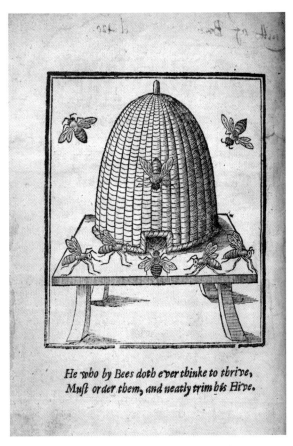

He who by Bees doth ever thinke to thrive,
Must order them, and neatly trim his Hive.

117 Straw skep, with a well-proportioned stool: frontispiece from John Levett, *The Ordering of Bees* (1634).

> Take a handful of straw and towards the one end bend it up againe, and there, within foure fingers of that end, I tie it fast with a rope-yarn or good Elme peeling, then do I taken another handfull, using it as before, and tie it fast to the other with a single knot between them, and so tie handfull after handfull, untill it will reach round about a hive: then do I tie the first handfull fast to the last handfull, and put it upon an empty hyve, which I have of purpose ready by me; and when the lower end that is so fastned together, is within some six inches of the ground, I gather all the upper ends of the strawes together, and tie them all fast together right above the crown of the hive, and as nigh as I can, and then cut the strawes away a foot above the place where you last tied it above the crown of the hive, and if any loose or short strawes stick out, cut them away with a paire of sheeres or such like. And thus can I make as many as I list, and afterwards at my pleasure in an evening or morning put them upon my hyves without troubling or molesting my Bees at all . . . And these kind of Coats will hold out raine, and Keepe the Bees both from the heat in the Summer, and from the cold in the Winter: and are done with little or no cost, but onely

a little paines taking twice or thrice in the yeere to renew such as decay, or to make new for the swarmes in swarming time, for once or twice a yeere at the least these must be viewed, and some of them amended or renewed as need shall require.

Moore favours folding the topmost straws into a sugar-loaf form and stresses the need for each hackle to be made to fit a particular hive: 'so that the skirts thereof must reach to the stool, or within half an inch of it round about, save only before where it may be parted somewhat shorter, that the Bees passage be not hindered'. In normal use the hackle would be 'girded close to the hive', though from time to time in good weather it might be removed and a search carried out for mice and insects. Hackles might also be applied to wicker skeps, in order to protect the insulating layer of clooming (see illus. 116). For the less punctilious, the skeps might simply be covered with a piece of sacking, held in place by an old ceramic pan inverted on the top, which also kept out the weather.

SITING THE APIARY AND INSTALLING THE SKEPS

[The bees] delight to live amongst the sweetest Hearbs and Flowers that may be; especially Fennell, and Walgilly-flowers, and therefore their best dwellings are in Gardens: and in these Gardens, or neer adjoyning thereunto, would be divers Fruit trees growing, chiefly Plumbe trees, or Peach trees . . . this Garden also would be well fenced, that no Swine nor other Cattell may come therein, as well for overthrowing their Hives, as also for offending them with their ill savours.

The idyllic setting proposed by Markham for the siting of the apiary was no doubt an ideal from which many fell short, but similar sets of features

were recommended in many of the earliest tracts on bee-keeping. A sunny spot sheltered from the prevailing wind was considered essential, but there were practical considerations too to be taken into account. Charles Butler's *Feminine Monarchie; or, A Treatise concerning Bees* of 1609 – extensively plagiarized by later writers – gives the following advice: 'For your bee-garden first choose some plot nigh your home, that the Bees may be in sight and hearing, because of swarming, fighting, or other sodaine happe, wherein they may need your presente help.' Butler, followed over the next century by others, further suggests a close-boarded fence for shelter on the north side and a hedge to the east to mask the early morning sun that might tempt the bees out of doors while the temperature was still dangerously low.

The skeps were to be carefully distributed so that their respective populations did not impinge overmuch on each other: Markham recommends that they be placed 'in orderly rows, one before another, keeping clear allies between them every way, so that you may walk and view each by itself severally'. Every skep was to be supported off the ground on a special platform, whose dimensions and materials were the subject of careful thought. Markham's specification was that three stakes should be driven into the ground in a triangle, projecting about 2 feet above the ground surface; over them would then be laid a broad, smooth paving stone, broader than the hive by some 6 inches on every side. The hive would then be placed on the platform with its door facing the rising sun or a little southwards. To keep them safe from 'tempestuous weather', he recommends that 'if you have sheds to draw over them in the Winter, it is so much the better'.

Needless to say, these details were argued over by other writers: Moore preferred four legs to three and a flat surface made of timber rather than stone, which he considered too hot in summer and too cold in winter; the surface was to be inclined so that water drained away from the door of the hive. As before, the bench needed to be broader than the diameter of the hive so that the pollen-laden bees had room to settle in safety before entering the hive; some experts favoured an additional settling platform leaning at an angle against the front of the stool.

Once it was set on its bench the base of the hive was to be sealed with cloom, so that the only way in and out was by means of the door, formed by cutting away a section of the lowest roll of straw and binding the ends – big enough to allow the bees to pass in comfort but not so wide as to allow the entry of mice or other predators. During the winter a wooden wicket might be inserted to reduce the gap to a minimum.

In some areas, at least, it was customary to have more permanent shelters within which the hives could be placed for their protection. Fraser interprets the very stable numbers of hives recorded at some manors in *Domesday* as evidence that even at this early date they may have occupied a bench of specific size under a penthouse roof. Samuel Cooke (*c*. 1780) advised the bee-keeper to make for every hive a cot or house of about two feet square and 2½ feet high on four legs 10 inches above ground and covered with boards or tiles to cast off the rain; the north side was to be close-boarded while the east and west sides were to be provided with doors, so that in summer it formed a penthouse and in winter could be closed up and straw put within the doors for additional insulation. Elsewhere hives might be grouped together under a common roof or pentice, in a manner that would not have been favoured by advocates of single hives on single benches, all of whom warn against placing the skeps in close proximity to each other. William Lawson's *Country Housewife's Garden* of

1618 shows eighteen hives closely packed in this way (illus. 118). Alternatively, recesses known as 'bee-boles' could be constructed within the walls of gardens, outbuildings or even in domestic residences, so that the skeps could be set within them and be sheltered from the worst of the weather; the tradition is one that can be traced back to the thirteenth or fourteenth century. Two hives at a time within such a recess represented the normal maximum, although numbers of bee-boles could be constructed in close proximity to each other. These structures seem to be unique to Britain and Ireland, where a combined total of over 1,200 sites has now been identified by Crane and others. From the late eighteenth century specially constructed bee-houses were created, characterized as windowless structures with numerous recesses like bee-boles, within which the hives could be placed during the most inclement winter months.

However well set up in their apiary, there were times when it might be advantageous for the bee-keeper to move his hives temporarily in order to exploit the seasonal flora on nearby moorland, for example, or in one the 'bee gardens' as identified by Crane in the New Forest – clearings with a rich flora that might be exploited during its brief flowering season but which would have had no permanent installation of hives. John Evelyn confirms this tradition and gives some useful advice on the best method of transportation of the hives:

> The best manner of carrying them is by tying the hives in a sheete, & bearing them on a Coal-staffe twixt two men. And of old we learne that they used to transplant their whole Apiaries as the Tartars do their heards of Cattell car[ry]ing their hives from place to place according to the season & for the benefit of the flowers.

118 A series of skeps within a protective pentice, from William Lawson's *Country Housewife's Garden* (1618).

SWARMING AND THE ORDERING OF BEES

The comparatively small size of traditional skeps placed a severe limit on the size of the colony it could contain, with the pressure on space increasing in proportion to the growing size of the combs built by the bees to store their honey. These pressures were relieved by periodic swarming, with part of the colony (necessarily including one or more queens) periodically migrating in search of new living quarters. While the necessity of having a queen was well understood, the precise nature of her role (and even her gender) remained quite unknown until comparatively recent centuries: as late as 1750, Robert Maxwell in his *Practical Bee-Master* can be found chastizing a certain Dr Warder who 'pretends to have dissected bees and . . . found a Conveniency in maintaining that this Soveraign was a Female' – Maxwell believing that Warder had cynically manipulated the conclusions of his work, which was dedicated to queen, while he (Maxwell) stoutly believed that the leader of the colony was invariably a male. In this belief he was by no means alone.

Left to its own devices, the colony would like as not take up residence in a hollow tree-trunk or some other natural feature. The regularity of this occurrence is reflected in legislative measures drawn up in early Irish, Welsh and Anglo-Saxon law-codes, establishing conventions for ownership of absconded swarms and placing a monetary value on them (on the eve of the Norman conquest the Welsh laws valued a hive of mature bees at 24d.). Unless prior ownership of a swarm could be proved by eyewitnesses to its migration from an existing hive, the swarm (and any honey it subsequently produced) was deemed to be the property of the landowner, along with the other natural resources of the forest. This was a principle that would survive throughout the medieval period.

In practice, the well-tended apiary was never left to its own devices and the tendency of the bees to form swarms was positively exploited and carefully regulated as part of the normal management regime. Whenever a new swarm formed, the beekeeper would take pains to ensure that it did not abscond but was directed into a specially prepared hive where it would form a new colony; in this way his stock was expanded and the production of honey and wax increased accordingly. Already in the late thirteenth century the *Husbandry* of Walter of Henley suggests that 'Each hive of bees ought to answer for two swarms a year as their issue, one with another, because some give nothing while some give three or four in the year.'

To the sensitive ear, the imminent formation of a swarm was revealed by a change in the pitch of the buzzing within the hive. Any time from May to mid-July swarms could be expected, and according to Cooke 'where there are store of Bees, there will sometimes happen three, foure, or five swarmes in a day, and within a very small time of one another', so it was necessary for the bee-keeper to be well prepared in advance. When the flight is imminent, Markham writes, after sunset the 'master bee' may be heard above all the others, 'in a higher and more solemne note'; some authors write more poetically of a bugling note being heard, calling the swarm together (see the passage by Evelyn quoted on p. 394). If the bees were seen to be having difficulty in getting into the hive, this too was taken as a sure sign that they would swarm before long. Too much sluggishness on the part of the bees (or too large a hive, so that the colony was not placed under pressure) might result in swarms forming too late in the season, for as Southerne points out:

> untill the Hives be full of Combes, they will not swarme, and then the Spring being far spente before they goe to breeding, the swarmes must needes come late, which dothe endaunger the swarme, and also the olde stocke, for that . . . the freshest flowers must needes decay before the bees begin to worke, whereof proceedeth many times such death of bees.

Having anticipated the swarm, the bee-keeper then had to ensure that it was efficiently captured. Any tendency for the swarm to rise in the air and fly off might be countered by throwing a little dust or hog's dung amongst them, which had the effect of making them settle. More questionable was the widely held belief that they could be made to settle by a process of 'tingling', that is, by beating on a metal vessel or a candlestick. Markham was one of those who subscribed to this method: 'When you see the swarm rise, take a brass bason, pan, candlestick and make a tingling noise thereon, and they are so delighted by music that they will settle on the branch of a tree.' So well ingrained

was this belief that it is represented on a silver cup in the possession of the Worshipful Company of Wax Chandlers, presented to the Company in 1683 (illus. 119), although many were rightly sceptical of its efficacy. Cooke estimated tingling

> a very ridiculous toy, and most absurd invention; and I assure you, if it worketh any effect, it is rather hurtfull than profitable to the Bees [for] all great noise doth disquiet and hurt them . . . for myselfe have had above forty swarmes in a yeere, and have not lost one of them, when my neighbours having a farre lesse number, and using this kinde of ringing and jangling, yet have lost divers.

If the swarm did manage to escape and could be located, the next problem for the bee-keeper was to persuade it to abandon the tree or other location in which they had settled for the security of a new hive. A great deal of effort was expended in scrupulously preparing the hive for which they were intended, as described above, and it might further have been rendered fragrant for its new occupants: Markham recommends that 'before you lodge any Bee in your Hive, you shall perfume it with Juniper, and rub it all within with Fennell, Isop, and Time-flowers, and also all the Stone on which the Hive shall stand.' (Other writers, notably Cooke, deny that any such preparation is necessary.) Once the swarm had formed a convenient cluster, the keeper was advised to proceed as follows:

> take a new sweet hive, well drest, and rub'd with hony and Fennel, and shake them all into the hive, then having spread a fayre sheete upon the ground, set the hive thereon, and cover it all clean over close with the sheete, and so let it stand till after Sunne-set,

119 Engraved ornament on the Wax Chandlers' Normansell cup, showing a swarm being enticed to settle by 'tingling' on a brass vessel. Although the ornament is drawn in Chinoiserie style, the cup was produced in England (*c.* 1683).

at which time the Bees being gathered up to the top of the hive . . . you shall set them upon the stone (having rub'd it with Fennell) and then dawbe it close round about with Lime and dung mixt together, leaving only a door.

The formation of swarms could to some degree be regulated by the keeper. If he wearied of waiting for one to form at its own pace he could speed up the process by a stratagem recommended by Cooke: 'Many ways have been attempted to cause bees to swarm, as by placing a large pewter plate under the cluster of bees as they hang out in the heat of the sun, so that it may strongly reflect the heat upon them, which will provoke them to swarm.' On the other hand, too many swarms from any one hive in a single season was considered undesirable and could be discouraged by easing the pressure on space within: the skep could be raised by 3 or 4 inches during the night and supported on bricks, the intervening spaces either being filled in with daub or an 'eke' could be inserted. This comprised a ring of straw, of the same diameter as the base of the skep and of perhaps four or five coils, which had the same effect of providing more room for the bees to build their combs downwards. The eke had the advantage that when the bees had filled this area too, it was possible to lift the skep and cut off the combs extending into the eke before replacing it.

BEE-KEEPING AND THE ENLIGHTENMENT

It was perhaps inevitable that the mounting taste for improvement would lead to an interest being taken in the husbandry of bees by certain scholars of an enlightened cast of mind from the later seventeenth century onwards. Among the inspirational figures of the early Royal Society (founded 1660) was John Wilkins at Wadham College, Oxford, who was visited by John Evelyn on 13 July 1654, as recorded in Evelyn's *Diary*:

We all din'd at that most obliging & universaly Curious Dr Wilkins's, at Waddum, who was the first who shew'd me Transparent Apiaries, which he had built like Castles & Palaces & so ordered them one upon another, as to take the Hony without destroying the Bees; These were adorn'd with variety of Dials, little Statues, Vanes &c: very ornamental, & he was so aboundantly civill, as finding me pleasd with them, to present me one of the Hives, which he had empty, & which I afterwards had in my Garden at Says-Court, many yeares after; & which his Majestie came on purpose to see & contemplate with much satisfaction.

Apart from being provided with glass panels so that the bee-keeper could observe the activity within, the crucial feature of this new generation of hives – carpenter-made from timber and box-like in construction – was their capacity to allow the honey to be harvested without interrupting the life cycle of the bees. Credit for the invention of this type evidently was a matter of some dispute, for in 1676 (by which time Wilkins had been elevated to the bishopric of Chester and subsequently had died) Robert Plot records in his *Natural History of Oxford-shire*:

the new sort of boxes, or Colony hives for Bees, first invented, I suppose, by the Right Reverend Father in God John Wilkins, late Lord Bishop of Chester; notwithstanding the pretensions of John Gedde Gent. and his seven years experience: for I find one of them set up in Wadham College Garden (where it still remains) when the said accomplish'd Bishop was Warden there above twenty years since.

The aforementioned Gedde is mentioned too in Moses Rusden's *Further Discovery of Bees* (1679), who records:

That his Majesty hath given and granted by letters patents under the Great Seal of England, to John Gedde, and his partners, the full and sole power, privilege, and authority, of using, practising, exercising, and enjoying the new art and invention for the improvement of Bees, during the space of fourteen years.

But there is yet another contender for the origination – or rather the introduction – of these box-hives (unless the reference is merely to the inclusion of glass panels in the hives), namely the Revd William Mewe of Eastlington (Gloucestershire), who, we learn from Evelyn, had had the benefit of seeing them in use on the Continent in the course of 'his exile or Eclipse during our unnatural Wars'. Samuel Hartlib, in 1655, referring to Mewe as 'the Father of the Invention', quotes a letter from Mewe to Nathaniel Angelo of 19 September 1653, in which he offers that 'If you desire the Model or Description, I shall give the same to you that I did to Dr Wilkins . . . who hath with great curiosity set one up in his garden, and, as I hear, is setting up another with augmentation'. Mewe evidently was as conscious of the symbolic significance as much as the practical value of his industrious colony, laid bare to inspection in its elaborate hive: 'I intended it first for a Hyeroglyphick of labour', he writes, 'upon which a gentleman bestowed a Statue of that form to crown't', although by the time of writing the statue had been replaced by a sundial and weathervane. Hartlib reproduces a drawing by Christopher Wren, showing the basic structure of Mewe's hive, though without its elaborate finial (illus. 120).

It may well have been one of Wilkins's hives (or certainly one inspired by them) that Plot later acquired for the Ashmolean Museum, where within a few years of its opening in 1683 the collections included 'A beehive with glass windows through which one can see the bees making their honey'. The same author's *Natural History of Stafford-shire* of 1686 reveals that the taste for experimentation had by that time penetrated deeply into rural England, as exemplified by his encounter with one John Whitehall of Pipe Ridware in that county, 'a most intelligent Bee-Master':

I was shewn great variety of hives most of his own contrivance: some being square, others round, both placed over one another, with drawers of wood between, like the Colony hives described in Oxfordshire: others he made out of hollow-trees, which are sawn asunder at due distances, which no doubt on't are as agreeable as any kind whatever, these being the first natural hives for bees, before they were brought under artificial regimen . . . But the hives he preferr'd to all the rest, he made of brick, on three sides, with windows behind and before to see their working: the fore-South windows in Summer, being cover'd with Matt to preserve the hony. Within these squares of brick he sets his frames of wood, for the bees to work on, which he can take away as they work downward. He makes use notwithstanding both of straw and wicker hives cover'd with Cow-dung and Lime, but neither of them made after the ordinary manner, Viz. not conical at the top, but cylindricaceous, and open at top and bottom, which he places first on the top of the brick-work, and underneath again to receive the bees at last so as to be conveyed again to the top of the brick-work as at first. Of which brick-hives he has some single, others many together: but the single he counts the best, because the most manageable.

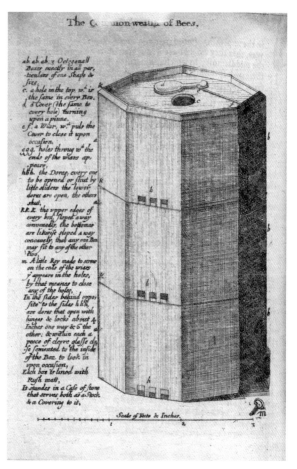

120 Drawing by Christopher Wren of Mewe's octagonal storied hive. From Samuel Hartlib's *Reformed Commonwealth of Bees* (1655).

Evelyn acknowledges the contribution of Moses Rusden, mentioned above, an apothecary with a shop in the Bowling Alley in Westminster, another proponent of transparent hives; these he describes as 'first shewed to us by Dr Wilkins . . . which have since received several variations and improvements by one Geddie, and since by myself'. Not only did Rusden's book of 1679 carry the accolade of being 'Published by His Majesties Special Command, and approved by the Royal Society at Gresham College', but he was himself appointed 'Bee-Master to the King's most excellent Majesty', a newly created office (acknowledged in the royal arms set over his frontispiece – see illus. 121) to which Evelyn claimed to have been instrumental in having Rusden appointed. His text sets out conveniently the advantage of the new box-construction hives:

> Now the keeping of Bees in Box-hives, called by the name of Colonies, to distinguish them from those kept only in Straw-hives, because all those young broods which are bred in the Spring, have room made fit for them, by the addition of another Box-hive, whereby they continue their labours without intermission, by working in those additional Box-hives, instead of swarming so that thereby all the labours of all the Bees, as well young as old, are united in one Colony . . .

Rusden had been responsible for the construction of a Royal Bee-House in St James's Park in the spring of 1677 and he now advised his readership 'that whosoever sets up this method' should first view either that installation or the hives which were kept conveniently for sale at his premises.

Evelyn wrote at length of the stacking frames featured in these hives in the pages of his *Elysium Britannicum*, compiled over the whole of the second half of the seventeenth century but not published until recent years by J. E. Ingram. The reader at whom Evelyn's text is aimed is essentially a gentleman like himself, for whom the cultivation of his garden and the bees which inhabit it are polite as much as practical pursuits, and his instruction is to proceed 'by prescribing some few directions in what is least knowne save amongst the curious, & how he may frame a Philosophicall Apiarie for Speculation, together with some briefe observations touching their Government'. The hives in which these experiments were to take place

recall those of Wilkins with their 'Dials, little Statues, Vanes &c', and in their richly allusory decorative and design schemes recall the attention lavished on other 'philosophical toys' and instruments of the age (illus. 122):

> The Place destin'd for the Apiarie shall have a Southern or Western aspect, The Hives framed of well seasoned Waine-Scott of Clapp-board, like Boxes of what shape you

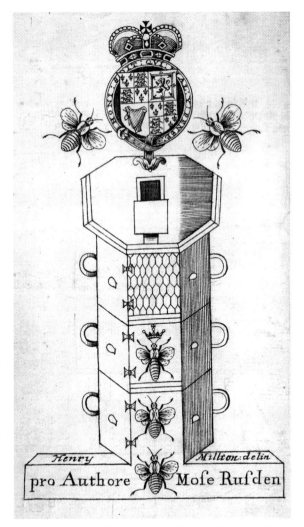

121 Frontispiece to Moses Rusden's *Further Discovery of Bees* (1679).

please, But the Hexangular seemes to be the most agreable because it resembles the forme of their cells, Let these Boxes be of capacity to containe about three pecks, and so exquisitely dovetayld & joynd that the weather may by no meanes separate or pierce them, to which purpose they may be layed in oyle with a white colour, and paynted with floures, Emblemes etc for the greater ornament. Of these you shall provide store made exactly of the same shape, with a flatt bottome or lid, which yet shall be so fitted as that 2 parts thereoff be separate from sides of the box almost halfe an Inch, For a reason to be hereafter shewed: and these spaces shall also have covers running in two groves to be drawne over them by wires at pleasure. The dores for the Bees to enter shall be made at the lower edge of the Hive, with little sliders of wood to open & shutt at pleasure. But the upper part of the box must advance above the lid to a full Inch, to be sloped away convexedly. The Bottomes concavely that being thus prepared they may mutually fitt, and applied fast & close to one another where you will connect two or three one upon another interchangeably. Lastly For the side opposite to the quarter where the holes and dores are, let there be a Window to open with hinges with lock & key. This may be about 4 Inches broad & five high within which fix a piece of Normandy glasse, exquisitely cemented to looke in upon occasion. All this don, mealt some store of Rosin & a little Benzoin & storax in a well glazed pott, & with a large brush of hogs haire anoynt it all over withinside, as they rosine their Canns for Beere, & this will long preserve your hives, & is far better then the matting of them which some use which rott & are a shelter for the mothes.

Now there must be a cover which may be removed at any tyme, taken off, & set upon the upmost hive. This should be made of a good thicknesse & with a concave Ledge to fitt the convex of the hive & to defend it from the Raine & other accidents of the weather, for which purpose let it be made of a pyramidall forme, & to project 3 Inches at the least, that the raine which dropps down may not wash the stoole which is therefore not to be above 2 Inches broader than the Circumference of the Hive, & to be supported on a single pedistall of two foote high. But you may contrive the Cover of what forme you will, & so as may most adorne your Apiarie for such we have made to resemble Palaces, Towers, & fortresses, or the hives may be placed under coverts of stone worke with a Dome or Cupola supported with Fower Corinthian pillars with Architrave & freezes, statues & busts, as you will have it more or lesse magnificent.

So constructed, with a minimum of two of the interlocking hexagonal elements (but preferably three), the colony of bees was to be installed in one of these units which would be set on top of the other; the doors on the upper unit would then be closed and the draw-boards separating it from the second unit opened, so that now the bees would enter by the door of the second stage and make their way up to the first. In time, the upper stage would be filled with honey and the bees would begin to colonize the second stage, at which point (determined by periodic checking via the window) the draw-board separating the two stages would be pulled closed, the uppermost element and its contents would be removed and a new lower element would be inserted so that the process could continue without interruption. In this

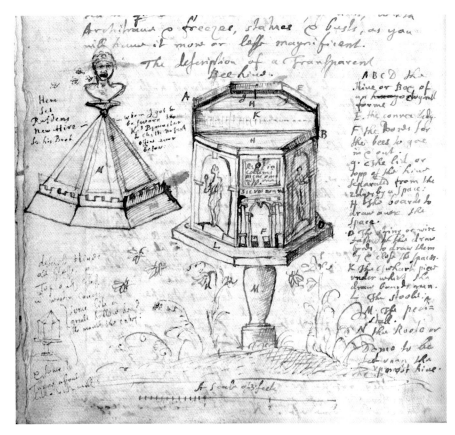

122 'The description of a Transparent Bee-hive', from John Evelyn's *Elysium Britannicum* (compiled *c.* 1650–1700). ABCD one element of the hive, of octagonal form (with painted ornament); E the convex lid; F the 'Doares for the Bees to go in & out'; G the lid of the hive separated from the edges by a space; H the boards to draw over the space; I the string fastened to the draw-boards; K the thwarts under which the draw-boards run; L the stool; M the pedestal; N the roof or dome to be set over the uppermost element.

way the imperative for periodic swarming was removed and (importantly) there was no need to sacrifice the bee population in order to extract the honeycombs.

An alternative form, 'more vulgar & lesse polite', is also offered, making use of circular elements resembling (and seemingly adapted from) empty casks 'well seasoned with canarie or Malaga, Raisins or Figgs'. Within these (as in the more elaborate version described above) are to be placed 'convenient supporters, for the Combs, which may be made of stickes to be let in, & rest upon holes made in the sides thereof' and on the outside two sets of handles are to be provided for ease of handling; communication between the elements is via a 'greate hole' in the head, for which a lead plug is provided when it occupies the uppermost

position in the hive. Otherwise the method of regulating it is as above.

Evelyn presents the introduction of the glass viewing portal in the more elaborate hive as a valuable means by which the keeper can gauge the productivity of his stock and quotes at length a letter from Mewe, who was proud that 'They serve . . . to give me an account of the daily income, and a diary of their Negotiations, whereby, if I spend half an houer after dinner or supper, I know what hath bin don that day.' In his judgement:

The Invention is a fancy that suits with the nature of that creature, they are much taken with the Grandur, & double their taske with delight. I tooke 14 quarts out of one of the transparent Hives, double their quantitie of others: etc . . . If every man of my ability, through the land cherished so many Hives as I doe it would be in the Commonwealths way 300000 *per annum*, which is lost by negligence, or ignorance of the use of that creature . . . Had we a hundred hives for one, when there are store of Oakes & Maples, the place cannot be over stored; So that if there were a statute for Parish Bees, as well as Parish Butts, and Parochial Apiaries designed for those places, where observed best to thrive I know not why a Parish may not make as much Hony as a Gent[leman] in Norfolk viz: 300lb *de claro per annum* . . .

Although more robust than the earlier straw skeps, it was recommended that box-hives too needed protection in the form of a shelter, not only to shield them from adverse weather but also because 'the sun, shining on the Box Hives hath more influence, and causeth greater heat in the inside than it doth shining on a Straw-Hive'. The best model, it was suggested, was provided by Rusden's Royal Bee-House at St James's (p. 405). Enclosing four colonies, it measured 10 feet by 2 feet 6 inches overall, with posts forming the corners and with a floor 1 foot off the ground. At the front were doors 3½ feet high, with the floor projecting under them some 4 inches for the bees to land on, sloping from side to side to avoid standing water; at the bottom of the doors were cut four holes, ½ inch high and 5 inches long through which the bees could come and go, the mouths of the hives to be aligned with the holes. At the back a second set of doors reaching up to roof level allowed the colonies to be removed when necessary and during the summer months could be opened to ventilate the interior. An octagonal rather than square format was preferred for the hives themselves, in order to avoid the honey in the corners

becoming spoiled; a height of 10 inches and a width of 16 inches was considered ideal. As well as sliding shutters to control access, as outlined above, the hives would incorporate 'two large glass windowes, one before, the other behind, with doors to cover the glasses', and handles to either side with which to lift them up. Internally there was a frame on which the bees might fasten their combs, which might be bought at Rusden's shop 'at as reasonable rates as anywhere else'.

NINETEENTH-CENTURY DEVELOPMENTS

Timber beehives of octagonal form and with glass viewing panels maintained their popularity up to the turn of the nineteenth century. John Fallowfield continued to promote them in his *Instructions for the Ordering of Bees* of 1791, quoting by now the imprimatur awarded by the Royal Society of Arts to one designed by Nathaniel Thorley. A late development, known as the Stewarton hive (from the place of its invention in 1819, in Ayrshire), retains the traditional octagonal structure, with access from one box to another being controlled by a system of sliding bars.

From the middle years of the eighteenth century, however, a new principle was being explored that resulted in the collateral box-hive – one in which a central brood-chamber was separated from honey-chambers arranged to either side – as first devised in 1756 by the Revd Stephen White. The idea was later perfected by Thomas Nutt who, in his *Humanity to Honey-Bees* maintained that while the 'piling of hive upon hive, or box upon box, (called storifying), and several other contrivances' had all failed to eliminate the destruction of at least a proportion of the bees in the process of retrieving the honey, various new forms, including the collateral hive, allowed the honey to be extracted in a humane and non-destructive manner.

His illustration (illus. 123) shows the hive partly disassembled in order to show its tripartite structure: the innermost walls of the two side boxes are pierced by slots that allow the bees to move between them and the central brood-chamber, on which stands a bell-jar full of comb honey (normally enclosed within a little pavilion of its own); below is a central drawer, devised for feeding the bees, while to either side are pivoting entranceways through which the bees gained access to the hives.

The idea of supporting the combs within individual, removable frames, spaced apart so as to avoid the bees building across the gaps and welding them together, was first explored by the Swiss naturalist François Huber, but it remained up to an American, the Revd L. L. Langstroth, to develop this into a working principle with multiple movable frames suspended side-by-side in a box-hive from which, simply by lifting a lid, they could be removed at will with a minimum of fuss. The use of dummies or dividers in these enlarged frame hives ensured that the efforts of the bees could be concentrated at will within particular sections according to the size of the swarm, and were not unnecessarily dissipated. By 1862, a decade after its development by

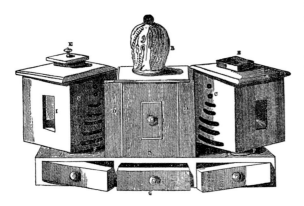

123 Thomas Nutt's collateral box-hive, opened up to show the means of communication for the bees. From Nutt's *Humanity to Honey-Bees* (1834).

Langstroth, the type was being imported into the British Isles, where it soon came to predominate. A myriad of different hives emerged in the course of the nineteenth century, all depending to some degree on this same principle. Although it tended to remain a cottage industry, the national production of honey had now stabilized into a highly efficient set of practices, informed by generations of earlier practical experience and now with a wide literature of its own. Books such as the immensely scholarly *Bees and Bee-Keeping; Scientific and Practical*, by Frank R. Cheshire ('lecturer on apiculture at South Kensington', where the Food Museum sought to promote improvements in the national diet), raised bee-keeping to the level of a science – albeit one that remained dependent on carefully cultivated personal skills and ultimately was at the mercy of the weather.

HONEY

The primary aim of all the activity hitherto described was, of course, to produce honey, whose principal uses in the centuries before easy access to sugar was as a sweetener in food and as the basis for mead. Although produced in untold numbers of gallons in the medieval period, mead was essentially brewed and consumed at a local level; it was also used by the more affluent in society in the preparation of clare, in which mead was added to white wine, honey and spices, or for piment, based on red wine and similarly spiced. Especially in clarified form, honey was also attributed an important medicinal value, being esteemed for cleansing, clearing obstructions, purging, nourishing and 'breeding good blood'.

At times it almost achieved the status of currency: it was the medium in which some customary dues were paid – sometimes wild honey was particularly specified – a practice widely observed at the time of *Domesday* but which was later generally commuted to cash payments, suggesting that honey was not always in plentiful supply. The quantities payable were often specified in barrels, the standard quantity for large amounts being the tun of 252 gallons. Retail prices of 3d. a gallon are typically found, although occasional references are also found to honey being sold in the comb.

In order to recover the honey, at the end of the season the bee-keeper would selectively harvest it according to the condition of the hives: those containing most honey would naturally be chosen, but so too would those poorly filled and occupied by colonies that would not be expected to survive the winter and which could therefore easily be sacrificed.

Removing the filled combs from a straw hive was not a task that could be undertaken progressively: the whole contents had to come out in one action. First the resident bees had been driven out, a process that could be achieved by inverting the skep with a second, empty skep suspended over it; rhythmic beating on the lower hive induced the bees to migrate into the other one – a rare-sounding skill but one that continued to be practised until recent times without, we are assured, serious danger to the operator. Other strategies involved driving off the bees with smoke, or (especially in the earlier centuries reviewed here) they might be killed off entirely. Some bee-keepers favoured drowning the whole colony in the hive, while others knocked the bees out of the skep held over a fire. Moore suggested that it should be suspended over a pit containing a brimstone match, the fumes from which would prove fatal to any occupants; Crane found sulphur darts still being used to this end in Yorkshire as late as the 1950s. From an early date, however, others were aware of the senselessness of this slaughter and argued against

such a course; Cooke maintained that 'it is not lawful for us, to use these silly creatures in such sort as they may be most to our benefit, which I take to be the right use of them and the very end of their creation'.

Once cleared of its occupants by whatever method, the whole hive had to be laid gently on its side, so that the widest dimension of the combs lay parallel with the ground; the splints or cross-pieces were then loosened from the wax and the combs were detached at any points where they might have stuck to the sides of the hive, after which they were removed one-by-one with the aid of a wooden spatula.

One alternative to the total evacuation of the skep was to fit it with an eke, as described above, while another more recent development of the skep involved making it in two sections, with a separate upper cap sitting on a discoid wooden top fitted to the main hive; holes were made in the wooden disc, large enough to allow the bees through in order to make their combs but small enough as to exclude the queen, so that no brood would be found there. Crane illustrates the type and mentions that the cap could be removed with its store of honey inside, ready to be sold intact. A more sophisticated development involved placing bell-jars over the communicating holes, so that when the bees had filled them with honey they could easily be removed (and sold at a premium).

Although it could perfectly well be eaten in the comb, comparatively little honey seems to have been marketed in this form: records of almost all early transactions are in liquid measures. In draining the honey from the combs the first flow, termed virgin honey, was deemed the best for quality and taste; the last drops of the bulk of the honey were extracted by pressing the comb, the remains of which would be reserved for processing, as described below.

Those colonies which escaped having their honey harvested at the end of the season might well have to be fed in order to survive the winter and to produce honey in the spring.

In some places one feeds the bees all the winter and in some places one does not give them anything to eat, that is to say the old ones which have remained in the hive one year or two. But the young ones which have been hatched during the summer do not know so well how to find food in winter, nor had they the time to save like the old ones who have worked throughout the year and therefore it is advisable to take more care with the young than with the old. And you may well support eight swarms all the winter with one gallon of honey and each swarm ought to yield one gallon of honey and wax per year.

And it is more profitable to leave them to work undisturbed for two or three years than to take away the wax and honey which they made each year; that way the hives and the bees will yield more in issue, wax and honey.

Markham recommends that overwintering stocks could be preserved by 'daily smearing their stone before the place of their going in and out with honey and rose-water mixed', this process to be continued until the flowers come in the spring. Others introduced the feed directly in dilute form, inserted by way of hollow reeds pushed into the hive through the entrance.

WAX

Almost as important in commercial terms as the honey produced by the bees was the wax from their combs, carefully recovered after the honey had been drained from it. Manorial estates might benefit from keeping bees through the wax they provided for lighting, but the largest noble households undoubtedly had to buy it on the market: in the year 1313–14 the housekeeping accounts for the Earl of Lancaster included purchases of '1,870 [pounds] of lights for Paris Candles, called Perchers' and 1,714 pounds of wax for seals, at a total cost of £314 7s. 4½d. At a national level, production remained insufficient to meet demand even during the Middle Ages, when large quantities of Baltic wax were sold at English fairs. Even in the royal household, candles were a valuable perquisite, specified as part of the maintenance to which courtiers were entitled and administered by the officers of the wax chandlery; normal practice was for the ends of used candles to be returned to the chandlery before fresh ones were issued.

The lower orders were unlikely ever to experience the luxury of beeswax candles and had to settle instead for those of tallow, made from animal fat and notoriously evil-smelling and smoky. Several instances are noted of the Company of Wax Chandlers having to investigate charges of wax being sold adulterated with animal fat – a prime offence within their own guild, in which candles had to be made 'of as good wax within as without'.

Churches and monastic establishments too made use of the best quality beeswax for liturgical purposes. Up to the time of the Reformation, white wax candles were burned at every service; the whole year's supply for the church was normally blessed at Candlemas. At times prodigious quantities were consumed: at the obsequies for the Bishop of London in 1303, wax candles weighing 1,200 pounds were consumed, although these may have been of yellow wax, which was normally reserved for masses for the souls of the dead. (Old stocks of bees were particularly suited to the production of yellow wax.) Dummelow records that in 1432 a pound of white beeswax sold for 6d., but in 1490 the price had dropped by a half; yellow wax sold for half the price of white.

At a domestic level, every bee-keeper would recover the wax from his hives as a matter of course. Cooke recommends draining the honey from the combs through a thin canvas cloth placed over 'a great earthen panne or such like', finishing by wringing the cloth to squeeze out the last drops. The crushed remains of the comb were then ready for reprocessing:

> melt the combs in boiling water and strain in a canvas bag shaped like an Ipocras bagge viz. narrow at the lower end, and straine as much as you can into a vessel of cold water. Gather the wax and melt it in a posnet on a soft fire and let it be made into what form you please, but if it be not purified at the first trying well enough then try or melt it againe, first having pared or scraped away that rosse that settleth at the bottome.

At a commercial scale the trade in wax and the manufacture of candles, torches, seal-blanks and other products was, from at least the late thirteenth century, in the hands of the Wax Chandlers, whose Company received its royal charter in 1484. Unlike some other guilds, the Chandlers never sought to exert influence on the producers of the wax they handled, but concentrated on its trading and processing into finished goods. Candles were formed either by dipping a wick (of twisted cotton, flax or hemp) in a vat of molten, purified wax and thereafter building up the thickness of the candle by basting, or alternatively the wick might be rolled in soft wax in order to gain in girth. Some candles were made in moulds, although the process is a difficult one with beeswax. As well as domestic candles (called 'sizes'), the chandlers produced larger square 'quarerres' and impressively tall 'perchers' for ecclesiastical and ceremonial use. Dummelow records that during the reign of Mary Tudor a single paschal candle weighing some 300 pounds was set up to mark the restoration of the shrine of Edward the Confessor in Westminster Abbey. As well as conventional candles, slender tapers (often sold in the form of long coils) were also manufactured, and for outdoor use torches were made of twisted tow or cotton soaked in resin and coated with beeswax

Up to the end of the medieval period a certain amount of wax was consumed in making up writing tablets, often in the form of two wooden elements linked at one side in the form of a book, each with a hollowed-out field on its inner face which was filled with beeswax to be written upon with a stylus, generally of bronze. This had the advantage that, when the 'page' was full, the script could be erased simply by reversing the stylus and drawing its spatulate head (suitably warmed) over the wax in order to regain a smooth surface. Writing tablets were widely used in schools and also as notebooks in the keeping of accounts and so on.

Wax was similarly consumed in large quantities in sealing formal documents. For official papers a slip of parchment might be threaded through the document, its ends clamped within a disc of beeswax, authenticated by impressing it within a matrix to produce the heraldic or other device of the appropriate authority. Uncoloured wax was used for seals of a general nature, green for those submitted to sheriffs and red for diplomatic documents. Verdigris and vermilion formed common colouring agents, and Venice turpentine was commonly mixed with the wax in order to improve its moulding properties. With the passage of time, and with the wider adoption of seals applied directly to paper for everyday correspondence, the wax might be mixed with shellac in order to render it hard and less prone to damage.

From the seventeenth century onwards, quantities of wax were also absorbed in the creation of waxwork figures. Although associated principally with somewhat scurrilous shows in the British Isles, wax modelling was raised to the level of a considerable art form in Italy and elsewhere, whether for portraiture or in the creation of life-sized anatomical figures of great complexity. Although a few talented figures in this field emerged in England, amongst whom Joseph Towne (1806–79), associated throughout his career with Guy's Hospital, deserves particular mention, it was never more than a minority activity in Britain. Beeswax was also esteemed as a medicament. Cooke writes:

As to its chirurgical, or physical virtues, it is reckoned a mean between hot and cold, between dry and moist, being the ground of all searcloths and salves; it molifies the sinews, ripens and resolveth ulcers; the quantity of a pea being swallowed down by nurses, dissolveth the milk curdled in the breast . . . The oil is of excellent virtue to cure wounds . . . And it is good for inward diseases, if you give one dram at a time in white wine, it will provoke urine, help stitches and pains in the loins, the cold gout, and all other griefs coming of cold.

As with honey, rents or portions of rents might be paid in wax, specified by the pound. Rights in wax might also be left by bequest, either by way of rent or as specified amounts to be rendered annually for the production of church candles. Fraser quotes the example of John, Archdeacon of Canterbury who, in 1137, left the rights and benefits of two properties in order to provide wax tapers to burn continuously on the altar at Rochester Cathedral.

124 E. M. Fox, *Two Longhorn Bulls*, 1833, oil on canvas.

FIVE

Animals on the Farm

CONSERVATIVE AND RADICAL PRACTICE IN THE COUNTRYSIDE

Popular perceptions of the progress of history have all too often been constructed on series of tableaux of significant events, centred around the strongholds of the aristocracy and later, with the growth of civic authority, within the burgeoning towns and cities. As little more than a background for the unfolding of these events lies the countryside, seemingly changing little from century to century and dragging its collective feet behind the progressive and opportunistic communities of merchants and industrialists. Undoubtedly, the succession of the seasons imposed a rhythm on the land that could not lightly be disregarded: the potentially catastrophic results of tampering with established routines, revealing themselves only after the investment of months of husbanding and likely as not at the start of a winter with the prospect of shortage if not famine hanging over an entire community, were enough to ensure that countrymen would settle for the devil they knew and would annually replicate the routines that had in the past proved most successful in seeing their animals and ultimately their families safely through to the following spring.

While some cautious progress was witnessed during the medieval period, it was only with a rising interest in the market for meat and other agricultural produce amongst a more entrepreneurial class, rich in capital and therefore not dependent in a life-or-death manner on the successful outcome of each innovatory idea, that the pace of change began to quicken. A significant shift came first with the emergence during the early 1500s of a new class of butcher-grazier, commonly based in towns but exercising wide influence in the countryside through the deployment of extensive flocks undergoing fattening at the hands of increasingly prosperous yeoman farmers, before final delivery for slaughter. From the following century, the increasing engagement of a further constituency can be detected as farming attracted more direct involvement by the major landowning classes: imbued with a spirit of philosophical curiosity that hitherto had made little impact on the countryside, they began to see themselves as engaged in a collective mission to materially benefit society while growing rich on the proceeds of a reformed agricultural economy.

The origins of this movement are reflected in the emergence of a new literary genre – the handbook or manual through which the curious landowner could begin to engage at some level with the theory and practice of farming, which hitherto he had been content to leave in the hands of his agent or bailiff. The first to make its appearance was the *Boke of Husbandrye*, attributed to Sir Anthony Fitzherbert (or just possibly Sir Anthony's brother John) and published in 1523, followed by Thomas Tusser's *Hundred Good Pointes of Husbandrie* of 1557 (expanded to *Five Hundred* in 1573) and a whole series of publications by Leonard Mascall from the 1570s onwards; during the first half of the seventeenth century Gervase Markham caught the spirit of this movement and his output amounted almost to a one-man industry, joined in the later 1600s by a flood of books conceived in the growing spirit of enquiry that gave rise to the broader programme of the nascent Royal Society, in which every educated man worth his salt aspired to engage in scientific investigation of one sort or another. None of these early texts was in itself innovatory or responsible for direct changes wrought in the field of animal husbandry, but collectively they helped give an identity to a new community of agricultural enthusiasts who would provide the means by which stiflingly conservative practices could begin to be overturned.

As a starting point for our review of the progress of animal husbandry, the *Domesday* survey of 1086 provides a valuable – if incomplete – picture of both the territory inherited by the new Norman overlords and, more obliquely, of the animal resources associated with it. From the detailed records of ploughlands, commons, heaths and forests, historians have extrapolated reasonable estimates of the animal populations which these resources might support in order to form a baseline from which later developments can be projected. Although all the principal animals of the present-day farmyard were already in place, the importance of each within the early medieval economy was markedly different from today.

By the end of the Middle Ages, at least, the population of England seems to have lived with a high expectation of meat as a regular part of its diet. Keith Thomas quotes the Elizabethan Thomas Moffet as claiming that 'our shambles' were quite simply 'the wonder of Europe' and by the middle of the following century Henry Peacham could claim that London 'eateth more good beef and mutton in one month than all Spain, Italy and a part of France in a whole year'. Needless to say, these claims were coloured by a strong streak of nationalism and are to be tempered by the remark of an early seventeenth-century theologian that 'Our poor country-people feed for the most part upon hard cheese, milk and roots.'

For those who could afford it, pigs had formed a major source of meat in the earlier medieval period (though from an assessment of excavated food bones Umberto Albarello concludes that beef predominated). The environment within which the pig population particularly flourished was the forest rather than the open field; considerable herds could be sustained under these conditions, often combining handfuls of animals belonging to several owners, for, to a greater degree than other farm animals, the ownership of pigs was characteristically dispersed amongst myriads of smallholders and peasant households (with others eking out a living in the yards of urban dwellers). Sheep were more widespread in the countryside, but mutton formed a less important element in the national diet than pork; their value was measured in milk and wool rather than meat. Even the importance of the sheep as a producer of dung to nourish the soil outweighed its value as a source of mutton at a time when the rotation of fields from grain to fallow and back again kept soils permanently on the verge of exhaustion. In the succeeding centuries, wool production would grow to a point where the sheep population represented perhaps the single most important national resource in England, although the picture was not a universal one. In Scotland, for example, the 'Black cattle' which by the late medieval period already formed a valuable export, would maintain their supremacy until the Highland clearances banished not only cattle but entire human communities to make way for vast flocks of sheep at the end of the eighteenth century. Cattle had been well represented throughout the countryside of Britain, but in the lowland zone, at least, were initially to be found playing their primary role as draught animals in the field: only at the end of their working lives might they be fattened for slaughter. Dairying too played a minor role, with much milk production ending up as butter and cheese and with consumption of cows' milk thought to have been at negligible levels up to the seventeenth century. This, at least, is the traditional view, although the passage already quoted in relation to the diet of the urban poor, combined with Sir Kenelm Digby's remark of 1658 that 'there's not the meanest cottager but hath a cow to furnish his family with milk; 'tis the principal sustenance of the poorer sort of people', suggests that a great deal of consumption went on below the historical radar. And with cattle providing most of the traction on the farm during these early centuries, horses were to be found playing only a minor role in agriculture, their rise to dominance taking many centuries to reach its climax.

Although the sizeable flocks of great estates placed them in a privileged position, in overall terms the bulk of all the stock lay in the hands of the peasantry. In place of demesne lands they had to make do with the produce supplied by their small plots and with common land that provided a principal resource for grazing. But while large numbers of animals could be sustained on the commons, they were hazardous places: herds were constantly at danger from cross-infection from every disease that might threaten densely populated land – murrain, liver-fluke, scab, and many others – and a great deal of attention is focused in the earliest manuals on these ever-present ailments.

In reality there were few responses that were in the least effective, beyond the application of tar to mitigate any non-lethal sores and the slaughter of beasts deemed beyond redemption. The effects of endemic disease played a major role in limiting the potential for improvement of the animal population, while a further check on progress resulted from the uncontrolled inter-breeding that was an inevitable consequence of the close cohabitation of stock, ensuring that no sense of purposeful intervention could ever hope to make a positive impact.

Far-reaching changes overtook the face of the countryside in the period following the Black Death of the mid-fourteenth century, when depletion of the human population brought about a breakdown in the manorial system of demesne farming. Many tenants now became leaseholders rather than bondsmen, as manorial service was replaced by a system of cash rents. A parallel change took place on the monastic estates, with many of the sheep-pastures being leased out; at the dissolution of the monasteries in the sixteenth century this trend was carried much further when wealthy graziers took over wholesale the former monastic estates. With a personal stake in the land they occupied, the new yeoman class set about defining their properties with a system of enclosures, investing effort in improving their assets in ways that had never been profitable under the medieval system of common grazings and open fields. An important corollary of this process was that flocks that had formerly lived in common began to enjoy a degree of separation that brought a number of advantages in its wake: farmers now found it worthwhile to plant fodder crops that would see their stock through the winter months; the animals themselves were protected to some degree from the everyday ailments of their open-field neighbours; and with less indiscriminate intermixture of flocks, owners found that (in theory, at least) the means of improving the quality of their stock was brought within their grasp.

It would take until the eighteenth century for the full implications of these possibilities to be realized. From this point a series of private Acts of Enclosure that would further transform the countryside began to unroll, culminating in the General Enclosure Act of 1845; this movement with regard to property was paralleled by (and in many ways made possible) a nation-wide interest in the 'improvement' of animals by selective breeding in a series of new and more rigorous programmes, a process that would revolutionize the appearance of livestock of every sort – particularly those destined to supply the growing urban demand for meat. A new sense of national interest emerged in the resources of the farmyard: with an outbreak in 1714 of 'infectious distemper' among cattle, the government of the day intervened with an unprecedented policy of compulsory slaughter of infected animals, linked with payments of compensation, and by mid-century national measures had been developed which could place controls on the movement of livestock and ban imports – completing a set of measures that today continue to form the basis of national responses to epidemics such as foot-and-mouth disease.

In the context of domestic herds, the fortunes of the human and animal populations were bound together in the closest manner. The relationship was, of course, an unequal and exploitative one, as it had been since the beginnings of agriculture, but it could never be mindlessly so: any concept of progress had to be founded on a degree of understanding and it may not be over-sentimental to suggest that there had been generally a shared sense of experience in the countryside that would be eroded when, for example, draught horses began to be brought in large numbers into industrial towns and mines. The proposition could easily be overstated, since domestic herds had no other end but a lifetime of service as back-breaking as that of the ploughman, or death at the hands of the slaughterman, or both, but it need not be predicated on mere sentiment: Keith Thomas observes that, 'as one late-seventeenth-century observer contemptuously put it, "farmers and poor people" made "very little difference between themselves and their beasts". They went out with them in the fields in the morning, toiled with them all day and returned home with them in the evening.' Even the successes of the great era of improvement in the eighteenth and early nineteenth centuries can be so termed only from a human perspective: it did no good to the pig population to be 'improved' to the point where the animals were smothered in their own fat, or for Longhorn cattle to be bred 'in-and-in' to the point of their near extinction as a breed; we might look with some pride at the perfect forms to which modern heavy horses have been bred from the unpromising material of the early medieval period, but when we remember that half a million of them were sent to die in World War One alone the question of whether this was an end that justified all that manipulation is hard to avoid. None the less, only a more dispassionate approach will serve as a basis for the following survey. Later, the progress through the centuries of each of the principal farm animals is reviewed in turn, but by way of introduction a number of themes that cross the species boundaries can be examined here.

OX VERSUS HORSE

Although the image of ox traction carries with it today inescapable overtones of primitiveness (illus. 125), the advantages to the farmer of substituting

Captabunt in animam iusti:+san
guinem innocentem condempnabut.

125 A four-ox plough-team at work in the mid-14th century. Note that the animals are yoked in pairs and that in addition to the ploughman there is a driver to control the team – a standard arrangement when working with oxen that survived until the 19th century. The plough itself is attached to the yoke by means of a rope or perhaps a leather trace. From the Luttrell Psalter (c. 1340).

horses in his plough-team – particularly the small-sized creatures of the early medieval period – for the cattle on which he had come to rely were by no means clear-cut, and even in later centuries the debate as to which was the more appropriate animal remained contested. Horses are mentioned in relation to the plough-team from the early decades of the twelfth century, but for hundreds of years their use remained both limited and scattered: only with the breeding of significantly more massive plough-horses in the eighteenth century (pp. 492-4) and the introduction of light iron ploughs soon afterwards did the ox-team became irretrievably redundant, with a few surviving long enough to be displaced directly by the steam plough and the tractor. Three principal considerations were at issue: the relative speed with which a team of oxen and a team of horses could each plough a field; the cost of keeping them during their working lives; and their respective values once they had outlived their usefulness.

Nominally, the horse was undoubtedly faster and on light soils invariably won the day, but it lacked the sustained pulling power of the ox that proved so useful on heavy loam. One alternative was to employ a mixed team, which might contribute the advantages of both (illus. 126). Early evidence for this practice emerges during the reign of Henry I from Ringstead (Norfolk), an estate of Ramsey Abbey (Cambridgeshire), where three ploughs each of four oxen and three horses are recorded. Anne Hyland notes that by the end of the twelfth century, fifteen of Ramsey's eighteen demesnes used mixed teams, and by this time evidence for similar practice can be found on a number of other monastic estates. At the turn of the thirteenth century, Walter of Henley concluded that 'with a team of oxen with two horses you draw quicker than with a team all horses', but added that 'a plough of oxen will go as far in a year as a plough of horses', for the reason that 'the malice of ploughmen will not allow the plough

126 '*Cain and his brood*' transported to East Anglia: ploughing with two oxen (in a yoke) and a donkey (in a breast-collar, with well-defined hames). From the Holkham Bible Picture Book.

[of horses] to go beyond their pace, no more than the plough of oxen'. (Walter's tract on husbandry forms the earliest English document on the subject, but Lynn White has observed that his text is not without a political agenda, and his assertions must be treated with caution.) The slightly later tract known as the *Seneschaucie* was open-minded on the question, suggesting that 'it is the office of every good Plow-man to know what Cattle [a term covering all domestic animals at this time] are meetest for his draught, as whether Oxen or Horse, or both Oxen and Horse', recommending that 'you shall sort your Plow or Team according to the fashion of your Country'. Ultimately the author again comes down in favour of the ox for ploughing, 'both in respect of the strength, stability, indurance, and fitness for labour', though advising the keeping of 'a Horse draught to do all your forraign abroad businesses'. In the end, the author reiterates, the terrain would determine which is most appropriate:

Now for the mixture of Oxen and Horses together, it falleth out oftentimes that the Plow-man of force must be provided with Cattle of both kind, as if he happen to live in a rocky Country, where the steepness of the Hills, and the narrowness of the ways, will neither suffer Cart, Wain, or Tumbrell to pass; in this case you shall keep Oxen for the Plow to till the ground with, and Horses to carry pots and hooks: the first to carry forth your manure, and the other to bring home your Hay or Corn-harvest, your fuel and other provisions, which are needful for your family, as they do both in Cornwal, and other mountainous Countries, where Carts and Wains, and such like draught, have no possible passage.

Although lack of proper feeding would prove a long-term factor in determining the poor quality of the medieval horse, it remained significantly more expensive to feed than the ox since it demanded an element of cereal in its fodder. Walter of Henley advised that plough-horses should be stalled for 25 weeks from 18 October to 3 May and fed every night with 'at least the sixth part' of a bushel of oats and with chaff – a ration that in practice was often exceeded several times over. Cattle, by comparison, were lucky if they got more than hay or straw, supplemented by foliage in times of shortage. John Langdon has analysed the costs tabulated by Walter and pronounced them not wholly accurate, principally on the basis that they exclude the cost of straw – a major expense in the case of the ox, whose true costs he estimates none the less at 70 per cent that of a horse. Shoeing added further demands: 1s. 1d. is estimated by Trow-Smith as the annual cost of shoeing the medieval horse, compared with only 3d. for an ox, where needed – notably on flinty soils where its hooves would be at risk, or when the ground became baked hard by the sun or reduced to a quagmire by seasonal rains. Closely datable ox-shoes are hard to find, but examples with wavy edges as illustrated by Sparkes correspond to the fashion in horseshoes in the early medieval period. According to Langdon they became more widely distributed in the later medieval centuries, although their adoption was neither universal nor rapid: excavated examples from this period include those published by Beresford from Goltho (Lincolnshire) and by Holden from Hangleton (Sussex).

Opinion over the respective merits of the two animals continued to be divided for 500 years and more. At the end of the eighteenth century George Culley regretted that there were by that time fewer oxen used in the draught and fewer still were kept to maturity: only in the north-east of England and the south of Scotland was the traditional practice maintained, the custom elsewhere being to sell the beasts by five years old at the latest. Culley himself favoured a mixed economy, with oxen reserved for the heavy draught work: he and his brother in partnership employed at that time about 150 oxen, some singly in carts, some in pairs for ploughing. The trend towards the horse was a pernicious one, he felt, adding that 'I heartily wish our legislature would take this matter into consideration, and give premiums to encourage the rearing and drawing of oxen.' Culley had no time for mixed teams, since 'the difference of the step is so very unequal'.

Even the harness of the horse was considerably more expensive than the rudimentary yoking system employed with the ox, although by the turn of the nineteenth century, at least, experiments were being made amongst 'practical men' to see if the pulling power of the ox could be improved by use of a structured collar as had transformed the tractive efficiency of the horse (see p. 15). Arthur Young, formerly secretary to the Board of Agriculture (founded in 1793) and editor of the influential *Annals of Agriculture* from 1784 to 1815, reports from Sussex in 1813, as follows.

The mode of working their oxen in this county has, from the earliest ages, been the established one of bows and yokes, both single and double. Oxen in collars are a late improvement . . . Some very sensible men, who have worked them in yokes, and afterwards with collars, have gone so far as to say, that three in harness are competent to as much work as four the other way . . . The Rev. Mr Davies, of Glynde, some few years ago, worked oxen singly in collars, and found it to answer exceedingly well. He worked them gently at first, and five in collars did the work of eight in yokes, and with equal ease.

Other instances are cited which had met with equal success, although a Mr Pennington, steward to Lord Ashburnham, found that while harnessing his oxen increased their efficiency, they needed so much additional nourishment to undertake the extra work expected of them that it cancelled out all the benefits. Pennington was led to conclude that 'in all severe or quick labour, horses are undoubtedly to be preferred, and oxen are only profitably employed in easy regular business, without any perceptible inconvenience'. By the time oxen reached the end of the road as traction animals, collars rather than yokes had become the standard method of harnessing (illus. 127).

On the matter of their longer-term value there was little competition, for the ox had the ultimate advantage that it could be retired to pasture for a few months' fattening before being sold for slaughter, while the horse simply declined in usefulness until ultimately it made little more than a dinner

for the local hunting hounds. The discrepancy in their respective values at the end of their working lives had been summarized by Walter of Henley: 'And when the horse is old and worn out then there is nothing but the skin; and when the ox is old with ten pennyworth of grass he shall be fit for the larder, or will sell for as much as he cost.' Although values changed over the years, the principles remained true. William Marshall calculated that for horses depreciation alone, calculated at £2 per annum, was costing the country at least £1 million a year, pointing out too that if all the work were done by oxen, the extra beef available would supply 100,000 people with an extra pound of meat each day. The matter had implications for the national economy and even for national security: writing in the year of the Battle of Trafalgar, Thomas Horne equates the growing taste for draught horses with the loss of supply of 'good beef for home consumption, and especially for the use of that meritorious class of subjects, the BRITISH SAILORS'. But while the Navy continued to welcome them, it might be observed

127 Harrowing with longhorn oxen in harness in collars, Aldbourne (Wiltshire), 1911. The team of ploughman and driver remained standard for as long as oxen remained in use.

that advances in the breeding of beef cattle had by this time rendered retired working animals much less palatable to the population at large, so that ultimately even this advantage was denied to the ox.

Wagons and Ploughs

As late as the turn of the nineteenth century, farm wagons remained in a fairly primitive state and absorbed inordinate amounts of horse power (or ox power) in their usage. Writing in 1790 Marshall condemns the typical Midlands wagon, 14 or 15 feet long in the body, for its 'awkwardness, clumsiness, unwieldiness, and all together, in the present state of the roads, its unfitness for a farmer's use'. A few years later Horne can be found bemoaning the continuing English predilection for large teams of animals pulling the biggest load possible: in these enormous vehicles, he points out, everything (including the wheels) had to be constructed on a massive scale so that the sheer weight of the wagon itself became problematic, both in cost of construction and in the weight it presented even in an unladen state for the animals to pull – animals that could have been more gainfully employed elsewhere.

Four-wheeled wagons seem to have been a novelty introduced to the farm from the Netherlands in the course of the second half of the sixteenth century, although they had been in more restricted use in aristocratic households for several centuries before that time (see p. 64). Two-wheeled carts had hitherto predominated on the farm – although they were by no means considered essential: many farmers used their horses simply as pack animals, with panniers slung across their backs or with saddles fitted with load-bearing frameworks: as late as 1796 William Marshall

could report from Devon that 'there was not a pair of wheels in the county'. In the uplands they remained of limited use up to the threshold of the twentieth century, the slide-car or sledge providing the principal means of moving heavy or bulky loads on the farm. Typical medieval carts, although made as lightly as possible, remained a considerable burden: more than one illustration in the Luttrell Psalter (*c.* 1340) shows three horses at a time harnessed to a cart, one between the shafts and the others in traces hitched to their collars (illus. 128).

Early wagons were even more fearsomely heavy and had the additional disadvantage of being extremely difficult to manoeuvre before the development in the seventeenth century of the movable fore-carriage, allowing the front axle to pivot. John Aubrey noted that in southern Wiltshire they had been almost unknown before about 1655, but that henceforth they were adopted with such enthusiasm that carts were now 'grown quite out of fashion'. A diversity of styles quickly developed, partly influenced by the landscape in which they were to operate, with larger versions predominating in East Anglia, for example, and smaller ones in the narrow-laned countryside of the south-west. Two principal types emerged, one with a box-like body supported on large (up to 6 feet in diameter) rear wheels and with smaller wheels at the front, challenged in some areas by more elegant bow-wagons as described by David Viner, in which the longitudinal timbers rise in a gentle sweep over the rear wheels.

More progressive farmers were by the early nineteenth century beginning to turn to what Horne calls the 'Irish cart', with a square bed and two small-diameter wheels with wide rims tucked in beneath the bed. He was also approving of the 'Cornish wain' – a flat-bed cart with arches over the wheels so that the sheaves or other loads could

phanasti in terra sanctuarium eius.
estruxisti omnes sepes eius : posu

128 Despite its unconventional driver, this illustration provides an impressively detailed record of a typical cart of the mid-14th century, with wattled sides and ladder extensions. The wheel-horse is harnessed to the shafts by means of a cart-saddle, while the others are in traces. Four centuries later Per Kalm noted that reins were seldom used in England even with six-horse teams, control being exercised by 'the various and particular calls of the driver'. From the Luttrell Psalter (c. 1340).

be built up over them. Within a few decades, however, the 'Scotch cart' with a bed that could be tipped-up to discharge its load began to predominate and remained the most popular and versatile form up to the twentieth century. The bigger carthorses of the era proved well adapted to these carts, but ultimately both were displaced with the advent of the tractor.

Ploughs were similarly characterized by a massive construction in timber up to the point at which light ploughs in iron came to be introduced at the turn of the nineteenth century. Wheeled ploughs were already in use by the time of the Conquest, as illustrated, for example, in the tenth-century Caedmon manuscript, but most were swing ploughs (without wheels), built around a solid oak beam – the Kentish variety, for example, was no less than 10 feet long. The earliest account of regional types is that included by Walter Blith

in his *English Improver Improved* of 1652 (illus. 129), where examples are shown of both double wheels and double mould-boards.

Along with the plough, harrows – for breaking up the earth turned over by the ploughshare – had been amongst the earliest implements associated with the horse. Early types had been made with wooden tines that could be hammered down progressively as they were worn away by friction; beyond being used in greater numbers – up to five sets being towed along together on the more purposeful farms by several horses – their principal refinement was to have the wooden tines replaced by iron spikes, latterly fitted to the timber baulks by screw-nuts. Alongside these a more primitive form survived, as recommended for improving grassland by Gervase Markham in his *Farewell to Husbandry* (illus. 130), whose antiquity can only be guessed at:

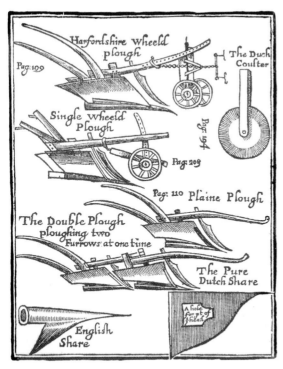

129 A range of regional ploughs: woodcut illustration from Walter Blith's *English Improver Improved* (1652).

You shall cut down a . . . Hauthorn-tree, and make sure that it be wonderful thick bushie and rough grown; which done you shall plash it as flat as you can, and spread it as broad as you can, and those branches or boughes which of necessity you must cut in sunder, you shall again plash and thrust into the body of the Tree, binding them with cords or withs so fast thereto, that may by no means scatter or shake out . . . and that all the roughness may be as in a flat level equally touch the ground; when you have thus proportioned your Harrow, you shall then take great loggs of wood, or pieces of timber, and with ropes bind them on the upperside of this rough Harrow, that the poise or weight of them may keep the rough side hard, and firm to the earth . . .

To the big end of this harrow, you shall fix a strong rope with a Single-tree with Treats, Coller, and Harness, and one Horse is fully sufficient to draw it round about the pasture or meadow: so with this harrow you shall harrow the ground all over, and it will not onely break all the hard clots to a very fine dust, but also disperse them and drive Them into the ground, and give such a comfort to the tender roots of the young grass, that newly springing, that it will double and treble the increase.

A similar implement made with sloes is mentioned by Per Kalm as being used on fallow land in mid-eighteenth-century Hertfordshire, principally for spreading manure over pasture. The type survived in use up to the nineteenth century, when Horne writes of it as being chiefly used for harrowing dung or seeds into grassland. In more structured versions of these harrows, thorn branches might be woven into a section of hurdling or into an old gate that had come to the end of its useful

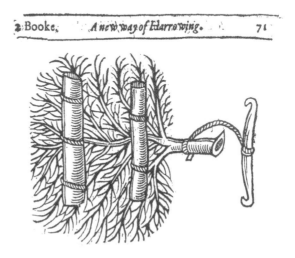

130 Bush-harrow with swingletree, from Gervase Markham's *Farewell to Husbandry* (1660). The branch is here weighed down by billets of wood, roped in place.

life, and two wheels might lift the forepart of the framework off the ground.

Horses were ever the favoured animals for harrowing, their brisk pace not only ensuring rapid completion but also causing the clods to be broken up more effectively than by the slower-moving ox. Industrialization caught up with the traditional implement with the development in the 1800s of zigzag harrows and disc-harrows, all made of iron.

The only other implements in early use were rollers, with which newly sown (or newly germinated) seed was compacted into the soil: Tusser writes that 'Some rowleth their barlie, straight after a raine, when first it appeareth, to leavell it plaine'. Early rollers were generally of timber, later replaced by iron.

With the advent of new methods of crop husbandry promoted by Jethro Tull, Charles Townshend and their contemporaries in the eighteenth century, a wider range of implements for mechanized tilling and planting came into use – all of them lighter in construction and favouring the use of the horse in their operation. Tull's system of 'horse-hoeing husbandry' depended on the planting of crops (particularly root vegetables) in orderly rows with the aid of his improved seed-drill, and the control of weeds thereafter with the aid of the horse-drawn hoe. An ever-increasing variety of drill-ploughs was added from this time onwards. Another era may be said to have opened with the invention in 1812 by John Common of Denwick (Northumberland) of the prototype of the modern mowing machine – provoking the hostility of his agricultural neighbours to such a degree that he was forced to emigrate to America; there, after further development work, it was patented by McCormick and brought back to the Great Exhibition of 1851, where it is said to have scored probably the greatest instantaneous success that any farm implement has enjoyed.

EIGHTEENTH-CENTURY IMPROVERS

From the early eighteenth century new attitudes to the improvement of specific types – and ultimately breeds – of livestock began to assert themselves. Up to this point only a very tenuous understanding of the principles of breeding had prevailed on the farm and the practice of always selling the best stock in order to maximize immediate returns – or of gelding the best animals for the draught – leaving only the poorer specimens to perpetuate the population, was a recipe for at best stagnation and at worst for a progressive loss of quality.

By the eighteenth century a constituency of dedicated improvers from widely disparate backgrounds had established itself, including notably Jethro Tull and Charles Townshend as already mentioned, and later in the century Robert Bakewell (illus. 131), Thomas Coke (later 1st Lord Leicester) and John, 15th Baron Somerville. The search for improvement proved an extraordinary social leveller, in which the aristocracy (and even the king himself) could be found vying with yeoman breeders to produce supreme animals. Amongst the latter the name of Bakewell, of Dishley Grange near Loughborough (Leicestershire), stands out in relation to the animal world, although his contribution was by no means unique and he undoubtedly built on improvements already instituted by others.

Prominent amongst those engaged in the early years of this movement was John Webster of Canley, near Coventry (Warwickshire), some of whose best Longhorn cattle were acquired around 1740–50 from the herd of Sir Thomas Gresley at Drakelow (Staffordshire). Bakewell's initial success has been attributed by some writers to his acquisition of breeding animals from Canley, although there is evidence that his own cattle were already

131 *Robert Bakewell at Dishley Grange*, by John Boultbee, *c.* 1785, oil on canvas. Represented as an unpretentious yeoman on his no-nonsense bay cob, only the group of Longhorn cattle in the background allude to Bakewell's prowess as a breeder and entrepreneur.

exceptional by the date in question. Others have observed that Webster's successes as a breeder were achieved before any means existed to publicize his improvements to the wider world, although his importance can be gauged from the numbers of later eighteenth-century prize Longhorns with Canley blood flowing in their veins. Robert Fowler of Little Rollright (Oxfordshire) also benefited from the introduction of Canley genes to his herd and in his use of inbreeding of close relatives he was said by Trow-Smith to have 'out-Bakewelled

Bakewell'. For a time his cattle commanded prices ten times that of the average. It is to Fowler that the principal accolades for the breeding of Long-horns is given: the dispersal of his stock by auction at his death is considered one of the most significant events in the annals of eighteenth-century improvement.

Bakewell remains, none the less, the most note-worthy breeder of his generation and may stand to illustrate the principal movements of the age. His work with sheep was most successful, although that too was supported by the work of others. The origins of his improved stock can be traced to Joseph Allom of Clifton (Nottinghamshire) who was, according to Marshall, 'the first to distinguish himself in the Midland District for a superior breed of sheep'. Bakewell's close friend and second cousin Thomas Paget is also deserving of recognition here: as well as meeting success with sheep-breeding, Paget was a breeder of much-admired bulls, one of which sold at his dispersal sale in 1793 for as much as 400 guineas. Several other cousins who were also prominent sheep-breeders are mentioned by Wykes, all of whom used Dishley stock for propagating: he comments on the advantages to Bakewell's self-promotion of this network of breeders, widening the gene pool of his stock and with it his reputation – a reputation deserving of closer attention.

The improvements Bakewell brought with his work on sheep, pigs and cattle (and to a lesser degree with horses) were not necessarily the most long-lasting of their kind or ultimately the most successful, but the mixture of natural intelligence and showmanship with which he was blessed has meant that his name is remembered when those of his less assertive contemporaries are largely forgotten. His talent for self-advertisement also found a ready outlet in the agricultural press that began to gain a foothold at this time; it was greatly to his advantage that he found timely support from talented journalists – enthusiasts such as William Marshall and Arthur Young.

In contrast to those farmers who turned their efforts to improving the general level of their herds, Bakewell's business lay strictly in first-class breeding stock, producing the best animals he could and then hiring them out at considerable profit to those who sought to enhance the blood-lines of their own beasts – a striking innovation in itself: Marshall described him as 'the only man

. . . who confines his practice solely to breeding and letting'. Bakewell's achievement lay not so much in innovation as in the successful application to his task of principles with which others were already experimenting.

Bakewell is said to have adopted from the breeders of racehorses in particular the techniques of 'in-and-in' breeding: Marshall certainly considered it a practice 'in a degree established by the gentlemen of the turf' at Newmarket, though doubt has been cast on this claim. The practice involved careful selection of strains displaying particularly desirable features, the animals possessing appropriate qualities then being repeatedly inbred with their own close relations in order to accentuate those features and to 'fix' them on a permanent basis. Improvements can be won more quickly by this method, and that which Bakewell sought in particular was 'a natural propensity to acquire a state of fatness, at an early age' – and at least cost.

Having mastered these principles, Bakewell assiduously applied the technique and marketed the services of his breeding males at a handsome profit. In this he was again following the lead of others, notably the sheep-breeders of Lincolnshire who were already in the habit of letting their rams to fee-paying farmers. Bakewell too earned most of his money from leasing rams for tupping, although he also popularized the practice for cattle. Letting in this way carried a number of advantages: being a specialist breeder with no interest in building a flock, he could afford to cull the least successful offspring in a way that no livestock farmer could contemplate; it also allowed the progeny of his beasts to become widely dispersed in a short space of time. After a slow start, prices for his rams gradually rose from under 10 guineas to 100 guineas; by 1789 he received 3,000 guineas in the space of twelve months, with his three best rams accounting for 1,200 guineas between them.

His greatest success came with the New Leicester breed (illus. 132), praised by Culley for its 'clean head, straight, broad, flat back, the barrel-like form of the body, fine small bones, thin pelt and inclination to early maturity', and contrasted by Marshall with the Old Leicester: had a naturalist encountered the latter on a mountain, Marshall suggested, he 'might have deemed him a cross between a sheep and a goat'.

Investors in all these expensively won genes, anxious to protect the value of their assets and to achieve similarly high repute for their own stock,

formed themselves into an exclusive club known as the Dishley Society, with the result that the valuable breeds Bakewell had succeeded in creating were propagated on an increasingly wide front and brought him the bonus of being able to observe the progeny of his animals in the flocks of others and to refine his methods of selection at minimal personal risk.

Unfortunately, his finances proved disastrously weak: his overheads (including the cost of feed and transport for the breeding stock) were excessively high, his wage bill was considerable and he

132 *Richard Meek of Dunstall Hall, with his prize New Leicester Ram*, by John Boultbee. The 'improved Leicester' was the most influential of Bakewell's experiments in breeding.

incurred a great deal of cost in entertaining potential customers (and the merely curious) on an overlavish scale; he was also plagued by many debtors in default. (Culley observed that due to his heavy expenditure Bakewell would never be rich till he earned £2,000 a year.) Eventually he was declared bankrupt and the stock at Dishley (as well as the premises themselves) were ordered to be sold. Fortunately, Bakewell managed to keep a good part of stock as well as a lease on Dishley: many of his greatest successes were indeed achieved after this period of crisis.

Neither was the method of breeding propounded by Bakewell achieved without cost to the animals, for in-and-in breeding carried with it the risk of perpetuating inherent weaknesses as well as strengths and in time these began to make themselves all too apparent. The success (at least at a regional level) that he achieved with his favoured Longhorn cattle, for example, in which he successfully improved the quality of the meat, the thickness of the hide and the weight of the skeleton, resulted also in a marked reduction in milk yield and a falling off in fecundity – a common result of inbreeding. Amongst the improved sheep and pigs too, improved times in reaching maturity (his New Leicester breed was ready for the butcher at 27 months instead of 39 months for its unimproved progenitors, saving 20 per cent of production costs) were bought at a cost in the quality of the mutton and pork, which proved so prone to fat that beasts had to be slaughtered young; wool quality also fell amongst the improved sheep.

Another blow to the immediate achievements of this talented generation of improvers came when the Longhorns on which they had lavished so much of their efforts fell from favour and within a few generations became virtually extinct. Shorthorn cattle, whose distribution in the eastern counties of central England initially had been complementary to that of the Longhorns in the west, began to find favour and to colonize those areas which proved amenable to their more delicate constitution.

By this time more general improvements were being brought about by increasing use of root crops for fodder and also by supplements such as imported cattle-cake. Improved diet as much as breeding was responsible for an increase in the average weight of beef cattle at Smithfield from 370 pounds in 1710 to 800 pounds in 1795. In the course of the following century reliance on imported grain and other foodstuffs became ever greater, ultimately precipitating a crisis as prices for home-grown products tumbled from the 1870s onwards: in the face of American and other imports of beef as well as foodstuffs, land values collapsed, although some stock breeders and dairymen in general continued to prosper.

RECORDING THE AGE OF IMPROVEMENT

Until the eighteenth century gave birth to an unprecedented wave of interest in domesticated animals, their place in the visual record had been largely symbolic, serving a (literally) marginal role, perhaps, in manuscript illumination, appearing in emblematic or generic form in the crude woodcuts that served to illustrate early tracts or as mere background ornament in seventeenth-century 'prospects' of aristocratic estates. In keeping with Enlightenment preoccupations with creating new, ideal forms for particular strains of animals that ultimately would emerge as formalized breeds, animal painting gradually emerged as a genre in its own right, spawning in turn a minor industry that disseminated its most famous images in the form of prints. These animal portraitists – largely distinct from the genre painters who recorded

133 *The Lincolnshire Ox*, by George Stubbs, 1790, oil on canvas. Prints were reproduced from this painting and sold wherever the animal (which stood 19 hands high) was exhibited.

countryside scenes for their own sake – ranged in ability from provincial amateurs whose naive paintings found a natural home in the farm cottage to skilled practitioners commissioned to celebrate the specific achievements of aristocratic or wealthy breeders or to illustrate the series of surveys of animal types that began to proliferate at this time. A high degree of documentary accuracy was expected from these representations: certainly the most purposeful records sought to distinguish the finer points of anatomy and physiognomy that separated one desirable breed from another. It was work that could be paid well enough: Elspeth Moncrieff quotes one painter, Ben Marshall, as quipping that 'many a man will pay me fifty guineas for painting his horse who thinks ten guineas too much for painting his wife'.

The majority of these works were a long way from the polished and sophisticated canvases of the likes of George Stubbs and others who specialized in the horseflesh that captivated race-goers of the day; Stubbs himself, however, was drawn into recording the 'Lincolnshire Ox' (illus. 133), one of the oversized prodigies that toured the country in his day, in addition to a range of disparate animals – wild as well as domestic – from elk to leopards. In contrast to the highly dramatized compositions favoured by Stubbs, which helped demonstrate his exceptional skills as an artist, the subjects represented by the rank and file of livestock painters

134 *Prize Sheep being fed with Turnips*, by W. H. Davis, 1838, oil on canvas. Compared with the naturalistic representation given in illus. 132, the scale and conformation of the sheep have here been enhanced to lend it an increased – almost menacing – presence.

are normally posed in a static manner, very often in profile, commonly with no more background than the stall or the farmyard but occasionally enlivened by a glimpse of landscape. A low viewpoint was generally favoured, since it threw the subject into dramatic relief. Amongst the less competent, perspective often presented difficulties – if it was not actively distorted in order to emphasize further bulk of the subject: human figures in attendance, whether representing herdsmen or owners, are often dwarfed by the principal subjects, even

when it might be a sheep rather than a carthorse (illus. 134). A few names call for special mention.

The reputation of the wood-engraver Thomas Bewick (1753–1828), whose own *General History of Quadrupeds* (1790) sold a remarkable 14,000 copies, led to him being commissioned to record animals for one of the Board of Agriculture's surveys. His insistence on veracity was noteworthy: he records that on one occasion it was represented to him by an aggrieved owner that he, Bewick, had not made the subjects fat enough in his image; he declined to amend his drawing on that occasion, but many of his fellows were certainly less scrupulous. His closely observed documentary work is exemplified by his comparisons of Old (or unimproved) and New (improved) Teeswater sheep (illus. 135).

James Ward (1769–1859) was a talented painter and engraver, elected to the Royal Academy in 1811; he was considered the greatest animal painter of his day. In his early career he produced genre scenes recalling those of his brother-in-law George Morland, but later was commissioned by the Board of Agriculture to undertake 200 paintings of all the native breeds of domestic livestock, to be prepared precisely to scale as accurate records. The project (financed by the publisher Boydell, who was to prepare engravings of each of the images) received the personal direction of Lord Somerville and the 5th Duke of Bedford (who provided the necessary letters of introduction); at their bidding he visited many of the most successful breeders of the day, starting with John Ellman of Glynde (p. 470) before undertaking extended tours in the south-west, the West Midlands and in Wales. Not infrequently he found his subjects (having already reached the peak of

their condition) were destined for imminent slaughter, requiring him to work all night by candlelight before they were dispatched the following morning. Sadly, the projected publication series fell through and his carefully prepared drawings and finished paintings, representing the most comprehensive survey of its kind ever undertaken, were dispersed. In a sense the collapse of this documentary project cleared the way for the development of his artistic success: a flood of private commissions followed which led to Ward continuing his itinerant career, though by now touring seats of aristocracy and the wealthy breeders. He was particularly valued by them as a reliable painter of horses; he undertook commissions for both George III and George IV.

Less well documented is John Boultbee, one of the painters sufficiently well regarded to meet the exacting needs of Robert Bakewell (see illus. 131), for whom he executed several paintings. He was also commissioned in 1802 to make a painting of the famous *Durham Ox* – an improved Shorthorn of enormous size – for its owner, John Day: the latter intended that a print should be produced from Boultbee's work, and within a year 2,000 copies had been sold.

135 Teeswater sheep in (a) unimproved and (b) improved form, by Thomas Bewick. Unlike some other artists prepared to indulge in a degree of flattery and exaggeration, Bewick's sheep have all the hallmarks of verisimilitude.

136 *Ram-Letting*, by Thomas Weaver, 1810, oil on canvas. In recent years the setting has been identified as the premises of Thomas Morris of Barton upon Humber (Lincolnshire). Following the success of Robert Bakewell's enterprise in letting his improved rams to farmers for breeding purposes, scenes such as these became commonplace.

Thomas Weaver, already mentioned, was a pupil of Boultbee's. Weaver, who lived in Shrewsbury, made a successful career as an animal painter, his subjects frequently being brought to his studio so that he could capture their likeness. He started out painting horses and dogs for the local aristocracy, but quickly became established in the more general field of livestock painting, recording several Shorthorns belonging to his patrons the breeders Charles and Robert Colling and to others in the field. Weaver's work took him from the Midlands as far as the Scottish border, often involving protracted stays at the homes of his aristocratic clients, who included Coke of Norfolk and the Earl of Bradford. His most ambitious conversation piece, his *Ram-Letting* in the Tate, is now identified as representing the premises of Thomas Morris of Barton upon Humber (illus. 136).

William Shiels (1783–1857) enjoyed success as a portrait painter in America for some years before returning to his native Scotland where he began to work with David Low, professor of agriculture at Edinburgh, in the production of a series of paintings of many local varieties of animals which were then on the verge of obliteration. The subjects were initially to be selected by Low and the paintings used by him as teaching aids; they formed the centrepiece of an agricultural museum he established, which by 1843 contained 100 of Shiels's paintings. The sheep, pigs and goats were drawn at life-size in this exercise (illus. 137), while the cattle and horses were recorded at a scale of 1:2. Over half of these were lithographed for publication in Low's two-volume book, *The Breeds of the Domestic Animals of the British Isles* (1842), which set out his ideas on preservation and breeding of these valuable indigenous species. Shiels, who had been brought up in rural Berwickshire, evidently became entrusted with a great deal of the final decision-making and on many occasions it was he rather than Low who made the final choice of subject.

Occupying a place of special interest amongst these artists is George Garrard (1760–1826). As a painter he was moderately successful, enjoying the patronage of several wealthy and aristocratic patrons, for whom he also produced relief sculptures of animal subjects; after becoming an associate of the Royal Academy in 1800, he exhibited there no fewer than 215 works, including numerous animal compositions in marble, bronze and plaster. These led in time to a more purposeful programme involving the production of accurate scale-models of domestic animals, which are of lasting scientific interest (illus. 138). It was evidently the enlightened members of the Board of Agriculture and like-minded improvers who steered him in this direction, to judge by a notice he placed in the *Annals of Agriculture* in 1798:

The Board of Agriculture having patronized several attempts at delineating Live Stock of different countries by Painting and engraving,

137 *A Berkshire Pig*, by William Shiels, *c.* 1835, oil on canvas. The Berkshire is here recorded in its 'unimproved' state, with a mottled colouration, before it became a uniformly black pig.

and it having occurred to the author of this work that a Picture (although it gives a most lively idea of colour, and general effect) rather exhibits a section or contour of the Animal than its real image, as ideas of thickness cannot adequately be conveyed with those of length and height, he was therefore induced to make proposals for executing Models of the Improved Breeds of British Cattle, in which the exact proportion, in every point, should be accurately preserved.

His plan was submitted to the Board of Agriculture, and had the honour of meeting with considerable encouragement, being referred by a Committee of that Board to the Duke of Bedford, and the Earl of Egremont .

Models were in consequence prepared from the best specimens that could be procured under the inspection of those noblemen, and being examined at a Committee of the Board of Agriculture, were much approved.

Garrard's seriousness of purpose was underlined for the reader:

These works are not intended merely as matters of curiosity, [for] they exhibit at once, the ideas of the best judges of the times, respecting the most improved shape in the different kinds of Livestock – Ideas which have seldom been obtained without great expence and the practice of many years. It is presumed that, by applying to works of this kind, the difficulty of acquiring a just knowledge upon the subject may be considerably removed; and also, that distant countries, where they may be sent, will be enabled to form very perfect ideas of the high state of cultivation in which the domestic animals are produced

138 Model by George Garrard of a shorthorn ox, probably the 'Durham Ox' of the Holderness breed, also illustrated in the same artist's *Description of the Different Varieties of Oxen* (1800).

at this day in Great Britain; and should further progress be made, these Models will shew what has already been done, and may be a sort of standard whereby to measure the improvements of future times.

The livestock models, prepared 'upon a scale from nature, of two inches and a quarter to a foot', were offered to subscribers at a price of 2 guineas plain or 3 three guineas 'coloured after nature'. Garrard anticipated that 'Some observations will be published with each number, descriptive of the cattle, and the soil where they are bred in the highest perfection, with other interesting particulars'; in the event, two volumes of aquatints were published in 1800 under the title *A Description of the Different Varieties of Oxen Common in the British Isles* (reprinted on several occasions, testifying to a wide interest), but no similar treatment followed for the other species. A permanent display was also mounted at the 'Agricultural Museum' he established at his home at Hanover Square in London, and where they were considered (a shade too grandly, perhaps) to rival 'the greatest statuaries of Greece'.

Juliet Clutton-Brock has surveyed the models known to have been produced by Garrard, examples of which survive at the Natural History Museum and at Woburn Abbey – the latter since diminished by a sale (Christie's, 20–21 September 2004, lots 200–208); Stephen Deuchar mentions others at South Hill (Berkshire). From completion of Garrard's first essays in this medium on 1 July 1799 until 31 May 1810 – the date incised on many of the surviving models – at least 21 breeds of cattle, sheep and pigs are found to have been represented in this way.

For these models alone the name of Garrard deserves to be celebrated, though his reputation as an artist never reached the heights to which he aspired, despite (or perhaps in some sense because

of) the over-ambitious scale of some of his works: his *Woburn Sheep-Shearing* of 1804, for example, is thronged with over 100 animals and 200 human subjects; he later published it as an engraving (illus. 139), together with a lengthy explanatory text. Garrard died without gaining the full recognition he craved, leaving an impoverished widow; many of his original moulds, as well as castings from them, were sold at auction by Martin & Johnson following the death of his heir in 1870.

ANIMALS ON DISPLAY

By the opening years of the nineteenth century some 30 regional agricultural shows were already in being. Their origins are to be found in meetings such as the annual sheep-shearings at Holkham

139 *The Woburn Sheep-Shearing*, etching by M. N. Bate after George Garrard, 1811. Garrard's original painting of 1804, though full of detail and with many individual portraits, is less easy to read at a small scale.

Hall, turned into a public event by Thomas Coke, and that at Woburn illustrated in illus. 139. These quickly came to include displays of finely bred animals and new developments in agricultural machinery; ploughing matches came to form a regular accompaniment. To these stimuli may be added the activities of the Society of Arts in London which had given premiums for deserving mechanical inventions since its foundation in 1754, as well as the formation of the Board of Agriculture in 1793 – the first organization dedicated to the national farming interest. More indirectly, it may be suggested that the growth of what might be called the cult of personality amongst both breeders and their prize animals served also to crystallize interest across the country.

The Board of Agriculture's first show was held at Aldridge's Repository in St Martin's Lane in April 1821 with a few dozen animals, mostly Shorthorn cattle plus some 40 pens of sheep. Unfortunately the government's grant to the Board was withdrawn thereafter, leading to its being wound up in 1822. In this year the Scottish Fat Stock Show was inaugurated by the Highland and Agricultural Society, followed six years later by the founding of the English Agricultural Society, soon to receive a charter as the Royal Agricultural Society, with the motto 'Practice with Science'. The Society held its first show in Oxford in 1839, when it attracted 20,000 visitors and had 247 entries. Competitors came from an astonishingly wide area: a group of Shorthorns famously made the three-week journey from Yorkshire on foot and still carried off several prizes for their owner. Twenty implement-makers took part, testifying to the burgeoning nature of this sector: by the time the show was held at Cambridge in 1840 one manufacturer, Ransomes, exhibited no fewer than 86 varieties of plough. As the Society's engineer reported two years later: 'The manufacture even of the common implements has already to a great extent passed out of the hands of the village ploughwright and hedgeside carpenter, and become transferred to makers possessed of great intelligence, skill and capital.' (The last Royal Show was held in 2009: visitor and exhibitor numbers had been falling for some years as interest once more became centred on regional exhibitions, with the Royal Norfolk Show, the Royal Cornwall Show and the Great Yorkshire Show each reporting rising visitor numbers of up to 200,000; having come full circle, interest is now refocused on regional responses to farming issues.)

ANIMAL BY-PRODUCTS

As well as their primary value as sources of food and traction (and in the case of sheep, of wool), a number of secondary industries came to depend on farming livestock for their raw materials. The skins of every animal from lambs to horses formed the basis of a country-wide leatherworking industry. Every town with a flesh-market was likely to support also a community of leatherworkers, often installed down-river on the edge of town so that pollution from their noxious processing operations was minimized. These involved the soaking of horse and cattle hides in lime to loosen the hair and to make fibres absorb the tanning solution; scraping and 'bating' in a vat of excrement from dogs or fowls in order to soften them; followed by months (or even years) of soaking in oak-bark solution in large pits. The tanners sold on their hides to curriers for softening, oiling, waterproofing with tallow, shaving to thickness, staining and graining, before the various leather trades took control of them.

Calf skins and sheep skins underwent a different process, being cured by a process of 'tawing' with gypsum that required no permanent installations as described above and evidently was carried out at a household level as well as by specialist workshops. This at least is the implication of the Act Touching the Transporting of Tawed Leather, made of Sheep-skins and Lamb-skins (1565) which mentions that 'great multitudes of the Queen's majesty's liege people have been set on work by converting of sheep-skins and lamb-skins into tawed leather and parchment' and which allows their products henceforth to be freely exported in order to contribute to their maintenance.

Tallow was also a major by-product, and sales to tallow-chandlers provided an important source of revenue for the butcher. Ideal cattle were considered to be those that had not only reached maturity as beef animals but which were also 'well tallowed'. In addition to having an important function in the production of candles (tallow candles outsold those of wax by a factor of 100 times in the early nineteenth century), it also provided a basis for soap, being mixed with olive oil and boiled for several hours with potash.

Having flayed the ox and found a buyer for its skin, the skinner had the task of separating its horns (normally left intact with the skin up to the point of sale). These would be destined for processing by the horner. After soaking in a pit for a matter of weeks or months (depending on the season) the membrane attaching the sheath of keratinous horn to its bony core would have decayed to the point where the horn could be pulled off with ease. If the horn was to be worked into a cylindrical beaker or a box, the manufacturing process might follow straight away, but commonly the sheath would be further soaked, warmed in water, slit and opened out into a sheet; large numbers of such sheets could be pressed flat under pressure between warmed metal plates, after which they were ready to be cut to form combs,

spectacles, fans or other implements, or further split and clarified to produce thin panes for horn lanterns (lanthorns) or for windows – a major industry in its own right. Horners formed a regular component of the manufacturing trades in towns up to the nineteenth century; all the industries relying on animals for their raw materials are reviewed in *Bone, Antler, Ivory and Horn* (1985), by the present author.

Even the bony horn-cores which had been discarded by the horners – dumps of which often reveal the presence of horners' workshops on archaeological sites – might find a use as building materials, being built up around garden plots and the like to form walls. Per Kalm describes seeing them, under the heading 'Fences or barriers around meadows, market gardens, &c., of Ox-horn':

An earth-wall is cast up in the usual way . . . When the earth has been cast up to a height of about six inches it is levelled all over the top. Thereupon they have ready to hand a multitude of the quicks or inner parts of Ox-horns; for the outer part of the horn itself, is taken off and sold to comb-makers and others who work in horn . . . The quicks are then set quite close beside one another over the earth that has been cast up for the wall, and this so that the larger and thicker ends of the quick, or that to which a portion of the skull is attached, is turned outwards or lies just in the face of the wall. In this way two rows of quicks are laid, viz.: one row on one side of the wall, and the other on the other, so that the small ends of the horn quicks meet in the middle. Over this is afterwards cast earth about six inches thick, when again in the aforementioned manner is laid a stratum of double-ranged ox-horn quicks,

140 Finely laid pavement of sheep's knuckle-bones at Endsleigh (Devon), built as a fishing lodge for the Duke of Bedford, 1810. The pavement (restored) was laid out as a polite version of a widely used functional type.

viz., so that one row turns the larger ends towards one side, and the other towards the other . . . It is thus continued alternately, with earth and ox-horn quicks until the wall has reached the desired height.

Bones make a further appearance as building materials in the form of floors or pavements made from the articular ends of metcarpals and metatarsals: the shafts of the bones are hammered tightly packed into a prepared bed of earth, so that a flat and durable surface is achieved. They are not infrequently found in cellars, and also in garden features such as covered walkways (illus. 140).

And finally, such animal waste as found no other function could be returned to the fields as fertilizer. This might include offcuts of skin (such as had escaped being boiled down to make glue),

hair scraped from hides by the tanner, burnt bones, blood, entrails and hooves; the latter could be chopped up or, as recommended by William Ellis in his *Practical Farmer* (1732), they could be left entire:

These [the farmer] sticks in the Ground about a Foot asunder, with their broad Ends upright, by first making a Hole with a piece of Iron or Wood . . . and thus be planted an Acre or two or more together. Now by planting these Hoofs upright in the Ground, they are capable of receiving and holding the Rain-Water that falls into them, which in time will corrupt, putrifying, run-over, and water all the Ground between the Hoofs, so that the Roots of the Trees and Hedges, as well as the Corn, will have the benefit of it.

In these ways, the farm animals that had spent their lives bound to the earth were returned to it in the most literal way. In thep following sections their fortunes are examined on a species-by-species basis.

CATTLE

As with other farm animals, the population of early medieval cattle was to be found partly in the ownership of great manorial estates but also distributed in small numbers amongst better off elements of the peasant population. While wealthy landowners might individually have held larger numbers of livestock, on a national scale their animals are likely to have been outnumbered by those owned by smallholders and cottars.

Only from the late thirteenth century can evidence be found for attempts to build up sizeable herds, and even then success proved elusive. Trow-Smith records how the De Lacy family in Lancashire embarked at this time on what he calls 'a major cattle ranching exercise', involving the leasing of land and livestock to keepers and the construction of 80-foot-long shelters of timber and thatch, but low yields, disease and even the depredations of wolves combined to bring about the failure of the project. The earls of Chester also proved innovative in developing at Macclesfield a centralized distribution centre for cattle which ensured that their dispersed estates were kept well stocked and their surplus disposed of in a controlled manner through the county fairs, but these large-scale enterprises remained extremely rare.

During the summer months cattle generally remained out at pasture: Walter of Henley had expected that on demesne farms 'every night the cowherd shall put the cows and other beasts in the fold during the season . . . and he himself shall lie

each night with his cows'. The character of such a fold was probably not very different from that described three centuries later by George Owen in his *Description of Penbrokshire*:

to their order of tillage they seldome use to carie any donge or mucke to their grounde, but use for the most parte a runninge fold of hurdels of cloven oake of about fowre foote heighe & five foote broade, havinge the two side postes sharpened at the lower endes. With an iron barre they make holes and with a woaden sleadge[-hammer] they sett these hurdells fast in the grounde, in such sorte as they are able to keape in any oxen Kine and horses . . . where they meane to till the next yeare, and therein drive their cattell everie night from mydd Marche till mydde November. For the rest of the yeare the nightes are too long & too cold for the Cattell to lie there.

Behind every plough-ox there would have been perhaps two females whose principal role was to produce calves to maintain the strength of the team, generating a little milk periodically and adding their own weight to the plough when not encumbered by the demands of reproduction. Many farms had no other cattle than that maintained for breeding for the plough in this way.

After selection from their progeny of potential breeding stock to maintain the plough-teams of the future, the remaining calves were gelded or spayed as appropriate at the age of about three months, when the cowherd's skill was once again called for: Mascall advises that he should 'tie up the cod with shoemaker's thread till the stones will consume and wear away' – a comparatively benign strategy contrasting with that favoured by the anonymous ['A. S.'] *Husbandman, Farmer, and Grasier's Compleat Instructor* of 1697, which recommends searing off the stones with a hot iron, after which the wound should be anointed with butter and sewn up with fine silk – though it seems doubtful that such a luxury was ever known by the majority of calves.

OXEN

Throughout the medieval period, the majority of cattle were to be found yoked to the cart or the plough, rather than grazing contentedly on the pasture. Traction was normally provided by the males which had been castrated: if this operation were performed before the animals reached maturity they would grow to be considerably larger, heavier and stronger than entire bulls; their horns would also grow longer and thinner. For the hard-pressed small farmer, however, it was not uncommon for breeding females to be pressed into service during the intervals between the production of calves. Thomas Horne recommended that bulls too should be put to the plough.

Thomas Tusser, in his *Five Hundred Pointes of Good Husbandrie* (1580) suggests that three to five years was an appropriate age for designated beasts to be put to work, although over the preceding years the judicious owner would have accustomed them to handling and to human contact by talking to them regularly in a reassuring manner. Some later authorities seem to have expected an earlier start to labour, but all writers agreed that (in contrast to the experience of the average horse) it was only with gentle treatment that cattle could be trained for the yoke; they simply did not respond positively to harsh treatment.

To begin to accustom the animal to its future role, the horns might be bound periodically in order to get it used to the sensation. When first put to the plough or cart, Tusser advises coupling the young animal with a gentle-natured ox; alternatively, it could be placed in a triple yoke with two experienced animals, one to either side, so that they might urge him on or slow him down as appropriate, and stop him lying down on the job. Either way, the work would be at first undemanding and slow in pace, after which the novice would be coupled with a succession of more spirited beasts; in the course of a month or six weeks he was expected to have been broken in, after which he would ideally be matched with animals of similar size and strength. Barren females and oxen alike could be used in the draught up to ten years of age, after which they would be fattened with hay, vetches, grain and pulses, and sold to the butcher. In practice, injury and disease probably reduced the working lives of many by half. The records of a Gloucestershire farm from as late as the 1840s, quoted by B.J.E. Mason, indicate that while a team of twelve working oxen was maintained, four animals would be retired each year and four more brought in to replace them.

Ox teams varied in size according to the soils on which they laboured: on heavy ground eight animals were commonly required to operate the massive beam-plough, a task that was achieved on lighter soils with only two or three. Trow-Smith reports that in Aberdeenshire the normal plough team was from eight to twelve cattle yoked in pairs, while at the opposite end of the country, according to Sir John St Aubyn, deep ploughing was carried out in Cornwall with a mixed team of fourteen oxen and seven horses. Mason suggests that teams of twenty oxen were not unknown. Before the general spread of larger farm units, it was customary – as with many tasks on the early medieval smallholding – for neighbours to collaborate in assembling large teams for seasonal work by pooling resources, each contributing one or more animals according to his ability.

141 Frontispiece from Fitzherbert's *Boke of Husbandry* (1523). The two-ox team and its method of yoking to the plough remain essentially unchanged from that shown in the mid-14th-century Luttrell Psalter (illus. 125).

The customary method of yoking oxen to the plough was commendably simple compared to that of the horse. The system illustrated in the Luttrell Psalter (see illus. 125) remained largely unchanged at the time it was recorded again – rather schematically – in Sir Anthony Fitzherbert's *Boke of Husbandrye* of 1523 (illus. 141). In both cases the plough is attached to a yoke spanning the shoulders of the two draught animals and anchored around their necks; the oxen might similarly be yoked to a cart by means of a single pole, rather than being harnessed within a pair of shafts as later became common. The principal alternative,

as illustrated by Lord Somerville in his *System followed during the two last Years by the Board of Agriculture* (1800), was to tie the beam of the yoke directly to the beasts' horns rather than attaching it round the neck. Use of the breast-collar and harness rather than the yoke, a development that improved the effectiveness of the ox no less than it had transformed the draught horse in the Norman period, is placed in the middle of the eighteenth century. Reviewing this development, Mason asserts that wearing the new design of harness the oxen walked straighter and with a steadier pull, though in addition to the ploughman a boy 'driver' continued to be employed to walk with and regulate the animals (see illus. 127).

Ultimately the introduction of the light iron plough began to tip the balance in favour of horse traction (see p. 424), while the rising price of beef in the nineteenth century turned many farmers in favour of breeding for the market rather than selling their stock only after it had given years of service in harness. Although they were not always used in the most efficient manner at first, by the turn of the nineteenth century the horse had ousted the ox in most areas, with the traditional plough lingering only on the heaviest soils.

BEEF AND MILK

Although it was recognized that some breeds made good milkers while others were better producers of beef (and others again were appreciated for their pulling power in the plough), the distinction was to some degree blurred in the earlier centuries when cattle of whatever persuasion were destined to end their lives with a short period of fattening followed by slaughter for the pot. Few distinctions as to types can be made before the early years of the eighteenth century; the term 'breeds' is certainly too specific at this time – most contemporary authors use the word 'kinds'. The following principal groupings are those observed by George Culley in the latter part of the eighteenth century.

Longhorns (see illus. 127) were the nearest thing to an indigenous, national type, their distribution stretching from northern Scotland down the western side of the country. Apart from their eponymous horns – typically spreading but frequently forming a tight downward curve towards the animal's nose – the principal characteristics of the breed were its thick hide with a long and close coat which might be any shade from red to black. Armitage suggests that from the late fourteenth century its size had been slowly increased by means of small but significant improvements in husbandry. By the time the improvers had finished with it, the Longhorn had become a more refined animal, with a lighter skeleton and thinner hide; its formerly dark and slow-maturing flesh had been bred to a paler form with yellow fat which recommended it to the cook, while its milking properties had been amended to produce a higher fat content, ideal for butter- and cheese-making. Although there were many regional varieties, they had in common rather small size and low (but high-quality) milk yields. Some of the best stock

came from the north-west of England (Culley refers to them as 'the Lancashire kind') and were to play a major role in early experiments at improvement (see pp. 426–7). Indeed, so assiduously were these animals bought up by the Midlands breeders that the supply became exhausted, leading Culley to comment that by his day 'the men of Lancashire had lost their valuable breed before they were sensible of it'.

Shorthorn types were more prolific on the eastern side of England from the border down to Lincolnshire and including several regional sub-types such as the Holderness (illus. 142) and Lincoln. During the seventeenth century, Dutch blood was introduced to good effect into this stock (hence Culley's label of 'the Dutch kind'), and Friesian crosses further improved it later in the 1700s (see below). Their particular strength lay in their capacity to produce high-quality milk, although their customary large size made them valuable for flesh too; Culley mentions, however, that through injudicious crosses some of it was for a time rendered 'as black and coarse as horse-flesh'. A great many regional varieties, from Hereford to Sussex, Gloucester and Devon, mingled the blood of both Longhorns and Shorthorns. The Devon kind were particularly esteemed as good traction animals.

142 George Garrard's aquatint of 'The Wonderful Ox', 1800, a prime specimen of the Holderness breed.

Hornless or 'polled' cattle formed the third major category. The Galloways of south-west Scotland formed an important group; the suggestion has been made that the Red Polls of East Anglia may have arisen from intermixture with Galloway cattle driven south for finishing, but in truth their respective origins remain obscure. The ancestors of today's Aberdeen Angus beef cattle also formed part of this group, as did the Ayrshires, which are milkers.

Culley includes among his principal types the Kyloes of the Scottish Highlands – a small, hardy breed well adapted to survival on the cold, exposed hillsides. These beasts were referred to more generally as 'Black cattle', although they remained until the nineteenth century markedly mixed in colour and race, some of them horned and others polled. They are to be related to the Welsh runts and Cornish and Irish cattle (which Culley thought might have incorporated some Longhorn blood). By his day these were being driven long distances in great numbers every autumn as stores for fattening in the lusher southern counties, particularly in East Anglia, whence they went on to form a mainstay of the stock reaching the London markets.

Other important contributions were made by the milking cattle from the Channel Islands, often referred to as Alderneys but including also the Jerseys and Guernseys. Culley refers to the comparative delicacy of these types, however, which made them unattractive to general farmers. Most were to be found initially at the seats of the seventeenth- and eighteenth-century nobility, where their high-quality milk found an appreciative reception.

So-called 'wild cattle' (see below) formed the last of Culley's groups, although they were thin on the ground. It was observed that these could be kept only within strong fences or stone walls (hence their alternative name of 'park cattle'), and consequently 'very few of them are now to be met with, except in the parks of some gentlemen who keep them for ornament and as a curiosity'.

DROVING AND STORING

Already in the thirteenth century the 'Welshmen who come from the parts of Wales to sell their cattle' were recorded as driving their stock via Ross-on-Wye to market in Gloucester, a trade that gained in momentum over the following centuries. By the 1500s the annual droves of cattle converging on London and the principal provincial cities had been swelled by beasts from as far away as Scotland, while Ireland too had begun to make a contribution via the Welsh ports. Such was the scale of these enforced migrations that the landscape became transected by broad tracks with grass margins termed drove roads that developed to accommodate them: while some of these perpetuated the lines of ancient trackways such as the Icknield Way, others related purely to the period of these mass movements. As frequently as possible, the drovers would follow their own routes through the least-populous parts of the countryside, avoiding the established road system – already overcrowded and, from the introduction of fee-paying turnpikes, increasingly costly for them to use – and establishing instead a network of 'green roads' where the only competition would come from other herds converging on the same destinations. In response to these movements, in which any one herd might easily comprise 200 cattle or more, markets and depots sprang up along the routes, together with blacksmiths offering shoeing services and also tanneries, horn-works and soap-boiling works to capitalize on those animals that could go no further. River crossings were normally swum in order to avoid bridge tolls, but even here charges later came to be introduced, as they were for crossing certain estates or entering towns or markets; fines might also be imposed on stray beasts, as attitudes hardened amongst countrymen towards the passage of alien herds through their territory, in a landscape marked progressively by enclosures whose entire *raison d'être* was at odds with the droving system.

In order to prevent losses when herds became intermingled, it was common for cattle to be branded with an identity mark; Bonser notes that farmers with properties bordering the drove routes would take care to isolate their own beasts as a drove passed by, although they might also rent fields for overnight stops, typically at the rate of ½d. a head. It was also common practice to fit cattle with iron shoes for their long journey, in order to avoid them going lame along the way; in the normal course of events, only oxen working on hard or flinty ground would be shod. The shoes favoured by drovers were comparatively light and crescentic in outline, and known as 'cues'; each hoof required a pair of them to match its cloven form. Other types of shoes said to be for oxen are occasionally found – in Wisbech Museum, for example, can be seen one resembling a flattened horseshoe and one forming a complete circle – presumably for wear by draught animals in marshy terrain. When the herd had been assembled at the start of a journey, the services of a blacksmith and his team would be called upon to shoe all of them: four such men could shoe 100 head of cattle in a day. Thomas Horne in his *Complete Grazier*, followed by Bonser, gives the following as the general course of events: a dozen beasts would be herded into an enclosure, where each in turn would be seized by the horns and secured to a post with a rope; a noose would be passed around the animal's legs and pulled tight so that it keeled over on its side; between either pair of legs a short Y-shaped brace was inserted, to which the feet were bound; one man would

trim the hooves and another fit the shoes. There was some regional variation to this routine: in the Vale of Pewsey, for example, each leg in turn was simply tied to a post or trevis while the shoes were fitted. In Wales, where Colyer reports the existence in the nineteenth century of shoeing specialists, who moved from fair to fair offering their services, the capacity to throw a beast – even one of the smaller 'runts' of the area – single-handed was regarded as a mark of particular prowess among practitioners. In Cardiganshire the approved method was to seize the beast by the muzzle with one hand and by the right horn with the other; with the thrower's foot braced against the animal's right foot, the head was given a sharp twist and the beast went down. Thereafter the thrower held the animal down by lying across its neck while his assistant fitted the shoes. Drovers might be equipped to carry out running repairs, or they could call on the services of a wayside blacksmith.

Once the animals reached the market, or perhaps their long-term feeding grounds, the shoes would be removed for return to their place of origin: Bonser reports the discovery at Barnard Castle of a pile of these shoes 'as big as a haystack', presumably marking the receiving point for such a consignment, awaiting recycling on the next herd heading south. Although they can scarcely have been matched to the hoof with the care expended on horseshoeing, some account would have had to be taken of size and also of the fact that those destined for the hind feet were generally of lighter construction than (and differently shaped from) those for the forefeet.

The drovers themselves operated under a system of licences in England from the second half of the sixteenth century and in Scotland from a century later. Their calling was one requiring a combination of physical resilience, a good business head, familiarity with perhaps hundreds of miles of territory and, above all, an understanding of the capacities of the animals they were required to deliver in good condition to their destination. Bonser contrasts the Scottish practice of the drovers generally buying their cattle before setting out on the journey, so that they undertook the whole of the risk, with that of the Welsh drovers who customarily received their animals from their respective owners on trust and paid for them with their profits on return. There were, as he points out, considerable risks involved in either system: from the reign of Edward VI, drovers were required to be married men and householders in order to qualify for a licence, a system designed to minimize the potential for dishonest dealing, either in the matter of the animals or in the various other activities such as message-carrying in which many drovers engaged.

Those drovers who could afford it would generally travel on horseback, although they might have a number of helpers assisting them on foot; whether they slept in a convenient inn or under a hedge was again a matter decided by status. It was prudent for them to be armed for their own protection and that of their animals: so essential were these measures considered that, even during the worst periods of Jacobite unrest in the eighteenth century, Scottish drovers were permitted to carry arms.

The beasts making up these driven herds might have started their lives hundreds of miles from their ultimate destinations, although most would spend a period as stores along the way, gaining weight and maturity in intermediate pastures; many would be in their fourth year before they would be considered ready for market, while others might pass years as milking or draught animals before completing their journey to Smithfield. The upland counties of Wales had long been a major source of such animals, being productive

of beasts but lacking the means to sustain them: in 1603 George Owen recorded that in Pembrokeshire cattle-breeding had much increased in recent years, although it was 'generallie not soe comodiouse for the comonwealth as the tillage, by reason it procureth depopulation and mantayneth lesse people at worke'. 'This trade of breeding Cattel', he continued, 'is used much in all partes of the shere but most in the welshe partes and neere the Mountaines, where their lande is not so apt for corne and where there is lardger scope of grounde.' So important had this trade become by the time of the Civil War that it resulted in a petition to the king from some gentlemen of north Wales, that 'there [be] many thousand families in the mountainous part of this countery who sowing little or no corne at all, trust merely to the sale of their cattle, wool and Welch cottons for their provision of bread'. Access to the markets was essential for them; their activities are reflected in the seizure by Parliamentary troops in 1644 of some 900 cattle from eighteen Welsh drovers at Gloucester market. By the Restoration, Welsh beasts were again making their way to markets in Middlesex, Essex and Kent – all doubtless passing through the hands of middlemen who would fatten them up before their final journey to London. Thomas Pennant estimated that in his day some 3,000 animals were exported annually from the Lleyn peninsula alone, and as many as 12,000 to 15,000 from Anglesey (although more cautious opinion puts the likely number at less than half that amount).

Irish beasts were also becoming more common in England by this time, most of them having been shipped through Liverpool and the Welsh ports. It was asserted in the House of Commons in 1621 that 100,000 Irish cattle came in to the country every year by this means. The trade was prohibited in 1667, a ban that would endure for the following century, until 1765.

In Scotland the Highland cattle were, if anything, worse off in their homeland than their Welsh counterparts. Martin Martin describes the inability of smallholders in the Western Isles to provide for their animals on a year-round basis:

> They have many large parcels of Ground never yet Manur'd, which if Cultivated, would maintain double the number of the present Inhabitants, and increase and preserve their Cattle; many of which for want of Hay or Straw, die in the Winter, and Spring; so that I have known particular Persons lose above one Hundred Cows at a time, meerly by want of Fodder.

Like the cattle from Anglesey, some of these island cattle began their journey to market with a lengthy swim:

> All the Horses and Cows Sold at the Fair [on Graddan], swim to the Main Land over one of the Ferries or Sounds called Kyles . . . They begin when it is near Low Water, and fasten a twisted Wyth about the lower Jaw of each Cow, the other end of the Wyth is fastned to another Cows Tail, and the number so tied together is commonly five. A Boat with four Oars rows off, and a Man sitting in the Stern, holds the Wyth in his hand to keep up the foremost Cows head, and thus all the five Cows swim as fast as the Boat rows; and in this Manner above a hundred may be ferried over in one day. These Cows are sometimes drove above 400 Miles further South; they soon grow fat, and prove sweet and tender Beef.

From as early as the sixteenth century, Scottish stockmen had orchestrated this flow of beasts from the Highlands to the south, a process that often involved a pause for a degree of improvement in lowland pastures before the droves braved the hazards of the border country (when it was not positively closed to them by hostilities). Trow-Smith records that by 1663 over 18,500 beasts were passing annually through Carlisle alone, and in that year customs barriers were finally removed. Although small in stature, these beasts formed part of a trade that gained in volume to the point where English producers along the way felt their livelihoods threatened by it. Their presence is recorded in the Fens where, by c. 1646, the *Anti-Projector* could claim that 'multitudes of heyfers, and Scots and Irish cattle' had been fattened there. A century later Defoe contributes the following observation on the method by which they came to be distributed: 'And this in particular is worthy remark, That the gross of all the Scots Cattle which come yearly into England are brought to a small Village lying North of the City of Norwich, call'd St Faith's, where the Norfolk Grasiers go and buy them.'

Fen pastures gave a wealth of fodder for winter, whether fresh or as hay, and new forms of foodstuffs being adopted elsewhere were treated there with scorn: 'What is Cole-seed and Rape', asked the *Anti-Projector*: 'they are but Dutch commodities, and but trash and trumpery . . . in respect of the fore-recited commodities, which are the rich Oare of the Common-wealth'. Such were the numbers of cattle grazing in close proximity on the Fens that it became customary to brand them with both the parish and the owner's mark according to a code of 1548.

English cattle too naturally participated in this trade, especially those from the upland areas or from those estates where farmers found themselves debarred from ploughing up pasture to provide root crops for their animals. The majority of these animals were fattened and finished on

143 *A Bird's Eye View of Smithfield Market*, an engraving of 1811, after Pugin and Rowlandson. This London market is shown working at close to maximum capacity; within a few years a more spacious cattle-market was opened at Islington.

pastures in the Home Counties. By the early decades of the eighteenth century the majority of farms in the southern half of England were growing turnips as fodder for their stock, as well as lucerne, sainfoin and clover, either to be eaten where they grew in the fields or stored to see the stock through the winter months. Later, cattle-cake would be added to the store of feedstuffs: manufactured from rape-seed and linseed oil, it was developed initially as a fertilizer, but in time it came to be fed to the cows whose dung then returned to the soil some of its goodness. The more sedentary lifestyle of these stall-fed cattle exacted a price in terms of their hardiness, however, and on their ability to survive being driven great distances to market.

The scale of this trade increased in proportion to the growth of the urban centres: by the end of the seventeenth century, John Houghton reported that some 88,500 cattle were being driven to London annually from every quarter of the country (illus. 143). The trade would peak in the first half of the nineteenth century, but thereafter the spread of dairying in the countryside and fear of infection from passing herds made life progressively more difficult for the drovers. Finally, they found themselves utterly displaced by the rapid service offered by the railway network.

J. H. Smith has produced an analysis of the progress of the cattle trade in Aberdeenshire in the nineteenth century, which doubtless was echoed in many comparable areas. Before the advent of sea transport for fat cattle, the bulk of the animals leaving the county had been driven south as stores for fattening in East Anglia and elsewhere. The hazards of droving (to which the beasts from north-east Scotland were subject in full measure) have been discussed above; here it may be added that the small farmers of the area found themselves in a particularly disadvantageous negotiating position with the drovers and agents, especially when poor weather led to shortages of fodder or when the drove roads to the south were rendered impassable by snow. Added to this, by the time the animals had completed their trek southwards of some five or six weeks, their condition would have deteriorated further so that good prices were even harder to come by.

With the introduction of a sea-going service from Aberdeen in 1828, the potential for a major shift in the economy was introduced. Now local farmers could fatten their own beasts and sell them directly to Smithfield at greatly enhanced prices. In the course of the next twenty years the numbers of animals travelling annually by sea rose from 150 in the first year to nearly 16,000 – even given that the journey could in foul weather take almost as long as it did by road. By 1850 a further major change came about with the opening of the Aberdeen Railway, carrying 12,000 live cattle to the markets in the south of Scotland and to London, and bringing in return cheap cattle-cake and other fodder that mitigated the rigours of over-wintering stock in the region, so that a whole economy aimed at producing fat cattle rather than potential stores quickly developed; beasts began to be brought to the region for fattening from as for north as Orkney and Shetland, from Ireland, and even from Canada.

Within a short space of time the full potential of the railway was realized when the export trade in live animals from the north-east was replaced by one in which it was carcasses that were transported to market, further enhancing the profitability of an area now able fully to participate in the national trade, despite its remoteness from the market centres.

DAIRYING

In the early centuries any distinction between milk and beef cattle is clouded by the fact that all dairy cows could expect to be fattened and sold for beef as their milk yield began to decline with age, so that the populations were not clearly distinguishable from one another. Until a developing taste for fresh cow's milk brought an increasing urban demand in the seventeenth century (a demand met partly by cattle stalled in the suburbs of many towns, so that deliveries could be made as speedily as possible), fresh milk had formed a more important component of the diet of the lower classes than the wealthy, with much of its consumption necessarily taking place at a local level. The bulk of the milk production, however, was destined to be turned into cheese, with whey butter being produced from the residual buttermilk. For the rural population, such milk consumption as there was generally took the form of skimmed milk, and calves and lambs might similarly be nourished with it after weaning from their mothers. Butter and cheese had the advantage of enjoying a longer shelf life, which allowed a considerable long-distance trade to build up: Daniel Defoe recorded that by his day some 14,000 tons of butter were sent annually from Cheshire to London, and a further 8,000 tons to Bristol. The keeping qualities in these manufactures are also implicit in the claims of the *Anti-prospector* that in the Fens 'we breed and feed great store of cattle, and we keep dayeries, which afford great store of butter and cheese to victual the Navy'. By the closing decade of the eighteenth century, the suburban cattle population on the Surrey side of London alone was estimated by James and Malcolm at some 700 animals. Meanwhile, some sizeable dairy herds had appeared in the countryside, with perhaps as many as 100 milkers; many such herds were still dedicated to butter- and cheese-making, with the whey going to support a mixed economy with pigs (see p. 486); this expansion went hand-in-hand with increasing enclosure of farmland.

From perhaps as early as the sixteenth century, far-reaching changes began to be registered in the composition of dairy herds, spreading westwards from the coastal counties stretching from Lincolnshire and the Fens as far south as Kent, as Dutch cattle made a growing impact on a population in which milk yields had hitherto scarcely improved since the medieval period. The appearance at this time of a 'pied' strain of cattle, with white splashes appearing on their coats, has been related to the arrival of these Dutch cattle, in which this is a regular characteristic. Gervase Markham was one of those who noted that the cattle in Lincolnshire 'are for the most part Pyde, with more white then the other colours, their horns little and crooked, of bodies exceedingly tall, long and large, lean and thin thighed, strong hoved, not apt to sorbate, and are fittest to labour and draught'. John Aubrey was struck by the same trait: 'I have not seen so many pied cattle any where as in North Wiltshire. The country hereabout is much inclined to pied cattle, but commonly the colour is black or brown, or deep red.' By 1707 Mortimer was describing these as 'the best sort of cows for the pail' and asserting confidently that they were 'the long legg'd, short-horn'd Cow of the Dutch-breed which is to be had in some Places of Lincolnshire, but most used in Kent'. The Kentish stock almost alone seems to have remained largely unmixed in an attempt to maximize yields: here, according to William Ellis, 'the fine Dutch breed . . . are still carefully kept up without Mixture in Colour, and . . . will yield two gallons at a milking, but in order to do this they require great Attendance and the best of Food'. By the time officially sanctioned exports from Holland and West Friesland are recorded at the beginning of the eighteenth century, there were said to be many cattle of the same general type already in England which had arrived by more informal means – themselves of rather mixed race at this time, but with the capacity to produce high-quality milk. Later Yorkshire and Durham would share in this benefice and Dutch blood quickly became absorbed into many British milking herds. Thomas Pennant commented that 'the large species that are cultivated thro' most parts of Great Britain are either entirely of foreign extraction; or our own Improved by a cross with a foreign kind'. He continues: 'The Lincolnshire kind derive their size from the Holstein breed; and the large hornless cattle that are bred in some parts of England come originally from Poland.' Curiously, by the time Boys carried out his survey of Kent at the end of the eighteenth century, he noted no trace of the formerly pure-bred herds of the county – a comment, perhaps, on the high cost of maintenance which had rendered them unprofitable.

Dutch influence can be traced in a wide range of British Shorthorn breeds, and indeed as this term entered common usage the contribution of Dutch cattle began to fade from view, if it was not positively obliterated. Although more prolific milkers than the Longhorn breeds, the large- and loose-framed Shorthorns were less noteworthy as beef animals until the work of certain breeders such as the Colling brothers of Darlington (illus. 144), who experimented with crosses made on Galloway and other Scots stock, brought about a more compact and profitable animal (though at the cost of milk

144 *A Shorthorned Heifer, aged Seven Years*, by an unknown artist after Thomas Weaver, *c.* 1840, oil on canvas. This famous white heifer, bred by Robert Colling, spent much of her adult life touring the country as an exhibition animal.

yield). Trow-Smith describes Ayrshires as the first modern milking breed, with Channel Islands and Suffolk cattle as their only serious competitors; Ayrshires too were the product of pragmatic commercial producers, not specialist breeders. The Friesian breed was added to this list around 1860, from which time further Dutch cattle began to arrive in significant numbers.

From this same period a great impetus was given to the dairy industry by the introduction of the railways, opening up markets in a major way. During the same decades mechanical milking machines began to be developed – mostly unsuccessfully, until the invention of the pulsator by Alexander Shields of Glasgow and incorporated in his Thistle Mechanical Milking Machine. By the late nineteenth century the framework for the modern specialized dairy industry was virtually complete.

MARKETS

A network of markets for livestock ensured their efficient transmission from the countryside to the major towns. Until the advent of steam transport, all animals arrived at their respective destinations on the hoof, to be slaughtered on the spot. In country towns, pens adjacent to the butchers' shops held animals until the hour had come for their dispatch. Edward III famously thought York the most malodorous place in England due to the stench from unregulated disposal of offal and eventually the butchers were compelled to carry their waste to the south bank of the Ouse, so that countrymen could carry it away for use as fertilizer. At Winchester the butchers persistently disposed of their offal by throwing it into the cathedral cemetery. Inevitably, the major flesh markets such as Smithfield in London were scenes of appalling squalor. David Farmer reproduces the findings of a jury in 1368 that:

> the butchers of St Nicholas Shambles and their servants were in the habit of carrying the said offal and filth to the bridge called 'Bochersbregg' near Castle Baynard, and there casting it into the Thames, making the water run foul, that in its passage through the streets some of the offal fell from the vessels in which it was carried, and that the blood of the animals slaughtered in the Shambles aforesaid found its way down the streets and lanes to the Thames, making a foul corruption and abominable sight and nuisance to all dwelling near or using those streets and lanes.

John Houghton records the method of felling cattle in general use at the turn of the eighteenth century:

> he is slaughtered by having a Rope put about his Neck and Horns, and drawn through a Hole in a Post, or a ring fastened to it, by which means he is pull'd close, and with a

Pole Ax, knock't on the Head, 'till almost or quite dead: Then his throat is cut, and the Blood let out. But I am told that at the King's Slaughter-House on Little Tower-Hill, the Butchers are so dextrous, that without tying, one Man will take an Ox by the Nose, another will take him by the Horn, and a third strike him on a certain place an Inch and a half above the Horn which, at one blow, will make him fall down immediately.

As mentioned elsewhere (p. 137), the baiting of bulls was considered not merely a sport but an essential preliminary to their slaughter for consumption. Houghton again records that 'that great Exercise makes his Flesh more tender, and so if eaten in good time (before putrefaction, which he is more subject to than if not baited) he is tolerable good Meat, although very red.' This long-lived belief had no basis whatever in fact, but was perhaps perpetuated on account of the sport it brought to the public.

VEAL

There was, it seems, comparatively little trade in veal before the sixteenth century: no mention of it is made in the manuals on husbandry referred to above. From that time, however – at least around London – veal rearing began to develop as a specialized industry, with Essex emerging as a main source for the London trade. The pre-eminence of the county is alluded to by Houghton, writing at the turn of the eighteenth century: 'There comes from Rumford in Essex to London weekly, about Thirty Carts or Wagons, bringing, one with another, about Twenty Calves each, which must amount to Six Hundred; and in the Year, upwards of Thirty Thousand.' Daniel Defoe similarly recognized the pre-eminence of Essex, where 'their chief Business is breeding of Calves, which I need not say are the best and fattest, and the largest Veal in England, if not in the World'.

Many of the most infamous modern practices were already in place by this date, with the calves penned up and crammed with cereals and pulses to supplement their mother's milk before being slaughtered at ten to twelve weeks. The treatment of the calves at this stage, as noted by Per Kalm, in 1748 confirms the reprehensible nature of the trade: in the search for the whitest (and most profitable) flesh, calves might be repeatedly bled before the last night of their lives, when 'they bleed him in the evening, allow him nearly to bleed to death, stop the blood, and slaughter him next morning'.

'WILD' AND PARK CATTLE

The true wild cattle of Europe, the aurochs (*Bos primigenius*), had vanished from Britain during the Early Bronze Age, some 3,000 years before the opening of the era considered here. Several historical accounts survive of encounters with 'wild' cattle, but all must relate to feral animals – incidentally, much smaller and less daunting than the 6-foot-high aurochs. George Owen, for example, in his *Description of Penbrokshire* of 1603 writes:

> I have alsoe seene good pastime in hunteing and killing the wild bull, wild oxe and wild calfe, by horsemen and footemen, whereof there is yett some store, reared upon the mountaines, thoughe lesse than heretofore, the owners findinge more profitte by the tame, then pleasure in the wilde.

In terms of high ancestry, the oldest herd to survive in unadulterated form is composed of the white cattle at Chillingham Park (Northumberland), which have avoided all penetration by other breeds since they were enclosed in the thirteenth century (and which in turn have contributed nothing to the development of the national stock during that period). Their wild demeanour renders them quite inimical to crossing with other breeds, so that their isolation now renders them of exceptional interest. Given their stable physical appearance, Bailey and Culley's description from the turn of the nineteenth century remains as good as any:

> Their colour is invariably white, muzzle black; the whole of the inside of the ear, and about one-third of the outside from the tip, downwards, red: horns white, with black tips, very fine, and bent upwards; some of the bulls have a thin upright mane, about an inch and a half, or two inches long: the weight of the oxen is from 35 to 45 stone; and the cows from 25 to 35 stone, the four quarters . . . The beef is finely marbled, and of excellent flavour . . .
>
> At the first appearance of any person they set off at full speed, and gallop to a considerable distance; when they make a wheel round, and come boldly up again, tossing their heads in a menacing manner: on a sudden they make a full stop, at the distance of forty or fifty yards, looking wildly at the object of their surprise; but upon the least motion being made, they again turn round, and gallop off with equal speed; but forming a shorter circle, and returning with a bolder and more threatening aspect, they approach much nearer, when they make another stand; and again gallop off. This they do several times, shortening their distance, and advancing nearer, till they come within a few yards, when most people think it prudent to leave them.

145 *Keepers stalking the Wild Cattle at Chillingham Park*, hand-coloured lithograph of *c.* 1840 by Hullmandel & Walton, after J. W. Snow. Culling animals from the herd had once been treated as a sport engaging the whole neighbourhood, but prudence born of many injuries led to the more discreet method illustrated here.

Conventional herding practices were of no avail with these animals. Bailey reports that the culling of a single bull had been until recent years a matter for general involvement of the entire neighbourhood; on horseback and on foot they would single out their target from the rest of the herd until he took a stand, at which point he would be killed by a fusillade of shots, though often not before he had made a final assault on his tormentors. Given the dangers inherent in this practice, it had become customary by Marshall's time for culling to be carried out by the park-keepers alone, armed with muskets that allowed them to keep their distance (illus. 145).

Bailey comments on other traits which seem to evoke the wild origins of the herd. The calves were hidden by their mothers in some 'sequestered situation' where they might be suckled in seclusion several times a day. From time to time bull calves would have to be castrated – a task especially fraught with danger. Culley reports that

the park keeper, having marked the spot where the calf had been hidden by its mother, would go there on horseback with an assistant, tie a handkerchief round the calf's muzzle to prevent its bellowing, perform the operation in the usual way and retreat with as much expedition as possible. He also claims that when a member of the herd was wounded or enfeebled by old age, the other cattle set upon it and gored it to death.

Somewhat comparable to the Chillingham cattle are the white park cattle originally reared at Chartley (Staffordshire). Judy Urquhart tells the story of the translation of the herd from its original home to Hedenham Hall (Norfolk), where they remain in possession of Lord Ferrers, whose ancestors once held Chartley. Having verged on extinction for a period, the herd was at one time bolstered by the introduction of Longhorn blood, the effects of which are now scarcely registered.

As early as the late seventeenth century there are records of Brahma cows being imported from India to England. Lord Rockingham established a herd of them at Wentworth Park (Yorkshire) in late 1770s. The bulls from India and Ceylon modelled by George Garrard (above) came from herds owned by the Duke of Bedford and the Earl of Salisbury – reminders of the degree to which wealthy landowners were willing to experiment at this period.

Sheep

No less impressive than the sheer numbers of sheep inhabiting almost the whole of the British Isles in recent times is the variety of breeds represented, each seemingly finely adapted to the terrain it occupies, whether windswept hillside, marsh or downland. The picture they present is, in fact, a highly evolved one, reflecting a long period of development. During the millennium concerning us here, nearly all the principal elements of the stock were already in place, with only the introduction of the Merino in the eighteenth century marking a significant intrusion of alien blood. Perhaps the most striking feature of this phase of the sheep's long history is its evolution through several phases of specialized production: from a primary role as a milking animal in the early Norman period, it came to be prized in the succeeding centuries as a source of wool so valuable as to form the cornerstone of the national economy; more prosaically, the fertilizing qualities of its dung were so cherished that an entire system of agriculture developed around it, before the growing national appetite for meat in the early modern period produced a further change of priorities that led to the sheep being re-engineered, as it were, as

an efficient producer of mutton. In the course of this complex history, many regional types emerged to flourish for a time; some vanished again due to the vagaries of the market while others were propelled into new breeds serving fresh demands, their characteristics progressively determined more and more closely by the increasingly professional practice of specialized breeders.

SHEEP HUSBANDRY IN THE MIDDLE AGES

As with other domesticates reviewed here, ownership of sheep was initially divided between, on the one hand, the great flocks of the seigneurial demesnes (and also, significantly, the monasteries) and, on the other hand, the smaller parcels of animals in the hands of villeins or bondsmen up and down the country. In lowland areas the sheep in these lesser flocks competed at times for the few wisps of grass provided by hard-pressed common grazings, but spent most of their lives on the fallow or stubble where their droppings could return valuable sustenance to the soil (see below); upland sheep tended to follow a different routine and in some areas seasonal transhumance continued to be practised throughout the Middle Ages (and indeed up to the threshold of the nineteenth century).

Shepherding constituted one of the major occupations of the Middle Ages, its practitioners ranging in status from flockmasters of the great monastic and demesne farms to common shepherds of the country villages, paid in pennies to care for handfuls of sheep in the possession of individual cottars and villagers, grazed as a single flock on the open fields and commons of the community. In addition to his wage, modest customary rights were widely enjoyed by the shepherd, typified by Eileen Power as a bowl of whey all through the summer and ewes' milk on Sunday, a lamb at weaning time and a fleece at shearing.

Additionally, he might have the right to keep a number of his own sheep with the flock under his control, a device designed, no doubt, to promote an identity of interest in the well-being of all the sheep, which he would protect from predators both human and animal, and would heal when necessary. He was bound to his flock in the closest possible way, to judge by the advice given in the early fourteenth-century *Seneschaucie*:

And he ought to sleep in the fold, he and his dog; and he ought to pasture his sheep well, and keep them in forage, and watch them well, so that they be not killed or destroyed by dogs or stolen or lost or changed, nor let them pasture in moors or dry places or bogs, to get sickness or disease from lack of guard. No shepherd ought to leave his sheep to go to fairs, or markets, or wrestling matches, or wakes, or to the tavern, without taking leave or asking it, or without putting a good keeper in his place to keep the sheep, that no harm may arise from his fault.

In the worst of the winter months the more fortunate flocks were brought under cover and hand-fed, initially with little more than hay but, as an appreciation of the importance of diet developed, with the addition of oats, vetches, tares or peas. Walter of Henley exhorted the prudent owner to 'see that your sheep are in houses between Martin-mas and Easter', while the *Seneschaucie* advocates the use of a hurdled fold, sheltered by a roof.

On the larger manors and on monastic lands a constant juggling of stock between individual properties went on, to ensure that the most appropriate (and most profitable) balance was maintained: on some such establishments breeding flocks alone would be kept, while on others only wethers (castrated males) would be farmed for

their wool. Hundreds of animals at a time might be moved around by this process, incidentally resulting in a great deal of intermixture of blood.

The increasing focus on wool was to have immediate repercussions in the composition of the flock. For one thing, ewes which initially formed the most valuable component of milking flocks now assumed the primary role of maintaining the stock of wool-bearing animals, the majority of which – since they produce better fleeces than ewes – were wethers; rams too were important primarily for their reproductive role, one ram generally serving between 35 and 55 ewes. Male lambs not destined for breeding would be gelded at some time between midsummer and Michaelmas. It was a perfunctory process: in the early seventeenth century Henry Best suggested that a competent man could geld 100 lambs in three hours, slitting them with a knife, drawing out the stones with his teeth and dressing the wound with tansy-butter to fend off flies and facilitate healing; a tally of his work was to be kept by nicks from his knife, registered on the bar of the gate. It was a process fraught with danger for the sheep, however, and Leonard Mascall's later observation that 'by cutting and gelding of them by unskilfull persons, many doe perish and die thereon' must cloak a legion of painful deaths over many centuries.

Shearing formed another major undertaking in the annual calendar, with land-holding tenants expected to contribute to the effort by sending a woman first to engage in washing the sheep and then to help with shearing – these duties lying beyond the personal responsibility of the shepherd; hired labour might also be brought in on the larger farms. The custom of washing the fleece before shearing developed as flockmasters realized that the higher price attracted by cleaned (and degreased) wool more than compensated for the extra effort involved in washing. It survived

146 The first plate of a series on woollen manufacture: the sheep are washed in the river on the right, before their fleeces are sheared. On the wall of the model farmhouse to the rear are two bee-skeps with a small pigeon-house above. *Universal Magazine of Knowledge and Pleasure*, 5 (1749).

long enough to be recorded in manuals and other texts from the seventeenth century onwards (illus. 146), from which time Henry Best's account of the routine is likely to reflect a practice little changed since the Middle Ages.

Washing would take place in the first half of June on a suitably 'faire and hotte day', Best writes, when one person would be required to deal with every 100 or so sheep to be washed. The washers would turn up around six in the morning in order to dam the stream chosen for the task, taking care to provide a dip with a depth of water up to thigh height; a pen would be constructed alongside, tapering somewhat towards the water, and washing would begin around 9 o'clock when the early morning chill would have dissipated. One man would single out the sheep from within the fold and another would launch them into the deepest part of the water; the shepherd would be on hand to detach any loose wool and place it in a sack, and the washers too would remove any easily detached parts of the fleece, while any wool that

escaped could be fished out downstream by 'children, boyes, and girles, with bushes and whins made fast to the endes of stickes'. As washing proceeded the size of the pen would be progressively reduced in order to keep the sheep within easy reach of the catcher, and when all had been washed they would be turned out on to some clean pasture so that the wool did not become dirty again before being sheared.

Shearing ideally followed during continuing good weather two or three days later when the wool had risen again, although some liked to leave it longer; once in this condition, the fleece would cohere in a natural manner. One shearer could clip perhaps 60 sheep in a day (or as many as 90, given an early start). With a view to preserving the cleanliness of the fleece, shearing would take place in a timber-floored shearing shed on the larger farms, or otherwise on a boarded platform within the shearing-pen. Each fleece would be rolled up with its whitest wool to the outside and the hairier wool within in order to make it look its best. A fortnight's fair weather was desirable for the now-vulnerable sheep, and in the case of stormy weather during that period they were to be brought inside. All the sheep were to be marked with the owner's device just as soon as they had been sheared: a pigment known as ruddle was normally used in marking, but some purchasers objected to wool permanently stained in this way, in which case lamp-black mixed with tallow might be used as an alternative. Other means of identification are less frequently mentioned, but Trow-Smith finds a reference to two strays described in the records of a manorial court at Appledram (Sussex) as having their 'right ears skagged and their left ears slit', practices that survived alongside marking the fleece well into the nineteenth century (illus. 147). Branding on the horns was also practised with

horned flocks, while those without sometimes suffered branding on the nose.

While struggling during clipping, sheep were always at risk from accidental cuts from the pointed shears, and it was common for each shearer to be provided with a dish of tar or salve with which to dress any wounds. Many other ailments threatened the well-being of the flock, but although the earliest manuals pay a great deal of attention to them there were, in truth, few effective remedies at the disposal of the shepherd. The ill-defined but lethal murrains that swept the country at intervals carried off livestock in significant numbers whenever they appeared; those whose sheep occupied the common grazings – and who were least able to stand the loss – were inevitably most at risk from cross-infection of their flocks. Scab (a mite

147 Two sets of wool- and ear-marks from north-west England, the marks overprinted on standardized engraved animals. Simon Prudea, Loweswater: 'Forked near ear, a red cross on the near side'; William Dixon, Loweswater: 'Punch holed both ears, a stroke from the top of the back to the shoulder, and one from that to the shank end on the near side'. From William Hodgson, *The Shepherd's Guide* (1849).

infestation), first recorded in 1275, resulted in the sheep casting its fleece; like the sheep-pox that first appeared in the following century, the condition was not in itself fatal, but both diseases resulted in the afflicted animals being slaughtered in order to safeguard the remainder. Sulphur and mercury might be applied to certain skin conditions, and Stockholm (pine) tar achieved the status of a cure-all, or at least a remedy of first resort whose reputation survived until recent years.

Even harder to treat were internal complaints of which liver-fluke was perhaps the most prevalent. Trow-Smith notes that in warning against allowing the sheep to eat 'the little white snails from which they will sicken and die', the *Seneschaucie* accurately identifies one of the hosts of *Fasciola hepatica* and recommends the slaughter of any animals showing signs of infection. The cycle was a difficult one to break, however, once the grazing had become infected.

The *Seneschaucie* recommends too that ewes and wethers should be inspected three times a year by men who know their business, when the least promising animals might be culled from the flock and sold. These cullings were to take place, respectively, after Easter 'because of the disease in May' (scab); before Lammas, when the old and weak were excluded; and by Michaelmas, when those that looked unlikely to survive the winter were removed. Whenever possible, a period of intensive feeding would ensure that the excluded animals would then sell to the butcher for the highest possible price.

MILK AND CHEESE

At the opening of our period, the sheep recorded in the *Domesday* survey were already so numerous as to outnumber all the other livestock together. The primary function of all these animals was to provide milk, all other considerations (including meat and wool) being at this period of secondary importance. For some estimate of the productivity of the ewes, Walter of Henley informs us that in his day five ewes would contribute the same amount of milk as a single cow. Their production, however, did not continue the year round – the lactation period began with the lambing season and ended perhaps six months later: the *Seneschaucie*, for example, advises the herdsman to 'let no ewes be milked after the feast of our Lady, for that they will mate more tardily another year'. The production of both wool and further lambs was also believed to be adversely affected by protracted milking.

The custom of milking sheep continued throughout the medieval period (illus. 148), even when wool production had taken over as the primary concern of the herdsman. The daily chore of milking was women's work and formed no part of the shepherd's duties. Manorial tenants of a certain standing generally were required to send a woman every day to help with the milking; in return they would receive a share of the whey or buttermilk remaining after it had been processed into cheese. The flocks of smaller owners might be milked in common, just as their sheep were often combined for convenience under a single shepherd.

The Essex marshes – heavily grazed by sheep – became one of the most productive areas for ewe's milk cheese for the London market, although it enjoyed no very high reputation for quality. Whey-butter, rather than the full-fat butter familiar to us today, was produced from the buttermilk left at the end of cheese-making. As well as providing nourishment and being much used in the kitchen, butter had a variety of uses as a salve, especially for a range of wounds and diseases suffered by the sheep themselves. Milk, of course, had only limited keeping qualities, and any not

148 Sheep milking (and shearing) taking place within a pen made from hurdles. From the Luttrell Psalter (*c.* 1340).

used in butter- and cheese-making was likely to be fed to the lambs.

After centuries of daily practice, by the nineteenth century the milking of sheep was confined to what Trow-Smith calls 'the more withdrawn parts of the country'. At the time he compiled his series of surveys of English husbandry (that is to say in the 1950s) ewe's milk cheese had become a rarity: the half century that has elapsed since that time has seen something of a renaissance in specialist cheese-making, and once again a healthy range of regional types is offered by specialist manufacturers.

THE HEYDAY OF WOOL

With appropriate pomp, the Ordinance of the Staple (1353) describes wool as 'the sovereign merchandise and jewel of this realm of England'. The prime position of wool in the medieval economy is undisputed, but it was a primacy that had to be worked at.

The imposition of Norman rule doubtless contributed to the impulse that enormously increased the importance of the sheep's wool-bearing role, with the growing influence of the monasteries – and especially the Cistercians, first established in England in 1128 – playing a major role in promoting wool-growing and in forging links with Continental markets. At an early phase, however, the wool-based economy was largely localized and closed in nature: carding or combing and spinning the wool were practices carried on in almost every cottage with the simplest equipment, notably the spindle and whorl (the spinning-wheel was invented only in the 1500s); woollen manufactories were widely dispersed, all of them dependent on supplies from their immediate hinterlands and there was only a limited market beyond these shores. By the mid-1100s there are signs of a distinct quickening of pace, with merchants and manufacturers in a number of towns petitioning for permission to form guilds in an attempt to develop (and of course to control) their markets.

The emergence of a significant export trade in woven textiles lay still some 200 years ahead, and for the present the commodity that was to underpin the medieval economy was raw wool.

Although small producers continued to contribute significantly to the volume of wool produced, the bulk of it now originated on demesne farms and on the great tracts of land under monastic control: in Yorkshire alone, the combined clip from all the monasteries is said to have exceeded 200,000 sheep. A median role between the producers and manufacturers was filled by a new class of middlemen who travelled the country negotiating the wholesale buying and selling of wool harvests. The trade took on an international dimension as agents of Flemish and Italian manufacturing houses entered the market, disposing of large sums of money. The entire year's clip might be purchased as seen, while still on the sheep, or increasingly it could be supplied under contract for several years in advance. Eileen Power finds that it became customary for monasteries to sell their entire production two or three years ahead – and sometimes as many as twenty years in advance. This arrangement could put large sums of money in the hands of monks eager to fund building projects or to achieve other ends, but it also held dangers of financial over-extension which led to the Cistercians in particular being forbidden to deal in this way.

Smaller producers, by contrast, were at first more likely to sell their wool at local markets and fairs, but by the thirteenth century mechanisms had emerged that brought their wool (termed *collecta*) within the organized market, with either a wealthy landowner (or perhaps a monastery) contracting for the whole district, or with one of the growing numbers of woolmongers from the market towns assiduously doing his rounds. Tensions developed between these entrepreneurs and the more commercially minded monastic communities, which found themselves accused by the merchants of 'carrying on business contrary to the honour of their order and to the impoverishment . . . of the King's market towns'. The latter complaint had issued from Lincoln, and by 1265 Henry III conceded to the burgesses of Shrewsbury that 'no wool merchant should make any purchases of wool anywhere in Shropshire save in market towns of the county'. With the decline in demesne farming in the later Middle Ages the importance of this community of middlemen increased in response to the growing role played by small owners. By the fourteenth century the size of the individual flocks in the hands of villein tenants also grew, with significant numbers of flocks reaching over 1,000 in number (though some of these, at least, may have been composite flocks incorporating sheep belonging to several owners).

The roads towards the south-coast ports are characterized at this period as being thronged with packhorses carrying wool to ports. Fleeces were packed for transport in large canvas sacks, tied at the corners and sewn with pack-thread along the seams. Over the centuries the trade suffered no end of royal interference as either imports or exports were periodically embargoed, as particular communities – especially the Flemings and Italians – were discriminated against and as the Crown sought to extract every penny it could in taxes or licence fees (and sometimes in wool), from whomsoever could bear it. By the turn of the fourteenth century, exported wool attracted tax at a rate of 33 per cent, but the wool merchants continued to prosper (see illus. 149).

The insistence of the large-scale industrial manufacturers that the wool they bought should be scrupulously stored helped bring about a general improvement in the standards of practice on farms, although doubtless the monasteries had little to learn in the matter of husbanding their assets: at

Crowland Abbey (Lincolnshire), for example, the Benedictines had great thatched wool-houses in which the clip was sorted and stored, while at Fountains Abbey (Yorkshire) excavations by Glyn Coppack revealed the putative remains of an extensive aisled woolhouse which was repeatedly enlarged in the thirteenth century and which by the late 1300s included also heated dying vats and a fulling mill, indicating that by now finished textiles were being produced on the site. Those farmers not reliant on capitalizing on their harvest every year also found it prudent to invest in good storage facilities so that they could sell when markets rose to their advantage.

In the course of the fifteenth century the indigenous textile industry underwent significant expansion, becoming dispersed through many of the smaller towns – specifically those with access to water to drive the new fulling mills with their water-powered beaters that rendered redundant many of the unskilled labourers previously employed in laboriously treading the cloth. Worsted and cheaper homespun cloth now began to soar in importance and to absorb a great deal of the native wool production; these employed the longer staple in which the principal wool-producing areas excelled, while demand for the finer, short-staple wools gradually fell away. While the export trade held up, it was now dominated by finished textiles rather than wool; a high point was reached in the later fifteenth century, when England's success was matched by a decline in the Flemish and Italian textile industries. Some indication of the new regard for longer wool is given by references to the export of sheep as well as wool – a practice that was, incidentally, seen as potentially damaging to English interests and was prohibited by law

in 1425. Gifts of Cotswold rams sent by Edward IV to Henry of Castile in 1464, and of further sheep sent in 1468 to King Juan of Aragón speak further of a period when a new regard for longwools buoyed up the industry, until English wool again lost its primacy under Henry VIII and the price of wool entered a period of decline from which it would never recover its former importance.

By this time, however, the beginnings of a new preoccupation with the sheep as a source of meat rather than of wool were beginning to make themselves felt, which from the seventeenth century onwards would become paramount. Typical late medieval long-wool sheep had tended to be coarse-boned with slow-maturing flesh of rather poor quality, but with rapidly expanding urban populations to be catered for efforts began to be made to refine the skeletal framework and the carcass while also bringing it to maturity at an earlier age – measures, incidentally, which brought about in the course of the sixteenth and seventeenth centuries a coarsening as well as a lengthening of the fleece. When Leonard Mascall came to write his *Thirde Booke of Cattel*, dealing with 'Sheepe, Goates, Hogges and Dogs', he was inclined to divide the sheep population into only two sorts, of which 'the better sort is those of the soft wooll, and the other the hairie wooll'. None the less, the sheep remained for him of all animals 'one of the chiefest and fruitfullest for the use of man', kept with little trouble except 'in keeping them from colde in winter, dagging in sommer, scab, bloud, and such other inconveniences that come unto them as well as to any other cattel'.

From the end of this period we have the thoughtful and observant testimony of Per Kalm, visiting England from Sweden in 1748 and looking at the sheep population (as much else) in their country setting with a fresh eye:

The little lambs had a long tail which reached nearly to the ground, but as soon as they were nearly six months old half the tail was cut off, which was said to be done partly because the sheep looked better, partly and principally because a great deal of dirt fastens on to the long tail . . . [the sheep] went day and night out on the pastures under the open sky, without having any house or roof to go under.

In one single place I saw that a boy went with them to pasture, but commonly and almost everywhere they were left without a shepherd, entirely by themselves. At home at the farms they had in some places small Skeelings, built of short posts and the roof of the skeel of straw, under which the sheep could go when it rained, or was bad weather. Some had also another outhouse, into which the shepherd, in such a case, and in some places every evening, drove in the sheep. Some farmers had in the middle of the farm-yard under the open sky erected as it were a crib or rack, of two narrow hurdles, which were fastened together at the top and bottom, and between which fine hay was laid of which the sheep went to eat in the night when they stood at home in the farm-yard.

By this point the demand for mutton had begun to exert its influence and, as well as the developments in sheep conformation described below, a taste for lamb – especially at Christmas time – had emerged in the increasingly important London market. Dorset and Wiltshire particularly were well placed to satisfy this demand; Dorset sheep, it seems, frequently lambed by September, and in the months leading up to Christmas the ewes would be sold at fairs convenient for London and their offspring brought up as house-lambs to be ready for the seasonal market: some thousands were being brought up in Surrey alone by the end of the eighteenth century, with one farmer alone fattening 500 lambs annually – 'and for this purpose the Dorsetshire ewes are the only sort he keeps'. Commonly the lambs would be housed permanently in sheds where they would be suckled alternately by 'nurses' and by their own mothers in order to ensure that they had achieved optimum fattening in time for the festive season.

FOLDING AND FLOATING

During this period of new preoccupations with food production from both arable and livestock sources, a very particular complementary relationship developed between the sheep and the soil, with well-thought-out routines to facilitate it. Appreciation of the beneficial effects of adding organic content to the soil by means of sheep manure had a long (if not precisely charted) history; by the sixteenth century it had become almost an article of faith, when Bishop Hugh Latimer (himself the son of a yeoman farmer) declared that 'A plough-land must have sheep . . . to dung the ground for bearing of corn; for if they have no sheep to help fat the ground, they shall have but bare corn and thin'. This was by no means a personal foible of the Bishop's, for in 1732 we find William Ellis, in his *Practical Farmer*, reiterating the belief that sheep's dung, described as 'of a hard, unctuous, saline and hot Nature', was a valuable source of enrichment that 'assists all Grounds more than any other'. Since the two-course system of rotation of the medieval period remained in place at this time, the benefits derived from manuring were all the more important in staving off exhaustion of the soil.

Effective delivery of this benison depended on a system of folding, in which the flock, having grazed all day on the pasture, was confined for the night in a pen composed of hurdles, erected on the bare arable land, so that their combined droppings would be deposited (and well trodden in) within a precisely defined area; the following evening the fold would be moved to an adjacent plot, and the process repeated until the whole of the designated area had been covered. The system worked only when the size of the flock was sufficient to deliver an effective charge of dung. For the smaller tenant farmers and villagers with a few sheep here and there, the critical mass – estimated at not less than about 400 animals – was achieved by placing their flocks in the care of a common shepherd; such a person would be elected or appointed by agreement and instructions would be issued to ensure that each of the land-holders in turn would benefit equally from the process of folding. It was customary for each tenant to provide a specified number of hurdles (commonly two hurdles and one post) for the fold, and for them to help with moving and re-erecting the fold each evening. It is estimated that a flock of perhaps 1,000 sheep would effectively dung an acre in a night; in practice the size of the fold would be regulated to ensure that the whole of the area to be manured had been covered before sowing time: while the tenantry fields remained unenclosed, the fold could move over the entire area in an uninterrupted manner, its direction of travel alternating year-by-year to ensure long-term even distribution.

Some smaller flockmasters owning no land of their own could also support their flocks of perhaps 30 or 40 sheep by folding them on land owned by their neighbours, where they might be paid for dunging; when no such opportunities presented themselves, their sheep would be fed on common land. Larger owners were able to operate independently, although at times even they might benefit from acting jointly with the community.

A valuable and detailed eyewitness account of folding in action (by now more of an individual than a communal exercise, it would seem, and operating within an extensively enclosed landscape), is provided by Kalm in 1748:

The hurdles . . . are about 8 feet long, and 3 feet 6 inches high, which hurdles are 'keyed' or looped, close together in a row, a post being driven down into the ground between each; and thus, according to the number of sheep, they made a larger or smaller fold. From the fold there commonly runs a narrow passage made of similar hurdles, to some one of the living hedges, by which the field is surrounded, that the sheep in bad weather may be able to go to such hedge and shelter there. In the sheep-fold there is mostly a 'sheep-crib' or 'sheep-trough', knocked together of two boards [at right angles] and a board-lap at each end, so that the fodder may not run out. When it is bad weather barley is laid in this trough, or oats, or pease, for the sheep to eat.

. . . Sheep dung and urine are here considered as the choicest manure for arable land, and the folding of sheep on fallow land is reckoned such a useful thing that it cannot be paid for in money. It is only through sheep that many a poor man has his food and the necessaries of life . . . he goes to a farmer and offers to fold his sheep at night on his fallow fields, if the farmer will give him a reasonable payment therefor. The farmer is quite satisfied with an offer which is so good for his fields, and agrees with the owner of the sheep to pay him a certain sum for every acre of land of his on which he folds his sheep . . . When the agreement is entered upon, the sheep-man drives his sheep in the day-time to pasture on the Common-lands and arable field pastures, or also on the farmer's own land, where he always has freedom to pasture them, because they by the droppings which they leave after them always pay for what they eat . . . Some assured us that when a man is owner of thirty or forty sheep he can, by only folding them on another man's arable, gain for himself in the year from £10 to £12 sterling. Others said that if a man has 150 sheep, he can in two weeks' time just manure an acre of land with them, and receives commonly from the farmer 16s. in payment for each acre of land he so manures.

The system was used to good effect on the southern downs which were, it seems, literally transformed by it. Daniel Defoe (who had been assured on an earlier visit to Dorchester that 'there were 600 Thousand Sheep fed within Six Miles of the Town') described 'the Down or Plains, which are generally called Salisbury Plain' in the following terms and anticipated that lessons could be learned from it at a national level:

[the Downs] were formerly all left open to be fed by large Flocks of Sheep, being judged to be a Soil almost incapable of producing Grain, but is now made to yield the most plentiful Crops; and that has been done by folding their Sheep upon the plow'd Lands . . . this, and this alone, has made these Lands, which in themselves are poor, and where, in some Places, the Earth is not above six Inches above the solid Chalk Rock, able to bear as good Wheat, as any of the richer lands in the Vales, though not in quite so great quantities . . . If this Way of folding Sheep upon the Fallows and plowed Lands were practised in some Parts of Britain, and especially in Scot-

land, they would find it turn to such Account, and so effectually improve the waste lands . . . that the Sheep would be more valuable, and Lands turn to a better Account than was ever yet known among them.

In fact, the system was adopted in widespread fashion in eastern England and in the Midlands, but little further. It survived well into the nineteenth century, with wheeled iron hurdles coming into use in the 1840s, partly to save the labour of constantly re-erecting the hurdles and partly because the heavy iron spike or 'drift' used by the shepherd to make holes for hurdle-stakes put at risk the tiled drains that by now were being laid in large numbers in order to improve drainage.

A second development, whose origins seem to stretch back to the late medieval period and which was described in the mid-sixteenth century by Rowland Vaughan and by Sir Anthony Fitzherbert before becoming more formalized in the late seventeenth century, was the 'floating' of meadows, in which landowners found a means to bridge the awkward weeks when winter hay was in short supply by engineering an earlier appearance to the spring grass. At the core of this scheme lay the controlled flooding of pasture meadows during winter, the carefully introduced body of water both protecting the grass from frost and irrigating it to the point where a lush crop would be produced during the early weeks of spring when flocks were in greatest danger of going hungry. Early methods made use of channels dug into the turf, but later wooden ducts were built to carry the water. This form of installation was comparatively costly, but the reward was a many-fold increase in the grass crop, delivered some weeks before it would otherwise become available for the ewes and their spring lambs. Either one of two methods might be chosen, according to local topography.

In the flowing (or bedwork) system, designed for low-lying ground bordering rivers, a weir or sluice was first constructed to dam the river in order to provide a reliable supply. A duct drew water from the river and delivered it to every corner of the meadow via a series of smaller channels or carriages branching to either side, with hatches or secondary sluices at intervals within the system to ensure an even distribution over the entire surface. Between each pair of carriages, drains were introduced which led the water to the other end of the meadow, where it was fed back into the river. These carriages and drains were constructed of timber, as were the hatches, sluices and stops. By these means the entire terrain would be covered with a sheet of water about 1 inch deep, which would be kept gently flowing for as long as the danger of frost persisted. Normally the meadow would be kept continuously covered, although during a mild spell it might be drained for a period in order to let it breathe.

By way of alternative, a so-called catchwork system was evolved for land lying on an incline and watered by streams: these would be tapped as above for their water, which would be carried along the contours by a similar series of ducts and allowed to overflow down the slope, the residue to be drained away at the bottom.

Meadows which had been floated in this way would be ready for the ewes by mid-March (wethers were never afforded this luxury), by which time a crop of grass about 6 inches high could be expected. The last of the water would be drained and the meadow allowed to air for a few days before the sheep were introduced; in order to avoid them scouring on the rich diet of grass, care had to be taken to feed them well on hay beforehand. Thereafter the normal routine was for the sheep to be brought in during late morning, after the last of any dampness had dissipated; they would

be driven off again to the fold in the late afternoon, so that their rich cargo of dung could be delivered directly to the arable. By the end of April the grass would have been cropped close to the ground, at which point the flow of water would be resumed for a few days before the meadow was put up for hay; again a crop several times that produced by a conventional meadow could be expected, and indeed two or even three crops might be won from it before the timber ducts had to be cleaned and made ready for the first of the winter floodwaters.

Eric Kerridge, in a useful review of the system of floating, describes it as one of the cardinal means to improvement of the late sixteenth to eighteenth centuries. He suggests that it was first introduced in Herefordshire, before being widely adopted on the thin soils of the chalk by the middle of the seventeenth century (John Aubrey places its introduction to Wiltshire to around 1635). It was a relatively costly undertaking, often carried out on a cooperative basis: Wade Martins identifies floating schemes as providing early examples of mutually beneficial collaboration between landowners and tenants, adducing examples for Dorset to Suffolk. Cutting and Cummings mention its adoption as far north as Scotland and estimate that a total in excess of 100,000 acres of watermeadows were constructed between the seventeenth and the nineteenth centuries. By the second half of the eighteenth century, however, floating had largely fallen from use, rendered redundant by the more easily won root crops that made the sheep's survival through the winter a less perilous business.

WOOL AND BREED TYPES

As early as the twelfth century, the higher valuations attributed to fine-woolled over coarse-woolled sheep mark the greater importance beginning to be attributed to the fleece and reflect the early

149 Monumental brass (detail) of a woolman, probably William Midwinter, *c.* 1500, in the Church of St Peter and St Paul at Northleach (Gloucestershire). His right foot rests on a sheep and his left on a woolsack bearing his merchant's mark; the sack is tied at the corners and stitched along the edge. Midwinter is known to have exported much of his wool to Calais via the London staple.

results of a growing export trade that would be in full swing in following century. The high quality of at least some of the native wool is indisputable, and on the Continent for a time English wool enjoyed a higher reputation than that of Spain. There were many competitors amongst the fine wool producers of the Continent, however, and in time the emphasis amongst English producers shifted to the production of longer wool, in which field they again began to excel. A final phase in this development saw a further shift to the production of finished textiles for export. Generations of wool merchants grew rich on this trade (illus. 149), the effects of which can be seen in the grandly built 'wool churches' of East Anglia and Cotswolds, and in the fine houses they built for themselves in market towns. A host of others besides the breeders and merchants won their livings from the backs of the sheep population, including carders, spinners, weavers, fullers and dyers.

Characterization of the medieval sheep population remains a difficult and imprecise task: no true breeds in the modern sense existed, although there were undoubted regional types: some of these already had established reputations and would become the progenitors of later true breeds in which their particular qualities came to be fixed by careful husbandry. Conformation remained of little interest to sheepmen at this time, their principal requirements being that the particular variety would flourish in the (often demanding) environment in which they were to lead their lives, and that they should produce the maximum amount of fleece of the best possible character.

Michael Ryder, who has written with unmatched authority on sheep through time and over much of the world, distinguishes three principal groupings amongst those of early medieval Britain: a native, brown-woolled, horned type akin to the present-day Soay and Shetland sheep, with fine, soft wool;

a white-faced type with some distant relationship with the Merino sheep of the Continental mainland; and a black-faced group with a rather hairy fleece occupying much of a swath from Northumbria and Yorkshire south-westwards to the Welsh border. Of these the first group is composed of descendants of the sheep present in the British Isles since the prehistoric period and making up the general population at the time of the Roman conquest of Britain; the second is thought perhaps to have been introduced by the Romans themselves; and from its genetic relationships with Scandinavian sheep the third group is thought to be a Viking Age introduction. The greatest economic impact would be made by animals in the second group, amongst which two principal sub-types arose – one with short wool similar to (but not identical with) the modern Ryeland breed, and a longer-woolled type somewhat similar to the modern Romney. The Ryeland type, thriving especially on the thin but dry pastures of the Welsh Marches and in the West Midlands, produced fine-quality wool that rivalled that of the Merino, while those characterized as of Lindsey type, centred on the grasslands and marshes Lincolnshire but stretching to Yorkshire and the Midlands, and of the Cotswolds (including Gloucestershire and Oxfordshire) – and to a lesser extent those of Leicestershire – came to dominate the export market in long wool. Through crosses with native breeds, this type had also produced the white- and tan-faced sheep characteristic of much of northern and western Britain. Somewhat coarser wools were produced on the chalk downlands; these fleeces were still of commercial value, but those of Devon and Cornwall were deemed too coarse for the export market.

THE EARLY MODERN SHEEP

The middle of the eighteenth century marked something of a watershed in ovine history, for it was from this time onwards that the modern conformation of the sheep was forged. Two principal agencies helped bring about these changes, namely improved diet and selective breeding.

Even if the long-held belief in a general autumn cull has been exposed as largely mythical, it remains true that the capacity to feed sheep (and other livestock) through the winter placed a limit on the size of the flock – and, indeed, on the size of the animals themselves. With the general adoption of winter feeding on turnips in particular (but also on other vegetables such as cabbages) this cycle was broken, and the numbers of animals able to be overwintered was increased: Youatt estimated that two or three times the number could be sustained in this way. At times the flock might be allowed to graze these crops where they grew, but routine harvesting of the crop and hand-feeding of the sheep further contributed to their wellbeing: Horne gives details of a device called the tumbril, an annular alternative to the trough, constructed of timber and wattle, into which the turnips could be placed so that sheep could feed in an orderly fashion. This regime-change brought to an end for the more fortunate flocks the rigours of winter pasturing and generated, incidentally, a new means of enriching the soil by introducing a third course of rotation. A price was paid by the older sheep (the 'crones'), however, whose failing teeth prevented them from participating in the turnip bonanza and who came in consequence to be routinely culled before they started losing body weight.

The impulse for improvement that permeated so many aspects of life in the later eighteenth century made itself felt in spectacular form in the sheep population through the efforts of two or three generations of dedicated husbandmen, amongst whom the name of Robert Bakewell of Dishley stands out as the most significant (see pp. 426–30). Others had already begun to take the first steps towards improvement by selective breeding before Bakewell came on the scene: the name of Joseph Allom of Clifton (Leicestershire) is invariably mentioned as one of these, and John Ellman of Glynde (Sussex) achieved successes with Southdown sheep which rival in a quiet way the achievements of Bakewell. Just as the Dishley blood would prove most valuable in bringing about successful crosses, the Southdowns too are notable for their success in bringing about the valuable Suffolk (Southdown/Norfolk cross) and Hampshire (Southdown/Wiltshire cross) breeds.

In the world of sheep Bakewell's supreme achievement was the isolation of the New Leicester breed – produced with the butcher rather than the wool merchant in mind. The progenitors of the new breed were drawn from the old, unimproved Leicesters and Lincolns – gangling, long-woolled animals whose fleece had declined in value as improved feeding turned it coarse, together with sheep from the West Midlands of Ryeland type. By repeated in-and-in breeding (p. 428) the New Leicester gradually emerged, now more readily fattened (although with flesh that was itself extremely fatty). When crossed with other breeds it had the advantage of transmitting its tendency to early maturity, which recommended it immediately to farmers everywhere.

Bakewell himself never set out to become the owner of an extensive flock, but concentrated his efforts instead on breeding first-quality rams which he then let out to flockmasters for a fee. When first recorded, around 1770, the prices he charged per ram were as low as 5 guineas for a season's use. The scheme got off to a rocky start, for Youatt reports that at first Bakewell 'had difficulty in inducing the farmers to act upon his plan. His

whole scheme of improvement was ridiculed and opposed, and most of all by those who lived in his immediate neighbourhood.' By the late 1700s, however, Culley could report that Bakewell had let tups, for one season only, for as much as 400 guineas each and had taken in ewes at 10 guineas each; in one instance, with a single ram named Two Pounder, he made a spectacular 1,200 guineas in a single season. By now Bakewell's rams were treated with extraordinary deference, being sent out to fulfil their contractual duties from mid-September onwards in well-sprung carriages, in order to ensure their comfort and well-being.

Fifteen years of careful breeding brought about for Bakewell an animal whose early-maturing carcass and short legs placed as much emphasis as possible on the production of flesh (see illus. 135). While he undoubtedly succeeded in this aim, Bakewell's achievements came at a cost: the quality of the mutton suffered, as did the fleece; sheep now had to be slaughtered at two years of age, otherwise they became too fat for refined tastes. (Until this time wethers had customarily been slaughtered at four or five years.) Also, the capacity of the ewes to produce lambs on an assured annual basis was inhibited: as much as any other factor, it was this lack of prolificacy that would be the undoing of the breed in its pure form. His contribution was none the less of an enduring quality, for his sheep formed successful crosses with many other breeds, perhaps most impressively with Lincolns and Cheviots, in which crosses many of the initial faults of the New Leicester were resolved. The formula was not an infallible one, however: neither the Cotswold nor Devon breeds in the south, the Ryeland of the Midlands or the black-face sheep of the Borders gained anything from interbreeding, although this scarcely inhibited the New Leicester from influencing flocks over much of the territory from northern Scotland to

Cornwall, at the expense of the old short-woolled Cheviots and the coarse-woolled Scottish types.

Apart from the matter of selection to improve the breed, other aspects of sheep husbandry received the attentions of the improvers at this time. Marshall, for example, experimented with putting the rams to the flock on his lowland farm at various dates from 20 September to 20 November, in order to ensure that the lambs arrived early in the spring – but not so early that fodder for the ewe was in short supply. Most breeders took Michaelmas (29 September) as the starting point for the tupping season; where the rams ran with the flock this activity might be controlled by 'clouting' or 'rugging' – fitting the ram with an apron that would frustrate his advances to the ewes – but in keeping with the desire to exert maximum control over the process, the most careful breeders would isolate the ram in a pen where the ewes could be brought to him in turn, one ram normally serving between 40 and 80 ewes in a season (although as many as 140 could be covered in this way). It was all a long

way from the kind of husbandry propagated by Markham in the previous century, when he advocated, for example, that

> If you would have your Ewes bring forth Male Lambes, note when the North Winde bloweth, and driving your Flocke against the winde: let your Rammes ride as they goe, and this will make the Ewes conceive Male Lambes; so likewise, if you would have female Lambes, put your Rams to the Ewes when the winde bloweth out of the South.

Some of the products of this intensive breeding for bulk, as recorded in contemporary paintings, look so grotesque to our eyes that we can scarcely believe the accuracy of the representation. On the other hand, the unquestionably accurate scale-model of a 'fat Leicestershire ewe' by George Garrard (illus. 150) provides objective confirmation that the natural conformation of the sheep was indeed distorted to such an unlikely extent.

150 *A fat Leicestershire Ewe,* a model in plaster by George Garrard (1760–1826).

By the nineteenth century the various disparate and highly localized varieties had been consolidated into perhaps twenty principal breeds, many of them enhanced with blood from the New Leicester and other improved sheep. These dominated the rich pasture lands of the lowlands, but space has prevented any detailed account being given here of the hill sheep that accounted for the bulk of the population in the highland zone. Culley records seeing sheep in Ireland in huge quantities but of little merit: 'I never saw such ill-formed ugly sheep as these', he writes; 'the worst breeds we have in Great Britain are by much superior . . . they are almost in every respect contrary to what I apprehend a well-formed sheep should be.' Their potential for improvement was, he apprehended, hampered by the fact that 'the same law is in full force against exporting sheep into Ireland, as into France, or to any of our national enemies on the Continent'.

Wales and Scotland would continue to breed their own hardy animals that would mature in the demanding environment of the bare hillside before joining the droves that converged on the growing urban centres of England, notably London, until the expanding railway system developed to the point where they made the journey as carcasses. In Scotland in particular, the vast flocks of sheep that displaced thousands of crofters and villagers in the era of the notorious Highland clearances of the later eighteenth century were drawn largely from the black-faced group originally confined to England but which throve in their new home to give rise to the modern Scottish blackface. On the furthest fringes of the western and northern isles the most primitive varieties, including the Soay and Orkney breeds, survived unaltered as they do to this day.

A reminder of the much harsher conditions endured by these upland animals is provided by the documented practice of waterproofing sheep to help them survive the rigours of the hillside. As practised in the northern counties of England and described by Houghton in 1728, the custom was to bring the sheep down from the hill in autumn, when the shepherd would have prepared a mixture of some 5–6 gallons of tar and 20 pounds of butter for every 500 sheep:

> he greases his sheep, opening the wool by platts, greasing and chafing it into the pelt or skin of the sheep, till he had greas'd him thus all over. A good man greaser will grease twelve sheep thus in a day; and if they were not greas'd they would not live three years, without dying of the rot and being pelt beaten, so that the wool would drop from their backs of it self.

Earlier, Henry Best in 1641 had advocated the late autumn greasing of lambs with tallow, similarly to repel the wet and to act as a salve against the attentions of lice and infection with scab. Ryder considers such treatments to have performed no useful function whatever.

THE MERINO INTERLUDE

Over the centuries while regard for English wool on the Continent rose and fell again, one breed was held in unwaveringly high regard – the Merino of the Iberian peninsula. Its genes became widely distributed through European sheep as breeders sought to improve the fleece quality of their own flocks, but it was not until the latter decades of the eighteenth century that it made direct impact in Britain (illus. 151). Writing in his *Observations on Livestock*, which went through several editions during those years, George Culley observed that the breed had 'a strong claim to public attention

151 *A Merino Ram and Ewe.* Attempts were made to establish pure-bred Merino herds in the later 18th century; at the same time an extensive programme of cross-breeding sought to improve the fleeces of native sheep. Lithograph after William Shiels, from David Low's *Breeds of Domestic Animals* (1842).

from the powerful influence it promises to have, in ameliorating the quality of our staple commodity, wool'. (It may be noted that the fineness of its wool, resulting from the meagre diet on which it had to exist, was regarded in England as the only point in its favour, for Spanish flockmasters had made no attempt to interfere with the 'very imperfect' form of its carcass, which remained totally unimproved and goat-like in character.) In its native country the flocks yielding the best wool were considered to be the *trashumantes*, which spent their entire lives in forced migrations from maritime winter grazing grounds to summer pastures in the mountains, a regime that had the

advantage of maintaining reasonably stable and temperate conditions for their development – conditions that would be impossible to reproduce even in the softer lowlands of southern England. Perhaps it was a certain nervousness at the potential problems of transplanting them that contributed to the length of time it took them to cross the Channel, and in any case Spain had imposed an absolute ban on the export of the live sheep that represented one of that country's most valuable assets.

These regulations were circumvented in 1785 when William Burton Conyngham of Slane Castle (Meath) clandestinely imported a ram and two ewes, evidently having been impressed by the breed on a visit to Spain two years earlier. Within three years Conyngham could boast 27 pure-bred Spanish sheep and had also crossed them successfully with native sheep of the Connaught breed. At about the same time, Sir Joseph Banks was presented with a single ram and a ewe from the experimental flock under the control of Louis-Jean-Marie Daubenton, then professor of rural economy at the French École Royale Vétérinaire. By the following spring a number of crosses had been successfully produced at Banks's estate near Hounslow; these experiments, involving Southdown, Herefordshire, Wiltshire and Lincolnshire ewes, as well as two from as far afield as Caithness, were continued until 1795, when Banks presented the remnant of his Spanish flock to Arthur Young at Bradfield Hall (Suffolk).

By this time Banks was already involved in a much larger project, having been commanded in 1787 to form a flock of Merinos for King George III. His first response had been to apply again to Daubenton, and by the following spring the first handful of Merinos had arrived at Windsor from Paris. Since the realization of Banks's ambition for a royal flock of some 200 sheep was clearly going to take some time by legitimate means, he eventually resorted to subterfuge: taking advantage of the animals' habitual winter movement to Extremadura, close to the Portuguese border, discreet arrangements were made for small numbers of them to be spirited over the frontier for trans-shipment to England via Lisbon. Even so, the numbers remained small and by 1790 there were still no more than 27 sheep in the royal flock, but a gift directly from Spain in 1792 brought the numbers up to about 100.

Thereafter new lambs gradually increased the size of the flock, although there were also severe losses due to poor management. Frustrated by the lack of close control, Banks arranged for the entire flock to be transferred from the grazing they shared with the other royal flocks at Windsor and at Kew to the royal park at Oatlands (Surrey), where they could be segregated and subjected to a more rigorous regime. The sheep were individually identified with identity tags (termed 'pastoral ear-rings') produced to Banks's specification by Matthew Boulton, and under closer scrutiny the flock began to fare better.

A primary ambition of the King was to introduce his Merino fleeces into the British market, and their first shearing had been eagerly anticipated. The wool was duly recognized by the manufacturers to be of the finest quality, yet at first none of them would offer a price equivalent to that commanded by Spanish wool, evidently being in doubt as to whether its superficial properties would survive the test of manufacture into cloth. Doggedly, the King decided to have it made up at his own expense, and continued to do so for several years until finally, in 1796, the excellence of the finished product was acknowledged – although he still had to accept at first a price below that of the Spanish wool. Thereafter it rose year by year – from 2s. a pound in 1799, reaching 5s. 6d. a pound in 1801 and peaking at 6s. 9d. a pound.

As surplus rams became available from the royal flock they were presented or sold off so that other entrepreneurs could explore the possibilities of the breed. Dr Caleb Parry of Bath began in 1792 to cross his Ryeland ewes with Merino rams ultimately from the royal flock and was gratified with an improvement in the quality of the wool which retained all the fineness of the imported animals; his flock eventually grew to some 300–400 sheep and lambs. Lord Somerville, who had proved an exceptionally imaginative and effective president of the Board of Agriculture, went so far as to journey abroad in order to acquire 'the whole system of sheep-husbandry as practised in Spain' and in

1801 brought home a flock of the finest *trashumantes*, which he crossed experimentally to such good effect as to receive 'sundry premiums from Bath and West of England Society and much profit'. By 1810 several hundred flocks are said to have benefited from an injection of Merino blood, with the South Downs and Ryelands, which had proved so rewarding for Lord Somerville, emerging as the breeds benefiting most rewardingly from crossing. A Merino Society was founded in 1811 with Banks as its first president and with no fewer than 54 vice-presidents drawn from the ranks of the aristocracy and from wealthy breeders.

Quite quickly, however, a plateau was reached beyond which it proved impossible to maintain the improvement brought by the breed (an experience common to many such enterprises) and interest in the Merino began to fall way as quickly as it had developed. On 16 March 1812 we find the Commissioners of His Majesty's Real and Personal Estate writing to Banks concerning overcrowding on the royal sheep pastures and suggesting that a sale of stock was overdue, to which Banks replied on the same day that while Merino sheep had been selling for £50 a head two years previously, 'now they are scarce worth a Mutton price & as there are from 4 to 6000 imported sheep now in the Country which cannot be sold even on Low terms . . . I do not see at present any hopes we can have of being able to dispose of any breeding sheep of that kind at any Rate whatever'. Within 30 years the situation had reached the point where there scarcely existed, 'except in the hands of the curious, a single flock of the mixed progeny from which so much was anticipated'. This was at one time considered to be perhaps an over-pessimistic view, their genes surviving to good effect in a number of fine-woolled British sheep. Most recently, however, Ryder has backed the contrary view, first expressed by Youatt who was inclined to deny that any such amelioration could be attributed to the influence of the Merino: neither foreign blood nor even the influence of the New Leicesters was responsible, he claimed, but rather the intelligent practice of the true principles of breeding, which ensured that 'the sexual intercourse of the sheep was no longer a matter almost of chance-medley'.

GOATS

Goats are much less visible in the historical record than sheep, but their hardy nature and milking qualities may have meant that they were quite widely distributed amongst the less well-documented peasantry even if largely absent from the more extensive demesne farms. Trow-Smith notes that in Norfolk the size of sheep and goat populations varied inversely according to whether properties lay in open pasture or in woodland, and the importance of topography to their distribution is confirmed by Gervase Markham's account of the goat, 'a beast of hot, strong, and lusty constitution; especially in the act of generation', given in his *Cheape and Good Husbandry* (1616):

Seeing Goates are not of any generall use in our Kingdome, but onely nourished in some wilde and barraine places, where Cattell of better profit can hardly be maintained, as in the mountainous parts of Wales, in the barrainest parts of Cornewall and Devonshire, on Malborne hils, and some few about the Peake . . . The profit that commeth from them is their Milke, which is an excellent restorative, and their Kids which are an excellent Venison . . . Some do use to sheare them, to make rough mantles of, but it is not so with us in England. The Goates would be kept in small stockes, or heards, as not above a hundred in a heard: as they must in the heate of the sommer have much shade, so in the winter likewise much shelter, for they can neither endure extreamitie of heate nor cold . . . Onely the unnatural excesse of their lust maketh them grow soone old, and so both past use and profit.

Thomas Pennant confirms that a century and a half later the goat remained confined to the mountainous parts of the country which, given its propensity to eating anything that grew, he evidently considered no bad thing: 'his most beloved food is the tops of boughs, or the tender bark of young trees; on which account he is so prejudicial to plantations, that it would be imprudent to draw him from his native rocks'. The inhabitants of Caernarvonshire, he continues, 'suffer these animals to run wild on the rocks during winter as well as summer; and kill them in October, for the sake of their fat; either by shooting them with bullets, or running them down with dogs, like deer'. (On the same principle that led to bulls being baited before slaughter, Thomas Moffet suggested that he-goat's flesh was improved by placing them under stress before killing them.) Their haunches could be salted and dried like bacon, while their suet made excellent candles, their skin fine gloves, and their hair the whitest periwigs.

PIGS

Although Swine are accounted troublesome, noysome, unruly, and great ravenours . . . yet the utility and profit of them, will easily wipe off those offences.
Gervase Markham, 1616

Until it began to engage the interest of improving breeders in the eighteenth century, the pig (*Sus*

scrofa) was essentially a poor man's animal, rarely if ever forming large-scale flocks in the manner of sheep or cattle but yet – singly or in small numbers, hidden away in innumerable yards and hovels across the countryside – challenging these other domesticates in terms of overall numerical supremacy. Native swine were by nature quite prolific: Walter of Henley anticipated that if the sows were allowed to forage for themselves and were helped through the lean months from February to April, they should farrow three times a year; although this was undoubtedly optimistic, their natural fecundity was none the less a pleasing characteristic, and a feature of the native stock that would prove difficult to sustain in the crossbreeds produced by improvers in the eighteenth century. A breeding sow might be expected to remain productive for six years; perhaps seven piglets in a litter could be expected, although the poor diet on which most had to subsist may have imposed a lower limit. Pigs destined to be fattened as hogs purely for the pot were neutered at about two weeks.

THE STOCK

At the time of the Conquest, the domestic pig population remained almost indistinguishable in nature from the wild swine that continued to inhabit the forests and which remained the subject of hunting rather than husbandry (see p. 133). One of the tasks of the swineherd would indeed have been to protect his sows from the unwelcome attentions of wild boars – no small mission – in order to prevent the stock from reverting to a totally wild state. As it was, the average domesticate, razor-backed and long-legged, with a bristly, reddish-brown coat and erect ears (illus. 152), remained little changed physically – except, perhaps, in point of size, being somewhat reduced

152 Swineherds shaking the branches for acorns, for the benefit of their typical forest pigs. From the early 14th-century Queen Mary's Psalter.

– from their wild cousins. In some areas, such as northern and western Scotland, this race (or some scarcely altered varieties of the same) flourished right up to the Victorian period: Youatt describes the 'immense herds' of them still being driven southwards on an annual basis until about 1800, when the trade faltered for a time before being restored to some degree with the wider availability of potatoes to sustain them. Reports of wild swine surviving in nineteenth-century Scotland are surely to be interpreted as indicating the presence of feral rather than indigenous pigs, although such an eminent naturalist as James Ritchie was inclined to derive them from the very earliest stages of domestication. This may introduce an unnecessarily long time-scale, however, when one considers the character of the domestic swine of Caithness, as seen 'tethered in every field' by Thomas Pennant in the late eighteenth century: these can scarcely have been distinguishable from their wild cousins, being 'short, high-backed, long-bristled,

sharp, slender and long-nosed [with] long erect ears, and most savage looks'. Escapees must have been all too frequent from such a population, retaining much of its wild and resolute character. In Ireland too the pigs most commonly encountered at this time retained many features of the unimproved stock (illus. 153), as they evidently did in parts of Wales, as described by Ritchie: these sound like fearsome animals, which, he says, 'resembled an alligator mounted on stilts, having bristles instead of scales . . . gaunt and with a remarkable extension of the snout'. From being the most common type in England perhaps as late as the eighteenth century, they survived in isolated pockets into the 1800s in the West Country, and in the form of 'forest pigs' in the thickly wooded areas of Hampshire – broad shouldered and high crested, dark in colour with a bristly mane and erect ears, as described by Youatt in 1846. These continued to differ little from the ancient stock, as confirmed by their fierce character, their resistance to fattening and extensive reliance on acorns and beech-mast in their diet. A somewhat idyllic picture of pig husbandry in Hampshire asserted that

Hampshire hogs are allowed by all for the best bacon being our English Westphalian . . . Here the swine feed in the forest on plenty of acorns . . . which, going out lean, return home fat, without care or cost to their owners. Nothing but fulness stinteth their feeding on the mast falling from the trees where also they lodge at liberty (not pent up, as in other places, to stacks of peas) which some assign the reason of the fineness of their flesh.

Such a pig utopia could scarcely have been imagined by the majority of the porcine population by this time and most pigs would have led a fairly miserable existence. Writing in 1796, for example, William Marshall records that it was common practice in Devon to 'shut pigs up in a narrow close hutch, in which they eat, drink and discharge their

153 Pig of the Irish Greyhound breed. Despite its primitive appearance and natural agility (it was said to be able to clear a five-barred gate) the lop ears suggest that some interbreeding has taken place with the Old English strain while the wattles at its throat may indicate the presence of some oriental blood. From H. D. Richardson, *Pigs: Their Origin and Varieties* (1847).

urine and faeces; which are formed into a bed of mud to sleep in, their bristly coats being presently converted into coats of mail; in which filthy plight they remain until they are slaughtered'. Such an abject picture must have been repeated all too often elsewhere in the country. Herds were seldom large, for once the numbers increased to the point where they exceeded the resources available from scavenging the pigs would have found themselves in competition for fodder with the cattle and horses maintained for traction and the whole balance of this finely adjusted economy would have been upset. Monastic pigs may have formed an exception to this rule, however, if we are to judge from evidence from Peterborough Abbey as presented by Kathleen Biddick: here, at the opening of the fourteenth century, the Abbey owned a total of 1,394 pigs distributed over eighteen manors, five of which had flocks of 100 or more animals; these were maintained on a diet including legumes and grains and were, it seems, mostly destined for consumption by the personnel of the Abbey itself.

By the time a domestic stock designated as 'Old English' began to emerge into the historical record, however, its characteristics were already markedly different from the rather primitive medieval type. Although widely distributed up to the seventeenth or early eighteenth century, the means by which the distinctive characteristics of this type were brought about remain essentially undocumented: while their larger size could have been engineered by centuries of careful breeding, their white coats and lop ears indicate that they derive from an unrelated stock introduced from elsewhere. Although further work remains to be done, current opinion favours the introduction – perhaps gradually over many centuries – of a Continental type of improved pig whose ancestry may stretch back as far as the Roman period. The form of this typical 'Old English hog' (illus. 154)

– which clearly was anything but indigenous – represented a variation rather than much of an improvement on the that of the native swine: it was characterized by Youatt as 'long in limb, narrow in the back . . . low in the shoulders, and large in bone; in a word, uniting all those characteristics which are now deemed most objectionable, and totally devoid of any approach to symmetry'. Clearly the improvers of the eighteenth century had a considerable task on their hands if they were to make an impact on this uncouth animal, but it was on this unpromising prototype rather than on native pigs that they would concentrate their efforts.

The pig was slower than other species to attract the attentions of those who set about trying to improve the level of British livestock by the application of some degree of scientific method – perhaps a reflection of its lowly status as primarily a countryman's animal. From the turn of the eighteenth century, however, more purposeful attempts to improve the stock resulted in the introduction of a variety of foreign breeds, not only from Europe but from much further afield. Imported animals from China would eventually transform the qualities of the native stock, adding greatly to their aptitude to ready fattening, earlier maturing and better flesh quality – all on a much lighter frame

154 *Old English Pig*. Although sturdily built, its long snout, lop ears and coat all distinguish it from the 'native' forest swine. Lithograph after William Shiels, from David Low's *Breeds of Domestic Animals* (1842).

than that of the notoriously big-boned 'Old English' types. Other exotic sources contributing new blood to British breeds at this time included Siam, India, Turkey, the Pacific Islands and Africa, as well as the West Indies; a number of German breeds were also experimented with, to which was added (from the early 1800s, at least) a type known as the 'black Neapolitan', itself the result of interbreeding Italian and Far Eastern strains. By the eighteenth century, however, such exotics were sought after not for their curiosity value but with the most serious intentions, namely to produce animals that would fatten rapidly, so turning a quicker profit. Gilbert White provides an eye-witness account of the success of one such cross-bred sow:

> my neighbour, a man of substance . . . kept a half-bred bantam-sow, who was as thick as she was long, and whose belly swept on the ground till she was advanced to her seventeenth year, at which period she showed some tokens of age by the decay of her teeth and the decline of her fertility.

For about ten years this prolific mother produced two litters in the year of about ten at a time, and once above twenty at a litter; but, as there were near double the number of pigs to that of teats, many died . . . At the age of about fifteen her litters began to be reduced to four or five, and such a litter she exhibited when in her fatting-pen. She proved, when fat, good bacon, juicy, and tender; the rind, or sward, was remarkably thin. At a moderate computation she was allowed to have been the fruitful parent of three hundred pigs: a prodigious instance of fecundity in so large a quadruped! She was killed in spring, 1775.

In their anxiety to introduce new blood which might improve the characteristics of their stock, breeders of pigs seem to have paid rather less attention than those experimenting with other animals to the potential of in-breeding, although here the name of Robert Bakewell (p. 426) again stands out. John Monk noted too in 1794 the close attention paid to diet in the experiments carried out at Bakewell's establishment at Dishley Grange:

> In one particular sty are appliances for measuring the food of the hogs, and also for noting down the results, which are done by a servant with a piece of chalk . . . until they zhelped to prevent mistakes and to give conclusive evidence for the experiments.

It took some time for Bakewell's efforts in this area to bear fruit, but by 1847 William Youatt could pronounce the resultant animal as definitely 'superior in value and beauty to the old stock'. As ever, beauty seems to have been very much in the eye of the beholder, for a less sympathetic observer describes Bakewell's improved pig as having 'its belly nearly touching the ground and its eyes and snout looking as if they were almost absorbed into the body'. It seems indeed to have been a general feature of these early 'improved' pigs that they had a tendency to run to fat: some of them weighed in excess of 1,000 pounds and were so burdened by fat that their whole race was in constant danger of suffocation. As outlined below (p. 487), the production of fat was not invariably looked on with disfavour as it would be today, but already the more discriminating consumers were seeking out smaller, leaner animals while leaving the 'snow-white bladders of lard' to consumption by the masses.

By the end of the eighteenth century a confusing plethora of pig types – the product of extensive cross-breeding and with little stability of character

155 *Pig of the Yorkshire Breed*, engraving by R. Pollard, 1809. This specimen weighed 12 cwt at the age of four, but the cost of feeding pigs of this type made them a poor investment.

– characterized the British stock: writing of the situation in Kent, John Boys observed that 'no two pigs are the same', and the same complaint might have been made of the country as a whole. On the other hand, there was evidently a readiness to claim a separate identity for particular races on very slender grounds, with pigs in one region being differently named from virtually identical animals bred at no great distance away. With a new generation of eight to a dozen piglets being produced in under a year, the changes wrought on the stock by experimental breeding were quick to be registered: Trow-Smith observes that in five years the progeny of a single crossed pair could amount to several million pigs.

The Berkshire type was one of the most successful, becoming widely distributed throughout the British Isles; Shropshire and Herefordshire pigs were also esteemed, although they have left little trace of their characteristics. The Yorkshire type, captured in an engraving by R. Pollard (illus. 155), although it might attain a prodigious weight, was characterized by Youatt as 'one of the most unprofitable for the farmer', being a greedy feeder and unsound of constitution, faults which evidently were redeemed by crossing with Leicestershires or with Chinese or Neapolitans. Throughout the country, an entirely new population of pigs was being forged, and in 1847 Youatt could write that

a systematic alteration is extending itself throughout all our English breeds of swine; the large, heavy, coarse breeds are almost extinct, and a smaller race of animals – most apt to fatten, less expensive to keep, attaining earlier to maturity, and furnishing a far more delicious and delicate meat – have taken their place.

In the latter part of the century a greater degree of stability had been achieved and a number of distinct breeds – several of them supported by their own breed associations – had now been established. In 1884 a National Pig Breeders' Association was formed with a view to bringing further order to pig production.

PANNAGE

As already mentioned, the Norman pig population (identical in every way with that of the late Saxon period, when pigs formed the very backbone of the pastoral economy) consisted essentially of animals of the forest and their presence there was a matter of significant economic importance: Julian Wiseman notes that in the *Domesday* survey woods were commonly classified according to the numbers of pigs they supported and he observes too that the revenue from pannage – controlled foraging within the demesne woodland, to be paid for either in cash or kind – might actually exceed the annual returns to the landowner from timber extraction or from charcoal. The comparison is all the more striking for the fact that pannage could be exercised only during a limited season, in order to protect the growing trees from undue damage: typically the season might run from the end of August to the end of December, but at times it could be more restricted – under Henry III for example, pannage could be exercised (in the royal forests, at least) only during the period from midsummer to Michaelmas – while it might extend under more liberal regimes to the point where spring growth began to manifest itself on the trees.

Amongst the resources most valued in pig feeding were acorns and beech-mast – the three-cornered fruits of the beech tree. The pigs were in their element searching these out amongst the fallen leaves on the forest floor. At times the swine-herd might be tempted into encouraging further nuts to fall from the trees by shaking the branches (see illus. 152) but the practice was strictly illegal, carrying as it did the risk of damage to the trees. (Unripe acorns were, in any case, potentially harmful to the pig: Per Kalm would later record on his visit to England in 1748 that a great many swine had been lost the previous year by being given acorns to eat before they had lain for any length of time; this could never have happened with beechnuts, he says, 'which they can eat without harm as soon as they fall down from the tree'.) Other dangers to saplings (and indeed to pasture and growing crops) arose from the animals' predilection to rooting in the ground with their specially adapted snouts – Mascall describes the pig as a 'hurtfull and spoyling beast, stout and hardy, & troublesome to rule' – so that regulations were introduced from time to time requiring all animals turned loose in the forest to be fitted with a ring in their nose in order that the undergrowth (and all the game that depended on it) should by protected. By the nineteenth century, at least, it was customary for the ring to be anchored separately to each nostril, generally by the village blacksmith; alternative strategies to ringing involved driving a peg of holly or similar wood through the membrane separating the nostrils or (as recorded by Youatt) trimming off the ridge of tough cartilage on top of the snout, all of which measures effectively limited the pig to feeding on the surface. Kalm again records that in Kent and Essex they were fitted with triangular wooden yokes round their necks to prevent them forcing their way through hedges and into the cultivated fields – clearly a matter of greater concern after the progressive enclosure of much of the countryside.

Access to the forest remained an important factor in pig husbandry up to the eighteenth and nineteenth centuries when more industrial-scale production began to take over. Without recourse to these natural resources, owners would have been saddled with additional costs in peas, beans or grain in order to bring their animals up to condition for the market. As late as the nineteenth century, Wiseman records that residents in the New Forest retained rights to pannage which resulted in some 20,000 pigs annually being seasonally nourished in this way.

Before leaving the matter of pannage, the point may be stressed that this most appealing aspect of the pig economy, being as we have seen strictly seasonal in its operation, could never have supported the pig population all the year round. During the long months when access to the forest remained closed, pigs had to make do with whatever green vegetation they could access, supplemented with such fodder – often of the lowest quality – as might casually be generated by other activities. Markham characterized its typical diet as follows:

> his foode and living is by that which would else rot in the yard, make it beastly . . . breed noysome smells, corruption and infection. From the Husband-man he taketh Pulse, Chaffe, Barne-dust, Mans-ordure, Garbage, and the weeds of his yard, and from the Huswife her Draffe, Swillings, Whey, washing of Tubs, and such like.

Pigs were in general less closely associated with arable economy than were other farm animals and would seldom have had access to extensive grazing: indeed, with the expansion of ploughland at the expense of the forest it seems likely that the pig population would have dwindled accordingly.

THE OFFICE OF SWINEHERD

There was seldom any question of pigs simply being turned loose and left to their own devices: standard practice involved the presence of a swineherd, both to protect the pigs from predatory animals (including any wild swine that might occupy the same forest) and to keep them under control. In the case of manorial estates with a sizeable population of pigs, a man might be employed specifically for this purpose. The early fourteenth-century *Seneschaucie* gives the following advice regarding 'the office of swineherd':

> The swineherd ought to be on those manors where swine can be sustained and kept in the forest, or in woods, or waste, or in marshes, without sustenance from the grange; and if the swine can be kept with little sustenance from the grange during hard frost, then must a pigsty be made in a marsh or wood, where the swine may be night and day. And when the sows have farrowed, let them be driven with the feeble swine to the manors and kept with the leavings as long as the hard frost and the bad weather last, and then driven back to the others. And if there is no wood or marsh or waste where the swine may be sustained without being altogether kept on the grange, no swineherd or swine shall be on the manor, except only such as can be kept in August on the stubble and leavings of the grange, and when the corn is threshed for sale, and as soon as they are in good condition and well, let them be sold. For whoever will keep swine for a year from the cost of the grange alone, and count the cost and the allowance for the swine and swineherd, together with the damage they do yearly to the corn, he shall lose twice as much as he shall gain, and this will be seen by whoever keeps account.

While the *Seneschaucie*'s unsentimental evaluation of the pig was couched in terms of manorial economy, the majority of pigs – at least until the agricultural revolution of the eighteenth century – were owned in ones or twos by small households and the normal practice was for a swineherd to be employed jointly by an entire community. It would be his (or her) task to gather all the animals from their individual homesteads every morning, and having assembled the flock to drive them all together into the forest, see to their safekeeping throughout the day and return the animals to their respective owners in the evening. Payment to the swineherd might be made in kind, perhaps with a sucking pig annually, with some minor parts (such as the tails or the entrails) at slaughtering time, or with some small sum of money – perhaps as little as a farthing – per head of the animals entrusted to his care. The swineherd could also form an intermediary in the payment of dues from the owners of the pigs to the landlords of the forest: Trow-Smith notes that in the *Exon Domesday*, compiled in 1086 and listing the resources of the south-western counties, 264 swineherds are listed, rendering rents in kind of 1,343½ swine, as well as 110 others rendering nothing.

PIGS IN THE AGRICULTURAL ECONOMY

Notoriously omnivorous by inclination, the pig more than any other animal was seen as a convenient and profitable means of disposing of virtually any kind of organic waste. Culley observed that 'they gather up, and greedily devour, what would otherwise be trodden under foot and wasted – The refuse of the fields, the gardens, the barns, and the scullery, to them is a feast'. There was an understandable reluctance among owners to squander more grain on them than was absolutely necessary, an error well appreciated by the writers of early texts such as the fourteenth-century *Seneschaucie*. On the other hand, Markham and others acknowledged that swill alone could not sustain a pig and recommended a regime in which a diet gained principally from grazing in the hedgerows, wastes and marshes played a major part. The owners of orchards too found a useful synergy in the rearing of pigs, for the animals could be relied on to clear the ground of windfalls (minimizing the risks to the fruit trees from pests), while enriching the soil with their dung. The Gloucester Old Spot was so closely identified with this practice that its alternative name was the Orchard Pig.

Pannage (as described above) formed a valuable contribution to the natural diet of the pig, both during its years as a store animal and in its finishing for the market. For those without access to woodland, pulses rather than grain formed the principal element in the supplementary diet of the pig and indeed the reputation as successful pig-rearing centres achieved by some areas – notably the Midland counties including Leicestershire and Northamptonshire – are ascribed to their capacity to produce these crops in large quantities specifically as fodder. In general, though, it was only in the final weeks of its life, while it was being fattened for slaughter, that the average pig would benefit from regular and substantial feeds of dried pulses, or when they might be turned loose briefly to gorge on peas or similar crops in order to prepare them for their appointment with the butcher.

The necessity of this final fattening stage was of crucial importance, and while almost every humble cottager could keep a pig at no great cost and ultimately could convert it into cash or eat it himself, William Cobbett shows that life was never quite that simple. Breeding piglets from birth was a stratagem he was absolutely against for the cottager, since the sow had to be copiously fed in order to nourish her offspring. Rather, he suggested, it made better sense for the pig to be bought in the spring time, already weaned and four months old, by which age it ought to be able to survive on anything that an old hog would eat; if the owner was a home-brewer of beer, he would have the advantage of grains to add to the wash. By the end of the year, however, the prospect of feeding the pig in order to keep it in condition would loom; at this point, he suggested, with the pig at a year old and fit for eating, it was better to slaughter it there and then, and to start the process again the following spring.

An engaging picture of a peasant society, rich in pigs if almost nothing else, is conjured up in Youatt's description of mid-nineteenth-century Ireland where, as he says, swine abounded in all parts: 'scarcely a peasant's cot but numbers a pig among the family; and the roads, lanes, and fields in the neighbourhood of every village, and the suburbs of every large town, are infested with a grunting multitude'. Moncrieff cites what must surely have been a geographically more restricted sight, as recorded by Thomas Pennant during his tour of Scotland in 1771–5: he writes that in Morayshire it was not unusual to see a cow, a sow and two young horses all yoked together in a plough. Controlling such a team must have taken all the ploughman's skill and it seems unlikely that pigs featured commonly in the draught elsewhere, although they are by no means lacking in intelligence: a few famous individuals were trained, for example, to substitute for hunting hounds, while numbers of porcine prodigies toured the country in Victorian funfairs.

The early entry of certain monasteries into the pig economy has already been mentioned (p. 478). Reviewing the evidence from Bolton Priory (Yorkshire), Annie Grant notes that whereas pigs formed only 3 per cent of the Priory's stock as recorded in the early fourteenth-century account books,

yet the animal bones recovered from the site indicate that 30 per cent of the carcasses consumed were from pigs. The discrepancy is, perhaps, a comment on the status of the pig as exclusively a source of food, the other animals being too valuable as providers of wool or of tractive power to kill until they could serve no further purpose.

The rise of towns carried with it no immediate imperative for this cottage economy to come to an end, and considerable populations of pigs were to be found in the back yards and waste plots of every town. The average urban pig would have had to subsist on an even less wholesome diet than its country cousin: household scraps were supplemented by waste from butchers' shambles, mills, skinners and other trades: Markham mentions that 'around York and London, they feed them Chandlers Graines, which is the dregs and offal of rendred Tallow, as hard skinnes, kils, and fleshy lumps, which will not melt, together with other course Skinnes of the Tallow, Suet, or Kitchen fee . . . mixed with warm wash' – a diet which, he writes, would 'puff them up', after which they were finished for a short period on dried peas to harden their flesh. Small wonder that as early as 1726 it was observed in the *Dictionarium Rusticum* of those allowed to forage in the forest that 'their Flesh will prove much better and sweeter than if fattn'd in a Stye'.

Until the advent of the railways, pigs – like all other livestock – are said frequently to have been driven long distances from their breeding grounds to market, a progress that might also involve a respite period as store beasts while they gained in weight and maturity and a 'finishing' period – quite possibly at a different venue – in which a concentrated diet of pulses and (after their widespread establishment) potatoes would ensure that the best price was gained from the butcher. There was, for example, a long tradition of Welsh pigs being driven to Gloucestershire for finishing as bacon, while Bonser records that in 1836 some 4,500 Irish pigs alone were recorded as travelling the turnpike from Bristol to London. These facts seem to fly in the face of present-day opinion that pigs were neither readily amenable to being herded nor possessed of the stamina necessary for long-distance droving. To a degree, the unimproved nature of the early pig may have suited it to marathon journeys of this sort which, as we shall see, could never have been contemplated by their more highly evolved cousins.

For the pig to make progress in its physical improvement, however, a more purposeful approach to feeding was demanded. Although its amenability would later recommend it for association with a number of industrial processes, the most long-lived practice was one in which natural resources played the principal role.

PIGS ASSOCIATED WITH OTHER ECONOMIES

It had long been recognized by those keeping dairy cattle that there was an economic advantage to having a pig that might be fed at little cost with the residues from butter- and cheese-making, and with the rise of larger-scale dairying (pp. 450–51), in which these resources became concentrated to an increasing degree, pigs provided a means of turning waste into a new source of profit on a significant scale. In 1817, for example, William Marshall reported as follows on dairies in the neighbourhood of Chelmsford (Essex):

skimmed milk is usually applied to the purposes of feeding porkers, or small pigs, for the London market . . . the milk is always sour before it reaches the troughs, but on that account there does not appear to lie the least possible objection; as the pigs are always

found to thrive extremely well, and their fat, from repeated trials of comparison, is firmer and vastly superior to that of hogs fattened upon peas or meal.

By the early nineteenth century the dairy waste from twenty cows was said to be sufficient to support twelve pigs, a number that later doubled as milk yields were progressively improved. Rural cider making, producing quantities of waste apple pulp, provided the basis for a further complementary relationship, while urban breweries, distilleries and starch factories, generating copious amounts of potentially nourishing waste, formed an industrial resource that by the eighteenth century had grown to the point where associated pig-rearing was regularly brought within the corporate plan. The origins of this practice are undocumented, but it may have emerged in the wake of the fashion for stiff ruffs, introduced around 1560. Joan Thirsk has found evidence for its regular practice in the early decades of the seventeenth century: in 1621, for example, Jacob Meade, starch-maker, was left with no way of feeding his 200 pigs – an extraordinary number – when he was restrained from making starch for a period of ten weeks, while the pigs belonging to Michael Francis, also a starch-maker, starved to death when he was similarly restrained. By 1748 Kalm reports that

in or near London, the Distillers keep a great many, often from 200 to 600 head, which they feed with the lees, and any thing that is over from the distillery: and after these animals have become fat enough, they are sold to the butcher at a great profit . . . In the same way, and with the same object, a great number of pigs are kept at starch factories, which are fed and fattened on the refuse of wheat, when the starch is manufactured. The house where the swine are kept, is cleaned and washed every day.

By its nature, this starch refuse was less nourishing than that of the brewing and distilling industries, so that dietary supplements of peas and beans were later introduced.

By the following century the scale of production had risen dramatically: on the evidence of James and Malcolm's *General View of the Agriculture of Surrey* (1794), some 600–700 hogs were being fattened at Randall & Suter's starch factory, while the distillers made even more impressive returns. Around 3,000 pigs were fattened annually by Messrs Johnson at Vauxhall, rather more by Benwell's at Battersea and rather less at Bush's of Wandsworth. An annual turnover of nearly 12,000 pigs was estimated for the five major distilleries and starch-works in the greater London area (and the pattern was repeated in provincial towns and cities), the animals being bought in at about fifteen months and sold on six months later. In this way pig fattening became as much an urban as a rural industry.

PIG PRODUCTS

In contrast to the fresh form in which most pork is eaten today, the problems of long-term preservation before the advent of refrigeration led to much of the production being salted. As mentioned above, from the age of improvement a great deal more fat was associated with the flesh, a characteristic that was positively welcomed by producers (though not by more discriminating consumers). Wiseman quotes a pickling process described by Abraham and William Driver in 1794, in which every vestige of lean meat and bone was separated from the fat, which formed a layer some 6 inches thick and which was salted down to become the staple fare of the labouring classes. Its keeping qualities also

recommended it for use on ships of the merchant marine and the Royal Navy, where it would keep for weeks packed in casks.

In 1828 William Cobbett, in his *Cottage Economy*, expressed the desirability that the cottager should pursue at all costs the goal of maximum fat content in rearing his hog:

> Make him fat by all means. If he can walk two or three hundred yards at a time he is not well fatted. Lean bacon is the most wasteful thing that a family can use. In short it is uneatable except by drunkards who want something to stimulate their sickly appetite.

This preoccupation with fat (see illus. 156) began to wane around the middle of the nineteenth century, partly in response to a growing public taste for leaner bacon and partly to the introduction of new methods of curing introduced from the United States, for which the presence of fat was less critical. Only the breeders showing their prize animals at increasingly popular agricultural shows seem to have been heedless of this trend, with the result that overblown animals which had less and less to do with the market continued to throng the show-tents up to the eve of World War One. Several of the smaller breeds had by this time literally been bred to extinction: Wiseman quotes contemporary references to the rapidly vanishing Small Whites as 'animated tubs of lard', frequently unable to stand for the judges, and finds an equally damning account of Black Dorsets from the pen of Sanders Spencer:

> to prevent accidents from suffocation the pigs were supplied with pillows made from round pieces of wood. These were placed by the pig-men under the snouts of the reclining beauties; whilst the effort to walk out of the pens

156 A pig of the improved Suffolk variety, aged one year, one month and a week, which 'took the prize at the Royal Agricultural Show, Battersea, 1862', painted by John Vine, 1862, oil on canvas.

to be examined by the judges was frequently so great that the attempt was often abandoned.

Even today the breeders' preoccupation with 'fancy points' and matters of coloration is sometimes at odds with the more prosaic demands of the market for tasty meat. A further trend which should have concentrated their minds was the increase in imports of pork from overseas, brought about by the advent of increasingly efficient refrigeration systems, so that British producers were by now having to compete with the best in Denmark, New Zealand and Australia, as well as with each other.

The situation was not one that was easily remedied, for some of the staple breeds were by this time said to have been ruined by inappropriate cross-breeding: the formerly much admired Berkshires, for example, had gone hopelessly to fat by the turn of the twentieth century, although

fortunately their close relations the Tamworths – the two names representing perhaps little more than regional labels applied to the same breed – had escaped 'improvement' and suddenly found themselves the subject of close attention as potential saviours of the national gene pool. The Large Whites also emerged into favour at this time, not least in recognition of the fundamental role they had played in establishing the Danish bacon industry as an international market leader.

HORSES

While the broad picture of horse usage is treated here in a separate section (pp. 21–99), it may be useful to single out the role of the horse on the farm for special consideration since it follows a trajectory somewhat distinct from that of the higher-bred mounts favoured by the equestrian classes. As might be expected, there is a greater identity of experience among the various communities of draught horses and packhorses, but the present chapter will allow for some reflection specifically on the history of the horse on the farm.

The earliest records of horses as farm animals show them mostly confined to the lighter work of harrowing rather than ploughing. Attention has been drawn already to the presence of a harrow-horse in the Bayeux Tapestry and others appear in the documentary record from the 1120s, so that by the time a splendid example appears in the Luttrell Psalter of *c.* 1340 (illus. 157) they are very well established – especially on the lighter soils of East Anglia. From the early decades of the twelfth century, horses also begin to make an appearance in the plough-team – usually in conjunction with oxen: a team of two oxen and three horses is noted at Bury St Edmunds, while six oxen and two horses were then in use at Groton (both in Suffolk). Fitz Stephen's account of London in 1174 includes the information that horses suitable for the plough

as well as the cart could be bought there. All the horses at this period were small in stature and effectively were not bred with any sense of potential for improvement.

As is well known, the ability of the horse to perform effectively as a traction animal was transformed with the general introduction of the shoulder-collar, fitting snugly (at least in theory) around the neck and allowing the strain to be taken by the shoulders rather than the neck. Padding helped spread the load: Tusser writes of 'Sedge collers for ploughhorse, for lightnes of neck', but straw became the most common form of stuffing. Spruytte dates the general appearance of the shoulder-collar in Europe to the tenth century, marking the beginnings of what he terms modern draught; on the evidence of the Bayeux Tapestry image, there seems little doubt that its introduction to Britain should be placed no later then the second half of the eleventh century, rather than the twelfth century as formerly held.

The long-contested debate on the respective merits of the horse and the ox as traction animals

157 A harrow-horse at work in the mid-14th century. The horse, in a padded shoulder-collar, is harnessed via a swingletree to a set of tined harrows. From the Luttrell Psalter (*c.* 1340).

158 Horse ploughing in East Anglia in the mid-14th century. From the Macclesfield Psalter (*c.* 1330).

in the field has been discussed elsewhere (pp. 418–23). Given even a minimally prepared road surface the horse could undoubtedly make a better pace and was less prone to going lame, but in the field it gained its place more slowly, gathering importance at first on the light soils of East Anglia and consolidating its position in the same area on those farms which went over at an early date to root vegetables and other fodder crops.

To judge from Blagrave's *Epitome of the Art of Husbandry* (1669), the primary role of the mare on the farm seems to have been akin to that of the cow to the ox-team, namely a means of producing male offspring, the majority of which would be gelded and set to the plough: 'A Husbandman cannot be without Horses or Mares, or both', he writes, 'and that more especially if he go with a Horse-plough, he must have both, his Horses to draw, and his Mares to bring Colts to uphold his stock'. Blagrave very sensibly doubted the counsel of those who claimed that the phase of the moon at the time of conception influenced the gender of

the foal, but beyond some words of warning on mixing the blood of horses of differing colours, he has nothing to contribute on their breeding.

In a gradual way, the horse eventually began to outstrip the ox as a traction animal (illus. 158), especially on light soils and in hilly and stony regions. Edwards finds that in the chalk country of Wiltshire by the turn of the seventeenth century, 65 farmers out of 100 possessing ploughs favoured horse-ploughs while only fourteen had specifically ox-ploughs; the remainder operated mixed teams of both animals. A similar trend surfaces elsewhere: for example on the Lincolnshire Wolds the average number of horses per farm rose from five in the sixteenth century to nine in the seventeenth. They were occasionally worked in pairs, but the long-favoured team of three in single file remained more usual. On farms retaining oxen for the plough, the horse began to be used customarily for cart-work and as a pack animal, as well as tackling the lighter agricultural tasks such as harrowing and (later) rolling.

In many farming communities, the advent of the carthorse was a very late development: such goods as warranted horse transport in the early medieval period generally went by packhorse. The harvest might long have been carried home by cart in some parts of the country (illus. 159), but at the turn of the eighteenth century Celia Fiennes encountered a more primitive survival in the south-west:

all over Cornwall and Devonshire, they have their carryages on horses backes; this being the time of harvest . . . I had the advantage of seeing their harvest bringing in, which is on a horse's backe with sort of crookes of wood like yokes on either side, two or three on a side stands up in which they stow the corne and so tie it with cords, but they cannot so equally poise it but the going of the horse is like to cast it down sometimes on the one side and sometimes on the other, for they load them from the neck to the taile and pretty high and are forced to support it with their hands; so to a horse they have two people and the women leads and supports them as well as the men, and goe through thick and thinn; sometymes I have met with half a score horses thus loaded, they are indeed but little horses, their Cavelles as they call them, and soe may not be able to draw a cart, otherwise I am sure 3 or 4 horses might draw three tymes as much as 4 horses does carry, and where it is open ground and roads broad, which in some places here it was, I wondered at their labour in this kind, for the men and women themselves toiled like their horses – but the common observation of custom being as a second nature people are very hardly convinc'd or brought off from, tho' never so inconvenient.

159 A well-laden harvest cart with iron-shod wheels, its carrying capacity extended by means of ladders. From the Luttrell Psalter (c. 1340).

For heavy duty in the field, it was only in the late 1700s that the use of horses was, in Arthur Marshall's words, beginning to 'creep in' in the south-west, although in the lighter soils of the flat-lands of East Anglia they had long been common, especially so since the seventeenth century when increasing familiarity with the wagons favoured by Dutch engineers engaged in draining the Fens coincided with the emergence of the sorrel horses for which the region became justly famous – the progenitors of the Suffolk Punch. None the less, panniers continued to provide an alternative means of transport, for example, for manure to the fields and, from the eighteenth century onwards, for gathering root crops such as turnips.

Per Kalm expressed surprise at the method of yoking horses to the wagon as practised in the country and the towns of south-east England in 1748 (see p. 60). His admiration for the size and strength of the horses at this period – that is to say, just before the era when it is perceived that the Shire and other horses went through a phase of intense improvement – suggests that the process was already under way by the time Bakewell and his contemporaries began their work. Greater size having been sought after by breeders for some time, by the 1830s Youatt could write that:

Farmers are now beginning to be aware of the superiority of the moderate-sized, strong, active horse over the bulkier, but slower animal of former days. It is not only in harvest, and when a frosty morning must be seized to cart manure, that this is perceived, but, in the every-day work of the farm, the saving of time, and the saving of provender too, will be very considerable in the course of a year.

In Youatt's day much of the country's horseflesh continued to come from the north, although he was at a loss to explain why this should be. In advising the small farmer to provide himself with a mare rather than a gelding for general use, he adds that 'wherever there are good horses, with convenience for rearing the colts, the farmer may start as a breeder with a good chance of success.'

Both Marshall and Culley were critical of the seeming profligacy with which great teams of horses were to be seen harnessed to wagons, Marshall lamenting that in the West Midlands the team 'is grown to a shameful height of extravagance' while Culley vented his scorn on the farmers of Berkshire where he had seen several times narrow-wheeled wagons pulled by as many as six stallions, one before the other, laden with bells and fringes. Chivers suggests that they may have been misled here, however, failing to enquire whether the offender might not be a breeder of stallions keeping his horses in trim or whether some of them were young ones being trained up and hardened for use in towns or docks.

The same author points out the error of assuming that all such carthorses not reared by the farmer himself necessarily came from the breeder: even horses worn out by years of drudgery in the towns could have a few years of useful farm life left in them – and they could be bought very cheaply. Many farmers around Bristol, he records, were used to buying such animals for perhaps £5 when their original cost to the townsman had been 50 guineas.

Horses of the Shire type (illus. 160) are generally accorded the status of the earliest English breed of true heavy horse, although it began to be so-called only in the nineteenth century: previously it was known only by the generic description of the Old English black horse. Trow-Smith notes that even when the breed society was first formed in 1878 it was with the title of the English Cart Horse Society, changing to the Shire Horse

160 *Old English Black Horse* (or Shire horse), by William Shiels, *c.* 1835, oil on canvas.

Society six years later. Conflicting claims for its geographical origins associate it broadly with the shire counties of central England stretching from the Midlands (Warwickshire, Staffordshire, Derbyshire and Leicestershire) to the Fens: some representatives of this type continued to be referred to as the 'Fen breed' into the nineteenth century.

The conformation of this venerable if imprecisely described type had been significantly improved in the eighteenth century by crossing with mares imported from Holland or Flanders: a number of breeders can claim credit for forwarding this process, among them the Earl of Chesterfield (believed to have brought back with him six Zeeland mares at the conclusion of his embassy to The Hague), the Earl of Huntingdon, Robert Bakewell and George Salisbury. Trow-Smith suggests that Flanders blood had probably been introduced to the type from as early as the thirteenth century, but it was only with the more purposeful programme adopted by breeders in the 1700s that a significant and permanent improvement was brought about and, as a result of their several efforts, the type had become fixed by the later eighteenth century. Like their earlier progenitors, some of the smaller of these horses had continued to serve as military mounts, but as they stabilized into a bigger frame they became almost exclusively draught animals, ideally suited to the heavy wagons of the day.

It may be that the early emergence of the type of horse that gave rise to the Suffolk Punch can be linked to the development in East Anglia of a light form of swing-plough that was suited to horse traction in a way that the heavier implements in use elsewhere never were. The early enclosure of large areas of Suffolk may also have provided the means by which horse-breeding could take place in a more controlled manner. By the eighteenth century these horses had become ubiquitous in the area. Looking back from the late 1700s, Arthur Young thought that in their *ur*-form they had been clumsy-looking animals, with 'short legs, great carcasses, large ill-made heads, slouching ugly ears, and low fore-hands', although he acknowledged that in the course of the 1770s it had been much changed to a 'handsomer, lighter and more active horse'. Culley was equally stinting in praise of its looks, conceding only that it probably merited 'more in constitutional hardiness than true shape, being in general a very plain made horse.' These (nowadays considered rather beautiful) sorrel horses were none the less held in high estimation for ploughing, and according to Culley, sold at greater prices than most other draught horses of their size.

The Cleveland Bay, which would emerge as the carriage-horse of preference for those who could afford them, largely displacing black horses of the Shire type from this role, was also successfully bred for greater weight in a way that saw it rise from modest beginnings as a packhorse and general farm animal to become the ideal plough-horse for the lighter soils of the north-east.

Competing claims for the ancestry of the Clydesdale are discussed elsewhere (p. 26): Chivers is surely right in describing its progenitors ultimately as Anglo-Flemish in origin, heavily interbred with the horses of Lanarkshire and the south-western counties of Scotland and sharing a great deal of background with the Shire breed. Certainly in the course of the nineteenth century there was a considerable amount of crossing between the Clydesdale and Shire, rendering the respective populations even more difficult to tell apart. Culley considered the Clydesdales high, strong, hardy and remarkably true pullers – 'as good and useful a draught horse as any we are possessed of'.

One final variety deserves mention, namely the Percheron – a very recent arrival by comparison with the others, two stallions and twelve mares having been imported from Normandy only in 1916, since which time over 4,000 pure-bred horses have been recorded in the stud-book for the breed. The trend masks the true story of the farm horse in the course of the twentieth century, however, when the population plummeted in inverse proportion to the rise of the tractor.

Donkeys and Mules

On the farms of northern Europe there seems never to have been much taste for the donkeys and mules on which agriculture and transport depended so much in the Mediterranean world. As mentioned on p. 97, donkeys became popular for a time in Ireland, especially during the eighteenth century when demand from the British military led to a general dearth of horses for domestic usage. The spread of donkeys there is all the more noteworthy since they appear to have been introduced only at the time of the Civil War, a few generations earlier, whereas their history in England was, Dent suggests, a continuous one from the Roman period onwards.

In a close survey of historical sources relating to draught animals, Langdon was able to find occasional reference references to the use of mules and donkeys in the plough-team, but numbers seem typically to have been less than 1 per cent of the total. Two English manuscript illuminations of the early fourteenth century can be added to the evidence he puts forward: the equid shown along with two oxen in a plough-team in the Gorleston Psalter is perhaps a mule rather than a horse, while another in the Holkham Bible Picture Book (illus. 126) must surely be a donkey. Later, the *Husbandman, Farmer, and Grasier's Compleat Instructor* of 1697 writes of the 'ass' – evidently meaning the donkey – that it is useful for 'drawing Burthens in a Cart . . . as also at the Plough, in light ground, or where there is no roots of Trees, stiff Clay, or large Stones'. Although there appears, therefore, to be some reason to believe that mules and donkeys may have had a greater currency in the countryside than the historical record reveals, their numbers undoubtedly remained small, never achieving the significance they held in the economies of southern Europe and the Mediterranean littoral.

161 Horse and tractor in unequal competition during harvest in 1938 at Aston Tirrold (Berkshire, now Oxfordshire), photographed by Eric Guy.

Epilogue

Almost a century has elapsed since the era of World War One, adopted here as marking something of a tipping point for many of the trends and processes whose earlier histories are charted above. Although the choice of any one cut-off date for the somewhat disparate trajectories followed by the various species considered here is inevitably arbitrary, there was a real sense in which the war itself brought major changes to the fortunes of many of them: the dynamics of society were significantly changed by the immense drain on human and monetary resources brought about by the conflict, and it was inescapable that the balance between the animal world and our own – artificially contrived to a high degree as it was by that time – should similarly have changed irretrievably.

Nowhere were these changes more striking than in the history of the horse in the twentieth century. Passenger transport was most rapidly affected: Barker estimates that by 1911 only 13 per cent of passenger vehicles were still horse-drawn, a figure that had dropped to 6 per cent by 1913. By contrast, 88 per cent of goods vehicles continued to be drawn by horses at this date, with only high-value freight and the posts considering the investment in motor transport worthwhile. The pace of change quickened markedly after World War One, with the numbers of horse-drawn vehicles in Britain dropping from 237,000 in 1922 to 12,000 by the eve of World War Two.

With the outbreak of hostilities in 1914, draught horses in particular found themselves suddenly in demand once again, for the terrain in the battlefields of Flanders proved quite beyond the capacities of most motor vehicles of the day: when war was declared the Army is said in any case to have had no more than 80 motor vehicles, compared with 25,000 horses. The latter figure was rapidly increased by requisitions, so that within two weeks the Remount Department had 165,000 horses at its disposal, joined later by large numbers of animals drafted in from America. One horse in four died on the Western Front and the veterinary field hospitals treated some 2½ million equine casualties in the course of the hostilities. No previous campaign had ever witnessed figures on this scale.

Meanwhile on the home front a concerted effort had been made to rebuild the much-reduced breeding stock, but the first products of this new initiative could scarcely have been in harness (and would certainly not have achieved maturity) when the armistice threw the whole process into reverse: within a few months of the peace, the Army is reported to have disposed of some 62,500 animals on the domestic market – just as the numbers of colts newly bred at home began to peak. To talk of the subsequent crash in the market and of new initiatives in mechanization in the post-war years (illus. 161) is to gloss over the enormous costs visited on the horse population, amongst which mortality levels must have been scarcely lower than during the war years. Thereafter a temporary lull in the dwindling fortunes of the horse was provided by World War Two, during which fuel shortages brought horse power once more into favour. The low numbers of animals now maintained for breeding purposes imposed severe limitations on the national ability to expand the horse population on demand and it was at this point that tractor sales began to accelerate dramatically: the horse population on farms, estimated at 650,000 in 1939 (compared with only 50,000 tractors), plummeted to 161,000 in 1955 and to 21,000 in 1965. These reductions were not to be achieved by anything so benevolent as natural wastage: 100,000 horses are said to have been slaughtered in 1947 and in 1948 respectively, nearly half of them aged three years or less. In the space of the following two decades, the formerly ubiquitous horse was virtually wiped from the map for all but recreational and sporting purposes.

The wider alienation of the human from the animal world which has been asserted here and which has formed the impetus for this volume is of course a construct proposed from the point of view of the urban majority and liable to be challenged by contented country dwellers. The face of the countryside itself, however, has been radically altered over the past hundred years – and especially so since World War Two – so that even where farm animals, for example, continue to form an everyday part of the landscape, they may be said to occupy an altered relationship to their keepers. Changes in food retailing, and especially the bulk-buying powers of supermarket chains operating in international markets, have made survival increasingly difficult for farmers wedded to traditional methods of animal husbandry, no less than for producers of fruit and vegetables: a few survive by making a virtue of following traditional methods, but many are swallowed up into ever-larger

economic units and others go out of business on an annual basis. Dietary supplements have long since rendered grazing on pasture only one food source among many available to the 'progressive' cattle farmer: at the extreme end of the scale, several zero-grazing schemes, in which literally thousands of cattle at a time will spend their entire lives in indoor industrial units, are currently at the planning stage. Such is the urban appetite for milk that, suppliers claim, demand can be met only by embracing large-scale industrialization of farming in this way, so that large tracts of grazing are likely to become increasingly thinly populated in years to come. The common sight of small family groups of pigs contentedly rooting in the hedgerows already gave way decades ago to sprawling high-density pig farms of many acres extent; current proposals could see these too replaced by zero-grazing units, so that in time pigs might vanish altogether from much of the landscape.

In more oblique ways, other forms of animal life have, over the last hundred years, fallen casualty of economics as well as of war and peace. The great country estates and sporting properties that accounted for much of the 'natural' landscape at the turn of the twentieth century – in reality artificially engineered to a great extent, as we have seen – experienced these changes in full. A generation of young men who had formed the basis of privileged country society went off war, leaving behind them clubs and hunts and indeed a whole rural economy that struggled to survive. With them went many of the gamekeepers who had played a major role in maintaining an arbitrarily prescribed balance in the animal world that favoured game for hunting and shooting at the expense of their natural predators or competitors. To the degree that these activities survived during the war years, they were carried on at a much reduced level from which many estates would never recover. The effects on the animal world were varied in kind, but the post-war decades saw the unfolding of the process of distancing of the human from the animal population to the point where the two would occupy, to a large extent, separate spheres.

For some species – martens and polecats, otters, raptors of all sorts, many of them already teetering on the edge of extinction – the respite of the war years gave them an opportunity to re-establish their numbers, although progressive loss of habitat in various forms blighted many such prospects. Some animals none the less went on to form robust populations that have held their own or have increased in the course of the twentieth century, but for others there were new challenges. The fortunes of four species – otters, rabbits, foxes and badgers – may illustrate some of the ways in which the fortunes of the human and animal populations continue to be interlinked, generally to the extreme disadvantage of the species concerned.

Otters were among the creatures that benefited from a period of comparative peace in the British countryside while war raged in Europe. Their numbers were calculated to have increased to not less than 6,000 individuals by 1918, a comparative abundance that was maintained in the inter-war years to the point where, in 1936, L.C.R. Cameron could judge that even the rising public antipathy to field sports seemed unlikely to dent its popularity: 'Attempts to have the sport suppressed are foredoomed to failure' he concluded: 'Otter Hunting is assured of a longer future than probably any other Field Sport.' Then from the mid-1950s a catastrophic decline set in, with alarm bells being first rung by an article titled 'Where are the otters?', which appeared in the *Gamekeeper and Countryside* in 1962. The author, Jack Iversen Lloyd, thought that at least part of the blame for the declining numbers of otters found by hunts could be attributed to the progressive destruction of habitat,

but once the scientific community began to focus on the problem it quickly became apparent that a startlingly steep decline had taken place starting in the years 1956 and 1957 (with the population falling by up to a half in those years), a profile that could not be reconciled with any gradual or progressive incursion into the otter's territory. The Mammal Society, the Nature Conservancy and a variety of other bodies and individuals (notably Chanin and Jefferies) undertook a series of surveys as a result of which the prime suspect was identified as a new group of organochlorine pesticides, particularly dieldrin and aldrin, which had been introduced precisely in 1955 for use in seed dressings, sheep-dips and some other purposes and which proved to have had an equally devastating effect on populations of sparrowhawks, peregrine falcons and other raptors.

Ultimately, dieldrin and aldrin were banned from use in dressing spring cereals in 1962, from sheep-dip in 1966 and from autumn cereals in 1975. The suppression of this family of noxious chemicals by no means brought about an early recovery of the otter population: animals that had not been killed outright by the effects of toxins entering the food chain were found to have had their capacity to reproduce adversely affected. Where populations had been severely reduced by the action of the chemicals, the surviving animals were at times too thinly distributed to support normal breeding activity. By the mid-1970s the otter had been totally wiped out from a large part of central England and elsewhere populations had been reduced to a fraction of their former numbers. Only Ireland seems to have escaped unaffected and indeed bounties were still being paid there for the destruction of otters when the mainland was in crisis.

Although the basis for a recovery had been established, it proved both a slow and an unpredictable process: clearly there were other factors at work. Water pollution on several fronts – industrial, agricultural and domestic – had resulted in a toxic cocktail of chemicals and heavy metals entering waterways, rendering them unfit for the otter and for many of the species on which it depended. Radical water-management initiatives and abstraction of water from rivers had resulted in a great deal of river clearance, with overhanging trees and intruding roots removed from the riverbanks and accumulated debris from periodic flooding swept away in a manner that turned many rivers into sterile and inimical habitats for the otter. The same period saw a marked increase in the recreational use of waterways, with boating, canoeing and fishing all expanding and with walkers, campers and fishermen making increasing use of the margins – all of these factors impacting on the tranquillity favoured by the otter. Even today, run-off from fields heavily treated with fertilizers remains a major problem, while water companies are continually criticized for polluting watercourses with raw sewage released into the river systems whenever high rainfall threatens to overwhelm inadequate drainage systems.

Even the activities of other animal species conspired to undermine the otter's quest for the quiet enjoyment of its habitat. Feral populations of mink and of coypu, having established themselves in large tracts of the river system during the 1960s and 1970s, became the subject of new and intensive extermination programmes that brought men and dogs into the very heart of its territory, causing increased disturbance and stress levels. Otter hunting came to an end altogether when, on 1 January 1978, legal protection was extended in England and Wales with the addition of the otter to the species listed in Schedule 1 of the Conservation of Wild Creatures and Wild Plants Act (1975). Nowadays the only bodies with a declared interest in the otter are those concerned with its well-being.

The Otter Society in particular has been responsible for the designation of some hundreds of miles of waterways as otter havens.

Even more dramatic than the experience of the otter were the circumstances that pulled up sharply the seemingly unstoppable career of the rabbit, with the introduction and spread of the virus *Myxoma* in the years 1953–5. Half a century of recorded history of the virus had preceded its arrival in England: myxomatosis had first been observed in a population of laboratory rabbits of European origin in Uruguay towards the end of the nineteenth century; some incidence of the disease was detected later on the west coast of North America but an enormous outburst took place in Australia in 1950 when, after a decade of laboratory testing, the virus was deliberately introduced into the proliferating population of rabbits (originally introduced from Europe), which in some areas had reached proportions that threatened the viability of the agricultural economy. It proved a devastatingly effective stratagem, reducing the population to one sixth of its former size within the space of two years. In 1952 a further chapter opened when (by private initiative rather than state intervention) the disease was brought to France, again with the aim of reducing the numbers in the wild, and within two years 90 per cent of the population had been wiped out.

The means by which it reached Britain are unclear, although the detailed characteristics of the virus indicate that it was identical to the strain that had spread throughout France. (The initiator of that outbreak had inoculated rabbits with virus obtained from a laboratory in Lausanne, Switzerland, and released them into the wild.) In Britain too official interest had been shown in the possibility that myxomatosis might provide an answer to controlling the size of the rabbit population: live testing had taken place in the 1930s on

Skokholm Island on the Pembrokeshire coast – incidentally, one of the island sites on which an early colony had been established, with a documented history going back to 1325. The experiments there proved inconclusive and the virus died out; further tests were being carried out in the Hebrides in 1952–3 when the course of events overtook these cautious scientific researches.

The disease was first recorded in England in October 1953, at Bough Beech near Edenbridge (Kent); within half a year it had spread to widely scattered locations throughout southern England and in Wales, and twelve months later its range extended to most of Britain. Some 90 per cent of the rabbits in the British Isles were dead within three years of its first being observed. Here and there small communities escaped infection, continued to breed and contributed to the maintenance of the population, but at a level fractionally the size of that which had formerly existed.

Throughout this horrific upheaval, public attitudes to the disease remained ambivalent. Both within government and in the population at large there were those who saw in it a final solution to the rabbit 'problem' and who advocated its encouragement by deliberately introducing infected animals to otherwise healthy colonies; others were appalled by these actions and objected to them on ethical and humanitarian grounds. The authorities struggled to find an appropriate response. At first, attempts were made to contain the disease by exterminating local rabbit populations, but even within the Advisory Committee set up to give guidance to the Minister of Agriculture on myxomatosis, opinion was split: in deference to strong public opinion, the Committee advised that there should be no deliberate spreading of the disease, but when the Pests Act (1954) introduced a legal sanction to this effect two members of the Committee resigned in protest.

Today the disease remains endemic and coextensive with the rabbit population, which now stands at much lower levels nationally than in former years and with no sign that it has developed any degree of immunity. Surveys of the nature and progress of the disease have included assessments of the effect of this loss of rabbits from the landscape: predators that had relied on the rabbit have found themselves under considerable pressure, with foxes being found to have turned their attentions to voles and mice, while owl and buzzard populations have diminished nationally. Equally dramatic has been the dietary change brought about in the human population, amongst whom the taste for rabbit has declined to minimal levels: today few people have any appetite for the creature that was once so carefully husbanded, while rabbit fur had already disappeared off the scale of desirability long before the wearing of furs in general became socially questionable. A century of anthropomorphization in children's books and films has also contributed to a process – not complete but largely so – that has seen the release of the rabbit from a millennium of human exploitation, even if if the casual effects of sharing the same habitat continue to prove no less hazardous.

The fortunes of the fox have followed a different trajectory from those of its principal prey, as it found itself pursued by increasing numbers of hunting packs up to the point where hunting with dogs was rendered illegal at the start of the present millennium. Reformers had succeeded in introducing the Protection of Animals Act in 1911, but at the expense of excluding blood sports from its terms of reference. The upheaval of World War One seemed to signal for a time the end of foxhunting, with the loss of so many able-bodied enthusiasts and with longer-term shortages of money and resources. Another World War and even greater privation might have finished it off completely, but with the resurgence of prosperity in the post-war years the numbers engaged in foxhunting instead began to soar: Emma Griffin calculates that by the mid-1970s there were 189 hunts active in England and Wales (some 40 more than had existed a century earlier), with 50,000 people (an increasing proportion of them women) regularly hunting on horseback – in addition to the fell-packs that continued to hunt on foot in the north. With a fox population that had reasserted itself in the lean years of hunting and with the growth of hunt supporters' clubs that regularly brought into the field hundreds or thousands of followers on foot, hunting now achieved an unprecedented level of support within country society. In the face of legislation that would outlaw foxhunting, the Countryside Alliance organized a march on Westminster in 2002 that attracted over 400,000 supporters, describing it as 'the largest civil liberties march in modern history'. Their efforts failed to avert passage of the Hunting Act (2004), however, but although in theory the Act should have signalled the end of hunting with hounds, the picture today remains unresolved: in a report in the *Guardian* at the end of 2007 hunt supporters are said to have claimed that more than 250,000 people attended 314 Boxing Day meets throughout the country, figures that were claimed by the Alliance to show that the ban had become irrelevant. Four years later and with a change of government – to a coalition dominated by a party with a majority of members opposed to the Hunting Act, and with a House of Lords similarly weighted against it – the future of foxhunting must be considered far from settled.

Even the inoffensive badger's troubles are perpetuated, despite the introduction of the Badgers Act of 1973. A national survey of the badger population undertaken in the 1980s found evidence that over 9,000 sets were still being dug annually,

while in 2007 Lovegrove found evidence of the continuing popularity of badger-baiting in south Wales, the northern counties of England and in central and southern Scotland, where audiences of up to 40 people at a time were reported. Only two years before the passing of the Badgers Act a more insidious threat reared its head, with the discovery of tuberculosis amongst the population. As a result, a new wave of officially sanctioned extermination was unleashed on suspicion that the spread of TB in cattle was directly attributable to the badger. The subsequent decades saw some stabilization of this position, largely due to the efforts of concerned naturalists who set to work compiling the first detailed surveys of the size, nature and habits of the populations concerned, gradually replacing with a factual body of evidence the subjective understanding of the badger that hitherto had prevailed, but at the present time, 40 years on, new regional extermination campaigns are being embarked upon whose ultimate effect can scarcely be foreseen.

These examples may serve to illustrate a few of the ways in which the human population continues to influence the fortunes of the animal world, whether directly or more obliquely and casually. Many others could have been chosen – the fate of the red squirrel population, devastated (even if unintentionally) by the introduction of the grey, for example – but the thrust of this text has been primarily historical and present-day concerns must remain beyond its scope. On a positive note, however, the interests of endangered domestic animals are now a matter of acknowledged concern: the Rare Breeds Survival Trust, founded in 1973, claims that no domestic breeds of livestock have been lost since its inception, compared with 26 breeds extinguished in the course of the previous 70 years; more specialized bodies like the Shire Horse Society, which traces its ancestry to 1878, and the Jacob Sheep Society, with half a century of history meticulously documented by Araminta Aldington, cater for individual breeds. High levels of current membership of societies concerning themselves with animal matters – the RSPCA with some 30,000 members, the RSPB with more than three times that number – speak of a healthy concern for and desire to engage with the animal kingdom, while the popularity of nature reserves and bird sanctuaries as recreational destinations speaks of a wider public sympathy for the natural world. Consideration for wildlife, as marked by the introduction of the Wildlife and Countryside Act (1981), is enshrined also in the operating ethos of major landowning bodies such as the National Trust and the Forestry Commission. These concerns already have a long history and are well rooted in society: the Sea Birds Preservation Act (1869) introduced a century and a half ago a measure of protection for wild birds exploited not only for sport and for food but also as a source of feathers with which to ornament hats, a frivolous practice that reached such proportions by the end of the nineteenth century that naturalists literally feared for the survival of certain species. There are still those for whom animal fur is the ultimate fashion accessory (and who will argue vigorously for its continuing use), but they are perhaps outnumbered by others who, to paraphrase Naomi Campbell, would rather go naked.

Through these evolving attitudes no less than formal legislative measures, society has reached a point where the well-being of the animal world is enshrined in the same administrative machinery that governs our own daily lives. The danger now, perhaps, is that animals can easily slip from our collective consciousness, generally until some new crisis hits the headlines – no one could have escaped being appalled by the outbreak of some 2,000 cases of foot and mouth disease in 2001 and by the consequent holocaust visited on the cattle population. Such disasters remind us that the destiny of the animal kingdom continues to be inseparably linked to our own: in some small way, the present essay may serve to supply some broad historical background to these continuing concerns, for directly or indirectly we live today with the legacy of a thousand years and more of human interaction with the animal kingdom.

Bibliography & References

Manuscript sources mentioned in the text

Bestiary: Oxford, Bodleian Library, MS Bodley 764 (English, *c.* 1220–50)

'De arte Piscandi': British Library, MS Sloane 1698 (English, fourteenth century)

'De nobilitatibus, sapientiis et prudentiis regum', by Walter de Milemete: Oxford, Christ Church, MS 92 (English, 1326)

Douce Apocalypse: Oxford, Bodleian Library, MS Douce 180 (English, *c.* 1265–90)

Gorleston Psalter: British Library, MS Add. 49622 (English, *c.* 1320–30)

Holkham Bible Picture Book: British Library, MS Add. 47682 (English, *c.* 1325–30)

Lambeth Apocalypse: London, Lambeth Palace Library, MS 209 (English, *c.* 1260)

Life of Cardinal Wolsey, by George Cavendish: Oxford, Bodleian Library, MS Douce 363 (English, 1578)

Livre de Chasse of Gaston Phébus: New York, Pierpont Morgan Library, MS M1044 (French, *c.* 1407)

Luttrell Psalter: British Library, MS Add. 42130 (English, *c.* 1340)

Macclesfield Psalter: Cambridge, Fitzwilliam Museum, MS 1-2005 (English, *c.* 1300)

Ormesby Psalter: Oxford, Bodleian Library, MS Douce 366 (English, *c.* 1280–1340)

Piers of Fulham, on angling: Cambridge, Trinity College, MS R.3.19 (English, late fifteenth century)

Queen Mary's Psalter: British Library, MS Royal 2 B. VII (English, *c.* 1310–20)

Romance of Alexander the Great: Oxford, Bodleian Library, MS Bodley 264 (French, twelfth century)

Taymouth Hours: British Library, MS Yates Thompson 13 (English, *c.* 1325–50)

'True form of keeping a session of ye swanmote': Oxford, Bodleian Library, MS Tanner 91

Printed sources

ONE: The Ubiquitous Horse

Allen, Tony, *Animals at War* (York, 1999)

Anonymous [1673], 'The Grand Concern of England Explained; in Several Proposals Offered to the Consideration of the Parliament', *Harleian Miscellany*, VIII (1811), pp. 547–82

Astley, John, *The Art of Riding* (London, 1584)

Barker, Juliet R. V., *The Tournament in England, 1100–1400* (Woodbridge, 1986)

Beresford, G. de la Poer, 'The History of Polo', in The Earl of Kimberley et al., *Polo*, Lonsdale Library XXI (London, 1936), pp. 17–26

Bird, Anthony, *Roads and Vehicles* (London, 1969)

Blackmore, David, 'The Horse at War', in Connor, *All the Queen's Horses*, pp. 48–50

Blundeville, Thomas, *The Art of Riding* (London, *c.* 1560)

—, *The Fower Chiefyst Offices belongyng to Horseman-shippe* (London, 1565)

Bracegirdle, Hilary, 'The Thoroughbred Horse', in *The Essential Horse*, ed. Bracegirdle and Connor, pp. 106–21

Bracegirdle, Hilary, and Patricia Connor, eds, *The Essential Horse* (London, 2000)

Brown, Jonathan, 'The Horse in Agriculture', in *The Essential Horse*, ed. Bracegirdle and Connor, pp. 37–49

Brown, J. Moray, *Polo* (London, 1891)

Browne, William, *Browne his fiftie Yeares Practice* (London, 1624)

Calendar of State Papers, Domestic Series, 109 vols (London, 1856–1913)

Calendar of State Papers and Manuscripts . . . Venice etc., 41 vols (London, 1864–1947)

Carew, Richard, *The Survey of Cornwall* [London, 1602] (reprinted Redruth, 2000)

Cavendish, William [1st Duke of Newcastle], *La Méthode nouvelle & Invention extraordinaire de dresser les Chevaux* (Antwerp, 1658)

—, *A New Method and Extraordinary Invention to Dress Horses and work them according to Nature* (London, 1667)

Chartres, J. A., 'Road Carrying in England in the Seventeenth Century: Myth and Reality', *Economic History Review*, 2nd series, xxx (1977), pp. 73–94

Chivers, Keith, *The Shire Horse: A History of the Breed, the Society and the Men* (London, 1976)

—, 'The Supply of Horses in Great Britain in the Nineteenth Century', in *Horses in European Economic History*, ed. Thompson, pp. 31–49

Clark, John, 'Medieval Horse-shoes', *Finds Research Group Datasheet*, 4 (n. p., 1986)

—, *The Medieval Horse and its Equipment, c. 1150–c. 1450*, Medieval Finds from Excavations in London 5 (London, 1995)

Cleland, James, *Ηρω-Παιδεια; or, The Institution of a Young Nobleman* (Oxford, 1607)

Clutton-Brock, Juliet, *Horse Power: A History of the Horse and the Donkey in Human Societies* (London, 1992)

A Collection of all the Publicke Orders, Ordinances and Declarations of both Houses of Parliament . . . 1642–1646 (London, 1646)

Connor, Patricia, ed., *All the Queen's Horses*, exh. cat., Museum of the Horse, Kentucky Horse Park (Lexington, KY, 2003)

Corte, Claudio, *The Art of Riding, conteining diverse necessarie Instructions, Demonstrations, Helps, and Corrections apperteining to Horssemanship* (London, 1584)

Crofts, J., *Packhorse, Waggon and Post: Land Carriage and Communication under the Tudors and Stuarts* (London, 1967)

Crouch, David, *Tournament* (Hambledon and London, 2005)

Dale, T. F., *The Game of Polo* (London, 1897)

—, *Polo Past and Present* (London, 1905)

Davis, R.H.C., *The Medieval Warhorse: Origin, Development and Redevelopment* (London, 1989)

De Lisle, General Sir B., 'The Horse in Sport', in *The Book of the Horse*, ed. Vesey-Fitzgerald, pp. 474–89

Dent, Anthony, 'Chaucer and the Horse', *Proceedings of the Leeds Literary and Philosophical Society*, IX (1959–62), pp. 1–12

—, *Donkey: The Story of the Ass from East to West* (London, 1972)

—, *Horses in Shakespeare's England* (London, 1987)

—, and Daphne Machin Goodall, *The Foals of Epona: A History of British Ponies from the Bronze Age to Yesterday* (London, 1962)

Edwards, P. R., 'The Horse Trade in Tudor and Stuart England', in *Horses in European Economic History*, ed. Thompson, pp. 113–31

—, 'The Supply of Horses to the Parliamentarian and Royalist Armies in the English Civil War', *Historical Research*, LXVIII/165 (1995), pp. 49–66

—, 'Les Écuries des monarques anglais aux XVIe et XVIIe siècles', in *Les Écuries royales du XVIe au XVIIIe siècle*, ed. Roche and Reytier, pp. 155–65

—, *Dealing in Death: The Arms Trade and the British Civil Wars, 1638–52* (Stroud, 2000)

—, *Horse and Man in Early Modern England* (London, 2007)

Evelyn, John, *Acetaria: A Discourse of Sallets* (London, 1699)

Fiennes, Celia, *The Journeys of Celia Fiennes*, ed. C. Morris (London, 1949)

Fitzgerald, A., *Royal Thoroughbreds: A History of the Royal Studs* (London, 1990)

Fitz Stephen, William, 'Description of the City of London, 1170–1183', in *English Historical Documents*, vol. II: *1042–1189*, ed. D. C. Douglas and G. W. Greenaway (London, 1953), pp. 956–62

Flavell, John, *Husbandry Spiritualized; or, The Heavenly Use of Earthly Things* (London, 1669)

Gerhold, Dorian, *Road Transport before the Railways: Russell's London Flying Waggons* (Cambridge, 1993)

Gilbey, Sir W., *The Great Horse*, 2nd edn (London, 1999)

Gordon, W. J., *The Horse-World of London* (London, 1893)

Grey, Thomas de, *Compleat Horseman and Expert Ferrier* (London, 1639)

Harwood, E., *The Advice of that Worthy Commander Sir Ed. Harwood, Collonell, written by King Charles his Command* (London, 1642)

Herbert Manuscripts, 'Herbert Manuscripts at Powis Castle, part II: Correspondence of Sir Edward Herbert, First Lord Herbert of Chirbury, 1614 to 1626', *Collections Historical and Archaeological Relating to Montgomeryshire*, XX (1886), pp. 1–282

Hewitt, H. J., *The Horse in Medieval England* (London, 1983)

Hey, David G., *Packmen, Carriers and Packhorse Roads* (Leeds, 1980)

Holinshed, R., *Holinshed's Chronicles of England, Scotland and Ireland* (London, 1987)

Hollis, F. H., 'The Horse in Agriculture', in Vesey-Fitzgerald, *The Book of the Horse*, pp. 160–83

Hyland, Ann, *The Medieval Warhorse from Byzantium to the Crusades* (Conshohocken, PA, 1994)

—, *The Warhorse, 1250–1600* (Stroud, 1998)

—, *The Horse in the Middle Ages* (Stroud, 1999)

Kalm, Per, *Kalm's Account of his Visit to England . . . in 1748*, trans. J. Lucas (London, 1892)

Langdon, John, 'Horse Hauling: A Revolution in Vehicle Transport in Twelfth- and Thirteenth-century England?', *Past and Present*, CIII (1984), pp. 37–66

Latham, Simon, *Lathams Falconry; or, The Faulcons Lure and Cure* (London, 1615)

—, *Lathams new and second Booke of Falconrie* (London, 1618)

Letters and Papers, Foreign and Domestic, of the reign of Henry VIII, ed. J. Gairdner and R. H. Brodie, 21 vols (London, 1862–1910)

Loch, Sylvia, *The Royal Horse of Europe* (London, 1986)

MacGregor, Arthur, 'Horsegear, Vehicles and Stable Equipment at the Stuart Court: A Documentary Archaeology', *Archaeological Journal*, CLIII (1996), pp. 148–200

—, 'The Royal Stables: A Seventeenth-century Perspective', *Antiquaries Journal*, LXXVI (1996), pp. 181–200

—, 'Les Écuries royales des Tudors et Stuarts: personnel et personnalités', in *Les Écuries royales du XVIe au XVIIIe siècle*, ed. Roche and Reytier, pp. 143–53

—, 'Strategies for Improving English Horses in the Sixteenth and Seventeenth Centuries', *Anthropozoologica*, no. 29 (1999), pp. 65–74

—, 'Le polo, de l'Orient au monde entier', in *À cheval! Écuyers, amazones et cavaliers du XIVe au XXIe siècle*, ed. Roche and Reytier, pp. 181–93

Major, J. Kenneth, *Animal-Powered Machines* (Oxford, 2008)

Malacarne, Giancarlo, *Il mito dei cavalli gonzagheschi:*

alle origine del purosangue (Verona, 1995)

Manwood, J., *A Treatise of the Laws of the Forest*, 3rd edn (London, 1665)

Markham, Gervase, *Discourse on Horsemanshippe* (London, 1593)

—, *Cavelarice; or, The English Horseman* (London, 1607)

Miller, E. D., *Modern Polo*, 2nd edn, ed. M. H. Hayes (London, 1902)

Morgan, Nicholas, *The Perfection of Horse-manship* (London, 1609)

Mortimer, John, *The Whole Art of Husbandry* (London, 1707)

Munby, Julian, 'Les origines du coche', in *Voitures, chevaux et attelages du XVIe au XIXe siècle*, ed. Roche and Reytier, pp. 75–83

Nicholson, Christopher, 'The Horse on the Road', in *All the Queen's Horses*, ed. Connor, pp. 51–3

Prior, C. M., *Early Records of the Thoroughbred Horse* (London, 1924)

—, *The Royal Studs of the Sixteenth and Seventeenth Centuries* (London, 1935)

Reese, M. M., *The Royal Office of the Master of the Horse* (London, 1976)

Roche, Daniel, and Daniel Reytier, eds, *Les Écuries royales du XVIe au XVIIIe siècle* (Paris, 1998)

—, and —, *Voitures, chevaux et attelages du XVIe au XIXe siècle* (Paris, 2000)

—, and —, *À cheval! Écuyers, amazones et cavaliers du XIVe au XXIe siècle* (Paris, 2007)

Russell, J. G., *The Field of Cloth of Gold: Men and Manners in 1520* (London, 1969)

St Quintin, T. A., *Chances of Sports of Sorts* (Edinburgh and London, 1912)

Sainty, J. C., and R. O. Bucholz, *Officials of the Royal Household, 1660–1837, part II: Departments of the Lord Steward and the Master of the Horse* (London, 1998)

Sherley, Sir Anthony, 'A True Discourse of Sir Anthony Sherley's Travel into Persia . . . by George Manwaring', in *The Three Brothers; or, The Travels and Adventures of Sir Anthony, Sir Robert, and Sir Thomas Sherley* (London, 1825), pp. 23–83

The Statutes of the Realm . . . from Original Records and Authentic Manuscripts, 12 vols (London, 1819–24)

Stokes, William, *The Vaulting Master* (Oxford, 1652)

Stow, John, *The Annales; or, Generall Chronicle of England* (London, 1615)

Taylor, John, *The Carriers Cosmographie; or, A Briefe Relation, of the Innes . . . where the Carriers, Waggons, Foote Posts and Higglers, doe usually come* (London, 1637)

Tegetmeier, W. B., and C. L. Sutherland, *Horses, Asses, Zebras, Mules and Mule Breeding* (London, 1895)

Thirsk, Joan, *Horses in Early Modern England: For Service, for Pleasure, for Power*, The Stenton Lecture, 1977 (Reading, 1978)

Thompson, F.M.L., ed., *Horses in European Economic History: A Preliminary Canter* (Reading, 1983)

Vesey-Fitzgerald, B., ed., *The Book of the Horse* (London, 1947)

Watson, J.N.P., *The World of Polo, Past and Present* (London, 1986)

—, *A Concise Guide to Polo* (London, 1989)

Worsley, Giles, *The British Stable* (New Haven, CT, and London, 2004)

Youatt, William, *The Horse, with a Treatise on Draught* (new edn, London, 1843)

Young, A., *Tudor and Jacobean Tournaments* (London, 1987)

TWO: The Art of Venery and its Adjuncts

Almond, Richard, *Medieval Hunting* (Stroud, 2003)

The Anglo-Saxon Chronicle, trans. and ed. M. J. Swanton (London, 1996)

Aybes, C., and D. Yalden, 'Place Name Evidence for the Former Distribution and Status of Wolves and Beavers in Britain', *Mammal Review*, XXV (1995), pp. 201–27

Barber, Richard, *Bestiary, being an English Version of*

the Bodleian Library, Oxford MS Bodley 764
(London, 1992)

Beckford, Peter, *Thoughts on Hunting* (London 1781,
and later editions)

Bert, Edmund, *An Approved Treatise of Hawkes and
Hawking* (London, 1619)

Bewick, Thomas, *A General History of Quadrupeds*
(5th edn, Newcastle upon Tyne, 1807)

Bingley, W., *Memoirs of British Quadrupeds* (London,
1809)

—, *Animal Biography, or Popular Zoology; comprising
authentic Anecdotes of the Economy, Habits of Life,
Instincts, and Sagacity, of the Animal Creation.
Arranged according to the System of Linnaeus*
(London, 1813)

Blackmore, Howard L., *Hunting Weapons* (London,
1971)

Blome, Richard, *The Gentleman's Recreation: in four
parts, viz. Hunting, Hawking, Fowling, Fishing*
(London, 1686)

Blyth, Edward, *The Natural History of Cranes*,
ed. W. B. Tegetmeier (London, 1881)

Browne, Sir Thomas, 'An Account of Birds Found in
Norfolk'; reproduced in *Sir Thomas Browne's Works*,
ed. S. Wilkin (London, 1835–6), vol. IV, pp. 313–24

Calendar of State Papers, Domestic Series, 109 vols
(London, 1856–1913)

*Calendar of State Papers and Manuscripts . . . Venice
etc.*, 41 vols (London, 1864–1947)

Cameron, L.C.R., *Otters and Otter-Hunting*
(London, 1908)

—, 'The Science of Hunting the Otter', 'An Otter-
Hunting Establishment', 'A Survey of
Otter-Hunting Countries' and 'A Glossary of Otter-
Hunting Terms', in *Deer, Hare and Otter Hunting*,
ed. the Earl of Lonsdale and E. Parker (London,
1936), pp. 113–82

Cantor, Leonard, *The Changing English Countryside,
1400–1700* (London, 1987)

Chanin, Paul, *The Natural History of Otters*
(London, 1985)

—, *Otters* (London, 1993)

—, and D. J. Jefferies, 'The Decline of the Otter *Lutra
lutra* L. in Britain: An Analysis of Hunting Records
and Discussion of Causes', *Biological Journal of the
Linnean Society*, X (1978), pp. 305–28

Clapham, Richard, *The Book of the Otter: A Manual
for Sportsmen and Naturalists* (London, 1922)

Cleland, James, *Ηρω-Παιδεια; or, The Institution of a
Young Noble Man* (Oxford, 1607)

Cockaine, Sir Thomas, *A Short Treatise of Hunting*
(London, 1591)

Colville, Robert, *Beagling and Otter-Hunting*
(London, 1940)

Conroy, J.W.H., A. C. Kitchener and J. A. Gibson,
'The History of the Beaver in Scotland and its
Future Reintroduction', in *Species History in
Scotland*, ed. R. A. Lambert (1998), pp. 107–28

Cooper, Anthony Ashley, 'A Character of Mr
Hastings of Woodlands, near Cranbourne, in
Dorsetshire, Anno 1656', *Gentleman's Magazine*,
1st series, XXIV (1754), pp. 160–61

Coventry, Earl of, 'Otter Hunting', in *Deer, Hare and
Otter Hunting*, ed. the Earl of Lonsdale and E.
Parker (London, 1936), pp. 105–9

Cummins, John, *The Hound and the Hawk: The Art
of Medieval Hunting* (London, 1988)

Daniel, William B., *Rural Sports* (London, 1801)

Davies, E.W.L., 'The Otter and his Ways', in *Hunting*,
ed. the Duke of Beaufort and M. Morris (London,
1885), pp. 286–320

Davis, H.W.C., *Mediaeval England* (Oxford, 1924)

Edward, 2nd Duke of York, *The Master of Game*, ed.
W. A. Baillie-Grohman and F. Baillie-Grohman
(London, 1909)

Elyot, Sir Thomas, *The Boke named the Governour*
(London, 1546)

English Historical Documents, vol. II: *1042–1189*, ed.
D. C. Douglas and G. W. Greenaway (2nd edn,
London, 1981)

Fairfax, T., *The Complete Sportsman; or, Country Gentleman's Recreation* (London, 1765)

Freeman, G. E., and F. H. Salvin, *Falconry: Its Claims, History, and Practice, to which are added Remarks on training the Otter and Cormorant* (London, 1859)

Gardiner, John S., *The Art and the Pleasures of Hare-Hunting* (London, 1750)

Gêlert [pseudonym], *Fores's Guide to the Foxhounds and Staghounds of England, to which are added the Otter-Hounds and Harriers of Several Counties* (London, 1850)

Goldsmith, Oliver, *An History of the Earth and Animated Nature* (London, 1774), vol. IV

Griffin, Emma, *Blood Sport: Hunting in Britain since 1066* (New Haven, CT, and London, 2007)

Gudger, E. W., 'Fishing with the Cormorant, I: In China', *American Naturalist*, LX (1926), pp. 5–41

—, 'Fishing with the Otter', *American Naturalist*, LXI (1927), pp. 193–225

Harris, C. J., *Otters: A Study of the Recent* Lutrinae (London, 1968)

Harrison, William, *The Description of England*, ed. G. Edelen (Washington, DC, and New York, 1994)

Harting, James E., *British Animals Extinct within Historic Times* (London, 1880)

—, *A Perfect Booke for Kepinge of Sparhawkes or Goshawkes, written about 1575* (London, 1886)

—, *Bibliotheca Acciptraria: A Catalogue of Books Ancient and Modern relating to Falconry* (London, 1891)

—, 'The Polecat, *Mustela putorius*', *Zoologist*, 3rd ser., XV (1891), pp. 281–94

The Inventory of King Henry VIII: The Transcript, ed. D. Starkey (London, 1998)

Issues of the Exchequer, being Payments made out of His Majesty's Revenue during the Reign of King James I (London, 1836)

Itzkowitz, David C., *Peculiar Privilege: A Social History of English Foxhunting, 1753–1885* (Hassocks, 1977)

Jackson, Christine, 'Fishing with Cormorants', *Archives of Natural History*, XXIV (1997), pp. 189–211

King, Angela, J. Ottaway and A. Potter, *The Declining Otter: A Guide to its Conservation* (Chard, 1976)

Kitchener, Andrew, *Beavers* (Stowmarket, 2001)

Langley, P.J.W., and D. W. Yalden, 'The Decline of the Rarer Carnivores in Great Britain during the Nineteenth Century', *Mammal Review*, VII (1977), pp. 95–116

Lomax, James, *Otter Hunting Diary, 1829 to 1871, of the Late James Lomax, Esq.* (Blackburn, 1910)

Longrigg, Roger, *The History of Foxhunting* (London, 1975)

Lovegrove, Roger, *Silent Fields: The Long Decline of the Nation's Wildlife* (Oxford, 2007)

MacGregor, Arthur, 'Animals and the Early Stuarts: Hunting and Hawking at the Court of James I and Charles I', *Archives of Natural History*, XVI (1989), pp. 305–18

—, 'The King's Disport: Sports, Games and Pastimes of the Early Stuarts', in *The Late King's Goods: Collections, Possessions and Patronage of Charles I in the Light of the Commonwealth Sale Inventories*, ed. A. MacGregor (London and Oxford, 1989), pp. 403–21

—, 'Deer on the Move: Relocation of Stock between Game Parks in the Sixteenth and Seventeenth Centuries', *Anthropozoologica*, XVI (1992), pp. 167–79

—, 'The Household Out of Doors: The Stuart Court and the Animal Kingdom', in *The Stuart Courts*, ed. E. Cruickshanks (Stroud, 2000), pp. 86–117

Manning, Roger B., *Hunters and Poachers: A Social and Cultural History of unlawful Hunting in England, 1485–1640* (Oxford, 1993)

Markham, Gervase, *The Art of Archerie* (London, 1634)

Martin, Martin, *A Description of the Western Islands of Scotland* (London, 1703)

Mascall, Leonard, *A Boke of Fishing with Hooke and Line* (London, 1590)

The Master of Game by Edward of Norwich (facsimile edn, Philadelphia, 2005)

Milbourn, Thomas, 'The Milbournes of Essex and the King's Otter Hounds, 1385–1439', *Transactions of the Essex Archaeological Society*, new ser., v (1895), pp. 87–94

Nature Conservancy Council, *Otter Survey of England, 1977–79* (Shrewsbury, [1981])

Noirmont, Le Baron Dunoyer de, *Histoire de la chasse en France*, 3 vols (Paris, 1867–8)

Oggins, Robin S., *The Kings and their Hawks: Falconry in Medieval England* (New Haven, CT, and London, 2004)

Pennant, Thomas, *British Zoology*, 4th edn (Warrington, 1776)

Rackham, Oliver, *Ancient Woodland: Its History, Vegetation and Uses in England* (London, 1980)

—, *The History of the Countryside* (London, 1986)

Roberts, Jane, *Royal Landscape: The Gardens and Parks of Windsor* (New Haven, CT, and London, 1997)

Round, J. H., *The King's Serjeants and Officers of State* (London, 1911)

Rowe, Anne, *Medieval Parks of Hertfordshire* (Hatfield, 2009)

Russell, Nicholas, *Like Engend'ring Like: Heredity and Animal Breeding in Early Modern England* (Cambridge, 1986)

St John, C., *Natural History and Sport in Moray* (Edinburgh, 1863)

Somervile, William, *The Chace* (London, 1896)

Special Catalogue of the Chinese Collection of Exhibits for the International Fisheries Exhibition, London, 1883. China, Imperial Maritime Customs, III, Miscellaneous series 11 (Shanghai, 1883)

Staunton, Sir George, *An Authentic Account of an Embassy from the King of Great Britain to the Emperor of China* (London, 1798), vol. II

Stonehenge [pseudonym], *British Rural Sports*, 17th edn (London, 1888)

Stringer, Arthur, *The Experienced Huntsman: Contain-ing Observations on the Nature and Qualities of the Different Species of Game* (Dublin, 1780)

Sykes, Naomi, 'Animal Bones and Animal Parks', in *The Medieval Park: New Perspectives*, ed. R. Liddiard (Macclesfield, 2007), pp. 49–62

Taplin, W., ed., *The Sporting Dictionary, and Rural Repository of General Information . . . appertaining to the Sports of the Field*, 2 vols (London, 1803)

The Tretyse of Huntyng, ed. Anne Rooney, *Scripta: Medieval and Renaissance Texts and Studies*, XIX (Brussels, 1987)

Turberville, George, *The Noble Arte of Venerie or Hunting* (London, 1576)

Twiti, William, *The Art of Hunting, 1327*, ed. B. Daniels-son, *Cynegetica Anglica*, 1 (Stockholm, 1977)

Walton, Izaak, *The Compleat Angler; or, The Contemplative Man's Recreation*, 3rd edn (London, 1661)

White, G. H., 'The *Constitutio Domus Regis* and the King's Sport', *Antiquaries Journal*, XXX (1950), pp. 52–63

Wilson, Charles, 'Notes on the Prior Existence of the Castor Fiber in Scotland . . . and on the Use of Castoreum', *Edinburgh New Philosophical Journal*, new ser., VIII (1858), pp. 1–40

THREE: Urban and Rural Sports and Pastimes

[Acton, John], *An Essay on Shooting* (London, 1789)

Adams, Joseph Q., *Shakespearean Playhouses* (Boston, MA, 1917)

Alken, Henry, *The National Sports of Great Britain* (London, 1903)

Alleyn, Edward, *The Alleyn Papers*, ed. J. Payne Collier (London, 1843)

Ashton, John, *Social Life in the Reign of Queen Anne Taken from Original Sources* (London, 1882)

Aston, M., ed., *Medieval Fish, Fisheries and Fishponds in England*, BAR British Ser. 182 (Oxford, 1988)

Atkinson, Herbert, *Cock-Fighting and Game Fowl*

*from the Note-Books of Herbert Atkinson of Ewelme,
together with the Life and Letters of John Harris, the
Cornish Cocker*, ed. Game Cock [pseudonym]
(Liss, 1977)

Baldiston, William A., *The British Sportsman; or,
Nobleman, Gentleman, and Farmers Dictionary of
Recreation and Amusement* (London, 1792)

Bentley, Gerald E., *The Jacobean and Caroline Stage*
(Oxford, 1968)

Bewick, Thomas, *A General History of Quadrupeds*,
5th edn (Newcastle upon Tyne, 1807)

—, *A History of British Birds* (Newcastle upon Tyne,
1797)

Bingley, W., *Animal Biography; or, Anecdotes of the
Lives, Manners and Economy of the Animal
Creation* (London, 1803)

Birkhead, Mike, and Christopher Perrins, *The Mute
Swan* (London, 1986)

Bitterling, K., 'A ME Treatise on Angling from BL MS
Sloane 1698', *English Studies*, LXII (1981), pp. 110–14

Blome, Richard, *The Gentleman's Recreation: in four
parts, viz. Hunting, Hawking, Fowling, Fishing*
(London, 1686)

Blyth, Edward, *The Natural History of Cranes*, ed.
W. B. Tegetmeier (London, 1881)

Borsay, Peter, *The English Urban Renaissance: Culture
and Society in the Provincial Town, 1660–1770*
(Oxford, 1989)

Braekman, W. L., 'The Treatise on Angling in the
Boke of St. Albans (1496)', *Scripta: Medieval and
Renaissance Texts and Studies*, I (1980), pp. 1–90

Brailsford, Dennis, *A Taste for Diversions: Sport in
Georgian England* (Cambridge, 1999)

Brown, A., R. Turner and C. Pearson, 'Medieval
Fishing Structures and Baskets at Sudbrook Point,
Severn Estuary, Wales', *Medieval Archaeology*, LIV
(2010), pp. 346–61

Brown, J. A. Harvie, 'The Past and Present Distribution
of Some of the Rarer Animals of Scotland, IV: The
Badger', *Zoologist*, 3rd ser., VI (1882), pp. 1–9, 41–5

Brunner, Bernd, *Bears: A Brief History*, trans. L. Lantz
(New Haven, CT, and London, 2007)

Bryden, H. A., *Nature and Sport in Great Britain*
(London, 1904)

Busino, Orazio, 'Anglipotrida', in *Calendar of State
Papers Venetian*, vol. XV, pp. 257–60

Chambers, E. K., *The Elizabethan Stage* (Oxford, 1923),
vol. II

Chute, R., *Shooting Flying: A Bibliography of Shooting
Books, 1598–1950* (Winchester, 2001)

Cook, W. A., and R.E.M. Pilcher, *The History of
Borough Fen Decoy* (Ely, 1982)

Cosimo de' Medici, *Travels of Cosmo the Third,
Grand Duke of Tuscany, through England*
(London, 1821)

Cox, Nicholas, *The Gentleman's Recreation* (London,
1677)

Creighton, Oliver, *Designs upon the Land: Elite
Landscapes of the Middle Ages* (Woodbridge, 2009)

Darby, H. C., *The Medieval Fenland* (Cambridge, 1940)

Darwin, C. R., *The Variation of Animals and Plants
under Domestication* (London, 1868)

Datta, Ann, et al., *Animals and the Law*, Otter
Memorial Paper 10, ed. P. Foster (Chichester, 1998)

Dawson, Giles E., 'London's Bull-Baiting and Bear-
Baiting Area in 1562', *Shakespeare Quarterly*, XV/1
(1964), pp. 97–101

Declaration of Lawful Sports, 'The King's Majesty's
Declaration to his Subjects, concerning Lawful
Sports to be used [1633]', *Harleian Miscellany*,
vol. V (London, 1810), pp. 75–7

Dennys, John, *The Secrets of Angling* (London, 1613)

Dugdale, [Sir] William, *The History of Imbanking
and Drayning of divers Fenns and Marshes*
(London, 1662)

Duncan, S., and G. Thorne, *The Complete Wildfowler*
(London, 1911)

Dyer, C., 'The Consumption of Fresh-Water Fish
in Medieval England', in *Medieval Fish, Fisheries
and Fishponds in England*, ed. Aston, pp. 27–38

Ellis, Edmund, '"The opinion of Mr Perkins and Mr Bolton, and others, concerning the sport of cockfighting . . .", Oxford . . . 1610', *Harleian Miscellany*, vol. VI (London, 1745), pp. 110–15

English Historical Documents, vol. II: *1042–1189*, ed. D. C. Douglas and G. W. Greenaway, 2nd edn (London, 1981)

Fairfax, T., *The Compleat Sportsman; or, Country Gentleman's Recreation* (London, 1762)

Fairfax Blakeborough, J., and Sir Alfred E. Pease, *The Life and Habits of the Badger* (London, 1914)

Fishwick, Henry, 'A Lancashire Cock-Fight in 1514', *Antiquary*, XLVI (1910), pp. 27–8

Folkard, H. C., *The Wild-Fowler: A Treatise on Fowling, Ancient and Modern, descriptive also of Decoys and Flight Ponds*, 4th edn (London, 1897)

Fretwell, Katie, 'Lodge Park, Gloucestershire: A Rare Surviving Deer Course and Bridgeman Layout', *Garden History*, XXIII (1995), pp. 133–44

Gardiner, S. R., *History of the Commonwealth and Protectorate, 1649–1656* (New York, 1965)

George, J. N., *English Guns and Rifles* (Plantersville, SC, 1947)

Gilbey, Sir Walter, *Sport in the Olden Time* (London, 1912)

Govett, L. A., *The King's Book of Sports* (London, 1890)

Graziani, René, 'Sir Thomas Wyatt at a Cockfight, 1539', *Review of English Studies*, new ser., XXVII (1976), pp. 299–303

Griffin, Emma, *Blood Sport: Hunting in Britain since 1066* (New Haven and London, 2007)

Gurney, J. H., *Early Annals of Ornithology* (London, 1921)

Hamilton, J. P., *Reminiscences of an Old Sportsman* (London, 1860)

Harris, John, *The Life and Letters of John Harris, the Cornish Cocker* (Ewelme, privately printed, 1910)

Harting, J. E., 'The Badger, *Meles taxus*', *Zoologist*, 3rd ser., XII (1888), pp. 1–13

Hawker, P., *Instructions to Young Sportsmen* (London, 1824 and later edns)

Heaton, A., *Duck Decoys* (Princes Risborough, 2001)

Heslop, R. O., 'Bull Ring on the Sandhill', *Proceedings of the Society of Antiquaries of Newcastle-upon-Tyne*, 3rd ser., III (1907), p. 100

Historical Manuscripts Commission, *The Manuscripts of His Grace the Duke of Rutland, K.G., preserved at Belvoir Castle* (London, 1889)

The History of the King's Works, vol. IV: *1485—1660*, ed. H. Colvin et al. (London, 1982)

Hodson, M. S., 'Bear Baiting in the River Wye', *Transactions of the Woolhope Naturalists' Field Club*, XXXII (1946–8), pp. 170–72

Hoffmann, R. C., 'Fishing for Sport in Medieval Europe: New Evidence', *Speculum*, LX (1985), pp. 877–902

Hosley, Richard, 'The Origins of the Shakespearian Playhouse', *Shakespeare Quarterly*, XV/2 (1964), pp. 29–39

Hotson, J. Leslie, 'Bear Gardens and Bear-Baiting during the Commonwealth', *Publications of the Modern Language Association of America*, XL (1925), pp. 276–88

Howlett, R., *The School of Recreation; or, The Gentlemans Tutor* (London, 1684)

Howlett, Robert, *The Royal Pastime of Cock-Fighting* (London, 1709)

Jenkins, Geraint, *Nets and Coracles* (Newton Abbot, 1974)

A Jewell for Gentrie: Being an exact Dictionary, or true Method, to make any Man understand all the Art, Secrets, and worthy Knowledges belonging to Hawking, Hunting, Fowling and Fishing (London, 1614)

King, H. H., *Working Terriers, Badgers and Badger-Digging* (London, n.d.)

Kingsford, C. L., 'Paris Garden and the Bear-Baiting', *Archaeologia*, LXX (1920), pp. 155–78

Kiser, Lisa J., 'Animals in Medieval Sports, Entertainment and Menageries', in *A Cultural*

History of Animals in the Medieval Age, ed. B. Resl (Oxford, 2007), pp. 103–26

Krebbs, John R., *Bovine Tuberculosis in Cattle and Badgers*, Report to the Rt Hon. Jack Cunningham, MP (London, 1998)

Laneham, Robert, *A Letter: wherein, part of the Entertainment untoo the Queenz Maiesty at Killingworth Castl . . . iz Signified* (London, 1575)

Longrigg, Roger, *The English Squire and his Sport* (London, 1977)

Lovegrove, Roger, *Silent Fields: The Long Decline of the Nation's Wildlife* (Oxford, 2007)

Lubbock, R., *Observations on the Fauna of Norfolk* (Norwich, 1845)

Machrie, William, *An Essay upon the Royal Recreation and Art of Cocking* (Edinburgh, 1705)

MacPherson, H. A., *A History of Fowling* (Edinburgh, 1897)

—, *A Vertebrate Fauna of Lakeland* (Edinburgh, 1892)

Madden, Frederic, 'Narrative of the Visit of the Duke of Nájera to England, in the Year 1543–4', *Archaeologia*, XXIII (1831), pp. 344–57

Malcolmson, Robert W., *Popular Recreations in English Society, 1700–1850* (Cambridge, 1973)

Markham, G., *Cheape and Good Husbandry for the well-Ordering of all Beasts, and Fowles* (London, 1614)

—, *Hungers Prevention; or, The whole Arte of Fowling by Water and Land* (London, 1621)

—, *Country Contentments; or, The Husbandmans Recreations. Containing the wholesome Experience, in which any ought to Recreate himself, after the toyle of more Serious Business*, 10th edn (London, 1668)

Marston, R. B., *Walton and Some Earlier Writers on Fish and Fishing* (London, 1894)

Mascall, L., *The Booke of Fishing with Hooke and Line: Another of Sundrie Engines and Trappes to take Polcats, Buzards, Rattes, Mice and all other Kindes of Vermine and Beasts whatsoever, most profitable for all Warriners, and such as delight in this Kind of Sport and Pastime* (London, 1590)

Maxwell, William H., *The Field Book; or, Sports and Pastimes of the United Kingdom* (London, 1833)

McDonnell, J., 'Inland Fisheries in Medieval Yorkshire, 1066–1300', *Borthwick Papers*, no. 60 (1981), pp. 1–42

Misson, Henri, *M. Misson's Memoirs and Observations in his Travels over England* (London, 1719)

Moffet [Mouffet], Thomas, *Healths Improvement; or, Rules Comprizing and Discovering the Nature, Method, and Manner of Preparing all sorts of Food* (London, 1655)

Moore, John, *Columbarium; or, The Pigeon-House* (London, 1735)

Mullett, C. F., 'Gervase Markham: Scientific Amateur', *Isis*, XXXV (1944), pp. 106–18

Neal, Ernest, *The Natural History of Badgers* (London, 1986)

Osman, A. H., *Pigeons in the Great War* (London, n.d.)

Payne-Gallwey, Sir R., *The Book of Duck Decoys: Their Construction, Management and History* (London, 1886)

Pease, Sir Alfred E., *The Badger* (London, 1898)

Pegge, Samuel, '"Ἀλεχ ρυόνων Ἀγών". A Memoir on Cock-Fighting; wherein the antiquity of it, as a pastime, is examined and stated; some errors of the moderns concerning it are corrected; and the retention of it amongst Christians is absolutely condemned and proscribed', *Archaeologia*, III (1786), pp. 132–50

—, 'A Dissertation on the Crane, as a Dish Served up at Great Tables in England', *Archaeologia*, II (1773), pp. 171–6

—, 'The Bull-Running, at Tutbury, in Staffordshire, Considered', *Archaeologia*, II (1773), pp. 86–91

Pennant, Thomas, *British Zoology* (London, 1768)

—, *Some Account of London, Westminster, and Southwark* (London, 1805)

Pepys, Samuel, *The Diary of Samuel Pepys*, vol. IX:

1668–1669, ed. R. Latham and W. Matthews (London, 1976)

Perkins, William, *The Whole Treatise of the Cases of Conscience . . . newly corrected* (London, 1632)

Peterson, H. L., *Encyclopædia of Firearms* (London, 1964)

Pevsner, Nikolaus, *The Buildings of England: Cornwall* (Harmondsworth, 1951)

Plot, Robert, *The Natural History of Stafford-shire* (Oxford, 1686)

Ray, J., *The Ornithology of Francis Willughby, in three Books* (London, 1678)

Rees, Abraham, *The Cyclopædia; or, Universal Dictionary of Arts, Sciences, and Literature*, 39 vols (London, 1819–20)

Reresby, Sir John, *Memoirs of Sir John Reresby*, ed. A. Browning (Glasgow, 1936)

Ritchie, James, *The Influence of Man on Animal Life in Scotland* (Cambridge, 1920)

Rowley, G. D., *Ornithological Miscellany* (London, 1877)

Rye, William B., *England as Seen by Foreigners in the Days of Elizabeth and James I* (London, 1865)

St John, Charles, *Short Sketches of the Wild Sports and Natural History of the Highlands* (London, 1846)

Saussure, C. de, *A Foreign View of England in 1725–1729: The Letters of M. César de Saussure to his Family*, trans. M. van Muyden (London, 1995)

Scott, George Ryley, *The History of Cockfighting* (Hindhead, 1983)

Seton, Walter, 'The Baiting of Bulls', *Antiquaries Journal*, IV (1924), pp. 413–14

Seymour, Richard, *The Compleat Gamester . . . to which is added The Gentleman's Diversion, in Riding, Racing, Archery, Cock-Fighting, and Bowling* (London, 1721)

Skinner, Paul, Don Jefferies and Stephen Harris, *Badger Persecution and the Law*, Mammal Society Occasional Publication, 10 (London, 1989)

The Sportsman's Dictionary; or, the Gentleman's Companion for Town and Country (London, 1778)

Stainthorpe, T. W., 'Ye ancient bull ring at Totnes', *Transactions of the Devonshire Association*, XXXII (1900), pp. 106–10

Steane, J. M., and M. Foreman, 'Medieval Fishing Tackle', in Aston, *Medieval Fish, Fisheries and Fishponds in England*, pp. 137–86

Stevenson, H., *The Birds of Norfolk* (London, 1870)

Stow, John, *A Survey of the Cities of Westminster and London* (London, 1598)

—, *The Annales; or, Generall Chronicle of England* (London, 1615)

—, *A Survey of the Cities of London and Westminster*, ed. John Strype (London, 1720)

Stringer, Arthur, *The Experienced Hunter*, 2nd edn (Belfast, 1780)

Stubbes, Philip, *Anatomie of Abuses* (London, 1583)

Taplin, William, ed., *The Sporting Dictionary, and Rural Repository of General Information . . . appertaining to the Sports of the Field* (London, 1803), 2 vols

Taverner, John, *Certaine Experiments concerning Fish and Fruite* (London, 1600)

Taylor, John F., *Fishing on the Lower Severn* (Gloucester, 1974)

Tegetmeier, W. B., *Pigeons: Their Structure, Habits and Varieties* (London, 1867)

—, *The Poultry Book* (London, 1873)

Topsell, Edward, *The Historie of Foure-Footed Beastes* (London, 1607)

Turberville, George, *The Noble Art of Venerie or Hunting* (London, 1576)

Turner, William, *Avium Præcipuarium . . . brevis et succincta historia* (Cologne, 1544)

Wallraff, Hans G., *Avian Navigation: Pigeon Homing as a Paradigm* (Heidelberg, 2005)

Wentworth-Day, J., *A History of the Fens* (London, 1954)

Whitaker, J., *British Duck Decoys of Today, 1918* (London, 1918)

Wildlife Link Badger Working Group, *Badgers, Cattle and Bovine Tuberculosis* (n.p., 1994)

Wilkinson, Robert, *Londina Illustrata* (London, 1819)

Willughby, Francis, *The Ornithology of Francis Willughby*, ed. John Ray (London, 1678)

Wilson, Gavin, Stephen Harris and Graeme McLaren, *Changes in the British Badger Population, 1988–1997* (London, 1997)

Wilson, George, *The Commendation of Cockes, and Cock-fighting: Wherein it is shewed, that Cocke-fighting was before the coming of Christ* (London, 1607)

Yalden, D. W., and U. Albarella, *The History of British Birds* (Oxford, 2009)

FOUR: The Living Larder

Andrews, Herbert C., 'Dovecotes', *Transactions of the East Hertfordshire Archaeological Society*, III (1905), pp. 297–303

Anon., *The Dove-Cote; or, The Art of Breeding Pigeons: A Poem* (London, 1740)

Aston, M., ed., *Medieval Fish, Fisheries and Fishponds in England*, BAR British Ser. 182 (Oxford, 1988)

Bailey, M., 'The Rabbit and the Medieval East Anglian Economy', *Agricultural History Review*, XXXVI (1988), pp. 1–20

Banks, Sir Joseph, 'Ordinances Respecting Swans on the River Witham, in the County of Lincoln: Together with an Original Roll of Swan Marks, Appertaining to the Proprietors on the said Stream', *Archaeologia*, XVI (1812), pp. 153–62

Barker, W. E., *Pigeon Racing: A Practical Guide to the Sport* (London, n.d.)

Best, H., *Rural Economy in Yorkshire in 1641, being the Farming and Account Books of Henry Best*, Surtees Society, XXXIII (London, 1857)

Bettey, J., 'The Production of Rabbits in Wiltshire during the Seventeenth Century', *Antiquaries Journal*, LXXXIV (2004), pp. 380–93

Birkhead, M., and C. Perrins, *The Mute Swan* (London, 1986)

Blomefield, F., *An Essay towards a Topographical History of the County of Norfolk*, 11 vols (London, 1805–10)

Bond, C. J., 'Monastic Fishponds', in *Medieval Fish, Fisheries and Fishponds in England*, ed. Aston, pp. 69–112

Bowyer, G., 'Letter to Sir Henry Ellis, Giving a Summary of the Old Laws Respecting Swans', *Archaeologia*, XXXII (1847), pp. 423–8

Bracton Henry de, *Henrici de Bracton, De Legibus et Consuetidinibus Angliae*, ed. T. Twiss, 6 vols (London, 1878–83).

Bromehead, J. M., 'Memoir on the Regulations Anciently Prescribed in Regard to Swans . . . and on an Original Book of Swan-Marks', *Memoirs illustrative of the History and Antiquities of the County and City of Lincoln*, Archaeological Institute of Great Britain and Ireland, Annual Meeting held at Lincoln, 1848 (London, 1850)

Butler, Charles, *The Feminine Monarchie; or, A Treatise concerning Bees* (Oxford, 1609)

Capello, F.], *A Relation; or, rather, a true Account, of the Island of England . . . about the Year 1500*, trans. and ed. C. A. Sneyd, Camden Society, XXXVII (London, 1897)

Cheshire, Frank R., *Bees and Bee-keeping: Scientific and Practical* (London, 1888)

Cockerell, S. C., ed., *The Gorleston Psalter: A Manuscript of the Beginning of the Fourteenth Century in the Library of C. W. Dyson Perrins* (London, 1907)

—, and M. Rhodes James, *Two East Anglian Psalters at the Bodleian Library, Oxford, the Ormesby Psalter MS Douce 366 and the Bromholm Psalter MS Ashmole 1523* (Oxford, for the Roxburghe Club, 1926)

Coke, Sir Edward, *The Reports of Sir Edward Coke, Knt*, new edn, ed. J. H. Thomas and J. F. Fraser (London, 1826)

Cooke, Arthur O., *A Book of Dovecotes* (London, Edinburgh and Boston, MA, 1920)

Cooke, Samuel, *The Complete English Gardener . . . to which is added the Complete Bee-Master* (London, [*c.* 1770])

Copeland, G. W., 'Devon Dovecotes', *Report and Transactions of the Devonshire Association*, LXIX (1937), pp. 391–401

Crane, Eva, *The Archaeology of Beekeeping* (London, 1983)

—, and Penelope Walker, 'Evidence on Welsh Beekeeping in the Past', *Folk Life*, XXIII (1984–5), pp. 21–47

—, 'Wall Recesses for Bee Hives', *Antiquity*, LXXIV (2000), pp. 805–11

Creighton, Oliver, *Designs upon the Land. Elite Landscapes of the Middle Ages* (Woodbridge, 2009)

Currie, C. K., 'The Role of Fishponds in the Monastic Economy', in *The Archaeology of Rural Monasteries*, ed. R. Gilchrist and H. Mytum, BAR British Ser. 203 (Oxford, 1989), pp. 147–72

—, 'Fishponds as Garden Features, *c.* 1550–1750', *Garden History*, XVIII (1990), pp. 22–46

—, 'The Early History of the Carp and its Economic Significance in England', *Agricultural History Review*, XXXIX (1991), pp. 97–107

Daniel, W. B., *Rural Sports* (London, 1801)

Defoe, Daniel, *A Tour through the Whole Island of Great Britain*, 2nd edn (London, 1738)

Dennison, E., 'Woodhall Rabbit Warren, Carperby', in *Archaeology and Historic Landscapes of the Yorkshire Dales*, ed. R. F. White and P. R. Wilson (Leeds, 2004), pp. 137–44

Dix, B., 'An Excavation at Sharpenhoe Clappers, Streatley, Bedfordshire', *Bedfordshire Archaeology*, XVI (1983), pp. 65–74

Dubravius, J., *A New Booke of good Husbandry, very pleasant, and of great Profite both for Gentlemen and Yomen*, trans. for G. Churchey (London, 1599)

Dugdale, Sir William, *Origines Juridicales; or, Historical Memorials of the English Laws . . .* (London, 1666)

Dummelow, John, *The Wax Chandlers of London* (Chichester, 1973)

Dyers' Company, *Swan Marking and Swan Upping* (London, n.d.)

Erskine, J., *An Institute of the Law of Scotland in Four Books*, 3rd edn (Edinburgh, 1793)

Evelyn, John, *Elysium Britannicum; or, Royal Gardens*, ed. J. E. Ingram (Philadelphia, 2001)

Fallowfield, John, *The Husbandman and Tradesman's Calendar . . . to which is added Instructions for the Ordering of Bees* (Preston, 1791)

Farmer, David L., 'Marketing the Produce of the Countryside, 1200–1500', in *The Agrarian History of England and Wales*, vol. III: *1348–1500*, ed. E. Miller (Cambridge, 1991), pp. 324–430

Fenner, F., and F. N. Ratcliffe, *Myxomatosis* (Cambridge, 1965)

Finlay, Michael, *Western Writing Implements in the Age of the Quill Pen* (Carlisle, 1990)

Ferguson, R. S., 'Culverhouses', *Archaeological Journal*, XLIV (1887), pp. 105–16

Fowler, J., *A Description of the High Stream of Arundel . . . Written . . . about the Year 1637* (Littlehampton, 1929)

Fraser, H. M., 'Beekeeping in the British Isles before 1500', *Bee World*, XXXVI (1955), pp. 177–86, 223–6

Frere, H. T., 'Norfolk Swan Fatting', *Zoologist*, IV (1846), p. 1250

Gilbert, J. M., *Hunting and Hunting Reserves in Medieval Scotland* (Edinburgh, 1979)

Giraldus Cambrensis, *Vita S. Hugonis*, Rolls Series XXI, vii, ed. J. F. Dimock (London, 1877)

Girton, Daniel [pseudonym], *The Complete Pigeon and Rabbit Fancier* (London, 1823)

Gurney, J. H., *Early Annals of Ornithology* (London, 1921)

Hansell, Peter, and Jean Hansell, *Doves and Dovecotes* (Bath, 1988)

—, *A Dovecote Heritage* (Bath, 1992)

Harris, A., and D. A. Spratt, 'The Rabbit Warrens of

the Tabular Hills, North Yorkshire', *Yorkshire Archaeological Journal*, LXIII (1991), pp. 177–206

Harting, J. E., *Recreations of a Naturalist* (London, 1906)

Hartlib, Samuel, *Legacy of Husbandry* (London, 1655)

—, *The Reformed Common-wealth of Bees, presented in several Letters and Observations to Samuel Hartlib Esq.* (London, 1655)

Haynes, R. G., 'Vermin Traps and Rabbit Warrens on Dartmoor', *Post-Medieval Archaeology*, IV (1970), pp. 147–64

Hayward, M., *Dress at the Court of King Henry VIII* (Leeds, 2007)

Herrod Hempsall, William, *Bee Keeping New and Old*, 2 vols (London, 1930–37)

Hickling, C. F., 'Prior Moore's Fishponds', *Medieval Archaeology*, XV (1971), pp. 118–23

Hope, W. H. St. J., 'A Palatinate Seal of John, Earl of Warenne, Surrey and Stratherne, 1305–1347', *Sussex Archaeological Collections*, LVII (1915), pp. 180–84

Humphrys, G., 'Ups and Downs for the Swan', *Country Life*, CLXXXI/30 (1987), p. 112

James, M. Rhodes, *The Apocalypse in Latin and French: Bodleian MS Douce 180* (Oxford, for the Roxburghe Club, 1922)

Jones, P. E., *The Worshipful Company of Poulters of the City of London: A Short History* (London, 1965)

Kear, J., *Man and Wildfowl* (London, 1990)

Klingender, F., *Animals in Art and Thought to the End of the Middle Ages* (London, 1971)

Lawson, William, *The Countrie Housewifes Garden . . . together with The Husbandry of Bees* (London, 1617)

Levett, John, *The Ordering of Bees; or, The True History of Managing Them* (London, 1634)

Linehan, C. D., 'Deserted Sites and Rabbit-Warrens on Dartmoor, Devon', *Medieval Archaeology*, X (1966), pp. 113–44

Loudon, J. C., *An Encyclopædia of Agriculture*, 8th edn (London, 1883)

Lovegrove, Roger, *Silent Fields: The Long Decline of a Nation's Wildlife* (Oxford, 2007)

MacGregor, Arthur, 'Swan Rolls and Beak Markings: Husbandry, Exploitation and Regulation of *Cygnus olor* in England, *c.* 1100–1900', *Anthropozoologica*, XXII (1996), pp. 39–68

Mansell-Pleydell, J. C., 'Decoys and Swan Marks', *Dorset Natural History and Antiquarian Field Club*, LXXXI (1886), pp. 1–8

Mantell, Gideon Algernon, 'A Few Remarks on the Discovery of the Remains of William de Warren . . . among the Ruins of Saint Pancras, at Southover, near Lewes, in Sussex', *Archaeologia*, XXXI (1846), pp. 430–36

Markham, Gervase, *Cheape and Good Husbandry for the well-Ordering of all Beasts, and Fowles . . . together with the Use and Profit of Bees . . .* (London, 1614)

Matheson, C., 'The Rabbit and the Hare in Wales', *Antiquity*, XV (1941), pp. 371–81

Maxwell, Robert, *The Practical Bee-Master*, 2nd edn (Edinburgh, 1750)

Mayo, C. H., 'Swans on the Salisbury Avon and the Dorset Stour', *Notes and Queries for Somerset and Dorset*, XIII (1913), pp. 297–312

McDonnell, J., 'Inland Fisheries in Medieval Yorkshire, 1066–1300', *Borthwick Papers*, no. 60 (1981), pp. 1–42

Minet, W., 'Two Early Seventeenth-Century Rolls of Norfolk Swan-Marks', *Proceedings of the Society of Antiquaries of London*, XX (1903–5), pp. 276–86

Moffet [Muffet], Thomas, *Healths Improvement; or, Rules comprizing and discovering the Nature, Method, and Manner of preparing all Sorts of Food* (London, 1655)

Moore, John, *Columbarium; or, The Pigeon-House* (London, 1735)

Moore, Sir Jonas, *England's Interest; or, The Gentleman and Farmer's Friend*, 3rd edn (London, 1705)

Moryson, F., *An Itinerary written by Fynes Moryson, gent. first in the Latine Tongue, and then translated by him into English* (London, 1617)

Mowat, George, 'Early Pigeon-Houses (Columbaria)', *Transactions of the St Albans and Hertfordshire Architectural and Archaeological Society*, new ser., II (1903–14), pp. 29–32

Munsche, P. B., *Gentlemen and Poachers: The English Game Laws, 1671–1831* (Cambridge, 1981)

Nicolson, William, 'Bishop Nicolson's Diaries', *Transactions of the Cumberland and Westmorland Antiquarian and Archaeological Society*, new ser., I (1901), pp. 1–51

Nishimura, M. M., and D. Nishimura, *Rabbits, Warrens and Warenne: The Patronage of the Gorleston Psalter*: www.cronaca.com/archives/003697.html, last accessed 3 July 2011

[North, R.], *A discourse of Fish and Fish-Ponds . . . done by a Person of Honour* (London, 1713)

Northcote, E. M., 'Morphology of Mute Swans *Cygnus olor* in Relation to Domestication', in *Animals and Archaeology, 2: Shell Middens, Fishes and Birds*, BAR International Ser. 183, ed. C. Grigson and J. Clutton-Brock (Oxford, 1983), pp. 173–9

Nutt, Thomas, *Humanity to Honey-Bees; or, Practical Directions for the Management of Honey-Bees*, 2nd edn (Wisbech, 1834)

O'Neil, H. E., 'Coney Warren on Elm Bank Farm, Cold Aston, Gloucestershire', *Proceedings of the Cotteswold Naturalists' Field Club*, XXXV (1966–70), pp. 156–8

The Orders Lawes and Ancient Customes of Swanns (London, 1632)

Paley-Baildon, W., 'A Sixteenth-century Account Book, with a Note on Swan-Marks', *Proceedings of the Society of Antiquaries of London*, XXV (1912–13), pp. 181–3

Peacock, E., 'Swan-Marks', *Archaeological Journal*, XLI (1884), pp. 291–6; XLII (1885), pp. 17–19

Pitt, W., *General View of the Agriculture of the County of Stafford* (London, 1796)

Plot, Robert, *The Natural History of Oxford-shire* (Oxford, 1676)

—, *The Natural History of Stafford-shire* (Oxford, 1686)

Poulson, G., *The History and Antiquities of the Seigniory of Holderness* (London, 1840)

Redstone, L. J., ed., 'The Cellarer's Account for Bromholm Priory, Norfolk, 1415–1416', *Norfolk Record Society*, XVII (1944), pp. 47–91

Roberts, B. K., 'The Rediscovery of Fishponds', in *Medieval Fish, Fisheries and Fishponds in England*, ed. Aston, pp. 9–16

Roberts, E., 'The Bishop of Winchester's Fishponds in Hampshire, 1150–1400: Their Development, Function and Management', *Proceedings of the Hampshire Field Club and Archaeological Society*, XLII (1986), pp. 125–38

Robins, E. C., 'Some Account of the History and Antiquities of the Worshipful Company of Dyers, London', *Transactions of the London and Middlesex Archaeological Society*, V (1881), pp. 463–76

Rusden, Moses, *A Further Discovery of Bees . . . with the Experiments and Improvements arising from keeping them in transparent Boxes, instead of Straw-hives* (London, 1679)

Sadler, P., 'Osteological Remains', in *Faccombe Netherton: Excavations of a Saxon and Medieval Manorial Complex*, 2 vols, ed. R. Fairbrother, British Museum Occasional Papers 74 (London, 1990), pp. 462–508

Scott, John, *Berwick-upon-Tweed: The History of the Town and Guild* (London, 1888)

Serjeantson, Dale, 'Birds: Food and a Mark of Status', in *Food in Medieval England*, ed. Woolgar, Serjeantson and Waldron, pp. 131–47

Sheail, John, *Rabbits and their History* (Newton Abbot, 1971)

Sheldon, Frederick, *History of Berwick-upon-Tweed* (Edinburgh, 1849)

Silvester, R. J., ''Pillow Mounds at Y Foel, Llanllugan', *Montgomeryshire Collections*, LXXXIII (1995), pp. 75–90

Southerne, Edmund, *A Treatise Concerning the Right Use and Ordering of Bees, newlie made and set forth according to the Author's owne Experience* (London, 1593)

Southwell, T., 'St. Helen's Swan-Pit', *Transactions of the Norfolk and Norwich Naturalists' Society*, V (1889–94), pp. 265–72; VI (1894–9), pp. 387–9; VII (1899–1904), pp. 579–81

Stamper, P., 'Woods and Parks', in *The Countryside of Medieval England*, ed. G. Astill and A. Grant (Oxford, 1988), pp. 128–48

Steane, J. M., 'The Royal Fishponds of Medieval England', in *Medieval Fish, Fisheries and Fishponds in England*, ed. Aston, pp. 39–68

—, and M. Foreman, 'Medieval Fishing Tackle', in *Medieval Fish, Fisheries and Fishponds in England*, ed. Aston, pp. 137–86

Stocker, D., and M. Stocker, 'Sacred Profanity: The Theology of Rabbit Breeding and the Symbolic Landscape of the Warren', *World Archaeology*, XXVIII (1996–7), pp. 265–72

Stone, D. J., 'The Consumption and Supply of Birds in Late Medieval England', in *Food in Medieval England*, ed. Woolgar, Serjeantson and Waldron, pp. 148–61

Suffield-Jones, N., 'Dovecotes and Gunpowder', *Surrey Archaeological Collections*, LXIII (1966), pp. 175–6

Taverner, J., *Certaine Experiments concerning Fish and Fruite* (London, 1600)

Thompson, H. V., 'The Rabbit in Britain', in *The European Rabbit: The History and Biology of a Successful Colonizer*, ed. H. V. Thompson and C. M. King (Oxford, 1994), pp. 64–107

Thompson, H. Yates, *A Lecture on Some English Illuminated Manuscripts* (London, 1902)

Ticehurst, N. F., *The Mute Swan in England: Its History, and the Ancient Custom of Swan Keeping* (London, 1957)

Tittensor, A. M., and R. M. Tittensor, 'The Rabbit Warren at West Dean near Chichester', *Sussex Archaeological Collections*, CXXIII (1985), pp. 151–85

Turner, E., 'The Marchant Diary', *Sussex Archaeological Collections*, XXV (1873), pp. 163–203

Veale, E. M., *The English Fur Trade in the Later Middle Ages* (Oxford, 1966)

Vintners' Company, *The Vintners' Swans: Swan Upping* (London, n.d.)

Walter of Henley, *Walter of Henley and Other Treatises on Estate Management and Accounting*, ed. Dorothea Oschinsky (Oxford, 1971)

Warner, G., *Queen Mary's Psalter: Miniatures and Drawings by an English Artist of the 14th Century, reproduced from Royal MS 2 B. VII in the British Museum* (London, 1912)

Williamson, T. W., 'Fish, Fur and Feather: Man and Nature in the Post-Medieval Landscape', in *Making English Landscapes: Changing Perspectives*, ed. K. Barker and T. Darvill (Oxford, 1997), pp. 92–117

—, *Rabbits, Warrens and Archaeology* (Stroud, 2007)

Willis, Robert, and John Willis Clark, *The Architectural History of the University of Cambridge and of the Colleges of Cambridge and Eton* (Cambridge, 1886; reprinted 1988)

Willughby, Francis, *The Ornithology of Francis Willughby . . . in Three Books*, ed. John Ray (London, 1678)

Wilson, C. A., *Food and Drink in Britain from the Stone Age to Recent Times* (Harmondsworth, 1984)

Woolgar, C. M., D. Serjeantson and T. Waldron, eds, *Food in Medieval England: Diet and Nutrition* (Oxford, 2006)

Worrall, V., 'Legal Aspects', in *The Rabbit*, ed. H. V. Thompson and A. N. Worden (London, 1956), pp. 199–210

Yarrell, W., *A History of British Birds*, 4th edn, ed. H. Saunders, 4 vols (London, 1844–5)

FIVE: Animals on the Farm

Albarello, U., 'Pig Husbandry and Pork Consumption in Medieval England', in *Food in Medieval England*, ed. Woolgar, Serjeantson and Waldron, pp. 72–87

Aldington, Araminta, *A History of the Jacob Sheep* (Ashford, 1989)

Armitage, Philip L., 'A Preliminary Description of British Cattle from the Late Twelfth to the Early Sixteenth Century', *The Ark*, VII (1980), pp. 405–13

A. S., *The Husbandman, Farmer, and Grasier's Compleat Instructor* (London, 1697)

Aubrey, John, *Aubrey's Natural History of Wiltshire*, ed. K. Ponting (Newton Abbot, 1969)

Banks, Sir Joseph, *The Sheep and Wool Correspondence of Sir Joseph Banks, 1781–1820*, ed. H. B. Carter (London, 1979)

Barker, T. C., 'The Delayed Decline of the Horse in the Twentieth Century', in *Horses in European Economic History*, ed. Thompson, pp. 101–12

Best, Henry, *Rural Economy in Yorkshire in 1641, being the Farming and Account Books of Henry Best*, Surtees Society 33 (Durham, 1857)

Biddick, Kathleen, 'Pig Husbandry on the Peterborough Abbey Estate from the Twelfth to the Fourteenth Century AD', in *Animals and Archaeology, 4: Husbandry in Europe*, ed. Grigson and Clutton-Brock, pp. 161–77

Blagrave, Joseph, *Epitomy of the Art of Husbandry* (London, 1699)

Blith, Walter, *The English Improver Improved* (London, 1649)

Bonser, Kenneth J., *The Drovers* (London, 1970)

Carter, H. B., *His Majesty's Spanish Flock: Sir Joseph Banks and the Merinos of George III of England* (London, 1964)

Chivers, Keith, *The Shire Horse: A History of the Breed, the Society and the Men* (London, 1976)

Clutton-Brock, Juliet, 'George Garrard's Livestock Models', *Agricultural History Review*, XXIV (1976), pp. 18–29

—, *Horse Power: A History of the Horse and the Donkey in Human Societies* (London, 1992)

Cobbett, William, *Cottage Economy* (London, 1822)

Collins, E.J.T., 'The Farm Horse Economy of England and Wales in the Early Tractor Age', in *Horses in European Economic History*, ed. Thompson, pp. 73–97

Coppack, Glyn, 'The Excavation of an Outer Court Building, perhaps the Woolhouse, at Fountains Abbey, North Yorkshire', *Medieval Archaeology*, XXX (1986), pp. 46–87

Colyer, R. J., '"No Foot, No Ox": Cattle Shoeing in 19th-century Wales', *Country Life*, CLIV (1973), pp. 991–2

Culley, George, *Observations on Livestock*, 4th edn (London, 1807)

Defoe, Daniel, *A Tour thro' the whole Island of Great Britain*, 2nd edn (London, 1738)

Dent, Anthony, *Donkey: The Story of the Ass from East to West* (London, 1972)

Deuchar, Stephen, *Paintings, Politics and Porter: Samuel Whitbread II (1764–1815) and British Art*, exh. cat., Museum of London (London, 1984)

Digby, Sir Kenelm, *A Late Discourse . . . touching the Cure of Wounds* (London, 1658)

Edwards, Peter, *Horse and Man in Early Modern England* (London, 2007)

Ellis, William, *The Practical Farmer; or, The Hertfordshire Husbandman* (Dublin, 1732)

Fiennes, Celia, *The Journeys of Celia Fiennes*, ed. C. Morris (London, 1949)

Finberg, H.P.R., 'An Early Reference to the Welsh Cattle Trade', *Agricultural History Review*, II (1954), pp. 12–14

Fitzherbert, Sir Anthony, *The Boke of Husbandrie* (London, 1523)

Grant, Annie, 'Medieval Animal Husbandry: The Archaeozoological Evidence', in *Animals and Archaeology, 4: Husbandry in Europe*, ed. Grigson and Clutton-Brock, pp. 179–86

—, 'Animal Resources', in *The Countryside of Medieval England*, ed. G. Astill and A. Grant (Oxford, 1988), pp. 149–87

Grigson, Caroline, and Juliet Clutton-Brock, eds,

Animals and Archaeology, 4: *Husbandry in Europe*, BAR International Ser. 227 (Oxford, 1984)

Hodgson, William, *The Shepherd's Guide; or, A Delineation of the Wool and Ear Marks of the different Stocks of Sheep in Lancashire, Cumberland and Westmorland* (Ulverston, 1849)

Hollis, F. H., 'The Horse in Agriculture', in *The Book of the Horse*, ed. B. Vesey-Fitzgerald (London, 1947), pp. 160–83

[Horne, Thomas H.], *The Complete Grazier; or, Farmer and Cattle-Dealer's Assistant* (London, 1805)

Houghton, John, *A Collection, for the Improvement of Husbandry*, 4 vols (London, 1692–1703)

James, William, and Jacob Malcolm, *General View of the Agriculture of the County of Surrey* (London, 1794)

Kalm, Per, *Kalm's Account of his Visit to England . . . in 1748*, trans. J. Lucas (London, 1892)

Kerridge, Eric, 'The Sheepfold in Wiltshire Meadows and the Floating of the Watermeadows', *Economic History Review*, 2nd ser., VI (1953–4), pp. 282–9

Lamond, E., trans. and ed., *Walter of Henley's Husbandry, together with an anonymous Husbandry, Seneschaucie, and Robert Grosseteste's Rules* (London, 1890)

Langdon, John, 'The Economics of Horses and Oxen in Medieval England', *Agricultural History Review*, XXX (1982), pp. 31–40

—, *Horses, Oxen and Technological Innovation* (Cambridge, 1986)

Markham, Gervase, *Cheape and Good Husbandry* (London, 1616)

—, *Farewell to Husbandry* (London, 1660)

William Marshall, *The Rural Economy of the Midland Counties* (London, 1790)

—, *The Review and Abstract of the County Reports to the Board of Agriculture* (London, 1817)

Martin, Martin, *A Description of the Western Islands of Scotland* (London, 1703)

Martin & Johnson, *Valuable collection of Works of Art . . . of . . . the late G. Garrard, Esq., ARA, 12–15*

December 1870

Mascall, Leonard, *The Governement of Cattel* (London, 1620)

Mason, B.J.E., 'When Oxen Pulled the Plough: The Disappearance of Draught Cattle from Britain', *Country Life*, CLVI (1974), pp. 320–21

Moncrieff, Elspeth, with Stephen Joseph and Iona Joseph, *Farm Animal Portraits* (Woodbridge, 1996)

Monk, John, *General View of the Agriculture of the Country of Leicester* (London, 1794)

Mortimer, John, *The Whole Art of Husbandry*, 5th edn (Dublin, 1721)

Owen, George, *The Description of Penbrokshire*, ed. H. Owen (London, 1892)

Parry, Caleb Hillier, *Facts and Observations tending to shew the Practicability and Advantage . . . of producing in the British Isles Clothing Wool, equal to that of Spain* (London, 1800)

Pennant, Thomas, *The British Zoology: Class I: Quadrupeds* (London, 1766)

—, *A Tour in Scotland* (Chester, 1771)

—, *A Tour in Wales* (London, 1778)

Power, Eileen, *The Wool Trade in English Medieval History* (Oxford, 1941)

Ritchie, James, *The Influence of Man on Animal Life in Scotland* (Cambridge, 1920)

Russell, Nicholas, *Like Engend'ring Like: Heredity and Animal Breeding in Early Modern England* (Cambridge, 1986)

Ryder, M. L., 'The History of Sheep Breeds in Britain', *Agricultural History Review*, XII (1964), pp. 1–12, 65–82

—, *Sheep and Man* (London, 1983)

Seneschaucie: see Lamond

Sinclair, Sir John, *Address to the Society for the Improvement of British Wool* (London, 1791)

Smith, J. H., 'The Cattle Trade of Aberdeenshire in the Nineteenth Century', *Agricultural History Review*, III (1955), pp. 114–18

Somerville, John [Lord], *The System followed during*

the two last Years by the Board of Agriculture (London, 1800)

Spencer, S., *Pigs. Breeds and Management* (London, 1897)

Spruytte, Jean, *Early Harness Systems*, trans. M. Littauer (London, 1983)

Thirsk, Joan, *Fenland Farming in the Sixteenth Century*, University College of Leicester Occasional Paper 3 (Leicester, 1953)

Thomas, Keith, *Man and the Natural World: Changing Attitudes in England, 1500–1800* (London, 1983)

Thompson, F.M.L., ed., *Horses in European Economic History: A Preliminary Canter* (Reading, 1983)

Trow-Smith, Robert, *English Husbandry from the Earliest Times to the Present Day* (London, 1951)

—, *A History of British Livestock Husbandry to 1700* (London, 1957)

—, *A History of British Livestock Husbandry, 1700–1900* (London, 1959)

Tusser, Thomas, *Five Hundred Pointes of Good Husbandrie* (London, 1580)

Urquhart, Judy, 'Chartley Herd of White Park Cattle',

The Ark, VII (1980), pp. 165–8

Walter of Henley's *Husbandry*: see Lamond

White, Lynn, *Medieval Technology and Social Change* (Oxford, 1962)

Wiseman, Julian, *A History of the British Pig* (London, 1986)

Woolgar, C. M., D. Serjeantson and T. Waldron, eds, *Food in Medieval England: Diet and Nutrition* (Oxford, 2006)

Wykes, David L., 'Robert Bakewell (1725–1795) of Dishley: Farmer and Livestock Improver', *Agricultural History Review*, LII (2004), pp. 38–55

Youatt, William, *The Horse; with a Treatise on Draught* (London, 1831)

—, *Sheep: Their Breeds, Management and Diseases* (London, 1837)

—, *The Pig: A Treatise on the Breeds, Management, Feeding and Medical Treatment, of Swine* (London, 1847)

Young, Arthur, *General View of the Agriculture of the County of Sussex* (London, 1794)

Acknowledgements

I have benefited for many years and in great measure from the kindness and friendly guidance of Juliet Clutton-Brock, whose close familiarity with and insights into the animal kingdom form a shining contrast to my own more distant acquaintanceship. Other friends who have contributed valuably but less directly include James Rackham, who guided some of my earliest enquiries into animals 40 years ago; Peter Edwards and John Clark, who have separately carried out much useful research on horses; Brian Dix, whose knowledge of the archaeology of parks and gardens has been shared with me on several occasions; Philippa Glanville, whose breadth of knowledge set me off on several unanticipated paths; Jane Roberts, who has proved much more knowledgeable than myself on several of the topics treated here and provided much valued support; Rowan Watson, whose gentle encouragement to look beyond the Welsh Marches invariably brought rewards; and the authors of the works quoted in the Bibliography in whose footsteps I have followed and to whom I owe the basis of the current book. Thanks are also due to Jean-Denis Vigne, under whose chairmanship of the scientific committee of *Anthropozoologica* I have been introduced to many admirable colleagues from across Europe and have learned some of the advantages of a multidisciplinary approach to the treatment of 'l'homme et l'animal': special acknowledgement goes to Cornelia Becker, Annie Grant, Marco Masetti, Joris Peters and François Poplin. I am also grateful to Daniel Roche and Daniel Reytier, under whose editorship I contributed to to the magnificent volumes they produced for the Association pour l'Académie d'Art Équestre de Versailles, and to Mrs Iona Joseph for generous permission to reproduce a number of transparencies in her possession.

The provision of publication grants from the Paul Mellon Centre for Studies in British Art to both the author and the publisher was a matter of enormous value, not only in enabling the volume to be illustrated more extensively and to a higher standard than otherwise would have been possible but also in the tacit acknowledgement of the important role played here by the images – not as incidental illustrations to the text as in many histories but as integral and complementary sources of evidence in their own right, to be accorded the significance to which they are fully entitled. I am grateful to the Advisory Council of the Mellon Centre for looking benignly on this project and trust that the final product justifies the confidence they have placed in it.

Photo Acknowledgements

From Rudolph Ackermann *Microcosm of London . . .* (London, 1808–10): 57; from Henry Thomas Alken, *National Sports of Great Britain* (London, 1821): 39, 61, 62, 66; from *The Archaeological Journal* (London, 1861): 54; photos courtesy of author: 92, 94, 96, 97, 98, 100, 114, 149; from Juliana Berner, *Treatyse of Fysshynge wyth an Angle . . .* (Westminster [London], 1496): 88, 102; from Edmund Bert, *An Approved Treatise of Hawkes and Hawking* (London, 1619): 51; from Walter Blith, *The English Improver, or a New survey of husbandry discovering to the kingdome that some land, both arrable and pasture, may be advanced double or treble; other land to a five or tenfold: and some to a twenty fold improvement . . . [Third Edition] The English Improver improved . . . The third impression, much augmented . . . With a second part, containing six newer peeces of improvement, etc.* (London, 1652): 129; 4; from Thomas Blundeville, *Fower Chiefyst Offices belongyng to Horsemanshippe, That is to saye, The office of the Breeder, Of the Rider, of the Keper, and of the Ferrer . . . Whyche bookes are not onely painfully collected out of a number of aucthours, but also orderly disposed and applied to the vse of this oure coutry . . .* (London, 1565): Bodleian Library, Oxford: 3 (MS Douce 88), 27 (MS Douce 363), 37 (MS Bodley 764); The British Library, London (photos © The British Library Board): 7 (MS Egerton 1269), 9 (Add. MS 42130), 17 (Add. MS 42130), 21 (MS Cotton Julius E iv), 33 (MS Cotton Julius E iv), 36 (MS Yates Thompson 13), 40 (MS Royal 2 B. VII), 50 (MS Yates Thompson 13), 59 (Add. MS 42130), 78 (MS Royal 2 B. VII), 103 (Add. MS 42130), 105 (Add. MS 42130), 109 (MS Royal 2 B. VII), 111 (Add. MS 78342), 112 (MS Yates Thompson 13), 122 (Add. MS 78342), 125 (Add. MS 42130), 126 (from *The Holkham Bible Picture Book, with explanatory texts in French, written and illuminated in England (c. 1327-35)* (Add. MS 47682), 128 (Add. MS 42130), 148 (Add. MS 42130), 152 (MS Royal 2 B. VII), 157 (Add. MS 42130), 159 (Add. MS 42130); The British Museum, London (photos © Trustees of the British Museum): 12, 20, 29, 41, 45, 52, 69, 73, 75, 77, 80, 85, 86, 139; photos © The British Sporting Art Trust, Newmarket, Suffolk / The Bridgeman Art Library, London: 43, 44; from William Browne, *Browne his fiftie Yeares practice. Or an exact Discourse concerning snaffile-riding for trotting and ambling for all manner of horses whatsoeuer, from one degree to another, till they be perfit both for the trot and amble, etc.* (London, 1624): 8; Calke Abbey, Derby (Photo © NTPL / Christopher Hurst): 2; Christ Church, Oxford (photo © The Governing Body): 35 (MS 92); reproduced by permission of the Clwyd-Powys Archaeological Trust, Welshpool, Powys: 61; College of Arms, London: 18 (MS M6); photo courtesy of Mr Phil Deller: 101; courtesy of Department for Environment, Food and Rural Affairs (reproduced under Open Government Licence): 63; East Sussex Record Office, Lewes: 108 (DAN 2097); photo © Edinburgh University Library: 14 (Laing MS III 283); from John Fitzherbert, *Boke of Husbandrie, [Here begynneth a newe tracte or treatyse moost profytable for all husbandemen: and very frutefull for all* other persons to rede] (London, 1523) (photo © The British Library Board): 141; Fitzwilliam Museum, Cambridge (photo © Fitzwilliam Museum): 158 (MS 1-2005); from G. E. Freeman and F. H. Salvin, *Falconry; its claims, history, and practice . . . To which are added remarks on training the Otter and Cormorant . . .* (London, 1859): 55, 56; Gloucester City Museum: 87, 89; photo courtesy of Guildhall Library, City of London: 15; drawing (by the late Barbara M. Frears, 1988) reproduced by permission of Dr Jean Hansell: 91; from Samuel Hartlib's *The Reformed Common-Wealth of Bees: presented in severall letters and observations to S. H. Esq. With the Reform'd Virginian Silk-worm. Containing many excellent and choice secrets . . .* (London, 1655) (photo © The British Library Board): 120; photo courtesy of Herefordshire Libraries: 116 (Alfred Watkins collection, no. 1654); Hertfordshire Archives and Local Studies, Hertford (reproduced by gracious permission of the Earl of Verulam): 110 (HALS: XIII/30); from William Hodgson's *The shepherd's guide, or A delineation of the wool and ear marks of the different stocks of sheep in Lancashire, Cumberland, and Westmorland* (Ulverston, 1849): 147; reproduced by courtesy of the late Gordon House: 95; photo © Huntington Library, San Marino, California: 6 (MS EL 26 C 9); from *The Illustrated London News*: 25 (vol. LXI, no. 1715 [1872]), 26 (vol. LXXVI, no. 2140 [1880]); Imperial War Museum London (photo © Imperial War Museum): 72 (photograph by 2nd-Lt D. McLellan, 23 December 1917, Q8391); reproduced by courtesy of Mrs Iona Joseph: 67, 124, 144, 156; Laing Art Gallery, Tyne & Wear Archives & Museums, Newcastle upon Tyne: 46 (B8130); Lambeth Palace Library, London: 38 (MS 209); from William Lawson, *The Country House-wife's Garden [A new Orchard and Garden. Or the best way for planting . . . and to make any ground good, for a rich Orchard . . . With the Country Housewifes Garden for hearbes of common use . . . As also the husbandry of bees]* (London, 1618): 118; Leicestershire County Council Museums Service, Leicester: 131; from John Levett, *The ordering of bees: or, The true history of managing them from time to time . . .* (London, 1634) (photo © The British Library Board): 117; from Michael Loggan, *Oxonia Illustrata* (Oxford, 1675) (Oxfordshire County Council Photographic Archive, Oxford): 13, 19; photo courtesy London Metropolitan Archives: 16 (SC/PZ/CT/02/1502), 58; from David Low, *The Breeds of the Domestic Animals of the British Islands . . .* (London, 1842) (photos © Natural History Museum): 151, 154; photo courtesy of Heather MacGregor: 140; from Gervase Markham, *Hungers Prevention: Or, The whole Arte of Fowling by water and land, etc.* (London, 1621): 79; from Gervase Markham, *Farewell to Husbandry* (London, 1660): 130; from Leonard Mascall *A Booke of fishing with Hooke & Line [taken from that by Dame Juliana Bernes] . . . Another of sundrie Engines and Trappes to take Polcats, Buzards, Rattes . . .* (London, 1590): 42, 48; Museum of English Rural Life, University of Reading, Berkshire: 145, 161; Museum of Lincolnshire Life, Lincoln: 134; photo © Museum of London: 49 (82.8/15); National Monuments Record (photo © Crown copyright): 115; courtesy of National Museums Liverpool (Walker Art Gallery), Merseyside: 133; The National Museum of Scotland, Edinburgh (photos © Trustees of the National Museums of Scotland): 137, 160; The National Trust, Mount Stewart, The Londonderry Collection, Co. Down (photo © NTPL / John Hammond): 24; photo © National Trust Picture Library / Oliver Benn: 90; Natural History Museum, London (photos © Natural History Museum): 70, 138, 150; from the Duke of Newcastle (William Cavendish) *Methode et invention nouvelle de dresser les chevaux par Guillaume Marquis et Comte de Newcastle, trad. de l'anglais . . . [A New Method and Extraordinary Invention to Dress Horses . . .]* (Printed in French, translated from Cavendish's English Manuscript, Antwerp, 1658 (reprinted in English in 1667)): 22; Norfolk Record Office, Norwich: 99 (MC2044/1), 107 (MC556/1); Nottingham City Museums and Galleries (photo © Nottingham City Museums and Galleries): 1;

from Thomas Nutt, *Humanity to honey bees: or, Practical directions for the management of honey bees . . .* (London, 1835): 123; from Sir Ralph Payne-Gallwey, *The Book of Duck Decoys, their construction, management, and history . . .* (London, 1886): 81, 82, 83; from Sir Alfred Pease, *The Badger: A Monograph* (London, 1898): 65; from Robert Plot, *Natural History of Stafford-shire* (Oxford, 1686): 68; photo © Portland (Welbeck) Collection, Nottinghamshire, 2011: 23; from John Ray, *The Ornithology of Francis Willughby . . . Translated into English, and enlarged with many additions . . . To which are added, Three . . . discourses, I. Of the Art of Fowling . . . II. Of the ordering of Singing birds. III. Of Falconry . . .* (London, 1678): 74; from H. D. Richardson, *Pigs; their origin and varieties, management with a view to profit, and treatment under disease; also plain directions relative to curing . . .* (Dublin, 1847): 153; copy of print provided by Rothamsted Research Ltd: 143, 155; The Royal Collection (photos © 2011 Her Majesty Queen Elizabeth II): 10 (RCIN 405800), 11 (RCIN 405794), 30 (RCIN 404440); The Royal Picture Gallery, Mauritshuis, The Hague: 53; from Moses Rusden's *A Further Discovery of Bees . . . with experiments . . .* (London, 1679) (photo © The British Library Board): 121; from John Speed, *The Theatre of the Empire of Great Britaine: presenting an exact geography of . . . England, Scotland, Ireland, etc.* (London, 1611): 31; from the collection of Mr and Mrs Edd Stepp: 132; Suffolk Record Office (from the 'Survey of the Island of Lothingland'): 84 (295/1); Tate General Collection (photo © Tate, London, 2011): 136; from George Turberville, *The Noble Art of Venerie or Hunting, etc.* (London, 1611): 32, 34, 64; from *The Universal Magazine of Knowledge and Pleasure* V (London, 1749) (photo © The British Library Board): 146; photo courtesy of Ken Upton: 104; Victoria and Albert Museum (photo © V&A): 60 (3690-1901); Westminster Abbey (photo © The Dean and Chapter of Westminster): 5; photo © Wiltshire Heritage Museum, Devizes: 127 (DZSWS: 1986.7314); Courtesy of the Worshipful Company of Wax Chandlers, London: 119.

Acts of Parliament

and other statutory instruments consulted in preparing the text

30/31 Hen. II: Assize of the Forest (1184)

13 Edw. I, cap. XLVII: Penalty for taking Salmons at certain Times of the Year (1285)

25 Edw. I, cap. I–XVI: Carta de Foresta (1297)

27 Edw. I, cap. I: Statute of Fines Levied (1299)

25 Edw. III, stat. 4 cap. IV: That new Weirs shall be pulled down and not Repaired (1350/1)

25 Edw. III, cap. II: Statute of the Staple (1353)

13 Rich. II, cap. XIII: None shall Hunt but they have a sufficient Living (1389)

13 Rich. II, cap. XIX: Touching the taking of Salmons (1389)

22 Edw. IV, cap. VI: Act concerning Swans (1482)

1 Hen. VII, cap. VII: Act shewing the penalty for Hunting in the Night, or with Disguising (1485)

11 Hen. VII, cap. XVII: Against taking Pheasants and Partridges (1485)

11 Hen. VII, cap. III: Acte agaynst Transporting of Horses and Mares beyond ye Seas (1495)

19 Hen. VII, cap. XI: Act for Deer-hays and Buck-stalls (1503)

14/15 Hen. VIII, cap. X: Penalty for unlawful Hunting of the Hare (1522/3)

23 Hen. VIII, cap. XVI: Felony to sell . . . to any Scotishman . . . any Horse (1531)

25 Hen. VIII, cap. VII: No Person . . . shall take any Fry, or Sawn of Eels, or Salmon (1533)

25 Hen. VIII, cap. XI: To avoid Destroying of Wildfowl (1533)

25 Hen. VIII, cap. XVII: Whosoever shall shoot in any Hand-gun or Cross-bow . . . shall forfeit £10 (1533)

27 Hen. VIII, cap. VI: Bill for the increase of Horses (1535/6)

31 Hen. VIII, cap. XII: A Felony to take in the King's Ground . . . any Faulcon &c (1539/40)

32 Hen. VIII, cap. XIII: Bill for the Breed of Horses (1540)

33 Hen. VIII, cap. VI: Acte concerninge Crosbowes and Handguns (1541)

3/4 Edw VI, cap. VII: Act of repeal of a Statute . . . touching the Taking of Wildfowl (1549)

2/3 P.&M., cap. VII: Act against the Buying of stolen Horses (1555)

1 Eliz. I, cap. XVII: Act for Preservation of Spawn and Fry of Fish (1558/9)

8 Eliz. I, cap. XIV: Act touching the Transporting of tawed Leather (1565)

8 Eliz. cap. VIII: Act for Repeale . . . of a Statute . . . for the Stature of Horses
whithin the Isle of Ely etc. (1566)

8 Eliz. cap. XV: Act for Preservation of Grayne (1566)

31 Eliz. I, cap. XII: Act to avoid Horse-stealing (1589)

43 Eliz. I, cap. XI: Act for the recovery of . . . Marshes (1601)

[27 April 1652] Declaration against transporting of wolfe dogges (1652)

[4 July 1654] Ordinance prohibiting Horse-races for six Moneths (1654)

[9 June 1657] Act for setling the Postage of England, Scotland and Ireland (1657)

16 Car. II, cap. VII: Act against deceitfull, disorderly, and excessive Gameing (1664)

22/3 Car. II, cap. XXV: Act for the better Preservation of the Game (1670/71)

3/4 W.&M., cap. XII: Act for the Repairing and Amending of the Highways (1691)

13 Geo. II, cap. XIX: Act to restrain . . . the Increase of Horse-races (1740)

28 Geo. II , cap. XVII: Act for the Amendment and Preservation of the Publick Highways
and Turnpike Roads (1755)

5 Geo. III, cap. XIV: Act for the more effectual Preservation of Fish in Fish Ponds . . .
and Conies in Warrens (1765)

9 Geo. III, cap. LXIX: Act for the . . . Prevention of Persons going armed by Night for the
Destruction of Game (1828)

1/2 W. IV, cap. XXXII: Act to amend the Laws in England relative to Game (1831)

5/6 W. IV, cap. LIX: Act to consolidate . . . Laws relating to the cruel and improper
Treatment of Animals (1835)

8/9 Vict., cap. CXVIII: Act to facilitate the Inclosure and Improvement of Commons etc. (1845)

12/13 Vict., cap. XCII: Act for the more Effectual Prevention of Cruelty to Animals (1849)

24/25 Vict. cap. XCVI: Larceny Act (1861)

25/26 Vict., cap. CXIV: Act for the Prevention of Poaching (1862)

28/29 Vict., cap. CXXII: Salmon Fishery (Amendment) Act (1865)

32/33 Vict., cap. XVII: Sea Birds Preservation Act (1869)

39/40 Vict., cap. XXXIV: Elver Fishing Act (1876)

43/44 Vict., cap. XLVII: Ground Game Act (1880)

1/2 Geo. V, cap. XXVII: Protection of Animals Act (1911)

13/14 Geo. V, cap. XVI: Act to consolidate . . . enactments relating to Salmon and
Freshwater Fisheries (1923)

2/3 Geo. VI, cap. XLIII: Prevention of Damage by Rabbits Act (1939)

10/11 Geo. VI, cap. XLVIII: Agriculture Act (1947)

2/3 Eliz. II, cap. LXVIII: Pests Act (1954)

21/22 Eliz. II, cap. LVII: Badgers Act (1973)

23/24 Eliz. II, cap. XLVIII: Conservation of Wild Creatures and Wild Plants Act (1975)

29/30 Eliz. II, cap. LXIX Wildlife and Countryside Act (1981)

52/53 Eliz. II, cap. XXXVII: Hunting Act (2004)

Index

Note: in keeping with the historical nature of the text, county boundaries observed in the index are those existing before the reorganization of 1974.